PETER THE GREAT

PETER THE GREAT

EMPEROR OF ALL RUSSIA

BY

IAN GREY

J. B. LIPPINCOTT COMPANY

Philadelphia & New York

To Wendy

To Wendy

CONTENTS

7

PREFACE

Peter the Great was one of the most creative, dynamic, and versatile rulers in history, and a man of exceptional character. Moreover, his reign is of paramount importance in the study of Russia. In fact, the eminent historian, Klyuchevsky, went so far as to state that "the whole essence of Russian history has been compressed into the single question of the significance of the work of Peter," and that question remains strikingly relevant to the understanding of Russia in the present century.

Nevertheless, few books have been published in English on the man and his work, and apart from B. H. Sumner's excellent but brief, *Peter the Great and the Emergence of Russia* (London, 1950), no worth-while study has been written in English since the biography by the American, Eugene Schuyler, was published in London in 1884. Even in Soviet Russia, where so much valuable work has been done in this field, historians, with one exception, have dealt only with aspects of Petrine Russia.

The present work is an attempt to portray Peter and his reign afresh, and particularly his transformation of Muscovy into the Russian Empire and, indeed, into modern Russia. It is based on Russian and contemporary sources. I have made full use of *The Letters and Papers of Emperor Peter* which reprints, in addition, all relevant material in the Russian State Archives. The first volume of this great compilation was published in 1889, and the latest in 1952, bringing the documents up to the end of the year 1709. Other contemporary material in Russian and English, together with the main secondary sources, is listed in the Bibliography.

I acknowledge my debt to the works of Bogoslovsky, Ustryalov, Solovev, and Klyuchevsky, on which I have leant heavily. Bogoslovsky's *Peter I: Materials for a Biography* (Moscow, 1940-48, 5 vols.), attempting as it does to give an almost day-by-day account of Peter's activities, has been indispensable, but unfortunately it breaks off at 1700. The histories of Ustryalov and Solovev have been especially valuable for the documents reprinted, which would not otherwise be available. Klyuchevsky's history has been useful on social and economic matters, but he is too often arbitrary, prejudiced, and misleading in his handling of Peter and his reign to serve as a guide; I have found Solovev's massive history to be a greater and more reliable work.

I have tried to avoid cluttering my pages with references and footnotes. The established facts will be found in the works of the four historians named above, and in other studies listed in the Bibliography. But at the end of the book will be found such explanatory notes and references as seemed necessary for each chapter.

It is usually stated that Peter was "repellent in his brutality, coarseness, and utter disregard for human life" (B. H. Sumner, *Survey of Russian History*, p. 103). I have not extenuated his barbarities, but have set them down as part of the man, his country, and his age, for it is in this context that he should be judged. Those who have been most censorious have tended to forget that his was a cruel age, when human life was disregarded, and nowhere more than in England, as the Bloody Assizes, the Glencoe massacre, and, later, the convict system bear witness.

Again many historians have dismissed Peter as a dynamic barbarian. I have found, however, that the more I have studied the man the more my admiration for him has grown, and not only because of his labours, so heroic in scale, but also for his humility, selflessness, and his dedication to the service of his country and his people. An autocrat wielding unlimited power, he was not corrupted by power. He avoided honours, except those due to Russia, and only for that reason did he accept the title of Emperor. He was the antithesis of Louis XIV. Indeed, it seems to me that his was a rare nature, and that he belongs among the very great princes of history.

Since it has been basic to my approach to this study, it is necessary to mention that I regard Russia as part of Europe and hold, with Catherine the Great, that "Russia is a European power." Some historians consider her to be Asiatic, or, at least, non-European. See, for example, H. A. L. Fisher, *History of Europe*, pp. 715-16 (London, 1936) and J. F. C. Fuller, *The Decisive Battles of the World*, II, 186 (London, 1955), while Dr. Arnold Toynbee in *A Study of History* (I, 63-67; III, 278-83) has sharply distinguished Russia from Western civilization. B. H. Sumner has examined these and other views in his valuable lecture, "Russia and Europe" (*Oxford Slavonic Papers*, II [1951]), as also has Prince Dmitri Obolensky in his paper on "Russia's Byzantine Heritage" (*Oxford Slavonic Papers*, I [1950]).

There is no satisfactory system of transliteration from the Cyrillic alphabet, but broadly I have followed the system adopted by the British Academy. Also, except where it would lead to confusion, as for example in using Pyotr for Peter, I have retained the Russian forms of Christian names, and have avoided translating Ivan into John, Mikhail into Michael, Alexei into Alexis, and so forth.

I should like to express my appreciation for the help and facilities I have received in the London Library, the British Museum, and the Library of the School of Slavonic Studies, University of London. Also for the assistance of friends in the British Embassy in Moscow, especially in obtaining Russian books for me. Finally, I must express my deep gratitude to my wife for her long support, patience, and confidence.

London
February 1959

By thy untiring labours and by thy sole leadership, we have stepped forth from the darkness of insignificance and ignorance on to the road of glory and have joined in equality with the civilized States of Europe.

——*Chancellor Count Golovkin in the Act conferring on Peter the Imperial title*

The more I learn of the character of the Tsar, the more I revere him.

——*Leibniz*

PETER THE GREAT

CHAPTER I

Muscovy in the Seventeenth Century

THE Muscovy into which Peter the Great was born in 1672 was a vast and troubled land. It extended from the White Sea in the north to the Caspian Sea in the south. In the east, embracing the whole of Siberia, it stretched to the Pacific Ocean, but the great expanse of land beyond the Ural Mountains was as yet unsettled. In the west, it stopped short at the Baltic provinces, which the Swedes held, denying the Muscovites access to the sea, where Novgorod had traded since the dawn of Russian history. Also in the west, White Russia and most of the Ukraine were part of the great kingdom of Lithuania-Poland. In the south the Cossacks and Crimean Tatars stood between Muscovy and the Black Sea. Thus, except in the north, where Archangel allowed some trade with western Europe, Muscovy was landlocked and isolated.

At the same time Muscovy was weak and troubled internally, and preyed on by her enemies. More than once during the seventeenth century the nation faced collapse and dissolution. Indeed, the century opened with the Time of Troubles, which had as its immediate cause the extinction of the old dynasty, and for fifteen years, while various contenders struggled for the throne, the country drifted perilously; unrest and rebellion went unchecked; Cossacks marauded at will; the Swedes invaded and plundered. The Polish occupation of Moscow had come as the final humiliation, uniting the Muscovites, and in a national rising they had expelled the invaders. But Moscow was still without a tsar and the empty throne remained a source of unease and distress. Finally summonses went out to all parts of the country, calling on the people to send delegates to the Zemsky Sobor

(Assembly of the Land). Early in 1613, this assembly elected Mikhail, the first of the Romanovs and grandfather of Peter, to the throne.

Tsar Mikhail gave his country a much-needed rest during his long reign. He made peace with Sweden and Poland, but at the price of terms that were a source of shame to all Muscovites. Internally he restored a semblance of order and quiet but it proved to be only the quiet before the storms that were to break upon his son and successor, Tsar Alexei. On the one hand, the discontent of all classes gathered strength as their burdens grew more oppressive; on the other, the country remained weak, impoverished, and unable to stand against its enemies, for by European standards it was backward.

The Russians had not always lagged behind the peoples of western Europe. In the tenth, eleventh, and twelfth centuries, before they had moved northwards and established Moscow as their capital, the Russians of Kiev and Novgorod had been closely bound by culture and trade with the countries of the West and had stood as their equals. But then for nearly two hundred and fifty years (1240-1480) they were under the yoke of the Mongol-Tatar khans; their intercourse with the West ceased, and they were isolated. They knew nothing of such great movements as the Renaissance, the Reformation, the explorations, and the scientific discoveries. Painfully in the sixteenth and seventeenth centuries, the tsars and some of the leading men at court became aware of the superiority of the West not only in war, but also in industry, trade, and education. A sense of isolation and vulnerability filled this small ruling circle with uneasiness. The realization that in the first half of the seventeenth century their country was farther behind the West than ever before in her history intensified their fears.

It was against this backwardness and isolation that Peter was to fight throughout his reign. His struggle was all the more difficult because Muscovy was sunk in lethargy; the people were lazy, ignorant, and conservative, and, encouraged by the church, they clung tenaciously to their way of life. But Peter wielded the power of the supreme autocrat and he wielded it ruthlessly. He was also helped by the gradual intrusion of Western influence. But most important of all in this struggle was the elemental force of his own will, energy, and dedication by which he was to transform Muscovy into the Russian Empire.

Moscow was the capital and centre of Muscovy and already in the seventeenth century it was a considerable city. Adam Olearius, an acute observer on the staff of the Holstein minister, considered it "out of all controversy one of the greatest cities in Europe,"[1] and the first sight of Moscow never failed to impress Western travellers. Captain John Perry, an English engineer, wrote that "whenever any traveller comes within a fair view of the city, the numerous churches, the monasteries, and noblemen's and gentlemen's houses, the steeples, cupolas, and crosses at the tops of the churches, which are gilded and painted over, make the city look to be one of the most rich and beautiful in the world, as indeed it appeared to me at first sight coming from the Novgorod road."[2] But to the Muscovites, Moscow was also the white-walled city of the Tsar and the centre of the Orthodox Church, and as such it was vested with divine majesty. They looked towards it in the spirit of pilgrims and saw it as a shrine. In most things, Moscow was also the epitome of the country to which it had given its name.

The Kremlin, set on a slight hill on the bank of the Moskva River, was its heart and matrix. Great walls enclosed this citadel and other districts outside it, while a palisade of logs marked the city limits. Moscow was, in fact, a walled city, and the massive walls were not relics of another age, but a necessary defence against invasion.

In appearance the city was neither Asiatic nor European, but distinctively Russian. Byzantine and, later, Italian and other European architects had contributed to its buildings and their styles had blended into a Russian style. The churches, most with one large and four small cupolas, typified it. The city contained over fifteen hundred churches, and the golden forest of gilded crosses and cupolas rising above the walls contributed overwhelmingly to the travellers' impression of Moscow's mysterious, fantastic, and savage character, and of her uniqueness.

With few exceptions all Muscovites from the Tsar to the poorest peasants, lived in log houses, which differed only in size and in the amount of decoration on their window frames, gables, and porches. Indeed, Moscow was built of logs, even the roads, where they existed, being laid with logs bound side by side. Consequently, both in winter, when the primitive stoves were burning in every house, and in summer, when the wood was tinder dry, fires were the scourge of Moscow. A few days before Olearius' arrival, a fire consumed a third of the

city, and he noted that it was a weekly occurrence for fires to reduce
whole streets to ashes. In the Great Fire of London, 13,200 houses are
said to have perished, but it may be estimated that in seventeenth
century Moscow, fires destroyed at least half this number of houses
every year.[3]

While the first sight of Moscow impressed travellers, it also sharp-
ened their disillusionment when they entered the city. The main
impression was one of squalor and the contrasts aggravated this impression. Churches and the palaces of boyars stood surrounded by
miserable huts. The magnificence of the Tsar's court and the opulence of the church and the nobility contrasted with the drab poverty
of the rest of the population.

Wearing long-sleeved coats of velvet or stiff brocaded cloth, which
reached to the ground, rich boyars and landowners rode on horse-
back or on sledges through the streets, escorted by suites of retainers.
They were usually fat and full of pride in the size of their bellies,
which, like the length of their beards and the profusion of their
servants, indicated wealth and station, and they moved against a
background of peasant-serfs, ragged holy-men, beggars and pedlars.

The *streltsi* or archers, a special force raised by Ivan the Terrible
and the only permanent regiments in the country, mounted guard
at the Kremlin gates and other points, and were both the city's
garrison and police. They wore bright kaftans and caps, yellow boots,
and richly embroidered belts, and they carried arquebuses and pole-
axes, the latter for fire fighting. Priests and church dignitaries were
a common sight. The simple priests were poor, and merged with the
peasant mass, while the dignitaries were resplendent in gold cloth
and belonged to the upper classes. Outside every church crowds of
beggars, tolerated as being almost holy, wailed for alms. Such were
the squalor and contrasts, and yet in spite of them the abiding impression of Western travellers was one of the magnificence of Moscow, and this impression derived chiefly from the Tsar and his court.

"The sole autocrat, only Tsar of the Christians" was vested with
sacred majesty. Western travellers marvelled at his power and the
servility of his subjects. "No people in the world," Olearius observed,
"have a greater veneration for their prince than the Muscovites, who
from their infancy are taught to speak of the Tsar as of God himself. . . ."[4] He appeared seldom to his people, and no common sub-

ject was allowed near his person. Within the precincts of the palace, barriers of ceremony kept the boyars and nobles at a distance; nor could his own family always claim direct access to him. To his people, high and low, he was a remote and majestic figure.

On festivals and other occasions, when he appeared in public, the Tsar was the centre of magnificent ceremony. Making a pilgrimage to a church outside the city, Tsar Alexei rode alone, preceded by officers who cleared the people from the streets, and followed by an escort of over one thousand horsemen.

Apart from church festivals, the great court occasions were the receptions of foreign ambassadors. The Muscovites attended closely to protocol and delighted in ceremonial. They were also anxious that in wealth and dignity the Tsar's court should never fall short of the courts of other rulers. Thus an escort of sixteen hundred horsemen met the Turkish ambassador at the gates of Moscow, and conducted him and his staff to the Kremlin where a lengthy ceremony of welcome followed. Again, at the presentation of the credentials of the Holstein envoy, the Tsar sat in a long robe embroidered with pearls and precious stones, wearing a fur cap on top of which rested his crown, while in his right hand he held a golden sceptre. Handsome young nobles stood on both sides of the throne, dressed in long coats of white damask, with caps of lynx-skin, white buskins, and with chains of gold over their chests; each held a silver axe as though in readiness to strike.

Nor was the Tsar merely a centre of magnificence and veneration. His power was real and absolute. He was chosen by God and responsible to God. Muscovy was his personal domain and he ruled it as unchallenged despot. For a time the extinction of the old dynasty and the bitter experience of the Time of Troubles had shaken the confidence of the Muscovites in the divine authority of their tsars, but they never entirely lost their habit of unquestioning obedience. And with the establishment of the Romanov dynasty the habit became more deeply ingrained than ever in their nature.

By custom the Tsar had consulted in his rule with the Council of Boyars, but this had become a formality. The council had, in fact, some legislative and administrative functions, and did at times appear to share supreme power. It might even have become a permanent body, aiding and restraining the Tsar in governing the country. It failed to do so because the boyars were riven by family rivalries and concerned only with securing their own privileges. They never became integrated as a class and so failed to meet the needs of the nation which had emerged under Moscow's domination.

These boyars were relics of the time when Russia had been a feudal land, split into apanage principalities. Like the barons of mediaeval Europe, they had served one of the grand-princes in return for grants of land or on the basis of personal contract. The boyars were now the subjects of the Tsar, but they cherished ideas of independence and voluntary service. When the Tsar was weak, they scrambled for power; but a strong tsar could keep them in check, and they never recovered from the savage assaults of Ivan the Terrible.

Moreover, as the tsars expanded and consolidated Muscovy, their need for officers and administrators grew more pressing, and they recruited them from outside the ranks of the boyars. This led to the growth of a new class of landowners—the men of service, who received grants of land which, at first temporary, gradually became permanent and hereditary. But the new landowners did not share the outlook of the old landowning boyars whom they largely supplanted. Soon they were serving in high office, wielding influence and power, and themselves acquiring the rank of boyar.

Tsar Alexei himself turned more and more to this new class, of whom Ordin-Nashchokin and Matveev were outstanding examples, and in his reign such new men were dominant in the inner chancellery which for all practical purposes took the place of the Council of Boyars. The Assembly of the Land also proved more of a hindrance than an aid to government, and was seldom summoned. Thus the Tsar ruled supreme and unchecked, relying only on advisers of his own choice.

Such were the autocratic power and position which Peter took for granted as his birthright, and in the same way he embraced without question the simple Orthodox faith of his fathers. But, while he was always to adhere to this faith, he was forced to recognize early in his reign that the church was a massive opponent.

The Russian Slavs received Christianity from Byzantium, and no factor played a greater part in shaping their subsequent history. The new faith took deep root among them, and subjection later to the Golden Horde did not hinder this process, for the khans were tolerant of other religions.

During these years the church became the centre of a vigorous religious life and of a great movement which led to the foundation of numerous monasteries, many in the lonely wilderness of the northern forests. These monasteries grew into powerful landlords, who, by the sixteenth century, held as much as one third of the land, and a great labour force of serfs along with it.

The Russian Church also played a momentous part in founding the Muscovite nation. It supported the Grand Dukes of Moscow in their policy of bringing the other principalities under their rule. In times of crisis it united the Muscovite people and, when the rulers were weak, it upheld the throne. Religious nationalism fired its outlook and, although Moscow acknowledged the primacy of Constantinople and the authority of the Greek Patriarch, it was reluctant to accept Greeks as primates of its own church.

Then, in 1453, the Ottoman Turks captured Constantinople, the centre of Orthodox Christendom. The Muscovites saw in this event a swift justice, punishing the Greeks who, fourteen years earlier at the Council of Florence, had betrayed Orthodoxy by agreeing to union with the Church of Rome. The Russian Church, now strongly independent and nationalistic, proclaimed its autonomy, and by the creation of the Russian patriarchate in 1589 signalized its final emancipation. At this time the idea of Moscow as "the third Rome" was born; inheriting the oecumenical role of Constantinople, Moscow had become the sole guardian of Orthodoxy.

The Russian Church always interpreted Orthodoxy to mean the preservation of the faith in pristine purity. Change of any kind was abhorrent, and this conservatism worked deep, dyeing the minds of a people who, untouched by the tides of new ideas that ebbed and flowed through Europe, felt no need for change. Encouraged by the church, Muscovite thought and life became equally petrified in its careful adherence to the faith and customs of the past.

From its earliest years the Orthodox Church imposed the pattern of daily life among Russians, shaping it with ritual, fasts, and holy days. They were a profoundly pious people whose religion was an integral part of their lives and often, because God was close and all-forgiving, and understood their needs and temptations, they took their punctiliousness to strange lengths. They were promiscuous, but no man would think of intercourse with a woman without first covering all the ikons in the room and taking her crucifix from around her neck. Robbers on the point of crime paused before their ikons to beseech blessing and protection. These and other anomalies pointed to the childlike simplicity of their faith.

By the middle of the seventeenth century the church had become enfeebled. Vitiating conservatism had drained its strength and its sluggish weight lay heavily over a people who were themselves infected by the same spirit of inertia. The church became like an ailing man who had suffered a stroke, and the stroke in this case was the Great Schism.

The immediate cause of the schism had been the correction of the liturgy and the sacred books, which provoked a storm of opposition throughout the country. It amounted to asserting the authority of the Greek over the Russian texts; most important of all to the simple believer, it made changes in the ritual, which was a part of his faith. To write "Iisus" in place of "Isus," and to cross oneself with three, not two, fingers was sacrilege. The schismatics or Old Believers refused to obey; excommunication only hardened their resistance. They banded together in a spirit of martyrdom, and in six years more than twenty thousand Old Believers perished by self-cremation. Crowded together in their wooden churches they would set the buildings alight on the approach of agents from Moscow, and, singing the old liturgies, men, women, and children allowed themselves to be burnt to death.

The fact that the Patriarch, Nikon, had enforced the hated revisions and that the church hierarchy and the state supported him convinced many Russians that the reign of the Antichrist had begun. It was even rumoured that Tsar Alexei himself was the Antichrist. The revolt against the church widened into a revolt against the state and in this the Old Believers were joined by runaway serfs, outcasts, and malcontents who rebelled for other reasons. Moreover, the schism widened the gulf that had already begun to separate the nobility and landowners from the rest of the people.

In spite of the widespread and bitter opposition, the ecclesiastical council confirmed the revision and anathematized all who continued to reject it. It also formally deposed Patriarch Nikon and exiled him to a distant monastery. He had been a virile and iconoclastic force in the church and his enemies were innumerable. But he was deposed because, hungry for power, he had dared to challenge the position of the Tsar, asserting the supremacy of the spiritual over the temporal power, of himself the Patriarch over Alexei the Tsar. It was a doctrine new to Moscow which had always accepted the Byzantine tradition of church and state, Patriarch and Tsar, working together as partners, and not struggling as rivals for power as in the West. Nevertheless, had Nikon combined with his other great qualities the statesmanship, tact, and patience of his French contemporaries, Richelieu and Mazarin, he might have indeed revitalized the church and established its autonomy. As it was his efforts only weakened it. The church was never again to exercise the same power and authority in Muscovy as before, and, instead of offering a strong opposition to Peter's reforms, it could only bow before them.

In the reigns of Peter's grandfather and father, Tsars Mikhail and Alexei, serfdom developed into the enslavement of labour that was to form the basis of Russian society well into the nineteenth century. Formerly, as in mediaeval Europe, peasants had enjoyed certain rights. But it became necessary, especially in the seventeenth century, to stabilize labour because peasants used their right of departure to evade both taxes and service. To counter this, they were by an inexorable process gradually tied to the land, their former right of departure was first limited and then abolished, and the time within which runaways could be reclaimed by landowners was extended. Thus, by the end of the century, about half of the peasants had become the absolute and hereditary property of landowners, while the other half were mainly state peasants, whose conditions were hardly better.

Inevitably they sought escape by flight and rebellion. Twice during the seventeenth century peasants' revolts, led and inspired by Cossacks, gathered such strength as to threaten the government. But usually the peasants, when driven to desperation, resorted to flight rather than rebellion. Some districts in central Muscovy even became deserted and the land lay untilled as peasants fled to the free lands in the south, or made for the virgin lands to the east, or joined the Cossacks.

These Cossacks were freebooters, hunters, and robbers inhabiting the lands to the south of Muscovy, and concentrated mainly on the Don, Volga, and Dnieper rivers. When not raiding and plundering, they spent their time hunting and fishing. They despised all labour, especially tilling the soil, as bondage, and took pride only in their buccaneering exploits by land and river, and in their freedom. The Don Cossacks observed their own law, and elected their own ataman, or headman,[5] but nominally they owed loyalty to Moscow. Tsar Alexei exacted a firm oath of allegiance from them, and regarded them as a useful frontier force, keeping the Turks and Tatars at bay. But they could never be trusted. Jealous of their freedom and quick to rebel, they allied themselves with the Tatars when necessary, and they had another ally in the Russian peasants. Even when the peasants cursed them for treachery, cruelty, and rapacity, their curses were touched with envy. The Cossacks acted as a magnet to all who were desperate and enslaved. Thus Stenka Razin, the Cossack leader who had dominated the Volga lands and defied Tsar Alexei for two years, had appeared as a champion of the peasants, and his revolt had spread uneasiness throughout Muscovy. At a time of crisis Peter had to put down a further Don Cossack revolt which threatened the security of the whole country. The Cossacks of the Dnieper were equally unstable and unreliable, and many of them were to play an especially treacherous role during his reign.

The people of Muscovy were lazy, corrupt, ignorant, servile, drunken, and immoral. All Western travellers agreed in painting them in these dark colours, which they applied not only to the peasants, who made up the mass of the population, then about eight millions, but also to the nobility, the landowners, and the clergy. They saw the Muscovites as a people sunk in the deepest barbarity and, while their judgments and understanding were often superficial, the general degradation was undeniable.

Drunkenness was the national vice. All classes from the Tsar down to the poorest peasant drank great quantities of spirits. Dr. Collins, Tsar Alexei's English physician, noted how the Tsar delighted in seeing his courtiers "handsomely fuddled" after drinking a beaker of vodka that would take away the breath of anyone not used to it.[6] To be drunk was accepted as part of normal living and a proof of hospitality. Women were no more abstemious than men. "They are often the first to become raving mad with immoderate draughts of brandy and are to be seen, half naked and shameless in almost all the streets."[7]

The state aided and the church abetted the people in their excess. The sale of alcohol was a state monopoly. At a time when the government's preoccupation was to stave off bankruptcy, this monopoly was an important source of revenue, and there could be no question of curtailing sales of vodka. The church did nothing to combat the evil and, indeed, drunkenness was common among the priesthood. The church was even more implicated because the most serious excesses happened during religious festivals; Muscovites believed that they showed respect to the saints by being drunk on their holy day.

"In the carnival before Lent," wrote Dr. Collins, "they give themselves to all manner of debauchery and luxury and in the last week they drink as if they were never to drink more. . . . Some of those going home drunk, if not attended by a sober companion, fall asleep upon the snow, a sad cold bed, and there they are frozen to death. . . . 'Tis a sad sight to see a dozen people brought upright in a sledge, frozen to death; some have their arms eaten off by dogs, others their faces, and others have nothing left but bones. Two or three hundred have been brought in after this manner in time of Lent."[8]

Immorality went with heavy drinking. To Olearius they were like beasts, "doing all things according to their unbridled passions and appetites. . . . They are wholly given up to licentiousness, even to sins against nature, not only with men, but also with beasts. . . . The postures of their dancing and the insolence of their women are infallible marks of their bad inclinations. We have seen at Moscow both men and women come out of the public brothel houses stark naked and incite some young people of our retinue to naughtiness by filthy and lascivious expressions."[9]

This immorality was, in part at least, a result of the Muscovite attitude towards women. The code of chivalry, which influenced European manners and particularly the position of women in society, never touched Muscovy, where women were chattels. Women of the upper classes had the sole function of childbearing, and in the gloom of the *terem* their lives were often dominated by boredom, drink, and fear.

Indeed, fear must have been a real and frequent emotion. Women were wholly at the mercy of their husbands and often treated with savagery. In all classes men beat their wives on the slightest pretext, and excited by drink they found pretexts readily. "Some of these barbarians will tie up their wives by the hair of their head and whip them stark naked," observed Dr. Collins.[10] Wife-beating was a national custom: but Olearius considered it not unreasonable, for the Muscovite women "have lewd tongues, are given to wine, and will not let slip the opportunity to pleasure a friend."[11]

Not infrequently the whippings were so severe that the women died. Death was then presumed to have happened in the course of correction, and the man went unpunished. Inevitably many wives, goaded beyond endurance, murdered their husbands, but this incurred a terrible penalty: the guilty wife was buried with only her head above the earth, and left to starve.[12]

Under these conditions crime flourished. No night passed without violence and murder. It was unsafe to be in the streets of Moscow after dark unless armed and escorted. The motive behind most crimes was simple theft, but the law punished all offences with such indiscriminate savagery that robbers usually killed both victims and witnesses to destroy all evidence.

Illiteracy was common even among the nobility, the gentry, and the clergy, and the peasantry was wholly illiterate. But the Muscovites, apart from a handful of boyars and churchmen, gave no thought to their abysmal ignorance. On the contrary, blinded by religious and national pride, they even protested their own superiority over other peoples.

Illiteracy and ignorance were open to reform, but corruption seemed ingrained in the Muscovite character. Cheating and lying were normal in every walk of life; extortion and bribery were the accepted methods of officials; justice was non-existent. The *prikazi*, or government ministries in Moscow responsible for administration, and the *voevodi*, or governors of each of the provincial districts into which the country was divided, were inefficient, indolent, but, above all, corrupt. Foreigners complained bitterly that they were a people with "no shame of lying, no blush for detected fraud," and Dr. Collins bluntly called them "false, truce-breakers, subtle foxes, and ravenous wolves."[13]

In short, Muscovy bore all the marks of a depraved and barbarous society and only the more observant foreigners noted the endurance, courage, and patience of her people. General Manstein, who spent most of his life in Russia, found them at least as intelligent as men of like station in other European countries.[14] Olearius considered that they were "very handy," and able to imitate anything they saw done, and that they were good soldiers, if properly led. But these were minor concessions.[15] Foreigners saw the country when it was stagnating and backward; they described this as its permanent condition, and, understandably, they saw no further.

But Muscovy in fact was a land of unlimited natural wealth, inhabited by a people of great strength and ability. Factors of history and geography had exposed her to frequent invasion and foreign occupation, retarding her development. In isolation from Europe, the people had failed to create new standards; they needed outside stimulus and instruction.

At last, however, in the seventeenth century the barriers of their western frontiers began to crumble, and the Orthodox Church, its great authority weakened, was no longer able to uphold so obstinately the conservatism that opposed all innovation. Western ideas and teachers began to flow a little more freely into Muscovy. In the reign of Peter, the flow was to become an overwhelming flood.

Western influence became an important factor in Muscovy only in the seventeenth century, although the policy of borrowing from the West began long before, when Ivan the Great (1462-1505) first engaged foreign architects, engineers, and soldiers. His successors continued this policy. But it was on a scale so small that it hardly disturbed the surface of Muscovite life.

The Time of Troubles, however, awakened the Tsar and his leading men to the fact that the old mounted militia was no longer a sufficient defence against Western enemies. They therefore enlisted foreign officers and soldiers, and began reforming the Muscovite army on Western lines. But, despite urgent preparations, Muscovy still suffered a further humiliating defeat at the hands of the Poles.

The government nevertheless persevered with Western reforms. Since mercenaries had proved unreliable, and the cost of importing arms was more than the treasury could bear, the policy in future was to concentrate more on the training of the Muscovites in Western methods, and on the manufacture of arms and equipment in Muscovy. Metallurgists and engineers were enlisted and special concessions attracted Western capital and *expertise*. Mineral surveys revealed rich iron ore deposits in several places. Andrei Vinius, a Dutch merchant, in 1632 set up foundries near Tula, which proved to be the beginning of Russian industry. In 1644 a Hamburg merchant, Marselis, established foundries in the basin of the upper

Volga, north of Moscow. Soon other industries were following in the wake of the foundries.

While military, industrial, and economic innovations came direct from the West with foreign experts, Western education and cultural influence reached Muscovy mainly through the Ukraine. South-western Russia, including Kiev, had long been under Roman Catholic Polish rule, although the population, except for the landowning aristocracy, was Russian and of the Orthodox faith. The Jesuits had a free hand, but their intensive missionary activity among the Ortho-dox Slavs won few converts. Zealously defending their faith and their way of life, these Orthodox Slavs were stimulated to intellectual activity. They adopted Jesuit methods, studied Latin, and absorbed elements of Western culture to such effect that in 1633 Peter Mogila, Metropolitan of Kiev, founded an academy which soon became the centre of Orthodox learning, but it was Orthodox learning revital-ized, and in part transformed, by Latin influence.

Moscow, therefore, turned to Kiev for teachers, and this marked the beginning of a new interest in education among the more ad-vanced men at the Tsar's court, and no one did more than a certain Rtishchev to encourage this interest.

A saint and a scholar, Rtishchev was also an able landowner and an intelligent man of affairs. Although he belonged to the old Mus-covite tradition, he acknowledged that Muscovy was backward and that the introduction of reforms from the West was inevitable. He considered education the first and most important field of reform, and with his own money he built a monastery near Moscow, where he assembled thirty learned monks from Little Russia, giving them the task of translating books into Russian, and teaching Greek, Latin, and other subjects. Even more important was the great moral authority that he lent to the new ideas of education in Muscovy.

In the latter part of Tsar Alexei's reign, Western influence at court became more pronounced. Permanent diplomatic residents were now maintained in some European capitals, and their des-patches, reporting the customs and entertainments abroad, were eagerly read by the Tsar and his ministers. Muscovites were still for-bidden under pain of death to travel abroad without express permis-sion, but a section of the nobility had begun to realize that Western societies enjoyed a comfort and grace of living that their own lives lacked. Certain nobles embraced Western style clothing; mirrors, clocks, and decorations appeared in their houses which had always been bare but for ikons. They seized on the trappings of Western life, without appreciating that these were the fruits of a vigorous society which had laboured and advanced, while Muscovy herself had stood still.

The change in Tsar Alexei's attitude towards Western entertainments was especially significant. Early in his reign he had issued an ukaz forbidding his subjects "to dance, play games, or watch them; at wedding feasts either to sing or to play on instruments; to give over one's soul to perdition in such pernicious and lawless practices as word-play, farces, and magic."[16] This was merely a repetition of the strict laws of earlier tsars, suppressing all gaiety as ungodly. Gradually, however, Alexei himself deviated from the letter and spirit of his own law. He appointed musicians to play to him, and even in 1672, having heard of the theatres in other capitals and of dramatic performances in the Foreign Quarter, ordered a theatre to be built at Pre-obrazhenskoe, and a play to be performed before him—appropriately it was in honour of the birth of Tsarevich Peter.

But the influence of Western ideas was still restricted to the Tsar's court, and the innovations, to which it gave rise in the army and in other fields, were still on a scale too small to make any real impression. The old boyars remained obdurately antagonistic to what they considered the corruption of Muscovy. The people reacted strongly against everything foreign. Religious bigotry, nationalism, and xenophobia had for centuries moulded their attitude towards the West and all that came from it. Throughout the country their powerful, though silent, opposition leant with massive weight against all change and reform.

Nevertheless, the government continued to look westwards. Tsar Alexei was often indecisive and inconsistent, but he at least supported the plans of his chosen advisers, especially Ordin-Nashchokin, Rtish-chev, and Matveev. Slowly the policy of westernization gained some momentum, and the existence, beyond the eastern limits of Moscow, of the Foreign Quarter added to it. This Foreign Quarter, or *Nemet-skaya Sloboda*, was sometimes called in English, the German Quarter, because *nemets*, from the Russian word meaning "dumb," was at first the name by which the Slavs described Germans, but the word early came to mean all European foreigners.

The Western soldiers, engineers, doctors, merchants, and artisans, who found their way into Muscovy in the seventeenth century, congregated in this Foreign Quarter on the banks of the stream, Yauza. The Quarter had existed in the time of Ivan the Terrible, but had been disbanded twice, the second time during the Time of Troubles. Early in the reign of Tsar Mikhail, the foreigners made their way back to Moscow, but xenophobic crowds molested them. When they took to wearing Muscovite clothes to avoid attention, an ukaz required them to wear their national dress, so that they might not enter an Orthodox church unobserved, and so that Muscovites might avoid the contamination of contact with them. Priests and others then raised an outcry that it was a profanation to allow heretics to live and worship within the precincts of Holy Moscow. In 1652, therefore, a further ukaz forbade the sale of houses in the city to foreigners, who were resettled at the original site beyond the city limits.

The Quarter, the population of which in 1652 was about fifteen hundred, grew throughout the reign of Tsar Alexei until it was about one fifth the total size of Moscow itself. The Dutch, English, Scots and Germans were its most numerous inhabitants. The Scots included such illustrious names as Gordon, Graham, Drummond, Dalziel, Crawfurd, Leslie, Bruce, Menzies, Ogilvie, and others which recur and leave their mark in each era of Russian history. Frenchmen were few; the Scots were the only Roman Catholics, and they were tolerated because Cromwell, whom Muscovites condemned as a regicide, had proscribed them.

Although multilingual and diverse in origin, the Westerners lived in harmony. They made use of the artisans among them to build a pleasant town. The streets were broad and lined with trees; the houses were attractive with steep gables in the Dutch style, and had gardens. The Quarter formed a contrast to Muscovite villages which were untidy and untended, and in which the houses stood until they fell or were burnt to the ground.

Within the Quarter the foreigners enjoyed wide freedom and, except for the Roman Catholics, even freedom of worship. Three Lutheran churches and two schools met their religious and educational needs. Their community fell naturally into an ordered society, reflecting the Europe of their origin. The numerous professional class gave it a large proportion of cultured and learned men, many of whom contrived to keep in touch with their own countries. General Patrick Gordon received the reports of the proceedings of the Royal

Society in London. The diplomatic representatives of England, Holland, Sweden, and other countries, who resided in the Quarter, received regular mail from their capitals. They were able to follow the politics and developments in science and literature of western Europe, and they made the Quarter an oasis of civilization in the mediaeval wilderness of Muscovy.

The influence of the Foreign Quarter on the course of Russian history is incalculable. It epitomized the life of western Europe and represented for the Muscovites a society that was both attractive and dangerous. Forbidden to travel abroad, they had little conception of other ways of living. The Quarter gave them new criteria with which to compare their own traditional way of life at a time when it was moribund. Slowly, by a process of attrition, the Quarter's example of the new wore away the authority of the old. But again only a small section of Muscovite society felt this insidious influence. West Europeans, if they mixed with the Muscovites at all, mixed with boyars and merchants. The peasants carried on their own traditional way of life, dominated by the soil and the seasons, by holy days and the demands of their masters, and they were untouched by the new ideas.

Of Tsar Alexei's chosen advisers three—Nikon, Rtishchev, and Ordin-Nashchokin—contributed notably to the preparation for Peter's reign. The importance of Nikon was that he seriously weakened the power of the church both in the country and in relation to the throne. Rtishchev gave early encouragement to education and lent a moral authority to the policy of reform and westernization. But the contribution of Ordin-Nashchokin was most important of all: he reformulated Muscovite foreign policy, and first gave expression to many of the reforms that Peter was to introduce.

Ordin-Nashchokin brought to the service of the Tsar a brilliant and original mind, vision, and humanity. He was born a member of the provincial nobility of the Pskov region. Bordering on the Baltic states, Pskov had always enjoyed frequent contact with Germans, Swedes, and other West Europeans, and this had freed the region from the suffocating conservatism of Moscow. Here Ordin-Nashchokin obtained a broad education, which included subjects considered heretical by the Muscovites. He first attracted attention in the reign of Tsar Mikhail; and Tsar Alexei, recognizing in him a man of outstanding ability, made full use of his services.[17]

Tempestuous, umbrageous, outspoken, and impatient, he made many enemies, but from his Tsar he had only sympathy and understanding. A close bond existed between them, and the quality linking the two men, and also Rtishchev, was their sense of humanity. In his policy and administration Ordin-Nashchokin's first consideration was for the Tsar's subjects. He thought of the governed not as pawns to be moved as required by state policy, but as fellow men for whom the state existed. It was an attitude well in advance not only of the ideas of seventeenth century Muscovy, but of seventeenth century Europe.

It was while head of the Foreign Office and chief minister that his restless mind had full rein and ranged over the whole machinery of Muscovite government. Diplomacy and foreign affairs were his main concern, but he also understood that military and diplomatic success needed the support of a healthy administration and a sound national economy. He stormed against the indolence and bureaucracy of officials, and against their corruption and nepotism. He constantly sought to develop trade and industry, and tried to open up trade routes with Central Asia and Persia and with the Far East. His proposals included the reorganization of the army, the establishment of a fleet in the Baltic and Caspian seas, a regular postal service, and the improvement of towns by the laying out of gardens.

In diplomacy, as in other fields, Ordin-Nashchokin was a man of high principles. Unfortunately these very principles finally brought him into conflict with Tsar Alexei, who refused to return Kiev to Poland, although the Treaty of Andrussovo called for the surrender of the city after two years. He petitioned for release from office, retired to a monastery, and died in 1680.

Ordin-Nashchokin became Foreign Minister and chief adviser to Tsar Alexei at a time when the conduct of Muscovite foreign policy was vacillating and confused. But the objectives were clear. Tsar Ivan the Great had formulated them when, having discarded the Tatar yoke, the Muscovites emerged from the Asiatic twilight to find that they had still to struggle, if they were to survive as a nation.

These objectives were two, and they continued as the basis of Russian policy into the twentieth century. First, Moscow was to bring under her rule the western territories inhabited by Orthodox Slavs. No less than four Russian lands formed part of the vast Lithuanian-

Polish state; they were Black Russia (the lands to the east of the Niemen River), White Russia, Red Russia (the region of Galicia), and Little Russia or Russia Minor or the Ukraine (embracing the lands between the Dniester and the Dnieper rivers). The second objective was to extend the frontiers of Muscovy to the shores of the Baltic and Black seas so that she might trade freely with the countries of western Europe and the Mediterranean.

The first objective involved Muscovy in war with Poland, and the second in war with Sweden and with the Ottoman Porte, and during the seventeenth century the Muscovites suffered constant defeat. But it remained a national Muscovite aspiration to recover access to the Baltic and, avenging the humiliations inflicted by the Poles, to recover at least White Russia and Little Russia.

In further campaigns against Poland in the reign of Tsar Alexei, Muscovy fared badly, but the Poles, too, were exhausted. The threat that the Ottoman Porte might enter the war made Muscovites and Poles come to terms. The Treaty of Andrussovo resulted in 1667, and from this date Poland declined, while Muscovy grew in strength.

This treaty also marked the beginning of closer relations between the two countries, although it did not erase the bitter enmity between their peoples. Further, the treaty was the first expression of the new Muscovite foreign policy, which was the work of Ordin-Nashchokin. To him the real enemy was Sweden who had, after many conquests, finally exacted Ingria from Tsar Mikhail, thus closing the Baltic to Muscovy. Ordin-Nashchokin, therefore, laboured to build up a coalition against Sweden, which would enable Muscovy to regain access to the Baltic. He gave this policy firm foundations, and it was to be adopted by Peter.

Throughout the seventeenth century, Muscovy remained weak and thwarted in her national aspirations. Internally the country stagnated. The discontent of the people began to give way to hopelessness. A more turbulent people would have demanded reforms, or have exploded in revolution. But reform in Russia has usually been imposed from above, and the Russian people have always been slow to rebel. Their religion and their inborn humility, their stamina and their patience, have led them to submit. Only when hope has gone and life has become insupportable have they rebelled. Then a dark destructive fury has surged through them and, like the blinded Samson, goaded beyond all endurance, they have sought to pull away the pillars of the society that filled their lives with suffering, and to destroy themselves with it. The fact that the century was a period of popular risings was a measure of the harsh misery that oppressed all but the few.

The continued absence of a strong tsar was another factor contributing to the dark mood of the Muscovites. The Romanov dynasty had popular support, but a curse seemed to lie over it. Of the first four tsars of this line, three were just sixteen when they ascended the throne, and one was fourteen; three were weak and sickly; and Alexei who enjoyed good health was not a strong ruler. Known to his subjects as *tishaishy Tsar*, the gentlest Tsar, he was in his upbringing, his piety, and his fondness for ceremonial, representative of the old Muscovite traditions so beloved by his people, but from which his son was to break sharply.

It was in his observance of his religion that Alexei came closest to the old Muscovite ideal. His day began at 4 A.M. with prayers in his private chapel, after which the Tsaritsa joined him and together they attended Matins in one of the palace churches. Since early morning the boyars, secretaries, and advisers had been gathering in the palace anterooms. All bowed to the ground several times "on first seeing the bright eyes of the Tsar," and, after brief discussion of the business of the day, the whole company went to late morning Mass in one of the many Kremlin churches. This service lasted two hours or more, and at convenient times during it the Tsar received reports and issued instructions. Even while conducting state affairs he was punctilious in carrying out the formalities of the ritual.

In Lent and at church festivals, Alexei spent nearly the whole day in church, standing for five or six hours at a stretch, and making as many as fifteen hundred prostrations to the ground during the service. He was equally strict in observing the fasts, which were frequent and rigorous. His piety was real and not limited to the forms of his faith. He belonged to the Orthodox tradition of selflessness and spiritual striving, from which the church had drifted. His was a way of life fit for a monk, however, and not for a tsar who bore the whole responsibility for the affairs of his country.

Discontent, rebellion, and mounting crisis marked his reign. The state of Muscovy demanded an extraordinary ruler, and he could not meet this demand. But he somehow held his tsardom from dissolution and, unwittingly, he helped prepare the way for his son's cataclysmic reign.

By the time of Peter's birth, the road ahead had been sign-posted, and the forerunners had outlined many reforms. But they were reforms that would have to be imposed from above on a stubborn people in whom they would arouse only hostility. In the vastness of Muscovy this was a task beyond the strength and capacity of ministers and of tsars—until the advent of Peter.

CHAPTER II

The Early Years

1672-1682

PETER was born in the Kremlin Palace in Moscow early on the morning of 30 May 1672. He was Tsar Alexei's fourteenth child and sixth son, but his birth was an event of exceptional importance: he was the first child of the Tsar's second wife, and he was an heir to the throne.

All five sons of Alexei's marriage with Tsaritsa Maria Miloslavskaya had proved weaklings. Three had died and of the remaining two, Feodor was sickly and Ivan was half-blind, defective in speech, and cretinous. Neither was expected to survive Alexei, who was just over forty years old. Muscovites of all classes feared that the Tsar might leave no heir, and on the death of Tsaritsa Maria Miloslavskaya it was the general hope that he would marry again; the announcement in February 1670 of his intention to take a wife was received with relief and enthusiasm.

It was through his chief minister, Artemon Matveev, that Alexei met his second wife. Matveev had married a Hamilton, one of the Scots family which had taken refuge in Muscovy at the turn of the century, and, as far as possible in Moscow, he lived as a Western European. This way of life attracted Alexei who, although it was almost unprecedented for the Tsar to visit one of his subjects, sometimes went informally to his house. On one visit he met Natalya Naryshkina, daughter of an impoverished landowner of Tatar origin, entrusted to Matveev's care and, falling in love with her on sight, he decided to marry her.

36

The young Tsaritsa brought a freshness into the somnolent formality of the Kremlin. Alexei was devoted to her and constantly at her side. His solicitude for her increased when she became pregnant, and the birth of a strong and healthy son completed his happiness. He spent the day of the birth in thanksgiving and the ceremonies continued for some days, culminating in the baptism of Tsarevich Peter in the Chudov Monastery on 29 June 1672, the holy day of his patron saint.[1]

Peter was a boisterous child and he developed rapidly. The luxury of the Muscovite court surrounded him. A suite of fourteen well-born women cared for his needs in the apartments specially built for him in the Kremlin. His nurseries were richly decorated and overflowed with toys. Six ikon painters of Kostroma made him a picture book. At the age of one he received a wooden horse, with a leather saddle secured with silver nails, and a bridle decorated with emeralds. He also had drums and then bows and arrows. Later more drums, cymbals, and other instruments bore witness to a love of noise which he never outgrew. When he was two, he had a toy boat, presented by Matveev who bought it from a foreigner. It was an unusual and portentous toy to be found at this time in the nursery of the Tsarevich.

Peter did not play alone, for the Tsarevich always had a group of chosen companions who bore the special title of *komnatnie stolniki*, or stewards. They included Andrei Matveev, son of the minister; Avtonom Golovin, and Gavril Golovkin, all destined to play important parts in the momentous years ahead. He also had a retinue of dwarfs, who served as escorts and even postilions.

The Austrian secretary saw him in a state procession in September 1675, and reported that chamberlains with two hundred runners preceded the Tsaritsa's carriage, "then followed the small carriage of the youngest prince, all glittering with gold, drawn by four small ponies; at the side of it rode four dwarfs on ponies and another behind."[2]

His father, the Tsar, made frequent journeys out of Moscow, either to observe religious festivals or to visit his country residences. He enjoyed hawking and hunting, and maintained vast establishments of hawks as well as stables containing hundreds of horses and a host of grooms to tend them. Usually in the autumn he made the journey of sixty miles to the monastery-fortress of Troitsa to celebrate the festival of St. Sergius, its founder. Tsaritsa Natalya could not accompany him in 1673, because she was expecting another child, and on 22 August she gave birth to Peter's sister, Tsarevna Natalya. But whenever possible Alexei took his Tsaritsa and his family with him.

Suddenly, when Peter was three and a half, the serenity of his nursery was disrupted. His father, normally so healthy and energetic, caught a chill. His illness at first aroused no anxiety, but then he grew worse and death was seen to be near. He gave his formal blessing to his eldest son, Tsarevich Feodor, as his heir and successor, and on 29 January 1676 he died.

Feodor succeeded to the throne without question. His mother's family, the Miloslavsky, who had been displaced by the Naryshkini on the Tsar's second marriage, at once set about restoring their fortunes. But the change at court was not dramatic and immediate. Although only fifteen years old, Feodor was by nature almost saintly, like his father, and he showed no desire to victimize his stepmother or her son. Nevertheless, he was a Miloslavsky and unable to resist for long the pressure of his family.

The first blow struck at Natalya and the Naryshkini was the exile of Matveev. The Miloslavsky, fearing his influence at court where he was popular, had turned the Tsar against him, and he was sentenced on a false charge to life imprisonment at Pustozersk in the Archangel province. It was an unhappy time for Natalya who remained in the Kremlin, filled with anxiety for the future of her son and herself.

Meanwhile Peter's upbringing took its normal course. In 1679, when he was seven, he was removed from the care of the women and entrusted to tutors. This was the stage when the Tsarevich normally started his formal education. But it is not known when Peter began lessons, although at the age of eight he was learning to read and write. His first teachers are also unknown, but from 1683 until 1690 Nikita Zotov, a clerk of one of the prikazi, gave him lessons. Legend relates that Zotov showed him pictures and told him heroic stories from Russian history that so fired his imagination that he vowed to place his country among the great powers of Europe. The legend may contain some truth. Certainly Zotov won Peter's affection and became one of his regular companions; he was also a great drunkard and later acted as Prince-Pope, president of the College of Drunkenness (All-joking, All-drunken Assembly).

Feodor reigned for less than six years. He was ailing and not the man to deal with the problems of Muscovy. He gave what time and strength he had to pressing ahead with Western reforms, and he advanced a little further the preparations for the reign of his stepbrother.

The death of Feodor on 27 April 1682 raised the problem of the succession to the throne. Muscovy had no law of succession, but it was the custom for the Tsar to present his eldest or chosen son to the people when he was nearly of age and to declare him formally as his heir. Feodor had, however, neither left an heir, nor named a successor. The two Tsarevichi, Ivan and Peter, remained with equal title to the throne, and the general preference was for Peter whose lively intelligence, glowing health, and fine physique gave promise of a strong tsar. Nor did the Muscovites overlook the fact that, since both Ivan and Peter were minors, a regent would rule, and they favoured Natalya, guided by Matveev, rather than a continuance of the Miloslavsky in power.

After the ceremony of taking leave of the dead Tsar, the boyars, meeting in the audience chamber with the Patriarch and the Church Council, decided that the Assembly of the Land should be summoned. Many provincial delegates were already in Moscow, having come earlier to consider certain taxation proposals; other representatives stayed more or less permanently in the city.

The Patriarch at once called them to the Kremlin and, although hastily convened, this assembly was a fairly representative body. Unanimously the delegates proclaimed Peter, and the Patriarch then blessed Peter as Tsar of Muscovy. The people dispersed to their homes relieved and satisfied that Tsaritsa Natalya would be Regent and Matveev would be her chief minister. They reckoned without Tsarevna Sofia.

Sofia, one of Tsar Alexei's eight daughters by his first wife, was a remarkable woman. She was at this time twenty-five years old, and she had the intelligence, strength of will, and vitality that her brothers lacked. Also she was fired with ambition and in revolt against Muscovite customs. She had emerged from the anonymity of the terem after the death of her father, and her influence had grown during Feodor's reign. The Miloslavsky had expected that Ivan would succeed Feodor, and that Sofia would be Regent in effect, if not in name.

The succession of Peter took them by surprise and it endangered Sofia's ambitions. She had always hated her stepmother as a rival, and she feared now that Natalya would insist on her retiring to a nunnery, which was the usual fate of the tsarevni. Stirred by this fear

and by her resentment, she fought desperately to displace Tsar Peter
and the Naryshkini.

At the funeral of Feodor she contrived to appeal to the people and
to unsettle popular opinion throughout the city. Natalya remained
inactive, alone, and afraid, in the Kremlin Palace. She did not understand how Sofia and the Miloslavsky had managed to inflame the
people against her and her family. Anxiously she waited for Matveev
to arrive. She had summoned him to Moscow immediately on the
proclamation of Peter as Tsar, and had been expecting him daily. But
two weeks passed before Matveev reached Moscow, and during this
brief period the Naryshkini antagonized most of the Muscovites, and
especially the streltsi.

The streltsi were a privileged force. They not only received pay,
food, and clothing from the Tsar, but also had the right to engage in
trade and, exempt from taxes, many grew rich. The main body of
the streltsi was always stationed in Moscow, occupying a special quarter outside the city. Their duties were not onerous. They mounted
sentries; they did some fire fighting; on state occasions they lined the
procession route and provided an escort. In time of war they acted as
a shield, while the Muscovite militia was mobilized. They served as
the spearhead of the army in attack and had distinguished themselves
in several campaigns. But privilege had corrupted them and discipline
had grown slack. Many among them were Old Believers and for that
reason in a rebellious mood. Their discontent had increased in the
reign of Tsar Feodor, and shortly before his death, one regiment presented a petition, alleging that their colonel had withheld their pay
and forced them to work on his estate even during Holy Week.
Prince Yuri Dolgoruky, their joint commander, ordered the strelets
who brought the petition to be knouted for insolence,[3] but his comrades attacked his guard and released him.

Knouting was a savage but common punishment in Muscovy. The
knout was a whip with a thick thong of leather some three and a half
feet in length, wielded by a skilled knoutmaster. For less serious
crimes the offender was lifted on the back of another man, and the
knoutmaster laid on the number of strokes ordered, each stroke flaying
the flesh and biting to the bone.

For serious crimes, the offender's arms were tied behind his back,
and he was hoisted from the ground by a rope tied to his wrists. To
make sure that his arms were pulled out of joint, a log or other weight

was tied to his feet. The knoutmaster then laid on to his bare back the strokes ordered, or he continued until ordered to stop, whereupon he took the offender down and put his arms in joint again. In some cases a man or woman might be subjected to this treatment three times in the course of three or four weeks, if it was considered that full confession had not been made. In extreme cases the victim was taken down and tied to a pole, held by two men; his back, raw from the lashes of the knout, was then slowly roasted over a fire, while he was examined further, and called on to confess. It is said that some survived this ordeal.

The rescue of this strelets by his comrades fired the whole streltsi quarter. Seventeen regiments combined to demand severe punishments for their colonels. On the day after the funeral of Tsar Feodor, they presented their petitions, and Natalya and her advisers took fright. Without any investigation, she condemned the colonels to be deprived of their rank and punished with *batogi*. These were rods, the thickness of a man's finger, which were used indiscriminately for minor offences, although sometimes they caused death. The offender lay with his back bare, his arms and legs extended, while two men wielded the batogi, one kneeling on his arms and the other on his legs.[4]

The streltsi took charge of the batogi, causing their colonels to be cruelly beaten, after which they returned to their quarter and dealt savagely with the regiments that had refused to join them.

Inflamed by drink and bloodshed the streltsi were in a dangerous mood. The one man who had any influence over them was Prince Ivan Khovansky, a braggart and an ambitious rogue, who at that time supported the Miloslavsky. He played on their fears, telling them they would be ill-treated by the boyars under the regency of Natalya, that their children would become slaves, and, worst of all, that foreigners would come to power and destroy Orthodoxy.

Sofia's plans depended on the streltsi. With her uncle, Ivan Miloslavsky, Khovansky, and a small trusted band of streltsi, she plotted to use them to bring about the downfall of her rivals. Already she had drawn up a list of the Naryshkini and their supporters who were to be killed. The next step was to harness the streltsi to her purpose, and it was not difficult.

Natalya had angered them by appointing certain new officers to their regiments. By planting rumours, Sofia and her confederates quickly turned their anger to fury. Soon all the streltsi were convinced that the Naryshkini had poisoned Tsar Feodor, and were plotting to murder Ivan. They were on the point of revolt, but still Sofia did not give the signal, for she was awaiting Matveev's return.

Matveev reached Moscow on 11 May to be greeted by the Tsaritsa as a father and saviour. With the exception of the Miloslavsky, all the boyars and representatives of the church and the merchants called to express their pleasure at his return. Of their own accord streltsi of all regiments conveyed their respects to him. For a moment the tensions of the city relaxed.

This welcome probably led Matveev to underestimate the dangers of the situation, or he may have thought that they would pass. Whatever the reason, he did not take the prompt action needed. Meanwhile Sofia and her party were again stirring up the streltsi, and the distraction caused by Matveev's return was quickly forgotten. The regiments were again ready to revolt, and the time was ripe.

CHAPTER III

The Revolt of the Streltsi

1682

ON the morning of 15 May 1682, two horsemen galloped into the streltsi quarter shouting: "The Naryshkini have strangled the Tsarevich Ivan!" The horsemen were Alexander Miloslavsky and Peter Tolstoy, both in close league with Sofia. Alarms sounded and the whole quarter stirred. Streltsi grasped their weapons and, with banners flying, marched towards the Kremlin, calling for the blood of the traitors.[1]

Within the Kremlin the day's business was proceeding normally. The Council of Boyars had met and Matveev was just leaving the council chamber when the news reached him that rebel streltsi were swarming through the outer suburbs and making for the Kremlin. He sent for the Patriarch, gave orders for the gates to be shut, and for the Stremyanny regiment, the duty regiment of the day, to stay at their posts to defend Tsar Peter and his family.

It was too late. The streltsi had already reached the Kremlin. They surged into the square in front of the Granovitaya Palace, sweeping with them the men of the duty regiment, who quitted their posts and joined the mob. They halted at the foot of the Red Staircase, the grand entrance to the palace, and demanded the heads of the Naryshkini.

Matveev, learning from their shouts the reason for the outbreak, advised Tsaritsa Natalya to show herself with the young Tsar and the Tsarevich Ivan. Natalya hesitated. It called for courage to face the howling mob, but she had no alternative.

43

Holding the hands of Peter and Ivan, she stepped out onto the staircase. A hush came over the square. She walked with the two boys to the top of the staircase and raising her voice called to them: "Here is the Lord Tsar Peter Alexeevich! Here is the Lord Tsarevich Ivan Alexeevich. Thanks be to God they are well and have not suffered at the hands of traitors!" The mob paused. A few, bolder than the rest, went up the staircase to Ivan, and, face to face with him, asked if he was truly alive and unharmed. He stammered a reassurance and, bewildered, they retreated down the stairs. Then a handful of streltsi started to clamour for certain boyars on the list which Sofia had prepared. The mob was growing unruly again.[2]

Matveev now stepped forward, accompanied by the Patriarch. The streltsi listened as he spoke quietly and paternally, referring to their great deeds in the past and asking how they could threaten violence to those surrounding their Tsar. He told them to disperse now that they had seen Tsarevich Ivan alive and well and realized that they had been tricked by lies. The Patriarch, speaking with all the authority of his great office, also admonished them. The revolt wavered and might have died away damply.

At this point Prince Mikhail Dolgoruky, head of the Streltsi Office and, jointly with his eighty-year-old father, commander of all the regiments, strode to the top of the Red Staircase. Dolgoruky was a fearless, foolish man. He roundly abused his troops, threatened them with the knout, and ordered them back to their quarters. His threats infuriated them. They rushed the staircase, seized him and, lifting him above their heads, threw him over the balustrade, to fall onto the pikes held by comrades below. Others then butchered his body, bespattering the mob with his blood.

No sooner was Dolgoruky dead than a band of streltsi, led by Sofia's agents, appeared from the shadow of the palace wall, shouting for Matveev's head. Tsaritsa Natalya dropped Peter's hand and threw her arms around Matveev to protect him. The streltsi tore him away and hurled him over the balustrade onto the pikes.

Lusting for more bloodshed, they then stormed the Red Staircase, sweeping Tsar Peter and his mother to the wall. They broke open the palace doors, calling for the heads of Ivan Naryshkin and other boyars. They raged through the rooms and desecrated the altars of the chapels in their search. They found a number of victims and, carrying them to the Red Staircase, cast them down. Other streltsi dragged the mangled bodies to the place of execution on the Red Square, where they hacked them to pieces. Only one of Natalya's brothers, Afanasy Naryshkin, lost his life on this first day.

Night began to fall and the mass of the streltsi withdrew to their quarters. They posted guards on the gates of the Kremlin, sealing off all escape, and swore to return next day for Ivan Naryshkin and Natalya's three younger brothers, Lev, Martemyan and Feodor. All four were hiding in the apartments of Tsarevna Natalya, Peter's eight-year-old sister, which had not been searched.

At dawn next day the streltsi streamed back into the Kremlin. But still Ivan Naryshkin and his brothers eluded them and, deprived of their chief prey, they grew more savage in their threats. The Danish resident, Butenant von Rosenbusch was involved in the search for one victim, and a detachment of streltsi conducted him to the Kremlin. He was in fear for his own life as he was led through the streets, littered with mutilated bodies. His escort took him to the Red Staircase, where Tsaritsa Natalya, Tsarevna Sofia, Prince Khovansky and others were standing. Seeing the resident, Khovansky turned to Sofia for instructions. She gave orders that he should be returned safely to his house, and to these orders he owed his life.[3]

Sofia was clearly in command, and she could, through Khovansky and Ivan Miloslavsky, have called a halt to the massacre. Matveev, whom she had feared most, was dead, together with a number of boyars whom she did not trust; Tsaritsa Natalya and Tsar Peter were at her mercy. But Ivan Naryshkin was still at large.

Returning on the third day the streltsi delivered their ultimatum: they would kill all the boyars in the Kremlin if Ivan Naryshkin was not surrendered. Sofia then approached Tsaritsa Natalya and, speaking loudly in front of the assembled boyars, said: "Your brother will not escape the streltsi. Nor is it right that we should perish on his account."[4]

It was a moment of tragedy and terror for Natalya. She had endured much during the three days of the revolt and now she was called on to sacrifice her own brother. The alternative was a massacre of the boyars, which might end with the murder of her son, Peter, and with her own death. Going with Sofia into the Church of the Miraculous Ikon, Natalya ordered her servants to bring her brother. He came and behaved bravely, as he received the last rites. Natalya then took from Sofia's hands the holy ikon of the Mother of God and, weeping bitterly, blessed him with it. Holding this ikon, Ivan walked to the church doors, and as he appeared the mob surged forward with a wild shout. For some hours they inflicted inhuman tortures on him, trying to extract confessions that he had murdered Tsar Feodor and plotted to seize the throne. He refused to answer. When he was nearly dead, his arms and legs broken and hanging grotesquely, they dragged him off to the Red Square where they hacked his body to pieces.

The streltsi now assembled at the Red Staircase again. They declared that they were satisfied, and that they would gladly die for the Tsar, the Tsarevich, and the Tsarevni. After further protesting their loyalty, they dispersed to their own quarters. But they had tasted power and could not resist the temptation to plunder and terrorize the city. Sofia alone was without fear, and they looked to her as their ruler. But she was determined to rule in name as well as in fact.

On 23 May the streltsi, prompted by Sofia's agents, sent spokesmen to Khovansky, whom she had appointed as their commander, with a petition that Ivan and Peter should occupy the throne together. The boyars assembled in the Granovitaya Palace to approve the proposal. The Assembly of the Land was hurriedly convened and it agreed formally that the two Tsars should reign jointly. Two days later, on another petition of the streltsi, Tsar Ivan was declared senior to Tsar Peter. No mention had yet been made of Sofia's regency. But, on 29 May, spokesmen informed the boyars that the streltsi wished Sofia to be regent during the minority of the two Tsars. The Patriarch and the boyars formally asked her to accept this office, and she thus achieved the supreme power.

During this turbulent period Sofia dominated the stage, overshadowing the tragic figure of Natalya who, thrust into the role of regent, had neither the courage nor the ability to support it. Contemporary accounts describe the parts played by others, but make no reference to Peter. One report stated that he stood quietly at his mother's side throughout the terror, his expression unchanging, and that his fearlessness impressed all who saw him, particularly the streltsi. But this report, based on hearsay evidence, was recorded some fifteen years after the event.[5] Peter was to show on several occasions in his early years that he could be frightened and that he could give way to panic. If he stood motionless with unchanging expression on the Red Staircase, it was probably because he was petrified with fear.

The revolt of the streltsi had a tremendous impact on him and proved one of the strongest formative influences in his life. He was at this time just ten years old, but advanced beyond his years physically and mentally. He undoubtedly realized what danger each day threatened his mother and himself. The experience shattered the happy security which had cradled him while his father was alive, and had continued during the reign of Feodor. It taught him the meaning of danger and fear. Moreover it was probably responsible for the mad rages that in later years would suddenly seize him, making it unsafe to be near him, and for the ugly twitching that contorted his handsome face throughout his life.

The revolt also awakened in him a hatred of Moscow, the ancient home of the Orthodox tsars, and the spiritual and temporal centre of Muscovy. He was never again to feel at ease in the city. He avoided it, and months, even years, were to pass when he did not set foot inside the palace. As he grew older, he turned his back on Moscow, and moved the capital to the new city, which he himself built, looking out over the Baltic Sea and to the West.

CHAPTER IV

The Regency of Sofia

1682

ON her proclamation as regent, Sofia at once appointed Prince
Vasily Golitsyn to the highest office. He was born of a
great noble family, lived in magnificence, and by Muscovite
standards he was highly educated. He belonged to the small group
of forerunners who looked to the West for guidance. Sofia had met
him at the sick bed of her brother and had fallen wildly in love with
him.[1] Their partnership now seemed full of promise for Russia, but
it was to prove neither fruitful nor lasting.

Sofia soon found that supreme power eluded her. She had assumed
that she could keep the streltsi under her control and, mistakenly,
she relied on Khovansky. As commander of the streltsi he now became the channel between them and the government, and he held
the real power in the land. At a meeting of the Council of Boyars he
boasted, "I am the one who holds up the throne and, if it weren't
for me, the people of Moscow would be up to their knees in blood."[2]
At court and throughout the city he was hated, but the streltsi followed him.

Realizing the insecurity of her position Sofia turned to the landowning gentry, the men of service, on whom her grandfather, Tsar
Mikhail, and her father had relied for support. And so on 19 August
1682, with the two Tsars and the court, she left the Kremlin for
Kolomenskoe. She then sent couriers into the provinces, alleging a
plot by Khovansky and his son to kill the Tsars, and calling on
boyars and gentry to rally to their defence with men and arms.

48

Meanwhile she moved with the Tsars to the Troitsa, the largest and most famous of Russian monasteries, and the stronghold which had withstood long siege by the Poles. From here she sent a detachment of troops who arrested and beheaded Khovansky and his son.

In Moscow the streltsi, learning of the army of the boyars gathering at the Troitsa, were at first rebellious, and then humbly petitioned for forgiveness and the return of the Tsars to the Kremlin. Sofia admonished them severely and placed her trusted lieutenant, Shaklovity, in command of them. They gave pledges of loyal service in future and wallowed in self-recriminations, until she felt that their repentance was sufficient. On 16 November 1682, attended by a strong escort, she made a triumphant return to Moscow with the Tsars, but she now had the formidable task of governing the country.

The record of Sofia's seven-year regency is disappointing. An able and vital woman, she favoured Western reforms, and Vasily Golitsyn was one of the most enlightened men of the day. For all this, her government was reactionary. She set out to restore the old order and to suppress all signs of discontent. She passed harsh laws punishing fugitive serfs, and made furious efforts to crush the Old Believers. She regarded the May revolt as a dangerous precedent, and issued an official version of the revolt as an attempt by Khovansky to overthrow the regime. At no time during her regency did she attempt reform, but concentrated on foreign policy and sought through alliances and war to distract attention from the general discontent at home.

It was usual for the Tsar, on ascending the throne, to confirm treaties made by his predecessor. As soon as Ivan was proclaimed Tsar, Sofia sent couriers abroad for this purpose, and she then made haste to despatch embassies to Stockholm and Warsaw. Both Swedes and Poles had shown interest in the revolt of the streltsi and, with good reason, she feared that they might yet again take advantage of Muscovy's internal discords.

The Swedes welcomed the embassy, whose mission was to confirm that the Tsars would pursue a policy of peace and make no attempt to recover the Baltic territories, surrendered by Tsar Mikhail. The embassy to Warsaw, however, met with no great welcome. Its object was to confirm the Treaty of Andrussovo (1667), which had provided for the exchange of embassies at intervals to negotiate a permanent peace, but each past attempt had failed. Sofia's embassy, on the accession of Ivan and Peter, met with no greater success, for King Sobieski again insisted on the return of Kiev to Poland.

At this time Poland and Austria were at war with Turkey, and both were anxious to secure Muscovy as an ally. A severe defeat at the hands of the Turks and the threat of Turkish invasion made King Sobieski of Poland desperate for Muscovite help, and this somewhat softened his obstinacy over the terms demanded. Finally, in 1686, he reluctantly agreed to cede Kiev permanently, and with this obstacle out of the way, an alliance was quickly signed. For their part the Muscovites undertook to declare war on the Sultan of Turkey and the Crimean Khan, to defend Polish lands against Tatar attacks, and to wage war in the Crimea in the following year. These were onerous conditions, but Sofia and her government, jubilant over the cession of Kiev, accepted them willingly.

Popular feeling in Muscovy ran high against the Turks and Tatars, who had frequently raided Russian towns, carrying off the inhabitants to sell into slavery. In fact, by the end of the seventeenth century Russian slaves were to be found chained to the oars of galleys in every harbour of the Mediterranean. For a time Moscow bought peace with the Tatars by regular gifts of money, but the peace was at best uneasy.

On learning of this alliance between Muscovites and Poles, the Crimean Khan promptly sent raiding parties into Little Russia. Sofia began preparing for war. But many months passed in muddle and confusion, and it was not until May 1687, that the Muscovite army of nearly one hundred thousand men began moving southwards. Prince Vasily Golitsyn was in command and he was so afraid the Tatars would take him by surprise that his army moved with a tedious caution that sapped morale. At Bolshoi Lug, not far from the Dnieper River, he smelt the acrid odor of burning grass and away to the south he could see clouds of smoke. Fires caught quickly in the tall feather-grass of the steppes and, fanned by the wind, they spread, leaving mile upon mile blackened and parched.

Golitsyn decided to retreat, but sent a despatch to Moscow, reporting that the Khan, seeing the ordered ranks of the Muscovite army, had fled in terror to the farthest corner of the Crimea. His rearguard had set fire to the steppe, but the Russians had pursued them almost to Perekop. Golitsyn, having lost over forty-five thousand men through hardships and inadequate supplies without, in fact, once sighting the enemy, returned to Moscow on 14 September 1687 to be hailed as a hero.

Meanwhile, among the retreating Muscovites, a rumour spread that the Cossacks, not the Tatars, had started the steppe fires. It gained ready acceptance in Moscow where Hetman Samoilovich was already suspect. He had expressed strong disagreement with Sofia's policy of alliance with Poland and war against the Crimean Tatars, for, aside from his fear of Tatar reprisals against Little Russia, he regarded Poland as the main enemy. He was outspoken, and did not suspect that he was playing into the hands of Ivan Mazepa, his chief lieutenant.

Mazepa has been named among the greater heroes of romance, but, as with most romantic heroes, neither the man nor his career bear scrutiny. Of obscure Cossack origin, he obtained a good education in Kiev, and served as a page at the court of John Casimir V, where he learnt Polish, German, and courtly manners. He was handsome, with a strong personality and an eloquent tongue, but he was also unscrupulous and deceitful, and frequently involved in quarrels.

It was as a result of a quarrel that he fled the Polish court, and he turned up fourteen years later among the Cossacks of Little Russia. There he won the favour of Hetman Samoilovich who advanced him rapidly. Mazepa realized, however, that the Hetman was falling from favour in Moscow, and he was ambitious to succeed him. Secretly he obtained the signatures of several Cossack elders to a denunciation of his benefactor, and this he presented to Golitsyn with the request that the Tsars might appoint a new hetman. Moscow replied promptly to Golitsyn's report with instructions to arrest Samoilovich and to appoint a successor, and while strictly only the Cossack elders could elect the Hetman, they did not ignore the advice of Golitsyn. Mazepa became Hetman of the Cossacks of the western Ukraine, and he was to play a dramatic and treacherous role in the years to come.[3]

CHAPTER V

Peter at Play

1682-1689

PETER was a healthy boy with tremendous energy. Eager curiosity enlivened his movements and showed in the quick expression of his face. The secretary of the Swedish embassy saw both Tsars at a formal reception in 1683. They sat side by side on their elaborate silver throne, wearing ceremonial robes which glittered with precious stones; on Peter they were impressive, but they seemed too heavy for Ivan. He had pushed his crown forward on his head, lowered his eyes, and sat motionless, seeing nothing. Peter was alert and upright. When the Swedish ambassador presented his credentials, and etiquette obliged both Tsars to stand together and speak, Peter did not allow time enough for his brother to rise with him. He leapt to his feet and rapidly spoke the customary greeting: "His Royal Highness, our brother Charles of Sweden, is he in good health?" Peter was then eleven years old, but to the Swedish secretary, he seemed in build and intelligence like a boy of sixteen.[1]

The seven years of Sofia's regency formed an important period in Peter's development. There is nothing to suggest that he was unduly restricted or unhappy at this time. Sofia was preoccupied with her own affairs and apparently paid no special attention to him. He carried out his formal duties as Tsar, which involved taking part in church festivals and numerous special services in honour of the saints and of members of his family. He spent countless hours fulfilling these religious duties, which formed the basis of his extensive knowledge of the Scriptures. He also made his appearance on diplomatic occasions. These functions completed, he escaped to pursue his own interests, and then he was more or less his own master.

Peter was now at the age when warlike games make their strongest appeal, and he delighted in the noise and excitement of playing at war. He had advantages and an incentive that other boys lack. In Sofia and the Miloslavsky he had the incentive of real, personal enemies to give keener edge to his battles. But it is impossible to determine how far these games, which were to grow into considerable military exercises, were inspired by motives, instinctive or deliberate, of self-defence, and how far they were the result of a boy's interest, which in Peter, who was wholehearted and constructive in everything he did, worked on a grand scale.

His advantages were that, without counting the cost, he could call on the resources of the state arsenal. Also, he was Tsar; he drew up the rules and disciplined his troops, and was not dependent on the co-operation and enthusiasm of the usual sort of playmates who might quit when the rules were not to their liking. He made full use of both advantages. Early in 1682 he had a small parade ground specially laid out near his quarters in the Kremlin, and here he drilled his companions. The records of the arsenal show that his demands for weapons were frequent, and what was not in store had to be specially made. In January 1683 he ordered two wooden cannon, their barrels lined with iron, and mounted on wheels to allow them to be drawn by horses. On his eleventh birthday he abandoned the wooden cannon and began playing with real cannon. To celebrate this occasion he arranged a special artillery display with a foreigner, Simon Zommer, in charge of a group of Russian gunners and trainees.

Since the death of Tsar Alexei, his mother had remained with her small court in Moscow. But the Kremlin oppressed her. She bitterly resented her stepdaughter's ascendancy and she was afraid that Sofia might shut her away in a nunnery and dispose of her son. These were real dangers, not chimeras inspired by the fear-laden gloom of the Kremlin. Away from Moscow, Natalya felt safer, and after 1683 she took to spending at least part of the summer at Preobrazhenskoe and other country residences. This suited Peter who needed the space of the countryside, for his games were growing in scale. In May 1685 alone he ordered sixteen pairs of pistols, and sixteen carbines with slings and brass mountings, and, shortly afterwards, he sent for another twenty-three carbines and sixteen muskets. He always wanted the weapons urgently and there was no question of his hoarding them

for future use. They were put into active service, and soon found
their way back to the arsenal with instructions for their repair. By
the time he was fourteen, Peter had made Preobrazhenskoe his military headquarters.

The small group of playmates appointed to the staff of the
Tsarevich had provided Peter with his first *poteshnie*, or play-soldiers,
as they came to be called. But soon he was drawing on the enormous
staff of grooms, falconers, and servants, that had been his father's,
and in 1687 he began recruiting in earnest. Sofia and Golitsyn were
taken up at the time with preparations for the first Crimean campaign, and he felt free to abandon secrecy. He publicly invited volunteers to join him, and soon had two regiments at full strength, the
Preobrazhensky and the Semyonovsky, named after the neighbouring
villages which were their headquarters.[2] He pitted his two regiments
one against the other in innumerable battles and, impelled by his
furious energy, they were untiring in their warfare.

At the same time Peter was taking a keen interest in various crafts
and trades. He was always happiest when doing something with his
hands, and he could never watch a craftsman at work without mastering the craft himself. The court account books show that in 1684,
when he was twelve, he ordered a set of stonemason's tools. A few
months later he was learning the trade of printer; shortly afterwards
he was engrossed with carpenter's tools, from which he turned to the
work of a smithy. His large nimble hands acquired a skill which they
never lost, and he continued throughout his life to master new
trades.

His formal education, however, received little attention during
these years. At the age of sixteen he could read and write, but with
difficulty. His writing, spelling, and grammar were execrable. But at
the age of sixteen the next stage in his education began through an
incident which brought out sharply the curiosity and the determination which were among his most striking qualities.

Before leaving for Paris as Russian envoy, Prince Yakov Dolgoruky told him about a special instrument for measuring distances.
Peter at once instructed him to buy one in France. But when Dolgoruky returned to Moscow triumphantly bringing an astrolabe,
Peter could not use it, nor could anyone among his own people reveal
its secret. He turned to the Foreign Quarter, and there found a
Dutchman, named Timmerman, who became his second tutor.

The astrolabe was unlike other things that he had mastered. It called for a knowledge of subjects of which he had barely heard and under Timmerman's guidance he set about learning arithmetic, geometry, and the sciences of fortifications and artillery. Pages of his exercise books have survived and they show how he started from elementary principles. On the first pages he wrote down the three arithmetical rules: addition, subtraction and multiplication, with sums worked out to illustrate them. On other pages he wrote out the rules concerning latitudes and for calculating the flight of a bomb fired from a mortar.[3] He applied himself with great industry, mastering the rudiments, and boldly pressing on to more advanced problems.

Shortly before his seventeenth birthday, an incident occurred which was to prove momentous in the life of Peter himself and of his people. With Franz Timmerman he was visiting a village some five miles from Moscow, where in a storehouse on the estate of a Romanov forebear, he noticed a boat quite unlike the flat-bottomed boats plying the Russian rivers.

"What kind of boat is that?" he asked Timmerman.

"An English boat."

"What's it used for? Is it better than our Russian boats?"

"Yes. If it had a new mast and sails, it would move not only with the wind, but against the wind as well," Timmerman answered.

Peter was astonished. It did not seem possible that a boat without oars could move against the wind.

"Is there anyone who can mend it and show me how it sails?" he asked eagerly and, on learning that Timmerman knew of such a man, had him sent for at once.[4]

Karsten Brandt, whom Timmerman introduced, repaired the English boat, and sailed it up and down the Yauza River. Peter then took the tiller, but the boat constantly went aground in the narrow stream. He travelled some fifty miles beyond the Troitsa Monastery to Lake Pleshchev, which offered a greater expanse of water, and the lake fired his imagination. Until a few weeks earlier he had never seen an area of water bigger than a village pond, and now, standing on the shores of the lake, his thoughts raced ahead. He had talked with foreigners about the sea, but it was too remote from his experience for him to imagine. Suddenly the English boat tacking against the wind had made it real; it was in this way that the English and Dutch merchantmen sailed to Archangel. In his imagination he saw his own

ships following the same route, and this vision became an obsession.
The boy, born hundreds of miles from the sea, Tsar of a nation of
landsmen and peasants, began to dream of being a sailor and of
creating a navy.

His enthusiasm aroused, Peter carried all before him. Even his
mother agreed, although reluctantly, to his request to go to Pereyaslavl, and he set out with Brandt and Kort, another old boatbuilder.
By the lake they built huts and a jetty, and the two Dutchmen
started work on two small frigates and three yachts. They worked
hard, but Peter soon realized that he could not remain until the
boats were finished, for his mother worried about him, and grudg-
ingly he returned to Moscow.

Natalya was possessive and anxious, and her son's games disturbed her. His latest enthusiasm for boats and water horrified her,
the more so because it brought him into closer contact with foreigners and took him away for long periods of time. Mistakenly she
thought that a wife would distract him from these pursuits. The
bride she chose was Evdokiya Lopukhina, daughter of a strongly conservative Muscovite family; Peter, behaving as a dutiful son, raised
no objection. The marriage took place quietly on 27 January 1689.
It was to be productive only of tragedy.

The honeymoon was hardly over when the ice on the river began
to break. Peter left his wife and hurried away to see how Brandt and
Kort had progressed with the boats. "Dearest Mummy, Your Majesty,
the Grand-Princess Natalya Kirillovna," he wrote soon after arriving.
"Your little son Petrushka, hard at work, seeks your blessing and to
hear of your health: we, thanks to your prayers, are in good health.
The lake cleared of ice on the twentieth, and all the vessels, apart
from the big boat, are being finished: we are waiting only for ropes
and in this I beg your kindness, to order these ropes, seven hundred
fathoms in length, to be sent without delay from the Artillery Department, for our work is held up for them and our stay here is prolonged. Meanwhile I ask your blessing."[5]

Natalya replied, not by sending ropes, but with instructions for
him to return to Moscow. The anniversary of the death of Tsar
Feodor was approaching and Peter's presence at the memorial service was essential. He tried hard to avoid going back. "Your unworthy son, Petrushka, sends his respects. And as to your instructions
to return to Moscow, I am ready to obey; only work—I have work

to do, and he whom you sent has seen it and will report to you about it."[6] His young wife, Evdokiya, wrote begging him to return and her plea had a ring of pathos.[7] His mother insisted and Peter left his boats, reaching Moscow only just in time for the memorial ceremonies.

A month passed before he was able to travel north again. He found the boats almost ready, and was soon sailing them on the lake. He snatched moments to write reassuringly to his mother. The fact that he now signed himself *Petrus* in Latin characters showed that Western influence had already begun to colour his mind.[8] Five letters written in the spring of 1689 to his mother have survived; they contain no mention of his wife.[9] In less than four months he had forgotten her.

Soon he was recalled for another memorial service, and arrived in Moscow four days too late. This time his mother impressed on him the need to remain with her, because the tension between his supporters and Sofia's party was growing. He obeyed, and he found it easier to obey at this stage. He had helped to build and learnt to sail his boats, and his thoughts were on future plans. Already he had passed beyond the little boat which he had found rotting in the storehouse, but it was destined to be preserved, so that generations of Russians to come could look on it respectfully, and call it, in Peter's own words, "the grandfather of the Russian Navy."[10]

CHAPTER VI

The Fall of Sofia

1689

IN Moscow a period of frantic diplomatic and military activity followed on the failure of Golitsyn's Crimean expedition. The Polish campaign of 1687 against the Turks had also failed, but the Austrians and Venetians had won resounding victories, which had aroused in the Orthodox Christians of southern and eastern Europe new hopes of liberation. These Orthodox Christians now implored the Muscovites to renew their campaign and their prayers were urgent for, much as they hated the Turkish yoke, they dreaded far more the Roman Catholic persecution which would hound them if Austrians and Venetians rather than Muscovites were their liberators. But Muscovy was in no position to answer their pleas.

At this time Sofia and her government were chiefly concerned that their allies should not make a separate peace. Fear of this led Sofia to reduce all other commitments. Desperate appeals for reinforcements were then reaching Moscow from the small band of frontiersmen in the Amur basin. The Russians, in their advance across Siberia to the Pacific Ocean, had reached the Amur River in 1643, where the might of China had halted them. For some thirty years they had been fighting to retain their foothold. But, instead of reinforcements, Sofia sent an embassy to make peace with the Chinese Emperor, and at Nerchinsk an agreement depriving Muscovy of the Amur basin was signed.

Meanwhile the Crimean Khan had renewed his raids. In the first three months of 1688, his Tatars had carried off sixty thousand prisoners to sell into slavery, and had advanced within striking distance of Kiev and Poltava. At this point Sofia learnt that the Polish King and the Austrian Emperor had opened peace talks with the Sultan, contrary to the terms of their alliance. Protests were made and Moscow proclaimed a new campaign against the Crimean Khan.

Peter took no part in these diplomatic and military activities. Sofia had excluded him from all but formal participation in state affairs and, despite his enthusiasm for military matters, he apparently showed no interest in the new campaign.[1]

By February 1689 the Muscovite army of 112,000 men had assembled, again under the command of Prince Vasily Golitsyn, and soon afterwards the march southwards began. At the Samara River Mazepa with his Cossacks joined Golitsyn but, as his army moved towards Perekop, a rumour that the Tatars were near by threw it into a panic, and the Muscovite troops remained in a permanent state of "disorder, irregularity, and confusion, with disobedience."[2]

Golitsyn's second campaign proved as abortive as the first. He returned to Moscow, having lost twenty thousand men killed and fifteen thousand taken prisoner by the Tatars, and nothing gained. But once more his despatches told of brilliant victories. Sofia accorded him a triumphal welcome, and drew up a proclamation, announcing rewards and decorations for all who had taken part. She took for granted that Tsar Peter would sign it, and was astonished and furious when he refused. Several days passed before he could be prevailed on to agree to it. Vasily Golitsyn's reports had not deceived him, and he felt deeply the disgrace of the retreat. When, after the proclamation had been made, Vasily Golitsyn arrived in Preobrazhenskoe to express gratitude for his rewards, Peter refused to receive him.

This public rebuff to her first minister and her lover incensed Sofia all the more because it was a sign of the increasingly independent spirit of the young Tsar. Moreover, her position was now anomalous; Peter had come of age, as his marriage had borne witness and, since, unlike Ivan, he was fully competent, a regent was no longer necessary. But she was determined to wear the crown of the Russian tsars.

Two years before, towards the end of August 1687, while expecting confirmation of a great victory over the Crimean Khan, Sofia had instructed Shaklovity to find out what the reaction of the streltsi

would be to her coronation. If their response was favourable, she
intended to be crowned on 1 September 1687, the Muscovite New
Year's Day. But Shaklovity found the streltsi reluctant to give their
support, and Sofia had to accept the unpalatable fact that the time
was not ripe. On several occasions Shaklovity tried to incite bands of
streltsi to kill the Tsaritsa and her brothers, the Naryshkini. Only a
handful of bloodthirsty extremists heeded him, and nothing further
happened. But tension between Peter's and Sofia's supporters was increasing. Each party was on the defensive, expecting the other to
attack; each was unsure of its strength.

Sofia held the advantage. The streltsi were behind her and, unreliable though they were, Shaklovity managed to control them. The
Patriarch supported her and the foreign officers, from General Patrick
Gordon down to the junior officers, had sworn allegiance to her. Peter
could claim no such support. Apart from his family, and his few advisers he had only his play-troops, who numbered less than a thousand
men. But, small though his force was, Sofia went in fear of it, and
whenever she moved outside Moscow a special troop of streltsi
escorted her.

Tension between the two parties continued to mount. On 31
July 1689, General Gordon noted in his diary that "the heat and
bitterness are ever greater and greater and it appears that they must
soon break out." A few days later he referred to "rumours unsafe to
be uttered."[3]

The explosion came early in August. Sofia had announced that she
would make a pilgrimage on foot to the Donskoi Monastery and had
ordered Shaklovity to provide a detachment of streltsi to accompany
her. Soon afterwards rumours of an anonymous letter began circulating in the palace. The letter purported to give warning that the play-
troops from Preobrazhenskoe would launch a surprise attack next
evening, with the intention of killing Tsar Ivan and all his sisters.
Shaklovity at once closed the Kremlin gates, posted streltsi at key
points, and sent scouts along the Preobrazhenskoe road to report
any signs of troop movements.

His preparations and the presence of large numbers of fully armed
streltsi filled Moscow with alarm. The streltsi themselves were uneasy. Among the men of the Stremyanny regiment, however, were
seven, led by Larion Elizarev, who had been close to Sofia, but had
had a change of heart. They now feared that an attempt would be

made on the life of Tsar Peter himself, and meeting nightly in Elizarev's house, they kept a horse saddled ready for one of them to gallop to Preobrazhenskoe, when the hour struck.

On the night of 7-8 August, they were at Elizarev's house, when duty streltsi brought orders for them to report at once to the Lubyanka Palace. They took these orders to indicate that Shaklovity was about to march on Preobrazhenskoe, and Elizarev decided to send an urgent warning to Peter.

All was quiet when, just on midnight, his messenger galloped into the village. Peter was asleep, but was immediately awakened and told that streltsi were even at this moment marching on Preobrazhenskoe. Terrified, he jumped from his bed, and, wearing only a nightshirt, ran barefoot to the stables, mounted a horse, and galloped to a near-by wood. There he hid until clothes were brought to him, and, having dressed with feverish haste, he galloped off on the road to the Troitsa Monastery. He was exhausted when he arrived, and had to be lifted down from his horse and carried to a cell, where the monks put him to bed. But he could not rest or sleep. Sobbing convulsively, he told the Archimandrite of his sister's dastardly plans to kill him and his family, and of his escape. Gradually his sobbing subsided, and he fell into a deep sleep of nervous exhaustion.

News of the Tsar's flight to Troitsa reached Moscow late next morning. Shaklovity and his accomplices showed indifference. Sofia alone understood its significance. Unwittingly Peter had taken a decisive step, for the Troitsa was more than an impregnable fortress, it was a place of special sanctity. Sofia herself had brought the streltsi to heel by going there, and she knew that in the minds of the people the fact that the Tsar had taken refuge in the monastery would mean that he was in danger. His flight to Troitsa would rally the whole of Muscovy to him.

Safe in this stronghold, where his family and the play-regiments had joined him, Peter took the offensive. On the day after his arrival, he sent a messenger to Sofia, demanding to know why she had assembled the streltsi in the Kremlin. She replied that she needed them to escort her to the Donskoi Monastery. He made no rejoinder, but sent instructions for Ivan Tsykler, Colonel of the Stremyanny regiment, to come to Troitsa with fifty streltsi. This was an ominous request, for Tsykler had been one of the ringleaders in the revolt of May 1682, and he enjoyed Sofia's confidence. If he were surrendered, it could only be for interrogation and punishment, and the thought of this made all of Sofia's supporters tremble. She hesitated and then allowed Tsykler to go. But she did not know that, having decided that Peter's star was in the ascendant, Tsykler had sent a secret message, promising to divulge all that he knew, if summoned to the monastery.

Peter's next step was to send written orders to eighteen colonels of the streltsi regiments to report to him by 18 August. Sofia summoned all colonels into her presence and, warning them against interfering in what was merely a quarrel between brother and sister, she ordered them to remain in the Kremlin. Her threats of punishment were enough to deter most of them, but they were uneasy.

Sofia realized now that the one way to avert catastrophe was to persuade Peter to return to Moscow. She was confident that she could handle him. She had only to bring him back to the capital, and then to dispose of his family to establish herself permanently. In the name of Tsar Ivan she sent two envoys to urge him to return to Moscow, but they had no success. She then appealed to Patriarch Ioakim to intervene on her behalf. Her hopes rose when he agreed and set out for the monastery, but they were shattered when, having reached Troitsa, he remained there. The Patriarch had supported Sofia, not as she assumed, because he favoured her cause, but because she held the power, and, like all Muscovites, he dreaded a weak tsar at the mercy of the boyars. But he did not accept her ambitions to wear the crown, and he hated the Western outlook of herself and Vasily Golitsyn.

Moscow was now in a turmoil. Many had already taken the road to Troitsa, and the Patriarch's defection encouraged others to follow. But the great majority of the streltsi and the people remained in the city, unhappy and hesitant, awaiting the next move.

On 27 August a second summons came from Peter, calling on all colonels and sergeants, with ten streltsi from each regiment to report to him without further orders, and threatening with death all who disobeyed. A similar summons called on representatives of the people of Moscow to go to Troitsa. These orders produced prompt results. Five colonels and over five hundred streltsi immediately set out from Moscow. Peter's next step was to send Colonel Nechaev to Moscow with a force of streltsi to arrest Shaklovity and certain others.

Sofia was now growing desperate, and on 29 August, escorted by her remaining supporters, she set out for Troitsa herself. She hoped by talking with Peter to settle their dispute. Some eight miles from the monastery, however, a chamberlain halted her party and informed her that it was the Tsar's wish that she should return to Moscow. Furiously Sofia dismissed him. Another envoy came, bearing the Tsar's decree that she was to be turned back, if necessary, by force. She had to retreat and arrived in Moscow on the evening of 31 August.

Colonel Nechaev reached the Kremlin a few hours after her on this same evening. At the Red Staircase, he handed to the clerk of the Streltsi Office Peter's order for the arrest of Shaklovity and others. News of the Tsar's order quickly circulated among the streltsi who, although they had not taken the road to Troitsa, and, at least nominally, were loyal to Sofia, began shouting for the surrender of the criminals. Sofia's closest supporters realized that the end was near. Vasily Golitsyn in a mood of despair retired to his country estate. Others fled, but Shaklovity did not dare leave the Kremlin for fear that the streltsi would seize him.

Sofia was alone and at bay, but her courage did not fail, and she did not admit defeat. She sent for Nechaev and her anger was magnificent. "How dare you take upon yourself such a duty!" she exploded, and Nechaev sturdily replied that he carried out the orders of the Tsar. In her rage she ordered his execution, but no executioner could be found.[4] Sofia then went out onto the Red Staircase and harangued first the streltsi gathered on the square, and then the townspeople of Moscow. She had all foreigners assembled in the palace, graciously receiving them herself and presenting them with wine. She also issued a proclamation, accusing the Naryshkini of innumerable crimes, and appealing to the patriotism of the people.

Meanwhile, the foreign officers were restive. General Gordon had declared that, without a decree from both Tsars, they would not stir from the Foreign Quarter. As foreigners they had to be especially careful to support the winning side, and Gordon was always cautious. Certain of them had already gone to join Peter. But, on 4 September, as night fell, Gordon and all the remaining foreign officers set out on the road to Troitsa. This was, as Gordon wrote in his diary, "the decisive break."[5]

Sofia's position was weakening hourly. The streltsi in Moscow were completely demoralized. A group approached her, demanding the

surrender of Shaklovity to Peter. They met only with her insistence
that they should not meddle in her affairs. But they now threatened
bloodshed, and Sofia was forced to yield.

Prince Vasily Golitsyn had remained at his country estate, hoping
still that Sofia might emerge victorious. But the arrest of Shaklovity
put an end to these hopes, and on 7 September he arrived at the
monastery. Expecting audience of the Tsar, he had prepared a statement of his services to the nation. But he was granted no audience,
and suffered the indignity of waiting with the crowd in the ante-
room, until a clerk to the council appeared, and read aloud the
Tsar's sentence, which was loss of the rank of boyar, confiscation of
all his estates, and exile with his family to the Arctic. It was a mild
sentence. His cousin Prince Boris Golitsyn, who was close to Peter
had interceded on his behalf, and he was spared torture and execution.
Peter also showed mercy to Sofia's other confederates. Gordon noted
that he was reluctant to have any of them executed, and only after
the Patriarch had pressed him, did he agree that Shaklovity and two
others, should lose their heads.[6] They were promptly executed outside the monastery walls.

Among the last to take the road to Troitsa was Hetman Mazepa,
and he nearly left it till too late. He had come to Moscow after the
Crimean campaign, and Sofia had showered honours on him. After
the Tsar's flight to Troitsa he had waited in the Kremlin and hesitated, uncertain whether Sofia would lose; only when nearly all her
supporters had gone over to Peter, had he followed. Nevertheless
Peter received him graciously. He listened sympathetically to Mazepa's vehement complaints against Sofia and Vasily Golitsyn, and he
fell under the spell of the Hetman's fluent tongue and persuasive
personality. When, after three days at Troitsa, Mazepa returned to
Little Russia it was with every mark of favour and friendship.

Peter's battle was nearly won. He wrote a letter to his brother,
condemning the evil deeds and ambitions of their sister, and proposing that she should no longer be allowed to interfere in affairs of
state; in future the two brothers would govern the country. He also
asked Ivan's permission to appoint new officials in place of many of
those now in power, without referring each case to him in advance.[7]

Ivan agreed to everything his brother proposed. He even agreed
that their sister should be expelled from the palace and sent to the

Novodevichi nunnery to end her days. Three weeks later she was escorted, protesting loudly, to the cells set aside for her. Peter had shown magnanimity, but for Sofia it was a cruel fate. She had fought boldly for power and for freedom and she failed because the Muscovites would not oppose their Tsar. The gates of the nunnery closed on her inexorably and finally.

CHAPTER VII

Peter's Western Tutelage Begins

1689-1693

ON 6 October 1689, Peter returned to Moscow. The bells of every church rang out to welcome the Tsar back to his capital, and for the Muscovites it was a great occasion. But the significance of their welcome was lost on Peter, whose mood was remote from that of his subjects. He returned to Moscow with reluctance. In part this was due to the deep aversion from the city that he had felt since the streltsi revolt; in part it arose from the fact that he was not interested at this time in ruling as supreme autocrat. Five years were to pass before he took into his own hands the reins of government, and in the meantime he left state matters to the small group of ministers whom he had appointed while at Troitsa Monastery.

Even now at the age of seventeen, Peter was a magnificent figure of a man. He was tall, nearly seven feet in height, and massively built. His face was round, his eyes open and intelligent, and his features were good; indeed, he would have been strikingly handsome had it not been for a certain distressing twitching of the side of his face and a habit of rolling his eyes, both marks of the horror he had experienced during the streltsi revolt seven years before. Already, too, he was beginning to display the two characteristics which were to mark the man and his reign; first, his energy which was dynamic and unquenchable, and, second, the grand scale on which he planned, laboured, and played.

At this time, unconcerned about the government of his country, he was in the midst of his education, studying on his own initiative and in his own way. He began frequenting the Foreign Quarter, because he found there the men who could help him. But for the first year after his return to Moscow he still had to exercise some restraint. His mother insisted on his carrying out the formal duties of Tsar and, anxious that he should retain popular support, she did everything to discourage his association with foreigners.

In Moscow, Peter found the formalities and religious duties of his Kremlin life unending. On 19 February 1690, he attended the special services celebrating the birth of his son, Tsarevich Alexei Petrovich. He did not, however, allow this to interfere with army manoeuvres that he had planned and the moment the services were over he rode away to Preobrazhenskoe. He was not greatly interested in this child, produced by a wife for whom he had no affection. Gradually his absences from Moscow became more frequent. But he behaved with some show of moderation while his mother and Patriarch Ioakim were alive. A conservative Muscovite, severe and venerable in aspect like an Old Testament prophet, the Patriarch was unrelenting in his hostility towards foreigners and with baleful eye he watched the young Tsar, whose association with Timmermann and others aroused his strongest disapproval.

Popular hatred of the foreigner had never been stronger in Muscovy than during the regency of Sofia. Partly religious and partly national prejudice, it simmered below the surface of daily life, ready to erupt the moment official protection faltered. Sofia's offer of asylum to the Huguenots and Vasily Golitsyn's patronage of foreigners had horrified Muscovites. They believed that the foreigners were gathering into their own pockets all the riches of Muscovy and keeping the people poor; their presence alone corrupted the Muscovite way of life and their poison was spreading at court. The fall of Sofia was the signal for a violent outburst of xenophobia.

Paradoxically, Peter's party was popularly regarded at first as the aristocratic and conservative party, which would cleanse Muscovy of the foreign blight. Immediately on Sofia's fall from power a frenzied mob seized a foreigner in Moscow and burnt him alive; no official action was taken to punish the malefactors. A strict decree was proclaimed, forbidding the entry of foreigners into the country, except with the Tsar's special permission. The hand of the Patriarch could also be seen in the movement to destroy the heretic churches in the

Quarter. But the foreigners were able to produce written permission, issued on the personal instructions of Tsar Alexei, and nothing further happened. The wave of xenophobia mounted, and then, with the death of the Patriarch, it subsided.

Patriarch Ioakim died suddenly on 17 March 1690. In his testament he enjoined the Tsar to avoid contact with heretics, Lutherans, Calvinists, and godless Tatars, to eschew foreign clothes and customs, and above all to appoint no foreigners to official positions. His injunctions were in vain. He had hardly been buried, when Peter ordered for himself a suit of German clothes. A week later he took the unprecedented step of visiting Gordon and dining with him. It was the first time that a Tsar of Muscovy had dined in the house of a foreigner, and it was an early indication of Peter's indifference to established custom and popular opinion.

The appointment of a successor to Ioakim was a matter of importance, for the Patriarch was second only to the Tsar in authority and popular esteem. Peter, supported by Boris Golitsyn and others of his Company, and by certain of the more enlightened clergy, expressed a preference for Marcellus, Metropolitan of Pskov, but Tsaritsa Natalya, the ordinary priesthood, and the whole of conservative Muscovy feared that, because he was learned, he would incline towards Catholicism. Their choice was the Metropolitan of Kazan, Adrian, whose ignorance and simplicity made him a strong candidate. Despite Peter's preference (he probably bowed to the wishes of his mother who had become increasingly devout), Adrian was chosen and consecrated Patriarch on 24 August 1690.[1] The experience of Ioakim's bigotry and the appointment of Adrian taught Peter a lesson which was to have important results for the church in later years.

At about this time Peter's Western tutelage began in earnest, marked by his close friendship with Gordon and Lefort. He had undoubtedly met them earlier, along with other foreigners, but it was in 1690 that his regular visits to the Foreign Quarter began and that his determination to learn about the West deepened.

Patrick Gordon was an honourable, conscientious, and courageous Scot, dignified in bearing. He was also intelligent, combining with his wide experience as a man of action the learning of a scholar. He enjoyed the respect of all who knew him, and he represented much that was best in western Europe at the time.

Born in Aberdeenshire in 1635, Gordon came of a distinguished family that was zealously Catholic and royalist. The future held no promise in England or Scotland for a young man of such background and at the age of sixteen, he sought his fortune in Europe. He spent two years in a Jesuit college in Brandenburg, and then, after serving with distinction in both the Swedish and Polish armies, he enlisted as a major in the Muscovite army for three years; on reaching Moscow, however, he found that his contract meant nothing and that he would never be released.

From the day of his arrival until his friendship with Peter, a period of some fifteen years, Gordon dreamt only of escaping. He married and had children, and when sent on a mission to England as the Tsar's envoy, he was forced to leave his family behind as hostages against his return. Several times he petitioned Tsar Alexei for leave to visit Scotland but, although he won favour and promotion to the rank of general, his petition was never granted.

Already in his mid-fifties, Gordon found a new interest in the companionship of his seventeen-year-old master. He took pleasure in instructing him, and in the active life he now followed in his company. Moreover, the respect and rewards he enjoyed as one of the Tsar's friends and senior commanders were some compensation for his continued exile.[2]

Franz Lefort, who was the son of a prosperous Genevan merchant, differed sharply from Gordon in character. He was pleasure-loving, high-spirited, but idle and irresponsible. In revolt against the dour Calvinistic way of life of Geneva, he had decided to seek adventure as a soldier. He enlisted in the army of the Duke of Courland, and then went to Muscovy, where he succeeded eventually in joining the Muscovite service and saw action under the command of General Gordon, who spoke highly of his bravery.

At Troitsa Monastery, Lefort, then in his early thirties, cast a spell over Peter, who had met no one like him before. The Muscovites, young and old, did not relax in pleasures. Their drinking habits were anti-social, aiming at drunken stupor. But Lefort was never stolid or dull; even in the Foreign Quarter, he was remarkable for his charm and gaiety, and for his irrepressible joy in life.

Lefort had had a good general education, and his quick brain and ready tongue masked his superficiality; his talk of the West, its ways of life, its science and institutions was always interesting. He had abundant energy, which enabled him to keep up with Peter, and as a drinking companion he had no equal. But Peter found in him something more; he found sympathy, affection, and understanding and a personality that both enlivened and calmed him. When anger seized on Peter, rising to a pitch of fury, distorting his features and his mind until he was dangerous to anyone near, Lefort alone could usually quiet him and avoid bloodshed. From the beginning of their friendship at Troitsa until Lefort's death, this bond of affection and understanding united the two men.[3]

In Lefort's house, Peter learnt to disport himself with foreign women, and began his affair with Anna Mons, a young flaxen-haired German beauty, the daughter of a wine merchant in the Quarter. His experience of women was limited to his mother and his wife, both of whom led retiring, prayerful lives. By contrast Anna Mons was fresh and vital. As with all who won his affection, he gave her rich presents, including a small palace of her own. Unlike Lefort, she was grasping and used her position to obtain further favours. But the affair was to last for over ten years.

In the way of life that Peter now began to follow, the "Company" supplanted the traditional court of the tsars. Ranging in numbers from eighty to two hundred members, it was a motley society, comprising men of many countries, faiths, trades, and tongues. Old Muscovites, for whom the Tsar was an almost divine creature, were aghast to see Peter hobnobbing and carousing with Dutch carpenters and boatbuilders, English and German merchants and soldiers, Catholic Scots, and with Muscovite grooms and ordinary soldiers. But Peter cared little for the traditional aloofness of the tsars. These were the men who shared and contributed to his interests and entertainments.

The inner circle of the Company included his favourites and the men whom he treated as colleagues. He confided in them, discussing his ideas and plans, and when the time came he called on them to bear responsibility. The leading foreigners in this inner circle were Gordon and Lefort; others were Andrei Vinius, von Mengden, Chambers, Adam Weide, and Jacob Bruce.[4] Of the Muscovites belonging to it, many were sons of old noble families who had grown up with Peter, or were older men on whose experience and maturity he could rely.

The Company went everywhere with Peter, and, in his restless energetic pursuit of military and naval experience, and of entertainment, his movements were unpredictable. Sometimes they dined in the Quarter, or went out to some country estate. Wherever they went, the chosen host found that at short notice he had to feast the Tsar and his Company. These banquets were lengthy, beginning at midday and lasting far into the night, often until dawn next day; on occasions the Company stayed two or three days, converting the host's house into a barracks, where they slept side by side on the floors and wherever else they could find space. They consumed gargantuan portions of food and drink, leaving the table to play ninepins, or bowls, or for archery matches and musket practice, then returning to eat again. More often than not these banquets degenerated into debauchery and drunkenness on a vast scale.

Most of all Peter liked to dine at Lefort's house in the Quarter. But this house was far too small to accommodate all the guests, and Lefort's pay could not run to such extensive hospitality. Peter, therefore, built him a palace with a banqueting hall to hold fifteen hundred people and, although it belonged to Lefort, it became a kind of clubhouse where the Company could gather.

Members of the Company needed the capacity to drink deeply. The young Tsar had a strong head and an iron constitution. All-night drinking bouts became one of his regular diversions and, while others were deep in drunken slumber after a night's orgy, he would rise at dawn to work furiously throughout the day as a carpenter, boatbuilder, smithy or gunner. It was a pace that many could not keep up. Usually Gordon took to his bed for two or three days after these bouts, and Peter visited him or sent medicines to help him on the road to recovery.

It was undoubtedly Lefort who introduced Peter to the habit of heavy drinking. He needed only the barest introduction, however, for he was not given to moderation. But the importance of the habit has often been exaggerated. It would have ruined the health of most men; it killed Lefort, and was probably one of the causes of the attacks of fever Peter suffered from time to time. But it did not abate the tremendous energy that erupted from him, nor did it prevent his doing the work of ten men throughout his life. For him, heavy drinking was a form of relaxation from his labours, releasing the great pressure of physical and nervous energy. The wild bacchanalia in which he indulged from the age of eighteen onwards did not leave him debauched or incapable, but refreshed him for the next day's work.

Fireworks were another fascinating discovery that Peter made at this time. He rejoiced in noise of every kind and when the flash of explosion was added, he found it irresistible. He had his first experience of fireworks in the Foreign Quarter, and he promptly began making them himself. As part of the Shrovetide celebrations in 1690, he organized a display of the first fireworks to be seen in Moscow. The display went on for five hours without a break. At one stage a five-pound rocket, made by Peter himself, failed to explode and, falling on the head of a boyar, killed him, but this did not impair the great success of the occasion.

In his enthusiasm he had to experiment, and several times he was fortunate in escaping serious injury. As he mastered pyrotechnics, his exhibitions became more elaborate. Thus, in another display, held in 1693, a triple salute of fifty-six cannon was followed by a white pavilion of flame on which the initials of Generalissimo Prince Romodanovsky appeared in fireworks, and then a picture of Hercules tearing open the lion's jaws.

Peter had an exuberant love of buffoonery and was at times a jokesmith of gross tastes. He seized on the occasion of the wedding of his jester, Yakov Turgeniev, for a typical outburst. The wedding feast was held in a magnificent tent erected in a field between the villages of Preobrazhenskoe and Semyonovskoe, and it lasted for three days. Numerous processions interrupted the feasting. In one procession the jester and his wife rode in state in the Tsar's carriage, followed by the leading boyars of the realm on foot. At another time members of the Company, wearing hats made of tree bark, boots of straw, and gloves of mouse-skins, their kaftans decorated with squirrel tails and cats' paws, followed the bridal pair in carriages drawn by oxen, goats, swine, and dogs. The festivities ended with the couple making a triumphal entry into Moscow on a camel.

Most of this elaborate buffoonery was offensive to his subjects, but Peter maintained it for many years as though part of a deliberate policy. His mockery of the church was the most significant example. He was deeply religious, although he did not follow the daily routine of worship of his father and did not share the bigotry of his subjects. In mocking the church he was giving expression to his deep impatience with its conservatism and incompetence, and the power wielded by its hierarchy. But it was the mockery of a high-spirited young tsar, hitting personally at something that angered him. As he grew older, he realized that the church had become a stagnant and retrograde force in Muscovite life; he then embarked on a campaign of reform.

This mockery took the form of a drunken assembly with its own patriarch, metropolitans, archimandrites, deacons and priesthood, who wore ecclesiastical vestments and performed special rites. He established this "All-joking, All-drunken Assembly," as it was called, some time after the consecration of Adrian as Patriarch. Peter's old tutor, Nikita Zotov, as president, or "Prince-Pope," of the assembly, took charge of the drinking bouts, and strictly enforced the rule that goblets must be emptied promptly; he also, by example, encouraged everyone to get roaring drunk.

Another of Peter's favourite jests was the elevation of Prince Feodor Romodanovsky to the position of "Prince Caesar" or "King." Peter himself played the part of a loyal subject, addressing him as "*Min Her Kenich*" (My Lord King) and "Your Majesty," and acknowledging his "Imperial decrees." Members of the Company were required to show him the respects accorded to royalty. Peter was to carry on this practice throughout his reign, often to the bewilderment of his subjects and even of members of his Company but, although begun as a jest, it became part of a deliberate policy of demonstrating to his subjects that he, too, served.

Even during these early years, however, banquets, buffoonery, and fireworks consumed only a very small part of his time and energies. He waited impatiently for the winter of 1689-1690 to pass, so that his play-regiments could take the field. Nor did he forget his boats, and he had begun to think of visiting the White Sea. Also Gordon was constantly in his company in the spring of 1690, planning manoeuvres. The first engagement between the two play-regiments nearly ended in tragedy. Peter was taking part in the storming of a village, when a clay pot filled with gunpowder, which served as a hand grenade, exploded near him, burning his face badly.

Throughout the summer of 1691, the troops prepared for "the great and terrible battle" to be waged in the autumn. This exercise was on a grand scale. Generalissimo Prince Romodanovsky's army comprised the Preobrazhensky and Semyonovsky regiments and other troops; the second army, commanded by Generalissimo Ivan

Buturlin, consisted of streltsi regiments. At dawn on 6 October, battle commenced. Bitter fighting raged all day, and ended with victory for Romodanovsky, and honours for Captain Peter Alexeevich—as the Tsar was known at this time—who saved his Generalissimo from capture during a counter-attack. But Peter was not satisfied; he ordered another round. The second battle took place in a high wind, rain, and mud on 9 October, and Romodanovsky's army was again victorious.

Early in the following month Peter went to Pereyaslavl, where Karsten Brandt, with a team of carpenters, was still working on the two small frigates and the three yachts. He ordered the erection of several new buildings to accommodate the court, and the reason for these preparations was ostensibly that Romodanovsky had, by his "Imperial decree," instructed Master Shipwright Peter Alexeevich to build a ship of war to be launched by the spring of 1692. This vessel absorbed him for the rest of the winter. With his own hands he laid down her keel, and worked from dawn until late each night, eating his food in the boatyard and sleeping only when tiredness overwhelmed him. He was oblivious of all but the work in hand. Lev Naryshkin and Boris Golitsyn had to hurry from Moscow to persuade him to return to receive the Persian ambassador. Reluctantly he laid down his tools, but within a week he was back at work again. At last, on 1 May, the ship was launched with all ceremony.

In July, Tsaritsa Natalya and the whole court went to inspect the flotilla and Peter enthusiastically conducted manoeuvres on water as well as on land. But soon after his return to Moscow he fell seriously ill with dysentery, and for weeks lay feebly on his bed. The whole of his Company was in a state of alarm, for they knew that if he were to die, Sofia would return to power, and exile or execution would be their fate. His strong constitution pulled him through, however, and by the end of January 1693, he was visiting the Quarter again. But it was not until the following month that he demonstrated his complete recovery by staging a magnificent fireworks display.

On 26 February Lefort gave a banquet in the Tsar's honour. At dawn next day, without having slept, Peter rode away to Pereyaslavl. He worked on his boats for two weeks, returning to Moscow because his mother was ill. In May he went again to Pereyaslavl; this was to be his last visit for twenty-four years. Boats and buildings rotted, and when he found them in this condition in 1722, he gave orders for the remnants to be preserved, but his orders were not carried out. One small boat survived through the efforts of the peasants of a near-by village.

Pereyaslavl and the flotilla he built there were only a short chapter in his naval education. Sailing his boats on the lake, he thought of the sea. Already, before his last visit to Pereyaslavl, he was planning to visit Archangel.

CHAPTER VIII

Archangel

1693-1694

PETER visited Archangel to satisfy his longing to see real ships
and the sea; he returned determined to create a navy. He had
intended to sail, soon after arriving, to Solovetsky Monastery,
situated on an island in the White Sea. Afanasy, Archbishop of
Kholmogory, was preparing to accompany him, when suddenly he
received a message that the Tsar would not visit the monastery
until the following summer.

Peter had heard much about Archangel, but nothing had prepared
him for the sight of so many ships or the bustle of a busy port. With
the first approach of spring each year, Archangel stirred. Everyone
prepared for the hectic activity of the summer when the Uspensky
market was piled high with goods, which had to be cleared before
the winter ice again closed the river and the sea to all traffic. As
soon as the ice broke, barges laden with wheat, caviare, hemp, tallow,
Russian leather, potash, pitch and fishglue crowded the Dvina River
on their way north. At the same time the first merchant ships from
England, Holland, Hamburg, and Bremen pushed their way through
the soft ice, bringing cargoes of silken fabrics, wool and cotton cloths,
gold and silver ware, wines and chemicals, and other products of
European industry. Archangel was then at the height of its importance as a centre of commerce.

Peter's immediate reason for postponing his visit to Solovetsky
Monastery was that a number of English and Dutch merchantmen
were preparing to sail in convoy, escorted by a Dutch warship. He

could not miss this opportunity to go to sea, and when, on 4 August, the merchantmen weighed anchor, he sailed with them in the *St. Peter*, a small twelve-gun yacht that had been made ready for him. The experience made a deep impression, and he had travelled nearly two hundred miles from Archangel before he reluctantly took leave of the merchantmen and returned to Archangel.

A letter from his mother, Tsaritsa Natalya, was awaiting him there. She reproached him for not writing to tell her the date of his return. But when the news reached Moscow that the Tsar had gone to sea, she was prostrated with worry. He wrote to her, but his letter upset her all the more because he intended remaining in the north until the arrival of certain Dutch ships.[1] She replied in tones of anguish, begging him to return.[2] But he was determined to wait for the ships, now three weeks out from Amsterdam, and he sent a member of his staff to Moscow to reassure her of his safety.

Meanwhile Peter was living on Moiseev Island from which he could watch the ships arriving and departing. He often attended services in the Church of Iliya the Prophet on Kegostrov. He did not neglect the various handicrafts which interested him; he forged iron bars and worked at a lathe; a chandelier of mammoth ivory which he turned at this time was later to hang over his tomb in the Cathedral of SS. Peter and Paul in St. Petersburg. He eagerly inspected the ships in the harbour, and spent hours questioning foreign masters about England and Holland. He was also busy with plans to exercise his troops at sea in the following summer. He had a wharf built at Solombala and with his own hands laid the keel of a new ship to be constructed during the winter. Next he sent instructions to Nicholas Witsen, Burgomaster of Amsterdam, to buy him a forty-four-gun frigate in Holland, to be delivered in the following summer.

Early in September, the expected merchantmen arrived, and Peter went on board, rewarding their masters for bringing them safely to port. Lefort gave a luxurious banquet in their honour, and the celebrations went on nearly a week, before Peter prepared for the return journey.

Bad weather prevented manoeuvres of the play-regiment during the autumn, but Peter was not idle. In his workshops at Preobrazhenskoe he turned blocks for the rigging, and cast guns for the armament of the ship under construction at Solombala. He also selected crews from the play-regiments for both ships. He usually sat late,

drinking and talking with members of his company, and after a few
hours' sleep he would go back to his workbench. But, on 25 January
1694, the death of his mother disrupted this routine.

Tsaritsa Natalya was not old, but she had never recovered from
the grief of early widowhood and the horrors of the streltsi revolt.
Peter was the centre of her life and thoughts, but as a son he gave
her little comfort. He loved and respected her, but was wild and
self-willed. He seldom showed her affection or consideration, except
in his letters, and then he was usually asking pardon for causing her
distress. On occasions she had restrained him and even exacted obedience, but such occasions had become rare. As he grew older, his passion for boats, mock-battles, and fireworks, leading to more frequent separations and exposing him to new dangers, had increased
her anxiety.

Natalya had been ailing since her visit to Pereyaslavl in the spring
of 1693, but when, in January of the next year, she took to her bed,
her illness did not seem serious. Peter went ahead with preparations
for his second visit to Archangel. On 21 January, while he was at a
banquet, a message that the Tsaritsa was failing interrupted the
merriment. On 25 January, not seeing Peter in the Kremlin where
he had arranged to meet him, Gordon hurried back to Preobrazhenskoe to find him "exceeding melancholy and troubled."[3] He had
been at his mother's bedside, and had realized for the first time that
she was dying. He had received her blessing and then, two or three
hours before her death, he had taken leave of her, hurrying away to
the privacy of Preobrazhenskoe.

The burial of the Tsaritsa took place on the next day with all
the sombre and magnificent ceremonial of the Muscovite Church.
Peter himself was not present, nor did he attend the service on the
next day at the nunnery for the repose of her soul. But later in the
day he went alone and prayed by her grave. He could not endure
the public services, and paid no attention to court etiquette. For
three days he was too overwrought to leave Preobrazhenskoe or to see
anyone.

Five days after her death, however, Peter was at work again. A
letter, written to Governor Apraxin on this day, began with a reference
to his grief "about which my hand cannot write in detail." It went on
to give exact instructions for a new ship to be built in Archangel.[4]
Soon afterwards he attended a wedding in the Foreign Quarter. Peter

was neither cold nor heartless by nature. He had loved his mother, but he could not stand still to grieve; he had to be active, and when he turned again to his plans for the summer he was immediately absorbed. But several times he made his way alone to the nunnery to attend the service for the repose of the dead. Thereafter his mother belonged to the past, while in all his thoughts and activities he belonged to the present and the future.

Tsaritsa Natalya had kept him in touch with the Kremlin ritual; after her death he ceased to take part in it. On 8 April 1694, he accompanied Tsar Ivan in the Easter procession, and this is the last reference in the court records to his participation in Kremlin ceremonies.[5] The Foreign Quarter became the centre of his interests, and his court moved between the Quarter and Preobrazhenskoe. He was creating new rituals and ceremonies and new ranks of nobility, which had only slight connexion with old Muscovy.

During the spring of 1694, Peter pressed ahead with preparations for his second visit to Archangel. This time he would have three ships, if the frigate from Amsterdam arrived safely, and naval manoeuvres in the White Sea were to be the highlight of the visit. He set out on 1 May, and from Vologda the party travelled in barges, making the voyage in fast time. On 20 May he launched the ship built at Solombala, and he now waited impatiently for the arrival of the frigate from Holland; the yacht *St. Peter* lay at the jetty, and the *St. Paul*, just launched, would be fully rigged and ready for sea within a month. Meanwhile he divided his time between carousals, visits to foreign ships, working on the newly launched ship, and attending the churches of Archangel, where he sang "in a bass voice with his imperial singers."[6] But he was longing to go to sea and, recalling his promise of the previous year, he decided to visit the Solovetsky Monastery.

Accompanied by Archbishop Afanasy, several boyars and a few soldiers, he sailed in the *St. Peter*. Some eighty miles out from Archangel, a gale burst upon them. The wind carried away the sails, and great waves threatened to poop the little vessel. The crew gave up hope and prayed for help; boyars and soldiers did likewise and the Archbishop administered the Last Sacrament to all on board. Peter, apparently unperturbed, was at the helm when the pilot advised him that the only way to avoid disaster was to make for the Unskaya Gulf. He turned the helm over to the pilot, who skilfully brought the ship to a safe anchorage near the Pertominsky Monastery.

Going ashore with his comrades, Peter gave thanks for divine protection; he presented rich gifts to the monks for the maintenance of their monastery, and rewarded the pilot. To commemorate his delivery from the tempest, he made a wooden cross ten and a half feet in height with the inscription in Dutch: *"Dat kruys maken Kaptein Piter van a cht. 1694"* (This cross was made by Captain Peter in the summer of 1694). He carried it on his own shoulders to the spot where he had first stepped on shore, and there erected it as a memorial.[7] As soon as the storm had passed, he put to sea again and reached Solovetsky Island where he spent three days and nights in the monastery in prayer, fasting, and veneration of the miracle-working relics of Saints Zossima and Savvatiya.

On 11 July, Vice-Admiral Generalissimo Buturlin commissioned the *St. Paul*. Peter had also received good news from Vinius, then Director of the Riga Post, who had heard from Witsen that the frigate had sailed from Amsterdam six weeks ago and was due in Archangel any day. Peter replied to Vinius at once, expressing his delight and going on to tell him of the completion of the "new ship on 11 July blessed in the name of Paul the Apostle and well hallowed with the incense of Mars, at which time Bacchus was shown worthy respect."[8]

Already Peter's thoughts were rushing ahead. He had two ships and expected a third any day, but now he wanted to build a fleet at Archangel. He instructed Vinius to obtain from Witsen in Amsterdam the exact measurements of Dutch ships, so that he could copy them at Solombala.[9] Witsen's reply was that it was not possible to give such measurements, adding that the frigate bought for the Tsar in Amsterdam was of good proportions and would serve as a model. This did not satisfy Peter, who retorted that he did not want a fleet of frigates. But, although he persisted, he was unable to obtain the information he wanted, and he did not understand why Witsen could not send it. It was probably this incident that gave him the idea of going abroad to study shipbuilding at first hand.

On 21 July the new frigate, called *The Holy Prophecy*, under the command of Jan Flam, anchored off Solombala. She was a sturdy ship, richly equipped and decorated, as was fitting for the Tsar of Russia. Peter and his suite gathered on board and in the midst of celebrating her arrival, he broke off to give Vinius the news. *"Min*

Her, I have nothing to write to you but to say that what we have long desired came to pass. . . . Jan Flam has arrived safely; in his ship are forty-four guns and forty sailors. Send your greetings to us all. I will write more fully by the proper post; but overjoyed as I am now I cannot write fully; also it is not permissible, for as always on such occasions Bacchus is receiving due respect and with his leaves he makes heavy the eyes of those who want to write lengthily." He signed himself "Skipper of the ship, *Holy Prophecy*," the rank which he took under Lefort who was captain; Jan Flam, an experienced seaman, who had already made over thirty voyages to Archangel, remained in actual command.[10] On the same night, he also found time to dictate a short formal letter to his brother in Moscow about this great event.[11]

The next week was devoted to refurbishing the frigate and provisioning all three ships. Peter had arranged that his little flotilla would sail with the English and Dutch merchantmen which were ready to depart. He called on Gordon one evening with a list of signals written out in Russian in his own hand and asked him to translate them into English, making a copy for each of the English captains. He also worked out the stations which the ships were to keep.

All was ready for their departure on 3 August, but there was no wind, and it was not until 14 August that the convoy cleared the mouth of the Dvina. Soon they had passed the point to which Peter had sailed in the previous summer, and on 17 August they reached Svyatoi Nos. Here the Admiral's ship fired five guns to indicate that the Russians would leave the convoy and, after exchanging farewell signals, Peter's three ships turned back. They arrived in Archangel four days later and Peter at once prepared for the journey to Moscow.

CHAPTER IX

The Azov Campaigns
1695-1696

O N his return Peter plunged into plans for autumn manoeuvres, which, known as the Kozhukhovsky Campaign, were to prove the prelude to real warfare. A few months later Peter himself, writing of their labours "below Kozhukhov, in the game of Mars," commented that, while nothing of the sort had been in his mind at the time, this game had been the forerunner of his expedition against the Turkish fortress of Azov.[1]

The two armies marched in solemn procession through Moscow, and the townspeople lined the streets to watch them pass. The procession was not without an element of the ridiculous. The Tsar's jester led a detachment of noblemen, armed with arquebuses and bearing on their banner, not the image of a saint, but the picture of a goat. A detachment of twenty-five dwarfs formed part of Romo-danovsky's army and marched boldly in front of a contingent of tall Cossacks. Each generalissimo cut a fine figure. But most staggering of all to the people of Moscow was the sight of their Tsar, marching on foot in front of the Preobrazhensky regiment as Bombardier Peter Alexeev.

The armies fought in two spirited actions, and Peter was delighted with their performance. He considered that they had shown marked skill in siege operations and that they had displayed the fighting spirit of a seasoned army. He now cast about for an opportunity to apply their experience in a serious campaign, and he found it ready at hand.

No armistice had been signed after Golitsyn's second expedition

to the Crimea, and Muscovy was still at war with the Turks and the
Crimean Tatars. It was not a state of active war, but the Russians
suffered constantly from Tatar raids. The Muscovite government, distracted by the games and entertainments of the Tsar, did nothing, but
it could not ignore these attacks indefinitely.[2] Meanwhile, bitter
complaints disrupted relations between Muscovy and her ally, Poland,
and with Poland's ally, Austria. The Poles, with justice, accused the
Russians of being inactive. The Russians suspected, with equal justice,
that the Poles and the Austrians were preparing to make a separate
peace with Turkey without thought for Russian interests. Also the
Zaporozhsky Cossacks were restless and Hetman Mazepa was urging
Moscow to send an army into the southern lands to remind the Cossacks of their allegiance to the Tsar.

Peter had another important incentive for waging war against
Turkey. Since his visits to Archangel the idea of creating a navy had
obsessed him. The White Sea, frozen for some nine months of the
year, was too distant from western centres of trade. The two seas on
which he could realize his ambition were the Baltic and the Black
seas, the former closed to him by Sweden and the latter by Turkey.
He was committed to some action against the Crimean Tatars or the
Turks, and he, therefore, decided to challenge the Turks at Azov,
which commanded access to the Sea of Azov from the north and
would provide him with the harbours which he needed.

The Ottoman Porte was a powerful enemy, but Peter had complete
confidence that his army, trained and led by foreign officers, could
capture Azov. He even planned ahead to the day when, with this
town in his hands, he would have harbours from which to seize Kerch
and to challenge the Turks in the Black Sea.

Preparations for the expedition against Azov began in earnest in
January 1695. The plan of campaign was that Boyar Sheremetev with
120,000 men and a detachment of Cossacks under Mazepa would
march against the Crimean Tatars. Their immediate objective was to
capture the Turkish fortresses on the lower Dnieper; their chief purpose was to divert the Tatars from aiding the Turks at Azov; Sheremetev's army was also intended to strengthen Moscow's authority
among the Zaporozhsky Cossacks.

For the campaign against the Turks at Azov, Peter reserved his best
troops, consisting of the play-regiments and others trained in Western
methods, together with chosen streltsi regiments. This force, num-

bering over thirty thousand men, was divided into three armies, under the commands of Generals Gordon, Lefort, and Avtonom Golovin. He appointed no supreme commander; the three generals meeting in council were to make all decisions, but in practice their decisions were subject to the approval of Bombardier of the Preobrazhensky Regiment Peter Alexeev.

A council of war, meeting in Moscow on 21 February, decided to send General Gordon in advance by land to Azov with ten thousand troops: nearly two months later the main force under the command of Lefort and Golovin embarked in the barges from the banks of the Moskva River, and set out on their journey along the Oka River and down the Volga as far as Tsaritsyn.[3] "The winds delayed us badly . . ." Peter wrote to Vinius from Nizhny-Novgorod on 19 May, "but most of all our delays have been due to stupid pilots and workmen, who call themselves masters, and who are as far from being masters as heaven is from earth."[4] Throughout this journey from Moscow, however, Peter was in high spirits, and his occasional outbursts of anger and impatience were fleeting. He was approaching the campaign in a lighthearted mood, as though setting out on manoeuvres with his play-troops.[5] The first Azov campaign was, in fact, to be the last of his games.

The fortress of Azov stood on the left bank of the river Don some ten miles from the sea. A mile above Azov the Turks had built two watchtowers with iron chains stretched across the river between them, which were designed to prevent the Cossacks sailing downriver to raid Turkish vessels and settlements. The Russian army took up positions before the fortress at the beginning of July and, despite disagreements among the engineers, built extensive siegeworks. But, without control of the mouth of the Don, their siege was ineffective, and Peter could only watch when, some days later, twenty Turkish galleys anchored close to the shore and delivered supplies and reinforcements. The Turkish garrison then launched attacks which the Russians fought off with difficulty. The Don Cossacks captured one of the watch-towers in a bold action, but Peter's pleasure was at once soured by the defection of Jacob Jansen, a Dutchman, to whom he had shown special favour. Jansen gave the Turks information on the Russian dis-positions and mentioned especially their habit of sleeping after their midday meal. At this time on the next day the Turks made a strong attack on the Russian centre which Gordon commanded, killing twelve officers and four hundred men, and wounding a further six hundred.

On Peter's insistence a massive attempt to take the fortress by storm was launched on 5 August, but, as Gordon noted in his journal: "This undertaking, begun prematurely and without sufficient thought, ended disastrously . . . some 1,500 men were killed, not including officers."[6] Gordon was the hero of the campaign and his efforts prevented even heavier losses. But he worked under difficulties. Both Lefort and Golovin resented his experience and his initiative, and withheld their support. Several times he was in the invidious position of opposing tactics which Peter himself favoured, and of being proved right in action.

The morale of the Russian troops was now very low. Their only encouragement, apart from the capture of the second watchtower, came on 19 August when reports were received from Sheremetev and Mazepa that they had captured the lower Dnieper fortresses. Nevertheless in September a council of war agreed, on Peter's insistence, to a second attempt to take Azov by storm, but, although pressed strenuously, this attack also failed.

It was then decided to raise the siege and retreat to Moscow. Heavy rain and cold delayed the army, which had the greatest difficulty in moving away at all. Enemy horsemen harried them, and annihilated one regiment. The morale of the Russian troops reached its lowest ebb and it was not until seven weeks after leaving Azov, that the remnants of the army reached Moscow.

Peter remained with his army during most of the retreat and took part in the march through Moscow. The seven months' campaign had made a deep impression on him. His games, although realistic, had not prepared him for the carnage of the battlefield. He had seen his troops wounded and killed, among them some of his closest comrades whom he mourned sincerely. He had been face to face with a real and resolute enemy; and had experienced the difficulties of moving troops long distances. Above all, he had tasted defeat; it was a new experience, and it was salutary. He acknowledged that the campaign had been a failure; he made no excuses, but threw himself into preparations for a new campaign to take place in the following spring. The experience of real warfare had matured him: at the age of twenty-three he became a responsible tsar and began his rule as supreme autocrat.

The three reasons for failure were clear. First, he had lacked skilled engineers. At Cherkassk, a few days after leaving Azov, he had sent instructions to Lev Naryshkin to write to Emperor Leopold of Austria asking him to send from six to ten competent engineers to assist in his new campaign against their common enemy, the infidel Turk; the formal request was sent in the Tsar's name to the Emperor towards the end of October. Similar requests were also made to Brandenburg and Denmark.[7]

Secondly, the Russian army had suffered through having no supreme commander. It is difficult to understand why Peter did not appoint a commander or himself assume the supreme command. For some reason he nearly always abdicated the formal headship of his own projects.

The third reason for failure was his lack of a fleet to prevent the Turks supporting the fortress by sea. He set about remedying all three defects before the new campaign in the spring.

The creation of a fleet was a formidable undertaking, especially in Russia where no facilities for shipbuilding existed, and the people, familiar only with the primitive barges on the Volga and the Don, lacked all experience of ships. Peter, however, seemed unaware of the enormity of the task. He had to decide where the ships should be built, establish shipyards, assemble timber, and other materials, find competent shipwrights and carpenters, and to train crews. By the standards of the time, the fleet that he planned was large. It was to consist of twenty-five armed galleys, and thirteen hundred river barges to transport troops and supplies to Azov, as well as some thirty seagoing boats, pinewood rafts, and fireships. Everything had to be done in five months of the winter of 1695-1696.

The town of Voronezh had direct access to the Don River, and was close to forests, providing oak, and other timbers. Peter chose it as the site of the main building yards which were to produce all the vessels, except for the galleys and fireships which were to be built in Preobrazhenskoe, and transported to Voronezh by sledge.

Peter himself made or supervised all these preparations. Through Witzen in Holland he had ordered a galley which sailed from Amsterdam for Archangel early in the summer of 1695, accompanied by Jan Petersen, a Dutch shipwright. At Archangel it had been dismantled and transported in sections to Preobrazhenskoe. This was the model for the whole galley fleet, and fortunately it arrived safely early in

January; the galley fleet was built and sent by land to Voronezh some three months later.

The main problem was shortage of skilled workmen. All the foreigners in the country were enlisted. Peter wrote to Archangel directing that all the ships' carpenters there should be sent to work on the galleys during the winter, after which they could return to Archangel in time for the opening of the White Sea.[8] Early in January 1697, twenty-four carpenters arrived and at once set to work in the shipyards. The supply of unskilled workmen presented less difficulty. An ukaz called on the province of Belgorod to provide 27,828 men to labour on this project, and all the towns of the province shared the obligation between them. Subsequently more labour was conscripted.

For the new expedition Peter appointed Boyar Shein as Generalissimo, and Lefort as Admiral of the Fleet. Neither was qualified for high command, but Peter probably regarded the appointments as honorary, for, in fact, he himself was in charge. He turned to his own regiments, the Preobrazhensky and the Semyonovsky, for crews for his galley fleet, and more than four thousand men were selected and divided into twenty-eight companies, each with a captain and a lieutenant in command. The Tsar himself commanded the fourth company as Captain Peter Alexeev.

The new campaign had been proclaimed within a week of Peter's return from Azov. All liable to serve had been summoned. Volunteers were also enlisted, and they were numerous from among the serfs, who could now obtain their freedom by military service. The Russian army for this campaign exceeded forty-six thousand men, and in addition there were fifteen thousand Ukrainian Cossacks, five thousand Don Cossacks, and three thousand Kalmyk horsemen, as well as other smaller contingents. The total force was over seventy thousand men, more than double the strength of the previous year.

During January and February 1696, Peter worked day and night on these preparations. A poisoned leg immobilized him for a time, and, although it meant that he could not work with an axe in the Voronezh yards, it did not prevent his directing the whole project, and driving it through at a tempo that was new to Russia.

On 29 January 1696, Tsar Ivan suddenly died. He had been ailing all his life and suffered from scurvy. He was buried next day with full ceremonial, and Peter attended the funeral. He had had a certain affection for Ivan, and, although since the death of his mother he had seldom visited Moscow and had seen little of him, he had usually written in a tone of almost tender respectfulness telling him about any event of interest. He now took Ivan's widow and family under his care, and provided generously for them during the rest of his life.[9]

By the end of January Peter's leg had improved enough to allow him to travel to Voronezh. He found there a scene of tremendous activity which delighted him. More than thirty thousand men at points along the Voronezh River were making barges and preparing timber, and work on most of the vessels was well advanced. He occupied a simple house, adjoining the building yards, and used it to snatch a few hours' sleep. In a letter to Moscow, he wrote with pride of his labours, claiming that "in obedience to the Lord's command to our Great-Grandfather Adam we are eating our bread in the sweat of our brows."[10]

The tempo of work at Voronezh mounted throughout March. The galleys, built in Preobrazhenskoe, were sent on their way by sledge at the beginning of the month, and several galleys accompanied by their captains had reached Voronezh by 15 March. But on the same day Peter was writing to Lefort to complain that the others had not arrived.[11] Lefort consoled him with news from Archangel of thirty-eight foreign sailors and two shipmasters, who had volunteered for the Tsar's service and had already reached Moscow. Peter himself wrote to the Danish resident in Moscow, asking when the party of Danish officers and shipbuilders whom he had requested would arrive.[12] Soon afterwards Vinius reported that two engineers and four gunnery experts were expected from Brandenburg by the end of April. Everything was moving towards Voronezh, and the second expedition against the Turks was nearly ready.

On 23 April, Gordon with his force sailed for Azov in 123 barges, followed two days later by Golovin with his troops. Next Generalissimo Shein set out with his staff, but Peter remained at Voronezh, until certain ships in which he was especially interested were ready. On 3 May he sailed, leading a squadron of eight galleys, and followed by three other squadrons at intervals of a week.

The voyage down the Don was uneventful, and at the end of May, all the galley squadrons and barges had reached the watchtowers at Novosergievsk. By 11 June, according to Peter's letters, twenty-two Russian galleys were anchored off the mouth of the Don, where they remained effectively blockading Azov.[13] Meanwhile other preparations went ahead. The Russian forces took up siege positions, and their morale was high. Work on the trenches went forward energetically and Gordon was satisfied with progress. The Tsar was no longer playing and his determination had given his troops a new and confident spirit.

Turkish prisoners taken in a skirmish on 10 June stated that a Turkish fleet of fifty ships was expected daily with reinforcements and supplies. Four days later the enemy fleet was sighted, and proved much smaller than reported. The Turks made halfhearted attempts to send troops ashore but, as soon as they saw the Russians weighing anchor, they gave up and put out to sea. Two weeks later the Turks tried, again unsuccessfully, to land troops. Without fighting a single action the Russians had gained command of the mouth of the Don.

The Russian artillery was now ready to bombard the fortress. Before opening fire, Peter called on the Turks to surrender, and they refused. The bombardment began, causing heavy damage to the town's defences. Peter himself served on the guns as a bombardier, but he went up to the front lines almost daily, and several times sailed out to the mouth of the river to visit his fleet. At the same time he kept up his correspondence with Romodanovsky, Vinius, and others in Moscow, telling them of the progress of the siege. Some of his letters were concerned with trivialities, such as the packing of an hourglass, or apologies to Romodanovsky who thought he had been slighted.[14] Alarmed by reports that he was running risks, his sister, Natalya, wrote asking him to take care of himself and not to go near cannon balls and bullets, to which he replied facetiously that "it is not I who go near to cannon balls and bullets, but they come near to me. Send orders for them to stop it. . . ."[15]

The bombardment continued. A Russian prisoner, who had escaped from Azov, stated that the Turks were divided between those determined to resist and those who were ready to capitulate. This report led Peter again to invite the Turks to surrender, offering them good terms, but the Turks only answered with gunfire. Meanwhile the Russians were making good progress with a wall of earth they were building around the fort, and moving forward so that it filled in the Turkish trenches and reached a height which allowed them to fire down into the fortress.

On 9 July, the Austrian engineers and gunnery experts, sent in answer to Peter's request, arrived at Novosergievsk. They inspected the siege positions and expressed amazement at the amount of work that the Russians had carried out. But they suggested improvements which, when introduced, greatly increased the effectiveness of the bombardment. Indeed, it was clear that, had the Austrians arrived earlier, the siege operations would have been far more advanced, and Peter bluntly expressed his regrets over their late arrival. He was then surprised to learn that, unable to obtain information from the Russian resident in Vienna, they had travelled slowly, assuming that operations would not begin until late in the summer. Peter at once made investigations and found that Ukraintsev at the Foreign Office had kept the Russian resident in ignorance about the campaign, as he considered it dangerous to send such information abroad, even to an allied court. Peter was furious, and expressed his anger in a letter written in his own hand to Ukraintsev's brother-in-law, Vinius, which closed on the threatening note: "Tell him that what he does not write on paper, I will write on his back"—meaning with the knout.[16]

A council of war fixed 22 July as the date for the general assault. But this proved unnecessary. A few hours after the council had met, the Turks began waving their turbans and lowering their banners to signal a cease-fire. They then sent an officer with a letter, stating that they would surrender if they could go in freedom with their wives and children and as much of their property as they could carry. Shein, in whose name the original offer had been made, confirmed these terms, but added the further condition that the Turks should hand over the Dutchman, Jacob Jansen, who had deserted the previous year.

Early in the morning of 19 July, the Turks began to leave the fortress. On the following day, Shein formally celebrated the capture of Azov with a banquet, at which he spared "neither drink nor powder."[17] A report signed by the Generalissimo was sent to Patriarch Adrian, and Peter's pleasure was reflected in his short joyful letters to Romodanovsky, Vinius, and others in Moscow.[18] All the members of Peter's Company in Moscow showered congratulations on him, but so high-flown and rhetorical were their praises that they probably gave him no pleasure. One letter that pleased him was from Vinius who wrote that he had sent reports of the victory abroad, and especially to Witsen, Burgomaster of Amsterdam, requesting him to inform William III of England, who of all the rulers in Europe was Peter's hero.[19]

On receiving news of the victory, Moscow gave way to rejoicing. The Muscovites had grown accustomed to defeats; a victory, especially over the great Ottoman Porte, was unbelievable. The Patriarch wept with joy as he read the official report, and then ordered the great bell to be rung.

Defeat of the Turks did not, however, herald a period of relaxation, such as had followed the play-exercises. Peter could not now afford the time. He gave immediate orders for the Russian siegeworks to be razed and for the rebuilding of Azov. His engineers, advised by the Austrians, drew up plans for its restoration and fortification, and work began five days later. He then explored the northern shore of the sea, for he needed a base for his navy; Azov itself was unsuitable, and he chose Cape Taganrog as the site of his new harbour.

Peter left Azov to return to Moscow in August. En route he sent orders to Vinius to erect a triumphal arch in Moscow to welcome the army home from its victory,[20] and the entry into the capital had to be delayed so that preparations could be made in accordance with his instructions and on the scale that he demanded.

The arch and other decorations bewildered the Muscovites, for they had seen nothing like them before. The holy ikons borne by church dignitaries, wearing their magnificent robes, and the solemn services in the cathedrals played no part; the religious character of the traditional Muscovite celebrations was absent. Peter's arrangements struck a new, secular note. The arch and its embellishments were classical in style, with columns, pediments, and allegorical statues. Massive figures of Hercules and Mars supported the arch, and at their feet were representations of the Turkish Pasha, and Turkish and Tatar prisoners in chains.

The procession, stretching several miles, marched through Moscow to Preobrazhenskoe. It opened with horsemen followed by carriages, bearing Prince-Pope Zotov, General Golovin, and others from the Company. Then, preceded by an escort of horsemen, came Admiral Lefort, in a gilded sledge drawn by six richly caparisoned horses. Peter wearing a German coat of black, and a white feather in his hat, followed the Admiral's sledge on foot and marched the full distance.

In the midst of the magnificent procession a simple wagon struck an incongruous note. In it sat the Dutch traitor, Jacob Jansen, wearing

Turkish dress, and around his neck a notice with the one word: "Evildoer." A small scaffold had been built in the wagon, and on it stood a gallows and two execution blocks, by each of which stood an executioner, surrounded with axes, knives, whips, pincers, leather thongs, and other articles of torture and execution.

It was an example of Peter's sense of humour at its most horrible. He may have had Jansen brought all the way from Azov and displayed as a warning to his people. More probably he was simply showing his satisfaction that the man who had betrayed him and caused so many of his troops to die was to be brought to justice. But also he was impelled by love of spectacle, for not only in Muscovy but in Europe at this time people took a strange pleasure in watching executions. Seven days later Jansen was knouted and tortured, broken on the wheel and, after execution, his head impaled on a stake, in the presence of a large crowd of spectators, no doubt including Peter.

CHAPTER X

The Navy

1697-1698

PETER returned from the capture of Azov with two great projects in mind. The first was the creation of a navy; the second, stemming from the first, was to send young Russians abroad to study seamanship, navigation, and shipbuilding, and to visit Europe himself for the same purpose. Both projects were revolutionary, and involved immense problems. But during the next five months of winter he gave to them such impetus that, by the beginning of March 1697, work on the navy was going ahead, and many Russians were already abroad, while his embassy was on the point of departure.

Peter was now twenty-four years of age. He towered over his subjects, but it was his vitality that set him apart from other men. A demon of energy possessed him. He did not walk, but rushed; his courtiers were usually forced to break into a run to keep up with him. Even at banquets he could not remain seated for long, but would suddenly get up from his chair and hurry off to another room. He travelled constantly, covering vast distances, and going to parts of his country where no tsar had ever been. His hands were horny and permanently calloused, but they worked swiftly and skilfully to master every new craft that caught his attention. His energy was not merely physical, it was also mental. He was always learning, planning, and building. And this energy, allied with an unshakable, single-minded determination, enabled him to drive the whole nation along a road that it was reluctant to follow.

In Peter's own words, "All his thoughts had been turned to the

93

creation of a navy," since his voyages in the White Sea.[1] He now had at Taganrog a site for a naval base; his next task was to create a Black Sea fleet. The vessels, built for the second Azov campaign, had been merely a supporting force. For his navy he required more than fifty warships, each armed with twenty-four to thirty guns. It meant nothing less than turning Russia into a sea power.

On 20 October 1696, Peter summoned a meeting of boyars at Pre- obrazhenskoe to consider the two important questions of the resettle- ment of Azov and the construction of the navy. The council promptly agreed to send three thousand infantrymen with their families from the Kazan region to colonize Azov, and subsequently sent three thousand streltsi from Moscow. It was also decided in principle that a navy should be built.

At a second meeting the council directed that a labour force of twenty thousand men should be assembled from the Ukrainian towns to build a town and harbour at Taganrog, and to start work not later than 1 May 1697. Next, it allocated responsibility for building and maintaining the ships. This was based on wealth and was an at- tempt to spread the burden evenly. The church and its monasteries were required to produce one ship fully rigged and armed for every eight thousand serf households attached to the lands they owned, while civil landowners were to produce one ship for every ten thou- sand households. The government was to provide timber, but the landowners had to find all other materials. They were to build their ships at Voronezh and have them ready for service not later than April 1698, a period of eighteen months. They were also responsible for maintaining and, if lost, replacing their ships. Landowners with not less than one hundred serf households were ordered to report to the Estates Office in Moscow by 1 January 1697, so that they could be inscribed in companies which were to be responsible for the con- struction of ships on the same scale as the great landowners. Con- fiscation of all property was the punishment for failure to report. Landowners with less than one hundred serf households were ex- empted from direct responsibility, but made a financial contribution. Merchants in the capital and the provinces were to provide twelve ships and, when they petitioned the Tsar to be relieved of this bur- den, the number was increased to fourteen.[2]

The ukaz allowed no exceptions. The Patriarch owned private estates containing 8,761 serf households; he was required to provide one ship for eight thousand households, and to join in a company, adding his remaining 761 households to those of two metropolitans, an archbishop, and twelve monasteries, to produce another ship. Peter's closest colleagues participated on the same terms; the Tsar's favour was never an excuse for smaller contributions. Landowners who failed to deliver on time were faced with heavy penalties, and most of them contracted with foreign shipwrights for the construction of their ships.

In July 1696, while still laying siege to Azov, Peter had instructed his minister to request the Doge of Venice "to send to Moscow for the purpose of our mutual Christian campaign, thirteen worthy shipwrights, able to build every kind of seagoing vessel."[3] The Venetian shipwrights arrived in the following January,[4] and others came from Holland, England, Denmark, and Sweden. In the first half of 1697 no fewer than fifty Western shipwrights reached Moscow and went on to work at Voronezh.

Still he faced the basic problem of insufficient skilled labour. He needed not only shipwrights, carpenters, and riggers, but also officers and crews. He had to enlist foreigners, but he regarded it as a temporary measure, for he had resolved to train his own people, turning landsmen into sailors, by sending them abroad to study.

On 22 November 1696, without warning, sixty-one young men of noble families received orders to proceed to western Europe at their own expense for naval training. Two weeks later in the Foreign Office, Councillor Ukraintsev announced that the "Sovereign has directed for his great affairs of state, that to the neighbouring nations, to the Emperor, to the Kings of England and Denmark, to the Pope of Rome, to the Dutch States, to the Elector of Brandenburg, and to Venice shall be sent his great Ambassadors and Plenipotentiaries: General and Admiral Franz Lefort, General and Kommissar Feodor Alexeevich Golovin, and Councillor Prokofy Voznitsyn."[5]

The unprecedented demands of the Tsar's shipbuilding programme, coming on top of the burdens of the two Azov campaigns, had distressed the boyars and gentry. But they were horrified to learn that their sons were to be sent to Italy, England, and Holland. To all but a handful of Muscovites, the countries to the west were unknown and sinister; the Tsar was dooming their sons to be corrupted and seduced from the Orthodox way of life.

This was not a danger that disturbed Peter who was concerned with their education and training, and in January 1697 he drew up a syllabus for their studies. Each Russian was to obtain a certificate of proficiency from the naval authorities with whom he had served; he was also to take one soldier with him and to see that he, too, received training; moreover, while abroad he had to hire and bring back to Moscow two skilled mariners.

If the Muscovites were shocked to learn that their young men were to travel abroad, they were stunned by Peter's decision to visit western Europe himself. The Tsar of Muscovy had never before gone beyond his own frontiers, except on very rare occasions of war. They did not understand why he should want to go. But already Peter was an enigma, the "Tsar-Stranger," who had discarded so many of the time-hallowed formalities with which they loved to surround the throne. Nevertheless, of all his violations of the customs of his fathers, the European tour shocked his people most. They felt that he was wilfully deserting them; they feared that he would disappear in Europe or suffer some deep change; and their horror had in it an element of pathos as though they were children about to be orphaned.

Peter's determination to visit Europe was not merely the self-indulgence of an autocrat. He saw himself as a forerunner, obliged to learn so that he could teach. Moreover, he thought it only natural that he should visit western Europe, "for a monarch would feel ashamed to lag behind his own subjects in any craft."[6]

The question was how to make this tour, for he could not travel abroad as he travelled in his own country. It may have been Lefort who suggested a formal embassy to the courts of western Europe and this suggestion suited his plans well. The capture of Azov was only the beginning of his campaign, and he knew that Muscovy alone could not conquer the Ottoman empire. He proposed, therefore, to form a great alliance of Russia, England, Denmark, Prussia, Holland, Austria, and Venice against Turkey. The negotiation of this alliance was the formal purpose of the embassy. It had the further advantage of allowing him to travel incognito and to avoid the lengthy diplomatic formalities which he found tedious.

All preparations for the tour had to be completed without delay. Peter directed the arrangements and received daily reports from Ukraintsev. He wrote out in his own hand what he required for the navy: his ambassadors were to enlist personnel, particularly ships' captains and officers, "who had themselves been sailors and had reached their rank by service and not other means," and to hire gunnery experts, ships' carpenters, and blacksmiths. They were also to purchase guns, blocks and tackle, anchors and navigating instruments.[7] The embassy grew rapidly until it numbered more than 250 persons, including a group of thirty-eight known as "volunteers" among whom Peter himself was listed under the name of Peter Mikhailov.

In the midst of this planning, he did not lose sight of his campaign against Turkey. In January 1697 he appointed Shein to command an army of 37,475 men to fortify Azov and Taganrog, and to build a fortress on the bank of the Don opposite Azov. He also sent a force of Ukrainian Cossacks to the Crimea to cut off the Tatars from the Turks. At the same time troops from the Novgorod and Ryazan provinces were despatched to the Polish frontier, for in Poland a stormy interregnum had followed the death of King Jan Sobieski.

Peter was now like a river in spate; his energies poured like torrents in several channels as he worked simultaneously on these diverse projects. He was approaching his first prime of manhood, and his confidence in his own powers was magnificent. He recognized no obstacles as insuperable, and it was typical of him that in the midst of these labours he should have found time to consider a proposal for linking the Volga and Don rivers by a canal, thus creating a waterway from Moscow to Azov. In the spring of 1697, he gave instructions for a labour force of twenty thousand men to work on this canal under the direction of Colonel Breckell, a German engineer.[8]

With so much on his hands, Peter was hardly conscious of his people. At this time he took them for granted as soldiers and labourers. When signs of revolt obtruded on his plans, his anger was harsh. Already at the beginning of January 1697 a small opposition group had been discovered. It had been meeting in the Andreevsky Monastery, and consisted of a few monks, medium-grade officials, and petty landowners, but their complaints were typical of the complaints of most Muscovites, as preserved in the archives of the secret police of the time.[9] The Tsar had, they said, lowered the dignity of the throne, especially by mingling with foreigners and walking on foot behind Lefort's carriage; he had forsaken the Kremlin and his Tsaritsa; in his games and campaigns he had caused hardships to all his subjects. Boldly but rather naïvely, they wrote a letter of protest.

They were arrested and, after examination under torture, were exiled to Siberia or to Azov.

On 23 February Peter was spending the evening at Lefort's house in the usual round of merriment, when suddenly a report of a plot on his life interrupted the festivities. The strelets, Larion Elizarev, whose warning had sent Peter fleeing to Troitsa Monastery eight years earlier, had informed against Tsykler. Although he had held high office several times and been promoted to the rank of councillor, Tsykler felt that he had not been advanced as he deserved, and he was now outspoken in his hostility towards the Tsar. He worked with energy to sow disaffection, and he had influence among the streltsi and the boyars, who longed for the old Muscovite ways.

The discovery of this plot stirred Peter to a fury. Even the sentence of death passed on the five ringleaders and the exile of their families to Siberia did not assuage his anger. He thought he had seen behind the conspiracy the idea of restoring the Miloslavsky to power and, as though it were a sinister spell, he devised a terrible means to exorcize it. He had the grave of Ivan Miloslavsky opened and the coffin brought to Preobrazhenskoe on a sledge drawn by swine. The coffin was then opened and placed under the execution block so that as the executioner cut off the arms and legs and finally the heads of the conspirators their blood flowed onto the corpse. It was a macabre spectacle, but Peter was still not satisfied. Next day a stone column was erected on the Red Square in Moscow, and the corpses of the executed men were brought from Preobrazhenskoe to be displayed on it, with a statement of their crimes, for all to see. For over five months the bodies remained on the Red Square as a warning to his people.

This conspiracy and the evidence of opposition in no way deterred him from going abroad. He was not easily deflected from what he wanted to do, least of all by his own people. Moreover, he took no special action to deal with outbreaks while he was away. Officially he was to be in Moscow and during his absence documents were issued and received in his name; the embassy itself sent all reports to Moscow addressed to him. But, while no governor or council of state could be appointed, Peter, according to Captain Perry, entrusted Boyar Lev Naryshkin, Prince Boris Golitsyn, and Prince Peter Prozorovsky with almost plenary powers to act in his absence. He also made Prince Feodor Romodanovsky Governor of Moscow.[10] Five days after the execution of Tsykler, he set out for the West.

CHAPTER XI

The Grand Embassy

1697

ALL Europe speculated over the reasons for the Tsar's journey. The Austrian resident in Moscow reported to his Emperor that the embassy was "merely a cloak to allow the Tsar to get out of his country and travel in freedom, and has no other serious purpose."[1] Another speculation was that he was fulfilling a vow to make a pilgrimage to the tombs of St. Peter and St. Paul in Rome. Other theories were advanced, but the real reason for the tour was simple, as were the reasons for most of his actions: Peter set out for western Europe to study shipbuilding and anything else that would help him to create a navy. The countries that he most wanted to visit were the naval powers—Holland, England, and Venice. He was curious to see Europe at first hand, and to learn something about her ways of living and government, but it was to examine her dockyards and ships that he made the journey. At first sight it was a narrow purpose, but the tour proved a turning-point in his reign and, such were the consequences, Macaulay did not overstate when he wrote that "his journey is an epoch in the history, not only of his own country but of ours, and of the world."[2]

The embassy left Moscow on 9 March. At Pskov, as it was about to leave Russian soil, the ambassadors sent a courier to the Governor of Riga, Governor-General Dahlberg, and without waiting for his reply, they crossed the Swedish frontier. They were within five miles of Riga when the formal letter of welcome reached them. Governor Dahlberg assured them that everything possible would be done "with

99

neighbourly friendliness" for the ambassadors of the Tsar, "bearing in mind the present condition of this land." His letter went on to say that he would have appreciated earlier notice of the visit.[3]

Livonia had suffered a disastrous failure of the harvest, and, although Dahlberg's letter was courteous, the arrival of two hundred and fifty Russians in time of famine faced him with serious problems. But he did what he could for his uninvited guests. Half a mile from Riga an escort awaited the ambassadors, and in a ceremonial procession they entered the town. The Russians were impressed and satisfied with their reception.[4]

The breaking of the ice on the Dvina River and the flooding of parts of the town compelled Peter to remain in Riga for seven days. He passed the time inspecting the defences of the town, but he showed little tact; on one occasion, as he measured the depth of the moat, a Swedish sentry threatened to fire on him. Learning of this incident the Governor sent his apologies, and Lefort, as first ambassador, acknowledged that the sentry had carried out his duties correctly, adding that he had instructed all members of the embassy to avoid giving rise to such incidents in future.

The enforced stay at Riga, however, annoyed Peter, and he particularly resented the restraints on his freedom. Another source of annoyance was the curiosity of the townspeople, who gathered in crowds to stare at him. The river was still swollen and floating ice made it dangerous, but on 8 April he managed to cross with a small party. He left in a mood of discontent, complaining of the "slavish way" they had been forced to live in Riga.[5] The embassy followed three days later, exasperated by the Swedish government's refusal to supply them with provisions, fodder for their horses, and with transport. Three years later, Peter was to make these incidents one of the main pretexts for declaring war on Sweden.[6]

From Riga, Peter with his small party travelled to Mitau, the capital of the duchy of Courland. The duchy was not rich, but Duke Frederick Casimir spared no expense in making his visitors welcome; "open tables were kept everywhere with trumpets and music, attended with feasting and excessive drinking all along, as if his Tsarish Majesty had been another Bacchus."[7] The Duke knew that the Tsar was present, and allowed him to remain incognito while showing him every honour. He had the satisfaction of meeting him more than once and of talking with him in private. But the Russians did not make a good impression. "I have not seen yet such hard drinkers," wrote Baron de Blomberg, . . . "though the attendants of this embassy are made up of chosen men; yet one soon discovers their brutish manner in many things." He learnt that the foreign officers with the embassy called the Russians "baptized bears"; it seemed a fitting description.[8]

On 2 May a yacht, chartered for his use by the Duke,[9] carried Peter to Pilau, the port of Königsberg. The Elector of Brandenburg, Frederick III, soon to become the first King of Prussia, was there at the time. He was keenly interested to meet the Tsar who had defeated the Turks, and anxious to negotiate a new treaty of alliance with Russia, directed against Sweden. When sure that the Tsar was with the embassy, he arranged a lavish welcome.

Soon after his arrival Peter had a private meeting with the Elector. He entered the palace by a back staircase to avoid being seen, and for an hour and a half they discussed ships, navigation, and gunnery. He declined, however, to receive a return visit on the ground that he wished to retain his incognito, but they met several times. At the castle of Friedrichsberg, Peter inspected the fortifications and the arsenal, impressing everyone with his military knowledge. He made full use of his time in Königsberg and Pilau to study gunnery under the Elector's artillery expert, and received a certificate proclaiming him a "Master of Artillery."[10]

The ambassadors reached Königsberg twelve days after Peter, and their stay was a succession of banquets, dinners, and entertainments. But the Elector kept in mind his need for a new alliance. The Muscovite tsars and the House of Hohenzollern had been joined in a defensive alliance for nearly two centuries, held together by fear of Sweden and Poland, and Peter's father, Tsar Alexei, had confirmed the alliance. Three days after their arrival, the ambassadors received the Elector's proposals for a new treaty. But Peter, who conducted the negotiations, although they were carried on in the name of his ambassadors, rejected the terms proposed, fearing they would lead to trouble with Sweden and Poland while he was still at war with Turkey. No agreement had been reached on 2 June when the ambassadors had their farewell audience but, on board the Elector's yacht anchored off Friedrichshof, Peter and Frederick met and for the first time negotiated directly. The clause in the alliance which Peter feared would offend Sweden and Poland was omitted, but he agreed orally with the Elector that they should help each other against all mutual

enemies, particularly Sweden. He would not commit himself to recognizing the kingly status of the Elector's representatives, but undertook to accord to them in Moscow the same status as the Elector
accorded to Muscovite representatives. This satisfied honour on both
sides, and the new alliance was concluded.[11]

Despite his impatience to reach Holland, Peter remained in Pilau
until the end of June so that he could follow the election of a new
king of Poland to succeed Jan Sobieski. Poland was now in decline.
Her vast sprawling territory, then embracing the great plain lying
between the Dnieper and Oder rivers, held together because her
neighbours were distracted in other directions or were too weak to
dismember her. The Polish republic was in fact a dual state, comprising Poland proper and the grand duchy of Lithuania; they had
King and Diet in common, but maintained separate armies, legal
systems, and certain high offices. Both were divided into provinces
and each province had its local Diet, which could freely refuse to
accept the decisions of the national Diet. Despite this incredible division of powers, Poland had enjoyed some semblance of government
due mainly to the authority of several strong kings.

In the sixteenth century two constitutional changes had further
increased the chaos. The first was the abolition of a hereditary for an
elective monarchy, the second was the introduction of a free veto
which any member of the Diet, composed exclusively of the powerful
landowning gentry, could exercise. Divided by petty jealousies and
selfish interests, the Poles used this veto to reduce the Diet to im-
potence. With such a system Poland's sole hope of order and unity
lay in a strong monarch. King Jan Sobieski had united the country,
but French intrigues had foiled his attempts to secure the succession
for his heirs. The candidates were numerous for the elections now approaching, but the Prince de Conti, a Bourbon and the nominee of
Louis XIV of France, and Frederick-Augustus, the Elector of Saxony,
were the most important.

Peter was prepared to invade Poland, if necessary, to prevent the
Prince de Conti being elected, for France supported Turkey against
the alliance of Poland, Russia, Venice, and Austria. With Conti on
the Polish throne, Poland would withdraw from this alliance and
might even aid the Turks; Kiev and the Ukraine, as well as his campaign against the Turks would then be endangered.

Already Russian troops had moved to the Polish frontier as a token of his support for Augustus of Saxony, and from Pilau, as he anxiously watched developments, Peter sent a stream of instructions to his resident in Warsaw. Finally he drew up a memorandum addressed to the Polish Rada, vigorously expressing his views.[12] It reached Warsaw three days before the elections began and made a strong impression. The electors were divided, but a majority supported Augustus of Saxony, who had already crossed the Polish frontier with his own army to enforce his claims. Only when his election was certain, did Peter make ready to leave Pilau.

Peter had wanted to travel on to Holland by sea, but the sea route was dangerous. He decided, therefore, to make for the nearest port in Brandenburg and to proceed by land from there to Holland. But he sent a party of seventy-one by sea to Lübeck and on to Amsterdam so that they could begin their training while awaiting the embassy's arrival.

With Holland almost in sight, Peter made haste. He stopped in Berlin only to eat. He was also at this time suffering acutely from his fear of being stared at. An incident in the small fortress town of Kustrin had upset him. A group of Frankfurt students had overpowered the guard and burst into the house where he was resting in order to see the Tsar of Muscovy; having satisfied their curiosity they had retired. He dreaded a repetition of this incident and, as he drove through Berlin, sat tightly in the corner of his carriage to avoid being seen.

On 27 July he stopped at the small town of Koppenbrugge, and there he met the Electress Sophia Charlotte. It was his first contact with the gracious, cultivated, and intellectual side of Western life. Sophia Charlotte, second wife of the Elector of Brandenburg, was one of the remarkable women of the day. At Versailles, where she had spent two years, her intelligence, beauty, and wit had attracted the attention of Louis XIV himself, and her teacher and close friend was Leibniz, one of the most profound thinkers of the time.

The first rumours of the visit of the Tsar of Muscovy had aroused Sophia's curiosity. Unable to accompany her husband to Königsberg, she asked one of the Elector's ministers to describe the visit in fullest detail.[13] Again she missed seeing Peter in Berlin and as soon as she heard that he would be travelling near by, she set out hastily for Koppenbrugge with her mother, three brothers and a considerable suite. She arrived only a few hours before Peter, who was as usual ahead of the embassy and she at once sent her chamberlain to invite him to dine.

Peter refused. He had seen the retinue of courtiers arriving and the local people crowding around the castle gates, and he recoiled from being the object of their curiosity. But Sophia was not to be baulked of her quarry. Her chamberlain pressed him to accept and he yielded on condition that the dinner be an informal family occasion. Sophia arranged that, apart from herself and her mother, those present would be limited to her three brothers, Crown Prince George-Ludwig, later to become George I of England, Prince Max, and Prince Ernst-Augustus, and the owner of the castle.

Peter entered the castle by a back staircase to avoid the crowd, and was welcomed by the Electress and her mother. It was an uncomfortable moment for him. Faced by these two poised and fashionable ladies, he lost his nerve, shyness overwhelmed him. He covered his face with his hands, and muttered in German "I don't know what to say!" Lefort had to speak for him.[14]

Sophia and her mother talked constantly to put him at his ease. He sat between them at the dinner table, but for some time persisted in using interpreters. Then his shyness passed and he conversed freely with them. He exchanged snuffboxes with Sophia, who was delighted with his company, although she noted that he was hardly conscious of her as a woman and showed no interest in flirtation.

Dinner lasted some four hours, and then he allowed the courtiers and their ladies to join the company. Sophia called for music and, in order to see how the Russians danced, asked Lefort to send for his musicians. Peter declined to open the dancing, saying that he had no gloves. But he was soon performing heartily, to the delight of the Electress and her mother. Peter amused them, too, when he exclaimed loudly as he danced and felt the whalebones in the corsets of his partner: "These German women have devilish hard bones!"[15] He was now enjoying himself enormously; his jester, catching the mood of his master, reduced the company to helpless laughter. Peter played with his favourite dwarfs. He gaily kissed the little Princess, Sophia's niece, and also her brother, the sixteen-year-old Prince George, who was to become George II of England. It was an occasion when Peter overflowed with high spirits and good nature and his happy mood infected the whole company.

Sophia and her mother observed him closely and were favourably impressed. He was extremely tall, strongly built, and handsome. His grimaces and facial contortions were not so bad as they had expected, but he was coarse and dirty in his eating habits; he did not know what to do with his table napkin, and a pitcher of water would have been useful after dinner. But they were completely won over by his natural easy manner. Far from being tired after their hours of conversation they would willingly have continued talking with him, instead of dancing. But Sophia was afraid that he might be bored, since, as she had learnt, social conversations were not the custom in Muscovy.

Both ladies considered that Peter was a remarkable man with a good heart and noble instincts. Sophia's final judgment, written some two months later, was that "he is a ruler both very good and very evil at the same time; his character is exactly the character of his country. If he had had a better education, he would be an exceptional man, for he has great qualities and unlimited natural intelligence."[16]

Peter enjoyed the company of the Electress, and he signified his pleasure by sending her a present of sables and brocade. But this contact with a woman who was both beautiful and highly intelligent, and a representative of Western European court life at its best, made no lasting impression on him. Now nearing Holland and her shipyards, he was impatient to set out on the last lap of his journey.[17]

CHAPTER XII

Peter in Holland

1697

IN the second half of the seventeenth century Holland was at the peak of her power and prestige. Dutch ships roved the oceans, claiming a large share of the world's trade. Amsterdam was the foremost port of Europe, although rapidly yielding primacy to London. The Dutch navy was a formidable force which at one stage was a match for the English navy. Above all, the prestige of Holland stood high because her people had defied the might of France and, led by William of Orange, had rallied the Protestant countries in opposition to the ambitious designs of Louis XIV. The ascent of William to the throne of England in 1688 as William III had carried Dutch prestige to its zenith.

Holland, as a naval and mercantile power with a great shipbuilding industry, naturally attracted Peter. At this time, moreover, the country held two further interests for him; the first was the presence of William III at Utrecht; the second was the Congress of Ryswyk which had brought to The Hague powerful embassies from the leading countries of Europe, thus facilitating his policy of forming a grand alliance against Turkey.

Peter left his embassy at Schermbeck on 4 August, and went ahead with a group of eighteen volunteers. Zaandam, then known as Saardam, was his destination. He hired boats to take him down the Rhine, and not even Amsterdam could deflect or delay him. He left twelve of his companions there to start training as shipbuilders, and himself pressed on, eager to begin his own studies.

Zaandam was then the centre of a flourishing shipbuilding district with more than fifty wharves, producing vessels of every type. But it was not the leading Dutch shipbuilding region that Peter thought it to be. Zaandamers in Muscovy, talking about their home with the nostalgia of expatriates, had given him the idea that it was the ship-building centre not only of Holland, but of the whole world.

A friendly encounter as he approached the town gave him great pleasure. His boat was moving along the canal when he recognized a Dutchman, fishing for eels. It was the blacksmith, Gerrit Kist, who had worked in Muscovy. Peter shouted to him, and it is said that Kist nearly fell out of his boat with surprise at seeing the Tsar of Muscovy in his native town. Peter was delighted with the meeting, for he liked familiar faces about him. A few hours later he was settled in Kist's tiny house which contained only two small rooms, two win-dows, a tiled stove, and a small airless closet for the bed.[1]

As it was Sunday, Peter had to spend his first day in idleness. His annoyance increased when the local inhabitants gathered to stare at him and his companions. Early next morning he bought carpenter's tools and on the same day signed on as a workman in one of the ship-yards. But rumours that the Tsar was among the foreigners soon brought crowds of people who stood around the house, waiting to see him.

Evidence came confirming the rumours. A Zaandamer received a letter from his son, then serving in Muscovy, which referred to the Tsar's European tour, mentioning his height, the way he shook his head and swung his right arm violently as he walked, and also the wart on his right cheek. The letter was read out in the local barber-shop. Soon afterwards Peter himself came into the shop and was rec-ognized. On the same day, when Peter was sitting in a coffee house, a shipmaster, who had made the voyage to Archangel several times, also recognized him.[2]

The news spread through Holland. Great crowds now shadowed him wherever he went. The burgomaster posted sentries, but the crowds pushed them aside. When he went sailing in the gulf of the Ij so many yachts and boats followed that Peter in desperation jumped ashore halfway to Haarlem and hid in a hotel, returning later to Zaandam under cover of night.

On the day that he had to go to Amsterdam to meet his embassy, the crowds were greater than ever. The burgomaster was powerless and it seemed that Peter would not be able to leave. Finally his yacht was brought nearer to his house and he managed to go on board. A high wind was blowing, but he insisted on getting under way and a few hours later he arrived in Amsterdam. He had spent only a week in Zaandam, but had seen enough to know that it could not give him the experience he sought.

The embassy reached Amsterdam on 16 August, and Peter took part in the ceremonial entry, marching among the junior officials. He was overjoyed at seeing Franz Lefort again. But the event of the day for him was his first meeting with Burgomaster Witsen.

Nicholas Witsen, who was wealthy and widely respected, was a patron of the arts and of science, but his great passion was ships. He had assembled a museum of models and articles used in shipbuilding and navigation through the ages and, as well as writing a treatise on *Ancient and Modern Shipbuilding and Management*, he had amassed a vast library on the subject. He had also written a book on *Northern and Eastern Tartary*, based on a visit to Muscovy in 1664 as a member of a Dutch embassy. He acted as an unofficial minister for Muscovite affairs, and the Tsar himself regarded him as a reliable agent through whom he could order ships and transact other business.

Peter and his ambassadors spent the next two days inspecting the buildings and institutions of Amsterdam. On 19 August a magnificent banquet was given in their honour, which concluded with a brilliant fireworks display. Both the banquet and the fireworks would normally have delighted him, but on this occasion he was anxious only to get away. He had explained to Witsen at their first meeting that the crowds made it impossible for him to stay in Zaandam; Witsen had suggested that he would find it more convenient and profitable to work in the yards of the East India Company and, as a director of the company, undertook to arrange it.

During the banquet he told Peter that the governing body of the company had passed a resolution earlier in the day accepting "an eminent person, living here incognito," to work on their wharves, allocating for his accommodation the house of a ropemaker and, so that he could go through the whole process of building a ship, directing that a new frigate should be specially laid down, 130 or 100 feet in length, according to his wishes.[3]

Peter could not restrain his excitement. He leapt to his feet as the last firework was burning out, and announced that he was going to

Zaandam for his tools. It was late, but attempts to dissuade him were useless, and early next morning he was back again in Amsterdam. He had already chosen ten comrades to work with him on the frigate, and had sent the other volunteers to learn to make masts, blocks, ropes, and sails. He started work himself on the same morning under the direction of the master shipwright, Gerrit Claes Pool; apart from occasional absences to attend official functions or to visit places of interest, he spent the next four months in the East India Company yards.

At the end of August, Peter laid down his tools to go to Utrecht for his meeting with William III, who had long been his hero. He had learnt about him from conversations in the Foreign Quarter and had taken constant interest in the progress of his war with France.[4] No report has survived of Peter's first meeting with William. It was undoubtedly friendly, although Peter declined his invitation to dine next day, probably because he could not spare the time from the shipyard. If they were attracted to each other, it was the attraction of opposites. William was cold, haughty, and restrained, while Peter was tempestuous, informal, and impulsive; William was an ailing, desiccated, joyless man, while Peter had the strength and energy of ten men, and overflowed with wild spirits. The two men contrasted in everything except their determination and their purposefulness, yet even here they diverged: William's objective—the destruction of French power—was negative; Peter's objective—the creation of a navy and, ultimately, of a new Russia—was positive and constructive.

Several times Peter left the East India Company wharf to visit the museum of the eminent anatomist, Professor Ruysch, whose work in preserving specimens and corpses fascinated him. It is said that he gazed for a long time at the body of a child which was so well preserved that it seemed to be alive and smiling, and in the end he could not resist kissing the little corpse.[5] He became so interested in surgery that he considered studying it under the professor and, although he could not find the time to do this, he always considered himself competent as a surgeon and readily operated on anyone ill and luckless enough to fall into his hands.

On 9 September, after nearly three weeks devoted to assembling materials, the keel of the frigate was laid down. Peter was excited and his mood was reflected in his letter written next day to the Patriarch in Moscow.[6] But on 16 September he had to leave the shipyard to go

with his ambassadors to The Hague for their audience, and to begin
negotiations with the Netherlands States-General.

The embassy made an impressive entry into The Hague, and eight
days later the ambassadors were received in audience by the States-
General. Both were occasions of pomp and intricate ceremony in
which the Dutch and the Russians played their parts with jealous
care. The Russians were especially anxious that they should receive
all respect due to them, for they were now watched by embassies
from the nations of Europe; their appearance at The Hague, in fact,
amounted to a diplomatic debut, and they acquitted themselves well.

Satisfied with their reception, Peter returned to his work in Amsterdam, breaking his journey to visit the island of Tessel at the mouth
of the Zuider Zee, where he watched the return of part of the Greenland whaling fleet. He examined the whalers closely and, unmindful
of the stench and of the blubber oil which permeated them, clam-
bered below decks to see how they were constructed. He again laid
down his tools on 24 September to travel to The Hague to witness
the second audience of the ambassadors by the States-General. By
1 October he was again hard at work in the East India Company
yards, but this did not prevent him directing his ambassadors in all
their business at The Hague.

Pleyer, the Austrian resident in Moscow, reported accurately to his
Emperor that "the hands of the embassy are completely tied; the
embassy fears and trembles before the anger and severity of the Tsar,
who directs everything himself."[7] Although abroad and serving as a
ship's carpenter, he was still Tsar of Muscovy and supreme autocrat,
wielding power of life and death. It was in Amsterdam that he suddenly clapped two noble members of the embassy suite into chains
and ordered their execution, because they had presumed to criticize
his behaviour. The burgomaster of Amsterdam pointed out that no
one could be executed in Holland without sentence of the courts,
and persuaded him to commute the death sentence. He agreed reluctantly, and only on the condition that the men were exiled to the
farthest Dutch colonies; one was sent to Batavia and the other to
Surinam.[8]

The ambassadors were fully occupied for nearly a month at The
Hague. They negotiated with the States-General; they received and
returned courtesy visits from the other embassies; they had frequent
discussions with the minister of the newly elected King of Poland,

Augustus II, about Russian assistance against French attempts to unseat him; they had to keep in mind the need to enlist skilled personnel for service in Russia; and they reported constantly to Peter.

One of their objectives was to obtain financial aid and naval equipment. Peter was confident that the Dutch would give, if not money, at least equipment since, to his eyes, it was to be found in abundance throughout the country. After the audience of the ambassadors, the States-General appointed a special commission, which had four meetings with the ambassadors, but their meetings were without result. The Dutch would concede nothing more than a vague assurance of help at some time in the future. The ambassadors had no alternative but to request their farewell audience.

Peter was disappointed by this refusal to help, and his disappointment was a measure of his lack of understanding of Dutch interests and of the European scene. He realized now that the Dutch would do nothing to endanger their trade in the eastern Mediterranean, and that they would not jeopardize the newly concluded Peace of Ryswyk by helping in a war against France's ally, Turkey. Not only Holland, but all Europe, except Russia, now wanted peace with Turkey, for the question of the Spanish succession was already paramount. Peter saw his dream of a grand alliance against the Turks fading; Louis XIV and the balance of power, not the infidel Turks, were the preoccupation of Western Europe.

This complete failure of the embassy's diplomatic mission did not, however, deflect him from his plans to establish a Russian fleet on the Black Sea. On the contrary, the Turks had, during the previous few months, suffered a series of defeats that confirmed him in these plans. On 2 September he had received news of Shein's victory near Azov over a force of Turks, Tatars, Kubantsi, and Kalmyks, who attacked from the Kuban.[9] This had been followed by Prince Eugene's brilliant victory on the Zenta, about which Peter wrote in detail to Moscow, with orders that it should be celebrated with full ceremony.[10] Towards the end of November he had news of a further success by his own troops near Tavan.[11] Turkey now appeared a far less formidable enemy than at the time of his first Azov expedition.

Since their arrival in Holland the ambassadors had been busily enlisting seamen, shipwrights, and technicians. Lack of skilled men was holding up Peter's plans. Every post brought letters from Vinius in Moscow, reminding him of the need for mining engineers. Peter replied with assurances that he was doing all he could and that he had asked Witsen to help, but service in Russia did not attract all the skilled labour required.[12] Another difficulty was that foreigners knew no Russian and often proved unable to learn it. Mainly for this reason Peter decided to seek in the Slav lands for suitable officers and sea-men, since they could quickly acquire a knowledge of Russian. A number of Slavs had already been enlisted in Holland; on 2 October he sent one of his officers, Captain Ostrovsky, to the Slav countries to enlist others, and Peter himself issued his instructions.[13] But Ostrov-sky went no farther than Vienna, and managed to hire only two ship-masters.

Meanwhile in Amsterdam the ambassadors were negotiating for the services of the distinguished Dutch naval officer, Cruys, a Nor-wegian by birth, who was at that time the Chief Inspector of Naval Stores and Equipment at the Netherlands Admiralty. He had been advising the Russians on naval equipment, but he showed no en-thusiasm for the Tsar's service, and he accepted appointment only after Witsen and others had persuaded him. They saw in him a permanent agent who would guide Russian orders into their hands, for already they were alarmed by Peter's changing attitude towards Dutch shipbuilding.

Peter spent most of November and December working on the frigate. It was launched on 16 November with the usual celebrations, but he did not even mention it in his letters to Moscow written on the following day.[14] Dutch shipbuilding had disappointed him. Dutch shipwrights worked by rule of thumb and had developed no basic principles. Neither his master, Gerrit Claes Pool, nor the many Dutch experts whom he met could answer the questions he put to them. He recalled that when he had been in Archangel he had in-structed Vinius to obtain the specifications of different types of ships so that he could build them in his new yards at Solombala. He now appreciated the reason why Witsen could not give this information, and so great was his disappointment in their unscientific methods that he sent instructions to his overseer in Voronezh that English, Danish, or Venetian shipwrights were to supervise all Dutchmen working there.[15] Thus, having completed his training as a practical shipwright in the East India Company yards and received a certificate of proficiency,[16] he had nothing more to learn in Holland. But, as his notebook showed, he still wanted to study the science of ship-building.[17]

Already his eyes were turning towards England and the magnificent and unexpected gift from William III of the new yacht, the *Royal Transport*,[18] intensified his interest. News of the King's gift first reached Lefort in a letter from Admiral Lord Carmarthen who wrote a further letter to the Tsar himself.[19] Carmarthen had designed the yacht and, as he pointed out proudly in his letters, she was a graceful, speedy, and luxuriously appointed craft, armed with twenty brass cannon. Peter was impatient not only to learn about his new yacht, but also to meet Carmarthen who seemed to have the technical knowledge he was seeking. A few days later he sent Major Adam Weide to England to report on the Russian victory near Azov. Weide was also to seek a private audience with the King and to ask for a written reply to the proposal made by the Tsar at The Hague; pre-sumably this proposal concerned Peter's visit to England. Four weeks later Weide returned to Amsterdam to report that the King had sent a squadron to carry the Tsar across the Channel.

Peter and his suite of sixteen went on board the *Yorke*, flagship of Vice-Admiral Sir David Mitchell, at Hellevoetsluis on 8 January, and early next morning the squadron, comprising two warships, two yachts, and a sloop, weighed anchor.[20]

CHAPTER XIII

Peter in England

1698

THE experience of being at sea in a large warship was new to Peter. The weather was stormy, but he stayed on deck throughout the voyage. He watched the handling of the *Yorke* with intense interest, asking endless questions, and could not be restrained from going aloft to examine the rigging.

The squadron sighted the shores of Suffolk on the morning of 10 January. A mile from the mouth of the Thames he went on board the yacht *Mary*, accompanied by Admiral Mitchell. The warships, *Yorke* and *Romney*, which could not navigate the river, fired salutes and made for Chatham, while the yachts, *Mary* and *Henrietta and Isabella*, moved up the Thames. Early on the following morning they anchored near the Tower of London, and Peter and his party were rowed under the bridge and upriver to a landing stage near York Buildings, off the Strand.

A house had been prepared for him in Norfolk Street, which at his express request was small, unpretentious, and had direct access to the river.[1] He hoped by living unobtrusively to avoid a repetition of the crowds that had distressed him in Holland. Soon after his arrival a chamberlain came with a message of welcome. Admiral Mitchell, who spoke Dutch, interpreted for Peter who usually relied on his broken Dutch and German while abroad. In fact Peter had already taken a liking to Mitchell and he was gratified when the King appointed Mitchell to attend on him.

Two days later William himself called, coming in a modest car-

114

riage so as to attract no attention. Peter was not dressed and received him in his shirt-sleeves in a small room where he slept with three or four members of his suite. The windows had been shut since their arrival; the air was so thick and stale that despite the heavy frost the King, who was asthmatic, was forced to ask for a window to be opened. On the following day, Prince George of Denmark, husband of Anne, the future Queen of England, called. These were the only formal visits that Peter, anxious to remain incognito, received in his first weeks in England.

At this time London was already one of the largest and wealthiest cities in Europe. Its population had more than doubled during the century, and the minor industrial revolution that had taken place in England had contributed to its vital throbbing life. It was a city of coarse and cruel pleasures, of bull- and bear-baiting and cock-fighting, where public hangings and whippings always attracted crowds of spectators. But it was also a city with an eager intelligent social life, centered on the coffee houses, numbering nearly five hundred, where men discussed shipping news and business, politics, religion, literature, and the new scientific ideas.

Greater London was also one of the most impressive cities of Europe. Louis XIV had diminished Paris by compelling his nobles to move to Versailles, but London had remained the home of the court and of the government and, because it was England's foremost port, the commercial capital of the country. The Great Fire of 1666 had destroyed the City between the Tower and the Temple, but so great were its vitality and wealth that within five years new mansions had risen from the ashes. Built now of brick in place of the old lath and plaster, the City had taken on an appearance of solid order and opulence. The genius of Sir Christopher Wren had had full play in designing and supervising the rebuilding of fifty-one churches, and, over all, St. Paul's Cathedral, his masterpiece, towered majestically. But the sign of the vigour and wealth of London that impressed Peter most strongly was the forest of masts of the ships moored in the Pool of London.

The winter of 1697-98 was severe and, as often happened until London Bridge was rebuilt, the upper reaches of the Thames were frozen. Partly for this reason Peter did not sail down the river soon after his arrival to inspect the navy at Chatham, but it was also because there was so much of interest in London. He went to factories and workshops, always demanding drawings, models, and specifications of what he had seen. He visited watchmakers and the manufacture of watches so fascinated him that he learnt to repair and to assemble them himself. He even found time to examine the construction of English coffins and bought a coffin to send to Moscow as a model.

In London he went nearly everywhere on foot. The people soon identified him by his great height, his convulsive movements, and his nervous twitchings. Again he found himself the object of curious stares from which he retreated. At the theatre he noticed suddenly that the audience was watching not the play but his box, and he quickly hid behind members of his suite. He went only that once to the theatre in London, and it is unlikely that the Restoration plays, performed in a language that he did not understand, appealed to him: in fact the theatre was never to attract him strongly, except as a means of educating his people.

On 23 January, accompanied by only two companions and Admiral Mitchell, Peter called at Kensington Palace to return the King's visit. The palace of Whitehall had been burnt down a few days before his arrival in England, and William III had moved his court to the palace extended and rebuilt for him by Sir Christopher Wren on the site of Nottingham House, in the countryside of Kensington. It was a dignified, homely, and delightful palace, to which William was much attached. Peter, however, paid no attention to the building or to the pictures and furnishings that adorned it; he was fascinated by a dial in the King's Gallery, operated by a wind-vane on the roof, which showed the direction in which the wind was blowing.[2]

At this meeting the King persuaded Peter to sit for Sir Godfrey Kneller, the most celebrated painter in Europe at the time. Kneller began the portrait on 28 January and produced what contemporaries considered a remarkable likeness. It shows a lively, open and handsome face with strong features and large dark intelligent eyes. There is something almost chivalrous and benevolent in this picture of the young Tsar, caught in a moment of calm, but it is a partial portrait, containing no suggestion of the savage anger, the fierce will, and the volcanic energy which were the essence of his character.[3]

Peter had come to England to study the principles of shipbuilding, and London had already distracted him long enough. On 9 February he moved to Deptford, which was the centre of important docks and building yards. The English government had provided accommodations for him and his suite at Sayes Court, the country house of John Evelyn, from which Admiral Benbow, to whom Evelyn had already leased it, had agreed to move. It was a fine house, beautifully furnished, and surrounded by woods and magnificent gardens which Evelyn himself had planned. But the important factor to Peter was that it adjoined the royal docks to which he had direct access from the garden through a private door.

This was the crucial stage of his studies when he was mastering the principles which underlay all that he had learnt by practice in Russia and Holland, and he spent many hours in the building yards. He did not sign on as a ship's carpenter or in any other capacity as he had done in Holland. But he could never stand watching others at work, and a journeyman-shipwright, employed there at the time, commented in later years that "the Tsar of Muscovy worked with his own hands as hard as any man in the yard."[4]

In his leisure hours he sailed or rowed on the Thames, or visited an inn in Great Tower Street, which came to be called "The Czars of Muscovy" as a result, where he took his ease smoking a pipe and drinking brandy.[5] His entertainment must also have included the usual drunken orgies, for the damage done to Sayes Court could hardly have been done by men who were sober.

Evelyn had complained that Admiral Benbow was not a "polite tenant," but nothing that the Admiral did prepared him for the barbarism of his new tenants. Evelyn's bailiff, who remained in the house while Peter was there, wrote to him that the house was "full of people and right nasty." After Peter's departure, the Treasury on the petition of Benbow appointed Sir Christopher Wren, the King's Surveyor, and two others to survey Sayes Court, and their report describes the destruction in detail. No part of the house escaped damage. All the floors were covered with grease and ink, and three new floors had to be provided. The tiled stoves, locks to the doors, and all paint work had to be renewed. The curtains, quilts, and bed linen were "tore in pieces." All the chairs in the house, numbering over fifty, were broken or had disappeared, probably used to stoke the stoves. Three hundred windowpanes were smashed and there were "twenty fine pictures very much tore and all frames broke." The garden which was Evelyn's great pride was ruined.[6] The report covers several pages and the Treasury paid out £350. 9s. 0d.—a large amount for the time—in compensation, but much of the damage was irreparable.[7]

On 15 February Peter received a formal visit from a group of Anglican churchmen, which included Gilbert Burnet, Bishop of Salisbury. It was a sign of the sympathetic interest and attraction that the Anglican Church felt then, and has always felt, for the Orthodox Church. Apparently Peter took a strong liking to Burnet who was a sincere, active, and godly man, and not only showed him special courtesy and respect, but called frequently for his company. Burnet himself had instructions both from the King and the Archbishop to attend upon the Tsar "and to offer him such informations of our religion and constitution, as he was willing to receive."[8]

Their meetings often lasted several hours and Burnet found difficulty in tearing himself away. They discussed the Scriptures and intricacies of doctrine. Burnet, who was mainly bent on proselytizing, was deeply impressed, as Witsen and others had been, by the Tsar's great religious knowledge. But he had every opportunity to expound Anglican doctrine and he found that Peter "hearkened to no part of what I told him more attentively than when I explained the authority that the Christian Emperors assumed in matters of religion, and the supremacy of our Kings."[9] Towards the end of February, accompanied by Burnet, Peter visited the Archbishop of Canterbury at Lambeth Palace. He had refused to attend the service in St. Paul's Cathedral for fear of the crowds, but willingly took communion in the Archbishop's private chapel, after which they breakfasted together and discussed church affairs.

In England Peter visited the churches freely and even went to Quaker meetings.[10] But the Established Church in particular interested him, because it was part of the English way of life, which manifested a spirit of enterprise and independence in contrast to the humility, submission, and inactivity inculcated by the Orthodox Church upon Russian life. The more practical and important reason for his interest, at least according to Burnet, was that the Anglican Church acknowledged the supremacy of the King, and its dogma was subject to Act of Parliament.

This was relevant to the antagonism that he had long felt towards the church hierarchy in Russia, and to his ideas, already crystallizing, on the reforms to be launched on his return to Moscow. The Orthodox Church was the guardian of the old traditions and, to Peter, it was a massive opposition party behind which was ranged the whole of his people. It was true that the church acknowledged his headship as Tsar, and that the one attempt by a patriarch to challenge the Tsar's primacy had failed. But the church still held a position of special authority enabling the Patriarch to criticize the throne; Peter foresaw that it would be an obstacle to his plans. The English had worked out a solution, and in these contacts with churchmen in England may be found the germ of his later reforms which finally broke the power of the Orthodox Church in Russia.

In all their meetings Burnet was favourably impressed by Peter, whom he regarded as potentially a great and Christian ruler. To one correspondent, he wrote that "the Tsar will either perish in the way or become a great man."[11] Subsequently when he came to write his *History of His Own Time*, his judgment had undergone a change. "After I had seen him often and had conversed much with him," he wrote, "I could not but adore the depth of the Providence of God that had raised up such a furious man to so absolute an authority over so great a part of the world. . . . Man seems a very contemptible thing in the sight of God, while such a person as the Tsar has such multitudes put as it were under his feet, exposed to his restless jealousy and savage temper."[12] The reason for this change in the opinion of the gentle Bishop was the massacre of the streltsi, which took place on Peter's return to Moscow and stories of which horrified Europe.

During these weeks Peregrine Osborne, Marquis of Carmarthen, was frequently with Peter. Carmarthen, son of William III's minister, Danby, later Duke of Leeds, was wild, brave, and a sturdy drinker, who introduced Peter to his favourite beverage of brandy laced with peppers; he was also an enthusiastic sailor and a gifted ship designer, which further recommended him to Peter. One of the fruits of their friendship was the grant of a monopoly to a group of English merchants to import tobacco into Russia.

The use of tobacco had been forbidden in Russia on religious grounds. But with the influx of foreigners the habit of smoking had spread. Tsar Mikhail had tried to suppress it by an ukaz making it illegal to smoke or trade in the "ungodly herb" under pain of death and confiscation of all property. In practice the knout, slitting of nostrils, and cutting-off of noses were the standard penalties, but they were not sufficient deterrents. Tobacco was still smuggled into the country and smoking became more popular. At an early age Peter himself had learnt to smoke and, despite the disapproval of old Muscovites, was to be seen in public with a long Dutch pipe in his mouth. Finally, on the eve of his departure for Europe he had issued an ukaz permitting the sale and use of tobacco.

English merchants had long regarded Muscovy as a valuable potential market for their tobacco, and news of the Tsar's European tour had attracted their attention. Growers in Virginia and Maryland had petitioned King Willaim in 1697 to use his good offices with the Tsar, and William had then instructed his ambassadors at The Hague to discuss with the Tsar's envoys the development of the tobacco trade and the granting of contracts to English merchants.[13]

Peter needed little encouragement. He enjoyed tobacco and probably welcomed the habit among his own people as a Western influence which would help break down conservative ways. But the most important factor in his mind was that tobacco could yield a bigger income at a time when he needed money—and he now needed it urgently.

The day-to-day expenditure of the embassy was heavy and already he had drawn on Moscow for large amounts. But he continued to buy instruments and other articles, and the ambassadors were busy enlisting naval officers, seamen, and technicians. Ready money was needed to pay the subsistence and salary advances of all these men. Moreover, the Dutch refusal of aid had meant buying naval and military equipment in large quantities. The contract with Carmarthen was timely. It yielded £12,000 or 28,000 rubles as an advance payment of customs dues, a sum far greater than the two earlier contracts had produced. Equally important was the fact that this money was available to him while still abroad.[14]

Peter was delighted with his tobacco deal, and his ambassadors, who had been waiting for news of it, were equally pleased. "On your orders," wrote Lefort, "we did not open your letter until we had drained three goblets, and after we read it we drank three more. . . . In truth I believe it's a fine stroke of business."[15]

William III went out of his way to be a considerate host. He was flattered by Peter's admiration and approved of his strong bias against the French. At the same time William knew that his active attempts to bring about peace between Austria and Turkey would anger the

Tsar and, anxious to retain his good will, he took pains to please him in other directions. He could not have made him a more acceptable gift than the *Royal Transport*, which was officially handed over by Admiral Mitchell on 2 March. He gave him the run of naval and military establishments in England and, finally, he invited Peter to inspect the fleet and witness naval manoeuvres in the Solent.

Peter set out on the Guildford road to Portsmouth on 20 March, and on the morning after their arrival, he went on board the warships, *Royal William*, *Victory*, and *Association*. Later in the day the fleet crossed the Solent and anchored in the lee of the Isle of Wight. Peter was now on board the *Humber* in which Admiral Mitchell flew his flag. Lack of wind delayed the manoeuvres, but finally, on 24 March, they took place. Peter was carried away with excitement as he watched the great ships manoeuvring, firing their broadsides, and veering to attack again.[16] After a second mock battle the squadron returned to Portsmouth, and all the crews gave three cheers and fired a salute of twenty-one guns in Peter's honour as he was rowed ashore. It was a memorable day for the young Tsar whose ambition it was to send a similar fleet into battle against the Turks.

On 2 April, soon after his return to London he visited the Houses of Parliament.[17] But Parliament, like Windsor Castle and Hampton Court, which he also saw, was of secondary interest to him. He attached greater importance to Greenwich Observatory, Woolwich Arsenal, and the Tower of London. He made several visits to Greenwich where he discussed mathematics with the Astronomer Royal, Flamstead.[18] Woolwich, as the main gunfoundry and arsenal, fascinated him and he found in the Master of the Ordnance, Romney, a man of charm and ability who shared his passion both for gunnery and for fireworks. The Tower of London[19] served then not only as an arsenal, but housed the zoo, the city museum, the Royal Society, and the Mint, and he was to spend many hours there.

The Mint in particular fascinated him and he made special visits to study the English method of coining, then the most advanced in Europe. For years the practice of clipping the silver coins of the realm had been undermining English economic life. Parliament had debated many remedies and, finally, in the Recoinage Bill of 1696 had enacted the scheme worked out by John Locke and Isaac Newton.[20] The reform was successful, and the new coins with their milled edges were handsome. The machinery of the Mint, which Peter watched in action many times, interested him all the more because Russia suffered from bad coinage; two years later he himself reformed it on the English model.

Peter spent much of Sunday, 3 April, discussing Quaker doctrine with William Penn and others, having attended one of their meetings for worship. Next day he was sight-seeing in London and climbed to the top of the Monument, erected in memory of the Great Fire of 1666. He was in Greenwich on the following day talking about mathematics with the Astronomer Royal, and the day after found him working in the shipyards at Deptford, whence he went direct to the University of Oxford.[21] On his return he visited the Mint again, and then spent two days at Woolwich.

In the midst of all these activities he found time to write regularly to his ambassadors in Holland and to his ministers in Moscow. His letters demonstrated that, far from being distracted by his new surroundings or by the novelties that western Europe had to show him, he kept his own needs and policy in the forefront of his mind. Thus, he patiently reassured Vinius, who wrote endlessly of the urgent need for mining engineers and ironworkers.[22] He gave detailed instructions to Shein about the fortifications and the harbour under construction near Azov, and about preparations for the forthcoming campaign against the Turks.[23] From Amsterdam he had sent orders to Romodanovsky about a ship to be moved down the Volga and had also written sternly rebuking him for withholding an officer's salary, and for being drunk and torturing Jacob Bruce, who had recently travelled from Moscow to join the embassy, and whose burnt hand Peter had noticed. In Deptford he received Romodanovsky's explanations and excuses to which he replied with a further rebuke.[24] He even wrote to P. M. Apraxin in Novgorod that he had taken two barbers into the Muscovite service "for purposes of future demands"; it was a minor but portentous incident.[25]

In another letter Peter gave Streshnev the delicate task of persuading his wife, Tsaritsa Evdokiya, to retire to a nunnery, which was the equivalent of divorce. He wrote also to Lev Naryshkin, and to the Tsaritsa's spiritual adviser with the same request.[26] No thoughts of remarriage were in his mind; he merely wanted to be rid of an encumbrance.

At the beginning of March, Lefort's elder brother, Jacob, and three nephews arrived in London with letters of introduction to the Tsar, who received them with particular favour. It was an act of kindness and a token of Peter's affection for his favourite. Describing their reception, Jacob Lefort wrote, "You know that the Sovereign is very tall, but he has one very unpleasant trait: he has convulsions, sometimes of the eyes, sometimes in his arms and sometimes in his whole body. At times he rolls his eyes so much that only the whites can be seen. . . . Then he also has spasms of his legs so that he can hardly stand still in one place. For the rest he is well built, dressed as a sailor, very simple in his tastes and he wishes nothing else than to be on the water."[27]

William III had given his approval to the hiring of Englishmen for service in Russia, and Golovin came over from Holland mainly for the purpose of making formal contracts with some sixty specialists whom Peter had engaged. They included Major Leonard van der Stamm, a ship designer who had been collecting plans for Peter, John Dean, a master shipwright, with whom Peter worked at Dept-ford, and for whom he developed a great affection,[28] and Captain John Perry, an hydraulic engineer who was to be responsible for con-structing a canal to link the Volga and Don rivers. Work had started on this canal, but the German engineer, Colonel Breckell, who was in charge, had suddenly fled.[29]

Peter had also hoped to engage in England the mining engineers whom Vinius pressed for in every letter. He found several who were willing to serve, but did not enlist them because their terms were too high.[30] But he did engage a mathematician from Aberdeen Uni-versity, named Henry Farquharson, who was probably recommended by Admiral Mitchell, himself an Aberdonian. Four days before leav-ing England, Peter instructed Dr. Peter Posnikov to inspect English schools and to find two teachers of navigation to serve in Russia. Posnikov enlisted Stephen Gwyn, aged fifteen, and Richard Grice, aged seventeen, two students of Christ's Hospital, who under the direction of Farquharson later established the School of Mathematics and Navigation in Moscow.[31]

Peter's visit to England was now coming to an end. On 18 April he paid a farewell visit to the King. Their relations were still cordial, although Peter's feelings had cooled after he had received news of William's efforts at mediation between the Emperor and the Turks.[32] Three days later Peter left London, but he was reluctant to go. On the day of his departure he could not resist paying a last visit to the

Mint though he had been there only the day before. His suite had already gone on board the *Royal Transport* and some hours later he joined them. The yacht sailed slowly down the Thames, but when they came to Woolwich he went ashore to visit the arsenal again. It was dusk when the yacht reached Gravesend and anchored.

Next morning they sailed past Sheerness and then made for Chatham. Carmarthen in his yacht, the *Peregrine*, had followed them downriver and reached Chatham shortly after the *Royal Transport*. Peter went on board the *Peregrine* and sailed around the harbour, inspecting the great ships of war that lay at anchor. He went on board the *Britannia*, the *Duke* and the *Triumph*, all three-deck ships and then went ashore to inspect the naval depot. It was not until later next morning, that he returned to the *Royal Transport* which had weighed anchor and was waiting for him off Sheerness. At 2 P.M. the yacht got under way and made for Margate where Admiral Mitchell was ready with a squadron of warships to escort him to Holland. Stormy weather delayed them further, but on 25 April the ships put to sea.

Peter had found England both enjoyable and profitable. In no other country had he met such men as Carmarthen, Mitchell, Romney, and others with whom he could drink deeply and talk for hours of ships and ship design, gunnery, and fireworks. He had wandered at will, examining warships and the machinery of the Mint. Most important of all he had been able to master the basic principles of shipbuilding at Deptford. He carried away with him a great respect for English engineers, gunners and, above all, for English shipwrights. He always acknowledged that in naval matters "if he had not come to England he had certainly been a bungler,"[33] and frequently remarked that "the English island is the best, most beautiful, and happiest that there is in the whole world."[34]

CHAPTER XIV

Vienna and the Return to Moscow

1698

P ETER arrived in Amsterdam to find his embassy surrounded by
men and equipment. More than seven hundred officers, seamen,
engineers, and artisans had been signed on and vast quantities of
arms and equipment purchased. All were assembled awaiting transport, and ten ships had to be chartered to carry them all to Russia.
The *Royal Transport* was also pressed into service; she sailed under
the command of Captain Ripley[1] for Archangel, carrying part of
Peter's collection of instruments and curiosities.[2]

Peter himself was in no hurry to leave western Europe, and
planned a leisurely journey back to Moscow with visits to Vienna
and to Venice. He would have spent more time touring Holland,
had not news from Moscow and from Vienna brought a note of
urgency to his travels. From Moscow the news was of another
streltsi revolt, which had arisen from his instructions, sent from
England, that four streltsi regiments wintering in Azov were to move
up to the Lithuanian frontier.

Several ministers wrote to Peter about this incident and their
letters, which reached him in Amsterdam on 8 May, made him
angry.[3] It was not the revolt so much as the ministers' behaviour
that angered him. Romodanovsky's letter showed that despite his
instructions he had only carried out a perfunctory examination of
the ringleaders. More serious, it showed that his ministers had been
on the verge of panic because they had had no news from him and
feared that he might be dead. Vinius had been so sure of this that

he had addressed his letters, not to the Tsar, but to Lefort: when, on 11 April, he received two letters from Peter his joy and relief were touching.[4] But Peter scolded him severely for his fears and castigated the others. If anything had happened to him, "in truth the news would have reached you more swiftly than the post," he wrote and continued, "I don't know why you should show the panic of old women!"[5] But the letters from Moscow satisfied him that the revolt had been put down.

The news from Vienna was that the Emperor and the Venetian Senate were discussing proposals for a peace with Turkey. Already in England he had had reports of these peace talks, but now he learnt that the negotiations were more advanced than he had thought. A few days later, on 12 May, he received a copy of the documents, which the Imperial government had sent to Moscow, notifying the Tsar of the Sultan's proposals and requesting him to appoint representatives to take part in a conference.[6] Peter's plans against the Turks were already well advanced, and this talk of peace threatened them. He therefore decided to go to Vienna as quickly as possible to persuade the Emperor to continue the war against Turkey.

On 15 May, Peter and his embassy set out from Amsterdam. On the road a petition for a printing monopoly submitted by Jan Tessing in Amsterdam, was reported to him.[7] Tessing had asked for a fifteen-year monopoly to print books, pictures, and maps in Russian, with the sole right to export them to Russia on payment of such customs duties as the Tsar imposed. Peter granted this monopoly immediately and gave instructions for his voevod in Archangel to be informed.[8] It was a proposal that he welcomed, for he knew that the old printing presses in Moscow could not produce the books and technical manuals which he would need for his schools and for instruction in the new navy and army.

At Cleve the embassy divided into two groups—an advance party, consisting of Peter himself, the ambassadors and sixteen of the volunteers, with the remainder under the command of Aleksasha Menshikov who was now rising rapidly in favour.

The reason for the advance party was that Peter had learnt, since leaving Amsterdam, of further progress in the peace talks with Turkey, and he hastened towards Vienna. He made few halts until he reached the territory of the Elector of Saxony, now Augustus II of Poland, who had given orders that all honours should be shown him.

Arriving in Leipzig, he spent the day in various entertainments, but Dresden contained more of interest to him. The burgomaster and councillors of Dresden had taken the greatest pains in the difficult task of paying the Tsar special respect, while observing his incognito. The ceremonial entry of the embassy took place on 1 June and Prince Fürstenberg, the Elector's representative, received them at the castle. Peter promptly complained that some people had stared at him, and he threatened to leave the city immediately if it happened again. Fürstenberg calmed him and, when he returned after dinner to discuss the programme for the next day, he found Peter in a good humour. He asked about the Dresden museum and, although it was after midnight, he insisted on seeing it. Fürstenberg and the curator accompanied him and he remained there engrossed in the mathematical and other instruments until dawn. Of all that he saw in Dresden, the museum impressed him most, and in later years, when he established a museum in Russia, it was on the Dresden model.

Peter dined next evening with Fürstenberg, and the dinner developed into a rowdy party of the kind that he enjoyed. When asked for music, his host summoned drummers, trumpeters, oboists, and flautists. Peter next requested the company of ladies. Fürstenberg invited five ladies, including the beautiful Countess Aurora of Königsmark, the mistress of Augustus II, and later the mother of Maurice of Saxony. No courtiers were present. Music was played and everyone drank heavily. Peter himself was in high spirits. He embraced Prince Fürstenberg and then, seizing the drumsticks, he beat the drums so expertly that he completely outdid the drummers. It was a highly successful party which ended only at 3 A.M.

On the evening of his departure Peter and his suite dined in the garden of the country palace. Again the music, drinking, dancing, and the same ladies combined to put Peter in a magnificent humour and it was dawn when he set off. He was well contented with his visit, and Fürstenberg, who was greatly impressed by the Tsar's knowledge and intelligence, but worn out by the pace at which he lived, was able to report to Augustus that his orders to make the visit both memorable and merry had been carried out to the full. Seven days later, having passed through Prague, Peter and his suite arrived at Stockerau, a village some nineteen miles from Vienna, and rode ahead independently; the ambassadors were forced to wait there for some time before making their formal entry into Vienna.

On arrival, Lefort advised the court chamberlain that the Tsar wished to meet the Emperor informally. He had to repeat this request three times before the meeting was arranged, and the protocol to be followed was agreed upon. Although informal, the meeting at the Imperial summer court, was to follow a strict pattern. The two monarchs were to enter the long room simultaneously from either end, each accompanied by a small suite, and they were to meet halfway, opposite the fifth window.

Once in the room, however, Peter forgot about these careful arrangements and bounded up to the Emperor, meeting him near the third window. The Imperial courtiers were shocked, but were soon mollified by the respect and deference that the Tsar displayed. The two monarchs drew apart and, with only Lefort to act as interpreter, they talked together quietly in one of the window recesses. They must have made an incongruous conversation-piece. Short, sickly, and ugly, with heavy moustache, a thick pendulous underlip, and a large wig hanging down over his narrow shoulders, the Emperor was dreamy and indecisive. In every way he contrasted with the tall energetic young Tsar. They exchanged compliments and vows of brotherhood for some fifteen minutes, and the meeting was over.

Peter had hurried across Europe to Vienna, only to encounter delays and the stultifying etiquette of the Imperial court. He was usually quick to resent such treatment, but far from being angry or depressed, he appeared from his letters to Moscow to be in good spirits, and proposed to spend some time in Vienna before going on to Venice.[9] Emperor Leopold was hardly a man to inspire respect or affection, and yet Peter showed him a deference that was the talk of the Imperial court. He even took a liking to him and spoke of him affectionately. When representatives of the Chamberlain's Office informed him that three thousand gulden weekly would be allocated for the embassy's expenses while in Vienna, Peter exclaimed that it was far too much for his "dear brother" to pay after waging long wars; he himself reduced it to three thousand florins per week.

His show of deference was not wholly disinterested; he was intent on winning good will, which would further his purposes. Nevertheless the imposing façade of the Holy Roman Empire overawed him and, paradoxically, the Imperial court with its cumbersome protocol impressed him, for it possessed a civilized dignity that Moscow lacked. Although he was to joke about it on his return, he did not forget the Imperial court; in later years he sought to emulate its dignity and gracious living in his own capital.

Peter had not lost sight of his purpose in coming to Vienna. But formal discussion of the Turkish peace proposals could not begin until his ambassadors had had audience with the Emperor; this, in turn, must wait until the gifts, which it was customary to present on such occasions, had arrived from Moscow. Meanwhile Peter opened unofficial discussions by bluntly asking Count Kinsky, the Imperial Foreign Minister, for a statement of Austrian intentions. Three days later Kinsky delivered a written reply in which he pointed out that the Turks, not the Emperor, had proposed peace, that the Turkish proposals had been sent to the Tsar and the other allies, and that the Emperor would accept a peace which permanently conceded his territorial gains. Peter considered this unsatisfactory; the principle of *uti possidetis* would, if accepted, mean only formal recognition of his capture of Azov, and he wanted more.

Finally, at Peter's request, Kinsky called for further discussions. Peter angrily arraigned the Imperial government for opening negotiations without the prior agreement of his allies. He played on their anxieties that the Turks might attack while the Imperial army was engaged in war over the Spanish succession, and that the Hungarians, who were the constant internal threat to the empire, would seize on this opportunity to revolt. Kinsky returned next day with an assurance that the Emperor would conclude no treaty with the Turks until he had discussed it fully with the Tsar. At this meeting Peter handed Kinsky a statement of his own proposals which included a demand for the surrender of Kerch to Russia.[10] Kinsky's reply was non-committal, merely suggesting that the Tsar had ample time to capture Kerch before the conference, so that the principle of retaining territorial gains would still be valid.

On this note Peter's discussions with the Imperial government ended. He had to recognize that his mission had failed. Not only had he been unable to inspire a general European crusade against the Turks, but he had found it impossible to prevent the existing alliance from collapsing. It remained only for him to take part in the conference, striking the best bargain that he could.

The discussions with Kinsky did not, however, take up the whole of Peter's time. He called on the Empress and on the King of Rome, the heir to the Imperial throne; he had several meetings with Father Woolf and other Jesuits in Vienna; he talked at length with the Serbian Patriarch, who pleaded with him to intercede with the Emperor on behalf of the Serbs who had resettled in lands to the north of the Danube. He also kept up with his correspondence with Moscow.[11] And yet he was subdued in Vienna, seldom displaying the gusto that had marked his visits to Holland and England. In the capital of the elderly Emperor, he was on his best behaviour. He had quickly learnt how to behave, and the various ambassadors in Vienna spoke of his "delicate and polished manners." The Spanish ambassador commented that "here he appears quite unlike the descriptions of other courts and far more civilized, intelligent, with excellent manners and modest."[12] He was already far removed from the young Tsar whom the Electress Sophia had thrown into confusion.

His political mission at an end, Peter became impatient to move on to Venice. He found little of interest in landlocked Vienna, and was looking forward eagerly to the galleys and shipyards of Venice. But he could not leave for more than two weeks. The Emperor wished to give a masquerade ball in his honour, and he had to remain in Vienna to attend it. He was also forced to delay his departure because his ambassadors had not yet been received in audience. Discussion of the procedure for this ceremonial audience, when begun, proved stormy and soon reached deadlock. But this did not affect the relations between the Emperor and the Tsar. At the masquerade ball they appeared to be on affectionate and brotherly terms. Prince Eugene of Savoy, who had not long returned from his victory on the Zenta, was presented to Peter during the evening, but no report of their meeting has survived.

Nowhere in Vienna had Peter's visit aroused more interest than in the Jesuit College. Reports of his curiosity about the Christian churches had circulated in Europe, and the Catholic hierarchy was hopeful that he might be converted. Father Woolf, the trusted confidential adviser to the Emperor, had studied Russian and dreamt of bringing about the union of the Orthodox and Catholic churches. On St. Peter's day the Tsar, after the Orthodox service conducted by his own priest, went to the Jesuit College, where Woolf celebrated Mass and preached a flattering sermon in which he referred to Peter as the scourge of the heretics. On 13 July Peter attended a special

Mass, celebrated this time by Cardinal Kollonitz, Primate of Hungary, and, after a simple lunch in the refectory of the college, he set off for Pressburg accompanied by the Jesuit. Hopes ran high in Catholic circles that Peter was firmly on the road to conversion. Rumours circulated that from Venice he would travel to Rome to be received into the church by the Pope himself. Preparations were even begun in Rome for his reception.[13] But Woolf's confidence was misplaced; Peter did not contemplate conversion. He may have had thoughts of the union of the churches, but from his later conduct this, too, seems extremely unlikely. His display of interest arose partly from the knowledge that both Cardinal Kollonitz and Father Woolf had the ear of the Emperor, and partly from the fact that he was genuinely curious about Roman Catholicism.

Returning from his farewell visit to the Emperor on the morning of 15 July, Peter was about to set out for Venice, when the post arrived from Moscow. It brought news of yet another streltsi outbreak. Romodanovsky reported that four regiments were marching on Moscow, and that he had sent troops under Boyar Shein and Gordon to meet them. The letter ended with the latest information, which was that the rebels had reached a town sixty miles from Moscow.[14]

This news disturbed Peter. The letter had taken a month to reach him. He had no idea whether the rebels had attacked Moscow or whether Shein had suppressed them. He was convinced that the Miloslavsky were behind the outbreak, and feared that his half-sister Sofia might already be on the throne. He decided to return to Moscow immediately; he wrote briefly and ominously to Romodanovsky: "Your letter of 17 June has been handed to me, in which your grace writes that the seed of Ivan Mikhailovich [Miloslavsky] is sprouting. I beg you to be severe; in no other way is it possible to put out this flame. Although we are very sorry to give up our present profitable business, yet, for the sake of this, we shall be with you sooner than you know."[15]

The next four days were given to hurried arrangements. The first two ambassadors were to accompany the Tsar. Voznitsyn was to remain in Vienna to act as Russian representative at the coming peace conference with the Turks. Most important of all was to arrange the audience of the ambassadors with the Emperor. It was important because the Russian representatives would labour under a grave handicap at the conference if the Tsar's ambassadors had not been received in audience in Vienna. The Imperial chamberlain's last word had been that he would await the Russian answer until 16 July. He was now, on 15 July, informed that the Russians accepted all his rulings, and the audience took place three days later.

Peter set out by post-horse on 19 July for Moscow. He made all haste, stopping only to change horses and to eat. But his haste proved unnecessary. Three days after his departure from Vienna, mail arrived with news that the revolt had been put down. Shein had scattered the rebels, carried out an investigation, executed 130 men, and was holding 1,860 men prisoners.

Voznitsyn immediately sent this mail on to Peter and it reached him about half a mile out of Cracow. Reassured about the streltsi, he thought of turning back to visit Venice, but then he decided to go on to Moscow. He had been away for a year and a half and now he had much to do. But he travelled at a more leisurely pace. On 31 July he arrived in Rawa, where he had his momentous meeting with Augustus.

Frederick-Augustus, Elector of Saxony, and now King Augustus II of Poland, made a strong impression on Peter, and he contributed greatly to the change in Peter's foreign policy that took place after his return from abroad. Two years older than Peter, Augustus was a tall, handsome, and powerfully built man. He could, like Peter, straighten a horseshoe with his bare hands and he had earned the nicknames of The Strong and Iron Hand. Unlike Peter, he seemed to have devoted most of his time to his mistresses and was said to have over three hundred illegitimate children. He was bluff and hearty in manner, but sensual, self-indulgent, deceitful, and cowardly by nature. On becoming Elector he had begun dreaming of winning military fame, but in two campaigns in Hungary had displayed no ability. His next ambition was to occupy the Polish throne; in this he was successful, owing to large-scale bribery, the presence of his Saxon troops, and the support of the Emperor and the Tsar.

Peter and Augustus became close friends on sight. A member of the Tsar's suite wrote: "I cannot begin to describe to you the tenderness between the two sovereigns."[16] But Peter, who was simple and honest in human relationships until, as so frequently happened, he was deceived, was soon to find that Augustus was a weak and treacherous ally.

Meanwhile at Rawa and then at Tomashov, where they inspected detachments of Saxon cavalry, Augustus succeeded in impressing his guest with his military strength, and Peter loudly praised the discipline and precision of the Saxon manoeuvres. In the evenings they drank and talked together. In public they discussed the war against Turkey and the perfidy of the Emperor in favouring peace. In secret they agreed between themselves to attack Sweden as soon as the time was ripe.[17]

In this meeting of Peter and Augustus at Rawa in August 1698, the Northern War had its beginnings. Peter himself confirmed this twenty-five years later in the introduction which he wrote to the official history of the war. The suggestion of war against Sweden, according to this account, arose from Augustus' request for Russian aid to suppress groups of rebellious Poles; Peter agreed on condition that Augustus help him to avenge the insults which he alleged he had suffered in Riga.[18] Augustus, anxious to establish himself more securely on the Polish throne by winning popular acclaim, was ambitious to recover the province of Livonia which the Poles had surrendered under the Treaty of Oliva, and he readily agreed the Tsar's terms.

The idea of a Northern league against Sweden was not new to Peter. Only thirty years earlier Ordin-Nashchokin, his father's great minister, had propounded it as a national policy. The Elector of Brandenburg had proposed it when Peter was in Prussia on his way to Holland and England, but at that time Peter would allow nothing to hinder his campaign in the south. Now, his grandiose plans for a crusade against the Turks having miscarried, he turned northwards. He was naturally eager to recover the lands seized by the Swedes, and there were the strong additional incentives that the Baltic ports would provide all the facilities he needed to create a navy, and would also give him direct access to the West. At some time in the future he would turn again to assert his claims to the Black Sea, but now he concentrated his strength against Sweden, and this policy was to dominate most of his reign.

Peter's tour was over. He had gained first-hand experience of Western politics, and had taken the first step towards challenging the Swedes in the north. More important was the deep, enduring impression that these eighteen months in western Europe had made on him. He had set out primarily to obtain the knowledge and experience he needed to create a Russian navy. With his intense, roving curiosity and his capacity to learn, he had gained a far wider technical knowledge, embracing engineering and astronomy, gunnery and coining, and other crafts and sciences. He had come expecting to see the technical superiority of the West, and it had exceeded his expectations. But also he had seen something of the wealth that trade and industry brought to these countries.

Finally, although he had paid scant attention to the social and cultural aspects of Western life, he had carried away with him a sense of the intellectual vitality, especially of London and Amsterdam, and of the culture and dignity of Vienna. Everything in the West contrasted with the spirit and conditions of his own country, where the people were harnessed by mediaeval traditions and, like blindfolded horses on a treadmill, plodded along the same tracks, unaware of anything different; they did not even want to move from the old ways which gave them a sense of security in the flat, timeless expanses of Russia.

Peter was now determined to make them change. His practical mind had translated his impressions into numerous plans which he was impatient to introduce. But, as he hastened towards Moscow, a cold savage anger consumed him. The streltsi, who had terrorized him and stamped his memory with the horrors of their revolt of May 1682, had again rebelled. Before he could go ahead with his plans, he must deal with them once and for all time. As a contemporary diarist in Moscow was to write: "It had come to pass that Muscovy was only to be saved by cruelty, not by pity."[19]

CHAPTER XV

The Beginning of the New Era
1698

THE entry of the old Muscovite tsars into their capital was always a magnificent occasion. The boyars and church hierarchy came in stately procession to pay homage, and the bells of Moscow rang out in welcome. But when Peter slipped into the city on the evening of 25 August 1698, he was not expected and no one met him. He did not remain in the Kremlin or see his wife and son. He accompanied Golovin and Lefort to their homes. He visited Anna Mons, and then went off to Preobrazhenskoe where he spent the night among his own trusted soldiers.

This informality did not prevent news of his return spreading overnight. At first light next morning, crowds of people made their way to Preobrazhenskoe to greet him. The habits of homage to the Tsar were too deeply ingrained to be put aside, even by his unprecedented behaviour, and the desire of everyone was to set eyes on him. He received them all, and when they prostrated themselves on the ground before him in the old fashion, he lifted them up and kissed them, for he disliked servile prostrations.

As his subjects crowded into the room, he revealed his surprise. Without warning he took a pair of scissors and began to cut off the courtiers' long beards. Shein was first to suffer, then Romodanovsky, and the others. Only the Patriarch and two old boyars escaped. Shein and Romodanovsky had long been close associates of the Tsar, but they cherished their beards and Muscovite clothing as much as the most conservative boyars in the room. The nobles were shocked; the simple people were horrified.

With this assault on the most powerful symbol of old Muscovy, Peter launched a new era in his country. It was an era when many old traditions were displaced and new ideas forcibly introduced, when the slow tempo of Muscovite life was accelerated, and the barriers against Western ideas and techniques struck down. It was an era of war and toil for everyone from the Tsar to the peasant serf. Peter did not spare himself, and it was his era, for he alone created it. The seeds of many of the changes had been planted long before his reign; in time, if allowed to grow, they might of themselves have borne fruit. But he could not wait, and he plunged his people into revolution.

The goal of his labours was to reform and revive Russia so that she would stand as a great power, accepted as an equal with the Western powers, especially Holland, England, and Austria, and as an equal not only in terms of military might, but also in trade and industry, in government and civilization. All his new projects, reforms, assaults on old Muscovy, and military and naval campaigns were harnessed to this objective. It involved him in constant war, and historians have repeatedly stated that it was war that inspired and compelled his reforms.[1] War was certainly the source of many reforms, and in the first decade of the new century it was to dictate or condition most of his legislation. But for Peter war was never an end in itself; it was an instrument of policy and no more. War was the unavoidable means to obtaining the access to the Baltic and Black seas that was essential to his basic policy. If he could have achieved his objectives without war, he would undoubtedly have done so. He was intensely interested in the weapons and techniques of war on land and sea, but he had no love of war, no hunger for military fame or personal glory, and this he showed repeatedly during his long duel with Charles of Sweden. By nature Peter was a builder and reformer; of necessity he became also a conqueror.

This grandiose vision of the role that Russia should play did not burst upon him suddenly while he travelled in western Europe. His very first contacts with foreigners had stirred in him the idea of revitalizing his country. He had seen that her backwardness was not only due to her inefficient government and her ill-equipped and untrained army, but, more basically, to lack of education among her people and to failure to develop her natural resources, found industries, and expand trade. But, while it did not inspire the policy to which he devoted his life, his experience of Western countries matured and crystallized his ideas. He returned ready for action on a scale that has rarely been undertaken by one man.

Peter was now like an elemental force. He was constructive, and converted every idea into prompt action, giving it an impetus that swept obstacles aside. Working much of the time under the pressure of war, he did not proceed calmly and methodically. He launched reforms and new projects one after the other, returning to them time and time again, modifying, cancelling, and then propelling them further towards fulfilment. It was a wasteful method; important factors were often forgotten, or overtaken in the rush of events. He had few ministers on whom he could rely; he had to supervise and direct everything himself, and he could not be everywhere. But he got extraordinary results. And when, during the final fourteen years of his reign, he was at last able to legislate after careful deliberation, he completely reorganized the structure of government, church, and society in Russia.

On his return from abroad Peter, having prohibited the wearing of beards, also set about changing the national costume, another powerful symbol of old Muscovy; and then he annihilated the streltsy. Simultaneously with the destruction of the old, he worked on the creation of his new navy and army, and issued decrees to finance them and the impending war against Sweden.[2]

The beard was a fundamental characteristic of the ancient Eastern faith, and one of the chief outward differences between Latin and Greek churches. Nevertheless among the Russian nobility the idea of shaving was not new. At the beginning of the century the fashion, introduced by foreigners, had appealed to many of the young courtiers. It had brought on their heads the fulminations of Patriarch Filaret, who had denounced it as "doglike foolishness," and Tsar Mikhail had legislated against it, but after his death the bolder spirits had begun shaving again.

The simple people cherished their beards more zealously. To them it was part of their Orthodoxy. When John Perry, the English engineer, met an old Russian carpenter, who had worked for him, coming from the barber, he jokingly told him that he had become a young man, and asked what he had done with his beard. The old Russian carefully put his hand under his shirt and produced it, explaining that when he went home he would put his beard in his coffin, so that it would be buried with him. On arriving in the other world, he would then be able to account for it to St. Nicholas.[3] All his comrades had taken the same precautions, for salvation was impossible without a beard. "God did not create men beardless, only cats and dogs . . . the shaving of beards is not only foolishness and a dishonour, it is a mortal sin," thundered the Patriarch Adrian.[4] The resistance shown by the mass of his subjects to losing their beards did not, however, deflect Peter from his policy. But a few months later, when he saw in it a source of revenue for his hard-pressed Treasury, he relaxed the ban to the extent of permitting beards on payment of a tax.[5]

Among the upper classes Western dress, like shaving, was not entirely novel. Tsar Feodor had introduced it at court, but the great majority of the nobility and all Russians of other classes continued to wear national dress. This costume with its full coat reaching to the ground, its capacious sleeves, and tall hat lined with fur, had no religious significance, but was hallowed by custom. On ceremonial occasions pearls and precious stones sewn on the brocades and velvets added to the richness of the dress of the nobles. Foreigners in Moscow admired this opulence, but considered it Asiatic. Russians, wearing it abroad, met with laughter.[6]

Peter disliked the national costume. It got in his way when he was working with an axe, marching with his troops, or clambering over the sides of his ships. He had early adopted Western clothes and, while abroad, he had normally dressed as a sailor or ship's master. He considered that his people would never become efficient while they wore the cumbersome Muscovite clothing. At a banquet, when he noticed a group of Russian officers wearing the old costume, he took a pair of scissors, and cut off part of their long sleeves. "See," he said, "these things are in your way. You are safe nowhere with them; at one moment you upset a glass, and then you forgetfully dip them in the sauce! Get gaiters made of them!"[7]

On his return to Moscow, Peter appeared to be in jovial mood. Boyar Shein gave a banquet on 1 September to celebrate the first day of the Muscovite New Year, and the cutting of beards continued, now carried on in a spirit of pantomime by the Tsar's jester, Turgeniev; no one dared to object. At another banquet given a few days later, Guarient, the Imperial ambassador, reported that he had never seen the Tsar in such a happy mood.[8] But beneath this joviality ran an undercurrent of angry impatience, for Peter was anxious to go to Voronezh to see how his shipbuilding programme had progressed. Two matters alone kept him in Moscow; the first was the disposal of his wife, Tsaritsa Evdokiya; the second was the investigation of the recent streltsi revolt.

Three days after his return Peter summoned his wife to his presence, presumably to tell her that she must retire to a nunnery. The marriage had been a failure from the start. He had married in obedience to his mother's wishes, and had never had any interest in Evdokiya. He had ignored her pleas for his company, or for letters, and, although always a regular correspondent with his friends and ministers, he had never written her a line. For this she blamed the foreigners, and especially Lefort. She became jealous and possessive, and her letters began to sound a note of reproach.[9] A typical product of the terem, she was narrowly Orthodox and conservative, and completely out of sympathy with all that Peter thought and did.

Evdokiya had resisted all past attempts to make her take the veil. When Streshnev, Naryshkin, Romodanovsky, and her confessor had pressed her to retire voluntarily to a nunnery, she had refused. Apart from her hope that the Tsar might change towards her, she dreaded separation from her son. Her second son, Alexander, had died in May 1692, aged seven months, and her family was in exile. The boy, Alexei, was her one consolation. Incarcerated in a nunnery, she might never see him again. Others would have charge of him, and probably they would be the heretic foreigners who enjoyed the Tsar's confidence. She had been brought up to regard obedience to her husband as the guiding principle of her life, but now she refused to obey.

The Tsar's will, however, was law, and her resistance was to no purpose. Shortly after their meeting, her son aged eight and a half, was taken from her and given into the care of Tsarevna Natalya, Peter's sister. On 23 September, a humble carriage carried the Tsaritsa away from the Kremlin to Suzdal Pokrovsky nunnery. No announcement had been made, but everyone in Moscow knew her fate and felt deep sympathy for her. Ten months later she took the veil under the name of Helen.[10]

Since his return Peter's temper had been more unpredictable than ever. "An inexplicable whirlwind troubled the gaieties," Korb noted in his diary on 18 October, "Seizing upon Mr. Lefort and flinging him upon the floor, the Czar's Majesty kicked him. He who is next to the fire is nearest to burning."[11]

At a banquet given by Lefort, Peter suddenly exploded with rage against Boyar Shein, who only three days ago had been his host, and his outburst nearly ended in bloodshed. In the presence of some five hundred guests Peter accused Shein of selling army commissions. Shein denied it, although, in fact, he and other ministers had indulged in this and every other kind of corruption. Peter then rushed out of the room and asked the sentry on duty how many officers Shein had created. He returned in a fury and, drawing his sword, shouted, "By striking thus I will mar thy mal-government."

Zotov and Romodanovsky tried to defend Shein. Peter struck out at both with his sword, wounding Zotov in the head and Romodanovsky in the hand. Lefort deflected a blow that would have killed Shein. Finally Menshikov managed to calm the Tsar. And a few minutes later Peter was taking part in the merriment as though nothing had happened.

The party went on until 5:30 A.M. with dancing and gaiety, but no one knew who would next fall foul of the Tsar. They did not dare withdraw and two young ladies who did creep away were stopped by the sentries at the door and on the Tsar's orders brought back to enjoy themselves.[12]

Peter's outburst on this occasion had another cause than the matter of army commissions—this was Shein's unsatisfactory handling of the streltsi rebels. His investigation had been perfunctory and, in executing so many of the ringleaders, he had also destroyed valuable evidence. Within a few days of his return to Moscow, Peter ordered Shein to assemble all those streltsi concerned in the rebellion whom he had not already executed.

In Preobrazhenskoe, fourteen torture chambers were then prepared. The procedure in these was that the accused was questioned and if, as usually happened, his evidence was considered incomplete, he was raised on the gallows, his arms disjointed, and he was lashed with the knout. Between strokes he was questioned further. In spite of this ordeal many streltsi proved stubborn and had to be further urged to confess by ordeal of fire. Other instruments of examination by torture were the rack and pincers of iron. Such were the normal methods of obtaining evidence.

The interrogation began on 17 September, and during the following weeks Preobrazhenskoe was bathed in a haze of fires and blood. It was Romodanovsky who examined the ringleaders, giving special attention to Vaska Zorin who had been interrogated five times already under torture by Shein; but on 17 September he divulged new evidence. He admitted that at Voskressensky he had handed an unfinished petition to one of Shein's officers with the request that it should be read aloud to the loyal troops. Zorin now confessed that he had composed the petition with the object of stirring up rebellion. He added that, on arriving in Moscow, the streltsi had intended going at once to Novodevichi nunnery to petition Tsarevna Sofia to govern once again. After this they had planned to stir the people to revolt, destroy the Foreign Quarter, and kill all the foreigners and certain of the boyars. Such was his new confession and others confirmed it.

The next day was a Sunday and the torture chambers stood empty. Peter prepared a list of questions to be put to the rebels in a mass investigation the following day. His questions concentrated on Zorin's petition and the subsequent plans to start riots in Moscow.[18] This interrogation took place on Monday, 19 September, when 164 streltsi were divided between ten torture chambers. Although under merciless examination, the great majority of them denied all intention of rebelling. Then one of the younger streltsi, named Maslov, broke down and confessed. The others were promptly re-examined and they, too, pleaded guilty.

The interrogation continued remorselessly on the following day, when two new batches of rebels were brought in. One of them after only three strokes with the knout, confessed that, if Sofia had declined to rule, they had planned to ask Tsarevich Alexei to ascend the throne, and that they had decided to stop the Tsar entering Moscow on his return from abroad. Two others later added that the streltsi had intended to kill him.

It was towards the end of this day that Peter obtained the evidence he had been seeking. One Vaska Alexeev, after being knouted and burnt by fire for the third time, confessed that the rebels had had a letter from Sofia, urging them to revolt and to go to her at Novodevichi nunnery. He stated that Vaska Tuma, who had already been executed, had brought the letter from Moscow to the streltsi at Velikie Luki and that another strelets, Mishka Obrosimov, had taken it from there to the streltsi at Torcpets.

Alexeev was re-examined the next day. He added that Obrosimov had read the letter aloud to the assembled streltsi, so that inevitably all knew of its existence. Obrosimov was brought to Preobrazhenskoe on that same day. He denied everything. Gradually, however, much of the evidence was wrung from him, although he did not confess all he knew. But Maslov, who had now admitted knowing about the letter, stated that Tuma had communicated with Sofia through a beggar woman, called Mashka Stepanova. Peter ordered that she should be found, and after a hurried search she was tracked down and brought to Preobrazhenskoe. There the chamber with its fire and gallows, its instruments of torture and the stench of burnt flesh terrified her. She uttered only a few incoherent words and fell into a faint. Soon afterwards, without giving evidence, she died.

The means of contact between Sofia and Tuma so obsessed Peter that he decided to examine the women surrounding Sofia in the nunnery. High- and low-born, these women received precisely the same treatment as the streltsi. Two chambermaids were stripped to the waist, raised on the gallows, and given each three strokes of the knout, while Princess Kasatkina herself received four strokes. But this ruthless examination revealed only that Sofia had indeed known that the streltsi were marching on Moscow, and that Marfa, her sister, had been heard to state that the rebels intended petitioning her, Sofia, to rule.

Peter himself questioned Marfa on that same day and although she divulged nothing new, she did implicate others. Instantly these, too, were savagely interrogated but without result. There now remained only one witness who had not been examined—Tsarevna Sofia herself.

On 27 September Peter rode to Novodevichi nunnery to interrogate her himself. The only record of this meeting is the bare official report that followed it.[14] But few meetings can have been more dramatic or more charged with hatred. Face to face with Peter, Sofia flatly denied either sending the letter or stirring the streltsi to revolt. She was not put to torture and, when she persisted in her denials, Peter did not examine her further. Abruptly he returned to Preobrazhenskoe and there gave all his attention to the re-examination of certain of the leading rebels.

On 29 September Peter absented himself from the torture chambers to attend the christening of the Danish ambassador's son. All the leading foreigners were present and Peter was in an affable mood.

But during the christening party his good humour suddenly vanished. He noticed Menshikov wearing his sword as he danced. This was an offence against court etiquette and because of it he knocked him down with a blow in the face which brought blood spouting from his nose. Colonel de Blumberg who was slow in taking off his sword, managed to beg the Tsar's pardon in time. In an evil temper Peter returned to the torture chambers.

The first of the mass executions took place the next day. Exactly one hundred of the first group of 341 men were under twenty years of age, and their youth saved them from death. Instead, they were knouted, their cheeks branded with the letter B for *buntovshchik* (rebel), and they were exiled to Siberia. Another forty rebels were kept in custody for further questioning. Five were summarily beheaded in Preobrazhenskoe.[15]

The remaining 196 rebels were seated in small carts, two to a cart, each man holding a lighted candle in his hands. In procession they then moved off slowly towards Moscow. At the main Preobrazhenskoe gate they halted, and there the Tsar was waiting, seated on his horse. A large suite of his ministers and of foreigners attended him, and all the ambassadors in Moscow were present by special invitation.

It was a solemn moment as the rebels, under the angry stare of their Tsar, heard the formal statement of their crimes and the sentence of death pronounced. Then the long procession of little carts continued on its way towards Moscow while wives and mothers and children of the condemned men stumbled along beside them, wailing plaintively and beseeching mercy. But there was no mercy in the Tsar's heart for the streltsi.

The people of Moscow watched morosely. Though their sympathies were with the rebels, though they had no understanding or love for their Tsar, nevertheless they feared him and were silent. Still followed by their families, the condemned men at last reached Moscow. There they were hanged from various gallows which had previously been erected at the gates of the city, at the barracks of each of the four regiments, and at certain other places.

On that evening Lefort gave one of his magnificent banquets at which were present many foreign officers and boyars. Peter himself came late, because he had been attending the funeral of a German colonel. To the people of Moscow it was fearful that their Tsar should apparently think nothing of executing more than two hundred of his own subjects, yet would publicly mourn the death of one hated foreigner. Peter, however, was not to be deterred by the horror of the people of Moscow.

Three days later, interrogations began again. Further groups of streltsi, making up the second party of 680 men, had by now been brought to Preobrazhenskoe. Of this party, eleven young streltsi divulged important new evidence. In the spring of 1698, they said, they had seen Vaska Tuma take a letter from a beggar woman on the Arbat in Moscow. Certain of them had also seen him receive another letter in a village some twenty-seven miles from Moscow, from an old woman who said that it was from Novodevichi nunnery. A woman called Anyutka Nikitina was found after a frantic search and at once the eleven streltsi identified her as the beggar seen with Tuma. She herself proved a reluctant witness—until put to the rack. Then she confessed that she had indeed handed the letter, sent from Novodevichi nunnery, to Tuma in Moscow. She confessed further that she had also served as a channel between the streltsi and Tsarevna Marfa.

On 6 October the interrogation of the beggar Anyutka was renewed. She now identified Anna Klushina, one of Tsarevna Marfa's bed-chamber attendants, as the woman who had brought her the letter to be delivered to Tuma. Anna Klushina, after being knouted, confessed that she had carried the letter.

Thus the main evidence had been extracted, but final proof was still lacking. In spite of this, further mass executions took place. On 11 October, 144 streltsi of the second group were hanged, the majority from beams projecting through the crenellations of the Kremlin walls. On the next two days 278 men were executed, many of them on gallows specially erected near the Novodevichi nunnery, where Sofia was held. Then for two days there was quiet.

This was broken by the second mass examination of rebels on 14-15 October, when 225 men were interrogated in the fourteen torture chambers. Peter had again prepared the list of questions, relentlessly seeking to extract still more information about the Tsarevna's letter, and to establish the origin of certain rumours. As before, the majority of the streltsi denied everything on first questioning, but eventually broke down under prolonged torture. Even then their evidence produced nothing new.

In Preobrazhenskoe 109 men were now beheaded over an open

trench. Peter not only attended, but even called on several of his suite to try their own hands as executioners. Lefort and De Blumberg declined on the ground that it was contrary to the customs of their countries, but it is said that Romodanovsky and Menshikov distinguished themselves at this task.[16]

Later, on the Red Square, ten men were executed. They included the Kalistratov brothers who were among the most stubborn of the rebels. They had denied everything, even under the most savage torture. Two of the brothers were thereupon broken on the wheel and left to a lingering death, meantime forced to watch the beheading of the third brother and then smeared with his blood. Both complained spiritedly at the injustice of their brother being despatched more rapidly than they were. At the same time many more streltsi were hanged from gallows specially erected in a square by the Novodevichi nunnery. Finally three streltsi were hanged directly in front of the window of Sofia's cell, and the man in the centre held, tied in his dead hands, a paper folded like a petition. Such was the mocking and gruesome symbol of the Tsar's vengeance.[17]

The main executions had now taken place. In all, 799 men had lost their lives by beheading, hanging, or breaking on the wheel. The winter had set in early and the frost had fixed in rigid permanence the horror of the Tsar's justice. For nearly five months Moscow was like a charnel house. Frozen corpses hung from the Kremlin walls and over all the gates through which the people passed on their daily business. On the Red Square, at the execution place, headless bodies lay grotesquely in pools of frozen blood, while on the wheel were bent those whom death had so slowly overtaken.

Peter was convinced that all the evidence had proved the guilt of Sofia who, although confined to the nunnery, had not yet taken the veil. He now ordered her head to be shaven, and she became a nun under the name of Susanna. A strong guard was mounted over her cell and in his own hand Peter wrote out the strict instructions that were to be followed by her guard at all times.[18] Five years later she died.

The investigation of the streltsi revolt did not end with these 799 executions. In January and February of 1699 and of 1700 there were further interrogations and more executions. In June 1699, Peter disbanded the remaining sixteen regiments of the Moscow streltsi. He confiscated their arms, houses, and land, and dispersed them throughout the country with their families, making it illegal for them ever to serve as soldiers again.[19] It was an inevitable decision. The streltsi had represented the old Muscovy, and formed the one armed opposition to the Tsar in the country. They were undisciplined and rebellious, and Peter himself held bitter childhood memories of their mutinous activities. They were never to challenge him again, and his own loyal guards regiments took their place.

Now, having dealt with the chief rebels Peter felt free to leave Moscow. He was impatient to see the new shipyards at Voronezh, and, on Sunday 23 October 1698, after the usual farewell banquet given by Lefort, he set out.

CHAPTER XVI

The Voronezh Fleet
1698-1699

PETER found Voronezh transformed from a small town into a sprawling shipbuilding centre. All along the river banks, shipyards bustled with activity. Shipwrights, captains, and seamen of other nations busily directed and helped with the work. Twenty ships had already been launched, and the storehouses were filled with naval supplies. Nevertheless Voronezh had many problems.

Protasyev, appointed in charge of shipbuilding, had written often to Peter in Holland and England, explaining his difficulties and seeking instructions. Suitable timber had proved hard to find, although the surrounding forests had been carefully surveyed. The various foreign shipwrights followed their own national designs, which differed considerably, and so they quarrelled among themselves. Peter's orders that Dutch shipwrights were to work under supervision had given rise to further confusion. The Russian administration was grossly inefficient.

It was shortage of labour, however, that had become the shipyards' chief problem. Hundreds of peasants had fled, and sickness had reduced the numbers of those who remained. At times the labour corps had fallen to a mere half the size needed. Not even harsh punishments could deter the peasants from flight; corruption, so deeply ingrained in Russian officialdom, had aggravated this problem, for many officials took bribes from peasants to allow them to flee.

In spite of all these troubles, however, work had progressed and, as he made his first hasty inspection, Peter was pleased. But his pleasure soon gave way to despondency, because on closer examination, many of the vessels already launched proved faulty. For a moment the magnitude of his task appalled him. "A cloud of doubt covers my mind," he wrote three days after arriving in Voronezh, "whether I shall ever taste these fruits, or whether they will be like dates, which those who plant them never gather."[1] It was typical of him, however, that he then put his doubts behind him and set to work. He personally laid down the keel of a sixty-gun ship, the *Predestination*.[2] He himself hurled orders at everyone, and he concentrated his tremendous energies on creating a navy.

Two months later, he was compelled to return to Moscow. Further interrogations of rebel streltsi were to take place and the negotiations for a northern alliance against Sweden had to be undertaken. Moreover, the question of peace or war with Turkey was again in the balance. As a background to all these problems, there was the urgent need to increase the national revenue.

Difficulties of finance had constantly plagued him. His predecessors, faced with such need to raise revenue, had simply increased taxes and imposed new monopolies, and, indeed, he himself resorted to these expedients. But his demands, so huge as to be unprecedented, had soon made the burden of taxation and special levies more than his people could bear.

Nevertheless he was in advance of his contemporaries in appreciating that Russia's national income depended on productivity and trade, with the result that he evolved an economic policy which was a combination of short-term projects, designed to meet the immediate costs of work in hand, and of long-term projects which would expand industry and trade.

One morning in January 1699, an anonymous letter in the form of a petition to the Tsar was found in the Transport Office. It contained a proposal that all formal documents should be engrossed on stamped paper, the duty thus levied being paid to the Treasury. The author of this letter, it was discovered, was one Alexei Kurbatov, a serf belonging to Boyar Sheremetev, who had risen by sheer ability to be his steward, and had even accompanied him on his visits to Italy and Malta in 1697. Peter promptly seized on this proposal. Four days later he issued an ukaz, fixing three rates of stamp duty, and making all agreements, petitions, contracts, and other documents, executed after 1 March 1699, invalid, unless on sheets bearing the official duty-paid mark of an eagle on the top left-hand corner.

Kurbatov, the former serf, was at once rewarded richly for his initiative, and he became the first of the "profit-makers" (*pribyl-shchiki*), a new class of official, whose task it was to evolve and administer schemes for increasing revenue.

At the same time Peter kept in mind the towns of western Europe, which as centres of trade, enjoying a large measure of autonomy, had impressed him. He had returned to Moscow convinced that such trade was the chief source of all national wealth, and that his nation could only flourish, if, as in Holland and England, his towns were also flourishing. Russian towns, however, laboured under burdens of bureaucracy and corruption.

To remedy this, Peter by an ukaz of 30 January 1699 abolished the jurisdiction of the military governors or voevodi over the merchant-traders. He then empowered the latter to elect their own councils which would have the function of collecting certain indirect and direct taxes, and of handling municipal affairs generally. A central department in Moscow, responsible for all these councils, was to be called the Ratusha or Burghers' Council, and it would answer directly to the Tsar. This reform had many good results. Thereafter, the collection of taxes became more efficient and equitable, especially for merchant-traders, and the Burghers' Council became, in effect, a second finance ministry. Within two years it was handling some two thirds of the national revenue.

Peter also directed merchants of Russia to form companies and to despatch goods abroad through Archangel, Novgorod, and Astrakhan. They had long complained that they could not compete with foreign merchants, who traded in companies, sharing both risks and profits, even though, many years earlier, Ordin-Nashchokin had urged them to join together to break this foreign monopoly. Left to themselves, however, they had taken no such initiative. In this, as in most other things, they had waited for reforms to be imposed, and now they had to labour to effect the changes demanded by their Tsar.

Furthermore, since his Azov campaigns against the Turks, Peter had been paying special attention to heavy industry. It was another field in which, though not an innovator, his achievements were spectacular. Industry had had its beginnings in Russia earlier in the century. Some twenty state or privately owned iron foundries were already working when Peter came to the throne. But these foundries were small and their output was wholly inadequate to meet the needs of Peter's army and navy. The Azov campaigns had brought this home to him. Already, therefore, he had sent samples of iron and silver ores to Holland for examination, and had ordered a series of surveys of mineral deposits in Russia. In 1696 Nikita Demidov, the great industrialist whose family was to dominate Russian industry for generations to come, set up foundries on the Tulitsa River. Others established foundries elsewhere. Further samples of iron ore, sent to Witsen in Amsterdam for analysis, brought the encouraging report that the ore was exceptional both in quality and yield.

On the very eve of his departure for western Europe, Peter had found time to give orders to Vinius, head of the Siberian Office, to conduct further surveys and to establish new foundries wherever possible. While abroad he corresponded constantly with Vinius about developing mining sites. In June 1697, he had given instructions for intensive prospecting to be carried out in the regions of Verkhoture and Tobolsk, and also the drafting of plans for both mines and foundries. These were the first steps in the development of heavy industry to which Peter eventually gave such impetus that it was able to supply all the armaments needed by his army and navy, and even make good the heavy wastage of his campaigns.

During the winter of 1697-1698 Peter had also found time for his usual wild relaxations. Thus he had revived in a more active and public form his "All-joking, All-drunken Assembly." On Christmas Day, the Tsar's mock patriarch, bearing the crozier, mitre, and other insignia of office, with a suite of some two hundred persons, made the rounds of Moscow in eighty sledges. They stopped at the houses of the richer Muscovites singing carols, and their chosen hosts had to pay dearly for this unsought pleasure.

At Epiphany, however, only a few days after this round of blasphemous carol singing, Peter attended the great Orthodox festival of the blessing of the waters of the Neglinnaya River. As though to demonstrate the absence of any firm policy of denigration of the church, he made this an occasion of even greater magnificence than usual. His three crack regiments, wearing their new uniforms, were present. More than five hundred church dignitaries took part. The people of Moscow crowded the streets and covered the roofs of the houses and the walls of the Kremlin, to catch a glimpse of the breaking of the ice and the solemn moment of benediction and the blessing of the Tsar with the hallowed water. The ceremony ended with salvoes by massed artillery, followed by a triple salvo of musketry. It was an impressive occasion, and no one present had behaved more devoutly than Tsar Peter himself.[3]

In Butter-week, or Maslenitsa, the week preceding the strict Lenten fasts, Russians traditionally abandoned themselves to heavy drinking and debauchery. "Then," observed Korb, "they have no shame of lust, no reverence of God, and most mischievous licentiousness is the order of the day."[4] In this year Peter celebrated Butter-week with an especially grotesque and drunken entertainment. This was the dedication to Bacchus of Lefort's palace, built for him by Peter in the Foreign Quarter. All the leading foreigners and diplomatic representatives in Moscow, and many of the boyars were invited in the Tsar's name to attend.[5]

It began with a procession in which the mock patriarch, Zotov, wore the vestments of an Orthodox bishop, and, although Moscow was in the freezing grip of winter, Bacchus, wearing only a mitre, "went stark naked to betoken lasciviousness to the onlookers; Cupid and Venus were the insignia on his crozier, lest there should be any mistake about what flock he was pastor of."[6] A rout of Bacchanalians followed him, carrying bowls of wine, beer and brandy, and great dishes of dried tobacco leaves. On arriving at the palace, they lit the tobacco so that its smoke filled the banqueting hall and other rooms. The mock patriarch then consecrated the palace, using for the purpose two long tobacco pipes, fixed in the form of a cross. This ceremony was followed by three days of banqueting.

Such events added to the bewilderment of the Muscovites. They had thronged to welcome their Tsar on his return to Moscow. They understood, loved, and feared him when he sat in magnificence in the Kremlin, or, by the river, received the blessing of the Patriarch. But he seldom went near the Kremlin and it was rare for him to take part in such ceremonies as the blessing of the waters. His travels abroad, his close friendships with foreigners, his mockery of the church, his wild habits, his passion for building ships, and his ferocious examination of the rebel streltsi were not the expected activities of a tsar of Muscovy. For this reason his subjects muttered among themselves about their "Drunken Tsar Stranger" and, shaking their heads forlornly, agreed that nothing good would come in the holy Russian land while he behaved as he did.

Filled with conservative prejudice, they could not understand that, for all his iconoclasm, his reforms, and his wild enthusiasms, Peter himself remained an Orthodox Russian and, in many respects, the embodiment of his country. His determination to purge and reform Russia and, by applying Western methods and machinery, to set her as an equal among the great Western powers, seemed to them to mean that he would convert her into a Western state, destroying her Orthodoxy, her way of life, and everything which in their eye made Russia unique. This was the gulf separating Peter from his people, isolating him, and compelling him to pursue his course alone, dragging them after him.

From now onwards, shunning the Kremlin which he loathed, Peter made his headquarters in the mansion which he had built for Lefort. There he received the Brandenburg envoy in farewell audience, and accepted the letter of credence of his successor. He then invited the new resident to dine with other foreign envoys and his boyars.[7] From this dinner Peter set out for another visit to Voronezh. He travelled rapidly, leaving behind him a Moscow where the debauchery of Butter-week had, almost incredibly, given way to the strict fasting of Lent.[8]

One evening during Lent, Lefort, who did not believe in abstinence at any time, caught a chill after a drinking bout. Debauchery had undermined his constitution and his condition quickly deteriorated. On 2 March, eight days after falling ill, he died, aged forty-six. Peter learning of his favourite's illness by letter[9] set out at once for Moscow, arriving on 7 March. He was staggered to find that Lefort was already dead. Grief overwhelmed him and, bursting into thick sobs, he muttered, "Now I am left without one trusty man: he alone was faithful to me: in whom can I confide henceforward?"[10]

Lefort received a state funeral of greater magnificence than that granted to any Russian, except only the tsars and the patriarchs. On Peter's orders, everyone of any importance was present. He himself wore deep mourning. When the moment came to move the body, he had the coffin opened and, weeping bitterly in the presence of the whole court, he kissed the corpse. He then led the first company of the Preobrazhensky regiment in the funeral procession to the Protestant church in the Foreign Quarter, and afterwards to the burial in the cemetery.[11]

Two days after the funeral, Peter returned to his shipbuilding. He had much to do and, as when his mother died, he would not stand still to grieve. He needed work and movement as he needed food and air. Also distracting him from personal grief, there was the problem of negotiating peace with the Turks.

Before his hurried departure from Vienna, Peter had given his representative, Voznitsyn, only hasty briefing for the coming peace conference, but Voznitsyn had understood well the terms that would be acceptable to his Tsar and did all he could by both diplomatic and undiplomatic means to achieve them. Peter required not only the formal surrender of Azov and of the forts on the lower Dnieper, already in his hands, but also of the town of Kerch, although he had instructed Voznitsyn to yield over Kerch if the Turks proved too stubborn.[12]

The peace congress met at last at Karlowitz on the Danube. There, in secret sessions, Lord Paget, the English ambassador in Constantinople, acting as mediator, established terms acceptable to Austria and Turkey, but particularly favourable to Austria.[13] Thus Voznitsyn found himself isolated. The Turks, having reached agreement with Austria, the only enemy whom they feared, were in no mood to make any further concessions.

As the negotiations dragged on, Peter grew increasingly impatient. This constant threat of war with Turkey was a serious drain on both his treasury and his army. He had for long been holding a force of twenty-two thousand men in readiness in the Ukraine and, when war seemed inevitable, he had not only concentrated a further eighteen thousand troops there, but had begun mobilizing an even greater force. At the same time he pressed boldly ahead with his navy, for it was at sea, not on land, that he planned to deliver the decisive blow.

On the other hand, the time was ripe to attack Sweden, and he was eager to free himself of commitments in the south. With this in mind, he sent special instructions to Voznitsyn to make concessions. But these instructions arrived too late. The congress had already ended, and Voznitsyn had managed only to conclude a two-year armistice on general terms.

In his report Voznitsyn advised that the Turks wanted a permanent peace, and that someone able, but not well known, should be sent to negotiate in Constantinople.[14] Following this advice, Peter appointed Councillor E. I. Ukraintsev[15] as his envoy extraordinary to the Sultan. He decided to send him to Constantinople in a warship and himself to escort him with his fleet as far as Kerch. In this way he could indulge his passion for naval exercises, train his men, and also demonstrate forcefully to the Turks that his ships could readily reach the Black Sea.

He now worked furiously on preparations for this voyage. His fleet was to consist of twelve warships, seven of which were not yet ready, and also four galleys, thirteen brigantines, and eleven galliots, while 117 barges would carry supplies. General-Admiral Feodor Golovin, who had succeeded Franz Lefort as senior naval officer, was to be in command. Golovin's naval experience amounted only to a voyage of a few hours in the Baltic Sea, and to two crossings of the English Channel, but he was no more than a figurehead, as Lefort had been. Vice-Admiral Cruys was second in command, and the captains of all ships were foreign masters with the one exception of the Tsar, who, as Captain Peter Mikhailov, was in command of a forty-four-gun frigate.

Azov, where the squadron arrived on 24 May 1699, had changed greatly in the three years since its capture. The town had been rebuilt and fortified, and was now an important stronghold. Satisfied with the work done there, Peter sailed on alone to Taganrog, where he inspected the new harbour and fort. Returning to Azov, he then led his fleet out to sea and by 29 June all his ships were riding at anchor off Taganrog.

The next stage was the voyage to Kerch. He appointed the forty-six-gun frigate, *Krepost* (Fortress), to carry his ambassador, Ukraintsev, on to Constantinople. He then ordered all his captains to overhaul their ships in readiness to sail for Kerch in twelve days. No one worked harder than the Tsar himself. He caulked decks, repaired rigging, and tackled any job, no matter how menial, that needed doing, but this was far from being his only occupation. Since leaving Moscow he had been in regular correspondence with Vinius, Weide, Bruce, Gordon, and others. From Vinius he demanded regular reports on developments in western Europe, especially concerning France and the Spanish succession. In Vienna, he had set Weide the task of studying the organization of the Imperial army and of drafting a new military code for the Russian army, and Weide now sent him draft sections of this code for approval.[16] To Jacob Bruce he wrote about gathering information on the law of inheritance in England, Scotland, and France.[17] He even found time to correspond with certain of the young Russians he had sent to study in Berlin.[18] At the same time he was closely supervising the preparations for Ukraintsev's mission to Constantinople.

His fleet sailed on 5 August, and thirteen days later triumphantly anchored outside the Straits of Kerch, firing a salute of three salvoes. Their unexpected arrival alarmed the Turks who only agreed after long hesitation to provide an escort for the Tsar's ambassador. On 28 August, however, the *Krepost* sailed through the straits, followed reluctantly by four Turkish vessels. Van Pamburg, the young Dutch captain of the *Krepost*, then clapped on all sail and left the Turks far behind.

On 6 September the *Krepost* anchored about a mile from Constantinople. Next day Pamburg managed to bring her to anchor under the very walls of the Seraglio, and the sight of a Russian frigate there disturbed the Turks. They could not understand how such a large ship had navigated the shallow waters at the mouth of the Don. The *Krepost* herself was an object of great curiosity. The Sultan and his ministers went on board and inspected her closely, while the people of Constantinople gathered in thousands to gaze at her. The frigate made a stronger impression than Peter could ever have hoped.[19] Nevertheless it was to take twenty-three meetings, held over a period of eight months, before Ukraintsev could reach agreement with the Turks.

CHAPTER XVII

Preparations for War with Sweden

1699-1700

RETURNING to Moscow from Kerch on 27 September 1699, Peter found awaiting him an embassy from the King of Sweden, as well as a secret mission from the King of Poland. The Swedish embassy, with its purpose of confirming existing treaties, was particularly unwelcome at this juncture, and the Polish mission was premature, for Ukraintsev was still negotiating in Constantinople, and Peter was determined to secure peace in the south before embarking on war in the north. To avoid arousing Swedish suspicions, however, he decided that he must receive the embassy and go through the pretence of endorsing the peace treaties. But while doing this, he was secretly concerting with General Karlovich, the Polish King's agent, a plan of campaign against Charles of Sweden.

On his accession to the Swedish throne in 1697, Charles XII had become king of a great power, supreme in the north. His empire embraced Finland, Karelia, Esthonia, Livonia, western Pomerania, Wismar, Bremen, Werden, many of the Baltic islands, and the whole of the Scandinavian peninsula, excepting only Norway. He controlled the mouths of the rivers Neva, Dvina, Oder, Elbe, and Weser, flowing into the Baltic Sea.

But enemies surrounded Sweden. The Norwegians, whom the Swedes had never been able to conquer, still menaced their flank. The Danes were their traditional enemies, and Swedish possessions in Germany involved frequent conflicts. The Poles had never resigned themselves to the Treaty of Oliva. In the east, a new Russia was rising under a tsar who was determined to cancel the Treaty of Kardis, which represented two centuries of Muscovite failure to reach the Baltic Sea.

The Swedes were understandably suspicious of all their neighbours and this new friendship between the Tsar and the King of Poland added to their fears, especially since now it was only a boy who occupied the Swedish throne. But Peter took pains to allay their suspicions by protestations of friendship. He received the Swedish ambassadors and at their farewell audience on 20 November gave them formal confirmation of his intention to honour his treaties with Sweden. They returned to Stockholm well pleased with their reception and confident of the success of their mission.

At this same time General Karlovich and General-Admiral Feodor Golovin were working together in Preobrazhenskoe. So great was the secrecy surrounding them that no one guessed that war with Sweden was near. Only those taking part in the negotiations knew it; apart from Karlovich and the Tsar's representative, Golovin, they were Shafirov, the interpreter, Heins, the Danish ambassador, and Johan Reinhold Patkul, a Livonian noble, who had come to Moscow with Karlovich, and who was one of the prime movers in the great war about to burst over northern Europe.

Johan Patkul was a remarkable man who flashed across the northern sky like a minor comet. He made his mark on the European scene, even though at the end of the seventeenth century it was crowded with outstanding men and women. Handsome, powerfully built, and possessing a strong personality as well as great courage and energy, he was a dynamic figure. He spoke several languages, could write gracefully in Greek and Latin, and was learned in the sciences of war and politics, as they were then known. By temperament he was ardent, single-minded, irascible, and hot-headed. He could be ruthless and arrogant, and he was indefatigable in pursuit of revenge.

Patkul was a member of the old Livonian baronage who, with the Hungarian nobility, were probably the most fiery, tough, and independent in Europe. The Livonian barons were the direct descendants of the Teutonic Knights who had held Esthonia, Courland, and Livonia until midway through the sixteenth century. On the dissolution of the Teutonic Order, Livonia had passed to Poland. But the Poles were harsh, dishonest overlords, and eventually the Livonians sought the protection of Protestant Sweden. A long struggle between Sweden and Poland ensued until, in 1660, the Peace of Oliva confirmed Livonia as a Swedish province.

Internal difficulties in Sweden were then centred on the nobles, who were powerful and rapacious, and hated by all other classes. Charles XI himself grew up with bitter memories of them and he was determined to break their stranglehold on his country. The Diet in Stockholm in 1680 voted him absolute powers, particularly to enforce the *reduction*, which meant the recovery of all crown lands, grabbed by the nobles in previous years. He applied the reduction with ruthless severity, not only in Sweden but also in her provinces. Even though, in 1678 he had solemnly affirmed the right of the Livonian barons to their inherited estates, he now in 1680 ignored his promises and confiscated certain of their lands. Patkul pleaded the Livonian cause with great eloquence before the King in the Swedish Diet. But the Swedes only affirmed the reduction as a national necessity.

On returning in March 1692 to his own country, Patkul reported to the barons at Wenden and there he drafted a petition. This was sent to Stockholm where it was held to be treasonable, and Patkul was sentenced to lose his right hand and his head.

A month before this sentence was announced, Patkul escaped. He wandered across Europe, studied Grotius and translated the works of Puffendorf on the duties of man and citizen: all the time he was watching for the chance of restoring his fortunes in Livonia. The death of Charles XI offered the opportunity. Discontent in Sweden, the hostility of her neighbours, and the apparent weakness of the government during the minority of Charles XII, made the time ripe, he felt, to free Livonia from Swedish rule.

In October 1698 Patkul had arrived secretly in Warsaw and set about persuading King Augustus to take the initiative in forming an anti-Swedish alliance. He showed him his secret correspondence with Livonians and others in Riga, who declared themselves ready to acknowledge Augustus as their King. He drew up detailed plans, setting them out clearly in two memoranda,[1] which made the project seem both simple and profitable.

Under Patkul's spell, Augustus grew more eager to launch the campaign, to which he had agreed in principle with Peter at Rawa. In July 1699 he requested General Fleming and a group of his most trusted advisers to consider how best to give immediate effect to Patkul's proposals. Fleming recommended that General Karlovich should go to Moscow to conclude a firm alliance with the Tsar, so that Russian forces could be unobtrusively drawn up along the Swedish frontier, ready to invade Ingria and Karelia at the end of December 1699.

At this stage Augustus' main problem was to obtain the support of the Polish Diet. Many Polish nobles still refused to acknowledge him as King, and others, suspecting him of seeking to make the throne hereditary, complained about Saxon troops being on Polish soil. Augustus instructed Patkul and Fleming to approach the Primate of Poland, Cardinal Radziejowski, who was the one man with sufficient authority to secure the approval of the Diet. Patkul by eloquence and bribery obtained the Cardinal's promise to persuade the Diet to allow a force of seven thousand Saxons to remain in Courland, ostensibly to garrison the port of Polangen. Having thus prepared for his attack on Riga, Augustus sent Karlovich to Moscow.

Peter needed little persuading. His enthusiasm had been mounting ever since the original meeting in Rawa. The memorandum which Karlovich now presented to him made the campaign seem especially attractive.[2] Probably written by Patkul, this paper showed an acute understanding of Peter's dearest ambitions. It listed all the advantages he would enjoy through possession of a Baltic seaboard, stressing the economic gains; he would be able to trade directly with Holland, England, Spain, Portugal, and in the Mediterranean, as well as to open the trade route from western Europe across Russia to the Far East, from which his profits would be inestimable. Moreover, the King of Poland had found a solution to his difficulties with the Polish Diet, and could now offer himself as a real ally. It was important not to let the opportunity pass. The Tsar should begin hostilities against Sweden not later than the end of December 1699.

Peter studied this memorandum and the plans submitted by Karlovich. He then discussed them with Heins, the Danish ambassador. A year earlier on his return from abroad Peter had found Heins waiting for him with a proposal from King Christian V of Denmark for an alliance against Sweden. He favoured such an alliance, but had acted with caution while unsure whether he would have war or peace with the Turks. After protracted negotiations and then delays caused by the death of Christian V and the accession of his son, Frederick IV, he had signed a formal treaty of alliance with Denmark.

Even in signing this agreement, Peter was breaking with the past. The tsars of Muscovy had never signed treaties or agreements; their ambassadors had signed and then, in the presence of the ambassadors of the country concerned, the Tsar had ratified the document by swearing on the Bible, placed on top of it, and by kissing the cross, that he would observe it.[3]

Heins now took part in the secret negotiations with Karlovich. No points of dispute arose. Augustus promised to support Peter in recovering the former Russian possessions of Ingria and Karelia, and in particular to divert the Swedes so that they would not threaten Russian operations from Livonia and Esthonia. For his part Peter agreed to open hostilities against Sweden at the latest by April 1700, and to send troops to support Augustus' Saxon army. But with his usual caution, he covered himself in Clause 13 of the agreement which stated that the Tsar would only open his campaign against Sweden on the signing of a peace or of a long armistice with Turkey. Both Peter and Augustus bound themselves to make no separate peace and to do all in their power to draw the Elector of Brandenburg into their alliance.[4] On the conclusion of this agreement Patkul was formally presented to the Tsar. He reported on the plan to take Riga by surprise and it seemed foolproof.

More impatient than ever to embark on his new campaign, Peter sent urgent instructions to Ukrainstev in Constantinople to make major concessions to secure peace with the Turks without further delay.[5]

Only at this late stage did Peter set to work to create an army with which to fight the Swedes. He had long realized that the old Muscovite levies of untrained, ill-equipped peasants, mobilized for a campaign, and then disbanded to return to their homes, could not face up to Western troops. But his navy and other matters had demanded his attention, and he had done nothing about the army. Now he had only a few weeks or months in which to enlist raw recruits, train, equip, and weld them into a force capable of defeating the Swedish army, which was respected throughout Europe. In this he made a grave miscalculation. Probably under the influence of Augustus, Karlovich, and Patkul, he overestimated the strength of the Northern alliance, and, like everyone else, underestimated the military prowess of the seventeen-year-old King of Sweden.

Once begun, the formation of the new army moved at a headlong pace. Within three months, twenty-nine new regiments, numbering in all some thirty-two thousand men, had been armed and to some extent trained as regular troops; according to two eyewitnesses, they made an impressive force.[6] The work had begun on 8 November 1699, when Peter issued a decree calling on freemen to volunteer for military service. He offered them pay at the rate of eleven rubles a year, with provisions and the same drink allowance as the guards enjoyed. These conditions made a strong appeal, and the flow of volunteers was heavy.[7] Peter next sent Prince Anika Repnin, a lieutenant-colonel of the Preobrazhensky regiment, to enlist suitable men from the towns along the lower reaches of the Volga River.

Civil and ecclesiastical landowners were the main source of recruits. An ukaz laid down that civil landowners had to provide one recruit for every thirty to fifty serf households on their estates, while ecclesiastical landowners were to provide one recruit for every twenty-five serf households. Peter also instructed them to send only those who were young and healthy and not gainfully employed. Rich landowners usually maintained a household staff of three hundred to five hundred serfs, while the monasteries were crowded with servants and hangers-on, and Peter, who always cut his own suite to the minimum, abhorred this waste of men.

During December and January, batches of recruits arrived in Preobrazhenskoe daily. General A. M. Golovin and Brigadier Weide were each responsible for forming and training a division of nine regiments, but Peter was present most of the time and took charge. He inspected recruits on arrival, allotted all who were suitable to regiments, and helped in their infantry training.

The colonels in command of the twenty-seven infantry regiments and of the two regiments of dragoons were foreigners, many of whom had seen action at Azov or in the earlier Crimean campaigns. They were experienced and reliable men. But most of the foreign junior officers proved incompetent, and had to be dismissed. General A. M. Golovin in a letter to Peter then in Voronezh suggested recruiting junior officers from among the Russian courtiers and officials, and especially those who had been sent abroad to study.[8]

Always ready to accept suggestions and to act on them, Peter summoned courtiers of certain grades, owning estates with more than forty households, to report in Moscow. The summer of 1700 passed in energetic training of these new officers. They showed such promise that he was delighted, and exclaimed, "Why do I waste my money on foreigners, when my own subjects know how to do all the same things that they do?"[9]

His new army was now in existence and under training. It was a regular army of thirty-five regiments, composed of troops who, unlike the streltsi, had no trading or other interests to distract them. The uniform was on the German pattern, with coats of dark green cloth, and a narrow three-cornered hat; the men were armed with muskets and bayonets. It appeared to be a smart and well-disciplined force.

In this hasty and strenuous work of creating an army, one man was absent, one who normally would have been at Peter's right hand. General Patrick Gordon had noted in his diary of 31 December 1698: "In this year I have felt a sensible failing of my health and strength— but Thy will be done, O my gracious God."[10] His last appearance was to command the Butyrsky regiment in the procession in honour of the Swedish ambassadors. A few days later he took to his bed and his strength slowly ebbed. Peter visited him several times. Towards the end of November, Gordon began to fail rapidly. Calling a second time on 29 November, Peter found him on the point of death. The Jesuit priest, who had given the Last Sacraments, moved away from the bedside as the Tsar entered. "Stay where you are, Father," he said, "and do what you think fit. I will not hinder you." Then he spoke to Gordon who did not reply. A moment later two slight convulsions stirred the dying man. Peter held a mirror to his face, hoping to detect some signs of breathing, and then said, "Father, I think he is already dead." He closed Gordon's eyes, kissed him, and, his own eyes filled with tears, left the house.[11]

General Gordon received a state funeral, and everyone of importance was present on the Tsar's orders. Many attended voluntarily, for the Muscovites respected Gordon, who had faithfully served three tsars and who, unlike Lefort, was a man of dignity. Tsarevich Alexei with his aunt, Tsarevna Natalya, were also present at the service, performed by an Austrian Jesuit. Peter showed every respect for the dead soldier. He was not overwhelmed by grief as he had been on the death of Lefort, but he mourned sincerely. The year had opened with the death of Lefort, and now at its end Gordon had gone. They were in their different ways the two most trustworthy colleagues that Peter had ever had, and he was always to miss them.

The new century began with a minor reform which heralded the new Russia. In two ukazi Peter changed the Russian calendar. In future the years, he decreed, were to be calculated, not from the creation of the world, but from the Birth of Christ, as was the practice in all Western nations. Also the year was to begin on the 1 January, and not on 1 September. Everyone had to celebrate the New Year of 1700 on 1 January, instead of waiting for 1 September and the new year of 7208.

It was the Julian calendar, which was eleven days behind the Gregorian calendar in the eighteenth century, that he introduced. He was no doubt influenced in this decision by the fact that the Julian calendar was in use in England at the time. The calendar introduced by Pope Gregory XIII in 1582 was suspect to Protestant and Orthodox alike as a papist invention; it was not adopted in England until 1752, and in Russia until 1918.

With his habit of organizing to the last detail, Peter instructed his subjects on how they were to observe the new year. Everyone should embrace and congratulate his neighbour on New Year's Day. On the Red Square a special display of fireworks and artillery fire would mark the beginning of the year and of the century. Houses were to be decorated with pine, fir, and juniper branches, which were to remain until 7 January. In the main streets bonfires were to be kept alight. Always ready to welcome a holiday, his people gave up their old calendar without opposition, and entered into the spirit of the occasion with enthusiasm.

During these months Peter could never be certain that a further war against the Turks would not compel him to postpone his proposed Swedish campaign. It was a difficult period of waiting, but he pressed on with his policy of breaking his people from their old customs and of introducing Western reforms. The most important of these were the currency reform, a new approach to the legal code, and his first steps in popular education.

Reform of the Russian coinage was long overdue, and it had been on Peter's mind ever since his visits to the Mint in London. The only Russian coin regularly minted in the seventeenth century was the silver kopeck, which was badly produced and easily counterfeited. Coiners were numerous and the death penalty did not deter them.[12]

Coins of smaller value had long ceased to be minted, and the people had taken to cutting the silver kopecks into two or even three pieces to meet their needs. Coins of higher value were also required. The unit of accounting was still the ruble, but this had not been minted for many years. Dutch, Spanish, and German coins were sometimes used in place of the ruble, but more frequently they were melted down to produce silver kopecks, because while the official exchange rate for an Imperial dollar, for example, was only forty-five kopecks, 110 kopecks could be coined from that same silver dollar.[13]

Lack of a suitable coinage was an obstacle to trade and complicated the collection of taxes. Peter's father, Tsar Alexei, had attempted a reform by substituting copper for silver kopecks, but when he did this all silver coins promptly disappeared; prices increased fifteenfold, serious riots broke out in Moscow, and eventually he was forced to restore the old silver kopeck. Peter did not repeat his father's mistake. He retained the silver kopeck and introduced copper coins of three smaller denominations. They were carefully minted and, by Russian standards, handsome coins, and they immediately won popular favour.[14]

The chaos of Muscovite legislation had attracted Peter's attention as early as June 1695. His father had promulgated a legal code in 1649, but nothing had been done to incorporate subsequent legislation, which often conflicted with the code itself. Each ministry had its own book of ukazi, but the books were not always complete, and there was no central registry. For this reason much of the more recent legislation remained unenforced. To remedy these defects, Peter appointed a special commission to prepare a new legal code.[15] It was a lengthy and complicated undertaking and the commission worked slowly. He had no time to supervise it and other developments overtook it, but in later years he was to return to this problem.

A scarcity of skilled men, especially shipwrights, engineers, gunners, and navigators, continued to handicap his new projects. The hiring of foreign experts was costly, especially since such foreigners were often the rejects of their own countries and incompetent to boot. In any case he had no intention of relying on outsiders one minute longer than necessary. He was determined to train his own people; having already sent a number of them abroad to study, he now gave attention to training even greater numbers at home.

While in western Europe, his ideas on education had broadened. The countries he had visited had made him realize more acutely than ever the ignorance and backwardness of his own people. He saw the need for popular education as well as for specialized training of technicians. Meanwhile the demands of his army, his navy, and of his other activities compelled him to concentrate on technical training.

Soon after his return to Moscow from Kerch, Peter called on the Patriarch and talked at length of his ideas for education.[16] He began by expressing his dissatisfaction with the illiteracy of the priesthood; an educated priesthood, he observed, was essential to teach the people, and also to convert heretics within his realm. As a first step, he proposed sending ten priests to study in Kiev. He then strongly criticized the one existing school in Moscow. This was the Slav-Greek-Latin Academy, founded during the regency of Sofia. The academy had done valuable work, although labouring under many difficulties, but after the departure of its founders in 1694 it had declined. However, even revitalized, it could not alone have satisfied Peter's requirements. He wanted a school with a wider curriculum, where his people could study military science, engineering, medicine, as well as the Gospels, and grammar, rhetoric and other literary subjects. He planned on a vast scale: it was not a school, but a university that he needed to carry out his programme, as he outlined it to the Patriarch.

At the time of this conversation, Henry Farquharson and his two young colleagues, Stephen Gwyn and Richard Grice, were in Moscow awaiting instructions. They had already waited a year. They could not obtain proper accommodation or the salary promised them, and in December 1700, weary of poverty and inactivity, they made a formal complaint to the Tsar. He had forgotten them! Now their complaint stirred him to action. On 14 January 1701 he issued a decree establishing the School of Mathematics and Navigation in Moscow.

This school, housed in the newly built Sukharev Tower, was modelled on the Royal Mathematical School of Christ's College in London. Henry Farquharson was the director and taught mathematics, while Stephen Gwyn and Richard Grice taught navigation. For fourteen years the school flourished in Moscow, but not without troubles. Young Richard Grice was reported to be "no good at anything, constantly unreliable, and full of mischief . . . and he indulges the pupils; the head teacher himself does not like him." He was, however, murdered in the streets of Moscow one night in January 1709. Farquharson and Gwyn were to teach for many more years, both becoming professors when the naval department of the school was subsequently moved to St. Petersburg, and named the Naval Academy. Indeed, Farquharson was always to be on very friendly terms with Peter, who had a fondness for Scots, and in addition to his teaching, he carried out many special duties, such as surveying a highway from Moscow to St. Petersburg, for which he was well rewarded.[17]

In committing himself to begin hostilities against Sweden not later than April 1700, Peter had not foreseen how protracted the negotiations for peace with Turkey would be. Although shaken by their defeats at the hands of Austria and themselves anxious for peace with Russia, the Turks moved at a leisurely pace. Not until three months after Ukraintsev's arrival in Constantinople, did negotiations begin in earnest. He presented a written statement of the Tsar's terms, the major demands of which were, first, that the principle of *uti possidetis* should be confirmed, which meant that the Tsar would retain Azov and the surrounding lands, as well as the lower Dnieper fortresses; secondly, that the Tsar's territories should be guaranteed against any further attacks by the Crimean Tatars and others owing allegiance to the Sultan; thirdly, that free trade should be allowed between the merchants of both countries and the right of Russian ships to free navigation in the Black Sea should be guaranteed; fourthly, the Sultan was to observe the rights of the Orthodox population in Turkey, and to hand over the Holy Places in Jerusalem to the Greeks; fifthly, the Sultan should acknowledge the Russian repudiation of the obligation to pay annual tribute in any form to the Khan of the Crimea; sixthly, the Sultan should concede to the Russians the right to maintain a permanent diplomatic representative in Constantinople. They were considerable demands and, although in the course of the months of wrangling that followed, Peter had to yield on several of them, he was to gain important advantages under the final treaty.

On two points the Turks were adamant. They would not grant any nation the right of free navigation in the Black Sea which they would always preserve as "a pure and immaculate virgin."[18] They would not concede Gazi-Kerman and the other fortresses on the Dnieper, which, they claimed, were an essential part of their communications with

Belgorodchin, Moldavia, and Wallachia. Both sides stood firm and the conference reached deadlock.

Ukraintsev now reported despondently to Moscow that he was expecting the Turks to declare the conference at an end. Fearing a revival of hostilities, Peter made preparations. On 18 February 1700, he went to Voronezh, where he worked furiously during the next three months, making his ships ready for war in the Black Sea. The sixty-gun warship *Predestination*, claimed much of his time. He took special pride in her and when, towards the end of April, she was ready for launching, he made it a splendid occasion.

Shortly before leaving for Voronezh, Peter had learnt of the miscarriage of Augustus' attempt to take Riga. It was a complete, almost musical-comedy failure. All had been ready for the assault on the agreed date, but General Fleming had gone off to Saxony to marry a lady of the noble Sapieha family. His second in command, Paykul, knew nothing of the plans against Riga and refused to advance. Reports of Saxon intentions reached Governor-General Dahlberg who promptly strengthened his defences. Peter was disgusted when he learnt details of this failure from F. A. Golovin, who attributed it to irresponsibility and the "pleasures of Venus."[19]

When Fleming returned from Saxony over a month later, confident that he could take Riga, he found Dahlberg's defences almost impregnable. He sent a detachment of troops under Karlovich to seize the small fort of Dunamunde at the mouth of the Dvina. The fort surrendered, but Karlovich was killed.

Peter was disinclined to believe that Dunamunde had been captured, until he received assurances from Augustus.[20] But his pleasure was tempered by news of the death of Karlovich, for whom he had respect and affection; he had even intended entrusting to him the education of his son, Alexei.[21] Meanwhile with Dunamunde in Saxon hands, he considered that the capture of Riga would not be difficult. But Fleming lacked siege artillery and dared not attack without it. He again left his army under the command of Paykul and went off to Warsaw. Peter now became openly critical of his allies and said bluntly that Augustus should be leading his troops instead of "diverting himself with women" in Saxony.[22]

While working in the Voronezh shipyards, Peter was also making further preparations for the Northern War. He had already decided on his plan of campaign. Novgorod and Pskov were to be the bases for operations. Troops were moved in readiness, but every precaution had to be taken to avoid awakening the suspicion of the Swedes. He could not rely on the small Saxon army to occupy Livonia and Esthonia and, while Narva was in Swedish hands, he could not hope to capture and hold Ingria and Karelia. He decided then to take the key points of Narva and Noteburg.[23]

News now reached Moscow that Frederick IV of Denmark had opened hostilities by invading the territory of the Duke of Holstein-Gottorp, Charles XII's brother-in-law. He had captured several important towns without difficulty, and was laying siege to Tonning. This news made Peter more impatient than ever to begin his own campaign. But news from the south disturbed and deterred him. He had had no further reports from Ukraintsev, and the Turks were rumoured to be preparing for war. He took these rumours seriously and even thought of diverting all his forces to the south. His overriding fear was still that he might find himself at war simultaneously with Turkey and Sweden and that, fighting on two fronts, he would suffer defeat, like his father and grandfather before him.[24]

On 17 April, Peter appointed three ambassadors to proceed to Stockholm to confirm the Treaty of Kardis. The Swedish embassy had already brought to Moscow the King's formal confirmation; the return embassy had not been thought of, because Peter had expected by this time to be at war with Sweden. To counter rumours of his military plans, he at once sent Prince Andrei Khilkov to Stockholm as his resident, and to anounce the early arrival of his ambassadors. Khilkov was to travel by way of Narva so that he could report on the state of the defences there.[25]

Peter's precautions succeeded. Various rumours of the Tsar's intentions were current in the capitals of Europe. The Swedes could not help being aware of his preparations for war, but his many gestures of peace allayed their suspicions. On the day after his return to Moscow from Voronezh, Peter himself called on Knipperkrona, the Swedish resident. He jokingly rebuked Knipperkrona's wife for writing to her daughter in Voronezh, where she was probably a member of Tsarevna Natalya's suite, that the Tsar intended invading Livonia and that all the Swedes in Moscow were living in a state of terror. "I could hardly calm your daughter, she was crying so bitterly," said Peter, and added: "You cannot think that I would begin an unjust war against the King of Sweden, and break an eternal peace, which I have just promised to preserve." Knipperkrona begged him to forgive his wife. Peter embraced him affectionately and swore that, if the King of Poland captured Riga from the Swedes, "I will tear it from his hands." In his despatch reporting this incident, Knipperkrona assured his government that the Tsar had no thought of aggression against Sweden.[26]

Peter and his allies, the Kings of Denmark and Poland, had previously agreed to do all they could to bring the Elector of Brandenburg into their alliance and it was apparently left to Peter to put this proposal formally, but his envoy did not reach Berlin until July. This belated approach was possibly due to Peter's expectation that the Elector would himself ask to join the alliance. Peter was so confident that he provided Prince Yuri Trubetskoy, his special envoy, with an agreement in duplicate—one copy in German for the Elector's immediate signature, and the other in Russian—which he had already signed in anticipation.[27] He saw this document as a simple development of the oral agreement which they had made three years earlier.

The Elector received Trubetskoy on 24 July, but to his proposals replied bluntly that he could not join the alliance. He presumed that the latest developments were not yet known to the Tsar. England and Holland were, he said, supporting Sweden against Denmark; the Swedes had attacked Copenhagen and the King of Denmark had had to sue for peace. If he, the Elector of Brandenburg, were to join the Tsar against Sweden, her allies would march against him and his lands would be laid waste. Further, he had received news from Vienna that the Turks would never agree to a peace with Russia, so that the Tsar would, therefore, be unable to help his allies. Trubetskoy's consequent report on the Elector's reply and on the Danish capitulation reached Moscow on 21 August. It was exactly twelve days too late to serve as a warning.

Augustus had returned to Warsaw from Saxony on 13 March, intent on obtaining active Polish support for his Swedish campaign. He needed a victory, like the capture of Riga, to rouse the Poles to see Livonia within their grasp. The capture of Dunamunde had given him some new hope, but still he could not attack Riga without more troops and without artillery. Since April, he had been pressing Peter to begin hostilities. He now sent Major-General Baron Langen to make further urgent representations to the Tsar. Langen reached Moscow on 15 July and was received informally next day. Peter "with tears in his eyes spoke of his bitter disappointment" that peace with

Turkey had not been concluded, although he had made great concessions. He promised Langen that as soon as his hands were free he
would go to the aid of his allies and he wrote specially to Augustus to
reassure him.[28]

Meantime, in Constantinople, Ukraintsev was having difficulty in
persuading the Turks even to reopen negotiations. Only after he had
sent five requests did they agree to meet again with him. At this meeting Ukraintsev carefully explained the new proposals brought by the
Tsar's special courier—that Gazi-Kerman and the other lower Dnieper
forts should remain in Russian hands for six or seven years, and then
be razed to the ground, the territory becoming neutral. This suggestion only aroused Turkish suspicions. Ukraintsev then made a final
proposal that the Dnieper forts should be razed to the ground on the
signing of their agreement, and the sites returned to the Turks. After
further argument, they agreed on condition that small unfortified
settlements could be built to assist travellers.

Another month passed in bitter disputes over other Russian demands. Ukraintsev was forced to yield on certain points, but at least
he succeeded in wringing from the Turks formal recognition of the
Russian refusal to pay tribute or presents to the Crimean Khan. He
had received express orders from Peter to secure agreement as quickly
as possible and he decided not to press for free navigation in the
Black Sea or for the return of the Holy Places in Jerusalem to the
Greeks. But he secured Turkish agreement that the Tsar should have
the right to maintain a permanent diplomatic representative in
Constantinople.[29]

The main points of dispute were now settled. But three weeks
passed without word from the Turks that they were ready to sign the
agreement. Eight times Ukraintsev sent his interpreter to demand its
completion. Each time the Turks made no reply. Then, on 12 June,
he was told that the Sultan approved all the clauses except one concerning the Azov towns. The Crimean Khan had reported that new
forts had been built around Azov with obvious aggressive intentions;
if the Tsar sincerely desired peace, he would also raze these forts to
the ground. The Sultan's new demand was not without justification,
but Ukraintsev delivered his ultimatum. He told the Turks that he
had received instructions that, if peace was not concluded within a
month, he was to break off all negotiations and return to Moscow.

Two weeks later the Turks agreed to waive their new demands. On 3 July the armistice for thirty years was signed.

Ukraintsev's report reached Moscow on 8 August. On the same day, unknown to Peter, Denmark had fallen out of the alliance. Charles XII had compelled the King of Denmark to sign the Treaty of Travendal, by which he conceded all demands of the Duke of Holstein-Gottorp and undertook not to help the enemies of Sweden. Russia's sole ally now was Augustus of Poland.

When, after all the months of anxious waiting, Peter at last found himself free to begin his campaign, he wasted no time. On 9 August, the day after Ukraintsev's news of peace with Turkey reached Moscow, the proclamation of war against Sweden was made from the Bedchamber Porch in the manner of the old Muscovite tsars. The proclamation was very brief: "The Great Tsar has directed that, for the many wrongs of the Swedish King and especially because during the Tsar's journey through Riga, he suffered at the hands of the people of Riga many obstacles and unpleasantnesses, his soldiers shall march in war on the Swedish towns with Field-Marshal and Admiral F. A. Golovin." It ended with the appointment of Generals A. M. Golovin, a cousin of the commander-in-chief, A. A. Weide, and Prince Repnin as the other commanders. This proclamation was, in Patkul's opinion, too brief. He was now secret military adviser to Augustus, and a man of great influence, who did not hesitate to take on further authority. In the name of the Tsar, whom he had not consulted, but to whom he sent a copy, he circulated to the courts of Europe a full statement of the Tsar's reasons for declaring war, and it was certainly an improvement on the cryptic Muscovite declaration.[30]

On the day that the proclamation was made in Moscow Peter wrote in his own hand to King Augustus, "his dearest brother, sovereign, and neighbour," to tell him of the armistice with Turkey, and that, true to his promise, he was launching his campaign without delay.[31]

Peter's mood was one of lighthearted impatience. The restraint he had laboured under had been removed. He was eager to recover Ingria and Karelia, and he saw no further than this immediate goal.

CHAPTER XVIII

Charles XII and the Northern War

1700

THE accession of a minor to the Swedish throne had emboldened the three allies to launch their campaign. They expected easy victory. But they were grievously mistaken. The eighteen-year-old King Charles XII was to prove an outstanding soldier even in an age that produced Marlborough, Prince Eugene, Vauban, and Turenne. Indeed, he dazzled Europe with his exploits. He believed he was invincible, and in the first years of the Northern War he gave every proof of it.

Soon the war resolved itself into a duel between Charles and Peter. Charles was contemptuous of his enemy. Peter, however, was to prove a greater monarch, a greater general, and a greater man. Slowly and inexorably he won through to victory. Russia was to become supreme in the Baltic; the Swedish empire was to fall, never to rise again.

Charles XII was the only son of Queen Ulrica Eleanora, a Danish princess, and of Charles XI of Sweden. His mother was a cultured and kindly woman, beloved by all, but she died when he was eleven years old. His father, whose influence on him was paramount, was ill-educated, harsh, and forbidding, but possessed by a stern sense of duty and great courage. He was not a man to attract the love of his people, but he compelled respect and his example inspired much of the thrift and industry which braced Swedish national life in the second half of the century.

From his earliest years Charles showed outstanding ability and

courage. He suffered as a child from poor health, but an active out-
door life soon hardened him. His father was his closest companion,
and in temperament and interests they were alike. Both were keen
horsemen and in their breakneck gallops they foundered many horses
under them. From his father, Charles learnt to live a simple spartan
life, despising luxury and display of feeling as weaknesses. But it was
in encouraging Charles in his passion for military exercises that his
father's influence was strongest. Like Peter's games, these exercises
were realistic and invariably ended, if not with deaths, at least with
numerous wounded. Charles always took an active part, throwing
himself into the thick of the fighting. But he never played with the
abandon and gusto of a high-spirited boy; a precocious self-discipline
and manliness marked his actions. He was fifteen years old when, in
April 1697, he lost his father, and, although so young, he at once
displayed an equal devotion to duty and a nature even more im-
perious than his father's. All Sweden was forced to recognize that
there would be no relaxation and that his would be a hard reign.

On the occasions of the visits to Stockholm of his kinsman, Frederick IV, Duke of Holstein-Gottorp, Charles revealed himself more
completely. The Duke first came to Stockholm for his marriage to
Princess Hedwig Sophia, Charles's favourite sister. During this visit
Charles went wild. For the first time he abandoned his self-restraint;
it resulted in such acts of wanton destructiveness and cruelty that this
period of his reign was known as the "Holstein Frenzy."

The King and the Duke several times rode full gallop through the
forests until they killed their horses. They coursed a hare in the
senate house. Bored at dinner, they smashed the glasses and plates,
and then the furniture, throwing the pieces through the windows.
They broke all the benches in the palace church and the congregation
had to stand for the service next day. The climax was reached in the
palace apartments when they vied with each other in testing the
sharpness of their swords and their skill in wielding them by executing
sheep, dogs, calves, and goats, and hurling the bleeding heads through
the windows onto passers-by. This game entertained them for
several days until the palace floors and the staircases ran with blood.
Finally, on one Sunday, three ministers preached on the same text:
"Woe to thee, O Land, when thy King is a child." Charles was
sincerely pious, and learning of these sermons sobered him. Soon

afterwards the Duke returned to Holstein and Charles resumed his routine of spartan discipline.

It is, indeed, difficult to avoid comparing the entertainments of the three chief participants in the Northern War; Charles riding horses to death, beheading sheep and goats, and waging war; Augustus, with his reputed 260 illegitimate children, straightening horseshoes and rolling silver plates with his bare hands; Peter building ships, making fireworks, mastering various crafts, and relaxing in marathon drinking bouts.[1]

A year later the Duke of Holstein again visited Stockholm. This time the cousins behaved with decorum, but Charles was wildly extravagant. Balls, masquerades, and other entertainments followed one after the other. For a brief period the royal court revived the brilliance and pageantry that it had known in the reign of Queen Christina.

It was then suggested that the King might be ready to take a wife. Ambitious mothers hastened to court with their daughters, but they journeyed in vain; Charles had no interest in marriage. Nor was he interested in the welfare of his country, for in the first two years of his rule he squandered the war-chest of over four and a half million thalers carefully saved by his father.

It was the news of Augustus' invasion of Livonia that put an end to these festivities. Charles at once embarked on what he considered the real business of life—war, to him a man's only true duty and pleasure. Reports of the Danish occupation of Holstein reached him soon after the news of the Saxon invasion of Livonia. He was eager to march on Augustus, but the Danish attack was nearer home and more dangerous; moreover, he had pledged himself to go to the Duke's aid, and he had to honour this pledge before dealing with his own enemies.

The Swedish ministers were alarmed by the prospect of being involved in war, not only because of the inexperience of their autocratic young King, but also because Sweden had been weakened by a three-year famine and her treasury was empty. Such obstacles, however, did not deter Charles, who swiftly mobilized his army and fitted out his fleet. He went to Karlskrona to supervise all preparations. He was just eighteen years old when he left Stockholm; he was never to see his capital again.

By the end of three months the Swedish fleet had sailed. Supported by English and Dutch squadrons, the Swedes landed on the Zealand shores. Charles was preparing to attack Copenhagen itself when a courier brought the news that the King of Denmark had capitulated and had already signed the Treaty of Travendal with the Duke of Holstein. It was a swift and bloodless victory.

Charles spent the next two months in Scania, preparing for his campaign in Livonia. His ministers and others urged him to make peace, for it was known through the French ambassador that Augustus was ready to discuss terms, despite his alliance with the Tsar. But Charles would not hear of it. The news of the Russian siege of Narva, which he learnt with great surprise while in Scania, made him even more determined to wage war. A few days later he sailed with his army in nine warships. On 6 October he reached Pernau.

Within two weeks of his declaration of war, Peter's troops had begun to move from Moscow. Narva, not Ingria or Karelia, was their destination, and this change in his plans filled Patkul and Augustus with anxiety. Baron Langen reported on 21 August 1700 to Patkul in Saxony: "I have done everything possible, with the help of the Danish ambassador, to distract him [the Tsar] from this intention; we found him so stubborn that we feared to touch any more on such a delicate subject, and must be satisfied with the Tsar's break with Sweden in the hope that in time Narva will not leave our hands."[2] Patkul, in a lengthy reply to Langen, expressed his fear that, having captured Narva, Peter would go on to take Reval, Dorpat, Pernau; before it was realized in Warsaw, he would have the whole of Livonia in his grasp. But, since attempts to turn him from Narva might antagonize him, Patkul counselled Langen not to press too hard.

The Russian army, which Peter had ordered to Narva under the command of Field-Marshal Feodor Golovin, should have numbered nearly sixty-four thousand, but several detachments were delayed, and the battle of Narva was over before they could arrive. In fact, the Russian army engaged in this action, amounted to less than forty thousand men.[3]

The guards, together with four other regiments, were the first to set out from Moscow, and the artillery and the detachments commanded by Generals Avtonom Golovin and Adam Weide followed. Peter with the rank of captain in the Preobrazhensky guards, accompanied his regiment as far as Tver. Here, on 26 August, he learnt from a courier sent by Augustus that the King of Sweden with a force of eighteen thousand men would shortly reach Livonia. It was unexpected and disturbing news. But he pressed ahead, confident that he could take Narva before the Swedes arrived.[4]

Reaching Novgorod four days later, Peter found the Duke von Croy waiting for him.[5] They had met two years earlier in Amsterdam when the Duke had offered his services, but, although favourably impressed, Peter had not then engaged him. The Duke now came as an emissary from Augustus to persuade Peter to send twenty thousand infantrymen to help the Saxon army take Riga. But Peter was not prepared at this juncture, when the Swedes were approaching, to weaken his army so drastically or to postpone his campaign. He promised, however, that as soon as he had taken Narva he would devote his whole army to helping Augustus in the capture of Riga.[6]

For eight days Peter waited in Novgorod for his other troops to arrive from Moscow. The autumn had set in early, and rains had reduced the roads, always bad, to deep furrows of mud. The difficulties of the march quickly revealed the inadequacy of the preparations for the campaign, and hardships decimated the ranks of many regiments.[7] Finally, on 8 September, having decided to wait no longer, Peter set out from Novgorod with his guards and a few other troops. Two weeks later he crossed the Narova River, and took up positions before Narva. Here, while waiting impatiently, he busied himself with the fortifications and moved the 10,600 troops already there into siege positions.[8]

The town of Narva, formerly called Rugodiv by the Russians, stands on the left bank of the Narova River at a point where it makes a wide bend ten miles from its entry into the Gulf of Finland. Founded in 1223, Narva had flourished as one of the chief Baltic ports in the times of the Hanseatic League. The grand dukes of Muscovy had always coveted it. Ivan the Terrible had captured it but the Russians had held it for only twenty-three years before the Swedes seized it again. Now, fortified with stone walls, nine bastions, and defence works, and with a garrison of fifteen hundred men under the command of Colonel Baron Horn, it was a stronghold.

At last, early in October, General Weide arrived with his troops, followed by the artillery, and then by Field-Marshal Feodor Golovin, with further detachments. These troops took up positions which cut off all approaches to Narva by land. Meanwhile Peter had appointed Lieutenant-General von Hallart, an engineer lent to him by Augustus.

to command of the siege operations. The artillery on arriving was posted in accordance with his plans, so that by 20 October all batteries were in position, and on the same day the bombardment of Narva began.

Russian hopes were now high. Hallart was confident that the town would soon fall. But the bombardment continued day and night for two weeks without reducing the garrison to surrender, and then it was found that nearly all Russian ammunition had been used up; the operation had to be suspended until supplies arrived. Meanwhile, two regiments, sent to take Ivangorod, the small fort on the opposite side of the river, were repelled with heavy losses. At this point Peter received disturbing news, first, of Augustus' decision to raise the siege of Riga, and then of the arrival of Charles XII at Pernau.

Augustus blamed Peter, writing bluntly that lack of the supporting forces promised by the Tsar had forced him to abandon his plans against Riga.[9] His envoy, Baron Langen, arriving in the Russian camp from Moscow, presented a memorandum from Poland, setting out Augustus' aims and pressing Peter "to reveal his intentions in a brotherly and friendly manner."[10] Langen also stated that Augustus was anxious to conclude an especially close alliance with the Tsar, so that they might operate together with complete confidence, and he asked the Tsar to state when and where they could meet.

The anxieties and doubts in the mind of Augustus, as thus revealed, disturbed Peter. He saw the danger of Saxony dropping out of the alliance and leaving Russia to face Sweden alone, whereupon Poland, unpredictable but staunchly Russophobe, might join with Sweden. It was a dangerous situation, and within a week Langen was able to report to Augustus that the Tsar had accepted all his proposals.

Peter was even more disturbed by the reports that Charles XII had landed at Pernau with a force of thirty to thirty-two thousand troops. He at once sent Sheremetev with cavalry to reconnoitre along the road to Reval.

In the Russian lines all were uneasy. The Swedes continued to make sorties from the fort, and in repelling them the Russians suffered heavy casualties. Their guns were now silent for lack of ammunition. Rumours that Charles XII would arrive any day further undermined Russian morale. At this point one of Peter's most favoured officers, Captain Jan Gummert, defected to the Swedes. His action, recalling the defection of Jansen before Azov, aggravated the uneasiness in the Russian camp.[11]

Three days after the defection of Gummert, Peter received word from Sheremetev that he had made contact with Charles's army and that he was falling back on Narva. It was now clear that the Swedish army would soon arrive and that a pitched battle was unavoidable. At this point Peter decided to leave his army and to go to Moscow.

On 17 November Baron Langen wrote to King Augustus: "The desire of the Tsar to meet your Majesty is so strong that I would be very unhappy if there were any delay in this meeting, which is of such importance to military success and to the alliance."[12] He went on to report the Tsar's plans, presumably as told to him by Peter himself, which were to proceed immediately to Moscow to receive the Turkish ambassador, from Moscow to hasten to Smolensk, and thence to the place proposed by Augustus for their meeting.

On the eve of his departure Peter appointed the Duke von Croy supreme commander of the Russian forces. The Duke was unwilling to take command of a foreign army, hastily entrusted to him as the enemy approached, but Peter persuaded him to accept.[13] Before dawn on 19 November, Peter set out with Golovin and Menshikov. Some eight hours later Charles with his small army attacked the Russian positions.

Peter's hasty departure gave every appearance of flight in the face of the enemy. It brought the charge of cowardice against him from many of his contemporaries, and historians have repeated the charge. To Charles XII it was contemptible behaviour. But Peter's criteria of conduct were remote from those of Charles. Pride, hunger for military glory, and craving for the excitement of battle dominated Charles, whereas they hardly touched Peter; certainly they did not influence his decision to leave Narva on the eve of battle. It is also improbable that he gave way to panic. Unlike Charles, Peter had known fear and, once or twice, complete panic, but he had learnt to control it and, when necessary, to face danger with great courage.

Several reasons for his departure have been given. Colonel Alexander Gordon, son-in-law of Patrick Gordon, believed that he had gone to "hasten up twelve more regiments of infantry."[14] The history of the Swedish war, compiled under Peter's direct supervision in later years, stated: "On 18 November the Sovereign left the army for Novgorod in order to hasten the arrival at Narva of the remaining regiments, and especially to have a meeting with the King of Poland."[15] Pleyer, the Imperial ambassador in Moscow, reporting to Vienna, came closer to the truth when he stated that "the Tsar had decided to remove himself from meeting a powerful danger."[16]

Peter was a realist and he had declared war on Sweden to gain certain objectives. No considerations of pride, glory, or chivalry could distract him from these objectives. He would have regarded it as sheer folly to risk himself in battle with Charles at this stage when his army was untried. Moreover, he was half expecting defeat at the hands of the Swedish veterans, and saw defeat not as dishonour, but as a stage in the development of his army and of Russia herself.[17] No doubt there was more than one reason for his hurried departure, but basically it was an act of prudence.

Prudence was never a factor in Charles's calculations. On arriving at Pernau, he had learnt that Narva was in serious danger and that Augustus had withdrawn his army from Riga. He was in a fury of impatience to march against the Russians. His generals and officers had misgivings; it was known that the Russians in entrenched positions outnumbered the Swedes by about five to one; the march from Wesenburg to Narva led through bogs and marshes of freezing mud and country already laid waste by the enemy. But Charles paid no attention to such obstacles, and the Swedes could only obey.

On 4 November Charles set out with his army of 8,430 men intent on making forced marches and taking the Russians by surprise. The conditions were appalling. At times the Swedes were up to their knees in mud and slush. During the last two days of their march they had no food.

Towards evening on 18 November, and shortly after Peter's departure, Sheremetev arrived in the Russian camp. His report that the enemy was not more than six miles away caused panic. The alarm was sounded, and the Duke von Croy gave orders for a special watch to be kept during the night.

Early on 19 November, the Swedes began moving. The infantry was in the centre with cavalry on either flank. At 11 A.M. the Swedish army moved out of the woods into the plain before the Russian positions. The Duke von Croy took it for the advance guard: it did not occur to him that Charles with such a small force would attack the whole Russian army.

The two armies exchanged artillery fire, but Charles was impatient to attack. He sent orders to his troops to make ready. At 2 P.M. two rockets, the agreed signal, were fired. The Swedish lines rang with the cry, "With God's help!" and the Swedes began to move forward.

At this moment the sky darkened and a violent snowstorm enveloped the scene. Visibility fell to twenty paces. The Swedish generals suggested holding the attack until the storm had passed. Charles would not hear of it. "Can't you see?" he exclaimed. "It's at our backs and blows into the faces of the enemy!" The Swedes advanced unobserved and then, attacking strongly, they took the Russians by surprise.

This sudden assault from out of the wall of swirling snow threw the Russians into disorder. Panic raced through the lines. Sheremetev was among the first to take to his heels. Followed by his cavalry, he threw himself into the Narova River and managed to swim to the other bank, but more than a thousand of his men were drowned.

The Preobrazhensky and Semyonovsky regiments were among the few that stood their ground. With them were the Duke von Croy, General Hallart, and Baron Langen, all of whom began to fear for their lives. In the general panic the Russian soldiers murdered their foreign officers, if they stood in their way. Watching the confusion, Von Croy gave up all hope of repelling the Swedes. He made his way along the river bank and surrendered to Colonel Stenbok. But the guards regiments continued to resist. Finally, the exhausted Swedes withdrew, intending to renew their attack next morning. It proved unnecessary.

Nightfall brought a respite during which the Russian commanders on the right flank sent an envoy to the Swedish camp with a proposal to surrender provided they could retire with their men to Russia. Early next morning the Swedish generals in the King's name agreed that the Russian troops could retreat with colours and weapons, but without artillery.

On the left flank General Adam Weide had stood his ground. He had repelled the enemy attack at the beginning of the battle, and, knowing nothing of the capitulation on the right flank, he was preparing to resume battle next day. Occupying a strong position and with sufficient ammunition, Weide might well have turned the tables by attacking in the early morning. The Swedes were exhausted and many were drunk from the spirits they had found in the Russian camp.[18] But, learning from Buturlin of the capitulation of the Russian commanders, Weide too, laid down his arms and went to the Swedish camp.[19]

On the morning of 20 November, the guards regiments and Avtonom Golovin's troops crossed the river followed by Weide's division. But, on the King's orders, seventy-nine men were held as prisoners-of-war. These included ten generals, ten colonels, and thirty-three other officers. Russian losses at Narva were heavy; the exact number is not known, but it was in the region of eight thousand men, while between 145 and 181 guns were surrendered. Swedish losses were about two thousand men.[20]

The Swedes treated their prisoners with scant consideration despite the senior rank of most of them. The Duke von Croy alone received good treatment from Charles. When the Baltic Sea opened to navigation in the following spring, the prisoners, still under strong guard, were embarked in eight ships and sent to Stockholm.

The Duke von Croy, Dr. Carbonari, the Tsar's physician and a few others were allowed to remain in Reval. They had no money and their position was not easy. The Duke was reduced to poverty. He wrote to Peter, to Feodor Golovin, and to Menshikov, offering to justify all his actions and asking for money. Peter instructed Golovin to send him six thousand rubles, which he received in due course, but he was soon again in need. His letters became pathetic. He feared that Peter was angry with him, and Golovin wrote to assure him that the Tsar had no complaint against him.[21] When in January 1702 the Duke died, the Imperial ambassador, Pleyer, reported to Vienna that Peter on receiving the news said: "I am sincerely sorry about the fine old man. He was in truth an able and experienced military leader. Had I entrusted the command to him fourteen days earlier, I would not have suffered defeat at Narva."[22]

In Sweden the Russian prisoners endured severe conditions. Langen, Hallart, and certain others were released in 1705, and Hallart entered the Russian service. But for some years the Swedes showed no interest in releasing prisoners except at an extortionate ransom, although Peter Lefort, nephew of the Tsar's deceased favourite, and Alexander Gordon were exchanged for Swedish officers in 1706 and 1708 respectively. After 1709, when the number of Swedish prisoners in Russian hands was very high, they showed more interest.

CHAPTER XIX

The Aftermath of Narva

1700-1702

THE months following Narva showed Peter at his best. Few monarchs have suffered a more crushing and humiliating defeat, and have risen to greatness out of it. The prestige he had won at Azov was instantly dissipated. Europe laughed at him. He had lost not only prestige, but all of his artillery, and the defeat had faced him brutally with the fact that his army was no more than a horde of untrained peasants, incapable of standing against Western troops.

But, although astonished by the magnitude of the disaster, Peter was neither depressed nor deterred. He indulged in no recriminations; he accepted the mistakes made as his own and he learnt by them. He had determination and courage and, when necessary, he had patience.

Meanwhile the defeat had whipped him into a frenzy of activity. He pressed on with his efforts to train and equip his army. He did not hesitate to apply every diplomatic and military expedient that might win him an advantage, no matter how small or temporary. To England, Holland, and Austria he protested his anxiety for peace; at the same time he made strenuous efforts to induce the Poles to enter the war against Sweden; he ignored all cost in binding Augustus to him in their alliance; he ordered his generals to lay waste Livonia, and they acted with terrible thoroughness.

His immediate fear was that Charles would follow up his victory by marching on Moscow. Nothing stood in his way; the whole of

Russia was open to him. Peter, therefore, set monks, civilians, women, and children to work digging entrenchments around Novgorod and Pskov, the two strongholds which might hinder Charles's advance. But it was soon clear that the Swedes would not invade Russia at this stage. A severe winter gripped the country; half of the Swedish troops were ill, and the other half were in no condition to march. But Peter's need to make haste was still acute; by the spring he had to have an army, supported by artillery, ready to meet the enemy.

From Novgorod, where he had received the news of the disaster, Peter had immediately sent a courier to intercept General Repnin, who was still on the road to Narva with his own division and the Butyrsky regiment. Repnin had already learnt of the defeat, and had himself turned towards Novgorod. There he received orders to re-form the troops who had fled and were straggling back into Russia. Within two weeks he was able to send a report to Peter, who had left for Moscow, that the total strength of the re-formed regiments was 22,967 men.[1] When these regiments were added to Repnin's force of 10,834 men and the Butyrsky regiment, it meant that Peter had an army of over thirty-four thousand men, to which the Cossacks, numbering 10,500, still on the road from Little Russia, would be joined.

On reaching Moscow Peter instructed Prince Boris Golitsyn to form ten regiments of dragoons, each consisting of one thousand men. Notices were published calling for volunteers between the ages of seventeen and thirty from all classes, excluding only streltsi of the disbanded regiments. The response was encouraging and six months later the new dragoon regiments marched to Pskov. In January 1701 Pleyer was reporting to Vienna that the Tsar's army was already twice as strong as before.[2]

Replacement of the artillery presented greater difficulties. Vinius, the Director of Posts, was in charge, with the title of Inspector of Artillery. Although now advanced in years, he had both energy and ability, which he applied to his new task. Moreover, Peter was behind him pressing for results and writing, "For God's sake speed the artillery!"[3]

The chief obstacles were lack of suitable metal and of iron founders, but neither was allowed to obstruct the work. Peter took the unprecedented step of ordering that "from the whole tsardom, in leading towns, from churches and monasteries, a proportion of the bells are to be collected for guns and mortars."[4] The order caused a popular outcry, for the bells were part of the lives of the people and as sacred as the churches in which they hung,[5] but, by the end of May 1701, over 1,450 tons of bell metal had been brought to Moscow. This metal without an alloy was unsuitable for guns, but somehow Vinius managed to find alloys. He had trouble with iron founders, two of whom were experienced and reliable, while the others were always drunk, and heeded neither his pleas nor whippings. A serious hold-up threatened through delays in delivery of the gun carriages. This drew anger from Peter, who wrote: "Tell the burgomasters, and show them this letter, that if through their delays the gun carriages are not ready, they will pay not only with money, but with their heads."[6] It was no empty threat, and the carriages began to arrive.

By the end of May 1701, twenty cannon had been sent to Novgorod, and a further seventy-six cannon of various calibres were ready. Vinius had also established a school to train gun founders and gunners. Peter wrote thanking him for his report on this progress. "It is good work done and necessary, for time is like death," he added.[7] By November 1701 Vinius had produced more than three hundred guns, and wrote proudly to Peter of their excellence and of the speed with which he had carried out the task. But with the development of the war, Peter's needs for artillery were greater than ever before. Shortage of alloys had thus become doubly serious, and he sent Vinius to Siberia in the following year to examine the suitability of ores found there.

Unfortunately for Vinius, the rich rewards and promotion that he was expecting did not materialize. For many years his peculations had been on a large scale and blatant. When he wrote complaining that he had been deprived of the office of Director of Posts sometime after being appointed Inspector of Artillery, Peter's reply was forthright: "You ask me if the post was not taken away from you so unexpectedly from some anger of mine. But does not your conscience accuse you at all? . . . The post was taken from you for no other reason than that, while you had it, it was not a profit to the state, but only to you . . . it has been given to another, from whom, also, if rumours are correctly spread, it will soon be taken away again."[8] The sentence of the Tsar's displeasure did not fall on him yet, for he was doing good work. But he was soon to slacken and grow careless in his labours.

In the midst of these frantic activities, Peter found time to launch a new scheme to join the Volga and the Don rivers, this time in their upper reaches by linking the rivers Upa and Oka. It involved draining Lake Ivan, cutting a canal through the Bobrikovskaya valley, and building some thirty sluices to raise the level of the water. He placed Prince Matvei Gagarin in charge and a number of Dutch canal engineers worked under him with an enormous labour force.

This was distinct from the canal begun four years earlier to join the Volga and the Don in the south. Work on this latter scheme had faltered. The Englishman, Captain John Perry, had taken charge after Colonel Breckell had fled. For three summers the work went ahead, but Perry complained of obstruction. The Governor of Astrakhan, Prince Alexei Golitsyn, was the main obstacle, for he considered "that God had made the rivers to go one way and that it was presumption in man to think to turn them another."[9] Obstruction of this kind was common even among Peter's closest associates, of whom Alexei Golitsyn was one. Against the background of such opposition and of the passive resistance of his people, Peter's achievements appear little short of miraculous.

Already from Novgorod, he had sent Prince Grigory Dolgoruky to Warsaw to inform the King of the disaster at Narva. Knowing that Augustus was a fainthearted and unreliable ally, Peter was uneasy that he might give up his campaign against Sweden as hopeless. He next sent Guards Captain Feodor Saltykov with a letter in his own hand, referring to Narva as "a certain unexpected and unhappy event."[10] Saltykov was to reassure the King that this defeat had not shaken the determination of the Tsar, who would never forsake his allies or give up his national heritage, and who was, therefore, still most anxious to meet Augustus to concert a winter campaign.

Dolgoruky reached Warsaw on 19 December and was received by the King next day. Augustus already knew about Narva and two days earlier had written to Peter commenting that "we ourselves do not know what after such a great reverse Your Majesty is thinking of undertaking."[11] Learning from Dolgoruky of the Tsar's determination, Augustus expressed a similar strong faith and proposed that they should meet at Dünaburg.

At the same time Peter was again making every attempt to gain the support of England, Holland, Austria, and Brandenburg. His efforts after Narva, however, met with even less success than before. In November 1700, Charles II of Spain had died, bequeathing his throne to Philip of Anjou, grandson of Louis XIV of France, who promptly declared his intention of supporting his grandson in his assumption of the Spanish crown. War between France and the maritime powers was inevitable. England and Holland wanted peace in the north so that they could concentrate on France, but the brilliant victories of Charles XII against the Danes and then against the Russians made both France and the allies eager for his support. In Stockholm and in Charles's camp the ambassadors of both sides busily competed for his favour.

Oxenstjerna, the sage Swedish Chancellor, urged on the King the advantages to Sweden of concluding an immediate peace with Saxony and Russia, and of taking up a neutral position in the War of the Spanish Succession about to break over Europe. Charles maintained an impenetrable silence for some days and then answered, "It would put our glory to shame if we were to lend ourselves to the slightest treaty of accommodation with one who had so vilely prostituted his honour."[12] He was referring to Augustus. He had already routed the Russians and he would deal with the Tsar at his leisure. Nothing could now turn him from punishing Augustus.

In September 1700 William III had offered through Lord Stanhope, his ambassador at The Hague, to mediate between Russia and Sweden. A few weeks later he sent a formal note to Peter, in which he pressed his proposal. From Moscow on 13 December, Peter replied, assuring William that he had not rejected his offer, and inviting him to appoint a suitable venue for negotiations.[13] But nothing came of the English offers, or of the approaches made to the Dutch for the same purpose. Danish promises of help also proved valueless.

At the beginning of February 1701, Prince Peter Golitsyn set out on a secret mission to the Imperial court with instructions to investigate the possibility of the Emperor interceding with the King of Sweden to secure peace. But Golitsyn found himself in a hostile city where the prestige of the Tsar had fallen very low. Seven weeks passed before he obtained an audience with the Emperor, who was courteous and unhelpful. He sought interviews with all influential ministers in Vienna, and it was a humiliating experience. "In no way can I arrange to see the ministers, no matter how I pursue them: they all avoid me and do not want to talk to me,"[14] he reported, and on another occasion he wrote bitterly, "They only laugh at us."[15]

The defeat of the Tsar at Narva had released a spate of rumours and hostile comment in Vienna. It was said that a revolution had taken place in Russia, that Tsarevna Sofia would soon displace the Tsar. Much of the criticism and rumour had as its source the former Imperial ambassador in Moscow, Guarient. Golitsyn, who had no diplomatic status on this mission, repeatedly requested the Emperor through Father Woolf to order Guarient to desist from spreading rumours and false reports, but without apparent results.

At this time Korb's Diary of an Austrian Secretary of Embassy was published in Vienna under Imperial licence and dedicated to Kaunitz, the Imperial Vice-Chancellor, who was responsible for foreign affairs. Containing a detailed account of Peter's annihilation of the streltsi, it seemed to confirm the worst reports made current by Guarient. The fact that Korb had been secretary in Guarient's embassy gave rise to the general belief that Guarient himself was its author. Golitsyn had a translation made and sent it to Moscow, where it aroused anger. Pleyer was instructed several times to request the Emperor to have it withdrawn from sale, and many copies were destroyed as a result.[16]

Meanwhile Guarient, learning of the Russian translation, hastened to write first to Feodor Golovin and Shafirov, and then to Peter, to justify himself and to protest that he was not the author of the diary or in any way to blame for its publication. He even added that "This lying report [that he was its author] has so distressed me that I have decided not to accept again the post offered to me of ambassador to the court of Your Majesty, so as to avoid meeting the anger of your eye and so as not to damage relations."[17] In this decision, at least, Guarient showed good sense.

Golitsyn's mission to Vienna was bound to fail in this atmosphere of ridicule and hostility. Moreover the imperial court was mainly concerned at this time with its own imminent war against France, although it could not wholly ignore the advance of Charles XII, since he threatened Roman Catholic Poland. Golitsyn managed to discuss with Count Kaunitz the question of the Emperor's mediation, but the terms on which Peter was prepared to conclude a peace were such as Charles would never accept. As a gesture, the Emperor sent a special courier to the Swedish camp to report the Russian proposals, but Charles showed no interest.[18]

While in Vienna, Golitsyn also received a proposal from the Empress, who apparently had been very favourably impressed by the Tsar during his visit to Vienna in 1698. This proposal, conveyed by Father Woolf, was that one of the Tsarevni should be married to her son, Archduke Karl, then aged sixteen. Golitsyn immediately sent a request to Feodor Golovin for instructions. Three months later he was able to report the Tsar's approval to the Empress. But the proposal languished through lack of Austrian support. In 1708 Archduke Karl married a German princess; their daughter was to be the Empress Maria Theresa.

The Empress also proposed marriage between Tsarevich Alexei, Peter's son, and one of the archduchesses. As a first step the Tsarevich was invited to study in Vienna where the Emperor would treat him as a son both privately and at court. Peter accepted this invitation and Golitsyn even discussed arrangements with the Imperial ministers. But for some reason, again nothing further happened. Fifteen years later, Tsarevich Alexei did appear in Vienna, but only as one seeking refuge from the anger of his father.

During the months following his disastrous defeat at Narva, Peter had yet another problem on his hands: the succession to the patriarchal throne. In October 1700, when standing before Narva, he had learnt of the death of Patriarch Adrian. Within two days Streshnev had written asking who should succeed, and reminding him that he had had Afanasy, Archbishop of Kholmogory, in mind for this office.[19] But Peter now had other ideas and proposals received a few days later from Kurbatov influenced him in the policy he finally adopted. Kurbatov advised leaving the patriarchate unfilled. He pointed out that the deceased Patriarch had been ill and ineffective and the affairs of the church were chaotic. He proposed the temporary appointment of Afanasy to direct spiritual affairs, while a layman should be placed in charge of the civil administration of the church, and especially its revenues.

Peter welcomed the suggestion to postpone the appointment of a new patriarch, and may even himself have already decided on this course. It was a crucial appointment, and he needed an energetic man who would bring order and efficiency to the affairs of the church and who would actively support him in his policy of reform. The Great Russian clergy were unlikely to produce the man he needed. The few Great Russian archbishops, such as Afanasy and Mitrofan of Voronezh, who were of the calibre for election to the patriarchate and who could be counted on to support him, he found inadequate for another reason: they were not learned men. He had to turn to Little Russia to find learned priests, and this was to cause strong resentment among the Great Russians, who considered the Ukrainian Church corrupt.

At the beginning of 1700, the Kiev Metropolitan had sent two abbots to Moscow, recommending the Patriarch to consecrate one of them Archbishop of the new see of Pereyaslavl. Stefan Yavorsky, one of these abbots, impressed Peter. He had studied at Lvov, Lublin, Poznan, and Vilno, and was a learned man of outstanding ability. Peter asked the Patriarch to appoint him to a see nearer to Moscow, and when the metropolitanate of Ryazan fell vacant, Yavorsky was told to prepare himself for consecration. He begged to be allowed to return to Kiev, but his pleas were rejected.

Yavorsky had hardly been consecrated when he found himself translated to a position of even greater responsibility. On 16 December 1700, a week after his return from Narva, Peter abolished the patriarchal chancery and distributed among various ministries its wide jurisdiction over laymen. Theological matters and questions of discipline within the church became the responsibility of Stefan Yavorsky, Metropolitan of Ryazan, who was appointed "Exarch of the most holy patriarchal throne, guardian, and administrator"; it was a position of acting-Patriarch. Peter had not yet decided on the abolition of the patriarchate itself, and may have intended this as a first step towards appointing Yavorsky. But he was acting with caution, first, because the immediate appointment of a Ukrainian might have given rise to another schism within the church, and, secondly, because he could not yet be sure of Yavorsky. In fact, his relations with Yavorsky were eventually to deteriorate, and he was never to appoint another Patriarch.

Within a month and a half, a second ukaz made Boyar Musin-Pushkin responsible for administering the estates of the Patriarch and the archbishops and the affairs of the monasteries. His first task was to draw up an inventory of all the monasteries and nunneries, lists of the monks and nuns, and also of all serfs and others living on these estates. Further, in December 1701, an ukaz fixed the annual food ration at ten rubles and ten quarters of grain for all monks and nuns, irrespective of rank. Excess revenue was to be allocated to re-

ligious charities, especially to poor and unendowed monasteries. But
the treasury took most of the surplus. The measure was, in fact,
tantamount to confiscation of a large part of the church revenues.

At the same time, Peter directed that the monastic rule should be
enforced more strictly. He pointed out that, unlike their forebears and
contrary to their religious orders, monks did not help to support the
poor by their labours, but themselves consumed labour; many monks
and nuns lived lives of great freedom and even licence, and some
enjoyed wealth and luxury. Moreover, monks had become lax in
handling their affairs and abuses had become common. In 1702 a
drunken monk beat another monk to death; on investigation it was
found that the murderer was a runaway serf, who had taken refuge
in the monastery and had become a monk without proper induc-
tion. The priesthood had become a refuge for many criminals and
fugitives. In future, servants in the monasteries were to be kept to a
minimum, and the church was to admit no novices under the age
of forty without the Tsar's express permission. Monks were to remain
in their monasteries and could only move to another on exceptional
grounds and with the written approval of the elder. In the past, laymen had often lived in monasteries, but this was now forbidden and
they could enter only to attend divine service. Nuns were also restricted severely.

Peter was not concerned with the church only as a source of
revenue and manpower. He recognized its place in Russian life.
Moreover, he had always considered that the church should be a
source of enlightenment as well as faith. He intended that it should
take responsibility for education and assist him in the task of banish-
ing illiteracy, ignorance, and superstition. Meanwhile he had made
Stefan Yavorsky "protector" of the Moscow Academy, with the task
of reforming it. He had then requested the Kiev Metropolitan to find
him a man of character and learning, who would serve as Metropolitan of Siberia. In the spring of 1701, the Abbot Dmitri, renowned for his devotional manual, *The Lives of the Saints*, was
chosen and sent to Moscow. But Dmitri, a saintly and scholarly man,
fell ill with distress on learning that he was to be translated to the
vast and primitive Siberian see. He begged to be allowed to continue
his studies in Moscow. Peter acceded to his request, and in due course
he became Metropolitan of Rostov. He found his new see in dreadful
straits, and the ignorance of both clergy and people appalled him.

He promptly set about restoring order; he also established a school, in which he himself energetically taught. To the formidable see of Siberia, Peter appointed another Little Russian, Filodei Leshchinsky, a man of great zeal, who was soon reporting to Moscow on the chaos that he had found, and demanding teachers, printing presses, and books for his schools. These were the men that Peter needed, but they alarmed the Muscovite clergy.

And yet among the Russian bishops, there were those who supported Peter. Afanasy, Archbishop of Kholmogory, had always shown him understanding and encouragement. Even more, Peter valued Mitrofan, Archbishop of Voronezh. Mitrofan had seen his labour in creating a navy, and had blessed it. He had urged the people to give all their support to their Tsar. He had gone further, handing Peter six thousand rubles of his own to help in the war. In subsequent years he always sent whatever money he had over from the expenses of the church and from his own modest needs to Peter or to the Admiralty, with the brief message, "for the troops." From his lonely position of authority, Peter treasured the encouragement of Mitrofan; on his death, he wept bitterly.

Towards the end of January 1701, Peter with a small suite set out from Moscow for his meeting with Augustus. It was midwinter, but he made all haste, reaching Birze on 15 February. The meeting of the two allies was an occasion for celebrations. The second day was devoted to a banquet, which lasted well into the night. Augustus drank so deeply that he overslept until dinner next day. But Peter rose early, as was his habit, and attended Mass alone in the Roman Catholic chapel. One of the Polish senators present remarked to him that it was within his power to unite the churches of Greece and Rome, to which he replied that "to monarchs belong only the bodies of the people; Christ is the monarch of their souls. For such a union general agreement is essential, and this is within the power of God alone."[20]

On the fourth day after his arrival, Peter talked with the Lithuanian Vice-Chancellor, Sczuka, and told him that Poland should take part in the war and win back Livonia. The Vice-Chancellor made it clear that the restoration of at least part of the territories, including Kiev, taken by Moscow in 1667 under the Treaty of Andrussovo, was the price of Polish participation. "It will be sufficient if I help you to

recover Livonia; Kiev is dear to us," Peter replied. Feodor Golovin
also had talks with him, but Sczuka insisted on the return of Kiev.[21]

After discussing their policy against Sweden, Peter and Augustus
on 26 February signed an agreement, confirming their previous alliance. The new agreement bound them to prosecute the war against
Sweden with all their strength, neither dropping out without the sanc-
tion of the other. The Tsar would send to the King at Dünaburg,
or such other place between there and Pskov, as the King decided,
between fifteen and twenty thousand trained and fully armed infantrymen, who would be at the King's disposal for operations in
Livonia and Esthonia. The Tsar agreed to send immediately on his
arrival at Smolensk one hundred thousand rubles and to pay this sum
annually for the next two years. The King for his part undertook to
harry the Swedes constantly in Livonia and Esthonia and by thus
diverting them to assist the Tsar's operations in Ingria and Karelia.
By a secret clause the Tsar agreed further to send the King by mid-
June the sum of twenty thousand rubles to buy the support of
Polish senators.[22]

Peter could not readily afford such aid to Augustus. But to fight
alone and to fight on two fronts were his abiding fears. He paid this
heavy price to keep his ally. After concluding this agreement Peter
made a further attempt to win the support of the Poles. He invited the Polish senators into his presence and offered them extensive aid for which he wanted no return, except their participation in
the war. At a subsequent meeting Golovin formally put to them the
Tsar's propositions, namely: 1) An alliance with Poland against
Sweden, and an eternal alliance against all enemies, together with an
undertaking that Russia would make no peace with Sweden except
with the approval of the Polish Senate; 2) Livonia and Esthonia were
to belong in their entirety to Poland; 3) The Tsar offered twenty
thousand infantrymen and forty guns with ammunition for the dura-
tion of the war. The Poles expressed appreciation of the Tsar's offer,
but merely repeated the reply of the Vice-Chancellor Sczuka, that
the return of Kiev was their price.

On 28 February 1701 the Tsar and the King agreed on their plan of
campaign. The King's army, assisted by the Russian auxiliary troops,
would lay siege to Riga in August; the Tsar's Kalmyk troops would
invade Finland, while the main Russian army would draw the enemy
troops to Pechora and the Narva region without engaging them in de-

cisive action. After the capture of Riga, the King's forces would help the Tsar to take Narva and, if necessary, to defend Moscow against the enemy. The plan reflected Peter's cautious outlook; he was not yet prepared to risk a pitched battle with the Swedes, and he knew that he might have to face a Swedish invasion.

Satisfied that he had bound Augustus to him, Peter returned to Moscow. Hot on his tracks followed Arnstedt, the Saxon Adjutant-General, to collect the money promised under the agreement. Peter found himself in difficulties, for his treasury was empty. A hurried search was made, and from many sources, including contributions from Menshikov and from the wealthy merchant, Filatyev, the required sum was collected and handed over.

The Russian auxiliary troops, Peter's other immediate obligation under the Birze agreement, set out from Pskov on 15 May under the command of General Repnin, and joined the Saxon army at Kokenhausen, seven miles from Riga. They made a good impression on their Saxon commander-in-chief, Field-Marshal Steinau. He noted that they marched well, worked zealously, and carried out their orders promptly. He praised them particularly because they had not brought with them either women or dogs, and he approved warmly of General Repnin's request "that the wives of the Saxon musketeers be forbidden to come into the Russian camp morning and evening to sell wine, because the Muscovites are greatly given to drinking and debauchery." Steinau was less impressed by the officers, all of whom were Germans, who were either old and incompetent, or young and inexperienced.[23]

On his return from Birze on 8 March, Peter stayed only ten days in Moscow, before hurrying away to Voronezh, where he spent three months. He had been a long time away from his shipyards, and he was anxious to prepare his fleet for war with the Turks, especially as rumours had reached him that the Turks, having ratified their peace with Venice, were about to open hostilities against Russia. While at Voronezh he also sent instructions to the Archangel voevod, Prince Alexei Prozorovsky, to strengthen the defences of Archangel and Kholmogory against a possible Swedish attack.

On 7 June Izmailov, the Russian ambassador at the Danish court, reported that the Swedes were hastily fitting out four ships in Gothenburg, ostensibly to hunt whales off Greenland, but in fact to attack Archangel. This report was passed immediately to Prozorovsky, with instructions to keep four hundred men in readiness and to hasten preparation of all defences. On the evening of 20 June the Swedish squadron of four warships, two frigates, and a yacht, all flying English or Dutch flags, sailed into the mouth of the Dvina. But in the action which followed one Swedish frigate and the yacht ran aground, while the rest of the squadron had to withdraw. Prozorovsky reported on the incident in glowing terms, and Peter, who took special pleasure in any successful action involving ships, ordered promotion and rewards for all who had taken part.

Meanwhile, after the battle of Narva, Charles had moved with his army into Livonia, taking up winter quarters at Lais, a castle thirty-three miles from Dorpat. Here he remained for five months, awaiting reinforcements from Sweden. They arrived nearly ten thousand strong, towards the end of the spring, marching first to Dorpat, thence with Charles to Riga. He had left a force of eight thousand men under Colonel Schlippenbach to defend Livonia and a small detachment to defend Ingria. He had also strengthened the garrison at Narva. Such was his contempt for the Russians that he made no other provision for the defence of the Baltic provinces.

At Riga, Charles found Steinau with his army of twenty-seven thousand men drawn up on the left back of the Dvina. He hastened to attack, crossing the river under the guns of the Saxons, whom he then routed. It was a resounding victory, and very satisfying to Charles, for the Saxons were veteran troops.

The four Russian regiments, standing in reserve, gave way to panic when they heard the first shots fired. They fled to Repnin, who with the other regiments was awaiting orders some twenty miles away. The Russian troops then returned to Pskov. The incident further confirmed Charles in his contempt for the Russians, who, he considered, would never fight as soldiers.

Craving movement and unable to endure Moscow for long, Peter had set out for Novgorod a few days after his return from Voronezh to see for himself what was happening on his western frontier. He was in Pskov when he learnt of the Saxon defeat. It was disturbing news. Charles was now free to march on Moscow and Russia was still wide open to him. Peter did not pretend to himself that his troops could hold the reinforced Swedish army and he anxiously waited for some sign of Charles's intentions.

On 22 July 1701, fresh from this victory, Charles sent orders to

Schlippenbach, standing near Dorpat with his detachment of eight thousand men, to take up a suitable position close to Pskov and within easy reach of Dorpat. From this it was clear that he planned to march from Courland into Russia. But he did not do so. Schlippenbach stated subsequently that his generals dissuaded him from embarking on the Russian campaign at this stage, and that later, realizing that their advice had been bad, Charles refused to pay any further heed to them.

It is unlikely, however, that Charles needed much persuading; he preferred to pursue Augustus, whose Saxon troops would fight, rather than the Russians who ran. Carried away by his belief in himself as the knight of the invincible sword, and in the infallibility of his own judgments, he grossly underestimated the Tsar and the Russians. He was to pay heavily for his mistake. Now was the time for him to have marched on Moscow, but instead he turned south and for the next six years bogged himself down in the Polish quagmire. Peter could not have asked for more. These six years gave him the chance he needed to establish himself in Livonia and Ingria, and to train his men. They also gave him victories which helped build up Russian morale and destroyed the myth of Swedish invincibility.

In this task Peter came to rely increasingly on Sheremetev who was soon one of the most prominent of his army commanders. A member of one of the old noble families, Boyar Sheremetev had served Peter's father faithfully, but without showing any special ability. He was, however, a brave and capable soldier, although often slow and lacking in initiative. In fact, he was another of those leading men of the period who served well and even achieved remarkable successes, but only because Peter himself was behind them, guiding, directing, and always driving them.

Within two weeks of the battle of Narva, Peter had instructed Sheremetev to winter in Pskov with his cavalry and the Cossacks, and to harry the Swedes. A few weeks later Sheremetev launched an attack on the fortress of Marienburg, but was repelled. When on 6 June 1701 Charles marched from Lais against the Saxons standing before Riga, Peter appointed Sheremetev commander-in-chief of the western frontier and ordered him to operate against the Swedes, using Pskov as his main base. The Russians were again repulsed in a skirmish at Rauga, but at least they were now attacking, although on a small scale. Schlippenbach, promoted to Major-General after this incident, was worried and, in writing to thank his King, he stated that he would rather have seven or eight thousand additional troops for the defence of Livonia than have personal promotion. Charles gave him a further 840 men and refused to do more. He then ordered a detachment of six hundred men to take up a position at Rapino near the Russian frontier. Schlippenbach's warning that they could not hope to survive was disregarded. On 4 September 1701 the Swedish detachment, completely outnumbered, was annihilated. This was the beginning of a series of Russian victories in Livonia.

In December 1701, Sheremetev launched a large-scale attack on Schlippenbach at Erestfer where he had taken up winter quarters. After heavy fighting, Sheremetev's army decisively defeated the Swedes and occupied Erestfer. Although a minor action, Swedish losses were three thousand killed and three hundred and fifty prisoners, and in the effect it had on Russian morale, it was to prove far more costly to the Swedes.

Moscow celebrated this victory with great festivities. A special banqueting hall was erected on the Red Square, for the Kremlin Palace had recently been destroyed by fire, and at night the city was illuminated by fireworks and shaken by cannon salvoes. Peter was jubilant and exclaimed on receiving Sheremetev's report, "Praise God. At last we are able to beat the Swedes."[24] He promoted Sheremetev to General-Field-Marshal and decorated him with the new Order of St. Andrew, which he had just created.

Then, on 18 July 1702 Sheremetev capped his triumph by inflicting an even greater defeat on Schlippenbach at Hummelshof. The Swedish infantry was annihilated and only part of the cavalry escaped. Livonia was now entirely without defences except for the garrisons in Riga, Pernau, and Dorpat, and small detachments in Wenden, Wolmar, Valk, and Marienburg.[25] Sheremetev captured these latter towns and for nearly two months Russian troops ravaged the land.

CHAPTER XX

Catherine

THE ancient fortress town of Marienburg had resisted stubbornly and had capitulated only after storming. The prisoners included many of the Swedish garrison and the citizens of the town with their wives and children. Among them was a seventeen-year-old Livonian girl of humble origin, called Catherine Skavron-skaya, destined to become the Tsar's mistress, then Tsaritsa and Empress and, finally, Catherine I, Empress of All Russia.

Catherine was born in 1685, in the village of Ringen in the Dorpat region of Livonia. She belonged to the family of the peasant Samuel Skavronsky, but was probably illegitimate. Her mother died three years after her birth, apparently leaving her alone and destitute, and the local pastor gave her shelter in his house. But he was a poor man with a large family of his own. Two years later, when the Lutheran pastor of Marienburg, Ernst Gluck, was passing through Ringen, the local pastor complained that he could no longer afford to keep her.

The little foundling attracted Gluck, who took her with him to Marienburg. Although he, too, was burdened with a large family, she lived in his house, helping with his children, and sharing the domestic work. From Gluck she received some education, but it was very scanty, for she could not read or write. It is surprising that he did not teach her more for he himself was a learned man. But, if he did not worry about the foundling's education, at least he gave her the security of a home.

Catherine was just seventeen years old when a Swedish dragoon, who had watched her in church and had fallen in love with her, asked her hand in marriage. She was willing. The pastor gave his approval, and the dragoon's commanding officer even promised to promote him to the rank of corporal on his marriage. It was at this time, however, that Sheremetev's army was approaching Marienburg. The dragoon, expecting daily to be called away, begged the pastor to perform the marriage ceremony quickly, and he did so three days later. It is not clear whether the couple had eight days of married life together or whether the dragoon was recalled to his troop during or immediately after the ceremony. In any case she was never to see him again.

Sheremetev laid siege to Marienburg, threatening complete destruction if the garrison did not surrender. The Swedish major in command knew that he could not hold the fortress and in desperation decided to blow it up. He kept his plan secret, but warned the pastor, Ernst Gluck, to escape in good time. Gluck gathered his family about him, including Catherine and a theology student, Gottfried Wurm, who was tutor to his children, and with the Slavonic Bible in his hand, he made his way to the Russian camp. He was taken to Sheremetev himself who received him with kindness and, approving his suggestion that he might serve the Tsar as a translator, sent him with his family to Moscow.

During Gluck's interview the Field-Marshal's eyes were constantly on Catherine. She was young, full in figure, dark, and strikingly attractive. Finally Sheremetev asked Gluck who she was. Learning that she was a foundling and that she had just been married to a Swedish dragoon, he replied, "That's of no importance. She will stay with me." For some six months Catherine kept house for Sheremetev. But then she came to the notice of Menshikov, already high in the Tsar's favour. Menshikov, too, was attracted and, much to Sheremetev's annoyance, he took her for himself. It was in Menshikov's house some months later that the Tsar made her acquaintance, and soon afterwards she became his mistress.[1]

Peter was not greatly interested in women. Romantic adventure and sexual indulgence played but a small part in his thoughts and activities; the beautiful Electress Sophia during her meeting with him had noted that he was hardly conscious of her as a woman. Shipbuilding, military training, the campaigns against the Turks, and now the Northern War absorbed him. These were the important things of life, and lovemaking belonged to times of relaxation. In fact he was strongly critical of Augustus of Poland because he devoted so much time to his mistresses.

There was no lack of gossip, circulating the courts of Europe, which attributed to Peter a sexual life as wild as it was insatiable.[2] He was dynamic, young, and absolute in his powers over his people, and diplomatists in Russia, especially those from Western courts, where love affairs were the staple of conversation, were always ready to believe, if not to invent, stories of debauchery involving him. But their stories remain unsubstantiated. Once introduced to sensual pleasures, Peter may well have indulged himself, but there is no evidence that he did so. In fact, he was monogamous by nature. Only four women played any real part in his life. There were others, although their number has been exaggerated, and they were of no importance. The four women were his mother, his sister, Natalya, with whom he felt a strong bond, Anna Mons, and Catherine who was to be his intimate companion for over twenty years.

It is not possible to fix the date of the first meetings and of the dawning affection between Peter and Catherine. Peter's letters in his own hand to his Little Mother (*Matka*) and Little Aunt (*Tyotka*), the names he gave to Catherine and to her friend Anisa Tolstaya, began in 1707. But two years earlier Catherine's name had appeared among those at the court of the Tsar's sister, to whose care he had apparently entrusted her.[3] She had become Peter's mistress long before this time, for in October 1705 she already had two children, Paul and Peter, of whom he was presumably the father; in a letter written at this time she asked his blessing for them. Probably Peter's affair with Catherine began soon after his break with Anna Mons.

Peter had met Anna Mons in the Foreign Quarter when he was only seventeen years old; she had reigned unchallenged as his mistress from that time, and he had openly bestowed his attentions upon her. Had she been more astute, she might have become Tsaritsa. But, as Alexander Gordon, who knew her well, observed, she was "an exceedingly beautiful young woman, endued with all the talents to please, except prudence and good sense."[4] She was foolish enough to become betrothed to another man, while still the Tsar's mistress.

Peter was constantly absent from Moscow and, although Anna sometimes followed him with the court to Voronezh, she did not accompany him in his frequent and rapid journeys all over Russia. Probably during one of these long separations she fell in love with the Prussian ambassador, Kaiserling who, according to Alexander

Gordon, prided himself on being the Tsar's rival and proposed to her. Anna accepted. Kaiserling then approached Menshikov to obtain the Tsar's consent to the marriage. In this he made a mistake. Menshikov had no time for Anna Mons and was anxious to see Catherine displace her. He told Kaiserling that he would gladly intercede with the Tsar, but first he must have confirmation in writing of Anna's wishes. She frankly avowed her love for Kaiserling and said that she would rather marry him than anyone else in the world. She willingly signed a written statement to this effect.

At the first suitable opportunity Menshikov slyly approached the Tsar and said, "You, Your Majesty, have always believed that Mistress Mons loved you beyond all mankind; what would you say if this were not so?" "Enough, Alexasha," Peter retorted. "I am so fully persuaded that she can love none but me that nothing shall convince me of the contrary unless she tell me so herself." Menshikov took her written statement from his pocket and handed it to him. Peter immediately went to see her. At first, without show of anger, he asked her if it were true. She admitted it. Peter then reproached her bitterly with faithlessness and folly. He took back the Dudino estate and also the portrait of himself, mounted in a diamond-studded frame, which were among the many presents given her, but allowed her to keep her palace and jewellery. She dropped instantly from eminence to the oblivion of disgrace.[5]

Catherine was both a more attractive person and a worthier mate for Peter, and fortune smiled on him in bringing them together. She overshadowed not only Anna Mons but also Tsaritsa Natalya and Evdokiya. She was not vivacious and witty, like Nell Gwyn, but merry and comfortable. Nell had grown up in the boisterous sensual world of seventeenth century London, winning acclaim on the Restoration stage by clever use of brain and body—Catherine in the stern calm house of the Pastor Gluck, a devout Lutheran. The Russian invasion of Livonia had thrown her suddenly into the world at the age of seventeen. She survived not only because she was a handsome young woman of opulent sensual charms, but also because she was kindhearted, generous, and good-natured. Alexander Gordon, who had talked with her often, considered that "the great reason why the Tsar was so fond of her was her exceeding good-temper; she was never seen peevish or out of humour; obliging and civil to all, and never forgetful of her former condition."[6] She provided a haven of affection and maternal care to which Peter could return from his travels and his furious activities, and from which he could set out again refreshed.

In all things Catherine appeared the ideal wife and companion for him. She had great physical stamina. Several times she accompanied him on campaigns, enduring hardships without complaint, and at the same time she bore him twelve children.⁷ Her amazing physical endurance was allied with a strong common sense and a simple honesty, which held her from being carried away by her new, exalted position, first as mistress, then as wife of the great Tsar. She had the same honesty in personal relationships as Peter himself. But, as he drove his people, punished corruption and incompetence, and pressed new ideas into practice, he was often blinded to the need for mercy, patience, and charity. Catherine did not forget them. Frequently she interceded with him to spare those condemned to death or to some other punishment, and she usually had her way.

Many Russians came to love her and she was the idol of the army, who saw in her not only the Tsaritsa, but the perfect commander's wife. She could review troops, speaking kindly to the men, awarding tots of vodka on special occasions, and showing both sympathy and understanding of the soldier's life. She accompanied Peter on his Persian campaign of 1722, and displayed great bravery under fire. It was on this campaign that, according to Campredon, the French ambassador, Peter gave orders for his army to march and then went to his tent to sleep. The heat of the summer was oppressive and had already taken heavy toll among the troops. On awakening Peter found that his army had not moved. He stormed and demanded to know which commander had dared overrule his orders. Catherine went to him and said, "I did it because your men would have died of heat and thirst."⁸

Peter became dependent on Catherine in many ways. He could rely on her to be at hand when he needed her. Often she appeared more as a mother than as a mistress and wife. When agonizing headaches presaged one of his insensate rages and everyone went in terror of him, Catherine alone was without fear. Firmly but tenderly she would call him to her, take his head in her hands and stroke his forehead until, lying against her bosom, he would relax into sleep. For hours she would sit motionless holding his head as he slept, and when he awoke the convulsions of face and body had passed and he was in the best of humours. Only Catherine could exorcise his furies and on these occasions she alone stood between the Tsar and his people.

The close companionship that quickly developed between them deepened with the passing years. Whenever separated, they wrote to each other, indulging in private jokes, and exchanging small presents, such as fresh lemons and figs, oysters, flowers, and clothes, and even mint. At first he usually addressed her as *Muder* or *Moeder* or Little Mother, and later affectionately, as Katerinoushka, referring to himself as the "old fellow," apparently alluding to some private joke about his sexual powers. From Karlsbad on his second visit to Europe, he wrote to her on 19 September 1711: "We, thanks to God are well, only our bellies are swelled up with water, because we drink like horses, and we have nothing else to do except . . . You write that on account of the cure I should not hurry to you. It is quite evident that you have found somebody better than me. Kindly write about it. Is it one of ours or a man of Thorn? I rather think a man of Thorn, and that you want to be revenged for what I did two years ago. That is the way you daughters of Eve act with us old fellows." Their letters frequently resound with an earthy coarseness which was in part a reflection of the manners of the day, but which also suggested that they were physically close and contented together.

Even when she became Tsaritsa, Catherine did not forget the people who had helped her. Pastor Gluck[9] died in May 1705, and in later years Catherine provided a pension for his widow. She also helped the Gluck children, two of whom became senior officials in the Russian service. When, more than ten years after the fall of Marienburg, she saw Gottfried Wurm again, she immediately recognized him and ordered that he should receive sixteen rubles a month from her income. At her request in 1722, Peter instructed his governor in Livonia to seek out the peasant Skavronsky and the rest of the family. Karl and Feodor Skavronsky, Catherine's brothers, and two sisters were found and sent to St. Petersburg. Karl was a groom at a post-station in Courland and the others held equally lowly positions. In St. Petersburg they were educated and, after the death of Peter, Catherine made them counts of the Russian empire.

CHAPTER XXI

Reforms: Peter in Archangel

1702

SHORTAGE of skilled men was one of Peter's most persistent problems. His people, although unwilling, were adaptable and quick to learn, but few among them could command in the army, and few possessed the technical knowledge to direct canal and shipbuilding, iron foundries, and his numerous other undertakings. For these projects he had to rely on foreigners, and his demands constantly outstripped supplies. The seven hundred officers, seamen, engineers and artisans, engaged in England and Holland, and sent to Russia in the spring of 1698, had long since been absorbed. His need for skilled foreigners was greater now in 1702 than ever before. Replacements for the senior officers he had lost at Narva were most pressing. When he learnt that Patkul had resigned from the service of Augustus, he was quick to invite him to Russia.[1]

Towards the end of March 1702, Patkul arrived in Moscow where Peter at once invited him to join the Russian service. He was delighted when Patkul accepted, for his ebullient personality, eloquent tongue, exceptional ability, and his ready flow of practical ideas on most subjects made him invaluable not only as military adviser and commander, but also as a diplomatic representative. Soon afterwards Peter requested his views on army organization and Patkul submitted recommendations in which he particularly stressed the need to attract foreign officers by offering certain basic conditions.[2] Peter was impressed and he adopted most of the proposals. Later Golovin was informing Patkul of Peter's desire to find an inspector of arsenals, also smiths, sword-masters, lawyers learned in Prussian and Saxon law, an experienced gardener who knew Polish, and a sheep-breeder, and to Patkul, who concentrated on the war, Peter's restless, wide-ranging enquiries were disturbing.

Patkul's advice on recruiting foreign officers resulted in a manifesto which caused a stir throughout western Europe. Proclaimed on 18 April 1702, it stated: "It is well known in all lands under our rule that all our endeavours are directed to the better condition of our subjects. To this end, attending to the internal order and the defence of our tsardom, we have introduced into the administration many changes for the education and industry of our people; most of all we have taken care for the better organization of the army. For the greater success in this and to encourage competent foreigners to join our service, we have ordered it to be proclaimed everywhere that: i. we confirm the complete abolition by us long ago of the ancient law forbidding to foreigners free entry into Russia, and that any wishing to enter our service, on the evidence of the Kommissar-General in Germany, will receive from the frontier governor, free transport for himself, his family, and for his luggage to Moscow itself; ii. we offer in our capital and in all our tsardom freedom of worship in all Christian faiths, which do not agree with our church, and no one in public or in private worship will be disturbed; iii. to allay fears of legal proceedings not in accord with natural territorial customs, we have ordered the establishment of a secret war council, composed of learned foreigners; this council will be responsible for all affairs concerning the foreign military establishment, together with the foreign war commissariat, the army paymaster, tribunals and courts-martial."

Jews were by implication excluded from this general manifesto. They were the one exception to Peter's wide tolerance of all races and religions. "I want to see around me," he said, "the best people of the Mohammedan and heathen faiths, rather than Jews. They are rogues and cheats. I am uprooting the evil, not multiplying it; there will be for them in Russia neither dwelling nor trade, no matter how hard they strive and no matter how much they bribe those close to me." But this prejudice was evidently not so strong in practice, for Shafirov and others among his close associates were Jews.[3]

During these three weeks in Moscow, Patkul won the confidence of his new master, and received many marks of favour. As Peter prepared to leave for Archangel, he entrusted Patkul with wide powers to negotiate with Augustus and with the Austrian court, and to engage certain senior officers and experts. Patkul acted in all these matters with his usual energy. He did not achieve great success in his political negotiations, but it is doubtful whether anyone representing the Tsar at this stage would have made greater headway. In the officers and experts, however, whom he induced to enter the Russian service, he showed great discernment.

Peter particularly wanted Lieutenant-General Fleming on his staff, but Patkul did not favour Fleming; he engaged in his place General Ogilvie, then in the Imperial service. He also enlisted Colonel Carl Evald Ronne, as a field officer, and Heinrich von Huyssen, a doctor of laws. All three men later served with distinction. Patkul had less success in securing other experts. "My task of enlisting capable men has proved very difficult," he wrote to Feodor Golovin from Vienna. "Many who decided to go to Russia have changed their minds; for what reasons, I do not know."[4] Apparently the generous terms and guarantees offered were not enough.

The main reason for this reluctance to enlist was that the descriptions of Russia, current in western Europe, dwelt with such lurid detail on the primitive conditions there and the xenophobia of the people, that only the adventurous and the desperate were prepared to serve the Tsar. The publication of Korb's diary had given added authority to the popular conception of Russia as a barbaric inferno.

This disturbed Peter, not only because it discouraged the foreign experts he needed, but for the more basic reason that it prevented acceptance of Russia as a civilized nation and an equal among Western powers. He resented the description of his country as barbaric and of his people as barbarians. At the same time he recognized that the widespread ignorance and superstition, and many of the old Muscovite customs still prevalent among his subjects merited the epithet. He had already taken some steps towards abolishing illiteracy by sending young men abroad to study and by establishing schools. But these measures were intended to produce technicians; he now wanted also to launch schemes for popular education, that would break down the narrow, isolated outlook of his people.

Meanwhile he was active in stamping out practices which gave ground for the charge of barbarism. He had taken the first steps in changing the status of women, and introducing social intercourse on the Western pattern by ordering that women should no longer be shut away in the *terem*, but should be invited to dinners and other social occasions. To the horror of his people, he abolished many of the marks of respect and deference, which they had always shown to the Tsar and which he considered servile. On 30 December 1701 he decreed that in future his subjects should not fall on their knees or prostrate themselves before him, or sign themselves with the diminutive forms of their names in petitions, or in winter take off their fur hats as a mark of respect in passing his Kremlin Palace, from which, in any case, he was invariably absent.

"What difference is there then between God and Tsar, when equal respects are paid to both?" he asked. "Less servility, more zeal in service, and loyalty to me and to the state—these are the respects to be paid to me."[5]

He took steps to put down the widespread robbery and violence which made Moscow and other Russian towns dangerous after dark and even by day. Drunken quarrels, especially frequent during church festivals, did little harm when the parties were unarmed, but many had begun carrying knives and other weapons which led to injury and murder. In 1700 Peter decreed that no one should carry daggers or pointed knives, or other weapons. A year later, he made duelling punishable by death.

Two practices, which had given rise to foreign criticism, concerned deformed children and marriage. Since pre-Christian days it had been the custom in Muscovy to kill deformed children at birth. Peter decreed that in future they should not be killed, and that their births should be recorded in the Monastery Office. The Muscovite system of arranging marriages was particularly iniquitous, because bride and groom had no voice in their union, and did not see each other until the marriage was solemnized. In 1693 the Patriarch Adrian had denounced the practice as evil in its effects on marriage and on the upbringing of children, but he could suggest no remedy. In April 1702 Peter decreed that marriage should be free and voluntary, that the parties should meet at least six weeks before their betrothal, and that each should be free to reject the other.

His reforms made for some improvement in Russian social life.

But other practices, abhorrent to foreigners, persisted. On 26 November 1706 Charles Whitworth, the English ambassador, ended a long despatch to Robert Harley, with an account of "the punishment of a woman of good quality, who with two of her accomplices lately murdered her husband, it being almost as dreadful, as the crime is abominable. On the 19 inst. a hole being dug in the ground in an open square, the lady was put in alive and the void filled up with earth to her shoulders, and then a block being laid just before her face, a maidservant, who assisted in the murder, was beheaded, and the other accessory, her steward, who had been her gallant, was hanged exactly over her head." The two bodies were left near her for twenty-four hours, but she remained alive in the bitter cold for five days and nights. The ground around her was then rammed in hard to hasten her death.[6]

Russia's reputation abroad for barbarity proved hard to eradicate, and certain incidents at this time aggravated it. Peter had intended sending his son, Tsarevich Alexei, abroad to study. His plans came to nothing, and in 1701 he appointed as his tutor in Moscow, a Dr. Neugebauer, whom Karlovich had recommended. It proved an unsatisfactory appointment. Neugebauer was soon writing to the Tsar and to Feodor Apraxin complaining of persecution. On 23 May 1702, the hostility between tutor and Russians exploded in a violent quarrel. Neugebauer lost all self-control and called those Russians present "pigs and barbarians." After an enquiry he was expelled from the country. Once back in Europe he took his revenge in a campaign vilifying Russia and the conditions in the Tsar's service, publishing a pamphlet full of malice and scurrility. Meanwhile from The Hague Matveev reported that similar stories about Russia were current in Holland.

This persistent denigration continued to worry Peter, and he himself let pass no opportunities to counter it. In Voronezh, towards the end of a wedding reception attended by a number of foreigners, he ordered a Russian soldier to be brought before the company. The soldier told how he and forty-five comrades had been captured by the Swedes who in cold blood had cut off the two first fingers of each man's right hand, and then had sent them back to Russia. Peter was greatly moved by this treatment of prisoners. He declared to everyone present that, although the Swedes represented him and his people as barbarous and unchristian, yet he appealed to all the world, and especially to the thousands of Swedish prisoners now in his dominions, to bear witness that he had never treated any of them with such cruelty and indignity.[7]

Meanwhile he decided to engage a special representative to counteract this disparaging attitude abroad, and chose Dr. Heinrich von Huyssen, who proved active and able, and gave exceptional service as a diplomatic representative, a propagandist, and as tutor to the Tsarevich.

On 18 April 1702, Peter set out for Archangel with a large suite and five battalions of guards; in all, his party numbered more than four thousand men. The purpose of this expedition was to defend the port against another Swedish attack, for Andrei Matveev had reported that the Swedes were hastily fitting out ships, and planned to send a greater force into the White Sea than in the previous year. The defences of Archangel had already been strengthened. But Peter was not satisfied. He could take no risks of his only port falling into the hands of the Swedes, who could then not only put an end to his foreign trade, but also make Archangel a base from which to attack him.

Peter remained in Archangel for nearly three months, supervising the defence preparations and working in the shipyards. Two frigates were launched, and the keel of a new twenty-six-gun ship was laid down, but lack of suitable timbers held up work on her.[8]

At the beginning of August, the first convoy, comprising eighty-six merchantmen, escorted by three warships, arrived in the White Sea. One of the warships brought a group of foreigners, including ten canal engineers, enlisted by Matveev in Holland. The convoy also brought news that the Swedes would not attack Archangel this summer.

Freed from the Swedish threat, Peter paid another visit to the Solovetsky Monastery, Archbishop Afanasy accompanying him part of the way.[9] Reaching the monastery safely, he spent several days in prayer at the tombs of Saints Zossima and Savvatiya. Early on the morning of 16 August, the flotilla sailed and in the evening anchored at Nyukhcha in the Bay of Onega.

This visit to the White Sea followed the pattern of his visit in 1694 so closely that he might have been deliberately retracing his steps, unchanged by the passing years. But, while his passion for ships and the sea, his unquenchable energy and curiosity, his drinking bouts and his religious devotion were as much part of him in 1702 as in 1693-1694, he himself had grown in stature. He was now thirty years old and during the eight crowded and dramatic years that had passed since his last visit to Archangel, the capture of Azov had encouraged him, the experience of England, Holland, and Austria had broadened and crystallized his ideas, and the opening of the Northern War had chastened him and forged his will. The years had transformed him into a responsible dynamic ruler. By the time of his second visit to Archangel, he had entered fully upon his heritage and had taken on his shoulders the massive burdens of a reformer.

His new sense of responsibility as Tsar showed in the greater interest he had begun to take in his son, Tsarevich Alexei. He was now treating him as his successor to be carefully trained in modern learning and techniques. His plans to send him abroad to study had come to nothing, and, distracted by the campaigns against Sweden, he had done little for the boy. Conscious now of his past neglect, he took Alexei with him to Archangel in 1702, both to remove him from the malignant atmosphere of Moscow and to begin under his own supervision the boy's training in the urgent, practical business of war and seafaring.

Alexei was not, however, to prove an apt or willing pupil, and it later emerged that the old Orthodox traditions had already struck deep root in his mind.

At Nyukhcha, Peter received Sheremetev's despatch reporting his decisive defeat of Schlippenbach at Hummelshof on 18 July. He was overjoyed with his news, and wrote promptly to *"Min Herr General Feltmarshaul,"* thanking him.[10] At Nyukhcha Peter also received a despatch from Peter Apraxin, whom he had sent with a force of men into Ingria. Apraxin reported that he had advanced down the Neva, laying waste the lands from the frontier to the river Lava, a distance of some sixty miles. He had then taken up positions on the Tosna River. The Swedish General Kronhjort was twenty miles away. Apraxin's letter ended: "We will advance against him, with God's help."[11]

Peter was not pleased with this report. "Min Herr," he replied to Apraxin: "We have received your letter in which you write of your advance against Kronhjort. (May God give you good fortune.) But, that on your advance you have destroyed and burnt everything, is not at all pleasant news to us; you were told, and it was included in your orders, not to disturb the land."[12] Livonia could be laid waste, and he had ordered Sheremetev to do so, but Ingria was part of the Russian tsardom, to be recovered with as little destruction as possible. On 13 August, however, Apraxin made amends for his mistake. He joined battle with the Swedes on the banks of the Izhora River and routed them. Kronhjort retreated to Dudorovshchina, and, although he still had a force of seven thousand men, he did not wait to meet the Russians again, but withdrew into Finland.

This was the propitious opening to Peter's Ingrian campaign. On 28 August he wrote hurriedly to Apraxin to express his pleasure. "We hope soon to be in Ladoga," he added.[13]

CHAPTER XXII

Conquest of Ingria

1702-1703

FROM Nyukhcha, Peter with his suite and five battalions of guards travelled south to Lake Onega, down this lake in boats, and along the river Svir. He was eager now to take advantage of Kronhjort's withdrawal which had left the Neva delta without defences, except for two small garrisons. From mid-stream in the Svir, he sent orders to Sheremetev in Pskov to make all haste to join him with his army. "The time is very ripe and should not be missed, and without you it will not be with us as we would wish," he wrote.[1] Harried by orders from his Tsar, Sheremetev made haste, and by the end of September his troops together with those of Apraxin, and a great array of artillery were concentrated against Noteburg.

This was a small fortress town on an island in the Neva River near Lake Ladoga. The citizens of Novgorod had built it at the beginning of the fourteenth century to defend their main trade route to the Baltic Sea, and had given it the name of Oreshka or Orekhova which, like the Swedish name of Noteburg, referred to the island's hazelnut shape. The Swedes had taken it once, but the people of Novgorod had quickly recaptured it. Thenceforward it had remained in Russian hands until 1611, when the Swedes had again seized the town, and the Treaty of Stolbovo had confirmed their possession. But it was a national Russian aspiration to recover it and the whole of Ingria.

The small garrison could not now withstand the great force that Peter had ranged against it, and on 11 October the Swedes surrendered on the generous terms offered them.[2] Peter, Sheremetev, and the Russian commanders then entered the fortress, and at once renamed it Schlusselburg. To the sound of cannon salvoes, a key, which the Swedish commandant had handed over, was fixed to the western bastion. It was a symbol of the town's importance as the key both to Ingria and to the Baltic Sea.

The capture of Schlusselburg gave Peter deep satisfaction.[3] He wrote of it immediately to many of his closer colleagues. He ended his letter to Vinius with the comment: "In truth, this nut was tough, but, praise God, we have truly cracked it. Our artillery carried out its work magnificently."[4] To Prince Feodor Romodanovsky, he addressed himself as a loyal subject. "Siir" (sic), he wrote, "I humbly report to Your Highness that the fortress of Noteburg, after a fierce and exceedingly difficult assault, surrendered to the name of Your Majesty on terms." He ended his letter, "With this victory I congratulate Your Majesty and remain Piter."[5] He found time to write five other letters on this first evening in Schlusselburg before giving himself up to celebrations.[6] In subsequent years, whenever he found himself in St. Petersburg, he always journeyed to Schlusselburg on 11 October to celebrate the anniversary of its capture.

Officers and men who had taken part in the campaign were promptly rewarded with promotion, grants of money, or land. But the rewards of Lieutenant Menshikov, who had shown outstanding spirit and ability in the final storming of the fortress, exceeded all others. He became Governor of Schlusselburg. From this time onward, he played his part in the centre of the stage at the side of Peter.

Menshikov's origins are as obscure as those of Catherine. In his own day it was popularly believed that he came of humble parents, and that as a boy he had sold pies in the streets of Moscow.[7] This is supported by an incident that happened in later years, when he was a prince of great wealth and power. It came to pass that he had incurred the anger of the Tsar, who sternly threatened to return him to his former trade. Menshikov rushed off to Catherine to beg her intercession. While she was soothing away the Tsar's anger, Menshikov found a pie-vendor and, putting on his tray, he returned to Peter's presence calling out his wares. Peter was highly amused and promptly forgave him. "But listen, Alexander," he added, "stop your mischief or you'll be worse off than a pie-vendor." Menshikov went after the Empress calling, "Hot pies! Hot pies!" Peter followed laughing, but he repeated, "Remember, Alexander!"

"I will remember, Your Majesty. I will not forget. Hot pies! Hot pies!"[8]

Others have stated that Menshikov came of a noble Lithuanian family. Peter may have believed, and he certainly abetted this story. The scroll conferring the title of Prince of Izhora on Menshikov mentioned this noble background as well as "the honourable service in our guard of his relative."[9] This relative was his father who had served as a corporal in the Preobrazhensky regiment.[10] But service in the guards, either in the ranks or as an officer, did not imply noble origin. Peter was concerned with abilities, rather than birth. The play-soldiers of his boyhood had included as many stable-hands as nobles. Among his closest associates in later years were men like Shafirov, who came from the humblest background. In his origins Menshikov was probably little better.

Menshikov's rise had not been rapid at first, although, as a bombardier, then as a sergeant, he had become one of Peter's associates, and known to everyone in the company as Alexashka. He had been one of the original play-soldiers, and had early enlisted in the Preobrazhensky regiment. In 1693 his name appeared in a list of the regiment's bombardiers and he took part in the Azov campaigns. When he went abroad with the Grand Embassy, he was a sergeant, and served for some time in this rank as a *denshchik* (orderly and personal attendant), taking it in turns to sleep on the floor at the foot of the Tsar's bed or in the adjoining room. He also acted as the Tsar's personal treasurer and was for a time in charge of the embassy.

After the capture of Schlusselburg, however, his advance was meteoric. Within five years he had become a count of Hungary, and a prince of the Holy Roman Empire, both honours conferred on him by the Emperor Joseph as a gesture to the Tsar, and Peter had created him Prince of Izhora as well as entrusting him with high office. In these few years Menshikov also acquired vast estates and enormous wealth.

This astonishing rise was in part due to his nature and striking abilities, and in part to the great affection that Peter had for him. Alexashka had the cheerful, optimistic, affectionate nature of Lefort. He was a lively and entertaining companion, who could banish weariness and raise low spirits. He was also energetic and extremely able. He alone of Peter's companions mastered the craft of ship-building; he developed remarkable ability as a field commander and he contributed greatly to subsequent Russian military successes against the Swedes. He gave his enthusiastic and unreserved support to Peter in all his activities, and to some degree he understood what Peter was striving to achieve.[11]

At the same time Menshikov was essentially a man who rose to success on the back of another. He could show initiative and understanding only within limits. He needed a master to command and discipline him, for in everything he was liable to be distracted by his own selfish, greedy ambition. At court and throughout the country, he was hated and feared. Only his ability and cunning, the support of Catherine, and Peter's affection saved him from downfall and even execution. Catherine was his chief ally, and her intercession sheltered him more than once from the full weight of the Tsar's anger. But squalls constantly disturbed his relationship with the Tsar, who "often kicked him publicly and beat him like a dog, so that by-standers concluded him undone, but always next morning, the peace was made up." Indeed, Menshikov was so adept in obtaining forgiveness that many believed that he employed witchcraft.[12]

Despite these trials, Peter's affection for him remained until the later years of his reign, when their comradeship became overclouded. He enjoyed Menshikov's company and when apart they exchanged frequent letters. Peter addressed him *Mein Herz* or *Mein Herzenkin* and, after 1704, *Mein Leibster Kamerad*, *Mein Leibster Freund* or *Mein Bruder*. He addressed his other officers and colleagues more formally in Dutch; to Sheremetev, *Min Herr General Feltmarshzal*, to Feodor Golovin, *Min Herr Admiral*; to Apraxin, *Min Herr Admiralteic Herr*, and to others simply, *Min Herr*.

Peter became even more attached to Menshikov than he had been to Lefort, who had always remained a foreigner and a drinking companion. Menshikov, in contrast, was a Russian and a comrade. He did not merely enliven parties; he also shouldered responsibilities and shared dangers. An element of family intimacy also united them. It centred first on the court of Tsarevna Natalya, then on Menshikov's house in Moscow, and later in St. Petersburg. Natalya's maids of honour included two sisters, Darya and Barbara Arsenieva, with whom Menshikov became friendly, and soon a deep affection developed between him and Darya. They wrote to each other when apart, and exchanged presents; usually Peter sent his greetings and sometimes a small present, for he encouraged their friendship, and later their marriage.

On his return to Moscow in 1703, Menshikov took Darya and Barbara to live in the large house which Peter had given him. A few weeks later Catherine joined them, and this house then became Peter's home during his brief visits to Moscow.

On 4 December 1702, Peter, returning from the capture of Schlusselburg, made a grand entry into Moscow. Three triumphal arches, celebrating his victory in Ingria and Sheremetev's victories in Livonia, had been erected at points in the city. The occasion recalled his entry into Moscow six years earlier after the Azov campaign. The arches and decoration were again allegorical, and still bewildering to the Muscovites who, with the habit of centuries, looked for the holy ikons and Orthodox ceremonial, and looked in vain.

During this visit to Moscow, Peter gave his attention to two ventures in popular education that he had had in mind for some time— a newspaper and a theatre. The Russian people lived in ignorance of what was happening not only abroad, but in their own country. Always in the past the tsars and their advisers received reports from ministers, voevodi, and ambassadors, and had extracts from foreign news-sheets read out to them, but they guarded all such information as a close secret, unsuitable for popular consumption.

Peter considered such secrecy harmful. He wanted news of events at home and abroad circulated as widely as possible. On 17 December 1702 he decreed that a gazette was to be published. All government departments were to send items of interest to the Monastery Office, which would pass them to the printing press. Three weeks later the first issue appeared under the title, "Gazette of military and other matters, meriting attention and remembrance, that have happened in the Muscovite State and in neighbouring countries."[13] This issue gave news of the victories in Ingria and Livonia, and of the number of cannon cast in Moscow. It declared that "by the orders of His Majesty, Muscovite schools are increasing in number, and forty-five pupils are studying philosophy, having already completed dialectics. In the mathematical-navigational school more than three hundred are learning. . . ."[14] The gazette also printed the number of male and female children born in Moscow, and reported that in China the Jesuits had fallen from favour because of their trickery. Appearing at irregular intervals, the gazette gave equal prominence to military successes, industrial developments, and events abroad. It was an important innovation, not only because it countered ignorance and isolationism in Russia, but also because through it Peter sought to explain and justify his reforms to his people.

With the same purpose Peter engaged foreign players and built a popular theatre. The restricted audience of his father's court theatre was not what he wanted. He had seen performances in Amsterdam and London which attracted crowds, and in the Ukraine and Poland the theatre was used for religious propaganda. He decided that in Russia the theatre should spread education and serve as a civilizing influence. In June 1702 a German, Johann Kunst, with his wife and seven players, arrived in Moscow. Peter was then in Archangel and in his absence Feodor Golovin had erected a theatre on Red Square, an act which horrified old Muscovites. Kunst was to train twenty Russian clerks as actors, but he had trouble with these apprentices, and even more trouble in carrying out instructions to celebrate in allegorical form the capture of Schlusselburg. He produced several plays, but in 1703 he died. His successor, Otto Furst, did nothing to further the venture. In this short period the theatre had made no appeal to the Russians who preferred their own *skomorokhi* or wandering minstrels, and so the Tsar's attempt to popularize it failed.[15]

As usual Peter did not linger in Moscow. He was eager to visit his shipyards at Voronezh, while he waited anxiously for reports from Prince D. M. Golitsyn, whom he had sent to Constantinople to ratify the peace treaty.[16] The return of Golitsyn some three months later with Turkish ratification was a great and unexpected relief. "We do not expect war with the Turks," he wrote jubilantly to Apraxin, "for the Sultan has ratified the peace willingly."[17]

One of the most important Russian gains under the treaty of 1700 was the right to maintain regular diplomatic representation in Constantinople. On 2 April 1702, a few months after receiving the ratification, Peter appointed Counsellor Peter Tolstoy to be his first permanent ambassador to the Sultan.[18] It was a difficult assignment, and Tolstoy, in the course of the thirteen arduous years he was to spend there, acquitted himself well.[19] But neither Turkish ratification, nor the arrival of Tolstoy in Constantinople made any real difference to relations between the two countries. Tolstoy was given a hostile reception. The Turks faced him with new demands that Russian ships should be withdrawn from Azov and Taganrog, and they muttered threats.

Tolstoy's reports disturbed Peter, making him even more impatient to put his fleet in order, and, accompanied by a large suite, he set out for Voronezh on 1 February 1703. He made all haste, but broke his journey at Lake Ivan to examine work on the canal. Since he had first thought of linking the Volga and Don rivers, his need for a system of waterways had become more pressing. While now engaged in Ingria and daily expecting Charles XII to march against him, he was again threatened in the south. In fact, the danger of attack by the Crimean Tatars and the Turks became so serious that he marched troops from the north to meet it. But he lacked both the resources and the trained men to maintain separate forces in the north and in the south. His answer to the problem was to develop water communications between Ingria and southern Russia so that he could readily move his troops to meet whichever of these threats materialized.

Peter and his party did not stop again until they reached the Stupinsky shipyards, twenty miles north of Voronezh, where he inspected ten vessels at the wharves. Arriving in Voronezh on 5 February he found fifteen ships at anchor in the river. It was a satisfactory result, but Peter was not satisfied. Nothing moved fast enough when he was away, and problems built up against his return. He now found the work delayed by a shortage of labour, caused partly by conditions in the Voronezh shipyards which were appalling, and by the mortality rate among the workmen which was disturbingly high.[20]

A problem, as urgent as the building of new ships, was the maintenance and preservation of those already built. Working under pressure, the shipwrights used unseasoned timber, which quickly warped and rotted. Captain John Perry was called to Voronezh to advise on refitting without careening, since the ships would suffer serious damage if laid on their sides. He built a system of sluices by which the ships were floated onto the land and kept on even keel. It was probably on this visit to Voronezh that Peter examined Perry's work and expressed himself well satisfied. He promptly instructed Perry to survey the Voronezh River for the purpose of constructing sluices to make the river navigable, so that ships could be launched and brought down the Don at any time of the year.[21]

Peter remained only a month in Voronezh, because news had come from Constantinople that attack by the Turks or Tatars was not, as had seemed probable, imminent. Anxious to complete his conquest of Ingria, he set out northwards for the Neva River almost immediately.[22]

Arriving at Schlusselburg on 19 March 1703, Peter was furious to find that the guns, ammunition, and other supplies that he had ordered, had not arrived. "Siir," (sic) he wrote to Romodanovsky, "I am informing you that here there is a great failure in the delivery of artillery. . . . Of this I have myself many times spoken to Vinius, who has answered me with the Muscovite 'Right away.' Kindly examine him as to why there should be such carelessness in so serious a matter, which is a thousand times more important than his head."[23]

Romodanovsky, himself a rogue guilty of serious peculations, questioned Vinius and reported, but Peter was not satisfied with his report. He ordered Menshikov to investigate. Anxious to retain his profitable Siberian Office, but to give up the onerous duties of the Artillery Office, Vinius tried to bribe Menshikov to recommend the change. For once Menshikov was not to be bribed.

Two months earlier Vinius had sent a memorandum listing all his services to the Tsar and petitioning for a reward. As Director of Posts and in developing heavy industry and the gun foundries he, more than any other minister, had carried out Peter's instructions with energy and ability, and for these reasons Peter had been patient with him. But he would not tolerate neglect of the urgent work in hand. Vinius had given way to carelessness, indolence, and gross corruption. He was deprived of all offices, heavily fined, knouted, and was fortunate indeed to escape execution. He had enjoyed the Tsar's trust and favour, but had betrayed both, and now he lost them irrevocably.

On 23 April 1703 Sheremetev, who had arrived at Schlusselburg from Pskov a few days earlier, advanced to the right bank of the Neva with an army of twenty thousand men. His orders were to capture the small fortress town of Nyenskantz at the entry of the river Okhta into the Neva. Peter joined him there,[24] and then on the evening of 28 April with seven companies of guards he sailed downriver past the fortress. He posted three companies at a point where they could give warning of any attempt by the Swedes to bring relief by sea. He then returned upriver to find that Sheremetev had by that time placed the siege guns and was ready to open fire. Two days later the Swedish garrison surrendered.[25] It was not an exciting or a major victory, but Peter attached importance to the town as a useful seaport, and, celebrating with the usual ceremonies, he renamed the fortress, Slotburg.

On the evening of 2 May, word came from the guard at the Neva mouth that enemy ships were approaching. Vice-Admiral Nummers with a squadron of nine ships, knowing nothing of the capture of the fortress, was sailing into the delta. Three days later he detached two small vessels to proceed to the fortress and they anchored off Vasily Island. Learning of this, Peter and Menshikov with both regiments of guards in thirty boats rowed downriver by night, hiding from the enemy on the other side of the island. Peter divided his force into two parts—one to attack from seawards and the other from upstream. At dawn on 7 May the Russians rowed silently towards the enemy and attacked. The Swedes tried to make for the sea, but could not get under way in the narrow channel. Firing their muskets and throwing hand grenades, the Russians boarded the vessels. They outnumbered the Swedes who, fighting fiercely, lost fifty-eight of their seventy-seven men before they were compelled to surrender.

On 8 May Peter returned to Slotburg with the two Swedish vessels. However minor, this was his first naval victory and his delight was unbounded. The Neva echoed with the sounds of triple salvoes of cannon and musketry, and he gave thanks at a special service. Admiral Feodor Golovin and Field-Marshal Sheremetev then formally invested Peter and Menshikov with the insignia of the Order of St. Andrew,[26] and all who had taken part were rewarded.

With his usual enthusiasm Peter hastened to share his news with his associates. He wrote on 10 May to Romodanovsky, Feodor Apraxin, and to at least seven others. He did not write boastfully, but factually of the victory as one belonging to all the participants. His letters unfortunately give no detail of the part that he himself played as the officer in command.[27]

For a moment pleasure in his naval victory seemed to obscure in his mind the fact that he had now regained Ingria—the objective for which he had declared war on Sweden. Russia once more had direct access to the West through the Baltic Sea. But menacing these gains and casting its shadow over all his plans was the stark fact that the Northern War was not yet won. Charles XII, after scattering the Russian army at Narva, had against other armies gone from one victory to another. He had created a legend of invincibility; his name alone struck terror in eastern Europe. But Peter could not think in terms of defeat. He expected to lose battles from time to time, but not to be defeated. It was a token of his great faith in the future that he now proceeded to found a city at the very mouth of the Neva.

CHAPTER XXIII

The Foundation of St. Petersburg
1703-1706

THE Neva is a turbulent river. It flows from Lake Ladoga into the Gulf of Finland, branching into four main streams at its delta. These streams—the Great and Little Neva, and the Great and Little Nevka—with their affluents form a broad and elaborate estuary, containing nineteen islands. Both mainland and islands are low lying, dank, and marshy: *neva*, a Finnish word, means mud.

At this time the estuary was desolate. The river frequently burst from its channels in flood. A few Finns fished the waters, but they abandoned their huts and fled whenever the river began to rise. The climate was unhealthy and harsh in its extremes. Fogs were frequent and the dampness pervasive. The winters were long, dark, and bitterly cold; the summers, breaking with hardly a warning of spring, were short and hot. The estuary was isolated. Approach was difficult by sea and by land. The delta of the Neva was an inhospitable wilderness. But here Peter chose to build his city.

At first he had no thought of a city. He wanted only a port and a fortress to guard the delta from attack. His plan was to rebuild the fortress of Slotburg at the mouth of the Okhta, but then he decided that a site must be found nearer to the sea. He considered Yanni-Saari, or Hare Island, on the northern side of the Great Neva, the most suitable. Here on 16 May 1703 he laid the foundations of the new fortress and port, to be called St. Petersburg, after his patron saint.[1]

This choice of Hare Island had every mark of an arbitrary and hasty decision. Peter had made only two short visits to the estuary, and knew nothing of the moods of the Neva. With far less labour and expense, he could have adapted other sites to his purpose, or made use of Narva, Riga, Libau, or Reval, all of which were to come within his grasp. Nor would he have found difficulty in building a naval base on the coast of Ingria or Livonia. But, if typical of Peter's impetuosity, the decision was also filled with the instinctive wisdom of a ruler deeply rooted in his country's history.

In creating St. Petersburg, Peter was in fact transplanting Novgorod to the Gulf of Finland, making the new city the heir to Novgorod the Great, which itself had been a starting-point of Russian history and the first centre of the Russian nation. During the Tatar conquest, Novgorod had survived as the most powerful and wealthy of Russian cities, controlling a vast trading empire. Ingria was part of this empire, and the bulk of Russian trade with merchants of the Hanseatic League had passed down the Neva. The whole province, which Peter had now recovered, was to him and his people an integral part of Russia and her history.

In the second half of the fifteenth century, Moscow had challenged and crushed Novgorod, which had nevertheless continued as the centre of trade and contact with the West. Moscow had turned from the West and in upon herself, partly as a result of the long isolation imposed by Tatar dominion, and partly because of her conservative and religious belief in her own self-sufficiency. In revolt against Moscow, Peter had turned again to the West, reviving the spirit of Novgorod and of Kiev. His new city, St. Petersburg, was to be the symbol and centre of his reformed and reorientated Russia.

The fortress of SS. Peter and Paul was designed with six bastions, and Peter decided that each one should be built under different supervision. He himself supervised the construction of the first bastion, and Menshikov, Golovin, Zotov, Trubetskoy, and Kirill Naryshkin the others. The whole fortress was of timber, and, although the Russians were skilled in using this material, the difficulties were great. Carpenters and labourers were drafted to the work from Novgorod and its surrounding villages, and soldiers helped them. But they lacked spades, picks, and tools of every kind. Earth was scarce on the island and the labourers had to carry it some distance "in the skirts of their clothes, and in bags made of rags and old mats, the use of wheelbarrows being unknown to them."[2] Despite these handicaps the fortress was well advanced five months later.

Across the river on the island of St. Petersburg the crown-work of the fortress was under construction. Here on the right bank of the Neva a small house of pinewood had been built in two days (24-26 May) for Peter himself. This little house was painted to look as though the walls were of brick and the roof of tiles. It had large windows with small panes of mica set in leaden frames. The three rooms were the dining-room, bedroom, and study, but the house had no stove or chimney, because Peter only lived there during the warm months, occupying it for short periods on and off during the summers of the years 1703-1708. From 1708 to 1763 the house stood vacant, although some work was done to preserve it. In 1784, however, Catherine the Great ordered it to be enclosed in a stone building, and with this protection Peter's little house has survived intact as a museum.[3]

The progress of these first buildings apparently satisfied Peter, who was already planning ahead. On 23 September 1703, he wrote from "Sankt Piterburkh"[4] to Romodanovsky, that he had enough skilled men; "at present the need is rather for several thousand thieves (and in fact, if possible, 2,000 men)" for the coming summer, and he gave instructions for all criminals sentenced to servitude in Siberia to be sent to the Neva delta.[5]

Although immersed in building plans Peter could not ignore the menace of the Swedes. Vice-Admiral Nummers with a squadron of nine ships, anchored off the delta, and Kronhjort with an army of four thousand men to the north at the river Sestra, constantly awaited their chance to attack the Russian settlements. Peter longed to sail with his own fleet to challenge them in the Gulf of Finland, but as yet he had no ships in the estuary. He could only post batteries on Vasily Island to defend it against attack by Nummers' ships.

On 7 July 1703, Peter advanced against the Swedish army. He had with him four mounted and two infantry regiments, in all about seven thousand men. Making forced marches through country believed by the Swedes to be impenetrable, they arrived on the following morning at the pass at Systerbek which the Swedes held. Colonel Ronne was detached with a regiment of dragoons and after fierce fighting he gained control of the pass. The Russian dragoons now led their horses along a narrow defile under fire. They then mounted and attacked. The Swedes fled into the forest, and retreated to Vyborg. It was a complete victory in which Peter claimed one thousand Swedes killed, while losing only thirty-two of his own men and 115 wounded.[6]

Writing his usual report to Romodanovsky, Peter did not mention the part that he had played in the victory. He had been constantly under fire and Patkul, who was present, had taken it upon himself to remind him that "he was also mortal like all men and that the bullet of a musketeer could upset the whole army and place the country in serious danger."[7]

Peter returned to St. Petersburg, but remained there only a few days. He then set out posthaste for Lodeinoe Pole on the banks of the river Svir, where he planned to build his navy and where his Baltic fleet, in fact, had its beginnings. In the spring of 1703, carpenters and labourers had felled trees, and under the direction of shipwrights, foreign and Russian, had begun building light vessels of various types. With Peter's arrival on 21 July, the work moved at a new tempo. Several vessels were launched in August, including a frigate, named the Shtandart (Standard). Impatiently, he helped fit and rig her, and on 8 September he sailed her to St. Petersburg. He was eager to explore the outlying shores of the delta, but had to wait because Vice-Admiral Nummers with his squadron still guarded the approaches. At the beginning of October, however, he received a letter from Menshikov, reporting that the Swedish ships had withdrawn to their winter anchorage at Vyborg. He immediately set sail and, although the ice was already gathering in the Neva, he put out into the gulf.

Eight miles from St. Petersburg and dominating the approach to the delta, Kotlin Island caught his attention. He sailed around it and, lead in hand, himself took soundings. He found it too shallow on the Finnish side for any but the smallest vessels. On the south side, he plotted a fairway, deep enough for ships of war and merchantmen. He decided to establish a strong fortress, later called Kronstadt, on the island, and at a gunshot to the south and in the channel itself, to erect another fortress. This would give St. Petersburg security from attack by sea.

During the following winter, while he himself was in Voronezh, Peter sent Menshikov detailed instructions, illustrated with his own drawings, for the construction of this channel fort. Following these orders, Menshikov had boxes made from tall trees. When thick ice covered the delta, the boxes, filled with stones, were dragged into position over the channel, and let down through holes in the ice.

Here they served as the anchorage and foundation of the wooden fortress. On 7 May in the following year (1704), Peter eagerly sailed out in the flute, Velkom (Welcome), to inspect it. He helped to mount in the fortress a battery of fourteen guns, which he had brought with him and then, with celebrations lasting three days, he named his new fortress, Kronslot. Having posted there a small garrison whose orders began: "Hold the citadel, with God's help, and, if necessary, to the last man," he returned to St. Petersburg.[8]

News of the Russian conquest of Ingria spread quickly in western Europe. Many governments were alarmed, and the reports circulated from Moscow by Feodor Golovin disturbed them further. To A. A. Matveev in London, Golovin had written that the Tsar would soon have in the Baltic a fleet of twenty warships and frigates, seventy-eight galleys, and a hundred brigantines, and that some of these ships were already lying off Kotlin Island and Kronslot.[9] At this time the frigate Shtandart, with two or three snows and only ten transports, represented the total strength of Peter's Baltic fleet. But on the banks of the Svir shipwrights were working furiously. Twice during 1704 Peter paid hurried visits to these shipyards. "Here, thanks be to God, all goes fairly well!" he wrote to Menshikov on 23 September. "Tomorrow and the day after, three frigates, four snows, a packet-boat, and a galliot will be launched."[10] Four days later he himself laid down the keel of a large ship, after which he went to pray at the Alexander Svirsky Monastery. He then sailed for St. Petersburg.

Peter took only three days on this voyage. The newly built ships that followed soon afterwards took nearly three weeks. Storms, driven snow, and high winds delayed them. Skirting the southern shore of the lake was particularly dangerous in stormy weather and several ships narrowly escaped being blown ashore. In July of the previous year, Peter himself had experienced the bad weather so common in this region. The voyage from the shipyards on the Svir to St. Petersburg was at all times hazardous, and he now became convinced that his main shipyards must be in St. Petersburg itself. On 4 November 1704, therefore, he laid the foundation of the Admiralty on the left bank of the Neva, opposite Vasily Island.[11] It was to be a vast establishment where ships could be built, launched, and fitted out, and where equipment could be stored and shipwrights could live. First the shipyards and wharves were built, and then work began on the walls to surround it. The first vessels were launched from the Admiralty yards two years later.

Meanwhile Peter had not forgotten that his city was to serve as a port as well as a naval base. The first merchantman had arrived by chance in November 1703, only six months after the foundation of the city. Learning of her approach Peter himself had sailed out and piloted her into port. Her master was astonished on being presented to his royal pilot, who rewarded him with a gift of five hundred ducats. Each sailor received thirty talers and the ship, renamed *St. Petersburg*, was granted exemption for all time from paying customs dues. Similar treatment was promised to the next two ships to arrive, and an English and another Dutch merchantman were able to claim these rewards.

Peter lost no opportunity to induce foreign merchantmen to use his new port. Several times he told Whitworth, the English ambassador, that he attached importance to English merchant ships using Russia's Baltic ports as well as Archangel. He reduced the dues payable in these ports to less than half the amount levied formerly by the Swedes, and also made them less than the Archangel dues. He tried to encourage English merchants in other ways. In the summer of 1705 Menshikov offered the English consul, Goodfellow, forty thousand kegs of pitch at a very low price, provided that he would send ships to load it at St. Petersburg. English merchantmen were soon calling regularly at the new port, together with the ships of Holland and other countries, and St. Petersburg developed quickly.[12]

Still the threat of attack by the Swedes hung over all these activities, giving to his plans a sense of impermanence which Peter found unbearable. Since he could not yet attack them by sea, he decided to deal with them again on land, and this time decisively. In May 1704 Russian troops began moving to Schlusselburg. Peter himself set out in boats up the Neva with his two guards regiments. His plan was to transport the whole army in boats northwards through Lake Ladoga to Kexholm, and to march from there down upon the Swedes.

Within a few hours of leaving St. Petersburg, however, he received an urgent despatch from Peter Apraxin that halted him. In May of the previous year, while work was beginning on the first buildings in St. Petersburg, Peter had sent Sheremetev and Major-General von Werden to complete the conquest of Ingria by taking the small fortresses of Koporie and Yami. He had greatly strengthened the latter, renaming it Yamburg, for it occupied a strong position a few miles from Narva and from the mouth of the Narova River. Three months later he had sent Peter Apraxin to winter in Yamburg with seven regiments. His orders were to hold the fortress and to prevent Swedish ships and supplies from reaching Narva. Apraxin now reported that a Swedish fleet of thirty-five ships had appeared and that Schlippenbach was expected to reach Narva any day with a large army.

Peter had originally intended making a second assault on Narva after his Kexholm expedition. But now Apraxin's report so disturbed him that he revised his plans. He decided that he must capture Narva as soon as possible, even if it meant leaving St. Petersburg for a time with inadequate defences. He therefore ordered his troops to proceed at once to Yamburg and thence to Narva with all speed.[13]

The force that remained behind to defend the Neva delta was small. Colonel Bruce, commandant of the fortress of SS. Peter and Paul, had at his disposal not more than six infantry regiments together with some detachments of Cossacks and Tatars, while the fleet at Kronslot comprised only seven frigates, built on the Svir the previous year, and a few galleys. But during 1704 Bruce nevertheless managed to repel two Swedish attacks by land and one by sea. In the spring of the following year, the Swedes fitted out in Karlskrona a fleet of twenty-two ships, which sailed under the command of Admiral Anckarstjerna,[14] and reinforced the army under the command of General Maidel. The Admiral was to capture Kotlin Island and destroy the Russian fleet, while Maidel was taking St. Petersburg. But their expedition failed completely.[15] Three years passed before the Swedes attacked again.

Under constant pressure from Peter, St. Petersburg grew. Difficulties only confirmed him in his ambitious plans. The Neva flooded once when Peter himself was in St. Petersburg. "The day before yesterday," he wrote to Menshikov on 11 September 1706, "the wind from west-southwest blew up such waters as, they say, have never been before. In my house, the water rose twenty-one inches above the floor; and in the garden and on the other side along the streets people went about freely in boats. However, the waters did not remain long—less than three hours. Here it was entertaining to watch how the people, not only the peasants but their women, too, sat on the roofs and in trees during the flood. Although the waters rose to a great height, they did not cause bad damage."[16]

Thus the first three years of St. Petersburg's existence had given Peter ample demonstration of the obstacles in the way of settling at the mouth of the Neva. The ground was marshy and, even when not reduced to a swamp by the flooding river, it was infertile. Apart from cabbage and turnips nothing would grow, and provisions brought from inland were expensive. Lack of fresh food resulted in outbreaks of scurvy, which, like diarrhoea, became a prevalent illness, and responsible for many deaths. Added to all these difficulties was the fact that the Swedes still threatened and that the permanence of the Baltic foothold depended wholly on the outcome of the Northern War. These were troubles and uncertainties enough to deter most men, but not the Tsar.

St. Petersburg had fired Peter's imagination. Perhaps as he took soundings around Kotlin Island in 1703, and plotted the fairway of the south, he had had a vision of a great port which might rival Amsterdam, where the Dutch had risen magnificently over similar obstacles of floods and marshy lands. Certainly he lavished all his attentions on his new town. In March 1704 he was writing to Tikhon Streshnev asking him to send from Izmailov flowering plants of all kinds, especially those with scent. He was delighted when some peony plants arrived and promptly wrote for mint, tansy, and other plants.[17] Soon he was referring to St. Petersburg as his Paradise and his Eden. He began a letter to Menshikov on 7 April 1706, "I cannot help writing to you from this Paradise; truly we live here in heaven." Even in the autumn of 1706, when describing the serious flooding and the twenty-one inches of water in his own house, he addressed his letter as "from Paradise or Sankpiterburg."[18]

Peter was fortunate to have at hand, soon after the founding of the city, an Italian engineer-architect, Domenico Trezzini, who had experience of the Dutch baroque style which Peter favoured. Trezzini, who was born near Lugano, had been employed by Frederick IV of Denmark on his palace in Copenhagen until April 1703, when he signed a contract to serve the Tsar as his Master of Building, Construction, and Fortification. Soon after his arrival, Peter summoned him to St. Petersburg, where he immediately took charge of the building of the SS. Peter and Paul fortress.

In employing a foreign architect, Peter was following long precedent. Italians and architects of other countries had designed part of the Kremlin and other buildings in Moscow during the previous three centuries. Peter's innovation was in the Northern baroque style which he wanted for his new city. Dutch influence was then strong in northern Europe and the small functional buildings in this style, which he had seen in Amsterdam, had attracted him. For the next nine years in charge of all building in St. Petersburg, and during his thirty-nine years in the Russian service, Trezzini gave effect to Peter's enthusiasm for this style, and was responsible for most of the important early buildings of that city.

Peter next decided that the city must be built of brick and stone, which, aside from greater dignity and permanence, would ensure that, unlike all other Russian cities, St. Petersburg would not be threatened by frequent fires. The fortress of SS. Peter and Paul was the first building to be reconstructed. On 30 May 1706 Peter laid a foundation stone of marble, engraved with his name, the day, and the year. Work began again immediately on Menshikov's bastion, and six months later it was well advanced.[19] But the rebuilding of the whole fortress took many years, and was not finished until after Peter's death.

As time passed, his vision of St. Petersburg expanded; his plans became more grandiose. By 1706 he had already begun to see it not merely as a fortress and a rich port, receiving ships from every part of Europe, but also as a great city. Later he was to make it his capital, supplanting Moscow. It was a conception that found favour with few of his people. The nobles, merchants, and the peasants hated his city. Tsarevna Maria, his half-sister, was to prophesy: "Petersburg will not endure after us: let it be a desert!"[20] Had it been an alien growth, grafted on to Russia by a ruthless westernizing tsar, divorced from the history of his country, it would have perished with its creator, and the prophesy would have come true. But St. Petersburg was not an alien phenomenon. It took root and grew with amazing rapidity. A century later, it was a world metropolis.

CHAPTER XXIV

Dorpat and Narva

1703-1704

THE capture of Yamburg and Koporie in the summer of 1703 had completed Russia's conquest of Ingria. Anticipating the cold weather, Sheremetev wrote to ask Peter where he should rest his troops and himself in winter quarters.[1] But Peter did not think of rest. "When the town [the fortification of Yamburg] is finished, it would be better, if you set out on some campaign," he replied on 24 July 1703 from the Svir shipyards.[2] On the same day he sent Menshikov to Yamburg to concert plans with Sheremetev. Three weeks later Sheremetev marched.[3]

The purpose of this expedition was to lay waste Esthonia and Livonia, and thus hinder any Swedish attempts to relieve the proposed seige of Dorpat and Narva in the summer of 1704. Sheremetev set out towards the end of August with twelve mounted regiments, and a collection of Cossacks, Bashkirs, Kalmyks, and Tatars. He crossed the Narova River and entered Wesenburg on 5 September. Within four days and nights his men had reduced the town to a vast mound of rubble. Meanwhile Schlippenbach had retreated to Reval, for with his small force, he could do nothing to stay the Russians in their fearful march. Sheremetev swept through Esthonia and Livonia scourging the land so terribly that only Reval, Pernau, Riga, Narva, and Dorpat, remained standing.

During the winter Peter gave Sheremetev orders to capture Dorpat in the spring,[4] and by mid-July, Sheremetev's army of twenty-three thousand men with forty-six cannon had taken up positions before this fortress town. Dorpat, or Yuriev, had been founded in the eleventh century by Grand-Prince Yaroslav Vladimirovich to subdue the Finns. The Teutonic Knights had captured it some two hundred years later, renaming it Dorpat. It had flourished as a trade centre, famed for its stone castle and its cathedral, but in the sixteenth century Ivan the Terrible had captured and destroyed it. Next the Poles and then the Swedes had taken it. But successive conquerors had strengthened its defences, so that Sheremetev now faced strong fortifications, manned by a well-armed Swedish garrison under the command of Colonel Skitte, who was renowned as a brave soldier. In fact, Sheremetev soon found Swedish resistance so spirited that he gave way to a mood of hopelessness.

At the approach of spring, Peter had also sent Apraxin, who had wintered at Yamburg, to the Baltic seaboard with twenty-five hundred men to guard the mouth of the Narova River. It had proved a wise precaution for by mid-May thirty-five Swedish warships were lying at anchor off the river mouth; it had been Apraxin's report of this concentration of enemy ships that had made Peter turn from Kexholm and hasten to Narva with his troops.

In May the Russian detachments moved to the same positions before Narva that they had occupied in 1700, while Apraxin remained at the mouth of the Narova, and the blockade of Narva was thus complete. But the siege could not yet begin for lack of artillery which had not arrived from St. Petersburg and Schlusselburg.

Meanwhile, sharp memories of their defeat four years earlier made the Russian troops uneasy. Rumours circulated that the Swedes were about to attack from Reval, and even that Charles XII was sailing from Gdansk personally to lead his men. Learning from captives taken in one of the sorties from the fortress that Schlippenbach was expected any day with a relief force six thousand strong, Peter sent Colonel Ronne with eight thousand troops to engage him. Schlippenbach retreated towards Reval, but Ronne overtook him and inflicted a crushing defeat on him.

While Ronne was marching to engage Schlippenbach, Peter set out with Menshikov for St. Petersburg to hasten the artillery and supplies. It was essential to capture Narva, not only to vindicate Russian arms, but also to secure Livonia. Already several weeks had been wasted through lack of artillery. His hurried journey produced prompt results, however, for on 1 July eight barges laden with ammunition

and supplies reached the Narova from St. Petersburg, having eluded
the Swedish fleet by hugging the coast. Ten days later the guns arrived and were at once moved into position.

On his return from St. Petersburg, Peter found that Field-Marshal
Ogilvie, whom Patkul had engaged, had arrived in the Russian camp
from Moscow. Ogilvie, who was of Scots extraction and had served
the Emperor well for more than forty years, was now in his sixties.
Reliable, skilled, and with the authority of long experience, he was a
senior officer of the type needed, and Peter at once entrusted him
with command of the army before Narva. But it soon became clear
that, although Peter made use of his knowledge, he did not like or
have confidence in him.[5]

Peter spent only five or six days with his army at Narva after his
return from St. Petersburg. He supervised the placing of the guns,
the construction of bridges over the Narova, and the building of approaches closer to the fortress. Frequent enemy sorties hampered
these operations, but, as one Swedish officer in the garrison observed,
the Russians "seemed resolved to carry on their works, however great
the loss might be."[6] Peter then rode with all speed to Dorpat. He
could not afford to have troops tied down by a long siege at Dorpat,
when he urgently needed them against Narva. Nor could he understand why Sheremetev was so dejected, and had so far failed to take
the fortress.

Reaching the Russian camp at Dorpat on 3 July, Peter found it in
a state of confusion.[7] He at once reorganized the approaches, con-
centrating on the vulnerable side of the fortress facing the river, which
Sheremetev had considered too difficult. Soon the artillery had made
three breaches in the fortress wall. Peter then built a bridge over the
river above the town, his troops crossed, and after fierce fighting occupied the outworks of Dorpat. The Swedes resisted desperately, but
were forced to surrender, and on 13 July the Russians entered Dorpat
in triumph: the siege had lasted five weeks, but the town had fallen
just ten days after Peter himself had arrived and taken over the
command.

At this moment, however, there was no time for celebrations. Menshikov had written to Peter, urging him to abandon the siege of
Dorpat and to hasten with all guns and cavalry to Narva.[8] His letter
had arrived two days after the capitulation of Dorpat. On Peter's

orders, Sheremetev posted a strong garrison in the fortress and himself hurried with the rest of his army to Narva.[9]

There preparations were well in hand, and on 30 July the bombardment began, continuing for ten days without cease. The wall of one bastion subsided, and at this point Horn, the commandant, was invited to surrender on generous terms. But he rejected the offer, and aggravated the effect of his defiance by sending an insulting message by word of mouth.

Narva was now doomed. At 2 P.M. on 9 August, five mortars fired the signal for the attack. The Swedes defended themselves furiously, but they could not hold the Russians. Within an hour grenadiers of the Preobrazhensky regiment had forced their way into one bastion. The Swedes retreated, fighting every foot of the way, and trying to throw up barricades. The Russians poured over the walls, and swept them aside.

Horn now saw that further resistance was hopeless and sounded the surrender. But it was too late. The Russians streamed through the fortress, slaughtering men, women, and children in the fury of battle. When Peter rode into the fortress after the storming, he found the streets running with blood, and Swedes and Livonians "butchered in heaps."[10] He ordered a trumpeter to sound the ceasefire throughout the town. But only with difficulty were the fighting and plundering stopped. Furious at this display of wanton destruction and insubordination, Peter himself decapitated one Russian soldier with his own sword for disobeying orders.

Peter at once sent for the enemy commandant, Horn. Angrily he demanded to know why he had not capitulated after the wall of the bastion had subsided; it had been clear then that further resistance was useless and would lead to unnecessary slaughter. He had Horn taken to the town prison and a few days later into Russia, where he remained a prisoner for fifteen years.[11]

The capture of Narva and Ivangorod was a victory of exceptional importance. Peter had not forgotten the beating he had received there four years earlier; he had now expunged the disgrace. During those four years he had welded his hordes of untrained peasants into an army: its infantry was, Ogilvie considered, better than German infantry, and inferior to none; he told Whitworth "that he never saw any nation go better to work with their cannons and mortars" than the Russians at Narva.[12] The capture of the fortress was also the climax of a series of victories, resulting in the occupation of the whole of Ingria and Livonia. Moreover, it strengthened the morale of Russian troops. They retained a special respect for Charles XII himself, but they no longer feared the Swedes in battle.

Peter celebrated the victory with gusto. He wrote immediately to tell Augustus II of this victory, "where four years ago our arms were disgraced," and sent letters, similarly worded, to Romodanovsky, Feodor Apraxin, to Stefan Yavorsky, and others. He was delighted to learn some eight days later from Romodanovsky and Streshnev, that the people of Moscow had celebrated the victory with great rejoicing, packing all the churches to give thanks in such crowds as Streshnev had never before seen.[13] When, four months later, Peter returned to Moscow, he marched with his army in a victory parade, grander than any before.

The year 1704 closed with good news from the south also. During his conquest of Ingria and Livonia, Peter had been anxiously studying reports from Turkey.[14] But on 10 December 1704 news came that put his fears at rest. "This minute," so he wrote to Menshikov, "we have received . . . from Peter Tolstoy, letters such as I had not expected; truly the hand of God lies over all."[15] Tolstoy's report was that the Ottoman Porte had decided to remain at peace with Russia.

CHAPTER XXV

Grodno

1705-1706

THE years 1705-1709 were for Peter the most critical of the Northern War. Instinctively he played for time and withdrew his army whenever head-on conflict threatened. But he knew he was merely delaying the fateful battle. Meanwhile discontent among his own people broke out in rebellion which exposed him to the danger of having to weaken his forces just at the time when the Swedes seemed about to invade. It was a period of strain for him, aggravated by bouts of illness which showed that even his tremendous strength was under severe pressure.

The chief source of Peter's tension and anxiety at this time was the unpredictability of his enemy, Charles XII. The Swedish generals themselves were bewildered by their young King, but, while he flouted their advice, his brilliance and speed of action brought him a succession of devastating victories, which added to his renown and his reputation for invincibility.

From defeating the Russians at Narva in November 1700, Charles had gone into winter quarters near Dorpat. Seven months later he had routed the Saxon army under Field-Marshal Steinau on the banks of the river Dvina. Next he had invaded Courland and then had moved into Lithuania, and from there had occupied Warsaw. After defeating Augustus's Saxon-Polish army at Klissow (1702), Charles had marched to Cracow, where Gyllenstjerna joined him with reinforcements, so that he then had an army of twenty-five thousand experienced well-equipped troops. In the spring of 1703 he yet again defeated the Saxon army under Steinau, this time at Pultusk, north of Warsaw. But then he spent the rest of the year laying siege to the fortress of Thorn. He took it in the end with the loss of only fifty men, but he had given both Peter and Augustus a further desperately needed respite.

While Charles was stubbornly besieging Thorn, Peter was completing the conquest of Ingria and founding St. Petersburg, and his army was growing in strength and confidence. Augustus, who had fled to Lublin after this defeat at Pultusk, desperately tried to win Polish support, but without success. His position was deteriorating so seriously that Peter sent Patkul to Poland to make a further attempt to persuade the Poles to declare war on Sweden.[1]

Patkul was soon immersed in negotiations. Several times the Poles reduced him to despair, but mainly through bribery he managed on 1 October 1703 to wring from the Grand Hetman, Prince Lyubomirsky, and from certain Polish magnates, an informal agreement to act against the Swedes. Nevertheless in January 1704 the Polish Diet, meeting in Warsaw on the orders of Charles and surrounded by Swedish troops, deposed Augustus and proclaimed an interregnum, and six months later formally elected Stanislas Leszczynski to the throne of Poland.

For over two years now the Poles had been maintaining the Swedish army and suffering the high-handed interference of Charles. The Lithuanians favoured alliance with Russia, and gradually the Poles, too, overcoming their Russophobia, began to accept this policy as unavoidable. In June 1703 ambassadors from Lithuania had made an informal agreement with Russia, binding their countrymen to fight to the death against Sweden, and in the following summer the Poles signed a formal alliance with the Tsar.

Peter now felt free to operate in Poland. He ordered Prince Repnin to advance with twelve regiments of cavalry and infantry across the Lithuanian frontier, where he was to co-operate with Augustus in harrying the Swedes, but he was not to take part in any major action. Peter then sent Sheremetev from Pskov into Courland to engage Lewenhaupt, who was rumoured to have an army of ten thousand men.

Charles was at this time in the south of Poland. Soon after the election of the new King of Poland, he had laid siege to Lemberg and, having taken it, had marched through the southern provinces. Meanwhile Augustus had captured Warsaw, where a Russian force of eleven infantry regiments together with Cossack auxiliaries and, soon afterwards, Field-Marshal Schulenburg with Saxon detachments, joined him. Augustus now had an army forty thousand strong, but, instead of keeping it together, he sent twelve thousand troops under Patkul to lay siege to Poznan, and the main army under Schulenburg to the Silesian frontier, while he himself with a small detachment moved to Cracow and thence to Dresden.

On learning of the capture of Warsaw, Charles had at once turned north, marching at a breakneck pace. He reoccupied the city, pursued the main Saxon army under Schulenburg, and routed it at Punitz in October 1704. With Poland once again completely in his grip, Charles then settled his troops in quarters along the Silesian frontier. He himself lived at Rawicz, where he remained for the winter and most of the following summer, menacing Saxony and cutting off Augustus from Poland.

Peter, after celebrating the capture of Narva, had spent a few weeks in Moscow and then had gone to Voronezh. Work in the shipyards there continued at full pressure, notwithstanding the fact that the Sultan had confirmed peace with Russia. Peter now decided to move his shipyards nearer to the Don and two miles from the mouth of the river Voronezh he laid the foundations of new shipyards and a fortress, to be called Tavrov.

While there Peter received a report that Charles was marching with his army into Lithuania. Alarmed by this news, he sent urgent instructions to his commanders, but then he learnt that the report was false. His fears quieted, he turned again to his plan of dividing his army, the cavalry under Sheremetev, and the infantry under Ogilvie, each to harry the Swedes in Courland and Lithuania. This reduction in his command hurt Sheremetev deeply. He complained to Menshikov, and wrote to Peter and to Feodor Golovin. "I have received your letter," Peter replied, "and from it see how distressed you are, for which I am indeed sorry, because it is unnecessary; this was done not in any way to cause you humiliation, but to provide more effective organization, about which your comrade [Menshikov] will report to you in greater detail. However, because of your distress I have called a halt to this reorganization and ordered the old arrangement to stand until I arrive."[2]

The army, which Peter joined at Polotsk at the end of May (1705) bore little resemblance to the hastily trained and equipped force that had laid siege to Narva five years earlier.[3] The infantry, forty thousand strong, and cavalry, twenty thousand strong, comprised in the main experienced troops, whose equipment was plentiful and up to date. The new foundries in the Urals and the expanded armament works at Tula had already begun to pour out small arms and artillery in impressive quantities and incorporating many new inventions. Peter had reorganized his grenadiers and seen to the mass production of grenades. The cavalry, which formerly had borne only sabres and pikes, was now armed with muskets, pistols, and broadswords. But the greatest change was in the artillery which was now standardized and becoming plentiful. He had also developed light artillery of three-pounders, which could more readily move up in support, and many of these light guns were already in service. Furthermore, by mounting his gunners he had made his artillery more mobile.

A new method of recruiting had been introduced in place of the ill-organized special levies of volunteers and serfs. In 1705, Peter insti-tuted a system of general levies, repeated annually until 1709, by which each estate or village provided one recruit for every twenty taxable households under its control. The recruits reported at muster-points in near-by towns in groups of five hundred to a thousand. They were quartered in barracks, where officers and sergeants in-valided from active service trained them. Peter had ordered that 168,000 men were to be enlisted in the first five general levies. Many defaulted, but the new rule that the estate or village responsible should replace any recruit who fled or was killed, reduced desertion considerably. Moreover, this system ensured that the army had re-serves of trained troops on which it could draw at short notice.

In a council of war Peter changed his mind about dividing the army into two parts, and decided to send Sheremetev with eleven regiments against Lewenhaupt who was now reported to be near Mitau. His orders were to cut Lewenhaupt's army off from Riga and destroy it, returning then to Grodno.[4] He himself prepared to march with the main army under Ogilvie's command to Vilno.

On the eve of his departure Peter visited a Polish monastery, not far from Polotsk, belonging to the Uniats. They formed a sect among the Orthodox, founded in 1596, and primarily the work of the Jesuits; the members retained much of their Orthodox rites and liturgy, but acknowledged the supremacy of the Pope. Peter's visit to this monastery was to prove an occasion of bitter memory. Showing his usual interest in other sects, he entered the church with a few companions. The Uniat priests behaved insultingly. He endured their hostility without comment. But, as he was leaving, he stopped in front of an image and asked who it was. "Our holy martyr, Josaphat, whom your fellow-believers—heretics, apostates, and tyrants all, just like yourself—murdered!" At this, Peter lost his temper, and ordered his suite to arrest the priests. They resisted and the Russians, drawing their swords, killed four of them; the fifth, a Russian subject, was sentenced to death and hanged the next day. The incident especially disturbed Peter because reports of it might inflame the Poles against the Russians at a time when his army was advancing into Poland. From Vilno, therefore, he issued a proclamation, explaining what had happened and stressing the provocation and disrespect shown by the priests.[5]

Peter had arrived in Vilno on 8 July, ahead of his army, and there he received bad news from Courland. Sheremetev had attacked Lewenhaupt's small army at Gemauerthof; the battle had proved obstinate and bloody, and in the end the Russians had fled, leaving behind all their artillery. Losses were heavy on both sides, and Lewenhaupt, finding himself too weak to hold Courland, had had to fall back to protect Riga.

News of this defeat angered Peter. "Min Her!" he wrote immediately to Sheremetev: "I have received your letter from which I have learnt of a certain unfortunate event; it was due to inadequate training of the dragoons, about which I have spoken many times!" He ordered Sheremetev to deal severely with those who had failed in their duty. Meanwhile Sheremetev was to remain at Birze and to obtain information on Lewenhaupt's movements.[6] Apparently, however, Peter felt that he had been too severe with his old general; three days later he wrote to him more gently. "Do not let yourself be too downcast over this past misfortune (for constant success has led many people to their ruin), but forget it and encourage your men."[7]

Peter's concern was still to cut Lewenhaupt off from Riga. He ordered Sheremetev to march westwards with all speed, and himself set out with the Preobrazhensky regiment and Repnin's corps in an attempt to outmarch Lewenhaupt. On 9 August, however, he learnt that the Swedes had already crossed the Dvina. He was disappointed, but ordered Sheremetev to take up positions on the left bank of the

river, opposite Riga. He himself laid siege to Mitau, which capitulated
on 4 September.

From Mitau, Menshikov went ahead to Vilno to accompany the
army under Ogilvie's command into winter quarters at Grodno. As
soon as he had ordered the defences of Mitau, Peter himself set out
for Grodno, and three weeks later Augustus joined him there. Encouraged by his ally's presence, and not expecting Charles to march
in the middle of winter, Peter entrusted his army to Augustus and,
departing on 7 December 1705, arrived in Moscow twelve days later.

Contrary to the rumours that had more than once disturbed Peter,
Charles had remained at Rawicz for most of the preceding summer.
There ambassadors from every part of Europe converged on his camp
with offers of alliance on terms that would enrich and strengthen
Sweden, but he waved them all aside. His immediate concern was the
coronation of his puppet, Stanislas, in Warsaw.

While preparations for this coronation were in progress, General
Paykul marched with an army of ten thousand Saxon and Russian
troops with the object of capturing Warsaw. This expedition was
simultaneous with Sheremetev's advance against Lewenhaupt in Courland, and it met with similar defeat. The Swedish general, Nieroth,
with a small force of two thousand men, boldly attacked Paykul's
army of ten thousand and routed it.

Annoyed by these attempts on Courland and Warsaw, and impatient at the delays in crowning Stanislas, Charles suddenly marched
from the Silesian border, leaving a small army under General Rehnskjold to hold the Saxons. At the beginning of August 1705, he
reached Blonie, four miles from Warsaw. He remained there for some
five months, and, after witnessing the coronation, he concluded a
close alliance with Stanislas against Russia and Saxony. Then, contrary to all Peter's expectations, he proclaimed a winter campaign.

Two weeks before Charles moved from Blonie, Menshikov wrote
to Peter that he had intelligence that the Swedes would march on
the Russian army. "From whom and can one believe it?" Peter replied sceptically on 23 December 1705. "How many reports of that
kind I have had!" But, if the intelligence was correct, Menshikov
was to arrange for special horses at each post-station, so that he could
join the army with all speed.[8] Menshikov's report was probably based
on rumour. Charles, deep in his usual reserve, had told no one of his
plans, and the Swedes themselves, as they crossed the Vistula, were

wondering whether they were marching against the Russians at Grodno, or against Little Russian forces at Lublin. When they advanced rapidly to the Western Bug River, however, they knew that Grodno was their goal.

Shortly after receiving Peter's letter, Menshikov wrote confirming that the Swedes were moving towards them, "but your Excellency should not be distressed; we are well prepared here. . . ." A few days later, Ogilvie wrote in the same confident mood.[9] Nevertheless, the news disturbed Peter; he was unsure of his army and its commanders; he also stood in awe of Charles. He replied at once to Menshikov, telling him to persuade Augustus to send a Saxon army against Rehnskjold, as a diversion. He himself would leave Moscow next day and join the army within a week. Before setting out he wrote again to warn them to take care that the Swedes did not cut off their retreat to the Russian frontier, and to stress that they must retire in good time. He was in poor health, troubled by a painful swelling on his right cheek. It was a cruel winter and his spirits were low. He wrote again to Menshikov on 12 January, telling him to set out and meet him on the road.[10]

The Swedes were already nearing Grodno, when Peter left Moscow. Charles had marched from the Vistula to the Niemen in two weeks, his troops performing amazing feats of endurance. The Russians did not believe it possible for them to move so rapidly in such weather, and took the Swedish army to be an advance party.[11] Menshikov wrote to Peter that Charles's route lay towards Minsk, but the next day he reported that the enemy was actually only three miles from Grodno.[12] It must have been soon after writing this letter that Menshikov, without a word to Ogilvie, his commander-in-chief, slipped out of Grodno and rode westwards to meet the Tsar.

Some three days before this, Augustus had called a council of war to consider what action should be taken. All except Ogilvie favoured retreat to Polotsk. Augustus sent an account of their deliberations by special messenger to Peter with the request that he should make "an immediate, categoric, and definite decision." Menshikov also wrote, doing all he could to undermine the authority of Ogilvie: "in truth, he is more of an opponent than a well-wisher" was his conclusion.[13] Peter was already suspicious of Ogilvie, and he heeded Menshikov's comments. But there can be little doubt that in delaying the retreat from Grodno, Ogilvie saved the Russian army from a major engagement in which it would probably have suffered defeat. On 13 January 1706, Charles came in sight of Grodno. He crossed the Nieman but, recognizing that he could not take the fortress, retreated to positions four miles to the north. Lack of provisions and fodder forced him to retreat further. Augustus seized the opportunity to get away from Grodno and, leaving Ogilvie in command, he hastened with four dragoon regiments to Warsaw. His plan was to meet the Saxon army, already marching against Rehnskjold, and to lead it to Grodno. Meanwhile the Swedes moved on in search of food and fodder, and finally camped at Zheludok, nearly fifty miles away.

Peter had travelled sixty miles beyond Smolensk before he learnt of the arrival of the Swedes. The news shocked him, and he was relieved to meet Menshikov at the village of Dubrovna. But he was anxious about his army and, during the following two months, he sent a stream of orders to Ogilvie to retreat to the Russian frontier. He constantly stressed that the one consideration was to save the army; nothing else mattered; if the artillery was a hindrance, they should throw the guns into the Niemen.[14] Ogilvie was obstinate and querulous, demanding several hundred camels and a force of twenty thousand well-equipped courtiers.[15] He was confident that the Saxon army, some thirty thousand strong, would defeat General Rehnskjold's force of eight thousand, and march to relieve them in Grodno. But at the beginning of March came news of Schulenburg's disastrous defeat at Fraustadt. Peter, infuriated by this Saxon failure,[16] sent new and categoric orders to Ogilvie to retreat immediately.[17] Reluctantly Ogilvie obeyed and at midnight on 24 March the Russians moved from Grodno. The bridge over the Niemen held and they retreated rapidly to Sokolka, where Menshikov met them.

Near Zheludok, Charles had built a bridge over the Niemen and was ready to hurl his army after the Russians the moment they left their fortified positions. But the breaking of the ice upset his plans. Heavy floes carried away his bridge. By the time it had been rebuilt, the Russian army was at Brest. Charles still hoped to overtake it. His troops marched with amazing speed, enduring terrible hardships as they plunged into the Polyese, a swampy region, made even more treacherous by the first thawing of spring. Charles reached Pinsk before he finally called off the chase.

From Brest, Menshikov had written to Peter that the army was retreating according to plan, and that they had no news of the

Swedes. His next letter, written on 17 April from Kolki on the river
Styr, confirmed that the army was in good heart and that they still
had no news of the enemy. "I have no doubt that your Excellency
will wish to join us, therefore when you are preparing to set out,
kindly order our girls to go to Smolensk," he added in a postscript,
referring to Catherine and to his wife, Darya. "Our route lies towards
Kiev, and from there, if the enemy does not come after us, we will
move to Bykhov so as to take up quarters between Kiev and
Smolensk."[18]

Peter was relieved and excited to learn that his army was safe. "*Min
Bruder!*" he replied to Menshikov on 29 April from St. Petersburg.
"With indescribable joy I received the old man from you with letters,
being then with the fleet at Kronslot on board the Vice-Admiral's
ship, *The Elephant* (*sic*) and that very minute, thanks be to God,
the whole fleet and the fortress fired three salvoes! And how joyful
we were at this news and then how noisy, the old man himself will
tell you. . . . We will set out from here in the coming month; kindly
let us know where to meet you."[19] But Peter did not set out in the
following month. Illness delayed him. His doctors bled him and prescribed a course of medicine lasting two weeks.[20]

Thus it was not until 16 June 1706 that he reached Smolensk,
where Menshikov met him. He went on to Kiev and there he remained for over a month and a half, daily expecting the Swedes
to invade.

Throughout these months when he was worrying over the survival
of his army at Grodno, Peter had yet another anxiety on his mind,
and one which might have developed into a danger as great as
Charles XII and his army. This new threat was the outbreak of rebellion in Astrakhan at the mouth of the Volga River. It had broken out
in July 1705 as a protest against Western innovations, the burden of
taxes, and against the extortions of their voevod. Apart from the local
streltsi regiments, many streltsi from the disbanded Moscow regiments had been sent to Astrakhan. Old Believers had also gathered
there in large numbers. Simple, fanatical people, they were united in
their horror of the Tsar's ukazi, and all were oppressed by the heavy
taxes and state monopolies. Rumours circulated that the Tsar was
dead and that their voevod and other officials had rejected the Christian faith. Then another rumour started that no marriages would take
place for seven years, because all their maidens were wanted for the

foreigners. Horrified, the people rushed to marry off their daughters and sisters among the local men. On one day, 30 July 1705, a hundred weddings took place in Astrakhan: on that day the revolt started. Drunk from celebrating, some three hundred rebels surged through the town, murdering officials and raiding government offices. On the following day they elected a leader, in Cossack fashion, and swore to resist to the end.

Although Astrakhan was more than a thousand miles away from the Polish lands, where his army was operating, Peter did not for a moment underestimate the seriousness of this outbreak. He knew well that it could spread to Azov and to the Cossacks of the Don and the Terek, and then sweep northwards to Moscow. The news from Astrakhan had reached him as he was planning to drive the Swedes from Courland. He at once put these plans aside, and sent Sheremetev with troops to quell the rebellion. So great was his alarm that he even wrote to Streshnev in Moscow, telling him to hide or send away to safety all state money and treasure, and to Feodor Apraxin, instructing him to defend Azov and Taganrog, and to watch the Don Cossacks.[21]

By the time his army had extricated itself from Grodno and reached the safety of Kiev, however, news had come from Astrakhan that the rebellion had collapsed. Peter was further surprised and relieved to learn that the Cossacks of the Don and the Terek had refused to join the rebels. Bearing in mind his desperate need for peace in the south at this time, he pardoned the rebels and hoped to hear no more of them.

Meanwhile Sheremetev had been complaining strongly about being sent to Astrakhan, and wrote asking permission to return to Moscow. Peter not only refused his request, but sent him new orders,[22] and Sergeant Shchepotev on the Tsar's special instructions, remained with Field-Marshal Sheremetev to see that they were obeyed. As he drew nearer to Astrakhan, Sheremetev learnt that rebellion had broken out afresh. He pressed forward and on 13 March 1706, after a brief exchange of fire, took the town by force, and put down the rising.

At this time, too, Peter had been concerned about Patkul. In October 1704 Augustus had sent him with nine Russian regiments, supported by Polish and Saxon cavalry, to take Poznan, and Patkul had been on the point of storming the fortress when he received orders to retreat with all speed, because Charles was approaching. He at once

sent the cavalry to join Augustus, and himself fell back with his Russian infantry across the Oder into Saxony.

Patkul then found himself with the Russian regiments on his own
hands. The Saxon ministers refused all responsibility, although, after
their hurried withdrawal, the Russians were in an appalling condition,
and threatened with starvation during the oncoming winter. Patkul
was indefatigable on their behalf. He wrote to the Tsar, to Feodor
Golovin, and to Menshikov for money and instructions, but they only
replied that he should march the troops from Saxony into Russia, and
this was impossible because they could not cross Poland, occupied
by the Swedes. To ensure their winter quarters and food, he then
asked permission to hire them to the Austrian government. Feodor
Golovin replied that the Tsar gave his approval, if it was a matter of
extreme necessity.[23] On 4 December (1705) Patkul made an agreement with the Imperial ambassador in Dresden, Count Straatman,
to transfer the Russian troops to the Emperor for one year.[24]

This agreement caused alarm among the Saxon ministers who
feared the anger of both the King and the Tsar. Their hostility
towards Patkul was of long standing, dating from the time when he
had been in the Saxon service and had been devastatingly outspoken
in his criticisms of the inefficiency and dishonesty of all at Augustus'
court. Their hatred of Patkul now became intense. Finally they decided that, acting on their own authority, they would arrest him, and
on 8 December 1705 he was taken into custody, handed over to the
governor of Sonnenstein castle, and assigned to his cell.[25]

The arrest of Patkul had caused a sensation not only in Saxony, but
also in the rest of Europe. In Dresden, the Danish and Imperial ambassadors protested strongly. The Imperial ambassador, Count Straatman, wrote the Tsar that he had seen Patkul's authorization to transfer the Russian troops, on whom the Emperor was counting.[26] Prince
Dmitri Golitsyn made an even stronger protest at this affront to his
Tsarish Majesty, and added that the ministers would be held responsible for all the consequences of what they had done. Alarmed at the
outcry and fearful that they had gone too far, the Saxon ministers reported to their King. From Grodno, Augustus sent word that he
approved their action.

Augustus had now turned against Patkul, and was determined to
ruin him. He wrote briefly to the Tsar that, to avoid damage to their
joint interests, his privy council had been forced to arrest Patkul. He

added that his chamberlain, Von Schonbek, would give a full account of Patkul's misdeeds.[27] The task of drafting this indictment fell to the King's Adjutant-General, Arnstedt, who did it with great reluctance and, despite the risks to himself and his family, wrote secretly to Shafirov in Moscow: "I am doing everything to save him. You must work to the same end. We must not and cannot allow such a fine man to perish. . . ."[28]

On receiving Straatman's letter, Peter wrote to Augustus requesting an early explanation.[29] Two days later, Von Schonbek reached Moscow and delivered the indictment. Nevertheless, Peter wrote again to Augustus, formally asking him to have Patkul with all his papers sent to Moscow so that the charges against him could be investigated.[30] But Peter was inclined to accept the Saxon allegations, and considered that Patkul had exceeded his authority in arranging, without further orders, to transfer the Russian troops to the Imperial government.[31] Meantime Patkul, imprisoned in Sonnenstein castle, could not defend himself. Finally he managed to write to the Tsar and in his letter, running into many pages, he answered in detail the charges made against him, and protested his innocence.[32]

It was the last letter that Patkul was to write to the Tsar or to his ministers. Peter received it at Orsha in February 1706, and wrote again to Augustus, stating that he had had no reply to his two letters, and demanding the return of Patkul.[33] Delays and evasions by the Saxons followed. He renewed his demands in March and again in August (1706) without result. Patkul was never to regain his freedom.

In Kiev, Field-Marshal Ogilvie received his release from the Russian service. He had asked to be allowed to retire on grounds of health, but he knew that he did not have the confidence of the Tsar, and the antagonism between Menshikov and himself had come to a head. Menshikov took a delight in thwarting and defying the old Field-Marshal, who wrote that "in all the years that I have served, never and nowhere have I been treated so badly as here."[34] He received his full salary, with which he expressed himself satisfied, and went to Saxony where he entered the service of Augustus.

Peter waited in vain at Kiev for Swedish invasion. Charles stayed at Pinsk for two months, destroying towns and villages in what was a region of Augustus' supporters. He then advanced into Volhynia, where he allowed his men three weeks rest before turning westwards and into Saxony. The Northern War dragged on.

CHAPTER XXVI

The Treaty of Altranstadt

1706-1707

THE approach of the Swedish army spread terror among the Saxons. Many fled over the frontier to seek refuge in the neighbouring states. But their panic was unnecessary. Charles marched into Saxony with the sole purpose of compelling Augustus to renounce the Polish throne, and in this he was so successful that he had no need to resort to arms.

From Cracow, where he had retreated after learning of the defeat of his army at Punitz, Augustus had moved with his small force into Lithuania. Here he received news of Charles's invasion of his hereditary electorate and his first thought was to come to terms. Secretly he sent two representatives, his secretary, Pfingsten, and Count Imhof, to the Swedish camp with proposals for peace on the basis of dividing Poland equally between Stanislas and himself. But Charles would not consider such terms. He ordered Count Piper, his chief minister, to lay down as his immutable conditions that Augustus should renounce the Polish throne for all time, denounce treaties of alliance directed against Sweden, and especially his alliance with the Tsar, and that he would surrender all Swedish traitors in his service, and in particular Patkul. They were humiliating terms, but Pfingsten and Imhof, knowing the temper of their King, accepted them.

Six weeks later, on 13 October 1706, at Altranstadt, where Charles had moved with his army, the peace treaty, incorporating these and other conditions, was signed in strict secrecy.[1] On the following day Charles sent trumpeters and drummers through the country to pro-

246

claim an armistice of ten weeks, but making no mention of the peace just negotiated. On the same day Pfingsten set out with the original treaty to obtain Augustus' confirmation.

Charles's camp had again become a centre of diplomatic activity. The Queen of England, the Emperor, and the Kings of Denmark and Prussia, had sent special ambassadors. Most came with offers to mediate between Charles and Augustus, and with expressions of readiness to recognize Stanislas as King of Poland. All had pressing orders to obtain information about the King's intentions.[2]

At Kiev, Peter had been greatly relieved to learn in August that Charles was again marching westwards. It gave him yet another respite, and he took full advantage of it. He sent Menshikov with a strong force into Poland to support Augustus and to harry the Swedes. He himself marched northwards into Karelia, intending to take Vyborg. He had no suspicions of Augustus' urgent efforts to come to terms with the enemy.

Before marching from Kiev, however, Peter was grieved to learn of the death of Admiral Count Feodor Golovin.[3] As Admiral, second ambassador in the Grand Embassy, and as head of the Foreign Office, Golovin had been one of his most able and dependable lieutenants. He had also been well liked by Russians and foreigners. Whitworth had written that he "indeed passes for the fairest as well as the most understanding man in all the country, and has always shown himself a particular friend to the English nation."[4] Feodor Apraxin was proclaimed Admiral in succession to Golovin, while Gavril Ivanovich Golovkin became head of the Foreign Office. But the pillar of the Foreign Office under Golovin and now under Golovkin was Peter Shafirov, a humble Jew from the Smolensk region, whom Peter had come across in Moscow and had promoted because of his intelligence and knowledge of languages.

It was late autumn, when Peter approached Vyborg with a small force. He found that Swedish infantry had manned two trenches in front of the town, and ejected them. Peter then marched on the town, and here he had his first disappointment. He found to his surprise that a canal surrounded it, and that without boats he could not attempt to take it by storm.[5]

In writing to Menshikov about this obstacle, he sent an account of a daring raid. His favourite sergeant, Shchepotev, had led a party in five boats to attack two Swedish sloops, which had been detached from the Swedish fleet to help in the defence of Vyborg. It was a highly successful action, but Shchepotev lost his life, and this distressed Peter deeply. He had his body taken to St. Petersburg, and buried with naval ceremony. For some weeks Peter, who had remained at Vyborg, was inconsolable, until Menshikov, Sheremetev, Golovkin, and Grigory Dolgoruky, joined in reminding him that war had always brought such sorrows, and that brooding on them served no purpose.[6] But when the town gave no sign of surrendering, he apparently lost heart, for he raised the siege and returned to St. Petersburg.

Meanwhile Menshikov had advanced from Kiev into Volhynia, and at the beginning of September, with a strong force of dragoons and infantry, he moved in the direction of Poznan. His objective was to destroy the force of eight thousand Swedes whom Charles had left under the command of General Mardefeld to maintain order in Poland. Peter had not anticipated that Menshikov would advance so rapidly and so far into Poland. On 22 September he had written warning him to be on guard against the enemy cutting him off from the Russian frontier.[7] But Menshikov did not share this cautious mood. At Lublin, Augustus joined him. He inspected the Russian troops and seemed satisfied, although Menshikov noted that he was less hearty than usual. But neither Peter nor Menshikov, although they both knew now of the armistice proclaimed by Charles, entertained doubts about Augustus' good faith.[8]

Augustus was caught in the web of his own duplicity. He dared not let Menshikov know he was now awaiting Charles's reply to his peace proposals. Meanwhile he was advancing with Menshikov to attack the Swedish troops under Mardefeld. At Pyotrkov, where Augustus arrived on 6 October, Pfingsten appeared and secretly reported Charles's terms. He at once sent Pfingsten back to Saxony to confirm that he would honour them in full. Augustus was afraid to divulge to the Russians that he had broken his agreement. It was not only a matter of fear, however, for he also clung to the hope that by some twist of fortune he would be able to maintain his alliance with Peter and to ignore the undertakings he had given to Charles. Meanwhile he had tried to extricate himself from his difficulties by sending messages to Mardefeld, advising him to retreat and to avoid battle. Knowing nothing of Augustus' peace with his King, Mardefeld merely dismissed his advice as a trick.

Menshikov, ignorant of these intrigues, was now advancing rapidly, eager to attack. On 18 October 1706, the two armies joined battle near Kalicz and, after three hours of bitter fighting, the Russians inflicted a decisive defeat on the Swedes, taking 1,760 prisoners, including Mardefeld himself and six colonels.[9]

The battle of Kalicz was the most complete victory that the Russians had yet won against Swedish troops. They had had a numerical advantage of more than two to one, but the Swedes had usually been successful against much greater odds, not only of Russian but also of Saxon and of Polish troops. For Menshikov, it was a special triumph; he had justified his first independent command as a general. He sent a despatch to Peter from the battlefield and, although it was a factual and soldierly report, it rang with pride and excitement. Peter received the news in the same spirit. He replied immediately "with indescribable joy" to congratulate Menshikov and his officers and men, and told of the numerous salutes and celebrations in their honour in St. Petersburg.[10]

On the day after the battle, Menshikov found himself involved in a dispute over his prisoners. Augustus demanded that all Swedish prisoners should be given up to him. Under pressure Menshikov yielded, subject to Augustus signing a declaration that he would within three months obtain the release of all the Russian officers in Stockholm in exchange for the Swedish prisoners taken at Kalicz. Augustus readily signed the declaration, and having obtained the prisoners, he released them all on parole into Swedish Pomerania.

From Kalicz, Augustus went to Warsaw. For the moment he apparently thought of continuing the war against Charles. But his fears for the safety of his electorate prevailed. From Warsaw, he wrote a letter to Pfingsten to be shown to Charles; in it he expressed his abject regret over the battle of Kalicz, and declared his readiness to make amends to the King of Sweden in any way that he thought fit. His letter was timely, for Charles was on the point of tearing up the new peace treaty and devastating Saxony. Augustus' protestations and apologies calmed his anger. Having received these assurances of good faith, Charles no longer delayed the announcement of the peace. On 15 November, 1706, the Treaty of Altranstadt was proclaimed.[11]

Early in December Peter left St. Petersburg for Narva, intending to travel from there to Moscow. But in Narva he received word from

Menshikov of Augustus' separate peace, and he at once turned southwards. Menshikov was now at Zholkva near Lvov, where he had retired from Kalicz. Sheremetev, Golovkin, and other Russian ministers
had also arrived there and all wrote pressing the Tsar to join them.[12]
Already many Polish magnates and churchmen had gathered in
Zholkva, and at a special meeting they had sworn to maintain the
alliance with Russia, and declared their wish to elect a new king in
succession to Augustus. Peter hurried southwards and on 28 December
reached Zholkva.

The news of the Treaty of Altranstadt sent a shock of amazement
through the courts of Europe. All recognized it as a crowning success
for Charles and a final humiliation for Augustus. But clause 11 in the
treaty aroused disgust. By it Augustus bound himself to deliver to
Charles all Swedish deserters and traitors in Saxony, and particularly
Johan Reinhold Patkul. Augustus honoured this undertaking, thus
displaying a degree of treachery equalled only by the vindictiveness
and inhumanity of Charles himself.

At the beginning of February 1707, Augustus sent Major General
Goltz[13] as special envoy to Peter to assure him of his continued friendship despite his treaty with Charles. Also, Goltz reported Augustus'
promise that Patkul would never be handed over to the Swedes.[14]
Peter did not believe these assurances. He himself sent notes to the
Emperor Joseph, to Frederick I of Prussia, to Frederick IV of Denmark, and to the Netherlands States-General in which he stated: "We
trust that the Swedish King will willingly yield to the intercession of
Your Majesty, and that in doing this he may gain before the whole
world the reputation of a great-hearted monarch, and not be partner
in a godless and barbarian business."[15] He also appealed to the foreign
ambassadors in Moscow, and especially to Whitworth, to entreat
their governments to use their influence with the King of Sweden
on Patkul's behalf.[16]

Nevertheless on 28 March, Patkul was handed over to General
Meyerfeld, who took him under strong guard to Altranstadt.[17] He
was kept there for three months, fastened to a stake by a heavy iron
chain. Finally, he was taken to Casimir, where in October 1707 a
court-martial, instructed by Charles to apply extreme severity, condemned him to be broken alive on the wheel and his body quartered.
The Swedes carried out this sentence with the utmost brutality.
Patkul's sufferings were such that he could only moan for them to

cut off his head. His arms and legs had been broken on the wheel, but when the final punishment was inflicted the executioner was inexperienced, and only after four blows with the axe did he manage to sever the condemned man's neck. Patkul's body was then quartered, and displayed on posts for all to see.

It was a cruel and tragic end to a remarkable man. Of obscure origins, he had risen by his own energy and ability to a position of such influence that kings and chancellors heard him with respect. He had taken the lead in forming the alliance and launching the war that transformed northern Europe. He was executed on a charge of high treason, and no doubt technically he was a Swedish citizen, but it was no more than a technicality. He had in fact fought against injustice and treachery suffered by himself and his fellow Livonians at the hands of the Swedish crown. He had devoted himself to breaking the might of Sweden, serving first the King of Poland and then the Tsar of Russia to further this aim. Had he escaped to live three years longer, he would have witnessed the achievement of his ambition.

CHAPTER XXVII

Discontent and Rebellion

1707-1708

SINCE his return from the West, Peter had created a new army and some of the light and heavy industries needed to equip it; he had captured the Baltic lands, founded St. Petersburg, and moved his army into Poland to support Augustus; he had built up his navy in Voronezh and laid the foundations of a new Baltic navy; he had begun to uncover and develop the vast mineral resources of his tsardom; he had continued his assault on the stubborn conservatism of old Muscovy, and launched reforms in the church and other fields. But activities on such a scale involve heavy cost and sacrifice.

The burden fell on the Russian people and, most heavily, on the peasantry. They were recruited in thousands into the army and as labourers. Sickness, famine, and the wastage of war killed off many. Those who survived had to face new taxes and other impositions, all gathered by those officials who permeated their lives. The patient endurance of the Russians was all the more heroic because at the same time they had to suffer the assaults of their Tsar on the old Muscovy in which they believed, and to bear his innovations which they hated as things new and heretical. Fantastic rumours circulated, and the simple peasants accepted them as the only explanations of the flood of misery, labour, and change that overwhelmed them. Discontent mounted. Many fled southwards to the no-man's-land of the Don and the Volga, yet even here the Tsar pursued them.

This discontent formed the background to Peter's work. The reports of secret police made him fully aware of his people's mood and complaints, and he made some attempts to better conditions, and counter foreign criticisms. In 1705, for example, he issued the first of a number of ukazi, designed to improve Moscow by paving and tidying the streets. He built a large hospital on the banks of the Yauza River in the following year to train Russian doctors as well as to care for the sick. Hordes of professional beggars besieged the traveller on every road to Moscow and at every church, and he tried to reduce their numbers by compelling them to go to almshouses to which he made grants from excess church revenues. In many other ways he showed concern for the burdens of his people. At the same time, he considered that only by creating a new Russia could they ultimately enjoy real amelioration of their hardships. Meanwhile he would allow nothing to hinder the policy of building and reform; everyone had to labour as he himself, their Tsar, laboured. Capable of kindness and understanding towards individuals, he was at times an inhuman force in dealing with his people. As the Northern War neared its most critical stage, and Charles was marching against him, the discontent broke out in a great rebellion, not in Russia itself, but in those Cossack lands, which were the traditional refuge of the oppressed, the desperate, and the untamable.

The Tsar demanded labour in a way that Russians had never before known. The army had priority. It had taken over three hundred thousand men in the first nine years of the Northern War. But desertion constantly threatened to undermine it. Out of the thirty thousand Russian dragoons in Poland, no less than fourteen thousand deserted; of eleven infantry regiments posted in Moscow to defend the city against Swedish attack, each regiment had lost two hundred or more men within two months of arriving; seven hundred men from one dragoon regiment fled during a march from Moscow to St. Petersburg. Though discipline was harsh, mass desertions persisted.

It was not only the army that consumed men. The fortifications of Azov and the naval base at Taganrog required over thirty thousand labourers in each of the three years from 1704 to 1706, and, although little more than half this number actually reported, it was still a serious drain on the districts from which they were levied. When Captain Perry was working on the Volga-Don canal, he complained that he had in the first two years only ten thousand workmen at his disposal, although he had asked for thirty thousand in each year. The new canals and the shipyards at Voronezh and on the Baltic also made heavy demands. St. Petersburg was soon to outdo the other projects in its consumption of men. Peter spared neither money nor men in building his city. In November 1706 he was writing to Streshnev to send fifteen thousand men in April-May-June, 1707, and a further fifteen thousand in July-August-September 1707; this was but one of a long series of such demands.[1] The city with its unhealthy climate and grim working conditions began to resemble an enormous graveyard.

A shortage of manpower soon made itself felt, and Peter was driven to take special measures. He decreed in 1701 that insolvent debtors should not in future be handed over to work for their creditors, but should be sent with their families to live permanently in Azov. Two years later, he decreed that only treason, murder, rebellion, and poisoning should be punished by death; the punishment for other crimes should be exile to Azov, not to Siberia. When he heard that in Bryansk the number of clerks and deacons employed had greatly increased, he promptly ordered that all who were suitable should be enlisted for the army.[2] But these and other measures did little towards solving the problem, which was a result not only of constant recruiting, but also of flight.

The one escape for the peasants from toil, from the tax-gatherer, and from the recruiting officer was in flight. The Russian peasant had a strong instinctive urge to wander, and to seek for new lands and freedom farther on. The great underpopulated expanse of Russia offered full scope for the colonizer and the wanderer, but this had made the labour force highly instable, and successive governments had passed measures tying the peasants to the soil which they worked. Persistently they sought to escape. Penalties were savage and runaways were hunted mercilessly, but still they fled in hundreds. In 1699, 330 families vanished from one Voronezh district. Villages in other parts of Russia fell deserted as peasants made their way southwards. Voevodi reported, and landowners petitioned, that they could not meet the Tsar's requisitions because their men had fled. Ukazi went out to the Cossack atamani, to voevodi in Little Russia, and to officials everywhere ordering them to seek out the runaways and return them. But the ukazi had small effect.

The Tsar's demands for money were equally insatiable. The cumbersome and inefficient Muscovite bureaucracy and the large-scale peculation of officials dissipated much of the national revenue before it even reached the Treasury. Peter had reorganized local government and finance in 1699 and his measures had produced some good results. But the national revenue was now wholly inadequate. The long war, his vast undertakings, grants to his allies, and the high cost of Russia's new diplomatic representation abroad had multiplied expenditure. Desperately he cast about for new sources of revenue. He had created "the profit-makers" (*pribylshchiki*) to help him in this task. Working side by side with them now were the "informers" or "reporters" (*donositeli*), whose function it was to submit proposals for improvements, changes and new projects, concerning everything which they considered worthy of the Tsar's attention. Peter paid close attention to their proposals and they were largely responsible for the plague of imposts that harried the people.

Some thirty new taxes were introduced, which bear witness to the ingenuity of Kurbatov and his colleagues. Taxes were imposed on leather and tanning, on baths, mills, lodging-houses, on drinking water, stovepipes, firewood, caps and boots, on the fares of cabmen, on the sale of provisions, on melons, cucumbers and nuts, on births and marriages, but not on deaths. They were, in fact, petty measures, invented by officials with more zeal than good sense; they added little to the national revenue but they seriously aggravated popular discontent. Gradually, as their yields fell, many of them lapsed, but the resentment lingered.

State monopolies were another source of revenue which aroused anger. Monopolies had long existed on such products as alcohol, resin, potash, and rhubarb. To these were added monopolies on tobacco, chalk, pitch, oak coffins, and salt, as well as on chessmen, playing cards, and other means of popular entertainment. The solid oak coffin, which was the last luxury of every aged Muscovite of substance, was taken over from the merchants, and sold by the state for four times the former price; when stocks of these coffins were consumed, the further use of oak for this purpose was forbidden. The salt monopoly, established by ukaz in 1705, was badly administered and particularly iniquitous. Many peasants, forced to eat without salt, fell ill and died.

The shaving of beards and wearing of Western dress continued to distress the people, but Peter persisted with both reforms. The ukaz of January 1700, forbidding old Muscovite dress, had at first been enforced strictly, and no one dared risk being seen by the Tsar in the familiar clothes. But the Northern War and other matters had come to absorb his attention, and gradually people reverted to the old costume. Kurbatov urged Peter to repeat the regulations, and a new ukaz was proclaimed. Anyone wearing long robes when passing into Moscow or other towns, was fined and had to kneel while his coat was cut even with the ground.[3] But this applied to the wealthier people. The peasants could not afford the new clothes, which they abhorred, and they clung to their old costume.

Already in 1700-1701 Peter had launched major reforms in the church. Further ukazi had applied them more rigorously. Some order was reappearing in the church's civil affairs; the Tsar's Treasury was benefiting from its excess revenues; the number seeking refuge in monasteries from military and labour service was falling. At the same time the Little Russian prelates were active in combating illiteracy and ignorance. The Great Russian clergy seethed with discontent, but without a patriarch and divided among themselves they could do nothing.

The people murmured, but they did not rebel. The innumerable complaints of landowners and voevodi about the flight of peasants made it seem that Russia had become a desert. In fact, the great majority stayed, served and laboured, and the tremendous impetus given by Peter to the reform movement carried them along with it. Their sufferings and discontent were heavy, but not enough to make them revolt. The habit of obedience to the Tsar was deeply rooted. Moreover, he had strong men and his guards regiments to support him, while they lacked a leader and a rallying point. But they found relief in complaining. Even in this they had to take care. The Secret Office of Preobrazhenskoe had its agents everywhere, watching, listening, and reporting.

The Secret Office was in part a new institution, and in part a successor to the Streltsi Office. The streltsi had maintained order in Moscow and, when Peter disbanded them, the Preobrazhensky guards regiment had taken over their police duties. The guards arrested robbers, drunkards, and anyone disturbing the peace. Gradually their responsibilities expanded to include all crime. In October 1702, an ukaz formalized the position, giving the Preobrazhensky Office jurisdiction in cases of treason, of "Word and Deed."[4] But the most important department of the office was the secret police, a sinister force with agents everywhere. Tsar Alexei and his predecessors had employed secret agents, but had not set up a special office or department. The Secret Office of Preobrazhenskoe was apparently the first organized secret police force in Russia.[5]

Romodanovsky, Peter's old colleague and "*Min her Kenich*," had charge of the Secret Office, and it was a sound appointment. He was a savage, drunken creature, but devoted to the Tsar. He could be trusted to deal with criminals and to investigate any suggestion of rebellion. The archives of the Secret Office of Preobrazhenskoe reveal only a few examples of treason,[6] but many innocent people were investigated under torture because of what proved to be a chance or distorted remark, or because they gave vent incautiously to their misery.

Complaints against the Tsar, embroidered with rumours and fantastic predictions, became frequent. "Since God sent him to be Tsar," the peasants muttered, "we have seen no bright days—the village is burdened with paying rubles and half rubles and with providing horses and carts; rest for us peasants, there is none."[7] The son of a boyar cried out, "What kind of a Tsar is he? He has dragged us all into the army, and taken away our people and peasants for recruits—nowhere will you escape him. Everything has been sold off, and he himself serves, and yet no one kills him; if someone should kill him, the service would cease, and it would be easier for the common people."[8] Peasant women and wives of soldiers wailed, "What kind of Tsar is he? He has destroyed the peasants, taken our husbands for soldiers, and he has made orphans of us and our children, and left us to weep for ever."[9] A serf foretold that "if he lives long, he will ruin all of us; I am full of surprise that they have not done away with him; he rides early and late at night, with few people or alone. . . . What kind of Tsar is he? He's the enemy of the peasants. He rides so often about Moscow, may he lose his head!"[10] Monks and priests complained and a beggar said, "The foreigners deceived him; a good hour comes—all is well, but the next hour comes—there is wailing and weeping, and now he has already attacked God—he has taken the bells from the churches!"[11] Another said, "Blood-sucker! He has eaten up the world!"[12]

The Secret Office recorded hundreds of complaints of this kind, expressing the widespread misery, and revealing the new popular attitude towards the Tsar. The old tsars had been godlike men, who appeared in dazzling raiment to the people on ceremonial occasions. They had been revered as beneficent figures aloof from the turmoil and hardship of their subjects' lives, but rulers whom those subjects could petition for justice and mercy. The reproaches of the Russian people had been directed previously at the boyars, rarely at the Tsar himself. But Peter had now destroyed this popular ideal. He appeared beardless, he dressed as a mere ship's captain, or, worse, as a bombardier, or a shipwright from the West, axe in hand, or smoking a pipe, as he mingled with the hated foreigners. No longer could they blame his ministers for their hardships, when they saw Peter himself giving orders and directing labour, examining recruits, and working as a shipwright. But still they were reluctant to abandon the old and popular ideal, which, like Orthodoxy, had always in the past given some comfort and stability to their meagre lives. They invented fables and fairy tales to explain away this new phenomenon. They asked: "Is this truly the Tsar?" and, if he was, why had he fallen under the spell of the foreigners?

The simple peasant women muttered among themselves that he was the bastard son of a foreign woman, substituted for the girl whom Tsaritsa Natalya had borne, because Tsar Alexei wanted a son. "He orders the wearing of foreign clothes—it's clear then that he was born a foreigner," they said.[13] The variation of this was that Peter was the son of a strelets or of Franz Lefort. The popular legends became more fantastic. It was noted that his spate of reforms had begun on his return from abroad; it meant, they said, that the Tsar himself had not returned. The foreigners had killed the true Tsar and sent back a foreigner to Muscovy to make apostates of them all.

More serious were the tales of the Antichrist. At the time of the schism, fanatic Old Believers had denounced, first, Patriarch Nikon, and then Tsar Alexei, as the Antichrist. But it was now clear to them that Peter was the real Antichrist. In June 1700 information was laid at the Secret Office, concerning a writer, called Grishka Talitsky, who was carving boards from which to print pamphlets for distribution among the people. Under torture Talitsky confessed that he had written in a letter that the end of the world was at hand, and that the Antichrist, meaning Peter, had come. Further, he had discussed the question of the Antichrist with Ignatyev, Bishop of Tambov, who sent him five rubles and instructed him to write it all down. Talitsky then implicated Boyar Prince Ivan Khovansky. Others gave evidence that Talitsky had threatened that he would raise a great popular rebellion in Moscow.[14]

The evidence was voluminous, and as a result of the investigation Talitsky and five fellow conspirators were executed; others were knouted and sent to Siberia; the Bishop of Tambov was unfrocked and imprisoned, and Prince Khovansky died while under arrest. But Talitsky's teachings were embedded in the memory of many people. Some even regarded him as a martyr. The legend of the Antichrist became so widespread that Stefan Yavorsky wrote a book to refute it, called *Signs of the Coming of the Antichrist*, but its influence among the clergy and the people, for the most part illiterate, was not great.

While the people of Great Russia endured their hardships, the Bashkirs and the Cossacks of the Don and the Dnieper rebelled. The Bashkirs suddenly felt Russian pressure too heavy upon them. To the north they saw a new industrial region growing at an alarming rate with towns like Verkhoture, Alapaevsksky, and Uktussky springing up, and they feared that this tide of development would sweep over their own lands. Already they were bearing their share of the hardships under the new policies, and already they suffered from the arrogance and rapacity of the Russian officials.[15]

By 1705 disturbing reports were reaching Moscow. The immediate cause of the unrest was the introduction in the autumn of 1704 of seventy-two new taxes, which further exasperated the whole people. By February 1708 they showed open resistance. They burnt down Russian settlements along the banks of the Kama and the Ufa rivers, and Tatars of the Kazan region and other tribes joined in the Bashkir raids, which grew in scale.

Peter was compelled to detach three regiments to deal with these rebels.[16] But he was anxious to avoid using force. At the beginning of 1708, he sent Prince Peter Khovansky to seek peace. All attempts to negotiate proving abortive, Khovansky marched from Kazan with troops. The threat of force succeeded where peaceful methods had failed; the Bashkirs declared their readiness to make peace and asked the Tsar's forgiveness for their misdeeds. Khovansky pardoned them, executing only their leader.

Farther to the east, the Bashkirs of the Ufa region remained unchecked. They were numerous and Peter could not at this stage detach further regiments from his army to restore order. His policy was to take advantage of local rivalries and to range Asiatics against Asi-

atics. He had already sent Counsellor Bakhmetev to persuade the
Buddhist Kalmyks to march against the Moslem Bashkirs. The
Kalmyks gave Bakhmetev ten thousand men for the purpose. In June
1708, learning that the Bashkirs had made an alliance with the
Karakalpaki, Kirgiz, and the Cossacks of the Don and of the Kuban,
Bakhmetev marched to prevent them joining with their allies. This
was enough to bring the Bashkir leaders begging the Tsar's forgiveness, and they swore on the Koran to live in peace. Despite these
protestations they continued to be restive and it was not until April
of the following year that they settled down.[17]

Far more serious was the revolt of the Cossacks of the Don and the
Dnieper. The Bashkirs had lacked a leader, and the bond of faith had
failed to bring the Moslems in the south to their aid. But the Cossacks had a leader, and were reinforced by the many Russians who
had fled to them. Their revolt threatened to unite all the Cossacks
to sweep northwards over central Russia.

Flights to the Cossack lands had been steadily increasing even as
Peter repeated his orders to the Cossack leaders that all runaway serfs
and deserters, who had joined them after 1695, should be returned.
They handed over an occasional fugitive as a gesture of obedience,
but did nothing further. In May 1705 Peter had sent instructions to
the Don that all new settlements, established without authority,
should be transferred beyond the Northern Donets River, and that
runaways in these settlements were to be returned to their places of
origin. His orders were ignored, and the settlements grew in size. For
a time, during the Astrakhan revolt, he relaxed his demands, fearing
that the Don Cossacks would join forces with the rebels. He was
relieved and grateful when they remained loyal, and in February
1706 he sent them new standards and other rewards. But he had not
forgotten his earlier ukaz. Soon he repeated it, and, when it brought
no response, he sent Prince Yury Dolgoruky to the Don with troops
to enforce it.[18]

Dolgoruky's mission alarmed the Don Cossacks, for it amounted to
a denial of their traditional freedoms. But the majority were reluctant to oppose the Tsar openly; they could not stand against his
troops, and they feared his punishments. They favoured a show of
obedience and evasion, which were the usual Cossack tactics.

At Cherkassk the Ataman, Lukyan Maximov, and the elders received Dolgoruky with respect, giving him guides to help in his search

for runaways. But Bulavin, the Ataman of Bakhmut, acted drastically; he made a surprise attack on the Russian camp on the bank of the Aidar River on the night of 9 October 1707, killing Dolgoruky and all his men. He then called on the Don Cossacks to join him in rebellion.

The more unruly elements rushed to support Bulavin. He strengthened his appeals by invoking the name of Stenka Razin, the Don Cossack rebel who had defied Tsar Alexei for several years, and whose name, as a popular leader of revolt against tyranny, was already a legend among the Russian people. Bulavin further proclaimed that he would capture Azov and Taganrog, free the labourers and exiles there, and in the spring march on Voronezh and Moscow. Meanwhile Maximov, learning of the massacre of Dolgoruky and his troops, and fearing the Tsar's reprisals, led a force of loyal Cossacks who defeated the rebels. But Bulavin escaped. Maximov then reported at length on this proof of his loyalty.[19] Peter received his letter in St. Petersburg, and wrote to Menshikov on 16 November 1707, expressing his relief that "this business by the grace of God has now completely finished."[20] He was soon to learn his mistake.

Bulavin had taken refuge among the Cossacks of Zaporozhye, the southern lands beyond the Dnieper rapids, which formed a buffer region between Russia and the Crimean khanate. The Zaporozhtsi, too, were not prepared at this stage to fight openly against the Tsar, but Bulavin quickly gathered a band of several hundred volunteers, and with them crossed the Dnieper.

From Azov a detachment of troops under Colonel Nikolai Vasiliev joined with Maximov, but as they advanced against Bulavin, they found that their men were deserting to the rebels. Bulavin attacked and destroyed the remnants of their force on 9 April 1708, only Vasiliev, Maximov, and a few others escaping.[21]

Now the revolt was growing dangerously. The rebels threatened Voronezh and the whole region of the upper Don. On 12 April 1708 Peter ordered one of his best officers, Guards Major Prince Vasily Dolgoruky, whose brother had been killed by Bulavin six months earlier, to proceed into the Ukraine with a strong detachment of infantry and dragoons "to extinguish this fire once for all."[22]

Peter wrote constantly to Dolgoruky, urging him to march with all haste. At the same time he ordered the Smolensk regiment to move from Kiev to Azov, and wrote instructing Ivan Tolstoy to prepare his defences. His letter showed that, in the event of Cherkassk falling to the rebels, he was unsure of the loyalty of the troops already in Azov.[23] At times his orders were contradictory and they bore witness to the strain and anxiety he felt as he watched the Swedish advance towards his western frontier, and followed the rebels' movements in his rear.

The possibility of Bulavin capturing Azov and Taganrog so alarmed Peter that he thought of hastening to the Don himself to conduct operations personally. "I do not need to take with me more than two or three battalions of my own regiment in order with God's help to extinguish this fire finally," he wrote to Menshikov on 27 May 1708.[24] At this time he was carefully following developments in Poland and calculating whether he could, in fact, risk leaving his main army while the Swedes were so near.

Meantime Bulavin's successes grew. On 30 April 1708 Cherkassk surrendered to him, and Maximov was executed. But his position was unstable. Already the Cossacks were plotting to overthrow him, and he had to surround himself with a bodyguard. At this point the Cossacks took a step that was typical; they drew up a petition to the Tsar, justifying their revolt on grounds of the injustices suffered at the hands of officials, and promising to serve as before, if forgiven the sin of rebellion.

Meanwhile in the north near the Bityug River, Bakhmetev with a force of only six hundred troops routed the rebels under Bulavin's lieutenant, Khokhlach. He sent his prisoners to Dolgoruky, who had arrived in Voronezh on 12 May (1708). A few days later Dolgoruky wrote to Peter of the severe punishments he proposed for them, but then he received a report that the Don Cossacks had surrendered, and he held his hand. Next a letter came from Peter, instructing him to behave mercifully. But he had no sooner received this letter than news came that Bulavin was threatening to march on Azov.

Peter was growing desperate. But at this point Bulavin weakened his position by dividing his army into three parts and dispersing it. On 1 July, Russian troops, sent by Dolgoruky, defeated one detachment in the north, while in the south a second detachment, advancing to attack Azov, was put to flight after savage fighting; rebel losses were heavy, and the survivors rushed back to Cherkassk, blaming Bulavin for the death of their comrades, and demanding his death in return. Bulavin killed the two Cossacks sent to arrest him. Apparently, however, he then lost heart, for he shot himself. Only one rebel force remained and in November Dolgoruky's troops cut it down without mercy, leaving more than three thousand rebels dead on the field of battle.

The revolt was at an end. Already in July, when Dolgoruky approached Cherkassk, the Cossack elders had come out to meet him, begging mercy, and swearing tearfully to honour their allegiance to the Tsar in future. Realizing the need for moderation, Peter on 15 August 1708 ordered Dolgoruky to "execute the worst rebel leaders and send other leaders to penal servitude; return all remaining Cossacks to their old places, and burn the new settlements as ordered before."[25] Along the Don tributaries unrest continued, but Dolgoruky quickly crushed it and he had two hundred rebels hanged from gallows placed on rafts which he sent drifting down the Don as a lesson and a warning.

The Cossacks, like the Bashkirs, were too irresponsible to maintain for long a united front against the Tsar. Local rivalries and indiscipline made them incapable of anything more than petty raiding. A leader of genius, like Genghis Khan, might have welded together all the Cossacks of the Dnieper, Don, Volga, Kuban, and Terek, and brought in the Bashkirs, Tatars, and other Asiatic races; this would have changed the course of Russian, and of European history. But no leader of greater calibre than Bulavin arose, and so the revolt died away.

Now Peter was free again to fight his real enemy, Charles of Sweden.

CHAPTER XXVIII

The Year of Diplomacy

1707

I T was the general expectation in Europe that Charles would invade Russia in the spring of 1707. Peter himself anticipated invasion then and he had hastened to Zholkva to make plans to meet it. But the prospect of this conflict made him uneasy. He was unwilling to gamble his Baltic seaboard, in fact, his whole policy, in a single battle or campaign, especially against Charles, undefeated and now at the peak of his fame. Anxiously he continued to seek mediation and peace. But he recognized the fact that "this war has now been left to us alone."[1] With only four months before spring, his orders rang with urgency.

His strategy was to avoid a major battle for as long as possible, and instead to wear down the Swedes by incessant minor engagements and by privations. To this end he did not hesitate to turn vast areas of his own country into desert. He instructed Apraxin to ensure that by the beginning of spring no grain or foodstuffs remained throughout a belt of land one hundred and thirty-three miles wide and deep, extending from Pskov and through Smolensk, the route which the Swedes would probably follow.[2]

Reports reached him in January that the Swedes were already marching towards the Russian frontier. Expecting attacks on Pskov and Polotsk, he reinforced their defences. He also sent three cavalry regiments to join General Hallart, writing that "I entrust to God's mercy and to your good management the defence of Polotsk and the other places."[3] He ordered Hetman Mazepa to be at Kiev with

264

his troops at "the very first grass in May" both to complete the fortifications there, and to protect the frontiers.[4] On the same day he directed Field-Marshal Sheremetev to bring his troops to full readiness.[5]

Every step that Charles took gave rise to new rumours. At the beginning of January, Peter wrote to Apraxin that "all here speak assuredly and letters arrive to the effect that the Swede is finally turning against the Empire [Austria]: may God grant that this be true."[6] But he was taking no risks and went ahead with preparations for the spring. It seemed hardly possible that Charles would allow him yet another respite. But this rumour proved correct and the year 1707 was to be taken up mainly with diplomacy.

Charles had quarrelled with the Austrian Emperor, and for twelve months he would not stir from Saxony. The points of dispute were unimportant, but Charles, eager to assert his new power and prestige, insisted on absolute satisfaction before he moved, and in the end he obtained it.

During these months Peter was active on several diplomatic fronts. In Poland he had first to displace Stanislas and to secure the support of the Poles who had formerly sided with Augustus, or, at least, to make sure that they did not go over to Stanislas and to the aid of Sweden.

In February a grand embassy from the republic of Poland arrived in Zholkva. The ambassadors announced at their first meeting with Golovkin that their purpose was to improve relations with the Tsar and to offer him greater assistance against the common enemy. Any encouragement that Peter may have felt on learning this was quickly dispelled when the Poles brought forward specific points for discussion. First, they demanded the immediate return of the Belaya Tserkov region of the Ukraine. Next they complained bitterly of the burden of maintaining Russian troops, and finally they pressed for the subsidies promised under the treaty of alliance, only part of which had so far been paid.

Negotiations dragged on for months. Peter found he could only raise twenty thousand of the fifty thousand rubles that he had offered to placate them. The Poles would not accept less than half of the full sum and renewed their demand for the return of the Ukrainian lands. Harassed by lack of money and unwilling to hand back the Ukrainian lands, especially at a time when Charles was expected in Poland at the head of his victorious army, Peter sent Ukraintsev to carry on the discussions in Lublin. By following a policy of judicious bribery, he won over the Polish leaders, who after all these months of wrangling finally accepted the original part-payment of twenty thousand rubles.

Meanwhile the Poles complained angrily of further plundering by Russian troops. Apparently the Russians could not resist the temptation to prey on their ancient enemies, and against this the Poles retaliated.[7] The Polish magnates drifted towards neutrality. They hated the Russians more than they hated the Swedes; on the other hand, they could not forgive Charles his high-handed behaviour. Among themselves they quarrelled and plotted for power; certain of them even had designs on the crown.

Peter had no false ideas about the attitude of the Poles and, as a Russian, he had no love for them. But he was consistent in his policy of seeking in Poland an ally. He renewed his efforts to dislodge Stanislas; at the same time he cast about him for a suitable candidate for the Polish throne. His first step was to send Prince Boris Kurakin as envoy to Rome. Pope Clement XI paid close attention to his representations.[8] The advance of the Protestant Swedes disturbed him and he answered Kurakin that he had not recognized Stanislas as King, and would not do so until the whole country had acknowledged him. He added that he had given this reply to the King of France, who had pressed him to accord recognition.

Rumours circulated that Menshikov had designs on the Polish throne; when Tsarevich Alexei was summoned to Zholkva to join his father, it was said that Peter intended him as the future King of Poland, and on learning of this story he immediately sent the Tsarevich back to Moscow. Peter was practical in his policies and, apart from the outlets to the sea in the west and the south, had no territorial ambitions. He wanted now a strong and friendly Poland on his frontier. His first choice for the Polish throne was Prince Eugene of Savoy. Peter had met him in Vienna in 1698 and, although their meeting was brief, had not forgotten him. On receiving the Tsar's proposal, Eugene wrote expressing his appreciation of the honour paid him, but explaining that he must leave the decision to his Emperor.[9]

The proposition held many attractions for the Emperor. But he was fully committed in the war against France; his relations with

Charles were causing anxiety, and he did not dare offend him further, even if his allies, England and Holland, would permit it, and in fact he had already recognized Stanislas in order to placate Charles. In June (1707) Huyssen reported from Vienna that the Emperor and Prince Eugene would gladly accept the Tsar's proposal, if the elections to the Polish throne were postponed until the war with France had ended.[10]

Peter could not wait so long. Anticipating the Emperor's reply, he had already approached Rakoczy, Prince of Transylvania, whom certain Poles were said to favour. This step involved a sharp change of policy. Peter had always sought to align himself with the Grand Alliance, and had consistently opposed French influence. Hungary, then part of the Austrian Empire, was in revolt against the Emperor, and Rakoczy, the leader of the insurgents, was in league with France. As King of Poland, he would have menaced Austria and sought to make an alliance between France and Poland. But, anxiously seeking to strengthen his position, Peter gave no thought to the longer term implications of his policy.

Rakoczy was interested, but he stipulated that he would only accept the Polish throne if freely elected by the Poles. On 4 September his representatives signed an agreement with Peter's ministers.[11] But the war was to intervene again before Rakoczy could advance closer to the throne of Poland.

A few weeks after this approach, Peter also sent another envoy to offer the crown to Jacob and, failing him, to Alexander Sobieski, sons of the great Polish King, Jan Sobieski.[12] Unwilling to shoulder such responsibilities and intimidated by the prospect of Charles's hostility, they each returned a polite refusal.[13]

Another factor complicating Peter's search for a King of Poland was Augustus himself. He had by no means relinquished the throne, except in his treaty with Charles, which he wished to forget. He constantly assured Peter of his friendship and his determination to stand by their alliance. Peter no longer placed any value on Augustus' word, but he did not reject offers of help, no matter how untrustworthy, and he wrote to Augustus of his continued brotherly affection.[14]

During the first four months of 1707, Peter had made Zholkva his headquarters. His main army, some seventy thousand strong, was in winter quarters in Volhynia, the dragoons near Zholkva, and the infantry around Dubno and Ostrog. All were ready to move at the first news of the Swedish advance from Saxony.

At the end of April, Peter moved to Dubno and then to Lublin. There he received a report that Charles was marching into Poland, where reinforcements would join him from Pomerania. It was the news that he was awaiting and he believed it, although the report was to prove false. He sent out a stream of orders, inspected the infantry regiments under Repnin's command in Dubno, writing to Menshikov that "here, praise God, all is fine,"[15] and detached troops to lay waste the regions through which the Swedes would march.

Expecting the Swedes to make direct for Moscow, Peter strengthened the defences of his capital. Rumours of the approach of the Swedes had already spread alarm in Moscow, and the orders to rebuild the city walls and to fortify the Kremlin added to the general distress. It was said that the Church of St. Basil at the head of Red Square was to be demolished altogether, with many other historical buildings, so that cannon could be trained on the enemy. The people were incensed. Korchmin whom Peter had placed in charge of these preparations[16] did not dare show himself in public without a guard. Fortunately the demolitions were not carried out. In October, Peter sent Tsarevich Alexei to supervise the work of defence. He reported to his father in some detail, adding that the Moscow garrison was twenty-five hundred strong, and that he had given orders to increase the labour force.[17]

After a month in Lublin, trying to persuade the Diet meeting there to oppose the Swedes as the common enemy, Peter went to Warsaw. He seemed in good spirits but his moods were unpredictable.[18] While in Warsaw he suffered again with a heavy fever that lasted ten days. He still had no further news of the Swedish army. The suspense of waiting and the endless preparations imposed a strain on him and he gave way to outbursts which he almost immediately regretted. On 3 August, he wrote furiously to Feodor Apraxin, asking why he had not dealt with the voevodi who had failed to deliver the full number of men to work in St. Petersburg, and accusing him of laziness.[19] His accusations upset Apraxin, and Peter hastened to apologize: "You are hurt because of what I wrote to you about the voevodi,—for God's sake do not let it sadden you, for in truth I bear no ill-will towards you, but in my way of life here even a small obstacle infuriates me!"[20] But at last, in the middle of

August, he learnt that Charles was moving from Saxony, and this time the report was accurate; the long period of waiting was drawing to a close.

In the midst of his preparations for invasion and of his efforts to find a king for the Poles, Peter still sought to come to terms with Charles. The signing of the Treaty of Altranstadt, depriving him of his last ally, had made him intensify his efforts. On 31 March he sent to Desalliers, the French minister at the court of Prince Rakoczy, a proposal that Louis XIV should mediate between Russia and Sweden. In return, Peter offered him Russian troops for use against the Grand Alliance.[21] Peter also pressed his offer through Besenval, the French ambassador at the Swedish court, and through the Marquis de Bonac at Danzig.

The French opened negotiations with Charles, and achieved nothing. Charles insisted on the return of all that Peter had won, and on the payment of full compensation for damage caused in the war; his terms were, as always, immutable. Peter was ready to give up Livonia, Esthonia, and Ingria, in fact everything, except Schlusselburg, St. Petersburg and a narrow strip of land on either side of the Neva River. But this line of the Neva was a vital artery of Sweden's Baltic empire, and Charles was determined to recover it.[22]

Already in January of the previous year (1706), Peter had proposed to van der Gulst, the Dutch resident in Moscow, that, if Holland and the allies could bring the King of Sweden to discuss peace with Russia on his terms, he would place at their disposal thirty thousand of his best troops for use against France. The Dutch had made no reply. Similar attempts to induce Prussia to mediate met with no success. But it was to England that Peter looked most hopefully.

Two years earlier, on 28 February 1705, Charles Whitworth had arrived in Moscow as envoy extraordinary from Queen Anne. The Russians received him warmly, and he soon realized that this welcome was largely due to their expectation that he had come with offers to mediate.[23] But he had been sent to work "for the mutual benefit of trade and commerce" between England and Russia, to protect English merchants, and to ensure the flow of the raw materials on which the Queen's navy depended. Whitworth's most pressing business was to obtain some relief for the English contractors to whom Peter, when in England, had granted the tobacco monopoly.[24] This monopoly had not flourished, and fault lay on both sides.[25]

But Whitworth managed to secure some concessions for the contractors. He was also able to obtain satisfaction on other grievances which he had listed in a note and handed to Golovin.[26]

One reason for Peter's conciliatory mood was his need for English shipwrights. Matveev, his ambassador at The Hague, had recently reported that Queen Anne had forbidden her subjects to enter the Tsar's service. Golovin summoned Whitworth and made strong representations, stressing that the Tsar intended the shipwrights, which he now needed urgently, to work in the Voronezh shipyards, and not in his new Baltic yards.[27]

Whitworth urged his government to meet these requests. He wrote to Robert Harley about the Tsar's great love of ships, adding that "he has taken a particular fancy for the English way of building, as much cleaner and lighter than the Dutch . . . he has such a passion for this art, that I am obliged to assure you, nothing can touch him so nearly, as the refusing leave for the shipwrights he desires may come hither, or recalling those who are now in his service."[28] The Tsar's requests were granted.

The other reason for Peter's friendly attitude was that he hoped to induce Queen Anne to mediate with Charles of Sweden. Golovin expressed deep disappointment when Whitworth finally admitted that he had brought no such proposals for mediation.[29] Golovin made it clear that the Tsar was prepared to conclude a formal treaty of commerce, highly advantageous to England. When this brought no offers of help, Peter drew the conclusion that his plans for a Baltic fleet were the obstacle. Golovin informed Whitworth "that the Tsar was ready to give Her Majesty the most positive assurances that he would never attempt to have a fleet of men of war on those seas [i.e., the Baltic], but only to have a door open that way for trade into his country, and to enjoy a province, which had been wrongfully taken from his ancestors in time of peace." Peter repeated this assurance several times, but it did not impress Whitworth.[30]

Negotiations with Whitworth in Moscow were achieving nothing and, at the end of 1706, Peter sent Matveev to England to press his proposals. By his instructions Matveev was to repeat the proposals already made through Whitworth, and to state that in return the Tsar asked only that England should compel Sweden to come to terms with Russia, if necessary using the threat of armed force. Matveev was also to consider whether presents might influence

English ministers, and especially Marlborough, Godolphin, and the head of the Northern Department in the Foreign Office. Opposite this clause Peter added in his own hand: "I do not believe Marlborough can be bought, since he is rich beyond measure; but you can offer him about 200,000 or more."[31]

Before leaving The Hague, Matveev had a meeting with Marlborough, who in a letter to Godolphin, wrote that Matveev had told him of the great esteem that the Tsar felt for the Queen; as a mark of this esteem he intended sending his only son, Alexei, to England, and asked that the Queen should appoint a house for his residence. Marlborough expressed the hope that this would be done, "for it is certain you will not be able to gratify him in any part of his negotiation."[32] But he said nothing to discourage Matveev, and went out of his way to be agreeable to him, even placing his yacht, the *Peregrine*, at his disposal. Matveev sailed for England, believing that his mission had Marlborough's support.

In London, where he arrived at the beginning of May 1707, Matveev was shown every respect. A few days later he wrote with some optimism to Golovin, but he explained, in anticipation of difficulties, that "here there is no autocratic power," for the Queen could do nothing without Parliament. He pursued his mission with great energy. But he could obtain no definite answer to the Tsar's proposals. On 1 September, he received orders from Peter to obtain the English reply without further delays. He had another audience of the Queen and further meetings, and still met with evasion.

On 23 November, just six months after his arrival in England, Matveev received a formal reply, accepting the Tsar's proposal to join the Grand Alliance, subject to the agreement of Holland and Austria as to the terms on which he joined. Further delays followed. In desperation Matveev, on 24 February 1708, sent a letter demanding a reply to all the proposals submitted in the Tsar's name. But already he knew that his mission had failed. He had heard rumours that England proposed to guarantee the Treaty of Altranstadt, and to recognize Stanislas as King of Poland. In April 1708, Peter wrote to Golovkin: "concerning Andrei Matveev, long ago we said that it was time for him to depart, for all there is tales and shame."[33]

Peter's last hopes of obtaining peace with Charles had passed. He had approached Holland, Austria, France, Prussia, Denmark, and

England. But all realized that there could be no mediation; Charles would never yield over the Neva and its delta, and Peter was equally adamant, being prepared to fight to the end to retain St. Petersburg. The war lay on Russia alone, and Peter could look to no one for help. All Europe expected that Charles would now annihilate the Russian armies and march to Moscow. All had given Peter up for lost.

CHAPTER XXIX

The March on Russia

1707-1708

CHARLES marched from Saxony on 22 August 1707, and again he belied all predictions. It was expected that, after twelve months of idleness in Saxony, he would be impatient to hurl his army into Russia. But he advanced eastwards without haste. For nearly two months he remained at Slupce, west of the Vistula, where reinforcements joined him from Sweden, bringing his army to full strength. It now comprised 8,450 cavalry, 16,000 dragoons, and 19,200 infantry, all well equipped and the majority seasoned troops. In addition he counted on Lewenhaupt's army, sixteen thousand strong, joining him from Riga. It was the finest army that Charles had ever commanded.

In Poland, he allowed his troops to live off the land, and they plundered the unfortunate Poles without mercy. Corrupt, inconstant, divided by petty jealousies, the Poles were, he considered, unworthy of attention. But he was taking no risks that Stanislas might be unseated, and when at the end of October he marched from Slupce, he left behind eight Swedish regiments under General Krassau to support the King.

As they advanced eastwards, Charles's troops began to suffer hardships. The Russians had laid waste the land through which they were passing. Heavy rains had turned the roads to quagmires, and severe frosts had followed the rains. By Christmas they had reached the Vistula River. The Russians had destroyed the bridges, but Charles, grown impatient and refusing to wait for the ice to thicken safely, marched his army across, and was fortunate to lose only a few men and horses by drowning.

From the Vistula, Charles did not press on by the most direct route to Russia, but turned northeast, marching near the Prussian frontier. This added to the hardships of his men. Forcing their way through bogs and thick forests, they had also to contend with a wild and hostile peasantry, who sniped at them and ambushed small detachments and any stragglers.

Soon after learning that the Swedish army had at last moved from Saxony, Peter left Warsaw to go to St. Petersburg. He travelled slowly, for he was waiting for some indication of his enemy's intentions. Charles might march northwards to recover the Baltic provinces and to destroy St. Petersburg; he might seek to capture Pskov and Novgorod and from there to advance on Moscow; he might strike at the heart of Russia by marching directly on Moscow. It was also possible that he would move into winter quarters near the Russian frontier and delay his campaign until the spring. Peter had no inkling what Charles would do and it worried him.

The Swedish generals were equally in the dark. They had misgivings over fighting an autumn or winter campaign in the vast Russian plain. They favoured reconquering the Baltic provinces as the first step. The King's Quartermaster, Gyllenkrook, had even worked out a plan of advance into the Baltic lands, and, moving northeast after crossing the Vistula, the Swedish generals assumed that they were following this plan. But Charles had neither accepted nor rejected it. With supreme confidence in his destiny, he kept his own counsels; to his own army, as to the Tsar, he was an enigma.

Peter had taken steps to meet each possible line of approach. At first he regarded a direct attack on Moscow as the most probable, and in August he had written instructing Korchmin to press on with the fortification of the city.[1] Meanwhile he had left Menshikov in command of the cavalry at Warsaw. Sheremetev was at Minsk with the main body of the infantry, while Generals Repnin and Chambers were at Vilno with detachments of infantry. Menshikov was to use his cavalry to harry the Swedes, especially at river crossings, and the infantry was to retire towards the Russian frontier, if the enemy moved in their direction.

From Warsaw, Peter travelled by way of Tilotsin, Grodno, and Vilno. He then went on to Merech, where Menshikov joined him with other commanders to reconsider the plan of campaign; the policy of falling back, leaving a waste land for the enemy to march through, and harassing him at every move, was confirmed. Returning to Vilno, Peter learnt that the Swedes had turned northeast, as though intending to attack Ingria. He set out at once for St. Petersburg, arriving on 23 October.

During his journey from Warsaw to St. Petersburg, Peter wrote nearly one hundred letters. Most of them were to his generals and especially to Menshikov about preparations against invasion, and he attended to everything in detail.

But also at this time and during the following months, he was giving close attention to the translating and printing of books. In 1707 a typefounder and two compositors arrived from Holland, bringing with them three specially designed type faces of the Cyrillic alphabet. He studied these new types, making changes to give certain letters greater strength and clarity. Books began to appear in the revised type in 1708; the first volume was a geometry manual, while the second was a handbook of polite forms of address. Technical manuals were the most pressing need and had priority, but he was also concerned to broaden the outlook and understanding of his people. He was himself interested in history, and ordered accounts of the Trojan wars and of the exploits of Alexander the Great to be printed in Russian. He also instructed a compositor, named Polikarpov, to write a history of Russia. Not only did he commission these books, he examined them personally and criticized them in detail. "We have read the book on fortifications which you translated," he wrote to the son of Zotov; "the conversations are good and clearly rendered, but in the sections teaching how to carry out fortifications it is darkly and unintelligibly translated. . . ."[2] His attention to detail and the tenacity with which he pressed ahead with certain reforms were never more striking than during this period of constant travel and of high tension, as his fateful battle with Charles XII drew nearer.

In St. Petersburg, Peter inspected fortifications, visited the fortress of Kronslot, spent hours working in the Admiralty, and drew up a building programme for the coming year.[3] At the same time he continued to pour out instructions for the approaching campaign. But he also relaxed in the company of Catherine, already mother of three of his children and in November 1707 in the Cathedral of the Holy Trinity they were privately, almost secretly, married.

On Menshikov's name-day, Peter took part in a banquet of the kind that he relished, and for which he now seldom had time and opportunity. He hastened to tell Menshikov about it. "Truly," he wrote, "since the death of Lefort up to this day there have been no days so merry. May God grant that we shall celebrate like this again with you here."[4] But news of the Cossack revolt and of the massacre of Dolgoruky and his battalion, received at the beginning of November (1707), threatened to cut short his stay in St. Petersburg. A few days later the report came that Maximov had routed Bulavin's rebel army.[5] He assumed that the revolt was over, and remained in St. Petersburg for several weeks longer before departing for Moscow.

Peter reached Moscow on 5 December. Two years had passed since he was last there and an accumulation of business awaited him. But his main concern was to prepare against the Swedish invasion. He gave orders for the training of an additional twenty thousand troops and also for calling up thirty thousand new recruits. He went into the question of army pay and provisioning. This led him to examine the national revenue, and all ministries had to submit accounts without delay. These showed that revenue from customs dues had dropped by half, although the duties had been doubled, and he appointed a committee to investigate the accounts and to report direct to him.

Peter also inspected the fortifications under construction in Moscow. The work was progressing with feverish haste. Twenty thousand men were engaged on it day and night. The cold was so bitter that they had to light great fires to thaw sods of earth to build the ramparts. Korchmin's plans included emplacements for "prodigious artillery of all calibres . . . near 2,000 pieces being designed for the walls and bastions."[6] Certain leading magnates undertook each to build a bastion, and the inhabitants were being formed in regiments to defend the city.

For the whole of the month that he spent in Moscow, Peter worked at furious pressure. He carried the full burden not only of the war, but of the government and of his own reforms. At times petty matters annoyed him and he showed his impatience. Whitworth chose this time to raise various minor grievances of the English merchants. Peter replied shortly that he would do what was possible, but that he could not attend to everything; he added that "God had given the Tsar twenty times more business than other people, but not twenty times more force or capacity to go through with it."[7]

On 6 January, he left Moscow to rejoin his army. He met Menshikov on the road to Minsk and, learning that Charles had nearly reached the Nieman River, he hastened to Grodno. He believed now that Charles would continue his march northwards and invade Russia at Pskov.

Charles was moving rapidly. It was his ability to advance at speed and to strike surprise blows that added to Peter's anxiety. In fact, it seemed that with dramatic suddenness Charles had already overtaken him at Grodno. On 25 January, Peter wrote to Admiral Apraxin, who was to have followed him from Moscow, that he should "make for Vilno, as rapidly as possible, and if you have already reached Vilno, go no farther, for the enemy has now come up with us."[8]

Nearing Grodno, Charles had rushed ahead with six hundred of his horse guards to reconnoitre the bridge over the Niemen. He found Brigadier Muhlenfeld defending it with two thousand Russian troops. He attacked, forced the bridge, and pursued the Russians to the walls of the town. But night had fallen, and he decided to make his attack on the town in the morning. Charles did not know that the Tsar was then in Grodno.[9]

Hearing the gunfire Peter thought that the whole Swedish army had reached Grodno. At dawn he hurriedly left with Menshikov, making for Vilno. At the same time Charles was advancing over the ice of the river; he entered the town just two hours after Peter's departure. Meanwhile, finding that a small detachment had taken the town, Peter sent Muhlenfeld with three thousand cavalry to recapture it. Muhlenfeld's men fought their way into the town. But the Swedish guards, supported by the inhabitants, compelled them to retire.

Charles stayed only five days in Grodno. He wanted to pursue the Tsar to force him to a decisive engagement. When several of his regiments came up, he at once set out towards Vilno. But he was soon compelled to give up the chase. The Russians had reduced the whole region to desert. The Swedes and their horses were nearing exhaustion. Charles turned from Vilno towards Minsk, and at Smorganie, where his army joined him, he allowed his men to rest.

At this point Charles revealed his plans. From Smorganie, he turned southeast, and took up quarters at Radoshkovichi, near Minsk, where he remained for nearly three months. His route now lay towards Smolensk and thence to Moscow. It was a bold plan to hurl his army at the heart of Russia and to dictate terms in the Tsar's capital.

Meanwhile in the north, General Lybecker in command of the Swedish army in Finland, prepared to recapture Ingria and to destroy St. Petersburg. In Poland, Stanislas, strengthened by Krassau's Swedish regiments, was to put down all Polish opposition. Charles may even have intended that, as he marched on Moscow from the south, Lybecker from the north and Stanislas from the west would attack simultaneously. It was a grandiose conception of the kind that appealed to him, although he would have scorned any suggestion that such a concentration of forces was needed against the Russians.

From Vilno, Peter at once moved his troops to meet the new threat. He placed the bulk of his army in entrenched positions along the Dnieper from Mogilev to Orsha. This gave protection to Smolensk and at the same time ensured safe lines of retreat. He also sent General Goltz with eight thousand troops to Borisov on the Berezina River to oppose the Swedish crossing. Mazepa was to march from the Ukraine with thirty thousand Cossacks, and to reinforce Goltz. With part of his army Peter himself moved to Polotsk, where some twenty thousand recruits joined him.

Taking advantage of Charles's halt at Radoshkovichi, Peter decided to go off to St. Petersburg again. On the eve of his departure from Polotsk, however, a severe bout of fever struck him down. By the time he reached St. Petersburg it had sapped his strength. On 6 April he wrote to Golovkin: ". . . I have always been healthy here, as though in paradise, and I don't know how I brought this fever with me from Poland, for I took care of myself in the sledge with clothing, but throughout Passion Week the fever has racked me, and apart from morning song and the Gospels I have attended none of the services through illness; now, thanks be to God, I am recovering, but still cannot leave my hut."[10]

Menshikov reported that the Swedes were building bridges over the rivers in preparation for their advance to the Russian frontier. But, on 14 April, Peter replied that he was not to be summoned back to the army, unless there was completely reliable information that the enemy was advancing. Distressed by his unaccustomed weakness, he added that, as Menshikov well knew, he "did not usually make requests of this kind, but if for five or six weeks I can remain here and take medicine, then I hope, with God's help, to come to you in health; but if there is absolute need for me to come now, kindly arrange to place relays for me. . . ."[11] But he could not remain ill for long in St. Petersburg, which was the symbol of all that he was fighting for. No man could have striven more impatiently towards recovery, and he gained strength with every day. By the beginning of May he had recovered and reports of the suppression of the Cossack revolt had lessened his anxiety, so that he no longer felt any need to go to the Ukraine himself. Such relief was timely, for Charles was ready to continue his advance towards Russia.

For nearly three months Charles had remained in camp at Radoshkovichi. His troops rested, but they were still weak from privations. Snow and bitter cold had been their constant companions, and they had marched through devastated lands where they found neither food nor forage, only the burnt ashes of villages, and broken bridges. Even in camp at the beginning of May, heavy snowstorms confined them to their huts. Nor did the warmth of spring bring them relief; it only unleashed disease and in their weakened condition men and horses succumbed readily. Rabies also struck them, and a number died in its terrible torments.

While at Radoshkovichi, Charles had summoned Lewenhaupt to concert plans for the spring campaign. Lewenhaupt had remained some six weeks with him, returning to his troops in Riga on 15 May. All was now ready for the invasion of Russia.

The Swedes were keen to march again: it was a sign of their hardihood and discipline and of the tremendous spirit which Charles inspired in them. But all, from Charles down to the trooper, laboured under several misconceptions, the chief of which was that on invading Russia the people would rise to support them as liberators. Another factor contributing to Charles's determination to invade Russia was Mazepa's apparent readiness, as declared in correspondence with Stanislas, to desert Peter, bringing with him the Cossacks and people of the Ukraine, and providing food and forage for the Swedish army.

On 6 June Charles broke camp and advanced to the Berezina River. Goltz, although well entrenched with eight thousand troops at Borisov, did not wait to oppose him, but made a hurried retreat to Mogilev. Charles continued his advance towards the Dnieper, hoping to overtake his enemy. But he could now make only slow progress over ground turned to bog by the spring thaw. On 30 June he came within sight of the town of Golovchina, or Holowczyn, on the little river of Bibich (Wabis) where he found the Russian army drawn up in positions that appeared impregnable. Although Peter had not yet rejoined the army, Sheremetev and Menshikov had decided to take advantage of the marshy banks of the Bibich to oppose the crossing of the Swedes.

Eager for action and fearing only that the Russians would retreat and rob him of a battle, Charles waited for his army to come up with him. When some two thirds of his troops had arrived, he decided to attack. On 4 July at the head of his foot-guards, he plunged into the river, wading breast-high in the water to the other side. They came under heavy fire from the Russian guns, but they advanced calmly and rapidly.

Without waiting for all his men to cross, Charles led a furious attack on the Russian left wing. Swedes and Russians were locked in a savage struggle for some hours. Certain of Repnin's regiments wavered and he rallied them. But the Swedes pressed their attack with such spirit that Repnin's wing broke and fled into the woods. Seeing Repnin fall back, Sheremetev with the main infantry force promptly retreated to Shklov on the Dnieper, posting part of his army in Kopeyes and part in Gorki.

Charles and his brave troops had won a further victory. News of it spread through Europe, adding to his renown and confirming the general belief that he would dictate his terms in Moscow. But it was a victory without decisive result. It had opened up the way to the Dnieper—but through utterly devastated and barren lands. The Russian army, except for certain of Repnin's regiments, had retreated in good order, and the fact that one wing had stood up for so long against the Swedes led by Charles himself, had a good effect on Russian morale. The Russians had also achieved their purpose of further weakening the enemy.[12]

Peter joined his army a few days after the battle. He was delighted with Menshikov's account of it, but later, when he learnt that certain regiments had fled, he ordered investigations and severe punishments for all who had failed in their duty.[13] He now concentrated his army in the region of Gorki to the east of the Dnieper, where he could guard the road to Smolensk and thence to Moscow. He was also in a position to intercept Lewenhaupt, whenever he should try to join the main Swedish army.

During July, Charles remained at Mogilev, where he had advanced from Golovchina, resting his men and waiting for Lewenhaupt with his troops and supplies. But finally craving action, he decided to wait no longer. He was now counting on Mazepa who had just concluded alliances with him and with Stanislas. Early in August, therefore, he marched his army to Chirikov on the Sozh River. All the way bands of Russian light-horsemen harried his men. Illness struck again among them. Their sufferings were terrible, but their courage was heroic, and with bitter humour they spoke of their three doctors as Dr. Vodka, Dr. Garlic, and Dr. Death.

Learning that Charles had crossed the Dnieper and was now marching southeast, Peter moved his own army to Mstislavl. Although still retreating and avoiding decisive action, he was gradually taking the offensive. His policy of scorching the earth was yielding results. Charles was losing the tremendous impetus which had always carried him to victory. As he marched, the Russians boldly attacked, and nearly succeeded in cutting off one of his divisions in the village of Dobry on the little river Chernaya Napa. From there the Russians made an orderly retreat, having inflicted heavy losses on the Swedes.

Peter was elated. He wrote to Apraxin, to Catherine and others about the action, as well as preparing a proclamation to his people.[14] In fact his enthusiasm seemed quite out of proportion; it had been only a minor and indecisive engagement. But he considered it important. He had watched his troops attack, fight bravely, and retreat in good order. They had behaved as disciplined soldiers, the equal of Western troops. Notwithstanding this he still acted with caution and retreated farther north.

Stubbornly Charles continued his pursuit, but it was no longer a chase. His men were so near exhaustion that he could make no sudden thrusts. Always the Russians fell back slowly before them, destroying and burning. Always the Swedes marched over charred ground. Always clouds of smoke from burning villages hung on the horizon, the smoke so thick that it filled their throats and nearly blotted out their sight of the sun. And in their weariness they never dared to fall behind, for bands of Cossack, Tatar, and Kalmyk horsemen waited pitilessly there to cut them down.[15]

At last Charles saw that they could no longer persist in his pursuit. He was at the Russian frontier now, but he did not attempt to cross it. He had believed that Peter would not dare to lay waste his own lands, as he had devastated Poland, for fear of revolt by his own subjects. Now, however, he saw beyond the frontier the same vista of smouldering grass and burning villages as had confronted him for so many weeks gone by. His great confidence in his destiny faltered then and he summoned a council of war. At this council his generals urged him to fall back to the Dnieper and there to join up with Lewenhaupt. Coldly he rejected their advice, refusing to consider any movement that resembled retreat. The one alternative remaining was to move southwards into the Ukraine. There he would have the promised support of Mazepa with his Cossack army as well as food and fodder in abundance. Once his men had recovered their strength, he would turn north again and take Moscow. On 14 September, Charles began his march southwards.

At this time Lewenhaupt was only three or four days' march away. On his return in May to Riga his instructions had been to muster all the troops that he could, together with three months' provisions for the whole Swedish army, and then to hold himself ready to join Charles on the Dnieper. He had hardly begun his preparations when he received orders to march at the beginning of June to the Berezina River; it was already 8 June when these orders reached him. By tremendous effort he managed to set out in July with a force of sixteen thousand troops and two thousand wagons of supplies. Although his men were fresh, he could only make slow progress, because muddy roads and a cumbersome supply train hampered him. Nevertheless he pressed ahead and reached Shklov on the Dnieper by mid-September.

Here Lewenhaupt was expecting to join the main Swedish army. He was staggered to receive further orders from a courier who had left the King only twenty-four hours earlier. The orders were to cross the Dnieper and Sozh rivers and to make for Starodub. Lewenhaupt knew that between the two rivers stood the Russian army; his orders seemed to condemn his small force and its great train of wagons to destruction. Loyally and bravely, however, he set out to obey.

On 21-22 September, the Swedish force crossed the Dnieper and made with all speed for the Sozh River. Lewenhaupt bribed a Jew to go to the Russian camp as a guide and to mislead them. The ruse nearly succeeded. The Jew assured Peter that the Swedes were still on the west bank of the Dnieper, and it was not until three days after the Swedish crossing that the Russians learnt their true position. Pflug first, and then Menshikov with cavalry, raced after Lewenhaupt, who was trying desperately to reach Propoisk. Once across the Sozh River, he would have a fair chance of reaching the main Swedish army with his force intact. But muddy roads and the supply train continued to delay him. His cavalry in the rear was now constantly skirmishing with the Russian cavalry. He pressed on until he reached the village of Lesnaya, a few miles from Propoisk. And here on 28 September, the Russians came up with him.

The Russian army had retreated farther north to Sobolev, for Peter was expecting Charles to attack Smolensk. He was astonished to learn on 10 September that his enemy had turned about and was heading for the Ukraine. At the same time he received news that Lewenhaupt had set out from Riga. At a council of war, he decided that Sheremetev with the main army should follow Charles into the Ukraine, while he himself remained in the north with an army of 11,625 to intercept Lewenhaupt.

Peter now moved southwest towards the Dnieper. He did not know where Lewenhaupt was or the strength of his army, although it was rumoured to be eight thousand men. As a precaution he sent orders to General Bauer, then with the main Russian army, to join him with reinforcements of three thousand dragoons.[16] For several days the Jew, taken as a guide, misled them. Then, learning that Lewenhaupt had crossed the Dnieper and was well on the way to the Sozh River, Peter rushed after him. He detached cavalry to take prisoners who could give intelligence about the enemy force. On 26 September, he learnt with surprise from captured Swedes that Lewenhaupt had sixteen thousand men. He at once sent further orders to Bauer to make all haste with his reinforcements.[17] On the next day further minor engagements took place and the Russians, moving swiftly, managed to outflank the Swedes. Lewenhaupt saw that battle was inevitable. He sent an advance guard of three thousand men ahead to Propoisk, and drew up his remaining troops in strong positions by a wood at the village of Lesnaya.

At 1 P.M. on the following day, 28 September, Russians and Swedes joined battle. It raged until late afternoon and, as Peter wrote, "all day it was impossible to see where victory would lie."[18] Soon after 4 P.M., General Bauer came up with his dragoons and reinforced the

Russian positions. About the same time three thousand Swedish cavalry arrived from Propoisk, whence Lewenhaupt had recalled them. The Swedish cavalry at once attacked, and the battle raged more fiercely than ever. "But then," Peter wrote, "by the grace of God, the giver of victories, the enemy was beaten and routed, so that over 8,000 of his dead were left on the field. The supply train of 2,000 wagons, sixteen cannon, forty-two standards, and the field of battle remained completely ours."[19]

Towards the end of the battle a snowstorm enveloped the field and in the darkness Lewenhaupt was able to retreat with the remnant of his forces. On the following morning, General Pflug with dragoons and with Cossack and Kalmyk detachments pursued the fleeing troops. He overtook them at Propoisk, where a further five hundred Swedes lost their lives, many more were taken prisoner, and the rest of the supply train was captured. Lewenhaupt himself managed to cross the Sozh with his surviving troops and to make his own escape.

Peter had always shown jubilation over battles from which his troops had emerged victorious or, at least, undefeated by the Swedes. At times his enthusiasms had seemed excessive, but throughout he had, in fact, remained clear-sighted. He had looked on all these actions merely as successive stages in the long process of creating an efficient fighting force. Of Lesnaya he wrote that "this may be regarded as our first victory, for we have never had a similar victory over regular troops, and then with numbers inferior to those of the enemy. Truly it was the source of all the subsequent good fortune of Russian arms. . . ."[20]

From the field of battle, he promptly wrote to his ministers and generals, and even to Augustus. As usual he made no mention of the part he himself had played, although he had been in command. The pursuit of the war in the Ukraine claimed his attention, but, as soon as he could, he drew up a detailed report and diagrams of the battle of Lesnaya, which he sent to Tsarevich Alexei in Moscow with instructions to have them printed in Russian and in Dutch.[21] He was losing no opportunity to publicize to the full among his own people and abroad this victory, which he later called "the mother of Poltava," his second and greatest victory which was soon to resound throughout Europe and to prove one of the most decisive battles of all time.

From Lesnaya, Peter went to Smolensk, entering in triumph to the sound of cannon salutes, and marching ahead of Swedish prisoners and colours captured in battle. Here he was soon to receive good news from Admiral Apraxin, in command of the defence of Ingria and St. Petersburg. Lybecker's attack from Finland was proving abortive. He had marched with an army of fourteen thousand men from Vyborg, but had not dared to attack the strong fortifications of St. Petersburg. He had advanced through Ingria, finally embarking in Swedish ships on the coast near Narva. His campaign had cost the Swedes more than three thousand men, as well as equipment and horses, and it had achieved nothing. Ingria remained in Russian hands and St. Petersburg stood inviolate.

Peter stayed for three weeks in Smolensk and then went to Bryansk and to Novogorodok-Seversky, near where he joined Sheremetev and the main army. Sheremetev had already had news of the victory at Lesnaya. The whole Russian army was now jubilant, and, like their Tsar, they felt a new spirit of confidence.

But at this very time of celebration, Peter received disastrous news. It came on 27 October in an urgent despatch from Menshikov. He reported that Hetman Mazepa had turned traitor and had gone over to the enemy.

CHAPTER XXX

Mazepa

COMING at a time when Charles's army had been seriously weakened, Mazepa's betrayal was a bitter disappointment and constituted a serious threat. Mazepa might even succeed in persuading the Cossacks of the Ukraine and the Zaporozhye to follow him. The Crimean Tatars, finding so strong a force arrayed against the Tsar, would not hesitate to join with them. The revolts among the Cossacks of the Don and the Volga, and among the Bashkirs, which had only just been quelled, would break out afresh. Such were the direct results to be expected from Mazepa's defection. But Peter's greatest fear was that the Ottoman Porte, seeing Russia challenged on nearly every side, would again declare war.

Peter at once took action to hold the Ukrainian and Zaporozhsky Cossacks from following Mazepa. He posted dragoon regiments where they could obstruct any movement to join the Swedes; he ordered Menshikov to assemble all Cossack elders and urge them to go to the Tsar's camp to elect a new hetman; he closed his letter with an order to Menshikov to come himself with all speed.[1] On the same night he summoned representatives of the Zaporozhsky Cossacks and the leading Ukrainian churchmen as well as the colonels of all Ukrainian regiments, to his camp.[2]

On the next day (28 October) formal ukazi were proclaimed designed to win the support of the Ukraine and of the Zaporozhye, especially by reviving fears of religious persecution by the Catholic Poles.[3] Similar proclamations were circulated to towns on the lower Don.[4]

After this spate of orders, Peter wrote to Apraxin to congratulate him on the retreat of Lybecker and his Swedish army from Ingria: "Although it is against my conscience," he continued, "that in reply to your good news I must write something bad, yet necessity compels me to tell you that Mazepa has become a new Judas, for, after twenty-one years of loyalty, now when nearly in his grave he has turned traitor and betrayer of his people." But the mood of his letter was one of strong confidence, and he assured Apraxin that Mazepa would have few followers.[5]

Peter never forgot or forgave treason, and Mazepa's betrayal was so treacherous and unexpected that it shocked him deeply. He had trusted the old Hetman implictly; he had in fact been overtrustful. Nineteen years earlier, Mazepa had been one of the last to ride to the Troitsa Monastery to pay homage to the young Tsar. Peter had shown him every favour, and with the passing years he had developed an affection for Mazepa, whose shrewd political sense, strong personality, and vitality made him a lively companion and a valuable ally.

In Moscow, the Hetman ranked with the highest dignitaries. He was the second to receive the Order of St. Andrew, and Peter had seen to it also that Augustus awarded him the Polish Order of the White Eagle.

On the other hand, the position of the Hetman was not easy. The Ukraine was in a constant state of ferment. Just over fifty years earlier, Bogdan Khmelnitsky had united the people in revolt against Polish rule. But this unity had since broken into antagonisms. The transfer of the Ukraine east of the Dnieper to Russian rule had given no satisfaction to most of the people, although they were now free to practise their Orthodox faith. The departure of the Polish landlords had not left the peasantry and the Cossacks free to enjoy the rich plenty of their lands. Instead a new Cossack officer class now scrambled for the land and built up large estates. The peasantry found themselves oppressed by the newcomers just as they had been by the old Polish landlords.

The simple rank-and-file Cossacks were strongly opposed to the new officer class. They resented the office of Hetman, and they were in close touch with the free-living Cossacks beyond the Dnieper rapids, who followed the true Cossack way of life and whose example and encouragement made them all the more restive. The townspeople of the Ukraine wanted only to live and trade in peace. They went in fear of the Cossacks and looked to Moscow for protection and stable government. But the Ukrainian clergy treasured their independence of Moscow and took pride in their cultural superiority and influence over the Great Russian Church.

At the head of this divided and discontented people stood Hetman Mazepa. He favoured the new landowning class, to which he himself belonged. He had amassed great wealth and estates, and even dreamt of making the hetmanship hereditary. But the landowners, jealous of their independence, resented his authority and held him to blame for the increasing encroachments of Moscow. To the peasantry he was the champion of their oppressors, the landlords. The simple Cossacks hated him as the appointee of Moscow. Beyond the Dnieper rapids, the free Cossacks opposed him for the same reasons. But Mazepa had always been careful to retain the Tsar's confidence and support.[6]

His enemies were numerous and they constantly plotted to bring him down. Soon after his election as Hetman in 1687, accusations were made that he was scheming to place the Ukraine east of the Dnieper under Polish rule again. Some three years later a fiery Cossack, named Petrik, who had Turkish support, sought to arouse the Zaporozhtsi and the Crimean Tatars to free the Ukraine from Moscow's rule. Mazepa won the support of the Zaporozhtsi by rich presents and fair promises; Petrik could raise only a small force among them, and Mazepa routed him without difficulty. In achieving this he not only saved his own position, but he earned the gratitude of Moscow where it was realized that Petrik's revolt might readily have spread to the scale of Khmelnitsky's rising. The revolt of Semyon Palei against Polish rule in the Ukraine on the right bank of the Dnieper in 1704 had placed Mazepa in an exceedingly difficult position. But he had extricated himself with territorial gains and his reputation with the Tsar stood higher than ever.

For a time no major incidents disturbed Mazepa's rule. But he was a man of unlimited duplicity and he soon brought upon himself a series of serious denunciations. His most persistent and bitter enemy now was Kochubei, the Judge-General, whose daughter, Matrena, he had disgraced. Fiery and amorous by nature Mazepa, although over sixty-five years old, had fallen in love with this young girl, who returned his love with wild abandon. Kochubei set his heart on destroying Mazepa, and went to great lengths to denounce him for plotting with the enemy and on other charges.

Early in March 1708 Peter had received reports of these denunciations. He had considered them mere mischievous attempts to cause
unrest in the Ukraine. On 10 March he wrote to Mazepa, assuring
him he did not believe the accusations and had resolved to put an
end to them. Kochubei and his confederates were examined. They
were unable to substantiate their charges, and were handed over to
Mazepa who had them publicly executed on 14 July 1708. It was an
event that horrified the Cossack elders, most of whom were in sympathy with Kochubei.[7]

At the time of these interrogations Mazepa was already plotting
with Stanislas to throw in his lot with the Swedes. In the past
Stanislas had made repeated attempts to turn Mazepa's allegiance.
In 1705 an envoy from him had brought secret proposals to Mazepa,
who sent the envoy in chains to the Kiev voevod. Mazepa then wrote
a flamboyant letter to the Tsar in which he listed three other attempts to corrupt him, which he had scorned. "For I, the Hetman,
and the faithful subject of your Tsarish Majesty, by my duty and my
oath of loyalty confirmed on the Holy Gospels, as I served your father
and your brother, so now I serve you truly, and as up to this time
I have remained before all temptations like a column immovable and
like a diamond indestructible, so now I humbly lay my unworthy
service at your sovereign feet."[8]

It was true that during his long service Mazepa had given practical
demonstration of his loyalty. Peter was particularly indebted to him
because in the previous year he had held his Cossacks from supporting Bulavin. Mazepa had even sent three thousand of his Cossacks
against the rebel Bashkirs at a time when it seemed that the Don
Cossacks might join forces with them. In the face of such proofs and
of his untarnished record of twenty-one years of service, Mazepa was,
by Cossack standards, a paragon of loyalty, and Peter's stubborn faith
in him was not surprising. But his allegiance was far from deep-
rooted, and he had long been disgruntled.

Mazepa was an arch-conservative and typical of his people. The one
bond between the Little and the Great Russians was their Orthodox
faith. Having rebelled against Polish oppression, they had sought the
protection of the Tsar as a lesser evil. They wanted only to live in
freedom and independence and while, as their great leader Bogdan
Khmelnitsky had realized, they could not stand alone, they were ever
ready to break from Moscow's rule with Tatar, Turkish, or even

Polish help, if they saw a possibility of greater independence. Under Mazepa they had remained loyal to the tsars, but already the burdens of the war had begun to lie heavily upon the Ukraine. Provisions and wagons were requisitioned and moved in a steady stream westwards across the vast steppes to the Russian strongholds. The Tsar's officers and officials took the peasants for recruits and for labour gangs, and often the Russians behaved brutally. Mazepa found himself in the centre of a storm of complaints. His people protested that, while they were serving with the Tsar's armies, Great Russians pillaged their homes, raped their wives and daughters, and drove off their horses and cattle.

The Tsar's westernizing policies filled Mazepa and his Cossacks with horror. Relations between Russian troops and Cossacks were a further source of trouble. In action the Cossacks were brave and cowardly by turns, and never dependable. The Russians set no great value on them and at times showed contempt. The Cossacks complained of the overbearing attitude of Russian officers and of maltreatment at their hands.

It was Mazepa's responsibility to see that the Tsar's orders were enforced and they aroused the hostility of his people. He sympathized with their complaints, but it was by no means on this score alone that he finally deserted to the Swedes. Personal jealousy and resentment, and his anxiety to be on the winning side played their part. Menshikov was the chief source of Mazepa's bitterness and jealousy. Away from Peter's presence, Menshikov displayed an arrogance as overweening as his ambition. He was hated and feared by everyone, and especially by Mazepa, whom he apparently humiliated on at least one occasion. While jealous of Menshikov's power and wealth, Mazepa also feared that he had ambitions to be Hetman himself. These fears came to a head through a letter that he received from a certain Countess Dolskaya, who was one of Stanislas' intermediaries. The Countess wrote that in Lvov she had sat between Sheremetev and Ronne at dinner. In conversation the Hetman's name had come up and she had spoken well of him. Ronne had then said: "May the Lord have mercy on this good and able gentleman; poor fellow, he does not know that Alexander Danilovich [Menshikov] is digging a pit under him, for he wants, having disposed of him, to be Hetman of the Ukraine himself." Sheremetev confirmed Ronne's statement, according to the Countess, who then asked, "Why do none of his good friends warn the Hetman?" To this Sheremetev replied, "Impossible! We ourselves endure many things and are compelled to remain silent."[9] This letter confirmed Mazepa's worst fears and probably helped harden his intention to go over to the Swedes.

Determination to be on the winning side was another factor in his calculations. He had gained deep respect for Swedish arms during his youth when the Swedes had invaded Poland, and he took it for granted, as did most of Europe, that Charles would defeat Peter. The resounding Russian defeat at Narva in 1700 had formed his estimate of Russian arms, and he did not believe that the new army would be more successful. Nevertheless he waited and watched, without acting. Premature action would only have brought the Russians into the Ukraine, laying waste the land. The battle of Golovchina convinced him of the ultimate Swedish victory. Still he waited. The fire and bold decision that had marked his career had grown dim; his caution had withered into hesitation.

Mazepa was playing a dangerous game. For some months he had been in secret correspondence with Stanislas, and had promised to join with the Swedes, while making it clear that he could not yet march against the Tsar. At the same time he had taken care not to break with the Russians, whose complete trust he still enjoyed, and on receiving orders from Peter he feigned illness and made excuses to avoid carrying them out. But in July (1708), while Charles was at Mogilev, Mazepa committed himself in treaties of alliance with Charles and with Stanislas, which were to be kept secret. The old Hetman was still not finally bound; even if the Russians came to hear of his alliance with the enemy, he could deny it. But Charles's unexpected decision to turn southwards and into the Ukraine suddenly faced him with the need to commit himself irrevocably.

On learning of this change in Charles's advance, Peter had sent orders to Mazepa to lead his Cossacks across the Dnieper to attack the Swedes in the rear. Mazepa replied that he was too ill to take part and that in any case he could not move from the Ukraine where he had no one trustworthy to leave in command. Peter accepted these excuses, particularly as he himself was worried about the effect that the Swedish approach might have on the Cossacks and Ukrainians.

On 13 October, shortly after the battle of Lesnaya, Peter summoned Mazepa to a council of war at Starodub, where he himself would arrive between the eighteenth and the twentieth of October.

Mazepa decided now to go over to Stanislas and Charles. To the Tsar he sent his usual excuses of illness and gave an exaggerated account of unrest in the Ukraine. Peter agreed that he should remain at Baturin, for, as he wrote to Menshikov, "his great value is in keeping his own people in check, rather than in the war."[10]

Menshikov was not far from Baturin and wrote to Mazepa that he was riding to see him. At this stage neither Peter nor Menshikov had any suspicion of his intended desertion. But Mazepa was terrified when he learnt that Menshikov was coming. He was convinced that the Russians knew of his plans, and that Menshikov would arrest or kill him. Hurriedly Mazepa sent his nephew, Voinarovsky, with a message that the Hetman was critically ill, and was going from Baturin to Borzna to receive extreme unction at the hands of the Archbishop of Kiev. Mazepa then instructed Orlik to write to Count Piper, declaring his support for the Swedes. Charles was still at Mogilev resting his troops after the battle of Golovchina, when Mazepa's letter reached him, and Count Piper replied on his behalf welcoming the Hetman's support.

Still suspecting nothing, Menshikov decided to go to Borzna. Mazepa had just received Count Piper's letter with the news that the Swedish army expected to reach the Desna River on 22 October. Shortly afterwards, Voinarovsky, who had slipped away from the Russian camp during the night, galloped into Borzna to tell Mazepa that Menshikov was coming. Learning this, Mazepa "fled like a whirlwind"[11] to Baturin, arriving late at night. He posted troops there with orders not to admit the Russians. He then galloped to the Swedes with an escort of some two thousand officers and horsemen.

Menshikov was on the road to Borzna when he learnt that Mazepa had gone to Baturin. He turned and found that the garrison of Baturin were manning their defences to oppose his entry. Then he learnt that Mazepa had crossed the Desna River, and he realized what had happened.

With all speed Menshikov rushed to Pogrebki on the Desna from where Peter with his army was following the Swedish advance. Peter at once called a war council which decided that Menshikov should take Baturin before the Swedes could reach it. The town was of special importance not only as Mazepa's capital, but also because it contained stores in vast quantities that would be invaluable to the Swedes. Mazepa, too, knew the importance of Baturin and wrote secretly to the Cossack Colonel Skoropadsky, urging him to hasten with his men to protect the town against the Russians. But Skoropadsky, whom Mazepa had counted on to defect with him, remained loyal to the Tsar. It was Menshikov who rushed to Baturin in a race to take it before the Swedes arrived.

Peter waited anxiously. The Swedes had not yet reached the Desna River, and he had already sent Major-General Gordon with a strong detachment to delay their crossing. He wrote several times to Menshikov to make haste and to be on guard against the arrival of the Swedes.[12] But Menshikov had wasted no time. On 3 November, he stormed Baturin and captured it without serious loss. The Swedes, delayed by Gordon's detachment, had not yet crossed the Desna. But Menshikov, expecting them to arrive at any moment, did not consider that he had time to garrison the fortress and prepare the defences against siege. Peter had left it to his discretion to hold or destroy the town.[13] He decided to destroy it. With cold ferocity his troops put to death the Cossacks and inhabitants, and destroyed all stores. They then razed the whole town, including its stone walls and castle, to the ground, setting fire to the debris. The Swedes forced a passage over the Desna on 4 November and, reaching Baturin a few days later, found only burnt ruins and rotting corpses, which fouled the air. Nothing else remained of the proud capital of the Hetman.

The destruction of Baturin sobered the Ukrainians. It was a rough and rapid stroke of justice which they understood. The events of the following three days also impressed them. Peter, after learning of the capture of Baturin, had gone to Glukhov, where on 7 November the Cossack officers and elders, assembled in answer to his summons, elected Skoropadsky, the Colonel of Starodub, to be Hetman.

On the following day the Metropolitan of Kiev and two archbishops arrived. With all the ceremonial of the Orthodox Church they pronounced the curse of anathema on Mazepa. The ceremony was soon afterwards repeated in Moscow and in all the churches of Great and Little Russia.[14]

CHAPTER XXXI

Poltava

1709

THE climax of the Northern War was approaching. Charles was eager to fight. In every pitched battle against the Russians he had triumphed, and he was confident in final victory. And Peter, who in the past had been reluctant to risk so much in a single battle, was ready now to meet the challenge. His strategy had won him a position of strength and he had a deep certainty of his ultimate success.

Peter was expecting to fight this action during the winter of 1708-1709. In secret instructions, drawn up at the beginning of December 1708 for his commanders, he wrote that ". . . it is essential and urgent this winter, with the help of God, to fight a general battle."[1] Meanwhile he moved his army eastwards so that it protected the road to Moscow.

Charles, after crossing the Desna, had advanced to Romny, where he found good quarters for his troops, and for the first time in many months they had food and forage in plenty. He had hoped to take up positions farther to the north at Starodub and Novgorod-Seversky, but the Russians, moving rapidly, had themselves occupied both towns.

During the past month Charles had suffered two more serious disappointments. First, Lewenhaupt had joined him on 13 October (1708) from Lesnaya, with less than half his troops and without the great baggage train on which the Swedes were depending. The second disappointment, coming some two weeks later, was the arrival of Mazepa. The Hetman normally commanded between twenty and

294

thirty thousand men, and Mazepa had undertaken to bring over not only his own army, but also the Cossacks of the Don. The Swedes, desperately in need of reinforcements, had been counting on this Cossack horde. They found now that they had won as an ally only a defeated old man, commanding not more than two thousand Cossacks. Mazepa nevertheless received every consideration in the Swedish camp. He charmed Charles and expressed his conviction that the Ukraine would join him.

On reaching Romny the Swedes found copies of Peter's proclamation to the people of the Ukraine. It appealed to their Orthodox faith and to their hatred of the Poles and the Uniate Church; it damned Mazepa as a traitor and called on them to support their new Hetman in the fight against the Swedish tyrant; finally, it offered rewards for Swedish captives on a scale of two thousand rubles for a general, one thousand rubles for a colonel, for other officers according to rank, and five rubles for an ordinary soldier, while three rubles would be paid for a dead Swede.[2] Peter had, moreover, set at rest Cossack fears that he intended abolishing their freedom and privileges.

At the end of November, Charles circulated a manifesto of his own in Latin to the people of Little Russia, but it had no effect. Even the Cossacks who had accompanied Mazepa to the Swedish camp changed their minds, and gradually most of them slipped away to be welcomed in the Russian camp. Mazepa, too, had second thoughts. At the end of 1708, he sent one of his colonels, named Apostol, to the Tsar with the oral undertaking that he would betray Charles into his hands, if Peter would restore to him his office of Hetman and confirm publicly his good will towards him. His proposals were confirmed by a secret messenger and then by the arrival of another of his Cossack colonels, Galagan, from the Swedish camp. Golovkin wrote to Mazepa on 22 December, but nothing came of his attempt to negotiate further. Apostol and Galagan remained in the Russian camp, leaving Mazepa, even more isolated, among the Swedes.

In November, Peter had concentrated his army at Putivl, Sumy, and Lebedin to the north and west of the Swedes at Romny. But he was no longer content to shadow his enemy and retreat. On 7 December he sent a large force southeast towards Gadiach, where Charles on the advice of Mazepa had posted a garrison, and, as

Peter had anticipated, Charles at once set out to engage this force, leaving Romny without adequate defence. Having thus drawn the Swedes from Romny, Peter sent Hallart to capture the town, which he did without difficulty.

The Swedes were on the march to Gadiach when a savage frost seared the land. It was the most bitter cold in the memory of men. The rivers of Europe were frozen and the canals of Venice were covered with ice. In the vast steppes of Little Russia the cold was yet more intense. Birds died in flight and fell to the ground; wine and spirits became solid ice; men's spittle froze before it reached the ground. The troops hurried to reach Gadiach in hope of shelter, warmth, and rest, but a cruel fate awaited many of them. On arriving they found that the town had only one narrow gate which was soon blocked with wagons, horses, and men. Most of the Swedes had to spend one and even two nights in the open air, and their sufferings were hideous. Sentries froze to death at their posts. Men feared to sleep, for they knew they would not awaken. Frostbite furtively destroyed ears and noses, legs and arms. Sledge-loads of frostbitten men passed constantly into the town. Every house became a hospital, where the air was soon heavy with the noisome stench of gangrene. Doctors crudely amputated arms, legs, hands, and feet. Few Swedes escaped injury of some kind and it was said that as many as three thousand lost their lives at Gadiach. The Russians also suffered, but, being properly fed and clothed, their losses were comparatively light.

The savage frosts continued, but still Charles craved action. As soon as he could he marched from Gadiach to Zenkov. At this point he decided to seize the small fortress of Veprik, where Peter had left a garrison. It was a position of little importance, but he was determined to take it, probably as a reprisal for the Russian capture of Romny. He was successful, but, so spirited was the defence of the garrison, his victory cost him over a thousand men and forty-six officers killed.

In mid-February the frosts broke with thunderstorms and heavy rains. Melting snow and ice made the ground marshy and the rivers began to flood. Troop movements were nearly impossible. Charles posted his army in quarters between the Psiol and the Vorskla, tributaries of the Dnieper.

The Swedish army was now but a shadow of the magnificent force over forty thousand strong, that had marched from Saxony in

August of the previous year. Hardship, sickness, shortage of food, and incessant fighting with an enemy who always led them on and refused decisive battle, had reduced their numbers and undermined their strength. Furthermore the Swedish generals knew well how dangerous their position was in the midst of the steppe lands, and they now urged Charles to retreat into Poland, where their troops could recuperate. Then, reinforced by Krassau's corps and by Polish troops, they could march on Moscow. Again Charles rejected their advice because it would mean retreating. He sent orders to Krassau to join him, bringing supplies. But Krassau was nearly a thousand miles away. Moreover, Peter had on 26 December sent Generals Goltz, Golitsyn, and Gordon with troops by way of Kiev to ensure that Krassau's reinforcements did not arrive.[3]

Charles also had strong hopes of support from close at hand. Mazepa had assured him that the Cossacks from beyond the Dnieper rapids, and the Tatars from the Crimea could be won over to his side. Peter had been alive to this danger,[4] for he knew that he could not count on the loyalty of Ataman Gordeenko, the leader of the Zaporozhtsi. In March the Ataman joined forces with the Swedes, and soon afterwards, he marched with six thousand Cossacks, defeated a small force of Russian dragoons, and occupied the town of Perevolochna on the Dnieper. But, although his appeals to the Ukrainian peasantry met with initial success, and as many as fifteen thousand men from the regions of Poltava and Mirgorod joined him, he could not arm them, and they were, therefore, of little use. Next, the Khan of the Crimea, moved by Mazepa's appeals, sent envoys to the Swedish camp. The Khan offered to join the Swedes subject to the approval of the Porte, and at this time Mazepa was in fact desperately trying to obtain Turkish support.

Against this Tolstoy was active in Constantinople. Golovkin had instructed him at the beginning of 1708 to do all he could to win over the Turks. Early in 1709 Tolstoy reported that the Grand Vizir had confirmed to him that the Turks would maintain peace with Russia, that they would not allow the Crimean Tatars to march, and that they would give Mazepa no encouragement. But in April Tolstoy was reporting on the arrival in Constantinople of Tatar deputies who urged acceptance of Mazepa's proposals, and also on the offers of rich presents made by Stanislas and by the Swedes in return for Turkish support. Tolstoy himself expressed confidence that the Turks would resist these seductions, and in this he was to prove correct.[5]

Peter was pleased with Tolstoy's reports. But the assurances of the Grand Vizir did not banish his fears entirely. He decided to show his fleet in the Black Sea in the spring, as the best means of deterring the Turks from war. Throughout the winter he was impatient to go to Voronezh, and a rumour that Charles intended marching to destroy the shipyards there increased his impatience.[6] He had written several times to Apraxin telling him to go to Voronezh to make the ships ready and to prepare reinforcements and provisions for Azov.[7] Although he had stated in November that he would set out soon, he was delayed in Sumy by the illness of his son, and he did not leave until the end of January.[8] But then, on arriving in Voronezh, he himself fell ill and wrote asking Menshikov to send a doctor to him without delay.[9] He took the medicines prescribed and expected to be well again by mid-May. However, only on 27 May was he able to rejoin his army.[10]

Far from accepting the advice of his generals to retreat into Poland, Charles early in April moved farther south into the Ukraine. He had now decided to take Poltava, a small but important commercial town on the western bank of the Vorskla River and on the Kiev-Kharkov route. He had intelligence that a Russian garrison of five thousand men under General Hallart occupied it, and that they had stores in plenty, which his army desperately needed. His intention was, apparently, to make Poltava his main headquarters, while awaiting reinforcement by the Zoporozhsky Cossacks and Crimean Tatars, and by Krassau from Poland.

At the beginning of May, Charles began his siege. Again he was acting in opposition to his generals; they pointed out that the Swedish army was now too small to invest a stronghold of this size. Moreover, Charles's intention of making use of the Zaporozhsky Cossacks did not arouse their enthusiasm. But Charles was inflexible. He still felt himself to be the conqueror and was even surprised that the garrison had not surrendered simply on his approach. The Russians, however, gave no sign of surrender and showed spirit in the defence of the fortress.

Charles was tireless in leading and encouraging his weary men; wherever there was trouble or action, he appeared and inspired new efforts. But the Swedish difficulties were mounting. The summer heat was oppressive and they had soon consumed the food and forage of the surrounding district. For six long weeks the siege continued, until the Swedes, weary with skirmishing and repelling sorties from the fortress, found themselves facing starvation.

Menshikov, always the most lively and daring of the Russian generals, had meantime shadowed the Swedes in the march southwards. Soon after Charles had begun the siege, Menshikov, acting on Peter's advice,[11] took up positions on the eastern bank of the Vorskla, opposite Poltava. Sheremetev was at this time with the main army by the Psiol River, and at the end of May he joined Menshikov.[12]

The Russian and Swedish armies were now ranged against each other in full strength. Menshikov judged that the time for decisive action had come. He reported on the position to Peter who was already on his way to rejoin his army. On 31 May Peter replied that he was making all possible speed, but that, rather than lose the vantage, they should, if necessary, act without waiting for him.[13] Menshikov waited.

In the three and a half months that Peter had spent at Voronezh and Azov, the threats from the south had faded. First, the opposition of the Zaporozhsky Cossacks had weakened as a result of the invasion of their lands and the destruction of the Sech, the historic stronghold beyond the Dnieper rapids, which Peter called "a nest of treason . . . an accursed place, which was the root of evil and the hope of the enemy."[14] Early in May, Colonel Yakovlev with a detachment of cavalry sailed down the Dnieper in barges, supported by Colonel Galagan, who moved with another detachment down the right bank of the river. Yakovlev recovered Perevolochna and, with Galagan, he scattered the garrison of one thousand Cossacks left by Gordeenko. The Russians then advanced to the rapids and razed the Sech to the ground, burning even its revered church. It was drastic action, which stunned the Zaporozhtsi, already disheartened by losses in skirmishing before Poltava and by the hard labour, to which they were unused, of building entrenchments. Next, Peter had news that General Goltz was already in Poland, where he had routed a large Polish force, and had compelled Krassau to retreat. Finally, he learnt from Tolstoy that the Sultan had forbidden Devlet-Girei, the fiery Russophobic Khan of the Crimean Tatars, to support Mazepa or the Zaporozhsky Cossacks.

On 4 June, Peter rejoined his army and at once assumed supreme command. This was unusual; he had so often in the past appointed one of his generals in command, taking only junior rank for himself. But now he was expecting the great trial of arms with Charles, and he had no thought of retreating. As he wrote to Apraxin on 7 June, "we have gathered close to our neighbours [i.e, the Swedes] and with God's help, we shall certainly this month have our chief affair with them."[15]

Within a few days of his arrival, Peter decided to cross the Vorskla and to entrench his army nearer to the Swedes, but their first attempt at a crossing had to be abandoned.[16] Meanwhile from their position on the eastern bank of the river, opposite Poltava, they fired messages in hollow bombs into the town; the commandant replied by the same method, and Peter learnt that the garrison was running out of gunpowder and that the Swedes were mining under the ramparts. In fact, it was only a matter of time before Poltava would fall. At a council of war, he decided to cross the Vorskla without delay and engage the Swedes.

In a general order to his troops on the eve of the battle he proclaimed that "the hour has struck when the fate of the whole fatherland lies in their hands; either Russia will perish or she will be reborn in a nobler shape. And they must not think of themselves as armed and drawn up to fight for Peter, but for the tsardom, entrusted to Peter by his birth and by the all-Russian people." Again towards the end of the order he stressed his role as a soldier, like themselves, carrying out his duty, declaring that "of Peter it should be known that he does not value his own life, but only that Russia should live, and Russian piety, glory and prosperity."[17]

On 19 June, the Russian army moved two miles north of the town and on the following day crossed the river. Five days later Peter marched his army south along the river bank to within a quarter of a mile of the Swedes. He reached the new positions at night, and during the same night the whole of the Russian entrenchments were built.

The Russian camp was a quadrilateral in shape. Of its four sides only the western side was open to attack. This side faced on to a plain which extended north and south between two woods. Peter had foreseen that the Swedes would have to advance through the gap made by these woods. He had therefore built a line of six redoubts across the gap, and had also ordered four more redoubts to be built at right angles to them. The approach was thus divided into two narrow channels. The redoubts were strongly manned and he placed cannon so that all routes of approach would come under heavy fire. He also posted cavalry in a line behind the redoubts. Sheremetev commanded the centre, Ronne the right wing, Menshikov the left wing, and Bruce had command of the artillery.

It was on 25 June, while supervising the entrenchment of his new positions, that Peter learnt Charles had been wounded. Charles had ridden to reconnoitre Russian troop movements in what the Swedes thought was a feint attack, made as a diversion while the Russian army crossed the Vorskla north of the fortress.[18] Charles, accompanied by Lewenhaupt, approached within musket range of the Russian position. Lewenhaupt's horse was shot from under him, but Charles refused to move to a place of greater safety. Then a musket ball pierced his boot, and, running through his foot, came out at the heel. Bones were broken and the leg swelled. Gangrene was the danger and the surgeons thought the foot should be amputated. Charles refused. He ordered them to cut away all infected flesh, and without flinching he himself held his leg steady during the operation. This prompt action saved his foot, but the loss of blood made a heavy toll on his strength and, in the intense heat, he was prostrated by fever. At this point, he received news that Krassau could not march to reinforce him and that the Sultan would give him no help either directly, or by allowing the Crimean Tatars to take up arms.

Despite his wound and fever, the proximity of the Russians and the threat that they would attack were more than Charles could endure. His whole approach to war was one of attack and he prepared to strike first. He appointed Field-Marshal Rehnskjold in command, ordering him to advance against the enemy on the next day. His generals urged him to concentrate all his troops for this battle, but Charles refused. He kept some two thousand men before Poltava, two thousand five hundred guarding the baggage, and one thousand two hundred men on the west bank of the Vorskla River. Rehnskjold had a force only thirteen thousand strong.

On the night of 26 June the Swedish army drew up in battle order, the infantry in four columns supported by the cavalry in six columns. Before dawn next day the Swedes attacked. The four redoubts divided the battle into two distinct actions. Attacking the

Russians' left wing, Roos' infantry met strong resistance and lost many men under heavy Russian gunfire. Roos pressed on, followed by Schlippenbach, and they became separated from the main Swedish army. Peter sent Menshikov with cavalry and infantry to cut off Roos' force, which had taken refuge in the woods. In the fighting that followed the Swedes were routed, and Schlippenbach was taken prisoner with many troops.

On the Russian right wing, Sparre's infantry column, supported by the cavalry under Creutz, captured two redoubts. Creutz then hurled himself at the Russian cavalry, driving them back. Ronne was severely wounded and Bauer took over his command.[19] Peter now ordered Bauer to withdraw with his cavalry to the right of the Russian camp, so that the Russian infantry could advance from the entrenchments into battle positions. In pursuing Bauer the Swedish cavalry and then Lewenhaupt's infantry found themselves exposed to withering fire from the Russian entrenchments. They fell back to the woods that bounded the plain on the western side. Peter moved up with his troops, and they quickly formed in battle order before the Swedes. It was a swift, efficient movement by the disciplined army that Peter had created.

At 9 A.M. the two armies in the open plain met in general battle. The Swedes fought with their usual spirit. But they were outnumbered and were now fighting against a brave and stubborn enemy. Throughout the battle Peter showed great courage. Everywhere in the Russian lines his tall figure was conspicuous. A musket ball knocked off his hat, another struck his saddle, while a third glanced off the metal crucifix that he wore around his neck. His example in the thickest of the fighting spurred on his men.

Charles, too, with his customary disregard for all danger, had himself borne on a litter among his troops. His presence raised their falling spirits. Twenty-one of his twenty-four bearers were killed. Then a cannon ball shattered his litter and he fell heavily to the ground. All the Swedes near by thought that he had been killed. The rumour flashed along their lines that the King was dead. But Charles had himself lifted onto a seat made of crossed pikes and continued to rally his troops.

Nevertheless the Swedes were near the end of their strength; their lines were beginning to break. The rumour that the King was dead had also done its damage. Rehnskjold galloped up to Charles and reported that their infantry was lost. "Lads, save the King!" he shouted and then led a desperate charge at the Russian lines, where he was quickly surrounded and taken prisoner. Charles himself was in danger of capture. He was saved by the sacrifice of one of his officers who gave him his own horse, and was soon afterwards cut down by Cossacks. Weak from fatigue and the bleeding of his wound, Charles lay on the neck of the horse, and ordered the retreat. By midday the battle was over.

The Swedes lost some three thousand killed and more than two thousand taken prisoner. Russian losses were thirteen hundred men. The Swedish prisoners included four major-generals, five colonels, and numerous other officers, as well as Field-Marshal Rehnskjold, and Count Piper who, separated from the King towards the end of the battle, had made his way with two chancery secretaries to the gates of Poltava, and given himself up. Led by Charles and Lewenhaupt, the remainder of the Swedish army, exhausted and demoralized, retreated southwards towards the Dnieper.

This was Peter's great moment of victory. The long tension and anxiety were suddenly released. He attended a service on the field of battle to give thanks. Then he celebrated. The Swedish generals and officers were brought to his tent and he sat them down at his side. He was exultant, but not arrogant. He showed consideration and great courtesy to the Swedes and especially to Rehnskjold, praising him for his bravery and presenting him with his own sword. During these festivities Count Piper was led in and promptly seated at the Tsar's table. Then to the roar of cannon salutes, Peter rose and proposed a toast to his teachers of the art of war. "Who are your teachers?" asked Rehnskjold. "You are, gentlemen," replied the Tsar. "Then well have the pupils returned thanks to their teachers," commented Rehnskjold.[20]

So great was Peter's excitement over this victory that he gave himself up to celebrating and talking with his prisoners. It was five o'clock in the afternoon before he thought of pursuing Charles and his retreating army. He then hurriedly sent Prince Golitsyn with the guards regiments and General Bauer with dragoons in pursuit. On the following morning Menshikov with cavalry joined the hunt. They came up with the Swedes at Perevolochna at the junction of the Vorskla with the Dnieper.

Charles and his generals had hoped to take the survivors from their shattered army across the Dnieper and into Moldavia. But they found Perevolochna in ruins and all boats and barges destroyed.

Charles himself was exhausted; Lewenhaupt and Creutz persuaded him to leave his army and make his escape in the two boats which they had found upstream. Charles went in one boat and Mazepa, clinging to two barrels of gold coin, went in the second. The Zaporozhtsi improvised rafts and enabled about one thousand of the Swedes to cross the river. Charles made his way to the Bug River closely pursued by the Russian cavalry. At one point they came up with him and captured part of his escort. But Charles managed to escape again and reach Bender.

Lewenhaupt and Creutz remained near Perevolochna with some twelve thousand men. The Russians were approaching, but Lewenhaupt could not rally the Swedes to fight. When Menshikov drew near with his cavalry, Lewenhaupt sent Creutz to negotiate their surrender. Menshikov offered honourable terms, from which the Zaporozhtsi were excepted, and Lewenhaupt had no choice but to accept.

"Thus, by the grace of God, the whole of the enemy's famous army, which during its sojourn in Saxony, had filled Europe with terror, fell into the hands of His Majesty the Tsar."[21] Including Lewenhaupt's detachment from Riga, the Swedish army had numbered nearly sixty thousand men. Half of his force had perished in the advance eastwards and into Little Russia. The remnants of the army, 16,947 in number, were taken prisoner in the battle of Poltava and afterwards at Perevolochna. The Swedish army no longer existed: Sweden had ceased to be the great Northern power.

No men could have served more loyally and bravely than the Swedish troops. They deserved better than to be sacrificed to the pride and obsessions of their King. Nor did Charles show any awareness of the devotion of his officers and men. In defeat he blamed his generals. He also refused to believe that the surrender at Perevolochna was unavoidable, and condemned Lewenhaupt, the most gallant and able of his officers.

After the battle Peter sent letters to Catherine and to his colleagues, giving them the tremendous news. To Catherine he wrote: "Little Mother, good-day. I declare to you that the all-merciful God has this day granted us an unprecedented victory over the enemy. In a word, the whole of the enemy's army is knocked on the head, and you will hear about it from us. Come here and congratulate us. Piter."[22] He also made a dutiful report to Romodanovsky, now elevated from King to Kaiser, congratulating him "on a victory such as has never before been heard of in this world," and adding: "Now without doubt Your Majesty's desire to have your permanent residence in St. Petersburg has been made possible by this final defeat of the enemy."[23]

But it was in his letter to Feodor Apraxin that Peter expressed most succinctly the chief reason for his great joy, and summed up the significance of Poltava for him. "Now," he wrote, "with the help of God the final stone in the foundation of St. Petersburg has been laid."[24]

On the return of Menshikov from Perevolochna, rewards and decorations were announced for the whole army. Peter himself received promotion. He had served in the rank of Colonel. At the request of the high command, officers, and troops he was now proclaimed Lieutenant-General in the army and Rear-Admiral in the navy.

In Moscow the news was reported in the Vedomosti, and many of the senior officials received letters from the army. The city gave itself over to celebrations. Peter was anxious to take full advantage of his victory to raise Russian prestige, and a stream of letters giving a detailed account of the battle went out from his camp to Poland and to all Russian ministers abroad, while on his instructions Menshikov wrote specially to the Duke of Marlborough about the victory.

At Poltava the Russian dead were buried under a mound marking the centre of the battlefield. Swedish prisoners were marched off, some to Kiev, Moscow, and St. Petersburg, and some to Siberia and other provinces. Swedish generals were treated with courtesy, and several were allowed to go to Stockholm to propose peace terms and to negotiate the release of Russian prisoners. Many Cossacks and Zaporozhtsi were executed for treason, but the majority received pardons.

By now Poltava had become extremely unhealthy. Two armies had stood there for some weeks, and rotting corpses added to the unbearable stench. On 13 July the Russians moved to Reshetilovka. From there, on 15 July, Field-Marshal Sheremetev marched with the infantry and detachments of cavalry to lay siege to Riga, while Menshikov with the bulk of the cavalry, advanced into Poland to operate with Goltz against Stanislas and Krassau. Peter himself set out for Kiev.

CHAPTER XXXII

The Aftermath of Poltava

1709-1711

NEWS of the Russian victory resounded throughout Europe. It was unexpected and its full significance was as yet imponderable. But most governments were quick to grasp the fact that a new power had arisen, changing the old balance of Europe. For the first time in history Russia had emerged as a major factor in European affairs. Peter had proved his new army and was building a navy, a force which Russia had never before possessed; with a navy and his new ports he threatened to dominate the Baltic. Suddenly western Europe as a whole watched the Tsar with suspicion and fear, an attitude which was to condition their policies in the years ahead.

The intoxication of victory did not distract Peter for long. He knew that Sweden would not readily capitulate, despite this overwhelming defeat. Meanwhile there was also the danger that Charles might advance into Poland or the Ukraine with Turkish, Tatar, and Cossack troops, and arouse the Ottoman Porte to declare war on Russia. With this in mind Peter was eager to revive his Northern alliance and to strengthen his foothold on the Baltic. He would then force the Swedes to sign a permanent peace, after which he could give his full attention to internal reforms. Later he would turn southwards again and compel the Turks to admit his ships to the Black Sea.

Reaching Kiev on his way from Poltava into Poland, Peter attended a service of thanksgiving in the Cathedral of St. Sophia. There the preacher was a certain Feofan Prokopovich[1] who in his sermon dwelt with patriotic fervour and eloquence on the might of Russia, making much play of the fact that the battle had taken place on the day of St. Samson, and likening Peter to a new Samson, who had torn asunder the jaws of the Swedish lion. It was a stirring sermon, proclaiming Russia as a strong and progressive power.[2] Peter had it printed in Russian and translated into Latin for circulation in western Europe. Nor did he overlook the preacher. Prokopovich was to become one of his most active and important supporters.

Peter had not intended staying in Kiev, but on 6 August he wrote to Menshikov that "sickness had for my sins stricken me . . . it's really an accursed illness, for, although not now accompanied by shivering and temperatures but with nausea and pain, it lays me low unexpectedly, and so I do not think I will be able to leave here because of weakness earlier than the 10th or on the holy day of the Assumption."[3]

It was not, in fact, until 15 August that Peter set out from Kiev. At Lublin an envoy from Augustus met him with fulsome congratulations. He reported that Augustus was marching from Saxony with an army fourteen thousand strong and that he was anxious to meet the Tsar at Thorn. Peter apparently had no hesitation in continuing to support Augustus, despite the Polish King's treachery and constant failure in the face of their enemy. On 29-30 September they renewed their alliance. Peter undertook to maintain Augustus on the Polish throne, and in a secret clause promised the duchy of Courland to him and his heirs as Elector of Saxony.[4]

While at Thorn, Peter received an envoy from Frederick IV of Denmark, who brought new proposals for a defensive and offensive pact against Sweden. Peter referred him to Prince Vasily Dolgoruky who had already spent months in Copenhagen vainly trying to negotiate such a pact. Then, however, the Danes had lacked money and been afraid of English and Dutch intervention. But now the news of Poltava gave them courage, and so Dolgoruky at last managed to conclude the alliance.[5]

From Thorn, Peter went to Marienwerder to meet the King of Prussia. Frederick was both jealous and afraid of this fellow monarch who had so unexpectedly emerged as the great power in the North and who, as a close neighbour, might seriously threaten Prussia. He nevertheless expressed warm brotherly sentiment towards the

Tsar, for he coveted certain Swedish possessions and, hoping to acquire them by diplomacy rather than by arms, was intent on pursuing his policy of friendship with Russia.

Within little more than three months of Poltava, Peter had thus renewed all his former alliances, for what they were worth. He turned now to the task of forcing the Swedes to capitulate.

The first step was to eject their garrisons from northern Europe and the Baltic states, and at the same time to guard against the return of Charles from Turkey. Accordingly Peter sent Menshikov to post troops on the Hungarian frontier to prevent Charles entering Poland. He also sent Major-General Nostitz to capture Elbing, held by a small Swedish garrison.[6] He himself set out across Prussia and Courland to join his army standing before Riga.

Reaching Sheremetev's camp in the early hours of the morning of 9 November, Peter at once inspected the siege positions. On 13 November he wrote to Menshikov: "Today at five o'clock in the morning the bombardment of Riga began and with my own hands I fired the first three bombs into the town, for which I thank God that I myself have been enabled to set under way our revenge of this accursed place."[7]

Riga did not, however, fall at once. Its defences were strong and the onset of winter made operations difficult for the siege force. But the town was completely blockaded and without hope of relief of any kind. Peter therefore ordered Sheremetev into winter quarters, and left Prince Repnin with only six thousand infantry and one thousand cavalry to maintain the siege.

On the day after opening the bombardment of Riga, Peter set out for St. Petersburg. It was to be a hurried visit, lasting just two weeks. He ordered the foundations to be laid of a new church dedicated to St. Samson, the patron of Poltava. He instructed his ministers, generals, and magnates to build for themselves in the city houses of stone, of good architecture, and with spacious gardens. He devoted much time to speeding up the building of docks, facilities for sailors, and warehouses for merchants. On 6 December he laid down the keel of a warship to be called the *Poltava*. He then went to Moscow for his triumphal entry into that capital, and this fittingly was more magnificent than any previous victory parade.

Peter remained in Moscow until mid-February, attending chiefly to civil affairs.[8] His main concern was for the finances of his tsardom which were growing steadily more critical. On 27 January (1710) he ordered a statement of the national income and expenditure for the years 1705-1707 to be drawn up. It was the first time that this had been done in Russia and it showed a deficit. Income was 3,113,879 rubles; expenditure was 3,834,418 rubles. And since 1707 expenditure had been rising sharply.

He was impatient to begin operations against the remaining Swedish strongholds in the Baltic states. Returning to St. Petersburg, he at once sent General-Admiral Apraxin with eighteen thousand infantry to lay siege to Vyborg which fell in the following June. In this he took special pleasure, partly because his earlier attempt had failed, but mainly because, as he expressed it in a letter to Catherine, this newly acquired fortress-town would provide "a strong pillow for St. Petersburg."[9]

After himself visiting Vyborg, Peter returned to celebrate the first anniversary of Poltava; he decreed that the twenty-seventh of June should thenceforward be observed as a national festival. Meanwhile envoys from the Duke of Courland had come to ask the hand of Tsarevna Anna, daughter of Peter's half-brother, Tsar Ivan. Peter welcomed a marriage which would further strengthen his position on the Baltic and he therefore accepted oncrous conditions under the marriage settlement. The wedding took place on 31 October in St. Petersburg, but two months later the young Duke suddenly died. Despite undertakings in the marriage settlement, Russian troops at once entered the duchy to ensure that it did not become a weak link in Russia's chain of defences.

During the summer of 1710 the Russians had further successes. Riga, its garrison weakened by hunger and by the plague, at last surrendered in July to Sheremetev. Pernau and Arensburg fell in August, and Keksholm and Reval in September. Thus the conquest of Karelia, Ingria, and the Baltic states was complete.

Peter spent most of the second half of 1710 in St. Petersburg. His city was now secure and he watched it grow under his urgent supervision. Some years earlier he had chosen a site on the southern bank of the Great Neva, almost opposite to the Petropavlovsky fortress, for a summer garden. It was a marshy waste, but he intended that ultimately these gardens would rival those of Versailles. He had a canal dug on the western side, so that with the Neva in the north, the Fontanka in the east, and the Moika in the south, water surrounded it. Following the fashion of the day, the garden was to be geometrical in pattern, with long straight alleys, pruned shrubs and hedges, and sylvan groves. He ordered flowering plants and limes, oaks, beeches, and other trees, especially his favourite—the fir, to be brought from all over Russia and from the West, and to be planted there. Rapidly a magnificent garden took shape.

Also in this year, Peter gave approval to plans for a summer palace to be built in this garden, and work began without delay. Domenico Trezzini designed a two-storey house in the simple Dutch style that Peter favoured. Around its walls twenty-nine terracotta bas-reliefs illustrated Russian victories in the Northern War. Finished in 1712, it was a home which suited Peter who, when in his city in summer, always occupied the ground floor, while Catherine had the second floor.[10] Also in 1710 he ordered a monastery to be built on the banks of the Neva, and dedicated to Alexander Nevsky, the Russian saint and hero who had defeated the Swedes there 470 years earlier, and whose victory Peter had now reasserted.

Only the deterioration of relations with the Ottoman Porte in the south cast a shadow over this sojourn in his paradise. Even though the Sultan had maintained peace during all the critical months leading up to Poltava, the dangers of a change in his policy were ever present. There were many in Constantinople, led by Devlet Girei, who were eager to march on Russia.

The sudden arrival of Charles XII and Mazepa in Turkish territory gave fresh strength and urgency to the warlike pleas of Devlet Girei's party. On 22 July 1709 Tolstoy, on receiving Golovkin's report of the great Poltava victory, had at once demanded that Charles and Mazepa should be held under guard pending their surrender—knowing that the Turks could not possibly accept this demand. In his despatches to Moscow he explained that, while no guests could be more unwelcome, the Turks were bound by their laws and religion to accord them hospitality. He added, moreover, that the Turks, who had always expected the Tsar to wage war against them eventually, were so convinced that in order to capture Charles, Peter would launch his campaign immediately, they had begun mobilizing their troops. A few weeks later the Grand Mufti warned Tolstoy that, while the Porte would not march on Russia in the autumn, he could not make the same promise for the spring of 1710.[11]

King Charles, meantime, had settled down near Bender on the

banks of the Dniester. His wound had healed and his supreme self-confidence remained unshaken. Shortage of money was his problem, for in Constantinople, more than anywhere in Europe at this time, the diplomat who came empty-handed was at a serious disadvantage. But a few months later Mazepa died, a broken old man, and at once his nephew handed over to Charles the dead man's treasure chest. Charles also received loans from Holstein and from the Cook brothers, the English bankers of the Levant Company. Furthermore Mazepa's secretary, Philip Orlik, had been elected emigré Hetman of the Ukraine, and he now worked tirelessly to bring about an alliance between Charles and the Sultan as a first step towards delivering the Ukraine from Russian suzerainty. Finally, Charles had the services of two able Russophobe agents in Poniatowsky, a Polish supporter of Stanislas, and in Neugebauei, the former tutor of Tsarevich Alexei, and the two men waged a bitter diplomatic battle with Tolstoy.

At first Tolstoy held the advantage and won Turkish agreement to renewal of the peace of 1700 and to the return of Charles to Sweden. But in January 1710 Poniatowsky managed to present direct to the Sultan a letter from Charles denouncing the Grand Vizir, Ali Pasha, as a traitor in Russian pay. At once Ali Pasha was exiled, and when his successor, although well disposed to Charles, was also reluctant to break with the Russians, Poniatowsky engineered his dismissal too. Baltadji Mahomet, a warlike vizir, succeeded him.

During all these months the indefatigable Tatar Khan had also been aiding Charles's agents, and arousing Turks in all quarters against Russia. In consequence most of the janissaries were demanding war and they were an unruly force, feared by the Sultan. Thus on 20 November 1710, a meeting of the Divan made a formal declaration of war. Tolstoy at once reported this to the Tsar and his despatch reached St. Petersburg on 22 December, by which time he himself had been flung into the dungeons of the Tower of the Seven Bastions.

Nothing could have been less welcome to Peter at this juncture. He still feared Swedish attacks; in his Northern alliance the Danes were fainthearted and the Poles unreliable. The Danes had won a brief success in Scania, but in February 1710 the Swedes had routed them. Russian relations with the Poles continued to be uneasy. The damage done by Russian troops stationed in Poland aroused special bitterness among the Poles, and their complaints on this score were apparently justified, for as Grigory Dolgoruky, the Russian ambassador, wrote to Golovkin: "You yourself know how our people behave towards the Poles, but now they are behaving even worse. . . ."[12]

On receiving Tolstoy's report of the Sultan's declaration of war, Peter at once began moving his troops. He ordered Prince Mikhail Dolgoruky, then in Poland with ten regiments of dragoons, to march to the frontier of Wallachia. He sent Sheremetev with twenty-two infantry regiments from Livonia towards the Wallachian frontier. Prince Dmitri Golitsyn, Governor of Kiev, was instructed to watch carefully for signs of unrest in the Ukraine and to station his troops at suitable points to prevent incursions by Turks and Tatars. Peter himself, appointing Menshikov in command of the defences of St. Petersburg, set out for Moscow, arriving on 21 January. While there he made further preparations for his war in the south; but typically he also devoted much of his time to what he considered urgent civil reforms.

The administration of Russia had been grossly inadequate when Peter came to the throne. He had introduced numerous reforms, but they were in the nature of palliatives. The fact that so many of his demands for money, men, and armaments had been met in the past was due solely to his own driving energy and determination. The fact remained that the unwieldy Muscovite bureaucracy always worked inefficiently and wastefully unless he put his shoulder to it, and he had long realized that an over-all reform was needed.

One basic fault in the government was its lack of a central executive. The Tsar was both the source of all authority and the chief executive officer. All action waited and depended on him. The old Council of Boyars had lost its authority and, since he created no new boyars, was dying out altogether. The various departments of state were unco-ordinated and sunk in sloth and corruption. Thus he did not even have legislative and executive organs to which he could safely delegate authority. Consequently he had to entrust his various projects to his special ministers and colleagues; even these he had to instruct carefully and watch constantly.

He could not attend to everything himself; ukazi remained in abeyance for lack of his supervision; matters requiring action were neglected; anomalies persisted. Nevertheless the amount of business that he despatched was staggering in its detail and scope, and it was his private chancery, a small personal staff attending him everywhere, that made this possible.

This chancery consisted of three secretaries appointed by himself. Of these, Alexei Makarov was by far the most important. Makarov was a humble clerk in Vologda when Peter came upon him and made him his cabinet-secretary. Modest, self-effacing, and discreet, he was always at Peter's side and, since he handled all letters and papers, deciding when they should be brought to Peter's notice, he wielded such power that the greatest in the land, including even Menshikov, sought his favour. The two other personal secretaries were Nikita Zotov, Peter's old tutor, and Osterman, an obscure Westphalian, son of a Lutheran pastor, who dealt with foreign correspondence and later became a prominent minister in the Russian service. Through the hands of these three men flowed a constant stream of papers.

As the Northern War dragged on, finance was Peter's desperate problem and it was in handling the national revenues that the ineffectiveness of the administration was most apparent. At the end of 1708 he had reorganized the whole country into eight vast governments, each with a governor at its head.[13] He gave extensive powers to the governors, especially in the field of finance. But this act of decentralization left a dangerous vacuum at the centre where a strong executive was needed. Confusion greater than before resulted. Governors, remote from all supervision in their vast territories, behaved like autocrats, and corruption was rife.

Now war with Turkey meant that Peter would not have the respite he had hoped for. It would take him away from the civil administration of his country for a further indefinite period; the government of Russia would lumber to a standstill. On 22 February 1711, therefore, he promulgated a brief ukaz, establishing a senate to govern in his absence, and appointing nine senators and a clerk.[14] Eight days later, on 2 March, a further ukaz was issued "to the Senate concerning its activity during the absence of the Tsar from Petersburg."[15] It was to be the central executive organ with control over the provincial governments; it would act as the supreme court of justice, and it was to have various special responsibilities.

This ukaz was promptly followed by yet a third, ordering all his subjects, irrespective of rank, to obey the ukazi of the Senate as the ukazi of the Tsar himself. The form of oath to be sworn by senators was laid down, and on 2 March in the Uspensky Cathedral both senators and governors swore to serve with honour, integrity, and diligence. On 5 March Peter issued regulations setting out the procedure to be followed by the Senate.[16] All senators were to have an equal vote and their decisions must be unanimous; all were to sign each ukaz and the absence of any one signature would invalidate it; any senator who opposed the passing of any ukaz had to give his reasons for so doing in writing.

Another of the more serious faults in the administration of Russia had always been its slowness. This was not so much a result of the vast distances separating the various provincial capitals from Moscow; rather it was the result of the dilatoriness of the governors themselves. This was something that had frequently exhausted Peter's patience. Now, in establishing the Senate, he specified that a *kommissar* for each provincial government should be attached to the office of the Senate and that special couriers should carry all correspondence between each kommissar and the governor of his particular province.

Of the many heavy duties imposed on the Senate, the efficient management of finance, and the control of all officials responsible for handling and increasing revenue, were paramount. Peter's instructions allowed no doubt on this score. The first two clauses of the ukaz of 2 March laid down that it was the duty of the Senate "throughout the tsardom to watch over expenditure and to check wasteful, but in particular unnecessary, expenditure, and . . . to collect as much money as possible for money is the life-blood of the artery of war."[17]

Peter at this time also established a new class of revenue officers, called by the foreign name, "fiscals." These formed a special force, spying and reporting on tax evasion, corruption, and maladministration. But, whereas the first profit-makers had been individuals hastily chosen and expected to produce quick results, the fiscals were established on a more permanent basis. Peter made them part of the administration and imposed on the Senate the task of appointing a chief fiscal who would be responsible directly to the Senate itself, and who would exercise control over those fiscals, numbering about five hundred, who operated in the provinces. Soon these officials were permeating Russian life, and earning the bitter hatred of all classes of the population.

In the midst of these reforms, Peter took part in a religious service in the Uspensky Cathedral on 25 February, and then declared war on the enemies of the Cross. During the next few days he ordered

General-Admiral Apraxin to prepare defences against the Turks in the Azov region, and also to instruct the Cossacks of the Don and the Kalmyks to be ready to support the Tsar's armies by the spring. Finally he sent orders to Major-General Buturlin and to the Ukrainian Hetman, Skoropadsky, to proceed with eight regiments to Kammeny Zaton which they were to defend to the last man. On 6 March, he himself, accompanied by Catherine, set out from Moscow for the Polish frontier on his way to the Pruth.

CHAPTER XXXIII

The Campaign on the Pruth

1711

PETER decided to carry the war deep into Ottoman territory before the Turks could invade Russia. It was a bold plan, but not new. For some years Orthodox Christian leaders in Moldavia, Wallachia, and the Balkans had been appealing to him to adopt this strategy. They had urged him to invade the Budzhak, capture the Perekop Isthmus, and seize Ochakov, which was more important even than Azov as a key to the Black Sea.[1] Despite their urging, Peter had in the past concentrated on building up Azov and Taganrog, and in 1700 had even welcomed the idea of the thirty-year peace with the Sultan because this would allow him to devote himself to the war against Sweden. But now he commanded a well-equipped and seasoned army; Poltava had given him prestige and confidence; and the power of the Sultan was no longer so intimidating. The plan to attack and invade first had strong appeal, even though it depended largely on the Orthodox Christians rising against their Moslem masters. This was a risk, but one that Peter felt he had to take if he was to avoid Turkish invasion of the Ukrainian steppes.

For the present the Ukraine was quiet. Hetman Skoropadsky had a few days after Poltava submitted detailed demands for confirmation of all Cossack privileges and rights, and for protection against Russian depredations.[2] Peter had promised irrevocably to honour his guarantees to the Cossacks, and had even, in January 1710, given Skoropadsky written confirmation of them.[3] At the same time, as a safeguard against any repetition of Mazepa's betrayal, he appointed a special

316

representative at the Hetman's court. This, though seemingly a formality, was in fact a step towards reducing the Hetman's rank and power. And even after these precautions Peter could not be sure that the Ukraine would remain loyal in the event of invasion from the south. Now that war with Turkey had been thrust upon him, he preferred to wage it in Turkish lands.

Since the beginning of Sofia's regency in 1682, the Orthodox Christians had been turning more and more to Moscow for help and protection. The Balkan Orthodox longed to be liberated from the Moslem Turks, but not by the Catholic Austrians. Indeed, the advance of the Austrian armies had filled the Orthodox in the principalities and the Balkans with alarm. The envoy of the Wallachian Hospodar, appealing for Russian help, wrote, "We all pray with tears for the sovereign monarch to save us from the Papists and Jesuits, who rage against the Orthodox more than against the Turks and Jews. . . . The secular war may finish some time, but the Jesuit war never."[4] The capture of Azov and the emergence of Russia as a major power had given them new hope of liberation by the Orthodox Tsar. Peter had built up closer relations with them and now, without thoughts of Panslavism or of launching a long-term offensive against the Ottoman Porte, but to meet the immediate challenge of the Sultan, he appeared as the champion of the Orthodox.

Even before he had left Moscow, Peter had issued a proclamation to Catholics as well as Orthodox Christians in Serbia, Slavonia, Macedonia, Bosnia, and Herzgovina to join him against the Turks, thus to ensure that "the descendants of the heathen Mahomet were driven out into their old homeland, the Arabian sands and steppes."[5] This proclamation and the agents, sent to stir the Balkan Christians to take up arms against the Turks, met with an enthusiastic response, especially among the Serbs. Several times in the past Serb leaders had come to Moscow to obtain help or offer their services to the Tsar, and they had always been eager to fight the Turks.[6] Even the hardy Montenegrins, locked in their mountain fastnesses, although they had only slight contact with Russia, now also rallied to the Tsar's summons.

Of the Christian peoples under Turkish rule or suzerainty, however, the Danubian principalities of Moldavia and Wallachia were by far the most important. The Balkan peoples were remote and could at best only make local diversions, but the Moldavians and

Wallachians were on the Danube, and could help with troops in strength and with provisions.

Brancovan, the Hospodar of Wallachia, had ruled for more than twenty years, accumulating wealth and building a strong army. It was to displace him that the Turks at the end of 1710 appointed Demetrius Kantemir as Hospodar of Moldavia, offering him at the same time the prize of being Hospodar also of Wallachia if he disposed of Brancovan. But Kantemir had made up his mind, supported by the majority of the Moldavian boyars, to go over to Peter, and the subsequent approach of both Turkish and Russian armies allowed him no chance to temporize. He therefore sent an envoy to Peter, who concluded an agreement whereby Kantemir swore allegiance to the Tsar and promised the Russians all possible help; in return, Peter undertook to restore to Moldavia its old frontiers, with the inclusion of the Budzhak, to exact no tribute, and to dismiss no hospodar except for treason or apostasy. He also bound himself to make no peace with Turkey by which Moldavia would remain under Turkish rule. Two further undertakings, which were to prove more relevant, were, first, that in the event of Turkish victory, Peter would give asylum to Kantemir with suitable grants of land, and, secondly, that Kantemir would be free to leave such Russian asylum at any time.[7]

From Moscow Peter went to Lutsk on the Polish frontier. There he fell dangerously ill and had to rest for several weeks. He wrote to Menshikov that since birth he had never suffered so severely; one seizure lasting a day and a half had made him despair of surviving.[8] This illness left him weak and depressed, but he dragged himself on to Yavorov and there his spirits revived.

News reached him here that the Tatars had invaded the Ukraine and had been expelled with heavy losses by Skoropadsky and his Cossacks. Next came reports that Orlik had advanced into the Ukraine at the head of the Zaporozhsky Cossacks, reinforced by Tatar troops. But the Tatars had given way to looting and had then deserted, while the Ukrainian Cossacks had expelled the Zaporozhtsi. These events put at rest Peter's fears over the loyalty of the Ukraine. He wrote on 3 May in a confident mood, giving Menshikov this news, mentioning also that "the poor Christians are joining us truly zealously."[9]

Another reason for his higher spirits was the brief period of merriment that he enjoyed in Yavorov. Local Polish magnates gave balls and other entertainments for the Tsar, during which they paid Catherine the attentions now due to her as Tsaritsa. She enjoyed her new position and took part with gusto in this round of pleasure which was a change from the hardships of travelling.[10]

Peter also derived satisfaction from the signing on 19 April of an agreement for the marriage of his son, Tsarevich Alexei and Princess Charlotte of Wolfenbüttel, whose sister had married the Emperor, Charles VI, three years earlier. Baron Huyssen had originally suggested the union, but the negotiations had dragged on for over four years. The Duke of Wolfenbüttel had at first had doubts about the security of the Tsar's position. Poltava quashed these misgivings, and the Duke was now enthusiastic about the marriage. Without further delay the agreement was signed "for the benefit, strengthening, and succession of the Russian monarchy." In this, too, Peter was departing from tradition, for the sons of the tsars had always married Russians; he was also establishing a precedent, for always in the future the tsarevichi were to marry foreigners.[11]

From Yavorov, Peter went to Yaroslavl, there to meet Augustus who had come specially to discuss operations in the north. The Swedes had reinforced their troops in Pomerania, and Augustus now proposed to engage them and to lay siege to Stralsund. Anxious that the Swedes should have no respite, Peter gave Augustus one hundred thousand rubles and placed twelve thousand Russian troops at his disposal for this campaign.

Peter had ordered Sheremetev to advance with his army and to reach the Dniester by 15 or 20 May. Meanwhile he had been receiving letters from Orthodox Christians in various parts of the Ottoman empire, proclaiming their eagerness to rise against the Turks and to support the Russians. Impressed by these letters Peter now began acting with an urgency more characteristic of him than his earlier depression. He sent strongly worded orders to Sheremetev, which he repeated, to have his army drawn up on the Dniester banks with adequate supplies by 15 May without fail.[12]

Knowing Sheremetev's tendency to proceed at a stubbornly slow pace, Peter on 7 May sent Prince Vasily Dolgoruky to explain in person to the old Field-Marshal why speed was essential. On crossing the Dniester and entering Moldavia, Sheremetev was to call on Kantemir and send word to the Wallachian Hospodar that they were to place their troops under his command. Meantime, he was not to halt or delay in his march towards the Danube, but if he had reliable information that the Turks had already crossed, he was to take up suitable positions behind the Dniester.[13]

Sheremetev duly crossed the Dniester, and Kantemir then declared for the Russians. These two developments pleased Peter.[14] The next despatch from Sheremetev, however, brought bad news: the Turks had already crossed the Danube in force and, equally serious, the Russian army was suffering from shortage of supplies, for drought had stricken the lands through which they were marching. Peter was angry. From Soroka on the bank of the Dniester, which he had just reached, he wrote accusing Sheremetev of allowing the enemy to outmarch him.[15] The lack of provisions caused him special anxiety. But he obtained promises of early delivery of supplies for the troops with him on the banks of the Dniester, and from Sheremetev he received reports that provisions for the whole army for a month would be ready in Jassy.[16]

Because long marches in the heat were arduous, Peter now arranged to send Catherine and the ladies with her to a place of safety in Poland. Catherine, however, begged him to allow her to accompany him. He could not refuse her request and, indeed, he welcomed her company. She remained with him throughout this campaign.

At Soroka, Peter called a council of war. The five-day march from the Dniester to Jassy lay through desert lands, and on joining with the main army under Sheremetev there was no real certainty of adequate supplies for his men. Hallart, supported by other foreign generals, urged that they should stop at the Dniester. But Ronne argued that the whole campaign depended on the Russian army advancing. Not only would the Orthodox peoples not rise against the Turks if the army halted on the Dniester, but they would also feel cheated in their hopes of liberation. Anyway the honour and prestige of the Tsar and of Russian arms required them to advance. The Russian generals supported Ronne, and Peter accepted their advice. But he still acted with caution. He wrote on 13 June to Sheremetev asking him to state categorically whether he now had, if not grain, then cattle enough to feed all the infantry for six weeks, and on receiving Sheremetev's assurance, he began moving south from the Dniester.

Reaching the Pruth, Peter left his guards and infantry regiments, and hurried to Jassy where Sheremetev awaited him, his army stationed near by. Kantemir with his chief boyars greeted him at the approaches to the town. Thomas Cantacuzene, an enemy and rival of the Wallachian Hospodar, arrived and told Peter that he had come without the knowledge of Brancovan, who, he alleged, was opposing the Russians; he stated also that the people of Wallachia were ready to rise as soon as the Tsar appeared there with his army.

In Jassy, moreover, Peter received Turkish offers of peace. The Grand Vizir had sent the Patriarch of Jerusalem to Brancovan to request him to enquire whether the Tsar was disposed to make peace, for he had the Sultan's authority to treat. Brancovan had sent an envoy to the Tsar to report this approach. But Peter rejected it. The display of timidity by the Turks, coming after Kantemir's affirmation of his support and Cantacuzene's assurances of Wallachian help, had encouraged him. After weeks of uncertainty and misgiving over this campaign he now felt confident.

Accompanied by Kantemir and Cantacuzene, Peter now rejoined his army on the Pruth, and at a council of war held on 27 June, the anniversary of Poltava, he made the fateful decision to advance south along the right bank of the Pruth and through the forests to the Serech River. He believed that the bogs at the lower reaches of the river would protect his army against the Turks crossing to attack. Moreover, numerous reports had convinced everyone in the Russian camp that the Turks had built up great magazines of provisions around Braila. Peter sent Ronne ahead with the cavalry to capture these provisions and to carry what they could to Galati where they would rejoin the main army. In the course of this expedition they were also to compel Brancovan to declare for the Tsar.

On 30 June Peter with his main army, preceded by an advance guard under General Janus, crossed the Pruth and moved southwards. Although he had received reports that the Khan with a large force had crossed the river behind them, he continued this advance until 7 July. On that day General Janus reported urgently that the Grand Vizir was on the Pruth and the janissaries were already crossing. Peter at once ordered him to fall back to join him. He also despatched messengers to recall Ronne and the cavalry. Janus promptly retired and rejoined the army with his force intact.

The Turks now attacked the Russian army. They were met with heavy fire, but pressed the attack until nightfall. Peter then summoned a council of war. He needed the cavalry, but there was no sign of Ronne returning from Braila. Moreover, he realized for the first time that the Orthodox Christians were not rising in force against the Turks, and further that his army was hopelessly outnumbered. The Turks had in all 119,665 troops, supported by 70,000 Tatars, while the Russians numbered only 38,246. The one decision that Peter and his generals could reach was to retreat, fighting rearguard actions.

Early on the following morning the Russian army began to withdraw towards the Pruth. The Turkish cavalry pursued, but was beaten off. On 9 July the Russians reached the village of Novoe Stanelishte. Here Peter posted the baggage train on the river bank and deployed his troops around it. The Turks came up with them towards evening. Next morning the Turks attacked with infantry and cavalry, but, although the fighting lasted all day, they could not broach the Russian lines. Peter's troops, and especially his guards, fought desperately. Turkish casualties were heavy, the janissaries alone losing seven thousand men killed. During the night the Turks maintained heavy fire on the Russian positions, while building new entrenchments in which they mounted three hundred cannon.

Peter was in despair. He was surrounded and outnumbered, and had provisions for only a few days. His troops were worn out by heavy fighting in the sultry heat. He had no hope of relief or even of making his way north towards the Dniester. The fearful humiliation of Turkish captivity faced him.[17]

But counsels of despair reigned also in the Turkish camp. The Vizir did not realize that the Russian army was at his mercy. The janissaries had suffered so severely that they refused to attack the Russian lines again and demanded that the Sultan's orders to make an early peace should be carried out. Further, the Vizir learnt that Ronne with the Russian cavalry had taken Braila in his rear, and he feared that Ronne would return to attack him.

On 10 July the Russians captured a few Turks who declared that the Vizir was ready to negotiate a peace. Peter sent a trumpeter with a letter in Sheremetev's name to the Turkish camp, expressing willingness to avoid further bloodshed and to discuss terms. It seemed hardly possible to the Russians that anything would come of this approach. When no answer came, a second letter was sent, threatening renewal of fighting. To this letter the Vizir replied that he was not opposed to peace, and invited the Field-Marshal to send an envoy of eminence to discuss terms. Peter chose Shafirov for this critical mission and at once sent him with three interpreters and two couriers to the Turkish camp.

Shafirov's instructions reflected Peter's desperation. He was authorized not only to surrender Azov and the fortresses Peter had built in the south, but also to offer to return to Sweden all the Russian conquests on the Baltic, even including the old Russian town of Pskov, but not Ingria, for Peter would not contemplate the surrender of his "holy land" and "beloved paradise"; Shafirov could also agree to the restoration of Stanislas to the Polish throne, and in other ways satisfy the Sultan so that he should not take up the Swedish cause too zealously. In addition Shafirov had authority to offer the Vizir 150,-000 rubles as a gift, and similar large sums for his officers. As a last resort, if the Turks were not content with these terms, Shafirov could agree that the whole Russian army would surrender at discretion and lay down their arms, if they could then retreat north along the river bank.

From the Turkish camp Shafirov sent a message the same day that, while the Vizir wanted peace, he was acting slowly. Long-drawn-out negotiations spelt starvation for the Russian army. Peter replied immediately to Shafirov that he should "concede everything that they want except slavery."[18] Later the same day Shafirov returned to the Russian camp to report the Vizir's terms. They were severe, but not nearly so severe as the Russians were expecting. The main conditions were that the Tsar would surrender Azov and destroy Taganrog and the other fortresses; that he would not interfere in Polish affairs in future, or disturb the Cossacks; that he would no longer maintain an ambassador in Constantinople; that he would allow the King of Sweden free passage to return to his own kingdom, and that both Russians and Swedes should endeavour to agree to a peace. Finally, until the fulfilment of these terms by the Tsar, Shafirov and Colonel Mikhail Sheremetev, son of the Field-Marshal, would be held as hostages.

Peter accepted promptly, and on the next day, 12 July, the agreement was signed.[19] Shafirov then sent word that the Russians were free to withdraw from their positions. Peter was relieved; he had saved his army and had had to surrender nothing of his northern conquests. But the peace was also a bitter disappointment. He had lost all that he had gained in his campaign of 1696 and had built up since then. There was also the humiliation of a bungled campaign.

He had led his army five hundred miles to the south of Kiev, where no Russian army had ventured for more than seven centuries, but he had neglected even to organize an adequate supply train, placing altogether too much reliance on the promises of the Orthodox to rise against the Turks. Admittedly Brancovan had built up supplies enough to maintain the Russians, but as soon as the Turks crossed the Danube, he had saved himself by handing all these supplies to them. And, perhaps most foolish of all, Peter had marched south from the Dniester without information about the size and the position of the Turkish army, only to find himself hopelessly outnumbered and outmanoeuvred.

Peter now wrote to Apraxin, for he was in command at Azov and it would fall to him to surrender the town. His letter ended strongly with the comment that "while this affair is not without sadness in that we are deprived of those places to which so much labour and expense have been devoted, yet I hope this loss will lead to great strengthening in another quarter, which will be an incomparable gain to us."[20] He wrote in the same sense to the Senate, to Menshikov, and others. He made no recriminations and, as always, his mood of despair was short-lived. Already he was taken up with plans for his next Baltic campaign.

Peter could not, however, simply turn his back on Turkey. Disputes immediately broke out over the peace terms, due to his own reluctance to carry out his undertakings. In forcing the Swedes to a permanent peace, he had been relying on Augustus' co-operation and on being able to move his own troops freely through Poland. Now the clause of the Turkish agreement by which he was not to interfere in Polish affairs cut across these plans. At the same time he feared that the Sultan, under pressure from Charles, might renew his war. He therefore instructed Apraxin at this stage not to give up Azov or to dismantle Taganrog until the Sultan had confirmed the peace and Charles had been ejected from Turkish territory.

Because of this, at the end of December, the Turks again declared war. Realizing then that he had gone too far, Peter ordered the surrender of Azov, whereupon, on receiving confirmation of this in April 1712, the Turks renewed peace. But bitter wrangling now bedevilled the negotiations for a treaty. The Turks insisted on the complete withdrawal of Russian troops from Poland and, when Peter did not comply, they declared war yet again. But still Peter refused to jeopardize his campaign against Sweden. This time the Turkish declaration did not move him. Instead he began preparing for a defensive war in the south.

His resolution impressed the Sultan who had been led to believe that Peter's position in Poland and even in Russia was so insecure that he could not risk another war. The Sultan now felt that he had been deceived. He also knew that war with Russia would be unpopular among his own people, and that, if unsuccessful this time, he would face rebellion and possibly lose his throne. In consequence he decided on peace and finally broke with the Swedes.[21]

Meanwhile, in March 1713, Shafirov and Tolstoy had been summoned to Adrianople and peace discussions began. The Turks again threatened war. But there was among them a real anxiety for peace with Russia because now they desired to challenge Venice and from them to recover Morea. The English and Dutch mediated effectively, and Shafirov, showing courage and dexterity in his negotiations and furthering his cause with liberal bribes, managed at last to secure Turkish agreement to a definitive treaty, which was based on the original agreement made after the battle on the Pruth.

This treaty required Peter to confirm the cession of Azov, Taganrog, and Kameny Zaton, and to undertake to build no new fortresses in this region; he had to withdraw his troops from Poland within two months; he also had to accept a new delimitation of the Ukraine, giving up all claims to the right bank of the Dnieper, except the Kiev enclave, and acknowledging a new Ukrainian frontier between the rivers Samara and Orel in the north. They were hard conditions, but Peter had become resigned to losses in the south, at least for the present while he secured his position on the Baltic. On 15 July (1713) Golovkin wrote from St. Petersburg to Shafirov that the Tsar approved these terms, and the Treaty of Adrianople was concluded.[22]

CHAPTER XXXIV

The War in the Baltic: The Battle of Hango

1711-1714

PETER marched from the Pruth determined to force Sweden to an early peace. He needed it to compensate for his losses in the south and to erase the humiliation of the Pruth campaign; he needed it, too, because he was tired of war and had much to do in his own country.

But peace still evaded him, and for the next ten years he was to struggle in the entanglements of intrigue and diplomacy. Had he concentrated all his forces on crushing Sweden, he might have won peace earlier. But he was now more than ever cautious and reluctant to act without allies, no matter how weak or unreliable these might be. He was also ambitious that Russia should play her part, as a European power, in the policies of the West.

Nevertheless, although Peter suffered countless frustrations and failures, these years were far from being a barren period in his reign. Indeed he was at this stage more active than ever and, released at last from all threats of invasion, he gave his attention increasingly to internal affairs. He worked on constitutional, fiscal, and administrative reform with a persistence and intensity that were all the more remarkable in a man beset with problems and responsibilities in so many other fields. His reforms affected every part of Russian life, and were no longer hasty improvisations, geared to the needs of the war, but the work of a careful legislator determined to introduce a new efficiency, wealth, and well-being into his country. To this

326

end he issued a stream of ukazi which, gathering in a tidal wave, surged over Russia, transforming her irrecoverably.

For the moment, however, the hardships and anxieties of the Pruth campaign had told on his health and he was suffering from violent attacks of colic. Leaving Catherine at Thorn, he went to take the waters at Karlsbad.

While there, he made final arrangements for the marriage of his son, Alexei, to Princess Charlotte of Wolfenbüttel. Word of the marriage of the Tsarevich to a Lutheran and a foreigner had aroused hostility among Orthodox Russians, and Alexei himself was reluctant to marry a foreigner. But Peter would brook no opposition, and decided that the marriage should be solemnized quietly at Torgau, the residence of the Queen of Poland. He arrived there on 13 October and the wedding took place next day. He was in a jolly mood and pleased that the marriage was "celebrated in a proper manner."[1] But it was to be a union devoid of happiness, dissolving early in the death of Charlotte.

In Torgau, Leibniz obtained the audience that he had been tenaciously seeking ever since Peter had first travelled through Europe. Then he had managed only to present a request for information on the genealogy of the tsars and on languages spoken in Russia. But he was keenly interested also in what he considered to be Russia's destiny, namely the expulsion of the Turks from Europe, and, after the introduction of European civilization into Russia, her role as the bridge between Europe and China. Peter's reforms in the intervening years had intensified Leibniz's interest. He had now drafted extensive plans for spreading education in Russia and for establishing an academy of sciences to direct education and research.

No account of this meeting has survived. But, as a mathematician, philosopher, and scientist of unlimited enthusiasm, Leibniz was bound to impress Peter, who took great interest in his proposals for magnetic observations and in his requests for linguistic material, promising that it would be supplied through his personal chancery.[2] In the following year Peter appointed him a councillor of justice in the Russian service with the special function of advising on educational, legal, and governmental matters, and promised him an annual salary.[3] In a letter to the Electress Sophia, Leibniz wrote that she would "find it strange that I am to be in a sense the Solon of

Russia, although at a distance."[4] He was to contribute notably to certain of the reforms that Peter later introduced.

From Torgau, Peter set out for St. Petersburg, arriving on 29 December 1711. There, while keeping the direction of diplomatic and military affairs in his hands, he worked on the development of his city, the functioning of the Senate, and numerous other matters, including trade. In relation to this he had directed the Senate to form a company of merchants to trade with China. The Senate had mishandled the matter and he had written angrily about it while abroad. He had also sent instructions for the expansion of trade with Persia and Armenia.

One reason why the Senate functioned so sluggishly was that it was in Moscow, remote from supervision, for Peter seldom went near the old city. Accordingly, in April (1712), he moved the Senate to St. Petersburg. There he himself for a time took part in its daily sittings and in his presence business moved more briskly.

Building was going ahead in St. Petersburg. At the beginning of May (1712) the foundation stone of the new Cathedral of SS. Peter and Paul was consecrated. Forestry was another of Peter's particular interests. He had to husband timber resources to maintain the steady growth of his Baltic navy. This spring he sent two men to survey the forests along the banks of the Volga, Oka, and other rivers, and himself spent many hours planting acorns in the neighbourhood of his city.

Next, concerned over the delay and cost of transporting merchandise to and from St. Petersburg, he ordered the Scot, Farquharson, to survey a direct road to Moscow, and soon afterwards work began on building it. At the same time he sent engineers to survey the rapids on the Msta River and also the rivers Mologa and Sheksna, tributaries of the Volga, for the purpose of building canals to enable barges to bring cargoes direct to St. Petersburg. The engineers were to submit plans to the Senate and work was to begin without fail in the spring of the following year.

On 19 February (1712) in St. Petersburg Peter publicly proclaimed and celebrated his private marriage to Catherine of November 1707 in a special ceremony in the new Church of St. Isaac the Dalmatian. It was a further token of his love for her and it was also a mark of his gratitude for her staunch support during the anxious years leading up to Poltava and during the Pruth campaign. Two years later (on 24 November 1714) he was to institute a new decoration, the Order of St. Catherine, her patron saint, which commemorated the part she had played in this campaign when she had behaved "not as a woman, but as a man."[5]

Meanwhile, from Bender Charles XII had ordered Stenbock in Sweden to form a new army, move it into Pomerania, and invade Poland, expelling both Russians and Saxons. Early in 1712 Stenbock managed to transport six thousand men with sixty cannon to Wismar.

Learning of this enemy movement, Peter reinforced his army in Pomerania and placed Menshikov in command. At the same time he made strenuous efforts to induce his allies to operate together, but this was to prove impossible. The Danes were the chief source of trouble. They were timorous, venal, and vacillating; they were suspicious of the Russians and Prussians; they stood in awe of England and Holland, and they were afraid of the Swedes. But Peter considered the Danish navy essential to the invasion of Sweden and so he continued to seek their co-operation.

Not only from Pomerania, but from Poland, the news that reached Peter was disturbing. Charles had sent a rebel Polish leader, Grudzinsky, with a force of Poles, Tatars, and Cossacks, to capture Poznan. But to Peter's relief, Vasily Dolgoruky soon afterwards routed Grudzinsky and his rebels. At this time negotiations in Constantinople were not going well and Peter ordered Sheremetev to post troops in the region of Starodub and Smolensk as a precaution. But it was the campaign in Pomerania that he was most anxious to advance and he decided to go there himself.

On 15 June (1712) after launching his new warship *Poltava*, Peter, accompanied by Catherine, set out for Pomerania. At Riga he learnt of the defeat of Grudzinsky. But bad news reached him from Matveev in Holland, who reported that the English and the French were drawing closer together in support of Sweden, and that they were insisting on acceptance of their mediation to bring the Northern War to an end, even threatening to enforce their terms with arms. Peter in his reply to Matveev pointed out that "this will not be mediation, but coercion,"[6] but he expressed willingness to negotiate on the basis of formal cession by Sweden of Russia's hereditary lands on the Baltic. Like earlier proposals of mediation, this, too, foundered on the obstinacy of Charles.

Peter reached his army, standing before Stettin, to find that Menshikov could take no action through lack of artillery. He at once
sent a letter of protest to the King of Denmark.[7] But, despite this
protest, the Russian army remained without cannon, while the Danes
pursued their campaign in Bremen. The failure of operations in
Pomerania disgusted Peter. He travelled restlessly from place to
place and in Wohlhast held a council of war with Augustus and
with the Saxon and Russian generals. But he was constantly thwarted,
and anxiety and frustration, coming on top of the fatigue of incessant
travel, told on his health.[8] On 28 September (1712) after celebrating
the anniversary of the battle of Lesnaya, he set out again for Karlsbad and Teplitz to take the waters, and travelling rapidly, reached
Karlsbad on 8 October.

On this journey Peter stopped at Wittenberg, where he visited the
house in which Martin Luther had lived. The curator showed him ink
stains on the wall of one of the rooms and related how one night
Luther had received a visit from the devil, and had thrown the ink-
well at him, thus causing the stains which had never faded. Peter
laughed and asked whether such a wise man could really have believed that he had seen the devil. He then examined the stains and,
when asked to write something in his own hand on the wall, wrote:
"The ink is quite fresh; and this story is completely untrue."[9]

After three weeks in Karlsbad, Peter set out to rejoin his army.
Menshikov had reported that Stenbock was marching with his troops
from Pomerania into Mecklenburg. Peter saw in this the chance to
unite his allies and to end the year of frustrations with a decisive
victory. He wrote to the King of Denmark, asking him to lead his
troops into Holstein and to join with the Russian army there. He
was so anxious to secure Danish co-operation that he wrote again
from Dresden, expressing the hope that he could count on the Danes'
help in this important operation, adding that he was himself hastening to join his army, "although my health demands quietness after
the cure."[10]

Reaching the Russian headquarters at Lago, Peter ordered his
army to follow him to Gustrow. Stenbock then marched to attack the
Danes and Saxons before the Russians could join them. Expecting
this, Peter had sent urgent messages to Frederick IV and to Field-
Marshal Fleming, to avoid battle until united with the Russian
forces. They ignored his warnings. Stenbock engaged and completely

routed them at Gadebusch. The Swedes then marched into Holstein and took refuge in the fortress of Tonning. Three months later, Stenbock capitulated.

Peter now decided to return to Russia, leaving Menshikov in command at Friedrichstadt. He had not abandoned hope of drawing the Elector of Hanover and the King of Prussia into the alliance, and on his way back to St. Petersburg he had meetings with both of them. Both the Elector and Frederick-William I, who had just succeeded Frederick I on the Prussian throne, expressed goodwill and showed eagerness to share in the spoils of the war, but not in the fighting.

Unable to wring further action from his allies, Peter, on reaching St. Petersburg, ordered immediate preparations for an invasion of Finland. He had had this project in mind for some months. In October in the previous year he had written to Apraxin from Karlsbad that, with Finland in Russian hands, "the Swedish neck will bend more easily."[11]

On 26 April (1713) the Russian galley fleet, comprising ninety-three galleys, sixty brigantines and fifty large boats, carrying in all 16,050 troops, sailed from St. Petersburg, with Peter as Rear-Admiral commanding the vanguard. General Lybecker, whose attempts to take St. Petersburg in 1708 had failed, was again in command in Finland and again proved ineffective. The Swedish garrisons and the Finns fled before the Russian army which during the summer captured Helsingfors, Borgo, and Abo, then the capital of Finland. The Swedes made a stand near Tammerfors, but the Russians defeated them. In an easy campaign Peter had thus captured the whole of southern Finland.

During this summer of 1713, Menshikov, supported by Saxon troops, laid siege to the Swedish fortress of Stettin. At this time he was strongly attracted by certain proposals made by the Holstein minister, Goertz, an arch-intriguer who was to play an important role during the next five years. Goertz had proposed that, after taking Stettin, Menshikov should allow Prussian and Holstein troops to occupy it on condition that they returned it to Sweden on the signing of a general peace; in effect it meant the cession of Stettin to Prussia. The advantage of this to Russia was that it might bring Prussia actively into the alliance against Sweden, and that, according to Goertz, Holstein would also join with Russia. Goertz's real purpose was to break up the Northern alliance, and in particular to isolate Denmark in the interest of Holstein and Sweden.

Peter was extremely wary of these proposals. "Although the Danes have been ungrateful and have acted both blindly and stupidly," he wrote to Menshikov, "yet it is a fact that they are the enemies of the Swedes, and to us, primarily at sea, they are very necessary, and on these new friends, the Holsteiners, it is difficult to place our trust."[12] But the possibility of Prussian help was attractive, and he told Menshikov as the man on the spot to make the decision, using all caution.

In September (1713) Stettin capitulated, and Menshikov agreed to its sequestration by Prussia and Holstein. The Danes were horrified and their worst fears proved justified when, shortly afterwards, the King of Prussia, prompted by Goertz, demanded the withdrawal of Danish troops from Holstein-Gottorp, and even threatened to eject them by force. Danish fears and anger reached such a pitch that the Northern alliance seemed at an end. Only the efforts of Peter kept it together.

Meanwhile England was obstructing Peter's plans. Earlier in the year the English ambassador at The Hague, Lord Strafford, had told Kurakin that "naturally England would never wish to see the Swedish crown ruined and powerless. England's intention was to maintain the balance between all powers in the north as it was before."[13] English merchants and ambassadors showed alarm over the Russian threat to trade and stability in the Baltic. Their barrage of hostility disturbed Peter, who reiterated his readiness to conclude peace on the terms he had so often stated.

Throughout these diplomatic exchanges Peter consistently pursued his plan for invading the Swedish mainland. He needed the help of the Danish fleet for this operation, but Frederick IV was under strong pressure, especially from England and Holland, to withhold it. Early in 1714 Peter sent to Copenhagen a certain Yaguzhinsky, whom he had elevated from lowly rank to be Adjutant-General. Yaguzhinsky and Dolgoruky presented a plan for a joint Russo-Danish landing. But Frederick IV refused to commit himself. Again Peter's hopes for allied action had come to nothing and he spent the summer completing his conquest of Finland.

The great event of the year for him was his first important naval victory. The Russian fleet, commanded by General-Admiral Apraxin and Rear-Admiral Peter, had put to sea from Kronslot in May (1714) to cruise in the Baltic. It was a large fleet of some twenty ships of the line and nearly two hundred galleys. Peter attached special importance to these galleys, realizing that they could get under way and manoeuvre easily in the Baltic, where islands and sheer cliffs could immobilize vessels depending on sail. It was also an advantage that galleys could be manned by troops, whereas warships required seamen.

At the end of June the Russian fleet anchored at Tverminne, some six miles to the east of Cape Hango, or Gangut, where stood the Swedish fleet of sixteen ships of the line, five frigates, and other smaller vessels. The Swedish ships barred the way to the Aland Islands and the Swedish mainland.

On 26 July 1714, Peter completely outmanoeuvred the Swedes off Cape Hango. Admiral Watrang found Russian squadrons bearing down on him from two sides and with his main fleet he managed to escape to sea. Then the Russian squadrons rejoined and pursued Ehrenskjold's ships which took refuge in Rilaks Fjord.

Peter, in command of the vanguard, led his ships into the fjord to attack on the following morning. The Swedes had superiority in cannon and skilled seamen manning their ships, but the Russians outnumbered them by more than three to one. Success, therefore, depended on getting alongside and boarding the Swedish ships.

Peter first invited Ehrenskjold to surrender on honourable terms, but, when the Swedes rejected this offer, the Russians joined battle. The fighting raged for three hours with heavy casualties on both sides. Gradually, ship by ship, the Swedes were beaten. Then, seeing that he had no hope of victory, Ehrenskjold in the frigate *Elephant* struck his flag. He himself tried to escape to the shore, but was taken captive by Captain Bredale, master of the thirty-gun *St. Paul*, an Englishman who had played a prominent part in the battle. The remaining Swedish vessels promptly surrendered. The Russians captured the *Elephant* and nine galleys, with 116 cannon, together with the crews and troops in each galley. But more important than these trophies, the Russians now held the Aland Islands.

Peter took tremendous pleasure and pride in this victory, which he considered equal in importance to Poltava. Then he had defeated Sweden's army; now he had defeated her navy. His dearest ambition had always been to make Russia a sea power: in the battle of

Hango he realized this ambition, and when early in September (1714) he returned to St. Petersburg, he celebrated with enthusiasm. His squadron anchored near the Admiralty and the victory parade, after marching under a triumphal arch, halted in front of the Senate buildings. Peter himself entered and asked permission to report to the Prince-Emperor (Romodanovsky). He presented his report and also a letter from General-Admiral Apraxin, his senior officer, praising the service he had rendered. The Prince-Emperor ordered both documents to be read aloud, and then promoted Peter to the rank of Vice-Admiral.[14] This promotion, won by action at sea, gave Peter great satisfaction, and writing to Apraxin about it, he expressed gratitude for the latter's recommendation.[15] All who had taken part were rewarded with promotion or medals and money.

CHAPTER XXXV

The War in the Baltic: Peter in Paris

1714-1717

ON 27 August 1714, as he returned to St. Petersburg, Peter learnt of the death of Queen Anne and the accession of George, Elector of Hanover, to the English throne. It was momentous news. George I was known to be anxious to expel the Swedes from northern Germany, and Peter was convinced that England would now join actively in the alliance against Sweden.

During the reign of Queen Anne, war with France had absorbed England's energies, so that she had remained emotionally detached from the Northern War except when it impinged on her own Baltic trade. She had only given diplomatic aid to Russia in Turkey, because it fell in with her policy against France. The Treaty of Utrecht and the accession of George of Hanover, however, unexpectedly to Peter, had reversed this policy. France became England's ally; George I felt himself directly involved in the Baltic. England, turning her attention to northern Europe, now decided that the Tsar was bidding not only to dominate Baltic trade, but also to make his new capital the emporium of commerce between East and West. Jealous, suspicious, and watchful, England, contrary to all Peter's hopes, was in no mood to help Russia to destroy Sweden.

Peter's reaction to the accession of George I was immediate and practical. He wrote on 30 September to Frederick of Denmark, proposing that he should draw George I into their alliance.[1] He was to write several letters and some months passed before he finally received news from Frederick that George had joined with Denmark

335

and Prussia against Sweden.[2] But the combined naval action that he hoped for did not result.[3] Nor could he secure the co-operation of the Danish fleet. When Dolgoruky pressed the Danes on one occasion, he received the reply that the Tsar with twenty-seven ships of the line could surely operate alone against the Swedes who had only nine. It was a fair retort. Peter indeed had ample forces on both land and sea to crush the Swedes, but still he chose to spend his time seeking allies and planning allied operations.

In December 1714, Charles XII reached Swedish Pomerania from Turkey, and took in hand the defence of the fortress of Stralsund. His arrival was unexpected, but it made no stir. He had reduced his country to exhaustion and he no longer commanded an army. But he still believed that he was king of a great power. It was by encouraging him in this belief that Goertz, the Holstein minister, won his confidence.

The year 1715 opened with the "English affair," as it was called, when the allies were negotiating with the new King of England, and a third coalition resulted. But it did not produce the action that Peter expected. From Copenhagen his ambassador, Dolgoruky, wrote that "although the English King has declared war, it is only as Elector of Hanover, and the English fleet has sailed to protect its merchants; if the Swedish fleet attacks the fleet of Your Majesty, it is not to be thought that the English will engage the Swedes. . . ."[4]

Dolgoruky's appraisal was sound. A squadron under the command of Admiral Sir John Norris sailed into the Baltic, escorting a large number of merchantmen, and Norris anchored his ships at Reval. Learning of this, Peter sent Osterman to invite him to stay until he himself arrived. But convoy duties and the weather prevented this. Not long afterwards Norris put into Reval again and this time found the Russian fleet at anchor. Peter happily entertained the visitors, and with Catherine took part in the dinners and balls given by Norris on board his ships.[5] But, despite this atmosphere of goodwill, Norris, holding to his instructions, refused to join in operations against the Swedes.

By the end of 1715 Peter had concluded treaties of alliance with Prussia, Denmark, and Hanover against Sweden. But, although bankrupt and exhausted, the Swedes still would not capitulate. Meanwhile, petty disputes between the allies prevented effective action. In July 1715, Danish and Prussian troops laid siege to Stralsund, defended by Charles himself. Both demanded Russian troops to help them. But on the urgent request of Prince Grigory Dolgoruky, who was alarmed by Polish demands for the withdrawal of Augustus' Saxon troops, Sheremetev held the Russian army in Poland. When on 12 December, Charles having escaped to Sweden, Stralsund finally surrendered, no Russian troops were present. Peter was extremely angry and castigated Dolgoruky. "I am truly astonished," he wrote, "that you have gone out of your mind in old age, and have let yourself be carried away by those constant tricksters and so have held the troops in Poland."[6]

At this time Peter was distressed by the problem of his son and the endurance of his work. He was also weak from illness, and his temper was short. At the beginning of November 1715 he had fallen gravely ill. For some days he was near to death. His ministers and senators remained day and night near his room, and those close to him trembled for the future. On 2 December he even received the Last Sacraments, but then he began to recover. The one event during this period which gave him pleasure was the birth on 29 October of a son to Catherine. Peter hastened to write to his officers. "I declare to you that this night God has given me a recruit, named after his father. I request that my congratulations be conveyed to all generals, officers, and others from the highest to the lowest, and that this be proclaimed."[7] To a naval captain he wrote: "I declare that this night God has given me a little seaman, who has received his father's name, and I congratulate you on this event."[8] On little Peter Petrovich, both father and mother lavished their affection and hopes.

On 24 January 1716, having recovered sufficiently, Peter set out from St. Petersburg. Dolgoruky in Copenhagen had been pressing Frederick IV to agree to a joint Russo-Danish invasion of Scania. But the Danes yet again refused to commit themselves. Peter felt that in person he would win co-operation in what was to him the obvious strategy. But he was not always skilful in diplomacy and the action he now took united northern Europe in its fears and suspicions of Russia.

Soon after his arrival in Danzig, on 18 February 1716, Peter began planning the marriage of his niece, Tsarevna Catherine Ivanovna, with Duke Karl Leopold of Mecklenburg. He was an overbearing, boorish man, embroiled in quarrels with his nobles, many of whom had fled and entered the service of other courts. Feeling the weak-

ness of his position, he had turned to the Tsar for protection. He saw
in this marriage a further guarantee of Russian support, while Peter
considered Mecklenburg a useful base for action against Sweden.

Peter had signed the marriage agreement in St. Petersburg two
days before his departure. From The Hague, Kurakin had sent a
strong warning that any guarantee to the Duke would be most unwelcome to the English court. At the request of Bernstorff, himself
a native of Mecklenburg, and a bitter enemy of the Duke, Kurakin
went to London where he received proposals for an alliance against
Sweden, but they were conditional on the withdrawal of the Tsar's
guarantees to the Duke.

Kurakin's warning and his report from London reached Peter in
Danzig. They came too late, and apparently Peter felt that he could
not retract his word even for alliance with England. He concluded
on 8 April 1716, the day appointed for the wedding, a further and
much wider agreement, guaranteeing the internal and external security of Mecklenburg and undertaking to place nine or ten regiments at the Duke's disposal.

Peter could hardly have done more to antagonize the courts of
England, Hanover, and Denmark. Bernstorff had great influence with
George I, who was himself furious about the Tsar's guarantees. In
March, however, Peter, unaware of the storm he had aroused, wrote
to Dolgoruky in Copenhagen expressing surprise that the King of
Denmark should be making no preparations for the invasion of
Sweden.[9] Finally, in an attempt to put an end to Danish obstruction
Peter set out from Danzig on 1 May for a meeting with Frederick
IV of Denmark and at long last managed to wring an agreement
from him for a Russo-Danish landing in Scania and on the east coast
of Sweden, covered by their own fleets, and, it was hoped, the English fleet as well.

Delighted with this agreement, obtained after such long delays,
Peter on 26 May hurried away to Pyrmont to take the waters, for his
health had been poor since leaving St. Petersburg. He had already
given instructions for assembling the force needed, and at the resort
he attended to other matters. He spent hours talking with certain
French artists, engineers, and artisans who were passing through
Pyrmont on their way to Russia. They had been recruited by Jean
Lefort, nephew of the old favourite, and Nikita Zotov's son, Konon,
whom Peter had sent to France in the previous year. Among the

Frenchmen engaged was a young Parisian architect, named Leblond, who impressed Peter strongly with his plans for St. Petersburg. During the next three years he was to make important contributions to the city.

While at Pyrmont Peter also had long interviews with Leibniz. They discussed the reorganization of the higher administration into colleges (boards),[10] and Leibniz also submitted plans for three projects: the establishment of an Academy of Sciences, the exploration of the boundary between Asia and America, and the introduction of magnetic observations.

In the course of these meetings Leibniz's respect and admiration for Peter grew. "I was struck not only by the humanity of this exceptional monarch, but also by his knowledge of affairs and his honest judgment," he wrote to one correspondent, and to another: "The more I learn of the character of the Tsar, the more I revere him."[11] In a further letter he wrote: "I can never cease marvelling at the liveliness and intelligence of this great sovereign. He gathers about him on all sides learned men, and when he talks with them, they are absolutely astonished at the knowledge he shows of their business. He studies all the mechanical sciences, but his great interest is concentrated on everything concerning seagoing, and so he also likes astronomy and geography."[12]

After taking the waters for three weeks Peter hurried off to Rostock where all his troops except the cavalry were awaiting transports. Leaving Catherine at Rostock, he himself sailed with his galley squadron to Copenhagen. Already obstacles to the campaign were appearing. It was not certain that the English fleet could be counted on, although Norris had confirmed that his squadron would take part. Peter nevertheless instructed Kurakin in London to strive for an alliance between Russia and England, which would ensure the future support of the English fleet, but Kurakin could make no progress, for the Mecklenburg affair cast its shadow over the negotiations.

Reaching Copenhagen on 6 July 1716, Peter was welcomed with ponderous ceremonial. He wrote to Catherine in Rostock, asking her to let him know when she would join him so that he could set out in time to meet her on the road. Soon he was restless and impatient over the delays and obstructions of his allies. This was the time to launch the invasion, but, as he wrote to Catherine: "We are only chattering in vain."[13] July passed without action and in August Peter

himself sailed near to Scania to inspect the coast at the points where
the landing was to be made. He found that the Swedes, well warned
of allied intentions, had built up formidable defences; Swedish
prisoners stated that as many as twenty thousand troops were concentrated to repel the invasion. The Swedish batteries opened fire on
the two Russian ships; Peter's ship received a hit, and the other was
seriously damaged.

Peter returned to Copenhagen with strong misgivings. A landing
in the face of such defences could only succeed if his allies would
fight in earnest. But since he had arrived in Copenhagen they had
merely intrigued and procrastinated. He feared, therefore, that he
would find himself fighting the Swedes alone. At the same time he
was reluctant to abandon an operation which might finally break
Swedish resistance. On 1 September 1716, he found his generals
unanimous in recommending that the landing should be put off
until the next year. He spent the rest of September in conferences
and discussions with Frederick IV and his generals. Finally he informed the Danes that the campaign must be postponed.

This decision caused a tremendous outcry and virtually destroyed
the alliance against Sweden. The Hanoverians and Mecklenburgers
alleged that the invasion plans had merely served as a cover while the
Tsar negotiated secretly with Sweden, and that he really intended to
occupy Denmark. Bernstorff and George I raged dangerously. But
Peter's decision was undoubtedly inspired by caution and by mistrust of his allies. Moreover, he was almost certainly right in postponing the invasion; faced with twenty thousand well-entrenched
Swedes, led by Charles and fighting on their own soil, it would probably have failed.[14] Meanwhile Peter, far from harbouring designs on
Denmark or engaging in secret negotiations with the enemy, was
impatiently considering how to compel the Swedes to an early peace.
On 13 October he wrote to the "Gentlemen of the Senate" in St.
Petersburg, explaining that the only course left was to attack Sweden
from the Aland Islands, and ordering all preparations to be made.[15]

Peter then set out for Holland and on 6 December 1716 reached
Amsterdam. Golovkin and Shafirov, as well as Prince Vasily Dolgoruky, Peter Tolstoy, Buturlin, and Prince Kurakin joined him
there next day. Catherine, who was pregnant, had to travel more
slowly. Peter had written to her about the bad roads and advised her
to wait in Mecklenburg; "however, do what you wish, and please

God, do not think that I do not want you to travel here, for you yourself know how much I wish it, and it is better for you to come than to be sad there; only I could not help writing to you, for I know that you cannot endure being alone."[16]

Catherine had to stop at Wesel, where on 2 January 1717 she gave birth to the Tsarevich Paul. Peter was overjoyed. "Yesterday I received your happy note in which you declare that the Lord God has blessed us, and given us another recruit . . . as soon as is possible I will come quickly to you."[17] He himself was ill with a fever that kept him from leaving immediately. But the next day brought bad news. The newborn Tsarevich had died, and Catherine herself was very weak. Anxiety over Catherine and worry about the behaviour of his elder son, Tsarevich Alexei, aggravated Peter's illness. He was prostrated and, although Catherine arrived on 2 February to look after him, it was not until some eight days later that he began to recover.

While ill in Amsterdam, Peter received a report from Veselovsky in London, which raised his spirits. It concerned the arrest of Count Gyllenborg, the Swedish minister in London, whose correspondence revealed a plot for the invasion of Scotland by twelve thousand Swedes in support of the Pretender. Peter was not aware that the English government had known of this intrigue for some time and was not alarmed.[18] He had not entirely given up hope of English participation in an invasion of Sweden in the following year. Before leaving Copenhagen he had sent a message to George I, proposing a meeting between them. On the road to Holland he had made another attempt to arrange a meeting; George I had declined. But now, assuming that Charles himself was involved in this Jacobite plot, Peter expected George to be better disposed towards him.[19] In this Peter was soon disappointed. Bernstorff informed Veselovsky, the Russian ambassador, that, while the King of England always desired the Tsar's friendship, he could not consider joining him in action against Sweden while Russian troops remained on German soil.

Veselovsky also reported another obstacle to the alliance. Certain of the papers found on the arrest of Gyllenborg implicated the Tsar's physician, Erskine,[20] a Scot and an ardent Jacobite. It was suggested in London that in this Erskine had the support of the Tsar. Peter ordered the immediate denial of these allegations. He expressed his confidence in Erskine, who swore on oath that he was not involved in Jacobite plots. The English government averred that they had never placed any credence in these Swedish insinuations, and Veselovsky again received assurances of the King's desire for the Tsar's friendship and the co-operation that would be possible on the withdrawal of Russian troops. But Peter now realized that he could hope for nothing from George I who, on the contrary, through his English and his Hanoverian ministers, seized on every pretext to arouse ill will against Russia.

Peter turned now to France. Throughout his reign he had found the French opposing him. But now Louis XIV was dead, and the War of the Spanish Succession had ended in the compromise treaties of Utrecht and Baden. Louis XV, the new King of France, was a delicate boy of seven, and the Regent, Philip, Duke of Orleans, guided by the Abbé Dubois, pursued a new policy of alliances with England and Holland, but he still needed a counterweight to the greatly enhanced prestige and authority of Austria, especially in the north.

Peter ordered Prince Kurakin to enter into negotiations with Châteauneuf, the French ambassador at The Hague. They were still meeting when suddenly Peter decided to go himself to France, believing that he would win more rapid agreement in Paris.

Another reason for his decision was his intense curiosity to see Paris and Versailles. His mind was full of plans for expanding and beautifying St. Petersburg. He had visited London, The Hague, and Vienna, but he had not seen Paris, the city most renowned for its buildings and its elegance, or Versailles, the royal court famed for its architectural splendour.

Châteauneuf's report of the Tsar's proposed visit aroused mixed feelings at the French court. The visit would certainly enable the Regent to reach closer understanding with the Tsar, to develop trade, and to ensure that Austria did not eclipse France in the north. But these possible advantages were more than offset by the fear that the visit would distress England and Holland. On the other hand, there could be no question of refusing to receive the Tsar.

The French made careful preparations. Peter was no longer merely an object of curiosity as during his first tour; he came now as a great and powerful monarch to whom all honours had to be shown. Protocol was important and involved special difficulties because of his practice of travelling incognito and of ignoring ceremony, except when he considered it a matter of Russia's prestige. Moreover the Russians had already acquired a reputation for being exceedingly difficult guests.

Peter moved at a leisurely pace through Holland, stopping to examine everything that caught his eye, and from Rotterdam he sent Catherine back to The Hague to await his return. At Dunkirk he was met by Monsieur de Liboy, a gentleman of the court appointed to attend on him. De Liboy had made extensive arrangements, but in spite of them he was soon receiving a stream of complaints from the Russians. "This little court is very changeable and irresolute, and all from the throne to the stable are extremely given to anger," he wrote in one despatch[21] and in another he exclaimed that no matter what was provided "these people will always demand more."[22] He also sent the special warning that "the whole of this court resents the name Muscovite and even Muscovy."[23]

Of Peter himself, de Liboy reported that he was "of very great stature, a little stooped, and with the habit of holding his head down. He is dark and there is a fierceness in his expression. He appears to have a lively mind and a ready understanding, with a certain grandeur in his movements, but with little restraint."[24] A few days later he wrote further that "the Tsar is rather exacting and irascible, and indecisive even in minor matters. He rises very early in the morning, dines about ten o'clock, drinks vodka before sitting down to table in the morning, wine after midday, and often beer. . . . He sups fairly lightly, when he has dined well; he sits down to supper at seven o'clock or a little later, and sometimes does not sup at all, and he goes to bed before nine."[25] In another despatch De Liboy commented: "I remain convinced of what I wrote about the character of the Tsar, in which one really meets seeds of virtue, but they are wild and extremely mixed with failings. In my opinion he lacks most of all consistency and constancy of purpose."[26]

Few men have in fact been more inflexibly constant of purpose than Peter, and yet the Frenchman may have had grounds for his impression. Peter was troubled during this journey by the flight of his son, Alexei, which faced him with the most intractable and tragic problem of his whole reign. If, when not restlessly examining harbour installations, factories, and other places, he was depressed, distracted, and more irascible than usual, it was probably for this reason.

On 26 April 1717, accompanied by Marshal de Tesse and an escort,

Peter entered Paris. He refused the apartments prepared for him at the Louvre, because they were too grand. He decided to stay at the Hôtel Lesdiguieres, which was also on the river but more secluded. Even this was too luxurious for his taste, and he slept on a camp-bed in one of the small dressing-rooms. On the following day the Duke of Orleans called. But, requiring that full respect should be paid to him as Tsar, Peter would not yet go out, despite his eagerness to see Paris. "I must tell you," he wrote to Catherine, "that for two or three days I must stay in the house waiting for the King's visit and other ceremonies, and for that reason I have still not seen anything here; but tomorrow or the day after I will begin looking at everything. From what I saw on the road, the poverty of the common people is great."[27]

Two days later Louis XV called. Peter met him at his carriage and, showing him a gentle courtesy, conducted him indoors. There the gigantic Tsar and the delicate boy King sat side by side in two arm-chairs, the King occupying the place of honour on the Tsar's right hand. Peter talked with him for a quarter of an hour, with Kurakin acting as interpreter. Then, after lifting him up and kissing him several times, Peter took his hand and led him back to his carriage. To Catherine he wrote that "the little King here, who is only a finger or two bigger than our Luke [his favourite dwarf], has visited me; the child is very handsome in face and build, and very intelligent for his age, which is seven years."[28]

Peter began exploring Paris on the next day, but at five o'clock in the afternoon he drove to the Tuileries to return the King's visit. Received with a full guard of honour, he jumped from his carriage as he saw the King coming to greet him, and taking him in his arms he carried him up the staircase. The courtesies exchanged satisfied both parties, and Peter's spontaneous manner made a good impression. Marshal Villeroi who was present on each occasion wrote to Madame de Maintenon: "I cannot express to you the dignity, graciousness, and charm with which the King made and received the Tsar's visit; but I must tell you at the same time that this Prince, said to be barbarous, is not so at all; he has displayed to us sentiments of grandeur, of generosity, and of politeness, that we by no means expected."[29]

Peter spent six weeks in Paris and the surrounding countryside. He rose each morning at 4 A.M. to set out on tours lasting all day. He studied the architecture of the royal buildings, bridges, churches, and squares. He visited glass factories and the botanical gardens. He went several times to the Gobelin tapestry workshops, which fascinated him, and a presentation of four large tapestries, one of them portraying a scene from the life of St. Peter, impressed him deeply. Six workers from the Gobelin factories had already joined the Russian service, and this visit strengthened his determination to start the manufacture of tapestries in Russia.

The Invalides, where some four thousand old or wounded soldiers were cared for, also appealed to him; he examined it carefully, even down to the kitchens where he sampled the food and drank a goblet of wine to the health of the inmates, whom he called "comrades."[30]

At the Mint he inspected the machinery and discussed with the director the techniques used. When during his visit a medal was struck, Peter was astonished to find it stamped with his own likeness and the words *Petrus Alexievitz Tzar. Mag. Russ, Imperat* on one side and on the other *Vires acquirit eundo* with an emblem of fame with two trumpets. He also paid special attention to the Sorbonne and to the Academy.[31]

Since his visit to England nineteen years earlier, Peter's interests had broadened. Then he had concentrated on shipbuilding and on scientific and mechanical subjects, and they still made the major claim on his attention. Now with St. Petersburg in mind he made repeated visits to Versailles, Fontainbleu, and St. Cloud, studying the architecture and internal decorations of the palaces and the planning of the magnificent gardens. When, on 3 May, he visited the royal library, he was delighted to receive twelve volumes, bound in morocco and richly gilded, containing engravings of the palace and gardens at Versailles and of the campaigns of Louis XIV. He not only made notes of all that he saw, but missed no opportunity to engage French artisans, and, before leaving Paris he instructed Dolgoruky in Copenhagen to charter a ship to transport over one hundred Frenchmen to St. Petersburg.

Peter made a strong and favourable impression on his French hosts. Marshal Villeroi and Marshal de Tesse, who saw him almost daily during these weeks, noted his dignity and grandeur, his vigour and his intelligence. There were also those who found these qualities mixed with a certain savagery and barbarism, and the behaviour of his suite, often drunken and quarrelsome, aroused disgust. But the general conclusion, as expressed by Saint-Simon at the end of his account of the visit, was that the Tsar was truly great, comparable with the greatest men of antiquity, and gifted with such a unique variety of talents that he would always be a monarch worthy of the profoundest respect and admiration even by remotest posterity, despite the barbarity of his country and of his upbringing; he had charmed France which would remember him as a prodigy.[32]

On 9 June, after exchanging farewell visits with the King and the Regent, Peter departed from Paris. His health still troubled him and, instead of travelling to Holland he went to Spa, where he spent five weeks resting and taking the waters. He then set out for Amsterdam where Catherine joined him. It was in Amsterdam that the agreement, resulting from the negotiations begun by Châteauneuf and concluded in Paris by Shafirov and Tolstoy with Peter's participation, was signed. It was a disappointing document.

Peter had come with high hopes of concluding a useful alliance. He had put his proposition to Marshal de Tesse bluntly: "I, the Tsar, want to take the place of Sweden with you; I will guarantee your treaties, and I propose an alliance with me, with Prussia, and with Poland, and I do not demand that you guarantee my conquests in return. I foresee that the growing power of the House of Austria must be a danger to us: put me in the place of Sweden and under that alliance I promise you all that you could count on from Sweden, and at the same time I will defend you against all that you may fear from the strength of the Emperor."[33]

The proposition was attractive to the French, for their fear of Austria was real. But the Regent went in greater terror of offending England and Holland, who were anxiously following the negotiations in Paris. The final agreement was a mere treaty of friendship between France, Prussia, and Russia, of some benefit to France and none to Russia. Under three secret clauses Russia and Prussia guaranteed the treaties of Utrecht and Baden, and France undertook to guarantee the treaty that concluded the Northern War; if one of the allies were attacked, the others would use all peaceful means to support him, and, if this were without result after four months, they would help with money and troops. The Tsar and the King of Prussia agreed to accept French mediation, while France undertook that on expiry of her treaty with Sweden in April 1718 she would make no new agreement contrary to the interests of Prussia and Russia.

One important result of the negotiations in Paris, although not included in the treaty, was the Tsar's agreement to withdraw his troops from Mecklenburg. He explained to de Tesse that he would have withdrawn them long ago but for the offensive behaviour of George I and Bernstorff. The withdrawal from Mecklenburg resulted at once in diplomatic approaches from England. Admiral Norris and Whitworth, now English minister at The Hague, entered into discussions with the Russians in Amsterdam. They expressed the King's desire for friendship with the Tsar, and especially for a trade agreement, and, since it affected trade, an early end to the war. They invited the Tsar's proposals. Peter demanded fifteen English ships of the line to be placed under his command so that, operating with the Russian fleet, they could cover a Russian landing on the east coast of Scania. This was more than England would concede, and the negotiations lapsed.

Peter had sought allies in the West and had failed. He had acted unwisely at times, especially over Mecklenburg, but he had also been the victim of suspicion and double-dealing. The King of Prussia had made a secret agreement with France behind his back; the French Regent had been reporting fully to George I on their negotiations. George I and Bernstorff had done everything in their power to counter his efforts to make allies and to bring the Northern War to an early end. There remained to Peter the one course of negotiating directly with Sweden. But at this time, overshadowing his disappointments and disillusionments in the West, the crisis in his relations with his own son demanded his attention.

CHAPTER XXXVI

Peter and Alexei

1717-1718

DURING these tremendous years of war and reform Alexei, Peter's elder son, had grown to manhood. Weak, craven, and with the outlook of an old Muscovite, he could not have grown more unlike his father. He had thus become the hope of those who hated the new Russia, and as Tsarevich he represented a direct threat to all that Peter had laboured to achieve. The conflict between father and son moved inexorably to a crisis, and its outcome was as inevitable as the falling of night.

Tsarevich Alexei, born in February 1690, had spent his first eight years in the care of his mother, Tsaritsa Evdokiya, surrounded by her family and supporters. All were embittered conservatives, hostile to the interests and policy of his father, and hating foreigners. They thought only of the day when the Tsarevich would succeed to the throne and live the life of the old Muscovite tsars.

On the return of Peter from the West in 1698, Alexei had been placed in the care of his aunt, Tsarevna Natalya. At first he had followed no consistent routine of study and training. Nikifor Vyazemsky, his Russian tutor since he was six years old, had taught him only reading, writing, and the theology that had always dominated the education of tsarevichi in the past. Vyazemsky was inadequate as a man and as a teacher, but it was probably he who first awakened in Alexei his love of religious reading and contemplation. Early in 1703 Baron Heinrich Huyssen, a learned, able, and likeable man, became his tutor, and his lessons had begun in earnest.

Peter did not intend, however, that his son's education should be limited to book learning. At the age of thirteen Alexei was present at the capture of Nyenskantz as a private in a bombardier regiment. Returning to his studies Alexei, who was intelligent and appeared eager to learn, made good progress. But after only five months Peter summoned him to Narva, where he witnessed the storming of the fortress.

At the beginning of 1705 Peter sent Huyssen abroad and he was away for nearly four years. Peter was taken up with the war and Menshikov was in St. Petersburg. Alexei lived at Preobrazhenskoe during this period without real supervision, giving full rein to his own tastes and inclinations. He acquired the habit of excessive drinking. He surrounded himself with monks and priests. His aunt, Tsarevna Maria Alexeevna, filled his mind with prophesies and superstitions. His maternal relations brought him into touch again with his mother, and themselves inveighed against all Peter's innovations. Another strong influence was Alexander Kikin, an orderly whom Peter had elevated to be head of the Admiralty. Kikin served with a show of zeal which hid a bitter hatred of the new policies. He won the confidence of the Tsarevich and further poisoned his mind against his father's work.

Alexei was readily influenced. He had no liking for war or reform, no ambition to build ports and ships, and no curiosity about Western science and learning. At the same time, far from yearning for the life of a monk, he was eager to succeed his father and to rule as Tsar.

Many among the people prayed for his accession. Already they looked on him as the hope of the future, the saviour of Muscovy who would lighten their burdens of taxation and service. The priesthood looked to Alexei, when Tsar, to restore the church to its former authority and glory. The old Russian nobility, resenting Menshikov and other upstart favourites, as well as the ubiquitous foreigners, felt confident that Alexei would recall them to their former eminence and dismiss the newcomers. When Alexei confessed that he had sinned in wishing the death of his father, Archpriest Ignatiev replied that "God will forgive you; we all wish his death for the burden on the people is great."[1]

Thus, for the first eighteen years of his life, except for brief periods, Alexei knew only the company of those who hated Peter and his work. And yet it is not clear that they succeeded in inspiring him with hatred of his father. Like so many of the people who complained of their burdens, but took pride in the new army and its victories over ancient enemies, Alexei held the Tsar in great awe, drawing comfort from his strong rule and, as his son, regarding him with special pride. At Narva Peter had exhorted him to "love all that contributes to the good and honour of our country and also true advisers and servants, be they foreigners or Russians" and never to spare himself for the general weal. Alexei had replied that "as an obedient son I will seek with all my strength to follow your activities and example,"[2] and he was probably sincere in wanting to emulate his father, for he dreamt of being a great monarch.

At first Alexei tried anxiously to please Peter. But a sense of his own inadequacy soon weakened his efforts. This feeling of inadequacy grew and with it dread of his father. He drank more heavily to escape his fear and weakness. He began resorting to cunning and feigned sickness to evade the duties and the burdens of responsibility which he could not carry. If as a boy he felt love and admiration for the massive strength and achievement of his father, these emotions were early numbed by terror.

Peter was harsh in his treatment of Alexei. He encouraged and helped those who tried conscientiously to carry out his orders, but he expected more of his son. Guided by his own dominating sense of service, he sought to harden the boy to the tasks ahead. Noting signs of submissiveness and timidity, he handled him with a Spartan firmness, withholding the warmth and kindness that he might have shown as a father. And when at last he tried to show sympathy and understanding, it was too late. Peter, titanic in strength and physique and relentless in purpose, overwhelmed his son without realizing it. He expected too much of a boy who was to prove weak in health, will, and courage, who broke under the weight of his demands, and who in the end was little more than a snivelling drunkard.

Early in 1707 Peter suddenly summoned Alexei to Zholkva. He had heard that his son was secretly visiting his mother and he had always feared that she might infect him with her conservative outlook, unfitting him for the labours to which he would succeed. In Zholkva he scolded Alexei for his deception. He then sent him to Smolensk to direct the preparation of army supplies and the mobilization of recruits. After five months at Smolensk, Alexei went to Moscow to take part in the meetings of ministers and to supervise the fortification of the city against invasion by the Swedes. His attitude towards these defences was completely defeatist. He wrote in one letter to a confidant that he did not believe anything could stop the Swedes and that he considered the Tsar's precautions useless.[3] But he did what he could to carry out his orders.

It was a time of tension and anxiety for Peter when he gave way to frequent outbursts of anger. At the end of 1708 he wrote charging his son with neglecting the defences and living in idleness. The letter reduced Alexei to a state of terror. He wrote tearfully three times to Tsaritsa Catherine, begging her to find out how he had failed and asking her to intercede for him. Peter's anger passed, whether with or without her intercession is not known. Alexei remained in Moscow, taking part in ministerial meetings and attending to certain business that arose from them. At the same time he had resumed his studies, presumably on Peter's orders. Vyazemsky reported at the beginning of 1708 that the Tsarevich had begun working at German, history, and geography; on the return of Huyssen in October he also renewed his lessons in French and arithmetic.

This burden of state business and study was beyond Alexei's strength. But the crisis of the war was now rapidly approaching and Peter sent him further orders to raise five regiments and march them into the Ukraine as soon as possible. Alexei led the regiments from Moscow and delivered them in Sumy on 19 January 1709. This was in the midst of that savage winter when several hundred Swedes froze to death. On reaching Sumy, Alexei fell ill, and for ten days his condition was desperate. Peter was anxious to go to Voronezh, but he remained at the side of his son and only on 30 January 1709, when the crisis of the illness had passed, did he set out. Two weeks later Alexei was well enough to join Peter in Voronezh and to accompany him to Tavrov. From there, probably because still weak from his illness, he returned to Moscow and so did not take part in the battle of Poltava.

At the end of the summer of 1709 Peter instructed Alexei to go abroad to complete his studies. He reached Dresden in the following spring, and a few days after his arrival he went to Karlsbad to take the waters. Not far from Karlsbad he had his first meeting with Princess Charlotte of Wolfenbüttel, who was to become his wife. She was at this time sixteen years old, a charming, natural, and dutiful girl, tall for her age and somewhat plain. She found the Tsarevich attractive; she told her mother that he was clever and chivalrous, and that she felt honoured that the Tsar had chosen her.[4] Alexei, too, was attracted, but he was strongly opposed to marriage with a foreigner and a Protestant. He did not, however, dare to express these misgivings or to oppose his father in any detail, but weakly hoped that he might be recalled to Moscow or that something else would happen to prevent this union with a heretic.

Nevertheless the marriage took place in Torgau on 14 October 1711. Four days later Peter ordered Alexei to go to Thorn in mid-November to organize army supplies and river transport. He set out three weeks after his marriage, and five weeks later his young wife joined him from Braunschweig. They remained together in Thorn for six months while he attended to his duties. Then he received orders to join the army for the campaign in Pomerania.

Charlotte went to Elbing to await his return. It had not been an easy time for her. Thorn and the surrounding country were desolate and she had lived in discomfort in a monastery. Moreover, no provision had been made for the expenses of Alexei and herself and they were often in difficulties. Menshikov on arriving there in the spring was shocked by their predicament; he wrote at once to Peter, mentioning that Charlotte, almost in tears, had had to ask his help so that she could travel to Elbing, and he had lent her five thousand rubles from army funds.[5]

In October 1712, while Alexei was with the army, Charlotte received instructions from Peter to go to St. Petersburg. She was afraid to travel so far alone and was frightened of the Russians, especially after the stories she had heard of their hatred of foreigners. Also, she was homesick and miserable. Instead of obeying the Tsar's orders, she fled to her old home in Braunschweig.

Peter himself went to Salzdahlen near Braunschweig in February 1713 to see her. He had already in the previous month written expressing disapproval of her behaviour, "for we would never have thwarted your wish to see your family, if only you had informed us of it beforehand."[6] She had replied excusing herself and asking forgiveness, which he had readily granted. At their meeting Peter was completely reconciled with his young daughter-in-law, and soon afterwards she set out for St. Petersburg.

A small palace, built in 1712 on the left bank of the Neva, was the home of Alexei and Charlotte. Living here, she now came to know her husband and her unhappiness deepened. The Imperial minister, Pleyer, had reported that the Tsarevich had "brought back from Germany little of German sentiment and manners; he passes most of his time with Muscovite priests and stupid people; moreover, he is given to drunkenness."[7] When drunk he was coarse and abusive; he behaved brutally towards his wife and spoke contemptuously of her to the servants. When at the end of the year it was found that Charlotte was pregnant, he took no interest, and continued to drink heavily. His health suffered and in the first half of 1714 he was constantly ill. The doctors prescribed the Karlsbad waters. Peter gave permission for him to go abroad for this purpose and showed considerable anxiety for his safety on the road, especially near Danzig, where he ordered special precautions to be taken. On 4 June 1714 Alexei, as an ordinary Russian officer, set out from St. Petersburg. Charlotte, then eight months pregnant, knew nothing of his plans until his departure when he abruptly bade her good-bye.

Meanwhile Peter had been growing increasingly disturbed about his son. He was passive, cowardly, and lazy; he had no interest in military or naval matters, and no sympathy with reforms.[8] At first Peter thought that with experience and training he would come to see the importance of all that his father was doing. His three years' absence from Russia and his marriage would also, Peter hoped, have changed him.

On Alexei's return to St. Petersburg in 1713 Peter greeted him affectionately. He showed interest in his son's impressions of the West and in his work. He asked what he had learnt, and then told him to bring drawings that he made in the course of his studies, presumably of geometry and fortifications. This request struck Alexei with an unreasoning terror. He was afraid that his father would ask him to make further sketches in his presence and that he would be unable to do them. He decided to evade this danger by maiming himself. Returning to his own house he took a pistol and tried to shoot the ball into his right hand. In his agitation he missed, but the powder burnt his hand badly. Later, noticing the injury, Peter asked what had happened. Alexei pretended that he had had an accident, and no comment was made. But Peter could not help seeing in the following weeks that Alexei, now twenty-three years old, was more unco-operative than ever before, and that fear alone made him carry out his orders. The supervision of shipbuilding timbers in Staraya

Rus and Ladoga in the summer of 1713 was the last task that Peter set him. Thereafter he no longer called on him to bear responsibility or to help. But he could not decide what to do with him.

Alexei returned from Karlsbad in December 1714. He had not written to Charlotte during this absence. She had borne him a daughter, named Natalya, a month after his departure, but he had enquired neither about the expected infant, nor about the mother. He showed some interest on his return and was for a short time affectionate towards his wife. But his earlier indifference and his failure to write from Karlsbad had hurt her deeply. Then she learnt that he was living with a serf girl, named Efrosinia; it was the final blow, but she was already pregnant again. She became sad and subdued as she waited for the birth of her second child. Some ten weeks before her confinement she fell while going upstairs. She complained afterwards of pains in the left side of her abdomen, and she had a slight fever. The doctors let blood, but she became worse and took to her bed. Early in the morning of 12 October 1715, she was delivered of a boy, whom she named Peter. After the birth of her daughter in the previous year she had, in writing, thanked the Tsar for his letter of congratulations, mentioned jokingly that with time she hoped to fulfill his wish by bearing a son; she took a sad pride now in having produced a prince.

For the next three days Charlotte seemed well. But on the fourth day she began to fail. The Tsar's doctors attended her, but they could do nothing, for, as they noted, she had no will to live. On 21 October she summoned Baron Lewenwald, a member of her suite. She told him that she was dying, consoled by the promise of Princess Ost-Friesland to remain with her children as a mother. She was confident that the Tsar would agree to this arrangement, for "he is very kind and will not refuse in the end if you inform him that I requested it on my death bed."[9] She feared that her death would be attributed to grief and unhappiness rather than to the failure of her health, and she directed the Baron to inform her parents "that I have always been satisfied and have rejoiced in the love of their Tsarish Majesties; not only has everything promised in the marriage contract been carried out, but in addition many kindnesses have been shown me. . . ."[10] She particularly regretted that the Tsar could not visit her, because he was ill and unable to leave his bed. But on the following day he came. She spoke to him about her children and her servants, and then took leave of him. During her last hours Alexei was at her side and so distraught with grief that he fainted three times. At midnight on 22 October 1715, Charlotte died; she was just twenty-one years old.[11]

The funeral took place six days later. In the presence of the whole court, except Catherine who was expecting to be delivered of a child at any hour, the coffin was entombed in the Cathedral of SS. Peter and Paul. Returning from the funeral, Alexei was given a letter which his father had written at Schlusselburg sixteen days earlier.

"A Declaration to My Son" was its heading and it faced Alexei with an ultimatum. After referring to the Swedes whom they had learnt to beat, the letter continued: "But, when considering this joy granted by God to our country, I think on the line of succession, a bitterness almost equal to my joy consumes me, seeing you unfit for the handling of state affairs (and God is not to blame, for he did not deprive you of intelligence, nor did he take away from you bodily strength; for, although not very strong by nature, still you are not weak); worst of all, you wish to hear nothing of military matters, through which we have come from darkness into light, and while before we were not known in the world, now we are respected. I do not teach that you should be eager to fight without cause, but to love this subject and in every way possible to further and learn it, because this is one of the two factors essential in governing, namely order and defence. . . . And having no desire, you do not learn anything of military matters and you know nothing of them. . . . You give weakness of health as your excuse for being unable to endure military hardships. But that is not the reason! For I do not desire labours, but willingness, which no illness can prevent. . . .

"Pondering all this I turn again to my first thought concerning you, for I am a man and subject to death; to whom am I to leave what I have planted and nurtured with God's help? To him who, like the lazy servant in the Gospel, buried his talent in the ground. Then, further, I recall what a bad stubborn character you have! How much have I not only scolded but beaten you for this, and think on how many years I have not spoken to you; but nothing has succeeded, nothing has made any difference; all is in vain; you want only to sit at home and make merry, although outside everything goes badly. . . . Considering with grief and seeing that in no way can I incline you to good work, I have written this last testament to you, deciding to wait yet a little to see whether *without hypocrisy* you will change. If not, then know that I will cut you off wholly from the succession, like a gangrenous growth, and do not imagine that because you are my only son I write this merely to frighten; in truth by the will of God I will do it, for as I have not spared and do not spare myself for my country and my people, how should I spare you who are useless? Better a worthy stranger than an unworthy son!"[12]

Alexei in a state of terror immediately asked Alexander Kikin what he should do. Kikin advised him to renounce the throne on the plea of poor health. Prince Vasily Dolgoruky, one of Peter's trusted men, who as a member of the old Russian nobility anxious for restoration of their former privileges was also a secret supporter of Alexei, gave the same advice. Both stressed that such renunciation could never be irrevocable.

On the day after the delivery of this ultimatum an important event took place: Catherine gave birth to a boy, also named Peter. Although delighted with his new son, Peter could not allow his hopes to rise too high; he had already lost three sons in infancy. To Alexei it seemed an ominous event. Kurakin had once said to him that "while your step-mother has no son, it will be all right for you, but once she has a son it won't be."[13]

Craven by nature, Alexei was anxious only to escape from his predicament. The advice of Kikin and Vasily Dolgoruky offered the easiest way, and the birth of a second tsarevich made his renunciation appear more genuine. On 31 October 1715, he replied to his father in a letter of cloying humility and hypocrisy.

"Most Gracious Sovereign—Father! I have naught to say save this: if thou art pleased to deprive me, because of my unfitness, of the succession to the crown of Russia—let thy will be done. I implore you most humbly, Sire, to do so—since I perceive myself to be unfit and incapable for this station, inasmuch as I am of quite poor memory, without which naught can be accomplished, for all my powers, mental and bodily, have become debilitated through sundry ailments, and have made me unfit to rule such a people, which hath need of a man less spent than I. Therefore, I have no pretensions to succeed to the rule of Russia after you—even though I had no brother; but all the more so since there is one now, for which God be thanked, and to whom God grant health; nor shall I have any pretensions in the future, in which I call God to witness to my soul;

and, as a true acknowledgment, I am ready to write this oath in my own hand. I entrust my children to you; as for myself, I crave nought save subsistence until my death. Your most humble slave and son, Alexei."[14]

Peter discussed this reply with Prince Vasily Dolgoruky who later told Alexei that his father was satisfied with his renunciation. He also claimed that by his advice he had saved Alexei's head from the block.[15] But Peter was in fact far from satisfied. He had demanded that his son should mend his ways and show goodwill towards his work; he had received in reply a plea of inadequacy and for permission to relinquish the succession.

For a month Peter was gravely ill and made no reply. Alexei visited him only once during this illness. He was terrified of his father even when he lay weak in bed. His supporters wished for the death of the Tsar and he, too, hoped that it would come to pass, for his troubles would then vanish.

On 19 January 1716, Peter sent Alexei "A further last warning." This letter reproached him for not replying fully to his first declaration and castigated him for ingratitude and opposition. "Everyone knows that you hate the works which I have carried out for the people of my nation, without sparing myself, and that finally after my death you will destroy them. And so, to remain as you desire, neither fish nor flesh, is impossible; thus, either change your nature and without hypocrisy be worthy to be my successor, or become a monk, for without this my soul cannot be easy, and especially since now my health is poor. And so, on receiving this, reply promptly by letter or in person, giving your decision. And if you do not do this I will treat you as a criminal."[16]

Alexei had hoped to be allowed to live quietly in the country until he could succeed to the throne. He did not want to be shaven as a monk and cut off from the succession. But he took comfort from Kikin's repeated advice that "to put on the cowl does not knock it into the head with a nail; it can be taken off again."[17] On the following day Alexei wrote stating that "I desire the monastic state and ask your kind permission thereto" and signed himself "Your slave and unworthy son Alexei."[18]

Peter was uneasy. He knew how simple it would be after his death for Alexei to put aside his vows, obtaining all necessary absolution. But there was no alternative to the monastery, except execution, and he would not contemplate such a step. He still nursed a faint hope that Alexei might mend his ways. He was now preparing to go to Copenhagen and he expected to be away for some months. Shortly before his departure he called on Alexei and found him in bed, feigning illness. He asked what his final decision was, and Alexei swore that he wanted only to be shorn as monk. "That's not easy for a young man," Peter said gently. "Think again without haste, then write to me what you want to do. But it would be better for you to take the straight road, rather than become a monk. I'll wait another six months."[19]

Relieved of his father's awful presence, Alexei relaxed in idleness and drinking. Seven months later Peter wrote to him from Copenhagen. His letter was restrained in tone. It recalled their meeting and his request that Alexei should make his decision in six months. "Therefore now, for you have had enough time for reflection, on receiving this letter, make your decision at once . . . for I know that you are only passing the time in your usual fruitless manner."[20]

Alexei could procrastinate no longer. Many times he had thought of flight. Two years earlier Kikin had urged him to flee after taking the cure at Karlsbad and to hide in Holland and then in Italy. But his nerve had failed and he had returned to St. Petersburg. Now he was desperate. A few months earlier Kikin himself had escorted Tsarevna Maria Alexeevna to Karlsbad, and before leaving he had said to Alexei: "I'll seek out some place for you."[21] Counting on this assurance, Alexei made his decision.

On 26 September 1716, he set out from St. Petersburg for Riga. He had with him his mistress, Efrosinia, her brother, and three servants. On the road from Riga and not far from Libau he met his aunt, Tsarevna Maria Alexeevna, returning from her cure. When Alexei told her he was going to join his father, she replied, "Good; it's necessary to obey him; that is pleasing to God. Whatever would have happened if you had gone into a monastery?" Alexei began weeping and said that he would be glad to hide somewhere. "Where could you go from your father; he would find you no matter where," she retorted. She then scolded him for not keeping in touch with his mother, and they departed without Alexei divulging more of his intention.[22]

In Libau he met Kikin. To his urgent question about a place of asylum, Kikin replied that he should go to Vienna, for the Emperor would not surrender him. This finally decided Alexei. He took the irrevocable step of flight, carefully covering his tracks, so that after passing through Danzig he disappeared.

Late on the evening of 10 November 1716, as the Imperial Vice-Chancellor, Count Schönborn, was about to retire, the Tsarevich burst in upon him. "I have come here," he exclaimed, "to ask the Emperor, my brother-in-law, to protect me, to save my very life. They want to kill me! . . ." He then began rushing round the room. Schönborn quieted him with difficulty and asked what exactly he wanted of the Emperor. Alexei again demanded that he should save his life. "I have done nothing to my father," he went on excitedly. "I know I am weak; but Menshikov brought me up like that. He deliberately undermined my health with drunkenness. Now my father says that I am of no use either for war or for government. . . . I do not want to go to a monastery. The Emperor must save me!"[23]

Alexei was again near to hysteria. Schönborn calmed him, and asked him to recount all that had happened, so that he could report to the Emperor. Alexei talked at length. He constantly blamed Menshikov and Catherine, alleging that they had inflamed the Tsar against him. He took care to contradict reports concerning his ill-treatment of his wife, sister of the Empress, for he was worried that they might prejudice his cause. Not he, but his father and Catherine had treated her badly, persecuting them both, because they might produce a son and heir to the throne.[24]

The Emperor summoned a secret council meeting to consider what to do with this overwrought and unwelcome guest. On its recommendation Alexei was informed that the Emperor would extend his protection and intercede with his father, but that he must remain hidden in the mountain fortress of Ehrenberg in the Tyrol. Meanwhile Alexei was taken to Weierburg near Vienna while Ehrenberg was made ready. The Emperor sent a minister to him in Weierberg to obtain an account of his relations with his father and again Alexei was only too glad to talk and to exonerate himself. At one time he said that his father was good in heart and just; at another time he said he was ruthless and blood-thirsty. He protested that he wished no harm to his father, whom he loved and revered, but he begged that he should not be given up, for then he would surely die.[25] On 27 November he set out under escort and, accompanied by Efrosinia whose disguise as a page the Austrians had not penetrated, travelled to the Tyrol.

In Copenhagen Peter was waiting for his son's answer. The courier, whom he had sent to St. Petersburg, met him on the road from Copenhagen to Lübeck, and reported that the Tsarevich was following after him. Two months passed and Alexei did not appear. Peter grew alarmed. On 9 December 1716, he sent secret instructions to General Weide in Mecklenburg to find his son. He summoned Veselovsky from Vienna to Amsterdam, and gave him a letter to the Emperor requesting that, if the Tsarevich appeared openly or secretly in his dominions, he should send him under an escort of officers to his father. Peter wrote this letter with difficulty and reluctance. He felt acutely the disgrace to himself as father and Tsar, and to Russia. Moreover his relations with the Emperor were strained at this time. But he had felt sure that Alexei would seek refuge in Austria.

The hunt began with Weide sending two officers to search through Germany. Veselovsky rode along the Frankfurt road, went to Prague, and then to Vienna without finding any trace of Alexei. The search continued into March 1717 when Guards Captain Rumyantsov with three other officers arrived in Vienna. Veselovsky had now found out that the castle of Ehrenberg was the hiding place. He sent Rumyantsov to the Tyrol and he returned early in April with confirmation that the Tsarevich was held there in such secrecy that no one even knew his name.

Veselovsky now began a siege of the Emperor and his ministers. On the day after Rumyantsov's return from Ehrenberg, Veselovsky was received in private audience by the Emperor, to whom he presented Peter's letter of 20 December. He mentioned that a Russian courier had seen members of the Tsarevich's suite at Ehrenberg and that the Tsarevich himself was living there, and begged the Emperor to deal frankly with the Tsar's request. Returning from this audience Veselovsky at once sent Rumyantsov back to Ehrenberg to follow the Tsarevich if he was moved to another hiding place.

The Emperor found himself in an acutely difficult position. If he withdrew his protection it would mean, so Alexei had convinced him, handing him over to his death, and he shrank from such a step. At the same time he was unwilling to interfere between father and son, and he was himself frightened of the Tsar and his armies.

At Ehrenberg Alexei had at last begun to feel safe. In January
1717 Schönborn had sent a copy of a despatch received from Pleyer
in St. Petersburg, reporting various rumours concerning his disap-
pearance. Pleyer also stated that the guards regiments and other
troops in Mecklenburg were plotting to kill the Tsar, incarcerate
Catherine in a nunnery, and entrust the government to the Tsarevich, and that the Tsar had ordered Menshikov to investigate this
plot. He added that in St. Petersburg "all is ready for rebellion."[26]

There were, in fact, no signs of rebellion and Pleyer was magni-
fying beyond all reason the grumblings of the people. But Alexei
treasured the report, keeping it with a few special personal papers,
for it gave him hope that he might not have to wait so long to return to Russia.

The sudden arrival of an Imperial secretary, however, reminded
him of his dangerous position. The secretary brought his father's
letter to the Emperor to show him, and asked him in the name of the
Emperor what he intended to do. Alexei read the letter and gave way
to hysteria, rushing from room to room, waving his arms, crying, and
talking to himself in Russian. The secretary calmed him and explained that, since his hiding place was known, it had been decided
to send him to Naples. On the next day the secretary set out with
Alexei and one servant, who was Efrosinia still dressed as a page. He
reported to Schönborn that "as far as Trento suspicious people followed us; all was well, however. I used all possible means to hold
our company from frequent and excessive drunkenness, but in vain."[27]
The "suspicious people" were none other than Rumyantsov, who
shadowed them all the way to Naples.

The pursuit of Alexei was dragging on. Already some nine months
had passed since his flight. Peter had travelled through Holland
and visited France, but the problem of his son was constantly hanging over him. The fact that he knew where he was but could not deal
with him, aggravated his impatience. Finally to put an end to the
Emperor's tergiversations, he decided to send Count Tolstoy to
Vienna. At the beginning of July 1717, at Spa, he gave Tolstoy and
Rumyantsov detailed instructions and a letter to the Emperor in
which he made it quite clear that he knew the movements and
whereabouts of his son, and demanded his surrender.[28] Tolstoy was
to let it be known that, if the Tsar's request went unheeded, he
would take the necessary steps, and the Imperial government, aware

of the nearness of the Russian troops in Poland and along the Silesian frontier, knew exactly what he meant.

Arriving in Vienna, Tolstoy at once began weaving his net around Alexei. First, he secured the support of the Duchess of Wolfenbüttel, mother of the Empress and Alexei's mother-in-law, by pointing out that the Tsar would lay a curse on his son if he did not return, and the Duchess was alarmed for her grandchildren. Next, at his audience with the Emperor, he faced him with the fact that efforts to hide Alexei were now not only useless but even dangerous. And the Emperor was by this time eager to use every means short of compulsion to return Alexei to Russia. He therefore acknowledged that the Tsarevich was under his protection, and promised to send a courier to induce him to return voluntarily. Tolstoy at once proposed that he himself should go to the Tsarevich, instead of a courier, for he had a letter for him from his father and verbal messages as well. The Emperor could not refuse, although he did send instructions to Count Daun, Viceroy of Naples, that, while it was essential that Alexei should receive Tolstoy, he should not be molested or threatened in any way.

In Naples, Tolstoy, supported by Rumyantsov, quickly won the confidence of the Viceroy who arranged for them to meet Alexei unexpectedly in his palace. Alexei trembled with fear as he set eyes on them. He was terrified—especially of Rumyantsov, a giant of a man nearly as big as the Tsar himself—and thought that he had come to kill him. Tolstoy calmed him and gave him the letter from his father.

"My son," the letter read, "it is known to all what disobedience and contempt you have shown to my wishes and that neither words nor punishment have made you obey my instructions, finally deceiving me and invoking God at your parting from me. Then what did you do? You ran off and like a traitor placed yourself under foreign protection. This has been unheard of not only among our children, but even among our true subjects! By this act what shame and grief have you inflicted on your father and what disgrace on your country! And so I am sending to you now for the last time a message which Messrs. Tolstoy and Rumyantsov will report to you. If you will obey me, then I assure you and promise before God and his judgment that you will suffer no punishment; but I will show you my best love, if you obey and return. But if you refuse, then as your father by the power given me by God I will curse you through eternity, and as your Sovereign I will declare you a traitor and I will neglect no means to bring you to justice as a traitor and vilifier of your father, in which God will aid me in my right. Remember that I have done nothing to you by force, and if you had so desired all would have been now as you wanted. What you wish, do!"[29] Tolstoy also gave Alexei a letter from his mother-in-law, urging him to obey. But Alexei was now in a state of high excitement and fear; he said merely that he would think over his plans, and hastily retired.

In the course of four meetings, Tolstoy drew his net more tightly. Noting that Alexei's resistance was based on his faith in the Emperor's protection, he bribed the Viceroy's secretary, who had access to him, to insinuate that this protection would be withdrawn. Tolstoy himself stressed to Alexei that in any case the Emperor would not go to war to protect him, and that the Tsar was prepared to march. The Viceroy, bearing in mind his instructions to induce Alexei to return voluntarily, asked the advice of Tolstoy who told him to threaten Alexei with the removal of his mistress, Efrosinia, whose disguise had now been penetrated. The possibility of losing her made him more desperate. She, too, was apparently pressing him to return to Russia, and she it was who restrained him from rushing off to seek the protection of the Pope. Meanwhile Tolstoy had told him that his father was coming to Italy. "Who can prevent him seeing you? . . . As you know, His Majesty has long intended visiting Italy; and now, because of this affair, he will certainly come soon."[30]

The threats of losing the Emperor's protection, of being parted from Efrosinia, and finally of having to face his father in Naples left Alexei no alternative. On 3 October 1717, in the presence of two Imperial officers, he told Tolstoy and Rumyantsov that he would go with them to Russia. He begged them to obtain his father's permission for him to marry Efrosinia, then four months pregnant, before they reached St. Petersburg. On the same day he wrote a letter of tearful humility to his father, and another letter to the Emperor.[31]

News of the return of the Tsarevich to Russia was received with relief at court, and by the people, who gave thanks that he was alive. But there were many who wished that he had stayed abroad. Of these his immediate supporters were the most alarmed. "That Judas— Peter Tolstoy has tricked him!" said Ivan Naryshkin.[32] Prince Vasily Dolgoruky said to Prince Bogdan Gagarin, "Have you heard that the fool of a Tsarevich is coming back, because his father has promised that he can marry Efrosinia? He'll have a grave, not a wedding!"[33] Meanwhile they waited with misgiving to see what the Tsar would do.

On 3 February 1718, three days after Alexei's arrival in Moscow, all ministers and nobles and the church hierarchy were summoned into the great audience chamber. Three battalions of guards were posted in the Kremlin. The Tsar appeared and, seated on the throne, ordered his son to be brought. Alexei came as a prisoner without his sword. Peter then denounced him for his feckless, drunken living, his ill-treatment of his deceased wife, his flight and his contemptuous behaviour towards his father. Alexei threw himself at his feet. "What do you ask?" said Peter. "My life and mercy!" was the tearful reply.[34] Peter promised to grant this, but now pardon was conditional on Alexei divulging the names of all who were close to him. Alexei readily agreed and went to a small adjoining room where he revealed the names of his friends and supporters. On his return to the audience chamber, Vice-Chancellor Shafirov read aloud a solemn oath of renunciation of the succession and recognition of Tsarevich Peter Petrovich as heir to the throne. The whole assembly then went to the Uspensky Cathedral where Alexei swore the oath before the holy relics.

Peter was still not satisfied. He suspected some conspiracy. He did not believe that without advice Alexei would have dared to act as he had and those who had advised him would be ready when the time came to persuade him to forget his oath and to ascend the throne. He decided that there must be an investigation to show the extent of the conspiracy. Already on the day of the solemn oath in the Kremlin, couriers had galloped to St. Petersburg with orders for the arrest of those named by Alexei. On the next day Alexei was told to answer in writing seven questions, prepared by Peter. He returned lengthy answers explaining his movements and implicating many people. Chief among those named were Alexander Kikin, Nikifor Vyazemsky, Prince Vasily Dolgoruky, Semeon Naryshkin, and Ivan Bolshoi Afanasiev. His answers were incomplete and in parts false, as when, from spite, he involved Vyazemsky, whom the court of ten ministers, which Peter had appointed, set free.

Alexander Kikin was now known as the chief offender. He had recently been found guilty of gross peculation and had been pardoned by the Tsar's special favour, but he could no longer expect mercy. Brought to Moscow, he admitted advising Alexei to flee abroad. He was given twenty-five strokes of the knout and examined on two further occasions, but he added little to what was already known. On 14 March 1718, the court of ministers sentenced him to a lingering death.

Prince Vasily Dolgoruky, who had been so high in the Tsar's favour, was also brought to Moscow in chains. His support of the Tsarevich was clear, but his family appealed for clemency in recognition of the long and honourable past services of the Dolgorukies. Peter bore in mind, as well, the services that Vasily Dolgoruky himself had rendered and, instead of execution, he deprived him of all honours and exiled him to Solikamsk.[35] Semeon Naryshkin was likewise exiled, and Alexei's personal servant, Bolshoi Afanasiev was executed.

At the same time another investigation was being made into the circle surrounding Evdokiya, Alexei's mother, for Peter suspected that she might be the centre of the conspiracy. On 4 February 1718, Guards Captain Skornyakov-Pisarev rode to the Suzdal Pokrovsky nunnery. There he found Evdokiya living in magnificence, not as a nun, but as a former tsaritsa. Investigations led to a number of arrests, and the examinations brought to light many interesting facts. Stepan Glebov was found to have been Evdokiya's lover, and she herself confessed her guilt. Since, however, she was no more than a stranger to Peter, he was not concerned with her immorality.[36] More serious was the fact that Glebov had sought to arouse the people against the Tsar. After cruel tortures he was impaled publicly and lingered for three days before he died.

Dositheus, Bishop of Rostov, was found guilty of uttering false prophecies concerning the succession of Alexei and of speaking against the Tsar. He was broken alive on the wheel and then beheaded. In all some fifty people were examined, but no conclusive evidence of a conspiracy against the Tsar ever emerged.

The investigations left Peter dissatisfied and suspicious, and he was still not sure what to do with his son. And so when he went to St. Petersburg on 18 March, he took Alexei with him and allowed him to live in freedom in a house adjoining Catherine's palace.

Here Alexei waited impatiently for the return of Efrosinia. He had left her with servants to travel at leisure, fearing that as she was pregnant the hurried journey with himself, Tolstoy, and Rumyantosov, would upset her. He had written to her frequently and made various arrangements for her comfort. Fear of his father and ardent love for his mistress were his two dominant emotions. As he waited for her to arrive, his one desire was that he might be allowed to marry her and retire to his country estate. At Easter, when paying his respects to Catherine in the traditional Russian style, he suddenly threw himself at her feet and implored her to obtain his father's permission to the marriage. He was never to achieve his wish.

Efrosinia reached St. Petersburg in the middle of April. She was taken straight to the Petropavlovsk fortress where presumably she gave birth to her child. Meanwhile her companions were examined, but their evidence added nothing to what was already known. Some four weeks later Peter travelled to his seaside palace, Peterhof, which the French architect Leblond was building on the shore of the Gulf of Finland. He took Alexei with him and gave orders for Efrosinia to be brought from the fortress secretly by boat on the following day. On her arrival he questioned her himself. He had no need to press for her answers or to cross-examine her. She spoke readily and openly, reporting everything that Alexei had said during their flight, their sojourn in Ehrenberg, and then at Naples. Whether inspired by hatred, contempt, or mere indifference, she could not have done more to damn him.

Alexei had, she said, written many times to the Emperor vilifying his father, the Tsar. When he heard the report of the alleged revolt among troops in Mecklenburg and of unrest near Moscow, he had said to her joyfully, "Now you can see how God acts in his own way."[37] Again when he read in a newssheet that Tsarevich Peter Petrovich was ill, he had rejoiced and made a similar comment. He was always talking of the succession to the throne which he ardently desired for himself. He had told her that when he was Tsar, he would live in Moscow and leave St. Petersburg deserted; he would not keep up the navy and the ships could rot; he would maintain an army sufficient only for defence, contenting himself with Russia's old frontiers.[38] Learning about certain portents seen in St. Petersburg he had commented that they were significant: "Perhaps my father will die," he said, "or there will be a rebellion," and he was confident that he would emerge victorious from a civil war.[39] On another occasion Alexei had written letters to the archbishops; they were not sent, but their purpose was to keep the churchmen on his side.

Efrosinia's evidence contained other similar details. All went to show that Alexei had lied. Far from being sincere in his renunciation of the throne and in his former protestations that he wished to enter a monastery, he was secretly but tenaciously clinging to his hopes of the succession. He would have no scruples about opposing his brother and breaking his oath, and once on the throne he would undo all that his father had wrought. This was what Peter had suspected, but so far evidence thereto had constantly eluded him and he had not been prepared to submit his son to normal examination by torture. Efrosinia, however, had now freely revealed Alexei's secret thoughts and hopes.[40] Confronted with his mistress, Alexei could only confess. He was placed under arrest and held in the fortress to await trial.

Peter was determined that he would not himself try his own son. On 13 July 1718, he issued a manifesto to the church hierarchy, asking their guidance on how a father should act towards this Absolom. The churchmen, headed by Yavorsky, returned an equivocal answer and evaded responsibility. Peter then issued a similar manifesto to senators, ministers, and senior officers, adding that they were to form a court and to judge the matter honestly, without fearing him, especially if they considered his son's crimes to deserve only mild punishment. In turning to his ecclesiastical and lay ministers Peter was no doubt taking care to avoid making Alexei a martyr, and was deliberately placing on them the responsibility for judging and punishing him. At the same time he himself felt unable to sit in judgment for, just as on many occasions he had shown special consideration for the sons of his generals and officers, so now he was not without paternal feeling as he brooded on Alexei's behaviour and his fate. He had shown no vindictiveness towards him and, despite Alexei's deceit and hostility, he might even now have required only that he should retire to a monastery, had not St. Petersburg and, in fact, his life's work been at stake.

The civil court formed to try Alexei consisted of 127 of the leading figures of the day. Following the Tsar's orders they treated the Tsarevich like anyone else charged with treason. The first examination took place on 19 June 1718, when Alexei was raised on the scaffold and received twenty-five strokes of the knout. Three days later Peter sent Tolstoy to the fortress to question him on certain points. The questions themselves suggest that Peter was anxious to probe the reasons for this failure in his relations with his son. Tolstoy was to ask why Alexei had never wanted to do what his father wished and why had he behaved unnaturally. Alexei blamed the influences of childhood, but he did not touch on his fears or the absence of the bond of affection and trust between father and son that had been crushed so early.[41]

On 24 June the second examination of Alexei took place, and he received fifteen strokes of the knout. On the same day the full court assembled and unanimously passed sentence of death on him for making false statements, plotting against the Tsar and wishing for his death, and for seeking the ruin of his country.

Alexei had so far suffered forty strokes of the knout in five days. He had been fearfully flayed, but on 26 June, despite the sentence of death already passed, he was apparently examined again with torture, this time in the presence of Peter, Menshikov, and others. Later in the day he began to fail and about 7 P.M. he died.[42] His body was placed in the Church of the Trinity in an open coffin with his face and right hand uncovered, as was customary, and people of all ranks who wished to take their leave of him were allowed to do so. On 30 June by the Tsar's ukaz the church hierarchy and all civil dignitaries attended with him and the Tsaritsa in the Church of the Trinity for the burial service, after which the body of Alexei was laid to rest in the Cathedral of SS. Peter and Paul.

CHAPTER XXXVII

The Treaty of Nystadt

1718-1721

ISAPPOINTED in his attempts to secure allied action, Peter had resolved to negotiate direct with Sweden, and at last he found Charles XII more tractable. At this time Charles was receiving overtures from George I, but he preferred to treat first with the Tsar for whom he had developed a certain liking and respect, which were, perhaps, no more than a reflection of the generous admiration that Peter had always expressed for him.

The congress opened on 12 May at Lafo, one of the Aland Islands. Peter instructed his plenipotentiaries, Bruce and Osterman, to propose as his basic conditions the cession to Russia of Ingria, Livonia, Esthonia, as well as Reval, Karelia, and Vyborg, and the return to Sweden of the whole of Finland. They were to show great friendliness towards the Swedes, and to cultivate Goertz, the Swedish minister, with flattery and presents. They were to inform him that the Tsar sincerely desired a close alliance with Sweden both for their own defence and "to maintain the balance of Europe"; moreover, if the King ceded the Russian conquests, the Tsar would bind himself to help him to obtain compensation in whatever quarter the King thought fit.[1]

From talks that he had already had with Kurakin in Holland, Goertz knew the Tsar's terms and that Charles would reject them. But he hoped ultimately to secure an acceptable treaty. Twice, during the subsequent weeks of wrangling, Goertz went to Sweden to report to the King. On 9 July 1718, he returned with a bold scheme which he had worked out and which, unknown to the Russians, was still awaiting Charles's approval. By this time, Goertz stated, the King would cede the Russian conquests, and the Tsar would restore Finland and part of Karelia. The equivalents required for these cessions were formidable. The Tsar was to help Sweden to conquer Norway and, if Great Britain interfered, Russia would join with Sweden in declaring war on her; finally, the Tsar would endeavour to obtain Mecklenburg for Sweden, compensating the Duke at the expense of Poland. Apart from refusing to use force against Denmark, Peter expressed himself satisfied. He was even prepared to support Sweden against Hanover, and this meant war with England. It was an onerous undertaking, but at this time he was confident that France would guarantee this Russo-Swedish treaty, and even join them in alliance.

Peter, who had been sailing off the Finnish coast with his fleet, now made for St. Petersburg. Believing that these terms already had Charles's approval, he thought that the peace treaty could be concluded without delay. Two weeks beforehand, however, Goertz had received Charles's rejection of his scheme. He had not divulged this fact, but with the passing of time the Russians realized that the King had raised objections. Peter was deeply disappointed and mainly for this reason he renewed his friendly overtures to the English government.

The Aland Congress had aroused great interest throughout Europe, but nowhere more than in England. The need to maintain the House of Hanover dominated English policy, not because of any esteem for George I, but because the alternatives were civil war and the restoration of Roman Catholicism. The Russo-Swedish congress contained threats of both alternatives and the English people, already disturbed by the advent of a new power in the Baltic, supported their King.

The first threat that roused the English was Charles XII's championship of the Pretender, and the fact that the Jacobites looked to him to lead them in another invasion of Scotland. Sweden could do nothing alone, but with the massive resources of the Tsar behind him Charles might seriously endanger the English throne. The second threat that brought George I the support of his people was the grandiose scheme of Cardinal Alberoni to revive the Spanish army and navy in an effort to return Spain to power in Italy and the

Mediterranean, and also to restore the Stuarts to the English throne. Knowing that England would support the Emperor, Alberoni began looking to Charles and Peter as allies, making approaches to both and urging them to conclude an early peace. For George I the position was menacing and he devoted himself to building up defensive alliances and preventing Sweden and Russia from coming together.

For this reason George responded promptly to Peter's overtures, made through Feodor Veselovsky in London. Admiral Norris sailed for St. Petersburg bearing messages of the King's strong desire for a friendly alliance. Captain James Jefferyes, who accompanied Norris, was to remain in St. Petersburg as English resident. But the mistrust of both parties ensured that these exchanges would be fruitless. Peter had consistently sought alliance with England and he expected now that in response to his overtures, Norris and Jefferyes were bringing firm proposals. When they brought only expressions of goodwill, his suspicions were aroused, particularly as he knew that George I, although he now denied it, had also sent two secret missions to Stockholm with proposals that Charles had rejected.

Meanwhile, after long hesitation, France had joined England, Holland, and Austria in the Quadruple Alliance, directed against Spain. Peter, seeing the collapse of his hopes of alliance with France, then began to reconsider the support he had promised Sweden against Hanover, for he saw that it would involve him in war against the whole of Europe, with only Sweden and possibly Spain as allies. He therefore instructed Osterman to propose holding over the undertaking against Hanover for three years, after which Louis XV would be of age, and he could hope for a change in French policy. Notwithstanding this instruction, however, if Charles insisted on the undertaking as a condition of peace, Osterman was to agree.

Early in December 1718 news of the death of Charles XII changed the whole position. He had been conducting the siege of the Norwegian fortress of Frederickshald and, exposing himself unnecessarily to danger, had been shot in the head.[2] He had made no provision for the succession and the candidates for the throne were now his nephew, the Duke of Holstein, whom Peter had cultivated, and his sister, Ulrica Eleonora, wife of the Prince of Hesse-Cassel. The Swedes, who hated the Holstein party, all the more because Goertz was a Holsteiner, made Ulrica Eleonora their Queen. Goertz, who had already been arrested, was beheaded.

Paradoxically, the death of Peter's great enemy only made peace with Sweden more remote than ever. The Swedes were impoverished and exhausted, but they were still not prepared to pay the Russian price. In February 1719 Bruce in the Aland Islands received a formal letter from the Queen addressed to the Tsar, expressing her desire for the continuance of the congress, to which she had appointed Count Lilienstedt in place of Goertz. From Count Gyllenborg, who had brought the Queen's letter, Bruce learnt that Lilienstedt's arrival at the congress would be delayed, and that the Swedes would certainly insist on the return of Livonia and Esthonia, as well as Finland.

Peter made strenuous efforts to bring the Swedes to terms. At first they procrastinated. Then they stated that, if they could not reach agreement, the Queen would be obliged to make peace with the other side. Finally they spoke ominously of plans against the Tsar that were already well advanced, and here they were referring to the machinations of George I.

Peter now determined to use the persuasion of force. Already in February 1719 he had given orders for operations in the summer. In July a Russian fleet landed Russian and Cossack troops on the Swedish coast where they caused extensive damage and left twenty thousand people homeless. At the same time Apraxin with another force landed only seven miles from Stockholm and ravaged the surrounding districts. Peter then sent Osterman to Stockholm to demand a final answer to his proposals. But Osterman brought back the report that the Swedes were still obdurate and that the Russian landings had only antagonized them further. In fact, it was as a direct result of these landings that Sweden signed a convention with Hanover.

On 21 August 1719, Peter instructed Bruce and Osterman that, if within one week of receiving his letter, their terms had not been accepted, they were to return to St. Petersburg. Informed of this ultimatum, Lilienstedt sent urgently to Stockholm for instructions. On 6 September he received the reply that the Queen rejected the Tsar's terms. The Aland Congress had come to an end without result. The Swedes, following the alternative plan of conceding their German possessions in return for help against the Tsar, were on the point of concluding a treaty with George, as Elector of Hanover. They were now confident that they would recover the Baltic provinces. Their confidence was sadly misplaced.

The death of Charles XII followed closely on the destruction of Alberoni's new Spanish fleet by Admiral Byng off Cape Passaro, and news of both events gave rise to joy and relief in England. George I, now secure on his throne, was able to concentrate openly on his policy of restricting Russian power in the Baltic. In the diplomatic war that he subsequently waged in Europe against Russian interests, he was successful in isolating Peter from all his allies. But it was an empty achievement.

Expecting the new Swedish government to favour peace with Hanover and England against Russia, George I dropped the pretence of seeking alliance with the Tsar. Veselovsky's position in London became difficult. In St. Petersburg Jefferyes, the newly arrived English resident, made trouble. Seeking to obstruct the Tsar, he seized on the idea of depriving him of his English shipwrights and naval officers, hoping thereby to maim the new Russian fleet which had aroused uneasiness in England, the more so because Russian ships could no longer be dismissed as primitive and ineffective, but were "as good as any in Europe."[3] Most of the English, however, were reluctant to leave Russia where they enjoyed great privileges and good conditions.[4] Jefferyes' second proposal was a ban on the employment and training of Russian apprentices in England. George I's government took action on both proposals.

These obstructions angered Peter and the hostility that they indicated disturbed him. But, influenced by his own fondness for English seamen and shipwrights and for England herself, he believed that George I was pursuing a Hanoverian policy which had no popular support. Also he thought that the importance to England of the Baltic would result in restraints on the Hanoverian faction. In London Veselovsky was extremely active in trying to arouse opinion against the government. He even went so far as to have printed and circulated in London a statement addressed to the King, which called forth a sharp reply, and aroused general resentment.

Relations deteriorated still further as George I developed his anti-Russian policy. His plan was that, in return for the cession of Swedish possessions in Germany, the allies—Hanover, Denmark, and Prussia—supported by the English fleet, and also by the Emperor and the

King of Poland, would compel the Tsar to restore his conquests to Sweden. All the countries involved had objections and when, after unremitting English and Hanoverian diplomatic pressure, they gave their support, it was halfhearted.

The first result of George I's anti-Russian policy was a treaty concluded in Vienna on 5 January 1719 between the Emperor, Augustus of Poland, and himself as Elector of Hanover. It proved abortive, but it was probably in Vienna that the ministers of these three countries worked out the general plan of offensive and defensive alliances designed to restore Sweden as a barrier against the Tsar who would be allowed to retain only St. Petersburg, Kronslot, and Narva.

The Vienna Treaty served as a warning to Peter. In England Feodor Veselovsky delivered a strong protest. George I replied that it was merely a defensive agreement, and gave assurances of his readiness to maintain friendly relations with the Tsar. Nevertheless at this time his diplomatic offensive against Russia was well under way in Copenhagen and Berlin.

Meanwhile, in July 1719, Lord Carteret, as British ambassador, and Colonel Bassewitz, the Hanoverian representative, had arrived in Stockholm to negotiate terms between Sweden and the allies. They met with strong opposition. The Swedes were particularly reluctant to cede territories to Prussia, Hanover, and Denmark. They declared that they would rather give everything to the Tsar, who had been a generous enemy by comparison with the Danes to whom they would give nothing.[5] But the Swedes were in no position to bargain, and the two subsequent Russian raids, causing serious damage and threatening Stockholm, brought this fact home to them. They promptly signed a convention with Hanover, ceding Bremen and Verden, which George I had coveted so long,[6] on the condition that the British naval squadron then at Copenhagen, would defend Sweden against further Russian attacks.

The arrival of Admiral Norris' squadron in the Baltic alarmed Peter. While Norris was still at Copenhagen, three Russian frigates came with a letter warning him that any approach to Russian ships or shores would be taken as a hostile act against which the Tsar would take all necessary steps. Norris expressed astonishment that the Tsar should feel himself threatened.

In September 1719, before leaving the Aland Islands, Bruce and

Osterman received letters addressed to the Tsar from Carteret and Norris, stating that the Queen of Sweden had accepted the mediation of Great Britain between her and the Tsar, and calling on him to cease hostilities. Carteret's letter ended with the threat that the British fleet had come to enforce mediation and that the King, together with France and his other allies, had taken measures to ensure its success. Bruce and Osterman rejected this "unusual and arrogant approach" and informed Carteret that they would not forward such a letter to their Tsar; they hoped that in a matter of such importance the King would himself write to the Tsar or communicate through his minister in St. Petersburg.[7]

Britain and Russia were thus near to war. Veselovsky reported from London on the widespread hostility towards Russia and the general agreement to defend Sweden so that the balance of power in the north would be maintained. At the same time he was assured at the beginning of 1720 that eight out of every ten Members of Parliament, whether Whig or Tory, were convinced that open war with Russia would be contrary to England's interests. Meanwhile George, as Elector of Hanover, had signed a formal treaty with Sweden, embodying the terms of the convention signed in July 1719. Two months later, as King of Great Britain, he concluded another treaty with Sweden, undertaking to pay an annual subsidy, to help her to hold Russian power in check in the Baltic, and to secure a favourable peace. Denmark had been compelled to agree to terms with Sweden. Frederick-William of Prussia, now fully reconciled with Hanover, took it upon himself to write to Peter, advising him to accept mediation, although it would involve giving up Finland, Livonia, Esthonia, and Reval. Peter refused to be intimidated, and promptly prepared to resist any attempts to deprive him of his Baltic conquests. He reinforced his regiments in Livonia and Courland, strengthened the defences of his ports, and made ready his galley fleet for new landings on the Swedish mainland.

At the beginning of 1720 the squadron, which Norris had sailed home to England in November of the previous year, was made ready to return to the Baltic. On 6 April Stanhope saw Veselovsky at court and told him personally, so that, as he said, the Russians would have no grounds for complaint, that Norris was sailing again to carry out the King's treaty obligations to Sweden, and that it was up to the Russians to decide whether to make peace or not, and whether to recognize the British as friends or enemies.

At the end of May, Norris anchored off Reval and, deciding that attack was impracticable, sent a letter to the commandant of Reval, Von Delden, enclosing a letter to the Tsar, which was promptly returned. While Norris at Reval was still pressing British mediation, a Russian force under Brigadier von Mengden landed on the Swedish coast and destroyed two towns and forty-one villages. Informing Yaguzkinsky of this raid, Peter wrote "the truth is that, although no very great loss was caused to the enemy, yet, praise God, it was done before the eyes of their allies, who could do nothing to prevent it."[8] The raid caused embarrassment to George I, and in Parliament the opposition made great play of this failure to defend Sweden.

Many factors were now undermining George's plans against Russia. In England sudden financial crises faced Parliament with the need to cut military expenditure; abroad, allies were falling away, divided and distracted by their own interests and rivalries. A serious breach came between George himself and the Emperor. Disputes began to divide Britain and France, who was also jealous of Austrian influence in the north and anxious over the improvement in relations between the Emperor and the Tsar. The King of Prussia sided with George against the Emperor, but refused to pursue a policy of hostility towards his powerful neighbour, the Tsar. Augustus of Poland, finding that George could not further his own ambitions, followed the course of the Emperor. He made overtures to Peter who, constant to his policy of keeping Poland always an ally, at once concluded a new defensive alliance with him.

Meanwhile in 1720 a Swedish adjutant-general had arrived in St. Petersburg to announce that Queen Ulrica Eleonora had resigned all royal power in favour of her husband, King Frederick I. Peter received the Swede with great courtesy and sent him back to Stockholm with assurances of his desire for the restoration of friendly relations between Russia and Sweden. In August 1720 he sent Rumyantsov, now Adjutant-General, to Stockholm. The Swedes welcomed him and proposed a renewal of negotiations, and discussions on the most suitable venue were begun.

Frederick I was now desperate for peace. The second Russian raid, carried out while Norris' squadron was anchored beyond range of the shore batteries of Reval, had been followed in August by a naval engagement in which the Russians had defeated a Swedish squadron, capturing four frigates. Peter was pleased with this exploit. "In truth, it is not to be considered a minor victory," he wrote to Menshikov, "because carried out under the eyes of the English gentlemen, who have defended the Swedes, their territory and their fleet alike."[9]

Further, it was clear that Sweden could now only be protected if land as well as naval forces were concentrated against the Tsar. George I had tried to bring this about, but none of his allies would face war with Russia. Even Great Britain, shaken by the financial crises of the South Sea Bubble, was now eager to shed her commitments under her treaty with Sweden. In October 1720, therefore, George himself advised Frederick I to make peace with the Tsar on the best terms he could get, offering him money to bribe Swedish senators to accept this policy. But the Swedes still considered peace impossible on the Tsar's terms.

In February 1720 the French minister, Campredon, arrived in St. Petersburg to further friendly relations between France and Russia and to help towards peace in the north. He found the Russians confident in their strength and obdurate in their terms. The Tsar had now secured a treaty of perpetual peace with Turkey, freeing him from threats in the south; he had a defence agreement with Augustus of Poland; he had assurances of neutrality from the Emperor and the King of Prussia. Moreover, his fleet, his massive army, and his great resources so impressed Campredon that his reports in Stockholm, where he arrived in April 1721 from St. Petersburg, made the Swedes realize that any thought of continuing the war would be madness.

Nystadt had now been agreed as the place for a conference. Peter again appointed Bruce and Osterman as his plenipotentiaries, while the Swedish representatives were to be Lilienstedt and Baron Stromfield. The conference opened at the end of April 1721. Once more, however, the Swedes demanded the return of Livonia and Vyborg, as well as Finland. Once more the Russians flatly rejected both demands and the negotiations approached deadlock.

In April 1721 Norris again sailed his squadron into the Baltic, and again a Russian force defiantly landed on the Swedish coast without opposition, causing widespread damage. This raid softened the obstinacy of the Swedes. They agreed then to cede Livonia on condition of the payment of compensation and of an undertaking by the Tsar that he would not take up the cause of the Duke of Holstein, who, as rival claimant to the Swedish throne, had now become a pawn in Peter's moves towards imposing a peace on Sweden. The Duke had, in fact, actually gone to St. Petersburg, where he received a magnificent welcome, and there were even strong rumours of his marriage with Tsarevna Anna, Peter's eldest daughter.

At Nystadt, however, the Russians accepted the two conditions attached to the cession of Livonia. The undertaking not to take the part of the Duke did not, it was considered, preclude his marriage with the Tsarevna. But the Swedes still fought for Vyborg and other disputes arose. On these, however, the Swedes had finally to give way, whereas the Russians granted only minor concessions.

It was in September 1721, when Peter was on his way from St. Petersburg to Vyborg to inspect the disputed frontier, that a courier from Nystadt overtook him with a letter, written on 30 August, from Bruce and Osterman. They reported that they had on that day signed the treaty of peace with Sweden, and on the Tsar's terms. The Swedes ceded to the Tsar in perpetuity the Baltic states of Livonia, Esthonia, Ingria, part of Karelia, and the Vyborg district, all of which he had conquered by his own arms. For his part the Tsar returned Finland, undertook to pay a large sum in compensation for Livonia, and granted to the Swedes certain rights to purchase grain free of duty in Riga, Reval, and Arensburg. He bound himself not to interfere in Swedish domestic affairs. He guaranteed to the inhabitants of the conquered provinces the rights which they had possessed under Swedish rule, and agreed to restore to all, who gave proof of ownership, their lands and property. Prisoners of war would be released without ransom and allowed to return to their homes, if they wished.[10]

Peter's delight at his triumph was unbounded. The Northern War had been a long and cruel struggle, but this treaty gave him all he had set out to win and even more. As he wrote to Prince Vasily Dolgoruky: "All students of science normally finish their course in seven years: our schooling has lasted three times as long, but, praise God, it has all ended so well that it could not be better."[11]

Peter now returned to St. Petersburg with all haste. He sailed into the Neva with drums beating, trumpets sounding, and guns firing.

The news was shouted to the shores and it flashed through the city. The people hurried to the Troitskaya wharf to greet the Tsar. The excitement and relief over the peace mounted as the crowd gathered and then walked with the Tsar to the Church of the Holy Trinity to give thanks. To the sound of gun salvoes Stefan Yavorsky conducted the service, after which General-Admiral Apraxin, all the flag officers, and all the ministers asked Peter to accept the rank of Admiral of the Red Flag. No honour could have pleased him more.

From the church Peter went out onto the square where the crowd had thickened, and mounting a small platform he said to them: "Rejoice and give thanks to God, Orthodox people, that the all-powerful God has brought an end to this war, so long drawn out and lasting twenty-one years, and has granted us a welcome and eternal peace with the Swedes."[12] Casks of wine were already being set up in the streets for the celebrations and he himself then took a beaker and drank to the health of his people, who roared their congratulations in reply.

Peter promptly busied himself with arrangements for the peace to be proclaimed throughout the tsardom, and decreed that it was to be thrice-celebrated, once immediately on receiving the news, a second time on 22 October and a third time on 28 January. He sent notes to all his ministers at foreign courts, congratulating them on the news, and instructing them to arrange banquets and suitable festivities. Also he wrote to Bruce and Osterman, congratulating and thanking them, "for the treaty has been made by your labours, although signed by us," and he promised that their work would not be forgotten.[13] He informed the Senate that as an expression of gratitude for God's mercy and bounty he would grant a general amnesty to all in prison, in exile, or serving sentence in the galleys, excepting only murderers and dangerous brigands; he would also grant remission of all debts owed to the Treasury and of arrears of taxes, accumulated from the beginning of the war up to 1718. On 10 September masquerades began and for a week people walked in the streets and rowed on the Neva wearing masks and fancy dress.

The date, 22 October, of the second celebration approached. At a joint meeting the Senate and the Holy Synod decided to petition the Tsar on behalf of the nation to take the title of Emperor and Great. Menshikov took their written request to Peter, who would only say that he would consider it. Receiving this answer the Senate and the Holy Synod sent two senators and the Archbishops of Novgorod and Pskov, who overcame his reluctance. It was not a feigned reluctance, but a reflection of the humility, piety, and modesty of the man. The Treaty of Nystadt was a magnificent climax in his reign, a victory that he had fought and laboured twenty-one years to win, and it was peculiarly his own achievement. But he claimed no special credit or rewards for himself. Replying to the acclamation he said: "It is for us to thank God with all our strength, but hoping for peace we must not grow weak in military matters, so that it does not happen with us as it happened with the Greek monarchy.... We must work for the general good, which God may grant us at home and abroad, and by which the burdens of the people may be lightened."[14]

On 22 October Peter with his family, his court, and all officers and ministers, attended service in the Church of the Holy Trinity in St. Petersburg, followed by the reading of the treaty and its ratification, which had now been received. The Archbishop of Pskov, Feofan Prokopovich, delivered an oration in praise of the Tsar. Then the whole Senate came before him and the Great Chancellor, Count Golovkin, on behalf of the Senate, the nobility, and all ranks of the people, spoke of the heroic deeds of the Tsar "through which alone and by your tireless labours and leadership we, your loyal subjects, have stepped from the darkness of ignorance onto the theatre of fame of the whole world, and, so to speak, have moved from non-existence to existence, and have joined in the society of political peoples—for that and for winning a peace so renowned and so rewarding, how can we render our proper gratitude? And so that we may not be with shame before the whole world, we take it upon ourselves in the name of the All Russian nation and of all ranks of the subjects of Your Majesty, humbly to pray you to be gracious to us and to agree, as a small mark of our acknowledgment of the great blessings that you have brought to us and to the whole nation, to take the title—Father of the Fatherland, Peter the Great, Emperor of All Russia!"[15]

Three times the senators shouted, "Vivat!" The crowds inside the church and outside took up the cry, which echoed through St. Petersburg and through Russia. All the bells rang, drums rolled, the cannon of the fortress and of the ships in the Neva roared their salvoes. The people of Russia, who had obeyed their Tsar so unwillingly, who had complained, but had endured their hardships and labours, had learnt and served, were now united in celebrating the fruits of their labours, and in paying tribute to the Father of their Fatherland, Emperor of All Russia, Peter the Great.

CHAPTER XXXVIII

Reform in State and Church

1714-1725

T HE years after Poltava formed the period of Peter's most thoroughgoing reforms. To his people they were the years of the greatest hardships, when their Tsar was like an elemental force upturning their lives. In many fields they thwarted his plans by their conservatism and laziness, evasion, and passivity. But he was unrelenting in pursuing his objective which was a well-ordered and wealthy country, standing secure and equal with the West, and one in which all his subjects would serve and share.

In this period war neither dictated nor conditioned his reforms, and they were no longer hasty improvisations. He worked under pressure, but it was now the pressure of the massive task to be performed, and not the urgent threat of invasion. He still tackled the task piecemeal; he had no grandiose over-all scheme. He was no theorist, but a practical man, working by trial and error, and burdened by countless other responsibilities.

In the past he had adopted military and other techniques from abroad. He now borrowed political institutions, mainly from Sweden. The fact that Sweden had been such a formidable enemy and that her government had continued to function so effectively while the King was absent had given him a deep respect for the Swedish system. But he did not copy blindly. He had no thought that the West was infallible; on the contrary he regarded it as a storehouse from which he took what was of use and adaptable to Russian needs. When in April 1718 he gave instructions for the drafting of certain new legislation by the Colleges, using Swedish models, he added that "those points in the Swedish regulations which are inconvenient or which are inapplicable to the situation of our government, shall be set down for my consideration."[1]

The Senate, which he had set up in February 1711 to govern in his absence, had continued as the chief executive organ. But from the start it had fallen short of what he required. In November 1715 he appointed Vasily Zotov to be "Inspector-General or Supervisor of Ukazi."[2] Zotov was to keep a register of ukazi, to see to their prompt execution, and to note and report senators who misbehaved or held up business in the Senate chamber.

An inspector-general was needed. Much of the confusion and delay in the Senate arose from friction between senators themselves and between the Senate and powerful governors like Menshikov and Romodanovsky. They complained and informed against each other incessantly, and Peter's patience was at times strained to its limits. He often took senators and the Senate as a whole to task, lecturing them on the need to despatch business without delay, to record their proceedings accurately, and to conduct themselves with dignity befitting legislators. He punished any who behaved badly, and in 1719 alone five senators were heavily fined.

At the same time he bore in mind that the Senate was under fire from every side. In 1718, while Zotov was reporting to him on its failure to collect fines and taxes, amounting to nearly a million and a half rubles, Peter was receiving bitter complaints from Romodanovsky and others about its harsh exactions, and the Vice-Governor of Kazan even petitioned to be relieved of office because he could not carry out its unreasonable orders.

Another equally serious obstacle to the proper functioning of the Senate was its heavy administrative burden. The old prikazi were neither suitable nor competent to handle the mass of new business and they could not relieve the Senate of routine administration. The administration of most countries in northern Europe at this time was based on the collegial system which in England was represented by the Board of Admiralty. The system appealed to Peter, because the collegial board, meeting under its president, reduced the dangers of corruption and of domination by one man and, as in a council of war, group decisions would probably be sounder than the arbitrary judgements of a single minister. For over five years he had considered the application of the system in Russia. He discussed it with Leibniz and others, and obtained information about Swedish, Danish, and German practices. By 1715 he had decided to abolish the prikazi and reorganize the whole administration of Russia in colleges. To do so, as with most of his reforms, he had to start from the very beginning.

First, he had to find experienced foreigners to establish the colleges and to train his own people. In August 1715 he instructed General Weide to engage foreigners for this purpose; they would have the rank of assessors, rent-free accommodation, a yearly salary of five hundred rubles, and a gratuity on completion of service.[3] The handicap was that they would have to carry out their duties through interpreters. A few months later Peter instructed Abram Veselovsky in Vienna to engage from each of the Imperial colleges, except the theological college, a civil servant not of senior rank, who was of Czech, Moravian, or other Slav race, and understood Slav languages.[4]

Veselovsky had small success in Vienna where anti-Russian feeling was always strong. In June 1717 from Spa, Peter sent instructions to the Senate to give all assistance to General Bruce who was also ordered to search for assessors.[5] In the following August he sent Izmailov to invite Swedish prisoners of war to volunteer for service in the colleges. But Izmailov could only find eighteen suitable volunteers. Meanwhile in January 1716 Peter had sent thirty-four young Russians to Koenigsburg to study "so that they may be better fitted for work in colleges, and a supervisor should be sent with them to see that they do not pass their time in pleasures."[6]

At the end of 1717 preparations were sufficiently advanced for nine colleges to be established, each with its president and vice-president.[7] With one exception the presidents were Russians and except in the college of foreign affairs, the vice-presidents were foreigners. But he imposed strict limits on the number of foreigners to be employed; of the staff of nineteen, excluding the president and vice-president, only three foreigners were allowed in each college.[8] He also wrote out in his own hand elaborate regulations designed to eliminate nepotism and corruption, while making his people take some responsibility for the appointments instead of leaving them entirely to him.

It was the usual story: unless Peter himself was present driving and supervising, everything was neglected. "Last December," so he wrote on 2 June 1718 to the Senate "before my departure I set up the beginnings of the colleges, intending that in the present year they would be brought to such a state that in the coming year of 1719 each would be ready to begin its work. But when I returned from Moscow I found that in certain colleges a little had been done and in the others nothing at all."[9]

Peter now appointed Yaguzhinsky to supervise these preparations and to report to him regularly. Four months later, finding that several of the presidents were still neglecting their colleges, he issued a further ukaz, requiring them to meet for the purpose every Tuesday and Thursday. "Also, having assembled both for this business and when in the Senate, there should be no unnecessary talking or chatter, but at this time there should be talk only of the matter in hand. Moreover, if someone begins to speak, another shall not interrupt, but shall allow him to finish, and then the other shall speak, behaving as is proper to honourable people, and not like wives trading in the market."[10] By 1720, when the General Regulation[11] was approved, the colleges had taken on their responsibilities.

Even allowing for the fact that this was a new and foreign institution, the colleges functioned sluggishly and with great confusion from the start. Disputes broke out between foreigners and Russians, and even more bitterly among the Russians themselves. A feud had raged for a long time between Golovkin and Shafirov, and now that they were respectively president and vice-president of the College of Foreign Affairs, it nearly brought business to a standstill. The Russians did not understand the new procedures and the foreigners were usually unable to explain them, either because they did not understand Russian, and the interpreters did not know the legal terminology, or because they themselves were ignorant of Swedish practice. Even less did the provincial offices understand the new system. Inevitably, then, in 1722 foreigners serving in the colleges were summoned to Moscow, and the majority were discharged. Peter also made some changes in the system, bringing it closer to Russian practice, which meant that many colleges gradually came to resemble the old prikazi and were under the thumbs of their presidents.

The introduction of the collegial system was, nevertheless, an important reform. It led to a more rational allocation of duties and responsibilities, and in this alone represented a distinct advance. Benefits were felt throughout the administration. The Senate was at first strengthened by the addition of the presidents of the colleges, who included Golovkin, Apraxin, Menshikov, and other powerful men who had in the past always opposed it. The colleges also freed the Senate of routine administration, so that it could now give its attention to supervision, to its function as high court of appeal, and, most important of all, to the legislation which Peter increasingly devolved upon it. He saw the Senate not only as the guardian of the law and of the interests of the state, but also as an adviser to the Tsar and the responsible organ for preparation of legislation. He himself turned to it from time to time and took the advice it tendered. In 1718, when worried over the Ladoga canal, he requested the advice of the Senate, and acted on its recommendations although they were contrary to his own views.

The Senate, nevertheless, still fell short of what he expected of it. He saw that it had been a mistake to make collegial presidents members of the Senate. Their double function meant that they performed neither properly; the collegial boards were even more reluctant to disagree with their presidents who were also senators; the presidents were thus able to run their colleges without restraint or opposition. Moreover, complaints against a president were usually dismissed by senators who rallied in support of their members against outsiders. By ukaz of 12 January 1722 Peter directed that, except in the two war colleges and the College of Foreign Affairs, new presidents were to be nominated for appointment to all colleges and that the presidents who continued as senators should attend the Senate only on certain specified occasions. His intention was that "senators should have no special business, but should ceaselessly work for the good order of the state and justice, and should supervise the colleges, while independent of them."[12] But this ukaz of 12 January 1722 did more than redefine the senate's position and responsibilities, it also set up the extremely important new office of procurator-general.

The Senate had continued to need the closest supervision. Peter had constantly found himself in the difficult position of having to correct and punish senators, while at the same time protecting and supporting their authority. Vasily Zotov as Inspector-General had lacked the authority and personality to press charges against the most powerful men in the land, and was succeeded by guards officers who did tours of one month on duty. But, apart from the incongruity of a captain or major of the guards being posted to see that the highest assembly in the land carried out its functions, the system was unsatisfactory because the officers did not understand the business of the Senate.[13]

Peter stormed against the general failure to observe and enforce civil laws, a practice "which nowhere in the world has been so strong as it is with us. . . ."[14] To ensure that, from the Senate, through the colleges, and down to the lowest branches of provincial and municipal administration, the law was respected and obeyed, he created the office of Procurator-General. Just as shortly before his departure for the Pruth he had instituted the Senate to act in his absence, so, as he prepared to set out on his Persian campaign, he now appointed Yaguzhinsky as the first Procurator-General. In the presence of all the senators he announced the appointment, saying: "Here is my eye, through whom I will see everything; he knows my intentions and wishes. What he considers to be for the general good, you are to do; and although it may seem to you that what he does is contrary to the advantage of me and of the State you should nevertheless carry it out and having notified me, await my orders."[15] As "the attorney of the Sovereign and of the State"[16] he would supervise the Senate to ensure that "it was worthy of its title and acted without deceit."[17] He was to maintain a constant check on the colleges through his own staff of procurators, attached to each college, and the fiscals came directly under him.

Yaguzhinsky had come to rival Menshikov as favourite. He possessed similar energy and initiative and, unlike Menshikov, he was completely honest. But even with the great authority of his office he proved unable to introduce discipline into the Senate. In 1722, after Peter had set out on his Persian campaign, a typical uproar showed that the Senate was out of hand. The Ober-Procurator, Skornyakov-Pisarev, complained to Catherine of his difficulties and then wrote to Peter. He was, he said, repeatedly sworn and shouted at in the Senate. Yaguzhinsky himself had set senators against him, but Shafirov's insults were worst of all. The quarrelling in the Senate became more strident and the feuds between senators came out into the open. Shafirov behaved so outrageously that the Senate passed a resolution reporting him to the Emperor. On his return Peter ordered an investigation, and as a result Shafirov was condemned to death,[18] Skornyakov-Pisarev was relieved of office, and both Dolgoruky and Golitsyn were reduced in rank. It was only gradually that the standards of conduct and work in the Senate improved.

Thus Peter had set up a central executive and an administration which gave some promise of efficiency. But he had also to think of the law to be administered. In 1700 he had appointed a committee of boyars to revise the code of 1649, but the task had never been completed. In the meantime he had decided that the old code promulgated by his father was completely out of date, and on 28 April 1718 he issued an ukaz to all colleges to prepare a new code.[19] A few days later the College of Justice was instructed to report to the Senate on setting up judicial centres, on the translation of the Swedish code and the preparation of a Russian code based on it.[20] In December 1719 he ordered the Senate to hold special sittings, as from 7 January 1720, to consider the draft code, which was to be finished by the end of the following October. The Senate was to report specially on points on which the Russian was preferable to the Swedish code, and in matters of real property the laws of Esthonia and Livonia were to be adopted.[21] In May 1721 he ordered members of the colleges to sit three days a week, in the mornings and from 3 to 8 P.M., working on the code, for he considered their progress slow and their attitude dilatory. From experience he knew that only by handling his administrators in this way could he obtain results.

The transformation of the government at the centre led to further reform of the provincial and municipal systems. He had in 1708 divided the country into eight, later to become eleven, vast governments. It had been a bold act of decentralization in a country that had developed from and depended on Moscow for everything.

In the period after Poltava, Peter made further changes. The eleven governments were divided into some fifty provinces, subject to the governors in military and judicial matters, but independent of them in all else. The provinces were sub-divided further into *distrikti* or districts and had a complicated system based on a rural chancellery with rural supervisors of tax collection, and other officials, while the districts were in the charge of a rural Kommissar.

By an ukaz of 24 April 1713 Peter made it clear that provincial government was the Senate's responsibility,[22] and imposed restraints on the powers of the governors by partially introducing the collegial system. Provincial landowners were to elect *landrats*, who would sit with the governors on all provincial matters. But the system did not take root and by 1719 the office of *landrat* had died out, probably through lack of suitable men.

Peter's attempts to reform provincial government were among his least successful measures. The system was too complex and too remote from the experience of his people. But in the course of this reform he made a bold attempt to separate justice from the executive. By an ukaz of 8 January 1719 he established judicial districts, each with a system of courts based on Swedish models. The courts were not subject to the local governor, but to the College of Justice, and the Senate was confirmed as the final court of appeal. It was a sharp departure from the Russian practice where justice was part of the administration. The experiment did not work, however, and early in 1722 it was abolished; justice was again made a responsibility of governors and voevodi.[23]

Peter's concern for justice and the rule of law did not stem only from his anxiety to produce an ordered society in which all honoured the law. He was also concerned about justice for individuals. He knew that in the midst of corruption and inefficiency the suitor without money or influence could not obtain justice or even a hearing, and that the petitioner who could not submit his petition to the Tsar personally, had small hope of securing his rights.[24] On a number of occasions he had proclaimed that petitions could be brought direct to him or to the duty guards officer, but he was often away and petitions reported by the guards to the relevant colleges were as often as not lost in the bureaucratic machine. In April 1720 he directed the Senate to set up the new office of General Master of Petitions (General Reketmeister) whose main duty was the scrutiny of petitions to ensure that they were honest and contained no false statements, to pass them to the proper college or chancery, and to see that they received prompt attention. Subsequently, in April 1722, he gave the General Master of Petitions further instructions to keep a constant watch that factory workers, manufacturers, prospectors, and foreigners were not oppressed or deprived of their rights.[25]

His municipal reforms were more successful. Peter had in 1699 freed the merchant-traders from the rapacious grasp of the voevodi and established the burghers' councils. In 1718 he instructed the Senate to draft a municipal statute based on those of Riga and Reval, where the merchants were strongly organized in guilds and managed their affairs with an efficiency foreign to Russian towns. Nothing happened for some months until Peter, who had been taken up with other matters, demanded action, and even then there were further delays. At the beginning of 1720 he instructed Prince Trubetskoy to establish a magistracy in St. Petersburg, which was to work on the collegial principle and serve as a model for other towns. In January of the following year it received its charter as the chief magistracy. At the same time the merchant-traders of the towns were organized into two guilds, according to wealth and station. Members of the senior guild could be elected to the board of the magistracy, which was responsible for the general administration and was a court of first instance in civil and criminal cases; it was also specially charged with the economic development of its town.

This municipal reform was, however, only a partial success. Though it brought some improvement into the administration of the towns and the affairs of the merchant-traders, it failed to develop the sturdy independent middle class which Peter had seen contributing to the wealth of England and Holland, and which he needed in Russia. The Russian habit of expecting orders from the centre stultified the growth of independence in the provinces. The chief magistracy in St. Petersburg at once established its dominance and the others were content to do as they were told.

Laziness and ignorance were two obstacles to reform, but even more serious was the corruption against which Peter fought throughout his reign. Bribery and corruption were common practices in Europe at this time, but in Russia they were carried to such extremes as to cripple the national life. Russians looked on service as a means of profit. Public officials were unpaid or received a nominal salary; they got their living by peculation and bribery, and those who were clever grew rich. It was accepted that everyone who could robbed the state; it was no matter for shame or disgrace. Corruption was so widespread that of the most senior and powerful men in the land on whom Peter depended, only six—Makarov, Osterman, Yaguzhinsky, Repnin, Rumyantsov, and Sheremetev—were said to be beyond reproach.

Peter was unrelenting in his campaign against corruption but was compelled to accept bribery in private business, for it was financially impossible to pay government servants proper salaries. When, in 1713 the clerks of the secret table of the Senate chancellery petitioned for an addition to their salary because they had no other income, he ordered that they should have care of all foreign and Stroganov affairs, from which they would be able to make some extra profits. But he would not accept corruption in any form affecting government property or diminishing the national revenues, condemning it not only because it damaged the interests of the state, but also because it was immoral and wrong. He was strict in his own handling of money. He regularly drew his naval pay and on one occasion he stated on receiving it: "I have earned this money, like other naval officers, by serving my country; so I am free to spend it as I wish; but by contrast money gathered from the people has to be spent on behalf of the State and for the benefit of the people, and at some time I will be obliged to render account of it to God himself."[26]

In August 1713 an ukaz proclaimed the Tsar's anxiety to lighten the burden of his people and to extirpate corrupt practices which brought many citizens, and especially the peasantry, to ruin. Shortly afterwards another ukaz called on everyone, knowing of cases of corruption, to report without fear to the Tsar himself in the period from October 1713 to March 1714. The reward of the informer was the property of the evildoer whom he denounced, but anyone informing falsely and maliciously would lose his own property. The people were impressed, but they did not properly understand what the rewards were for; they had always accepted bribery, peculation, and embezzlement as part of the order of things. In December of the following year Peter issued a further ukaz, forbidding those holding official positions to be parties to contracts with the government and threatening those who disobeyed with severe punishments, even death. This ukaz also made failure to inform punishable, and required all concerned in public business or trade to sign the ukaz so that they could not subsequently plead ignorance.

A flood of anonymous letters showed that people were willing to inform, especially against those in high office. But they would not inform in person either because they could not prove their accusations or because they feared the revenge of their victims. Many gave vent to their spleen by laying false charges. It was not the kind of information that Peter wanted and in an ukaz, proclaimed at the beginning of 1715, he condemned anonymous letters, written by those who "beneath a show of virtue put out their venom."[27] This ukaz stressed that there was no danger in making an honest denunciation and so he "who is a true Christian and an honourable servant of his sovereign and his fatherland, may without any misgiving report verbally or by letter to the Tsar himself or to the duty sergeant at his court."[28] The ukaz referred to the example of the fiscals "who constantly report not only on the lowly but also on the most eminent without any fear, for which they receive reward."[29]

The fiscals had indeed brought numerous malpractices to light. The majority were indefatigable in tracking down and reporting every form of corruption, but with few exceptions all succumbed to temptation themselves in the end. They were the most hated men in Russia. Stefan Yavorsky, in a sermon on 17 March 1712, strongly denounced them, because their powers put everyone at their mercy while placing them beyond the law; he expressed the feeling of the whole country.

Hostility surrounded them in their work, not only in the provinces but even in the Senate. In April 1712 three senior fiscals—Nesterov, Zhelyabuzhsky, and Shepelev—complained to Peter that the Senate ignored their reports, and that it was dangerous for them to be near Senators Yakov Dolgoruky and Grigory Plemyannikov, who called them "Antichrists and rogues."[30] These attacks and Yavorsky's sermon impressed Peter who acknowledged that the office of fiscal was both heavy and hated. He did not abolish it; fiscals were necessary, but subsequently he restricted their powers and functions.

The most zealous of the fiscals was Alexei Nesterov. He was the most fearless in accusing those in high office and his zeal was often spiced with malice. He laid charges against Prince Yakov Dolgoruky, Musin-Pushkin, and the Archbishop of Kholomenskoe, but his most striking denunciation concerned Prince Matvei Gagarin, the Governor of Siberia since 1708.

Remote from control and supervision, Gagarin ruled like a monarch. He built up a vast fortune, mainly by illegally trading with China when the China trade was a government monopoly. He lived and entertained magnificently and was loved by everyone in Siberia, including the Swedish prisoners of war, for he wielded his power without arrogance and to the benefit of others as well as himself. Moreover, he achieved much in developing Siberian trade, mineral resources, and industry. Rumours of Gagarin's corruption came to Peter's ears in 1711, but not until Nesterov began investigating was evidence obtained. Nesterov's first report was made in 1714. This and a subsequent report to the Senate were deliberately overlooked, for Gagarin was both wealthy and influential. Nesterov obtained further evidence and took advantage of Peter's presence in Moscow in 1717 to submit his case. Under investigation Gagarin confessed his guilt and begged to be allowed to end his days in a monastery. His eminence and services were such that all believed that he would be pardoned. But the persistence of corruption in defiance of his ukazi had angered Peter. He determined to make an example of Gagarin, who was stripped of all honours and property, and was publicly hanged in St. Petersburg in 1718.

Peter had now realized the extent to which even those closest to him were involved in malpractices. He had every charge investigated, usually by his trusted guards officers, and was merciless in punishing the guilty. At the end of 1714 the officials of the Ingria, the St. Petersburg, and the Admiralty offices, including the Vice-Governor of St. Petersburg, Korsakov, the head of the Admiralty, Alexander Kikin, and the chief Minister for Building, Sinyavin, were arrested, as well as two senators, Volkonsky and Opukhtin. All were found guilty of corruption in various degrees. Korsakov was publicly knouted; his property was confiscated, and he was exiled to Siberia. A number of officials were condemned to death and at the gallows their sentence was commuted to exile. Peter made a terrible example of the two senators. He called Volkonsky a Judas because, entrusted with investigating an accusation, he had accepted bribes and made a false report, and in addition had been found guilty of gross peculation himself. Both he and Opukhtin were severely knouted and then, for breaking their oath as senators, their tongues were burnt out with red hot irons, and they were exiled. Alexander Kikin, who had been one of Peter's favourites and for whom Catherine interceded, was pardoned, but as the chief accomplice of Tsarevich Alexei he was to meet a terrible end two years later.

Menshikov's peculations and interests were on such a grand scale that for over ten years his affairs were constantly under examination. He had amassed enormous wealth and his influence reached out to every part of the country. Peter had always treated him with generosity, rewarding him for his services, usually with grants of land and serfs, as when in 1709 he gave him the vast estates of Mazepa at Baturin. But Menshikov was insatiable in his greed. Astute in business and unprincipled, he used his position to accumulate further wealth. It was even said that he had hidden away over a million rubles in banks in London and Amsterdam.

Peter first censured Menshikov in 1711, when he learnt of his extortions in Poland; Menshikov justified himself on the ground that he had only taken from Poles. But on his return from the Pruth campaign, Peter found evidence of Menshikov's malpractices even in St. Petersburg. At the beginning of 1712, Peter warned him again: "I'm telling you for the last time: mend your ways if you don't want to suffer great misfortune. You are going now into Pomerania; don't imagine that you will behave there as you did in Poland; you will answer to me with your head if I receive the smallest complaint against you."[31] At this very time, when Menshikov was promising to mend his ways, the Dutch resident, De Bie, reported to his government that Konon Zotov was exacting fees from the foreign merchants and sharing the proceeds with Menshikov.

At the beginning of 1715 Menshikov was charged, first, with obtaining grossly excessive profits from army contracts, made before the ban on officials contracting with the government, and second, with misappropriating government property to the value of a million rubles or more. Peter had the contracts investigated and while it was found that he had not overcharged in all cases he was judged to owe the Treasury 144,788 rubles. He was able to give satisfactory explanations of the items under the second charge, except for two or three involving the repayment of 202,283 rubles. Menshikov's position was, however, exceptional, since the government itself was indebted to him for services and loans of money. He had been Governor of St. Petersburg since its foundation, but had received no salary. He had the duty of receiving and entertaining foreign ministers, and he must meet the expense from his own pocket. Furthermore, Menshikov had on many occasions made timely advances to the government. In July 1714 when Peter was abroad, Admiral Apraxin had written desperately from Finland that his troops were starving. Menshikov demanded action from the Senate. But the senators disclaimed responsibility, on the ground that they had no money to purchase provisions. It was on such occasions that Menshikov showed his worth. He promptly requisitioned supplies to the value of 200,000 rubles on his own account from merchants' warehouses, had them loaded on ships which sailed immediately and thus saved Apraxin's army.

Peter found that many of the charges against Menshikov were

matters of irregular accounting rather than peculation. He was, therefore, more lenient and, protesting his innocence, Menshikov paid part of the sum owing while the remainder was cancelled. In 1718 new charges were brought and he appeared before a court-martial which also tried General-Admiral Apraxin, Prince Yakov Dolgoruky, and others. Menshikov and Apraxin were sentenced to dismissal and loss of all honours. Apart from consideration of their services, however, Peter recognized that he could not do without them, and he soon afterwards restored them to their ranks. But then investigations of charges against Kurbatov, and the Solovev affair, again implicated Menshikov.

Kurbatov, first of the profit-makers, had risen to a position of high authority. In 1711 Peter had appointed him Vice-Governor of Archangel. It was an important post, for Archangel was then still the chief port. But Kurbatov felt that he had been reduced in rank and disgraced. He wrote begging to be made governor. "Build three ships and you'll be governor!" was Peter's reply.[32] Five years later Kurbatov wrote to Makarov that he had built not three but seven ships and, far from receiving the governorship, he had been relieved of office and left in poverty. It was true, and the reason was Kurbatov's peculations and his involvement in the affair of the Solovev brothers. This affair had wide repercussions. Of the three brothers Solovev, one was the chief Russian agent and banker in Amsterdam and his recall and trial destroyed the credit of Russian merchants in Holland; the second brother was kommissar for government trade in Archangel, where he quarrelled with Kurbatov; the third was manager of Menshikov's estates. The affair involved bitter recriminations between Menshikov and Kurbatov, who had formerly been in league. Kurbatov died in 1721 before the charges against him were finally decided, although he had undoubtedly been guilty of fraud and embezzlement. His activities had, however, been less inspired by the malice that made Nesterov so hated that no one would speak to him. Nesterov, too, was found guilty of corruption and despite his age was broken alive on the wheel and then beheaded.

The extent of the malpractices, especially among those close to him, disgusted Peter.[33] He thundered against corruption and savagely punished the guilty. He could not stamp it out, but his efforts were not wholly without result. Formerly accepted as a normal part of the life of the country, and arousing no comment, it now became a crime and a sin, which men confessed.

At the same time Peter regarded corruption not as an isolated evil, but as part of the general backwardness of Russia. Standards of conduct inevitably declined among a people sunk in ignorance, barbarism, and sloth. Social reform and education were essential to raise them. He had always considered that in this the church had the most important part to play, but first he had to stir the church from its lethargy and cleanse it of abuses.

Begun in 1700, the reform of the church waited over twenty years before Peter gave it final shape. During these years his own personal faith remained unchanged. It was the simple Orthodox faith, rooted in wide knowledge of the Bible and of the liturgy, which he had learnt as a boy. He had discarded the exaggerated ceremonial that had hedged the lives of the tsars, but he had not neglected the normal observance of his religion, which was as much part of his life as it was of the lives of his most devout subjects. He felt the hand of God over everything and he acknowledged with humility the divine will. After victory his first thought was always to give thanks; in danger or disaster he offered prayers for God's protection and blessing. When abroad he had shown eager curiosity about the doctrines of other Christian sects. He had impressed Anglicans, Quakers, Lutherans, and Roman Catholics with his theological knowledge, and the latter, in particular, had entertained hopes of his conversion. But at no time had he contemplated forsaking the faith of his fathers or interfering with the Orthodoxy of his subjects.

Many among his people considered him irreligious because of his tolerance. He not only showed a sympathetic interest in other faiths, but also allowed Russia to be contaminated by their churches and worship. He guaranteed freedom of worship to Lutheran churches in the captured Baltic provinces; he permitted the erection of Lutheran and Roman Catholic churches in Moscow and elsewhere; he allowed Jesuits to preach in Moscow and to pass freely through Russia to the Far East on missionary errands.[34] Eventually his example and the stream of foreigners whom he brought into the country led to some relaxation in the bigotry of his church and people. Roman Catholics and Protestants were no longer damned as unbaptized and their heresy was thus of lighter hue. More important, the marriage of Russian girls to non-Orthodox foreigners was permitted by the church, with the result that foreigners and many Swedish prisoners in Siberia married Russians and settled there. But these were merely the beginnings of tolerance among a people still bigoted and xenophobic.

Peter was even forbearing in his treatment of Old Believers whom the church had anathematized. In the Olonets region they had settled in large numbers, developing a community with its own hierarchy. In 1702, when they learnt that the Tsar himself would be travelling through their region to the Neva, they gave way to panic and prepared to burn themselves to death in their wooden churches. But Peter, passing by their settlements, merely said, "Let them live there."[35] On another occasion when told that the Old Believers were honest and diligent merchants he said, "If they are truly so, then so far as I am concerned, let them believe what they wish, for when it is impossible to turn them from their superstition by reasoning, there is obviously no use in fire or sword; and to make them martyrs is stupid—neither are they worthy of that honour, nor would the state derive any benefit."[36]

The greatly expanded iron foundries in the Olonets region depended on Old Believers who proved reliable workers. In return, Peter granted them freedom to live in peace and to worship according to the old books. They were not, however, free from persecution by the church. Henning, the able Dutchman, who contributed so much to the development of Russian industry, wrote to Peter complaining that the Archbishop of Novgorod had arrested a leading Old Believer who was one of his best workmen. The Archbishop of Novgorod was Job, a dauntless powerful man whom Peter humoured because of his zeal for reform and education, and he was not prepared to upset him on behalf of a heretic. While the church actively persecuted them, Peter sent a priest among them to persuade them back into the fold.[37]

The Old Believers who laboured in the new iron foundries were exceptional. The great majority were ultra-conservatives and the most obdurate enemies of reform. They had fled in crowds to live in the forests and deserted places, thus depriving the state of revenue and recruits. For this reason Peter regarded them with suspicion. In February 1716 he ordered a census of all Old Believers and imposed on them a double tax. But many evaded the census and the tax proved hard to gather. Gradually he was forced to adopt more severe measures and to treat them as enemies of the state.

Peter regarded himself as holding the throne on trust from God to whom he would have to render strict account. His duty to God was to serve honestly and to the best of his ability. This was equally the duty of the church. By its teaching and the example of the clergy it should inspire the people to live Christian lives of work and service, and because it failed to do so he introduced numerous reforms.

The appointment of a new patriarch had remained in abeyance. Peter had probably not at first decided to abolish the patriarchate but was acting cautiously over an appointment which might become a focus of opposition. He had made Stefan Yavorsky "Exarch of the most holy patriarchal throne, guardian and administrator," imposing on him the responsibility of raising the standards of conduct and education among the clergy and of cleansing the church of various abuses. But Yavorsky belonged by nature to a monastery; he longed for a quiet devotional life in his native Ukraine, and constantly begged to be released from the turmoil of his life in Russia where enemies surrounded him. Gradually, too, he found himself in opposition to Peter. On a number of occasions he criticized him directly or indirectly as when, in March 1712, he denounced the fiscals and spoke of Tsarevich Alexei as "our sole hope."[38] He had also accused Peter of committing adultery, failing to reverence holy ikons, and had even declared him worthy of expulsion from the church. He was always quick to repent his outspokenness and to beg forgiveness, as he put it, "by writing writ with tears not with ink."[39] Peter showed forbearance, although disappointed in his failure in the work of reform. But in 1716 he admonished him to mend his ways, especially to consider more carefully before excommunicating anyone, "to deal with enemies of the Holy Church sensibly, correctly, and with tenderness," and also to avoid certain abuses of power of which he had been guilty.[40]

After Poltava, Peter turned increasingly to Feofan Prokopovich. Unlike Yavorsky, who in his jealousy had denounced him as a heretic, Prokopovich had no fear of enemies and threw himself into a struggle with zest. He was, moreover, in the fullest sympathy with the reforms in the church and in other fields, and he supported Peter personally. When the church hierarchy stood aside from judging Tsarevich Alexei, Prokopovich thundered from the pulpit against the

Tsar's enemies. Peter had at last found in him the man whom he needed to help in the final reform of the church. But, still respecting Yavorsky for his learning and ability, he retained him in the highest post. In 1718, after the consecration of Prokopovich as Bishop of Pskov, he brought Yavorsky to St. Petersburg and entrusted to Musin-Pushkin the task of bringing the two men together. It was an uneasy peace but, suffering from a dearth of able men, he was determined to retain both of his chief ecclesiastical advisers.

Peter had now decided on an ecclesiastical college as the best form of government for the church. Yavorsky strongly opposed it. Prokopovich favoured it, and it was he who composed the Spiritual Regulation which, after detailed revision by Peter himself, was proclaimed in January 1721. It established a "spiritual" college, later called the Holy Governing Synod, which took the place of the patriarchate and was responsible for the affairs, spiritual and temporal, of the church. A manifesto, proclaimed at the same time, and the first part of the regulation itself explained why the collegial form of government had been adopted. A spiritual college would be less likely to fall into errors of prejudice and bigotry; its pronouncement would have more authority than those of one man; "from collegial government the fatherland has no need to fear revolt and disturbance such as arise from the spiritual government of a single man, for the simple people do not know how to distinguish the spiritual power from that of the autocrat, but struck by the glory and splendour of the highest pastor, they think that he is a second sovereign with like powers, or even with greater powers, and that the spiritual rank is a different and higher state. . . ."[41]

Peter made Yavorsky president of the Holy Synod and appointed eight other members. Prokopovich was third in seniority, but his influence was probably greater than that of the others. Since the Holy Synod was as liable as the Senate to be disrupted by quarrels and negligent in attending to its business, Peter also appointed a procurator-general who was a layman with duties analogous to those of the procurator-general in the Senate.

The Synod took time to settle down. Yavorsky, until his death in the following year, was quarrelsome, and mainly through him the Synod was soon involved in sharp conflict with the Senate. This gave rise to difficulties because Peter intended it to be superior to the other colleges and equal with the Senate; and the two bodies were to de-

cide matters of dispute between them by meeting together in joint
session. But the system finally took root. The patriarchate was not a
long-established institution or an essential part of the church, and
Peter by his elaborate mockery, had undoubtedly dissipated much of
the popular reverence formerly shown to the person of the Patriarch.[42]

The second part of the Spiritual Regulation defined more specifically the functions of the Holy Synod. It was to combat superstition
and spread knowledge of the Gospels, composing and publishing
manuals for the purpose. Education was to be one of its chief concerns. Bishops were to establish schools for the training of the priesthood; within four years forty-six schools had been opened. Bishops
themselves were, incidentally, enjoined to behave with humility, not
with pride and arrogance.

The regulation even defined the syllabus for church schools. It
embraced grammar, history, geography, arithmetic and geometry,
logic and dialectics, rhetoric and poetry, physics and metaphysics,
politics and theology. Not narrowly utilitarian, it reflected the
breadth of Peter's own outlook.

The church schools were an important step in the improvement of
the quality of the priesthood, to which he attached so much value.
Both the "white clergy," the seculars who were allowed to marry, and
the "black clergy," who were celibate, had degenerated. The children
of the white clergy had almost automatically followed their fathers
into holy orders, although often wholly unsuitable. Recruiting for
the army and navy had given rise to a rush to holy orders by young
men who saw in it a means of evading service. One of the first tasks
of the Senate, in consultation with the church hierarchy, had been
to put an end to this form of evasion both for the benefit of the
church and of the armed forces, and to regularize certain hasty measures that Peter himself had taken in the early years of the war. An
ukaz of March 1711 had severely limited admission to holy orders;
in future men under twenty-five could not become deacons and men
under thirty years of age could not become priests, while the numbers
in both categories could not be increased. These and other stringent
regulations were confirmed in 1718 when it was decreed that the
children of priests could only take holy orders if they proved themselves worthy by study and conduct. Other ukazi required priests to
carry out their duties properly, and to show zeal in their calling.[43]

At the same time Peter insisted that the people should be more punctilious in their devotions. Learning that many did not go to church, even during the great religious festivals, he issued a decree to be proclaimed in towns and villages that all who were not sick should worship twice or thrice on Sundays and holy days. Priests were to report those who failed to attend, and a scale of fines was laid down. When in church they were to stand silently during the liturgy and those who talked or misbehaved were also liable to fines. Proper attendance at church had special importance because new laws and regulations were read out from the pulpit—often the only means of informing the peasantry in distant villages. But these measures were also introduced in the belief that regular worship and thanksgiving were Christian duties.

The reform of the monasteries and of the "black clergy" was also a massive task. In 1700 there were over 557 monasteries and nunneries and a census taken later in Peter's reign accounted for 14,534 monks and 10,673 nuns. For the most part these monasteries were wealthy, possessing vast estates and thousands of serfs, but they grossly mismanaged their affairs. They had ceased to be houses of learning and devotion and had become places of superstition and pious frauds, the refuge of runaway serfs and deserters from the army, of hordes of laymen and servants.

Peter did not attempt to confiscate their estates, but he required efficiency in their management. In 1701 he had revived the Monastery Office, appointing a layman, Boyar Musin-Pushkin, to administer their affairs. He had also sought to eliminate waste, corruption, and luxury by limiting monastery expenditure. But he was not concerned only to introduce order and efficiency into the affairs of the monasteries. He respected the monastic ideal, as he had shown in his visits to the Solovetsky Monastery and by himself establishing a great monastery near St. Petersburg, but he considered the number of monasteries and of monks excessive. He was also determined to raise the standards of learning and conduct of the monks themselves, so that they should honour their vows in their daily lives. First he decreed that monasteries with less than thirty monks should be turned into schools or used as churches, their monks being transferred to other houses. This eliminated a number of the small unendowed monasteries which he considered superfluous. He next placed further severe restrictions on the reception of novices.

Many have held that in the fourteenth and fifteenth centuries the

Orthodox Church had developed in Russia a Christian ethos far in advance of anything produced by the Western churches. By the seventeenth century, however, it had sunk into a morass of bigotry, corruption, and lassitude, and it proved unable to reform itself. Peter had had to shoulder this task and in the process he had swept away the patriarchate. Inevitably this led to a weakening of the position of the church in relation to the autocrat, but it did not change their relationship. There was no collision between state and church as in the West. The church had always worked with the state, acknowledging the authority of the Tsar who convoked the church councils, accepting or disregarding, as he thought fit, their advice and rulings. The Tsar had always selected those to be appointed to high office, or at least had confirmed the appointments, including that of Patriarch, proposed by the church councils.

Peter's incursions into the affairs of the church, therefore, aroused no popular outcry, and his changes provoked no real opposition, except among the Old Believers and certain ultra-conservative sections of the Russian clergy.

The reforms produced a revolution in the church, but it was a revolution of customs and institutions, not of doctrine and ideas, and did not offend against the national faith. Quickly absorbed into the life of the church and of the nation, most of these reforms endured.[44]

CHAPTER XXXIX

Social and Economic Reforms

1714-1725

THE revolutions in government and in the church were matched by a revolution in Russian society. By his social and economic reforms, Peter broadened the composition of the landowning class, regularized the position of the peasantry, and reorganized the merchant-traders. His reforms were designed to strengthen the nation by giving it an efficient administration, by maintaining its armed forces, by developing its natural resources, and by establishing new industries. They did not lighten but added to the burdens of the people, and their effect was to widen the gulf between the landowning class and the peasant masses, which had appeared early in the previous century, and which was to lead to the complete isolation of the upper class and to revolution.

Russian society was based on the contract of service. The nobles had the right, shared only with the church, to own land and the serfs on it, and they in turn owed service to the Tsar. Originally they had been divided between those holding their estates in perpetuity and those holding them on a service basis, but gradually during the seventeenth century, all estates had become hereditary. In 1714 Peter gave legal recognition to this change; the distinction had no validity when he required all without exception to serve. The nobles had grown lax in meeting this obligation, but service was the driving principle of Peter's life, and he exacted it from his subjects on a scale more extensive and onerous than his predecessors had ever expected.

To the landowning class service meant military service. While they had disliked the old militia from which they had been dispersed to their homes after each campaign, they hated the new standing army, for in it the duties were heavy and from it there was no release except on grounds of old age or injury. And if they disliked the army, they detested the navy.

Peter regarded the landowning class as the source of officers, and he carefully prescribed their training. From the age of fifteen the young landowner, if of noble family, served either in a guards regiment, or in a regiment of the line. All had to serve initially as privates. By his ukaz of 26 February 1714 he absolutely forbade the commissioning of anyone who had not trained in the ranks. At one time, in fact, some three hundred princes of the most illustrious families were serving as privates in the one guards regiment, living in barracks, receiving a soldier's food and pay, and carrying out normal duties. Likewise training in seamanship was the first stage in the career of those drafted into the navy.

Meanwhile the greatly enlarged civil service also needed recruits, and the landowning class was again the main source. This was the one popular form of service, for government offices could be lucrative and work in them was less arduous. But Peter laid the rule down that not more than one third of the members of any one family could serve in civil departments, the others being compelled to serve in the army or the navy.

Attempts to evade these duties were common, although constant revision of the old service registers and summary enrolments made evasions increasingly difficult. In 1712 all minors of the landowning class, whether living at home or attending schools, were ordered to report to the Senate in Moscow, whence they were sent to St. Petersburg for inspection, and divided into three age groups; the youngest were sent to Reval to learn seamanship, the middle group went to Holland for naval training, and the eldest were drafted into the army. Again in September 1714 the sons of landowners between ten and thirty years of age, not already serving, had to report to the Senate for enrolment. Failure to report was punished by confiscation of all property. When this deterrent proved insufficient, an ukaz condemned all who failed to report to be outlawed which meant that they could be robbed, injured, or killed with impunity; the public executioner proclaimed their names and anyone, even a serf, who brought in such a person, could claim half his property.

Occasional enrolment, even enforced by such punishments, was not enough to keep track of all the sons of this class, and in 1721 Peter set up the office of Herald or *Geroldmeister*.[1] His duties were to compile and keep up to date lists, showing where and in what capacity each member of the nobility and gentry was serving, who was not serving, and what male children were alive.[2]

A more fundamental reform was introduced by an ukaz of 14 March 1714 changing the Muscovite law of inheritance by which estates were divided equally among all sons of the family. It was a bad practice which impoverished the less wealthy landowners by the subdivision of estates and which encouraged their sons to live in idleness. Some sixteen years earlier, when in England, Peter had been impressed by the fact that the eldest son normally inherited while the younger sons had to make their own way in the armed forces or in commerce. He did not adopt the rule of primogeniture, but decreed that the estate should be left to only one son. The ukaz set out the reasons for the reform, which were to facilitate the collection of taxes by keeping the property in the hands of one person, to enable a family to retain its wealth and position, and, most important of all, to oblige the younger sons to seek useful employment.

Service and ability were the two criteria by which Peter had always rewarded and promoted men, and he gave long consideration to applying these criteria throughout the army, the navy, and the civil departments. The result was the Table of Ranks, introduced in 1722, which transformed the social and service conditions of the landowning class. This table separated the military from the civil branch and classified all officers and officials in fourteen parallel grades. Everyone had to start in the bottom grade and earn promotion by length of service and by ability. All precedence was based on rank and, while titles of nobility were not abolished, they now became distinctions carrying no rights or privileges, so that, even at court, rank gained by service had precedence over other titles. Furthermore, all persons, whether Russians or foreigners, could acquire on a hereditary basis the privileges of the nobility by reaching a certain grade in the hierarchy of ranks. Inevitably the old landowning class resented the measure and complained bitterly about the lowborn newcomers who took precedence and command over them. But it was

Peter's purpose to attract these newcomers and to broaden the composition of the landowning class in the interests of the state.[3] In this he was successful and the Table of Ranks endured, revitalizing the serving class, although in later years it was to develop all the faults of a bureaucracy.

It was not enough for people to serve. They must give efficient service and for this education and training were required. Education was also necessary to raise Russian society to equality with Western society. Those young nobles sent to Holland to learn seamanship and navigation early in 1697 were the first of a stream of young men sent abroad to study. Mainly they went to train in Western armies and navies, but many learnt new trades and crafts, and studied the sciences, even though it was always a problem to control them and to ensure that they attended to their work. Indeed their behaviour called forth official complaints wherever they went. In August 1717, for example, Konon Zotov reported that in Toulon Russian midshipmen had so disturbed the peace by their incessant quarrelling that the French authorities had confiscated their swords. An even worse failing of these students was their laziness. Trainees rebelled against the discipline and hard work required of them. The Russian resident in London, Feodor Veselovsky, complained bitterly in September 1718 that the most recent batches of apprentices refused to work. They paid no heed to his instructions and ignored his threats of punishments, relying on the fact, as he wrote, "that I cannot punish them without the authority of Your Majesty and that, by the custom of this nation, punishment is not permitted except by order of the court."[4]

The foreign officers and experts engaged in such great numbers to serve in Russia had as their main duty "to teach the Russian people without reserve and diligently,"[5] and although there were cases of foreigners refusing to reveal the secrets of their trades, most honoured these terms of service. And the Russians were quick to learn from them in every field so that Peter was soon able to rely on Russian ships and armaments, and increasingly on Russian manufactures of various kinds. At home as abroad, however, laziness and reluctance to learn were widespread. The Tsar's attempts to introduce elementary education met everywhere with passive resistance and evasion.

Although the first Russian secular school, the School of Mathematics and Navigation, founded by Henry Farquharson in Moscow in

1701, and removed to St. Petersburg and renamed the Naval Academy in 1715, had flourished, and although the Slav-Latin School had expanded, the new schools in Moscow and St. Petersburg and those attached to monasteries in other towns, attracted few pupils. The new engineering school with only twenty-three students was typical. When this small enrolment came to Peter's notice in January 1712 he directed that additional Russian teachers should be engaged and that the number of students should always be between one hundred and one hundred and fifty, of whom two thirds were to be the sons of landowners. But he had to repeat these instructions in November of the same year and only then presumably did the school expand as he had required.[6]

Recognizing that voluntary schools had failed, Peter then tried to make elementary education compulsory. On 20 January 1714 he decreed that teachers from the schools of mathematics should be sent to all governments to teach the children of landowners figures and geometry, "and the following penalty shall be imposed, that no one shall be allowed to marry until he had learnt this."[7] The ukaz aroused strong opposition and, hastily and arbitrarily devised as it was, it failed to produce results. In 1716 he revoked it and decreed that the children of landowners should go to one of three special schools in St. Petersburg—the Naval Academy, the Engineering Academy, and the Artillery Academy—which were open only to them. This system won acceptance and was more successful in imposing education on the landowning class.

Also in 1714 Peter took steps to make elementary education compulsory for the middle class. He decreed that children of clerks, priests, and monastery servants should learn figures and geometry. For this purpose two teachers were to be sent into each government to establish schools which would be administered by the Admiralty College. The ukaz excused children of merchant-traders who did not volunteer, because they usually worked with their fathers and, if taken from this important work, the state revenues might suffer.[8] But still these schools had small success. The vast distances of Russia, shortage of teachers, the impossibility of proper supervision, and, finally, the evasion of both parents and pupils were insuperable obstacles. Accordingly towards the end of his reign, Peter abolished them, devising in their place special garrison and naval schools for children of this class.

Peter himself collected books all his life and his personal library was to provide the foundation of the library of the Russian Academy of Sciences. Whenever in Europe, he eagerly bought books, and his library included works on a wide variety of subjects, among them history, medicine, military and naval subjects, science, law, and religion. This library was housed first in the Summer Palace and then, as it outgrew the small residence, sections were kept in the Winter Palace, Peterhof, and other places. It was his policy throughout his reign, to increase the circulation of books among his people.[9] The Tessing brothers under their concession had printed books in translation and sold them in Russia at fair prices. But the Russian presses were themselves mainly responsible for the sharp increase in the number of books in Russian and the reformed alphabet, introduced by Peter in 1707, facilitated their work. During the whole of the seventeenth century the output of these presses had amounted to only 374 volumes, of which a mere nineteen were secular works; in the twenty-seven years after Peter's return from his first tour of the West, they produced seven hundred books, of which no less than three hundred were secular. Nor were they all manuals of military and naval practice, geography, and mathematics. Peter's policy was not so narrowly utilitarian. He gave particular attention to history and to explanations of his own policy. The *Book of Mars*, published in 1713 in St. Petersburg, contained an heroic account of the feats and victories of the Tsar's armies. The *Razsuzhdenie* or *Dissertation*, published four years later, explained and justified the war against Sweden, and Peter himself made a cogent contribution to it.[10] In fact he was most eager that his people should know more of their own history. To this end he had some time earlier commissioned Polikarpov, a printer, to write a Russian history, but he was far from satisfied with the work when finally it was submitted, and so directed Makarov to rewrite it. Meanwhile, in readiness for the time when an historian would appear, he ordered that in monasteries throughout the tsardom historic manuscripts, books, and papers of interest should be assembled and preserved. He also directed that a history of Europe should be translated and published, and entrusted to Feofan Prokopovich the task of writing the history of his own reign.

Once the Holy Synod was established, he made it responsible for the translation of books into Russian, pending the setting up of the Academy of Sciences which he was planning. From Astrakhan in July 1722, he wrote to the Synod: "the book about the Slav people which Sava Raguzhinsky translated and the other one about the Mohammedan faith which Prince Kantemir translated, if printed, should be sent to me here without delay; if not ready, order them to be printed quickly and sent here."[11] Again, in October 1724, he wrote to the Synod: "I am enclosing a book by Puffendorf, in which are two treatises: the first is on the duty of man and citizen; the other about the Christian faith: but I require only that the first should be translated, since in the other I do not expect anything of use to us."[12] He was constantly watching for books which might be translated for the purpose of educating his people, of broadening their outlook, and stimulating their curiosity.

This spate of books, procured by Peter, was the more remarkable because Russia as yet had no literary language. Church Slavonic, used only for religious works, was not readily understood by most Russians; the written language in official use was meagre and incapable of expressing the new ideas. But Peter demanded clarity and directed that translations should be made "not into high-flown Slav words, but into simple Russian language."[13] Thus translators laboured against terrible difficulties, of which not the least was that Peter himself was a severe critic. One translator, named Volkov, faced with rendering into Russian *Les Instructions sur les jardins fruitiers et potagers* of de la Quintinye gave up in despair and, cutting open his arteries, committed suicide![14] Many of the translations that did appear were a strange muddle of Russian, Church Slavonic, and foreign words. But in spite of obstacles Peter did, by compelling the translation of so many foreign works and by insisting on the use of simple language, make possible the forging of modern Russian.[15] During the last years of his reign, a boy named Lomonosov (1711-1765), the son of a White Sea peasant, was growing up, who was to weld Church Slavonic and popular speech into a strong, flexible literary language; a century later his work would be completed by Pushkin.

While ensuring that the landowning class rendered service and was, moreover, mentally equipped to render it effectively, Peter also gave close attention to the peasant class on whom the burdens of war and reform fell most heavily. They paid the taxes, provided recruits and on them fell most of the labour. Peter, by increasing the powers of the landowners, by subjecting them to army supervision, and making escape more difficult, extended their bondage.

The twenty-one years of the Northern War had imposed a severe strain on the finances of the country, with no temporary alleviation of the burdens through foreign or domestic loans, for throughout Peter met the whole costs of the war from current revenues. He had increased the revenues from taxation until, even allowing for his depreciation of the currency, they were nearly four times as great as on his accession. But revenue did not keep up with expenditure. At times the Treasury could not even meet the salaries of government officials who were paid in furs and other goods.

Evasion of taxes and corruption, as well as mass flights by peasants, even led to a falling off in the revenues. In an attempt to remedy this, Peter had in 1710 ordered a new census, but returns were falsified on such a scale as to make it useless. Drastic measures were needed and Peter, probably influenced by the taxation system in force in France during his visit in 1717, decided to introduce a poll-tax in place of the old tax on households. But before this tax could be levied another census was necessary.

The census, decreed on 26 November 1718, was a major undertaking. It was to be completed in twelve months, but on his death, six years later, Peter still had not seen the final results. The ukaz ordered that all males of the peasant class and of most classes in the towns were to be listed. The instructions were confusing, but the chief difficulties again were evasion and false returns. Landowners, hearing that the census portended new and heavier taxes, withheld large numbers of serfs. The few returns which were delivered on time were incorrect. The Senate then ordered the guards to put in chains all governors and other officials responsible, and to hold them in chains until they had sent their returns to St. Petersburg. But even such drastic measures had little effect. It was only by the savage punishments of knouting, confiscation of property, and execution that towards the end of 1722 the census was at last completed. It accounted for 5,794,928 males—still far from accurate, and what was virtually a second census had then to be carried out by the army.

Without waiting for the final results, Peter imposed the new poll-tax for the first time in 1724. Levied on some five and a half million peasants and townsmen, known as "souls," it was the taxpaying unit of the "soul" or *dusha* that made the tax more manageable than a land or household tax. The first levy of the poll-tax produced a sum equal to more than half the total revenue, although corruption, evasion, and non-payment were as rife as ever. Peter had intended it as a permanent tax for the maintenance of the army and the amount levied was based on estimates of army expenditure. Although in many respects an unjust tax, it proved so lucrative that the Russian Treasury was to depend on it for more than a century to come.

The immediate effects of the census, the poll-tax, and other financial measures was to simplify and strengthen the structure of the peasant class in the interests of the state. Through them Peter removed anomalies and greatly increased the number of taxpayers. He abolished the small class of slaves, whose condition was little different to that of the serfs, but who paid no taxes. He required free peasants, who were mainly freed serfs, to become serfs again or to serve in the army or navy. He also dealt with the large amorphous group which belonged to no class, paid no taxes, and rendered no services. This group comprised vagrants and beggars, who formed an exceptionally large parasitic section of the population, as well as monastery and church servants, and the numerous children of the clergy.

By an inexorable process all peasants were brought more completely under control of the landowners, and subjected inescapably to the demands of the tax-collectors and recruiting officers, and to the supervision of the army. As a further safeguard against flight Peter decreed in 1722 that no serf could move from his master's estate without his written permission, and thus he initiated the passport system which continued into the twentieth century. But it was the supervision of the army that most aggravated the misery of the peasants.

The army, now settled in permanent quarters by the ukaz of 26 November 1718, had many policing duties in addition to its military training. The colonel and his officers in each region were responsible for pursuing thieves and robber gangs, for preventing flight by peasants and catching runaways, for supervising local officials and even governors. The peasants suffered most. They could not move without army approval in addition to the written permission of their masters, and in countless other ways their lives were entangled in bureaucratic restraints. The collection of the taxes which came every third year and lasted for about two months was an occasion which every village awaited with terror. The officers acted harshly, ordering knouting and even execution for failure to pay or being in arrears. In many villages the peasants hated these officers more than the tax itself. Some fled or tried to flee, and there were occasional local revolts, but they were always small in scale and quickly put down. Though voices were raised against their inhuman lot, the peasantry as a whole endured their conditions, labouring and serving with an incredible fortitude.

Peter himself was aware of their hardships, and considered them unavoidable. To the end of his reign he struggled against major corruption, tax evasion, and other malpractices. He could give no thought to important relaxation of the people's burdens until these problems were solved. But in many measures he sought to improve their living conditions and to give some protection to the sick, the aged, and the weak. He built hospitals, almshouses, and orphanages and showed special care for officers and men, retired because of wounds, illness, or age, and for their widows and children.

Hospitals and the training of doctors were always matters of importance to him. In 1706 he had given orders for his first hospital to be built in Moscow on the bank of the Yauza River, opposite the Foreign Quarter; it opened in the following year and was primarily a training hospital. A Dr. Bidleau was in charge with two assistants, and medical students were provided from the Monastery Office. Bidleau was apparently a zealous teacher, for five years later he was reporting with some pride that out of fifty students thirty-three had qualified as surgeons.[16] Peter next built a large military hospital in St. Petersburg, but he was anxious to provide medical facilities for civilians as well as servicemen.[17] In 1715 he decreed that in all towns in Russia hospitals were to be built, attached to the churches. The number of hospitals that resulted was probably small, especially as the shortage of doctors remained acute. The advance was nevertheless striking, for on his accession to the throne there had not been one doctor among his subjects and hospitals were unknown.

The problem of illegitimate children also exercised him. The practice had been widespread of killing unwanted babies. Peter, condemning this as an offence against the laws of God and of the nation, decreed that anyone found guilty would be executed without hope of mercy.[18] In 1715 he decreed that in all towns in Russia homes should be established in which experienced women were to care for unwanted infants. Moreover, he provided that since these children were illegitimate and a source of shame, each of these homes should have a special window through which mothers could put their babies without being seen.[19]

Fires were the scourge of every Russian city and town, but the people were so fatalistic they gave no thought to the most obvious precautions. Peter drew up and enforced certain fire regulations. Impatient to build St. Petersburg without delay and held up by the shortage of stone masons, he placed a ban in 1714 on all building in stone throughout Russia, until such time as the necessary buildings had been erected in his city. But this was a temporary measure. Four years later he decreed that in the Kremlin and Kitaigorod of Moscow all buildings should be of stone and that roofs should be of tiles; houses were to be erected in streets and not grouped around courtyards. In other parts of the city timber could be used, but builders were to observe his fire regulations, which applied to all towns as well as to the two cities. Stoves were to be built to certain specifications and with pipes large enough for a man to crawl through for sweeping; the ceilings of rooms were to be of clay or plaster, and roofs to be tiled or of shingles, instead of the customary rough wood with loose bark which so readily caught fire. He went further and even designed houses. In certain places, such as Vasilevsky Island, building had to follow these designs.

But regulations such as these were of no use unless properly enforced. In each city the Ober-Kommandant was at first responsible for carrying out strict inspections of all buildings and for punishing offenders. But Peter considered this to be part of the general task of municipal administration. In June 1718 he appointed a general policemaster in St. Petersburg, whose main duties were to see that all buildings were erected in accordance with regulations, that river banks were high enough and sound, that streets and bridges were swept and in good order, that every inhabitant kept the front of his house clean, and that canals were not cluttered with rubbish. He was responsible for quarterly inspections of buildings to make sure there were no fire dangers, and his men had to help in fighting fires. He also had the responsibility for keeping the peace, arresting criminals, scrutinizing newcomers, and mounting guard posts throughout the city. In January 1722 Peter appointed a senior policemaster in Moscow with similar duties, and responsible to the General Policemaster in St. Petersburg.

In the last years of his reign Peter gave much thought to principles of good citizenship and an ordered society based on law and honest service rather than on custom, superstition, and self-interest. But, like so many of his innovations, these were merely the beginnings which he did not live to establish firmly. They illustrate, nevertheless, the breadth of his ideas, some of which were in advance of his time, and the ideal which he sought for his people.

In his economic policy Peter followed the practices common to most Western countries. He laboured to build up Russia's wealth and strength by utilizing her mineral resources, by accumulating precious metals and preventing their export, and by increasing her productivity and trade. His achievements in these fields were remarkable. At his death he left 233 new industrial undertakings, ranging from large-scale ironworks to a factory for manufacturing needles, and Russia's foreign trade had quadrupled in value with a large active balance in her favour.

Peter established heavy industry in Russia. He had begun developing iron foundries early in his reign, primarily to equip his army. Twenty or so small state and private foundries at Olenets and around Moscow were working at his accession and he expanded several of them. His achievement, however, was to set up a further fifty-two foundries, including thirteen large well-equipped works which opened up the important industrial region of the Urals. From this industry and his arms factories, Peter was able to equip his army and navy with cannon and other weapons, and at his death he had sixteen thousand cannon in reserve.

Equally striking was his use of the mineral resources of his country. Even before his first tour of the West he had ordered a survey of the ores in the Urals and right up to his death he did everything to encourage prospecting and to promote mining. "Our Russian state," he wrote in one ukaz, "abounds in riches more than many other lands, and is blessed with the necessary metals and minerals, which up to the present day have been sought without diligence. The reason for this has been that our subjects have not understood mining and partly because they have not wanted to devote money and labour to it."[20] He saw to it that both money and labour were available. One of the original colleges, set up in 1717, was the College of Mining and Industry with its first duty to encourage and supervise prospecting and the working of new mineral sites. In

December 1719 he decreed that everyone had the right, whether on his own land or that of another, to prospect, wash, and smelt minerals; landowners on whose land minerals were found had the first claim to work the deposits, but if they would not, others could obtain permission from the college to do so, paying the landowner a third of the profits; any landowner concealing mineral deposits on his land or obstructing their development, was liable to knouting, and even execution. The college was also instructed to give every encouragement and facility to foreigners to conduct surveys. In addition to the rich iron ore deposits of the Ural region, copper, and other minerals were discovered and worked. Russia even began exporting pig iron of high quality to England, but Peter by numerous regulations and punishments forbade the export of precious metals, and even made provision for the import of gold and silver.

In light industry his efforts were also at first directed to meeting the needs of his army and navy. He established textile mills and as early as 1705 he was writing enthusiastically to Menshikov about their output.[21] In 1712 he ordered the erection of further mills which would within five years produce sufficient cloth for uniforms for the whole army and navy. Similarly he established factories to produce sailcloth and ropes, and he organized the lumber industry, equipping it with numerous sawmills, to supply his rapidly growing navy.

Once the pressure of the war had eased, Peter with the rich variety of Western industry in mind set about establishing and encouraging other manufactures. Glass crystal, and china works were set up in St. Petersburg in 1715; a stocking factory, silk, velvet, and other textile works, brickworks and paper mills were also established.

Many of these enterprises flourished, but many failed through lack of skilled workers or bad management. The tapestry workrooms, inspired by the Gobelin works in Paris, stood idle for lack of proper wools. The silk factory, set up by Apraxin, Shafirov, and Tolstoy, failed through bad management. Peter himself sometimes issued contradictory ukazi or interfered unwisely, as when he prohibited the manufacture of Russian leather tanned with birch bark, ordering the use of tallow instead, and again when, with his eye to exports, he decreed the weaving of linen at least a yard wide instead of the narrower widths to which his people were accustomed.

The impetus and initiative behind all these developments came from Peter himself. His people showed little enterprise, and the upper classes had always looked down on trade and industry. But by rewards and persistent propaganda Peter gradually overcame their prejudice. He also offered inducements, in the form of loans, subsidies, monopolies, and exemptions from tax.

On more than one occasion he remarked of a new project that "although it be good and necessary, if it is new our people will not do it without compulsion."[22] Thus trading companies of the Western type were new to the Russians and he had to resort to ukazi ordering his people to form them and to build factories. At the same time he gave every encouragement to trading and industrial enterprises. They were made the equivalent of state service and carried similar privileges. The most important privilege was the right to own serfs, granted by an ukaz of 18 January 1721, which meant that manufacturers could acquire compulsory factory labour, and that a new category of serfs—the industrial serf—was created. Peter even relaxed the ruthless campaign that he had always conducted to recover fugitive serfs, decreeing that factory serfs who had been runaways were not to be surrendered. Also he established the College of Manufactures which watched over factories, and was empowered to help any that were failing through lack of capital. But, while these measures had considerable success as the new industries bore witness, they did not overcome the reluctance of the landowning class to invest capital in undertakings which were subject to the arbitrary power of the state. Often, therefore, to get industries established, Peter had to start them at treasury expense and then turn them over to individuals or to companies on special conditions.

Agriculture received less of Peter's attention than industry, although it was the main occupation of his people. In the interest of efficiency he decreed that peasants should reap with scythes and not sickles, but apart from this and other minor decrees, any changes and developments in agriculture during his reign were the result of decrees primarily directed to other ends. For example the main development of his time was the great increase in land under cultivation, and this was a direct result of the poll-tax which, being unconnected with the land and productivity, gave both peasants and landowners an incentive to cultivate a greater acreage. More positively Peter directed the Senate to set up stud farms for breeding horses, and to import stud horses from Silesia and Prussia. Sheep breeding and the improvement of fleeces were encouraged, to supply the new textile industry. Increases in the production of tobacco, hemp and flax were other measures designed to help industry, expand exports, and reduce imports.

The development of trade had been one of Peter's foremost concerns ever since his first visit to Archangel in 1693. By various reforms, culminating in the chief magistracy, he had tried to strengthen the merchant-trader class. He had also persevered in his policy of increasing the volume of trade, and especially of making his exports exceed imports, and in this he had considerable success.

This new trade was mainly with the West, and in it the Baltic ports, for which he had waged the Northern War, played an important part. Formerly Russia's foreign trade, apart from the over-land trade with China and the silk trade with Persia, was concentrated on Archangel. Peter now transferred his European trade to St. Petersburg, doing it gradually, for Russian and foreign merchants alike hated the new city. In 1724, 240 merchantmen sailed into St. Petersburg and in the following year, excluding Pernau and Kronstadt, his Baltic ports received 914 merchant ships from all parts of Europe.

Also in the interest of trade, as well as defence, Peter tried to develop his internal communications. Early in his reign he recognized the value of Russia's great network of rivers and ordered canals to be built linking them. Thus, while Azov was in his hands and he was cherishing plans to trade in the Black Sea, he had begun two canals, joining the Volga and Don rivers at different points. But after the loss of Azov the work was abandoned. Later, with the foundation of St. Petersburg, he planned to link it by waterways with Moscow and the interior. A short canal built at Vyshnevolotsk, provided a link through tributaries between the Volga and the Neva, but because the flat-bottomed boats used in the canal could not survive the stormy passage through Lake Ladoga, he decided to by-pass the lake by cutting a second canal through the swamps to the south. In his enthusiasm for this project he even thought of applying his whole army to it, but threats of war prevented this. On 19 September 1718 ukazi went out to all governments, requiring them to assemble labour for the project on the basis of one worker for every twenty households. The first batches of labourers were to be delivered by April

1719 and released in the following year, when the second batch would be delivered, and so on.

From the start misfortune plagued the work on the Ladoga canal. Disease and food shortage, due to maladministration, led to the death of many thousands of labourers. But the work continued. Eventually it began to progress so well that he planned ahead to the day when he could travel from St. Petersburg to Moscow by water. He did not live to make this journey, but twenty miles of canal were completed at his death, and the project was completed soon afterwards. Nor did Peter realize his other great plan of joining the Baltic, the Black, the Caspian, and the White seas by means of canals linking the great Russian rivers. Nevertheless this was achieved in the following century, and the vision of it had been his.

CHAPTER XL

Trade, Exploration, and the Persian Campaign

1721-1722

ALTHOUGH engaged in the West during most of his reign, Peter was always keenly interested in the countries to the east and south of Russia. The fabulous Cathay of which foreign merchants and seamen talked so much fascinated him. He had stored up in his memory tales of the wealth of India, and had long cherished plans to develop the rich silk trade of Persia, bringing it entirely into Russian hands. Once the danger of invasion by the Swedes had passed, he turned his attention increasingly to China and Persia, and to Central Asia as the gateway to India.

Tsarevna Sofia had sent an embassy to Peking in 1689, when the Treaty of Nerchinsk had been made, depriving Russia of the lands of the Amur basin which her frontiersmen had been struggling to hold for nearly fifty years. Their withdrawal was, however, timely, for China was strong and united, and Russia was then in no condition to challenge her. The treaty had made some provision for continuing the Siberian caravan trade, mainly in furs, silk, and tea, but the Chinese did not take such trade seriously.

Peter himself made several attempts to increase this trade. He met with obstacles on both sides of the frontier. First, he had made such trade a state monopoly with the purpose of developing it. But Gagarin and others, dealing on their own accounts, undermined the monopoly. Next, Peter appointed Guards Captain Lev Izmailov in 1719 as his envoy extraordinary to the Emperor of China. Izmailov was well received in Peking. But when he raised Peter's proposals—that trade between their countries should be free, that Russian merchants should have their own church in Peking, and that the Tsar should maintain a consul-general in Peking, and vice-consuls in important towns—the Chinese merely replied that "our sovereign does not trade; whilst you value your merchants highly, we scorn commerce. . . ."[1] Izmailov could obtain no concessions and after his departure Russian merchants suffered new restrictions. At this stage Peter was even prepared to resort to arms. However, the death of Emperor Kiang-hi in December 1722 halted his plans, for he expected, wrongly as it proved, more favourable treatment from the new Emperor.[2]

Although frustrated in his hopes of China trade, Peter pressed on with exploration of the Pacific coast to the north. He had already annexed Kamchatka and the Kurile Islands and in January 1719 he sent two geodesists to chart their shores as well as the coast of the Sea of Okhotsk. They had the further task of establishing whether Asia and America were joined. It was a problem that had always fascinated him and in the last year of his reign, land expeditions having failed to solve it, he sent Captain Behring on the voyage which resulted in the discovery of the Behring Straits.

Meanwhile he had not lost sight of his plans to establish routes to Persia and India. He was interested primarily in trade and had no grandiose plan of conquest, but the dividing line between developing trade routes and territorial expansion is often fine. Indeed, his instructions to the leaders of expeditions into Central Asia and his policy towards Persia both showed that he was always ready to annex territory wherever he could do so without difficulty. Moreover, he was determined to keep the Turks from the Caspian Sea and anxious to compensate himself for the surrender of Azov by taking other lands farther to the east which held promise of trade with India and Persia.

Inevitably then his advance into Central Asia and Persia was seen by others as part of a policy of conquest. He thus found himself involved in sporadic conflict with Asiatic nomads and in a campaign in Persia which nearly resulted in a renewal of war with Turkey.

Peter looked on Central Asia primarily as a gateway to India, but reports of mineral deposits, especially of sands of pure gold near the town of Erket, had aroused his interest in the region itself.[3] In 1714 he sent an expedition under Colonel Buchholz with instructions to build a fort at Lake Yamysh, to capture Erket, find the golden sands and explore the mouth of the river. Buchholz reached the lake and built the fort, but his presence alarmed the Kalmyks. They laid siege to his fort and in April 1716, forced to accept their terms, he razed it to the ground and withdrew along the Irtysh River to its junction with the Om, where he built a new fort which became the town of Omsk.

Still eager to find the gold sands, Peter in 1719, when sending General Likharev to Siberia to investigate charges of corruption against Gagarin, instructed him to erect a fort at Lake Zaisan and to send a party to explore as far as Erket, but without taking any risks. Likharev had no success in finding the golden sands, but he built the fort, and these two expeditions firmly established Russian authority on the upper and middle reaches of the Irtysh.

Peter instructed Likharev to take no risks because he had recently had reliable news of the disaster that had overtaken Prince Bekovich Cherkassky who had led an ambitious expedition intended to extend Russian power over the Khivan and Bukharan khanates. Peter had long nursed this plan. Twice the Khivan Khan had appealed to him for protection against his rival, the Bukharan Khan, and on each occasion, because of the Northern War, he had been able to do nothing. But in 1714 he instructed the Senate to send a formal embassy to the Khans of Khiva and Bukhara, and at the beginning of 1716 after many difficulties Bekovich Cherkassky set out down the Volga.

Peter's detailed instructions for this expedition revealed his purpose in pressing forward into this region.[4] Bekovich was to erect a fort at the former mouth of the Amu-Darya River. He was then to send an envoy to Khiva, who should study the route carefully. This envoy was to induce the Khivan Khan to accept the suzerainty of the Tsar and, if the Khan showed goodwill, he was to ask for guides to escort a party of Russians up the Syr-Darya to Erket. He should also request boats to enable another party to proceed along the Amu-Darya into India. While at Khiva, Bekovich was also to persuade the Khan of Bukhara to swear loyalty to the Tsar or at least to enter into friendly relations.

In the autumn of 1716 Bekovich with surveyors and engineers, four thousand regular troops, and a force of Cossacks reached the

Caspian Sea. He established two forts on the eastern shore of the sea and in February of the next year returned to Astrakhan. He was warned that the Khans of Khiva and Bukhara would attack him, and the envoys whom he sent ahead also reported hostility. Nevertheless, in the spring of 1717 with five hundred Russian dragoons and some three thousand other troops he marched overland to Khiva; nothing more was ever heard from him.

The fate of the expedition was learnt many months later from a Cossack Tatar who had escaped. He related that after repelling attacks by the Khivan Khan for three days, Bekovich had accepted his overtures for peace and his invitation to go to Khiva. Approaching the town, he had allowed the Khan to persuade him to divide his force into five parts, which were soon afterwards overpowered, the officers killed and the men sold into slavery.

Concurrently with these expeditions, Peter was pursuing closer relations with Persia. In 1715 he appointed Volynsky as his envoy to the Shah. His detailed instructions required Volynsky to obtain information on land and water routes and especially, as he added in his own hand, "to what places one may travel by these rivers from the [Caspian] sea, and whether there is not some river from India that flows into this sea."[5] Once in Persia, Volynsky was to gather intelligence on the Persian army and on the Shah's relations with the Sultan. He was to suggest that Turkey was the great enemy of Persia, whereas Russia was her friend. He should persuade the Shah to order the Armenians, in whose hands the silk trade was largely concentrated, to transport their silk through Russia which offered convenient waterways all the way to St. Petersburg, instead of by camel through the Turkish territories; if unsuccessful in this, he should consider bribing the Shah's ministers, and he should also find out what obstacles could be put in the way of Turkish trade through Smyrna and Aleppo.

Volynsky reached Isfahan in March 1717[6] and soon afterwards was confined to his house under strong guard. Reports of Russian power and of the Tsar's expeditions into Central Asia had alarmed the Persians, who believed that Russian troops were massing to attack them. The Shah's immediate concern was to get rid of this envoy before he could learn how weak and vulnerable Persia then was. But Volynsky managed to stay until September and he reported fully to Peter on the state of the country, advising that he could take what he wanted without difficulty. Forced to spend the winter in Shemaha on his return journey, Volynsky gathered more evidence of Persian weakness and while there he received an envoy of the Georgian prince, Vakhtang Leonovich, who, also believing that the Tsar was about to invade Persia, was eager to declare his support.

On his return Volynsky, appointed Governor of Astrakhan, was tireless in urging that the Persian campaign should be launched without delay. But Peter's policy was to hasten the collapse of Persia by encouraging revolts by her subject peoples and enlisting their support, and Volynsky was instructed to work to this end. Peter continued to show caution until, in September 1721, an incident took place that decided him on action.

Daud-Bek, leader of the Lesghian mountaineers of Daghestan, who had asked for Russian help and had been refused, decided that he was strong enough without it to attack the Persian provinces. On 7 August he captured Shemaha, at this time the main centre of Russian trade with Persia. At first the Russian merchants were not worried, having been assured that neither they nor their goods would be touched. But Daud-Bek was unable to hold his men who plundered and destroyed Russian stores to the value of half a million rubles. Volynsky at once reported to Peter and pressed him to send troops with all speed on the pretext of defending Russian trade and protecting the Shah against his enemies.[7]

"I have received your letter," Peter replied in December 1721, "in which you write of the Daud-Bek affair and . . . I answer that this is clearly an opportunity which should not be allowed to pass, and we have already ordered a fair number of troops to march to quarters on the Volga, whence they will go to Astrakhan in the spring. . . ."[8]

At the beginning of 1722, when in Moscow, Peter received reports from his consul in Persia, Semeon Avramov, that made him hasten his preparations. The news was that the Afghans had put the Persian army to flight; the Shah Husayn had abdicated, surrendering the capital to the Afghan leader, Mir Mahmud; Tahmasp, the heir of the Shah, was at Kazvin, trying to raise an army. For Peter the danger was that the Turks, finding the total collapse of Persia imminent, might forestall him in occupying the shores of the Caspian.

On 13 May Peter himself set out from Moscow, going by land to Kolomna where Catherine, Admiral Apraxin, Tolstoy, and others joined him. They then travelled in galleys along the Oka and down the Volga. Peter stopped frequently to inspect towns, receive petitions, and to examine local officials. At Nizhni-Novgorod on 30 May he celebrated his birthday and was richly entertained by Baron Stroganov who with his two brothers had done much to develop Russian industries. He spent some days at Kazan, where he found a government textile mill functioning badly while another mill, owned and run by a local merchant, was flourishing; after examining both mills closely, he gave the government mill to the merchant on condition that he ran it as efficiently as he was running his own.

Arriving at Astrakhan Peter found his army assembled. It was far greater than the modest force that Volynsky had proposed, and comprised twenty-two thousand infantry, nine thousand cavalry, with Cossacks, Kalmyks, and Tatars in strength. On 18 July with his infantry he sailed into the Caspian Sea. The cavalry travelled by land towards Derbent, and proclaimed a manifesto, calling on the local peoples to acknowledge and support the Russian Emperor. When at the beginning of August the cavalry joined up with the infantry, Peter continued his advance southwards towards Derbent.

One of the mountain rulers did not come to make his obeisance, killing the three Cossack couriers sent to summon him, and even attacking a detachment of Russian troops. His small army was routed and his capital, Utemish, was razed to the ground, but the knowledge that the wild Lesghians of Daghestan were likely to attack from their mountain strongholds made special precautions necessary. Derbent, where Peter arrived on 23 August, offered no opposition. The Naib, or Vice-Governor, greeted him at the approaches to the town, fell on his knees, and presented him with two silver keys to the gates.

From Derbent Peter wrote to the Senate, giving an account of the advance. He was in good spirits, although worried about lack of provisions and by the heat. His intention was to send a garrison to occupy Baku "and thus in these regions with the help of God we will have gained a foothold."[9] But he had now decided that he himself with the main army would advance no farther. His troops were enduring many hardships. A fleet of supply barges from Astrakhan had not arrived; the troops at Derbent were already on short rations, and many had fallen ill from the heat and from eating melons and other fruits to which they were not accustomed. The Caucasian people were wild and treacherous. Above all else Peter feared a repetition of the Pruth campaign when he had suddenly found himself without provisions and surrounded by the Turkish army. He was now even farther south and equally close to the Turkish frontier. Although at peace with the Sultan, he was uneasy. He ordered further precautions against sudden attack and the army retreated north to Astrakhan, where he himself arrived on 4 October.

Peter spent a month there before returning to Moscow and most of the time he was ill. He suffered from strangury and stone, ailments which had probably been afflicting him in some degree over the years, but which now became serious and were soon to cause his death. He was fifty and despite his tempestuous life there was no diminution in his energies and his capacity for work, but his bouts of illness were more frequent and more serious.

The Persian campaign had so far proved disappointing. He had intended originally to march to the Kura River, flowing into the Caspian south of Baku, and to establish there a stronghold which would dominate Indian, Persian, and Caucasian trade; he had proposed travelling then along the Kura to Tiflis to ensure the loyalty of Vakhtang and to bring the Georgians back into the Christian fold, which under Turkish pressure they were gradually forsaking. The heat, illness, and the hostility of the Daghestan mountaineers made him give up these plans, but he continued the campaign. In November he sent a force under Colonel Shipov to capture Resht at the southern end of the Caspian. By February 1723 Resht was secure in his hands and in July Major-General Matyuskhin captured Baku, which Peter considered "the key to our whole campaign."[10]

Meanwhile Peter had been applying diplomatic pressure in Isfahan. From Astrakhan in June 1722 he had instructed Semeon Avramov to represent to the old or to the new Shah or to the person in power that the Russians were advancing not against Persia, but against her enemies who had damaged Russian interests, and that the Tsar was ready to rid Persia of these enemies if the Shah would concede certain provinces by the Caspian Sea; if Persia remained weak and disrupted, the Turks would undoubtedly conquer her and this would be contrary to Russian interests; he would, therefore, be obliged to seize these provinces if the Shah rejected his proposal. In Kazvin, Tahmasp, desperate for help against the Afghans, agreed to send an ambassador to Russia to negotiate. Izmail-Bek was appointed and on 23 September 1723 he signed a treaty in St. Petersburg whereby the

Tsar undertook to expel the Afghans, restore order in Persia, and secure Tahmasp on the throne, while in return the towns of Derbent and Baku with their surrounding territories, as well as the provinces of Gilyan, Mazanderan, and Astrabad would be conceded to Russia.

Peter thought that he had thus gained all that he wanted from Persia. But the treaty had yet to be ratified. Lieutenant Boris Meshchersky, whom he sent to Isfahan for the purpose, found on his arrival in April 1724 that the Afghan, Mahmud, was now in power and, as he did not recognize the treaty, Meshchersky returned empty-handed.

Meanwhile Peter went ahead with strengthening his hold on the provinces. In May 1724 he sent instructions to Matyushkin to reinforce the defences of Derbent, Baku, and of the province of Gilyan, to prepare defences in the provinces of Astrabad and Mazanderan, and to survey the Kura River. He was to use every means to attract Armenians and other Christian peoples, and unobtrusively to get rid of as many Mohammedans as possible. He was to gather information about the copper and oil deposits, as well as the production of lemons and sugar. But hanging over all these preparations was the threat of Turkish intervention.

When preparing to set out on this campaign Peter had received a report from Neplyuev, his resident in Constantinople, that the Lesghians had asked for the Sultan's protection. The Armenians and the Georgians were appealing for Russian support to free them from the Turks. But the rivalry between Russia and Turkey did not develop into a struggle for the lands occupied by their co-religionists. Peter treated the appeals and offers of support from the Caucasian Christians with caution, remembering the failure of the Christians to rally to him on the Pruth. He was, moreover, primarily concerned with the Persian provinces and the trade which he could develop through them. The Turks were less interested in Persia, but they were determined that the Russians should not have Armenia and Georgia as bases from which to attack them.

In Constantinople the Persian affair was soon entangled in diplomatic intrigue. The French ambassador mediated as a friend of both Turks and Russians, and he might have brought about an early agreement but for the English ambassador who was making strenuous efforts to persuade the Turks to declare war on Russia. The great fear of the English government was that Peter would become active in the north, if not tied down by war with Turkey. But the Sultan wanted peace. His Vizir even let Neplyuev know informally that if the Russian advance went no farther than Shemaha, they would offer no opposition; if, however, the Russian Emperor pressed his intention of taking eastern Georgia under his protection, the Sultan would be forced to declare war, as it was his firm policy to bring this part of Georgia under his rule, especially as western Georgia was already Turkish.

News of Peter's return from Derbent to Astrakhan quieted the anxiety of the Turks. But they took advantage of his withdrawal to inform Daud-Bek at Shemaha that the Sultan recognized him as his subject with similar status to that of the Crimean Khan, and that he was to make all effort to bring the neighbouring Persian provinces under his rule.

Knowing nothing of the Sultan's latest move, Peter had sent instructions to Neplyuev to endeavour to reach some agreement. In February 1723, however, the Grand Vizir informed Neplyuev that there was nothing to discuss. Mir Mahmud, the Afghan leader, who was, he alleged, about to accept Turkish suzerainty, had occupied Isfahan and most of its provinces; Daud-Bek had occupied Armenia; all these lands were therefore under Turkish protection. The vizir closed with the warning that, if the Russians marched again into Persian territory, the Sultan would be compelled to send his armies to defend his subjects.

Peter refused to be ejected from the Caspian provinces and the Caucasus by threats. On 4 April 1723 he ordered preparations for war with Turkey. He appointed Prince Mikhail Golitsyn in command of the Ukrainian army; Russian and Cossack troops were released from various labour projects and assembled in readiness. To Neplyuev he sent instructions that "our interests in no way permit that any other power, no matter which, should become established on the Caspian Sea. . . ."[11] Russian troops moved to Baku, but the Turks did not declare war as expected. Meetings continued between Neplyuev and the Grand Vizir with the French ambassador mediating. On 2 January 1724 Neplyuev was informed that the Turks were about to declare war. Meanwhile the French ambassador was impressing on the Vizir the dangers of a war, which was in any case unnecessary since the Porte had no real interest in the Caspian provinces and was concerned primarily that the Russians should not occupy Armenia and Georgia. The Turks had second thoughts and in a private audience the Vizir proposed to Neplyuev the division of the Persian provinces between the Porte and Russia. Neplyuev urgently requested new instructions which reached him from St. Petersburg in May 1724. Conferences began at once, and after lengthy disputes the treaty was signed on 12 June 1724. By its terms Shemaha remained under the rule of Daud-Bek, but Turkish troops would not garrison it, unless local revolts made this necessary. The Russian Emperor undertook to induce Tahmasp to give up to the Sultan the provinces occupied by Turkish troops, whereupon they would help him to recover his throne. The Caspian provinces from the Russian frontier near the Terek River along the western and southern shores of the sea, including Gilyan and Mazanderan, were conceded to Russia.

Peter sent Rumyantsev to Constantinople to exchange ratification of this treaty. He also gave him instructions to negotiate agreement on the Russian and Turkish frontiers in the Caucasus and to obtain detailed information concerning the routes to Armenia and Georgia and the military strength of both countries. Peter was still determined to bring both Armenians and Georgians under his protection. But the Turks were equally determined that he should not have footholds so close to their frontier. They overran and occupied eastern Georgia and strengthened their grip on Armenia. For the time being Peter had to be content with his Persian provinces.[12]

CHAPTER XLI

Emperor Peter the Great

1722-1725

PETER felt keenly the loneliness which is the greatest afflic-
tion of power. It was his nature to work as captain of a team,
directing and himself a member of it. But in the years after
Poltava, when he might have expected to share the fruits of victory
with proven comrades, his isolation was, in fact, greatest.

Many of his officers and colleagues had died in action. Some, like
Gagarin and Kikin, had been executed for corruption or treason.
Others had grown old and died, like Romodanovsky, or were near to
death like Prince Boris Golitsyn, who had become a pathetic figure,
having lost his only son and being crippled with arthritis and gout.
For him Peter found time to make a chair with his own hands, in
which the invalid could be carried out of doors. Sheremetev was
ageing and querulous, and in February 1718 he died.

Of those who were living many, like Menshikov, the family Dolgoruky, Vinius, and Shafirov, had all through dishonesty or greed or
other good reasons lost Peter's confidence. He had sent them away
from him or, recognizing their ability and experience and having no
one to put in their places, he had kept them in office, but under his
disappointed and watchful eye.

The trial of Tsarevich Alexei had been a crisis in Peter's isolation. He had seen his own son and the heir to the throne grow to
be the very focal point of opposition to himself and to his work, and
he had not failed to sense the silent but massive popular support

429

behind Alexei. At this time Peter found some consolation in Tsarevich Peter Petrovich, on whom he lavished affection, but in April 1719, at the age of three and a half years, he too had died. Within a few days of escorting Sheremetev's coffin to the Nevsky Monastery, Peter had found himself making the same journey behind the coffin of his little son.

Neither grief nor disappointment, however, distracted him from his tasks and he continued to throw himself into work. He now took pride and pleasure in the support of the many young men in his guards regiments and the navy, who were devoted to his ideal of service and who regarded him in a special sense as their father.[1] He also in these years turned more and more to Catherine who gave him companionship and understanding and a family circle in which he could relax. In her company and in his own work he found his consolations.

With the passing of the years the relationship between Peter and Catherine had matured and deepened. When he had married her privately in November 1707, his old company of comrades in arms and diplomacy was already breaking up. He had acted cautiously in this marriage, perhaps recalling the deception of Anna Mons, but Catherine did not betray his trust. He found in her a partner of great energy and even greater stamina than himself. She often travelled with him at his own headlong pace. Even when pregnant she sometimes stayed by him, although it would doubtless have been wiser had she remained quietly in St. Petersburg. But she accompanied him on her own insistence, overriding his anxiety for her health and safety, and soon he came to count on having her at his side. Between them a close bond had grown, wrought by mutual trust, by their children, and by grief shared over the infant sons they had lost. They enjoyed being together and disliked the frequent separations that disrupted their lives. "Praise God, all is merry here," so Peter wrote from Reval in 1719, "but when I come to a country house and you are not there, I feel so sad." Again in another letter he wrote, "But when you state that it's miserable walking alone, although the garden is pleasant, I believe you, for it's the same for me; only pray God that this is the last summer we'll spend apart, and that we may be always together in future."[2]

Catherine was in fact a remarkable woman. She gave little thought to wealth or even to comfort, and was always ready to put up with hardships from which others would have shrunk. She was adaptable and good-tempered under all conditions and, although some among the old nobles resented her elevation to the throne, she had no enemies. As the person closest to the Tsar she was constantly receiving requests and petitions to use her influence with him. At one time or another all the ministers and leading persons of the day turned to her to secure some special attention for their pleas, to settle quarrels between them, or to beg the Tsar's mercy. She used her influence to bring peace or to soften Peter's anger.[3] Menshikov, for example, regarded her as his chief ally and she had frequently interceded on his behalf, obtaining pardon or a reduction in the fines imposed on him, or sheltering him from the full weight of Peter's anger. Tsarevich Alexei, who might well have hated her for standing in his mother's place and for producing a rival to the throne, turned frequently to her to shield him from his father.

Catherine had won Peter's gratitude during the campaign on the Pruth. Again during the Persian campaign when the heat and the hardships of the march were taking heavy toll among the troops, she was at Peter's side, sharing difficulties and discomforts, and behaving with bravery under fire. He had already acknowledged his love and his debt to her in the public celebration of their marriage and by establishing the Order of St. Catherine in her honour. But after the Persian campaign he decided to acclaim her services to him and to the nation more completely.

On 15 November 1723 he issed an ukaz, stating that "our best beloved Spouse, Consort, and Empress Catherine has been a great support to us, and not only in this, but also in many military operations, putting aside womanly weakness, of her own will she has been present with us and has helped in every way possible, and especially in the Pruth battle with the Turks, when our troops were 22,000 in number and the Turks had 270,000 men, and it was a desperate time for us, she acted as a man, not as a woman, which is known to our whole army and through it without doubt to the whole nation; and so for these labours of our Spouse we have decided that by virtue of the supreme power given us by God she shall be crowned which, God willing, is to take place formally in Moscow in the present winter. . . ."[4]

A serious bout of strangury compelled him to postpone the coronation. At the beginning of March 1724, he went to Olenets to take the waters and from there he travelled direct to Moscow for the ceremony, appointed to take place on 7 May. Elaborate preparations were made and Peter, who was always careful in his expenditure on himself, spared no expense for this occasion. Catherine's robes had been ordered from France and her cloak was embroidered in gold with the double-headed eagle. Her crown shone with priceless jewels. Peter formed a special horse guard for her, picked men of great stature and handsome appearance. Orders were sent out summoning the Senate, the Holy Synod, and all people of eminence to Moscow for the ceremony.

The coronation procession set out from the Red Staircase where as a boy, forty-two years earlier, Peter had stood with his mother in mortal terror of the rebel streltsi. Now in the evening of his reign the violence of his feelings against Moscow had calmed. Catherine was being crowned not in the new capital but in Moscow; the procession followed the route of the old tsars of Muscovy on their coronation. During the service in the Uspensky Cathedral he took the crown and placed it on the head of his Empress. He then retired to the palace, while Catherine went on to the Arkhangelsky Cathedral where she prayed at the tombs of the Muscovite tsars. The procession then escorted her back to the palace where a great banquet began. Late into the night the Emperor and Empress feasted their guests. Towards the end of the banquet Menshikov distributed medals, bearing on one side portraits of Peter and Catherine and on the other the scene of Peter placing the crown upon her head and the words: "Crowned in Moscow 1724."

The coronation of Catherine was taken by many to mean that Peter intended her to succeed him on the throne. The succession was already a matter of anxious speculation. On 5 February 1722 Peter had by ukaz abolished the old Muscovite custom whereby the Tsar had presented his chosen son as his heir, and, invoking the example of Ivan the Great, he had provided that the Emperor should in future appoint as his successor whomsoever he thought best suited.[5] He instructed Prokopovich to write an explanation and justification of the measure and also required his subjects to swear to honour his choice. This ukaz caused widespread unease and even minor revolts, for it was feared that he might appoint some foreigner to sit on the throne of Russia. There was resentment, too, over the exclusion of Tsarevich Peter Alexeevich for it was clear that Peter had no intention of allowing his grandson to succeed him.

Peter's ukaz thus did nothing to quiet popular anxiety. Tsarevich Peter Alexeevich was the sole surviving male Romanov, but he was still a boy and, if he did succeed, it would mean a regency for several years. Of the family of Ivan, Peter's half-brother, two daughters were living—Catherine, Duchess of Mecklenburg and Anna, widow of the Duke of Courland. Of Empress Catherine's children only three daughters were living—Anna, Elizabeth, and Natalya. But Russia had never had a woman on the throne, and the prospect of one to come was far from popular. Peter did not, however, share this prejudice, and may well have intended, in promulgating his ukaz of 5 February 1722, that Catherine should rule after his death, and herself appoint one of their daughters to succeed her. Meanwhile anxious conjectures grew among the people and abroad, for the succession to the Russian throne was now a matter of high importance in Europe.[6]

Peter was still working with the furious intensity of a man racing against time. John Bell noted that "he could despatch more affairs in a morning than a houseful of Senators could do in a month."[7] In St. Petersburg he rose at four o'clock in the morning, and sometimes earlier, going direct to his cabinet where Makarov and his assistants were in constant attendance. Having worked through the morning he went to the Senate or to the colleges to supervise, give instructions, and signify approval to new ukazi. After dinner he would inspect new buildings or the Admiralty shipyards, often working there himself. When he had on hand a task of special importance, his hours were even longer; in November 1721 when revising the draft of the naval code he consistently worked at it in his cabinet for fourteen hours a day.[8] He allowed his hours of rest to be interrupted only in case of fire. It was a standing order that he was to be awakened on the outbreak of fire anywhere in the city, and then he was usually the first on the scene, taking charge of operations and remaining until the fire was out.

Wherever he went he carried a notebook with him and wrote down at once any idea or suggestion that caught his imagination so that he would not forget. His notes covered a vast range of subjects. "A short history of present day and ancient affairs for instruction of young people after the alphabet," "Despatch to Siberia for information on Kamchatka," and "Send officers to observe in the Imperial forces" were typical.[9] Sometimes the notes were so brief that only the subject on his mind was clear.[10] It was by harnessing his tremendous energy, concentration, and capacity for detail in such rigorous habits of work that he was able to accomplish all that he did.

Foreign relations continued to be one of his major preoccupations in these last years. Prussia, Holland, and Sweden had now all recognized his imperial title, but the other great powers had withheld recognition, although they feared and respected his strength. Indeed, from The Hague, Kurakin reported in November 1723 that all Europe was following closely the progress of the Persian campaign, hoping that it would continue for several years, thus distracting Peter from any activities in the north.[11]

George I of England was still leader of this anti-Russian bloc, and was still doing everything possible through his ambassador in Constantinople to persuade the Turks once more to declare war on Russia. He was especially afraid of Russian policy in Holstein and Mecklenburg. Frederick IV of Denmark shared his fear and was also alarmed by Peter's demand for exemption of his ships from paying dues in the Sound. But Frederick's main concern was to retain Sleswig, which had formerly belonged to Holstein, and he refused to concede the Tsar's Imperial title until Peter had guaranteed his possession of Sleswig and broken off relations with the Duke of Holstein, then in St. Petersburg. Both George I and Frederick IV sought by every means to bring Sweden into their anti-Russian alliance, but their efforts failed.

The Duke of Holstein was both the key and the pawn in these diplomatic intrigues. He had arrived in St. Petersburg in 1721 to seek the hand of Tsarevna Anna and to obtain Russian support for his claims to the Swedish succession. The Swedes had exacted an undertaking under the Treaty of Nystadt that Peter would never take up the Holstein cause, but later Mikhail Bestuzhev, as Russian resident in Stockholm, found that in fact a strong party opposed the then King of Sweden, and favoured recognition of the Duke's right of succession. In 1723 a Diet agreed to recognize the Tsar's Imperial title and to concede the title of Royal Highness to the Duke, despite the protests of the King and the Queen, but it made no decisions concerning the succession. Bestuzhev also had instructions to propose a defensive alliance of Russia with Sweden. This the King opposed, but again his policy was overruled. The Diet approved the alliance which was signed in February 1724, and which also contained a secret article that both countries would now undertake to persuade Denmark to restore Sleswig to Holstein. The way was now clear for Peter to give his approval to the marriage of his daughter Anna to the Duke.

Another possibility much in Peter's mind at this time was a marriage between his daughter Elizabeth and a member of the French royal family. He was anxious to improve relations with France so as to counterbalance the hostility of England and Austria. Moreover, if it could be arranged that the French prince, married to his daughter, should succeed to the Polish throne, then this would secure Russian influence in Poland as well as French support in the wider sphere of Europe.

The French prince mentioned was the Duke of Chartres, son of the Regent. The proposal appealed to the Regent, for, with his son on the Polish throne, France would at last be able to count on Poland as an ally against Austria and Prussia. But there were also many objections to the proposal and, further, neither the Regent nor Cardinal Dubois were prepared to risk offending England. After much equivocation Dubois finally proposed that the election of the Duke of Chartres to the Polish throne should be a condition precedent to the marriage, and that a defensive alliance should be concluded between France, Russia, and England, in place of Prussia.

Campredon, the French ambassador, reported these proposals on Peter's return to Moscow from the Persian campaign. Peter objected, insisting that the marriage should take place at once. Campredon, therefore, tried to persuade his government to accept the marriage without delay. He reported that Tsarevna Elizabeth was attractive and that, although less well educated than Anna, she had the intelligence to make good this defect. But for months he could obtain no reply to his despatches and when eventually Dubois did reply, it was merely to state that difficulties had been raised in England and that he would send further instructions. In fact, both Cardinal Dubois and the Duke of Orleans died in 1723, and Peter's designs for uniting the royal families of Russia and France came to nothing.

Relations with Poland were, as always, complicated. Peter persisted in his policy of holding Poland either as an ally or so disrupted by internal disputes as to be an ineffective enemy. He maintained his alliance with the King of Prussia, but resisted proposals to partition Poland. Moreover, he had now withdrawn his support finally from Augustus and opposed his ambition to make the Polish throne hereditary. The health of Augustus, undermined by years of debauchery, seemed to be breaking and the succession to the Polish throne had become an urgent matter. Meanwhile Peter's minister in Poland managed, by bribery, to thwart Augustus' attempts to have his son adopted as his successor.

On the other hand the loss of Kiev and the other lands made over to Russia in the previous century continued to rankle with the Poles, so that they refused to recognize the title of Emperor of All Russia because it could be taken to include these former Polish provinces. Courland was a further matter of dispute. This duchy was a fief of Poland, but by virtue of the marriage of the Duke with Tsarevna Anna it had come under Russian protection. The subsequent death of the Duke had not, however, led to any withdrawal of Russian troops; on the contrary Anna continued to live in Mitau and the duchy remained a Russian dependency.

One new factor in Peter's policy towards Poland was his protection there of the Orthodox and other non-Catholics. Many Russians lived in the eastern provinces of Poland, refusing either to embrace Catholicism or to accept the Uniat Church. Polish nobles and priests vied in persecuting them, despite the undertakings given in the Treaty of Moscow in 1686, and the Orthodox appealed to Peter for protection. Protestant Poles, suffering similar oppression, turned to the King of Prussia who also asked for Peter's help. Promptly on both scores Peter took vigorous action. He informed Augustus that he was sending a commission to investigate disputes between Orthodox, Uniates, and Catholics, and to this Augustus reluctantly agreed. Peter also pressed for articles to be included in the Polish constitution, guaranteeing the liberties of the Orthodox.

In 1724 Catholics mobbed and killed a large number of Protestants in Thorn, and Peter was so incensed that he publicly denounced the Polish Catholics and demanded the death penalty for the guilty. Religious antagonisms and the persecution of the Orthodox were to be thorny matters of dispute between Russia and Poland for many years to come, but Peter stood throughout on strong ground in demanding tolerance and respect for the rights of other faiths abroad, for these were no more than the rights that he had himself introduced and enforced in his own empire.

St. Petersburg had grown rapidly. Until 1715 Peter had had only a general idea of the plan of his city. His intention originally was that it should reach out into the sea and he had therefore looked on Kotlin Island as its most suitable centre.[12] But towards the end of 1715 he decided that Vasilevsky Island should be the centre.[13] In 1716 Trezzini drew up a plan making Vasilevsky Island the heart of St. Petersburg and by planning intersecting canals he gave shape to Peter's ideal of a city like Amsterdam.

At first, building on Vasilevsky Island was slow, and in 1719 Peter decided that the work must be accelerated. An ukaz imposed on all landowners possessing more than forty serf households the obligation to build a house on the island and to live there themselves. Landowners with between one hundred and fifty and four hundred households were ordered to erect two-storied houses of stone, while those possessing between forty and one hundred and fifty households had to raise one storey buildings of timber.

In January 1724, following on the census, he issued a new scale, based on the ownership of "souls" instead of serf households, and made the punishment for failure to build more severe. Results again fell far short of what was expected. But all the time St. Petersburg grew; in 1717 there were some forty-five hundred permanent houses and by 1725 the number was in the region of six thousand. Although unpopular because living there was expensive and the climate unhealthy, the city was nevertheless the home of the court, the centre of the government, and the chief port; inevitably the population increased. Moreover, the city had begun to take shape architecturally, arousing some pride in the inhabitants and admiration in foreigners. St. Petersburg had already struck deep roots and was asserting itself as the heir to Novgorod the Great.

By tremendous feats of organization Peter had set up the industries necessary to provide bricks, timber, tiles, and other materials necessary for building the city. However, it was not materials, but labour which was the serious obstacle to more rapid construction. From 1704, the annual labour force demanded had been about forty thousand men, but frequently the demand was less, and evasion, flight, and illness usually reduced the actual numbers to half.[14] Although the peasants were required only to work for two (later, five)-month periods mainly in the summer, this requisitioning of labour was a cruel system. Able-bodied men were torn from their families and villages, driven north by the hundreds, and compelled to labour for a pittance in the damp heat of the city and under fearful conditions. Administrative incompetence often gave rise to shortages of food, and epidemics, including plague, struck among them.[15] Peter was fully aware of their hardships and of the high mortality rate, but to him this was the price that had to be paid.

Like the navy, the city was his own special creation, a symbol of much that he had laboured to achieve, and he took a personal pride and pleasure in making it grow. Whenever he returned to it after even a short absence, he impatiently inspected every part to see what progress had been made. He never refused an invitation to lay a foundation stone. He enjoined on the inhabitants the need to keep their houses clean and to cultivate gardens and trees, and he himself was constantly planting trees, especially fruit trees. The Nevsky Prospekt, a magnificent broad avenue, which Swedish prisoners had laid down and paved with stone, was swept by them every Saturday. All this was not merely a matter of his own pride in his city, it was also a part of his determination to teach his people the needs for order, cleanliness, and good administration.

As Governor of the city, Menshikov had made important contributions. He had the capacity for getting things done and he realized that new works in St. Petersburg would win him favour.[16] When in 1713 Andreas Schlueter, Director of the Berlin Academy of Arts, with four other architects arrived in St. Petersburg, Menshikov took two of them, Schaedel and Schwertfeger, who worked almost exclusively for him. A rivalry developed between his architects and Trezzini and Leblond. Schaedel built Menshikov a palace on Vasilevsky Island and a country palace called Oranienbaum, on the shores of the Gulf of Finland some twenty-five miles from the city, both of which became renowned. Peter generally had no fondness for magnificence, but his city was an exception, and he encouraged Menshikov and others to build opulently.

In 1722 he approved plans, prepared by Trezzini, for twelve great buildings, running side by side along the shore of Vasilevsky Island, which were to house the colleges. Work began on them at once, but it was a major undertaking which took ten years, and Peter did not live to see the imposing façade of the colleges or of the neighbouring building of the Academy of Sciences which he also decreed.

During this period Peter not only worked, but he also relaxed in St. Petersburg. His greatest pleasure in summer was to sail on the Neva, his own hand on the tiller. He was eager that his people should learn to be at home on the water, like the Dutch and English, and it was in fact essential, for communications in summer between the islands was by water. He provided that all inhabitants should receive rowing or sailing boats at the expense of the Treasury. He also appointed a kommissar who inspected all boats at regular intervals and necessary repairs were carried out at the expense of the owner. On Sundays and special holidays, when signals were flown from masts at certain points all the people and the court had to gather in their boats. Then, led by Peter and Catherine, the people of St. Petersburg sailed or rowed up and down their river to the sound of music.

An exceptional occasion was the salute to the little boat which Peter had found rotting at Izmailov and which was now known as "the Grandfather of the Russian Navy." In the summer of 1723, while Peter was engaged in naval manoeuvres in the Baltic, the boat was brought to St. Petersburg. At the beginning of August, he returned with his fleet to Kronstadt, where the boat was carried with great ceremony on a galliot, escorted by two hundred galleys. The fleet took up positions in the harbour. The little boat was then placed in the water and, flying the Imperial standard with Peter steering and the four senior admirals rowing, she passed slowly by the twenty-two ships of the line, the galleys, and the innumerable other naval vessels, all of which fired cannon salvoes in its honour. The ceremony triumphantly proclaimed the fact that Russia, a nation of landsmen, possessing no seagoing vessels, had within the span of his reign become a naval power.[17]

To the end of his life Peter retained his love of fireworks, of boisterous banquets and celebrations which ended in drunkenness on a massive scale, and even took a renewed interest in the All Joking-All Drunken Assembly which he had set up in his youth. But he enjoyed such occasions less and drank far less than in the past. At Calais, for example, a Frenchman attached to his court, had reported to Paris that "today is the day of their Easter and to celebrate the mystery with greater dignity they are all drunk, except his Tsarish Majesty who, it is said, never drinks to the point of clouding his brain."[18] John Bell who had lived in St. Petersburg and had accompanied Peter on the Persian campaign even considered him abstemious, and noted that "he had an aversion to all sots and to those given to too much drink."[19]

His great weakness, according to John Bell and others, was for women.[20] Allegations of his immorality, usually in general terms, but sometimes specific, persisted throughout his reign. It was said that Marie Hamilton was his mistress,[21] and that certain of the eminent men of the next generation were his illegitimate children.[22] But these statements are usually nothing more than the gossip of the courts. More credible, although also hearsay, was the evidence given under investigation in 1718 by Bolshoi Afanasiev, the personal servant of Tsarevich Alexei. He revealed that the clerk, Voronov, had said to him, "I have heard that the Sovereign has a mistress and that the Tsaritsa knows about it. When she arrived in Holland, she began weeping in front of His Majesty who asked her, 'Who told you?' 'The Colonel's wife told me and Plato [a servant] told her about it,' she answered. And the Sovereign gave Plato a beating for that."[23]

Peter was indeed indulgent towards immorality among his people and this may well have been a reflection of his own weakness. He was not given to restraint and may have been promiscuous, but, if so, it is clear that such affairs were never more than matters of the moment to which he attached no importance and gave no further thought.

Peter liked nothing better than to hold receptions and celebrations in the Summer Garden. The anniversary of Poltava was always a great occasion. The company gathered at 5 P.M. and on the Tsaritsyn Lug, a broad field adjoining the garden, the Preobrazhensky and Semyonovsky guards regiments were drawn up. Peter himself always handed out to his guards the wooden beakers of wine or beer in which to drink in honour of the day. Catherine with her family and her court gathered in the garden by one of the fountains. Her court, by contrast with the austerity of Peter's few attendants, was richly dressed and numerous. The nobility, who had quickly taken up European fashions, made these festivities events of splendour. But always the drinking followed the old Russian custom of frequent toasts from which no one was exempted. Groups of guardsmen carried beakers of wine to the guests who had to drink the healths of their colonels. Everyone became merry, including members of the church hierarchy who were as assiduous in attending as they were in drinking their fill. Later, on a galley moored at the northern side of the garden, dancing began. Then firework displays lit up the

Neva and, as the night wore on, the merriment grew more hilarious until the alcohol which had been consumed in such vast quantities at last claimed its many victims who then littered the garden, sunk in profound and drunken sleep.

The new feature of these and other occasions was the presence of women. Peter had emancipated them completely from the prison gloom of the terem, and he was insistent that they should play their full part in social life. To accustom his people to mixing as in the Western countries, he had decreed in November 1718 that assemblies should be held at frequent intervals and laid down the procedure to be followed. A list of hosts was drawn and the host appointed to hold an assembly was obliged to open his house to guests and their wives from 4 or 5 P.M. until 10 P.M., providing rooms for dancing, smoking, cards and forfeits, and conversation. He had no obligation to greet or look after his guests or to provide drinks apart from tea and cold water. The rules were few and the guests, from the most senior to the most junior officers and civil servants mingled with merchants and the more prominent artisans, and departed when they wished within the prescribed hours. The assemblies, awkward at first, were soon part of the life of the city.

Peter spent most of the year 1724 in St. Petersburg. His health was deteriorating. Agonizing bouts of strangury weakened him, although usually he kept up the same pace of living and working. But he also had periods of depression when he would withdraw into himself, and show a strange disinterest in matters that always in the past had absorbed him.

During January and February he was busy on further reforms in the church, setting up a special college, responsible to the Holy Synod, for the administration of church revenues, and revising an important ukaz on the position and functions of monasteries and on monastic discipline. He also decreed that the Academy of Science should be established and made provision for the erection of a vast building to house it. Since before his visit to France in 1717 he had been thinking and talking about this project which embraced not only an academy, but a university as well.[24]

Towards the end of the summer his attacks of strangury became unendurable. Blumentrost anxiously consulted with other doctors and on their advice Peter agreed to submit to an operation. An English surgeon, named Horn, performed it, making a perforation in the bladder from the lower abdomen, from which blood and urine flowed freely. Peter endured the surgeon's probing with fortitude, although the two doctors at his side during the operation had their hands crushed and bruised as he grabbed them in spasms of pain. But the operation secured only temporary relief. Renewed attacks kept him to his bed in the following weeks. Then suddenly medicines gave him relief. He began to think that he was cured and impatiently planned to visit the Olonetsky ironworks and the Ladoga canal. Blumentrost hastened to warn him of the dangers of such a strenuous journey, but he was not to be deterred and sailed at the beginning of October.

The progress on the Ladoga canal gave him great satisfaction and he not only inspected the ironworks at Olenets, he even worked there, forging with his own hands a band of iron 180 pounds in weight. Then, arriving back in St. Petersburg on 5 November, he sailed at once for Lakhta on the Gulf of Finland there to inspect an ironworks and an armament factory. Approaching Lakhta in stormy weather and noticing a boat which had run aground and was in danger of capsizing, he sent a skiff manned by sailors from his own yacht to refloat it. He watched impatiently and then angrily as their efforts failed. Several men were washed from the grounded vessel, to be dragged half-drowned from the water, and waves threatened to overturn her. Unable to watch any longer, Peter went himself in another skiff to help. When he could not get alongside he jumped into the angry shallows and waded across to her. He then directed the work, secured the ropes, and with his own hands helped to refloat her. He gave orders for the twenty men, whose lives had thus been saved, to be taken off and accommodated in peasant huts on the shore.

Peter changed from his wet clothes, intending to spend the night at Lakhta and to go on from there to Sestrebek next morning. But he had spent some hours up to his waist in the freezing waters of late autumn, and suddenly he was wracked with fever and convulsions of the stomach. And so he returned to St. Petersburg.

There an unfortunate incident distressed him and aggravated his condition. Somehow it came to his notice that Catherine's chamberlain, William Mons, and Matrena Balk, one of her ladies-in-waiting, who were brother and sister of the Anna Mons who had beguiled him in his youth, were guilty of serious corruption, especially in taking bribes and extorting large sums of money from petitioners before allowing them access to the Empress. Catherine herself may well have been aware of these practices, but if so, easygoing by nature, she had avoided stirring up trouble.

Peter, however, was enraged by the extent of their corruption, and when Makarov, his apparently incorruptible secretary, was also implicated he was beside himself. Under examination Mons further confessed that he had converted to his own use the revenues of several estates belonging to the Empress. His crimes were especially villainous in Peter's eyes because they involved the abuse of a position of trust. Catherine begged him to pardon her chamberlain and lady-in-waiting, but he could not be moved. Mons was executed, Matrena Balk was knouted and exiled to Tobolsk,[25] and Peter promptly issued an ukaz condemning to death without mercy all those who, holding positions at court, used them for gain, especially by extorting bribes for permission to petition the Emperor or Empress.

During the next few weeks Peter contrived to attend to state business, but his strength was already ebbing. His illness had grown steadily worse and on 16 January 1725 it attacked him so savagely that he cried out in agony. His doctors gathered and conferred, but could do nothing. A private chapel was installed in a room adjoining his bedroom, and priests prayed for his recovery. Several senators were in constant attendance and Catherine never left his side. His tremendous strength and energy had always in the past served to carry him through such crises. But now his condition grew hourly worse.

A long reign was nearing its end. It had been a hard reign for the whole nation, aggravated in these last years by famine. The people were near to exhaustion, but they held Peter in awe as their Emperor and their father, and the approach of his death stunned them. On 26 January the Senate, members of the colleges, the army high command, guards, and naval officers gathered at the palace to keep vigil. Many were in tears. A hush came over St. Petersburg. Once Peter rallied enough to give orders for the release of those sentenced to hard labour and of other criminals, except those guilty of murder or treason. In the evening, when all hope had gone, the archbishops of the Holy Synod administered the last rites. But still Peter clung to life. On the following morning he gave further orders for clemency to be extended to certain classes of criminals.

Then at about 2 P.M. he called for pen and paper and began writing; but what he wrote was indecipherable except for the words: "Give all to . . . " and his pen fell from his hand. He asked for Tsarevna Anna, his eldest daughter, to whom he could dictate, but when she came to his side he was unable to speak. Thus he lingered, unconscious most of the time, until six o'clock on the morning of 28 January. On that morning the silence that had lain over St. Petersburg for days on end was broken by the suddenly whispered news: the Emperor Peter the Great was dead.

BIBLIOGRAPHY

The following are the main sources and studies consulted. I have omitted several works available in English which are in my opinion of no value, and I have not included the many articles, published in Voprosy Istorii, The Slavonic and East European Review, and other periodicals, which I have found most useful, and which I have referred to in the notes to each chapter.

An asterisk (*) indicates that the work is available only in Russian.

Adlerfeld, G. The Military History of Charles XII. London, 1740. (Tr. into English.)

Allen, W. E. D. The Ukraine: A History. Cambridge, 1940.

*Andreev, A. N. (ed.). Peter I: A Symposium. Leningrad, 1947.

Bain, Nisbet R. Charles XII and the Collapse of the Swedish Empire, 1682-1719. New York, 1895. Peter the Great and Pupils. London, 1897. Charles XII and the Great Northern War in The Cambridge Modern History, Vol. V. Cambridge, 1907. Slavonic Europe. Cambridge, 1908.

Barrow, J. A Memoir of the Life of Peter the Great. London, 1832.

Bell, J. Travels from St. Petersburg into Russia to Diverse Parts of Asia. 2 vols. Glasgow, 1763.

Blomberg, Baron de. An Account of Livonia. London, 1701.

*Bogoslovsky, M. M. Peter the First; Materials for a Biography. 5 vols. Leningrad, 1940-8. *Peter the Great and His Reform. Moscow, 1920.

Bridges, C. A. G. (ed.). The Russian Fleet During the Reign of Peter the Great by a contemporary Englishman. Navy Records Society, 1899.

Browning, O. Peter the Great. London, 1898.

Bruce, P. H. Memoirs . . . containing an account of his travels in Germany, Russia, Tatary, etc. London, 1782.

Buxhoeveden, Baroness Sophie. A Cavalier in Muscovy. London, 1932.

Chance, J. F. George I and the Northern War. London, 1909.

Collins, S. The Present State of Russia. London, 1671.

Godley, E. Charles XII of Sweden. London, 1928.

*Golikov, I. I. The Works of Peter the Great. Moscow, 1788-97. 10 vols. with supplements.

445

Gordon, Alexander. *History of Peter the Great, Emperor of Russia*. 2 vols. London, 1755.

Gordon, Patrick. *Passages from the Diary of General Patrick Gordon of Auchleuchries*, edited for the Spalding Society by J. Robertson. Aberdeen, 1859.

*Grekov, V. D., Bakhrushin, S. V., Lebedev, V. I. (eds.). *From the Most Ancient Times to the End of the 18th Century*, being Vol. I of the *History of the U.S.S.R.* Moscow, 1947. 2nd ed.

*Guerrier V. *The Relations of Leibniz with Russia and Peter the Great*. St. Petersburg, 1871.

Hallendorf and Schuck. *History of Sweden*. Stockholm, 1929.

Imperial Russian Historical Society, the Collection of: Vol. XXXIX (St. Petersburg, 1884). Vol. L (St. Petersburg, 1886). Vol. LXI (St. Petersburg, 1888). (A collection of diplomatic despatches, both foreign and Russian, printed in their original languages, with notes.)

*Kafengaus, B. B. *The Foreign Policy of Russia in the Reign of Peter I*. Moscow, 1942. *Russia in the Reign of Peter the First*. Moscow, 1955.

*Klyuchevsky, V. *Course of Russian History*. 5 vols. Moscow-Petrograd, 1923. 2nd ed. (The English translation is unreliable.) *Stories by Foreigners About the Muscovite State*. Petrograd, 1918.

*Knyazkov, S. *Sketches from the History of Peter the Great and His Time*. Moscow, 1709.

Korb, J. G. *Diary of an Austrian Secretary of Legation at the Court of Tsar Peter the Great*. London, 1863. (Translated from the Latin by Count MacDonnell.)

*Luppov, S. P. *History of the Building of Peterburg in the First Quarter of the Eighteenth Century*. Moscow-Leningrad, 1957.

Manstein, C. H. *Memoirs of Russia, 1727-44*. London, 1773. (2nd ed.).

Mavor, James. *An Economic History of Russia*. 2 vols. London, 1925. (2nd ed.).

*Mavrodin, V. *Peter I*. Moscow, 1949.

Merezhkovsky, D. *Peter and Alexei: A Novel*.

Mottley, J. *The History of the Life of Peter I. Emperor of Russia*. 3 vols. London, 1739.

*Murzanova, M. N., Bobrova, E. I., Petrov, V. A. (eds.). *Historical Outline and Review of the Contents of the Manuscript Department of the Library of the Academy of Sciences of the U.S.S.R.* Number I. Eighteenth Century. Moscow-Leningrad, 1956.

*Nikiforov, L. A. *Russian-English Relations in the Reign of Peter I*. Moscow, 1950.

Olearius, Aadam, *The Voyages and Travels of the Ambassadors sent by Frederick, Duke of Holstein, to the Great Duke of Holstein to the*

Great Duke of Muscovy and the King of Persia, begun in the year 1633 and finished in 1639. London, 1662.

*Pekarsky, P. Science and Literature in Russia in the Reign of Peter the Great. St. Petersburg, 1862.

Perry, John. The State of Russia under the present Tsar. London, 1716.

*Peter the Great, Gallery of, in the Imperial Public Library. St. Petersburg, 1903. (A catalogue of portraits of Peter with numerous illustrations.)

*Peter the Great, Emperor, Letters and Papers of. St. Petersburg-Leningrad, 1887-1952. 9 vols. (Containing all documents up to end of 1709; subsequent papers have yet to be published.)

*Platonov, S. F. Peter the Great. Leningrad, 1926.

*Pylyaev, M. I. Old St. Peterburg. St. Petersburg, 1887.

Schuyler, Eugene. Peter the Great. 2 vols. London, 1884.

Shcherbatov, M. M. (ed.). Journal de Pierre le Grand depuis l'année 1698 jusqu'à la conclusion de la paix de Neustadt. Berlin, 1773. (Tr. de l'original russe.)

*Shubinsky, S. N. Historical Essays and Sketches. St. Petersburg, 1903.

*Solovev, S. M. History of Russia from Earliest Times. 29 vols. St. Petersburg, no date. 2nd ed.

*Spiridonov, E. V. The Economic Policy and Economic Opinions of Peter I. Moscow, 1952.

Staehlin-Storcksburg, J. V. Original Anecdotes of Peter the Great. London, 1788.

Stanley, A. P. Lectures on the History of the Eastern Church. London, 1861.

Sumner, B. H. Survey of Russian History. London, 1944.
Peter the Great and the Emergence of Russia. London, 1950.
Peter the Great and the Ottoman Empire. Oxford, 1949.

*Tarle, E. V. The Russian Navy and the Foreign Policy of Peter I. (Moscow, 1949).

*Ustryalov, N. History of the Reign of Peter the Great. 8 vols. St. Petersburg, 1858.

*Vasilev, M. The Siege and Capture of Vyborg by the Russian Army and Navy in 1710. Moscow, 1953.

*Venevitinov, M. A. The Russians in Holland: The Grand Embassy 1687-8. Moscow, 1897.

*Voensky, K. Peter I in Karlsbad in 1711 and 1712. St. Petersburg, 1908.

de Vogue, E. Melchior. The True Story of Mazepa. London, 1884. (Tr. by J. Millington.)

Voltaire. Historie de Russie sous Pierre le Grand. Paris, 1719. (Oeuvres complètes). Histoire de Charles XII. Paris, 1719 (Oeuvres complètes.)

*Voskresensky, N. A. (ed.). Legislative Acts of Peter I. Moscow, 1945.

*Vyatkin, M. P. (ed.). Outlines of the History of Leningrad: Volume I, The Feudal Period, 1703-1861. Moscow-Leningrad, 1955.

Waliszewski, K. Peter the Great. 2 vols. London, 1897. (Tr. by Lady Mary Lloyd.)

Weber, F. C. The Present State of Russia. London, 1722. Memoires pour servir à l'histoire de l'Empire Russien sous le regne de Pierre le Grand 1700-20. Par un ministre étranger. La Haye, 1725. Das Veränderte Russland. Franckfurt, 1721.

*Zabelin. The Domestic Life of the Russian Tsars and Tsaritsas. Moscow, 1862-69.

*Zaozerskaya, E. I. Manufacture in the Reign of Peter I. Moscow, 1947. The Development of Light Industry in Moscow in the First Quarter of the Eighteenth Century. Moscow, 1955.

*Zhitkov, K. G. History of the Russian Navy: Petrine Period 1672-1725. St. Petersburg, 1912.

NOTES

ABBREVIATIONS USED IN NOTES

Adlerfeld	Adlerfeld, G. The Military History of Charles XII. London, 1740.
Bogoslavsky	Bogoslavsky, M. M. Peter the First; Materials for a Biography. Leningrad, 1940-48.
Golikov	Golikov, I. I. The Works of Peter the Great. Moscow, 1788-97.
Journal	Shcherbatov, M. M. (ed.). Journal de Pierre le Grand depuis l'année 1698 jusqu'à la conclusion de la paix de Neustadt. Berlin, 1773. (Tr. de l'original russe.)
Korb	Korb, J. G. Diary of an Austrian Secretary of Legation at the Court of Tsar Peter the Great. London, 1863. (Tr. by Count MacDonnell.)
P & B	Letters and Papers of Emperor Peter the Great. St. Petersburg-Leningrad, 1887-1952.
Sbornik I.R.I.O.	Imperial Russian Historical Society, The Collection of. St. Petersburg, 1884-88.
Solovev	Solovev, S. M. History of Russia from Earliest Times. St. Petersburg, no date. 2nd ed.
Staehlin	Staehlin-Storeksburg, J. V. Original Anecdotes of Peter the Great. London, 1788.
Ustryalov	Ustryalov, N. History of the Reign of Peter the Great. St. Petersburg, 1858.
Voskresensky	Voskresensky, N. A. (ed.). Legislative Acts of Peter I. Moscow, 1945.

449

Chapter I · Muscovy in the Seventeenth Century

1. Adam Olearius, The Voyages and Travels of the Ambassadors sent by Frederick, Duke of Holstein, to the Grand Duke of Muscovy, 57.

2. John Perry, The State of Russia, 237.

3. In 1619 fire destroyed the Tsar's Kremlin Palace, which was at once rebuilt. In 1626 a serious fire destroyed not only the new palace, but also the Tsar's stables and treasury, and other buildings in the Kremlin. It was after this fire that, with the encouragement of Tsar Mikhail, a few more buildings of stone and brick were erected. In 1635-36 Tsar Mikhail ordered a residence of stone to be built for himself and his family: it was an important innovation, but even the Tsar's example made little headway against Muscovite conservatism; log houses, like the fires, continued to be traditional.
Zabelin, Domestic Life of the Russian Tsars, 56-57.

4. Olearius, op. cit., 95.

5. The headman of the free Cossacks in Little Russia was known as the Hetman. In Poland and Lithuania the commander-in-chief was called the Grand Crown Hetman. Both Hetman and Ataman are said to derive from the German Hauptmann.

6. Samuel Collins, The Present State of Russia, 63.

7. Korb, I, 100.

8. Collins, op. cit., 22.

9. Olearius, op. cit., 80-81.

10. Collins, op. cit., 71-74.

11. Olearius, op. cit., 93.

12. Ibid., 123-124.

13. Collins, op. cit., 128.

14. C. H. Manstein, Memoirs of Russia, 416.

15. Olearius, op. cit., 86, 89.

16. History of the Russian Theatre, ed. by V. V. Kallash and others (Moscow, 1914), I, 17-18.

17. Collins, op. cit., 107-09.

Chapter II   The Early Years, 1672-1682

1. Among the old customs was the "birth measure," an image of the child's

450

patron saint painted on a board of cypress wood to the size of the child, which was carefully preserved, and eventually hung over his tomb. The ikon painter, Simeon Ushakov, was ordered to paint the Apostle Peter to the measurements of the Tsarevich and, when he fell ill, Feodor Kozlov completed it. This cypress board, showing his measurements soon after birth to have been 19¾ inches long by 5¼ inches wide, was later hung over the tomb of Emperor Peter the Great in the Cathedral of SS. Peter and Paul in St. Petersburg. The birth board has since been moved, presumably during the Second World War when many antiquities were evacuated.

2. Bogoslovsky, I, 30.

3. Perry, op. cit., 217-19. These were the punishments of a cruel age, not only in Russia, but in Europe: the cat-o'nine-tails then in common use in the British army and navy often resulted in death, and was not in fact abolished until 1881.

4. Ibid., 217.

Chapter III   The Revolt of the Streltsi, 1682

1. Report of the Danish resident, Butenant von Rosenbusch, on the revolt of the streltsi in May 1682, printed by Ustryalov, I, App. vi, 330-46.

2. Ibid.

3. Ibid.

4. Bogoslovsky, I, 44.

5. Ustryalov, 61.

Chapter IV   The Regency of Sofia, 1682

1. Descriptions of Sofia conflict. Some praised her beauty, and the Englishman, Captain Perry, called her "a handsome young lady." But he had never seen her, while the Frenchman, La Neuville, who had, described her as having "a shapeless body, monstrously fat, a head as big as a bushel measure, hair growing on her face." Perry, op. cit., 143; La Neuville, Relation curieuse et nouvelle de Moscovie (A La Haye, 1699), 151. Quoted by Ustryalov, I, 273-74.

2. Ustryalov, I, 79.

3. Mazepa's fame as a romantic hero rests mainly on Byron's dramatic poem, describing how an enraged husband had him seized on his way to a secret meeting with his wife. Servants of the husband stripped him naked and bound him on the back of his horse which they terrified by firing pistols and whipping until it galloped away through bushes and thickets. The disgrace of this incident compelled him to flee from the Polish court.

Mazepa lacks a biographer. Russian historians have usually damned him as a traitor; Ukrainian nationalists have portrayed him as a hero of the Ukrainian separatist movement. Melchior de Vogue has written an interesting essay on the romantic legend of Mazepa, created by Voltaire, Byron, and others, and has given an account of his life. (Melchior de Vogue, The True Story of Mazepa.) Probably the most objective and understanding account of his subsequent fall is that given by Solovev in his History of Russia. W. E. D. Allen in Ukraine: A History, contains valuable bibliographical notes on Mazepa, and most of the facts of his life.

Chapter V   Peter at Play, 1682-1689

1. Bogoslovsky, I, 53-55.

2. The Preobrazhensky was the senior regiment and until 1917 remained the first regiment of the Imperial Guard, of which the Tsar was commander. Peter himself served in it as a bombardier and by gradual promotion was to reach the rank of Colonel. By tradition the first volunteer, enlisted in the Preobrazhensky regiment, was a brawny, twenty-year-old groom, named Sergei Bukhvostov, whom the arsenal records mention in 1683 as being a member of Peter's play-troop. In 1715, when the Russian army had won renown, Peter ordered Rastrelli, the Italian sculptor, to cast a life-size statue of Bukhvostov as the first Russian soldier. Golikov states that this statue was kept in the Museum of the Academy (Golikov, VI, 74). Others mention that it was placed in a prominent position in St. Petersburg. The present whereabouts of this statue are not known.

3. P & B, Nos. 1-3.

4. Ustryalov, II, App. i.

5. P & B, No. 6.

6. Ibid., No. 7.

7. Ibid., No. 9.

8. Ustryalov, II, 29.

9. P & B, I, Nos. 5-9.

10. This account of the birth of Peter's love of ships and the sea has been taken from his own autobiographical introduction to the Naval Code published in 1720 and reprinted by Ustryalov (II, App. i). Bogoslovsky states (I, 66) that "the recollections of the Tsar, written thirty-two years after the events related, are fully accurate and confirmed by other documents."

Peter's little boat was moved to St. Petersburg in 1723, where it has been preserved. It is now in the Central Naval Museum on Vassilevsky Island.

The English origin of the boat is disputed. It is claimed by some that Dutch carpenters built it with the Orel in 1668 at Dedinovo on the river Oka. Others hold that it was a gift from Queen Elizabeth to Tsar Ivan the Terrible.

Chapter VI   The Fall of Sofia, 1689

1. P & B, I, Nos. 5-9.

2. Ustryalov, II, 222.

3. Bogoslovsky, I, 80.

4. Ustryalov, II, 70.

5. Ibid., 74.

6. Op. cit., II, 83. Passages from the Diary of General Gordon, 166.

7. P & B, I, No. 10.

Chapter VII   Peter's Western Tutelage Begins, 1689-1693

1. Peter himself related subsequently that his subjects petitioned at the time in great numbers, alleging that Marcellus was unsuitable, because he spoke barbarous languages (Latin and French), because his beard was not worthy of a patriarch, and because his coachman sat upon the coach seat and not upon the horse, as was usual. Blomberg, An Account of Livonia.

2. Patrick Gordon kept a diary, which is an invaluable source of informa-

tion on Muscovy under three tsars. It is preserved in six large quarto volumes in the Russian State Archives, from which unfortunately some parts are missing, notably the years 1667-77, and 1678-84. A German translation was made by Posselt and published in 1849-52. E. Schuyler, who presumably consulted the original diary in St. Petersburg, states that this translation is in some places unreliable. Extracts from the diary were published by the Spalding Club at Aberdeen in 1859 under the title *Passages from the Diary of General Patrick Gordon of Auchleuchries.* The commentary linking these extracts is highly inaccurate.

3. The abilities of Lefort and the extent of his influence have been exaggerated by many historians. Nisbet Bain, for example, wrote that "it was Lefort who put 'Peter the Bombardier' in the way of becoming 'Peter the Great.' " It has been claimed that he first awakened in Peter a desire to learn and to study Western methods and that he inspired him with determination to visit the West. But Peter's curiosity and urge to learn were inborn and certainly in evidence at an early age, while the West had cast a spell over him long before he met Lefort. But it remains true that Lefort exerted some influence, and that he encouraged Peter in his pursuit of Western ideas.

Voltaire, probably more than any writer on Peter, may have been responsible for this misconception. But, while Voltaire could be misled at times into making wrong judgments, mainly due to limitations on the materials available to him, his biographies of Peter and of Charles XII remain among the most readable and sound studies available. R. Nisbet Bain, *Peter the Great and His Pupils;* Ustryalov, II, 5-23; G. P. Gooch, "Voltaire as Historian" in *Catherine the Great and Other Studies* (London, 1954).

4. Andrei Vinius was born in Muscovy. He was the son of the Dutch merchant who in the reign of Tsar Mikhail had set up iron foundries near Tula, and, having married a Russian, settled in Muscovy. Andrei Vinius knew Dutch and Russian, and Tsar Alexei had appointed him a director of postal services.

Von Mengden was a colonel of the Preobrazhensky regiment; nothing is known of his origin or how he came to be in Muscovy.

The Scot, Chambers, was born in Moscow and was a colonel in the Semyonovsky regiment.

Adam Weide, the son of a Dutch colonel who settled in Muscovy, began studying medicine but turned to engineering and soldiering, and became a major in the Preobrazhensky regiment.

Jacob Bruce was also born in Moscow, and won Peter's notice by his ability as an engineer and gunner.

Ustryalov, II, 125-28.

Chapter VIII   Archangel, 1693-1694

1. P & B, I, No. 14.
2. P & B, I, p. 490.
3. Ustryalov, II, 161.
4. P & B, I, No. 21.
5. Bogoslovsky, I, 176.
6. *Ibid.*, 181.
7. This cross was transferred to Archangel Cathedral on 29 June 1805, on the petition of the citizens of Archangel. It is not known whether the cross is still there. Ustryalov, II, Note 45; P & B, I, 495.

8. P & B, No. 27.
9. P & B, I, Nos. 28, 29 and 500-01.
10. Ibid., No. 29.
11. Ibid., No. 30.

Chapter IX   The Azov Campaigns, 1695-1696

1. P & B, I, No. 36.
2. B. H. Sumner, Peter the Great and the Ottoman Empire, 15-16.
3. Now called Stalingrad.
4. P & B, I, No. 38.
5. Ibid., Nos. 37-38, 40-42.
6. Bogoslovsky, I, 245.
7. P & B, I, 543.
8. Ibid., No. 71.
9. Without realizing it, Peter was also providing for his successors; three of Tsar Ivan's five daughters survived; Anna became Empress of Russia, while Catherine became Duchess of Mecklenburg, and her grandson ascended the throne as Ivan VI for a short time.
10. P & B, I, No. 72.
11. Bogoslovsky, I, 293.
12. P & B, I, 551.
13. Ibid., Nos. 93-95.
14. Ibid., Nos. 96-98, 100.
15. Ibid., No. 99.
16. Ibid., No. 108.
17. Gordon's Diary quoted by Bogoslovsky, I, 333.
18. P & B, I, No. 111, Nos. 112-14.
19. Ibid., I, pp. 597-99.
20. Ibid., I, No. 122.

Chapter X   The Navy, 1697-1698

1. Ustryalov, II, App. i.
2. Bogoslovsky, I, 362.
3. Ustryalov, II, 309; P & B, I, No. 104.
4. P & B, I, No. 285.
5. Bogoslovsky, I, 367; Ustryalov, III, 6.
Feodor Alexeevich Golovin, the second ambassador, should be distinguished from Avtonom Mikhailovich Golovin, who held commands in the Azov campaigns.
In all, seven Golovins served Peter; four of them had the christian name of Ivan. They belonged to three families, which were related, although not closely. Avtonom Golovin and Feodor Golovin won eminence, and are distinguished by their christian names in these pages.
Prokofy Voznitsyn served in the Foreign Office, gaining wide experience under Ordin-Nashchokin and Matveev. He also travelled to Constantinople to negotiate the conclusion of the Treaty of Bakhchi-sarai in 1681. On the fall of Sofia, he left the Foreign Office and attached himself to Boris Golitsyn, through whom he became known to Peter.
6. Ustryalov, II, App. i.
7. P & B, I, No. 140.

8. Ustryalov, III, 633.
9. Bogoslovsky, I, 385-86; Ustryalov, III, 387-88, 637.
10. Perry, op. cit., 156; Bogoslovsky, II, 14.

Chapter XI   The Grand Embassy, 1697

1. Ustryalov, III, App. xi.
2. Macaulay, History of England, Chap. 23.
3. Ustryalov, III, 25-26.
4. P & B, I, No. 147.
5. Ibid., No. 149.
6. The Swedes had behaved with strict correctness and even with forbearance. Under the terms of the Treaty of Kardis (1661) Sweden and Russia were obliged to provide appropriately for embassies appointed by one to the court of the other. A Russian embassy passing through Swedish territory was only entitled to "friendly assistance." The Swedes might have been less stiff in their behaviour; the Governor knew that the Tsar was with the embassy and, while respecting his incognito, could have shown him special courtesy; but it was the Tsar's presence that caused him to exercise the forbearance that he did. Riga was a frontier town and only forty years earlier Tsar Alexei had laid siege to it without success. Dahlberg had every reason to be suspicious of the close interest that the Tsar took in its fortifications. Peter had already advised Vinius that he would write in invisible ink between the lines of his letters and, as Dahlberg suspected, his reports manifested not the curiosity of a tourist, but the interest of a military commander. P & B, I, Nos. 145-46, 149.
7. Blomberg, op. cit., 295.
8. Ibid.
9. P & B, I, Nos. 154, 156, 161.
10. Ustryalov, III, 32-33; Bogoslovsky, II, 58-59.
11. P & B, I, Nos. 170-71 giving terms of the secret verbal agreement and of the formal agreement between the Tsar and the Elector.
12. This memorandum was dated 31 May in Moscow, but was in fact dispatched from Pilau on 12 June. P & B, I, No. 166.
13. Bogoslovsky, II, 113 14.
14. Ibid., 115-16.
15. Ibid., 118.
16. Ibid., 121.
17. In Minden, Leibniz was waiting for the embassy. He had tried without success to be presented to the Tsar in Koppenbrugge and had been received only by Lefort's nephew. He had raced ahead hoping to be presented, if not to the Tsar, at least to the first ambassador in Minden. His anxiety to meet the Tsar was not merely a matter of curiosity. With his usual enthusiasm he saw in Peter the great ruler who, having defeated the infidel Turks, would now spread enlightenment among the peoples of the East. He also hoped to obtain through the Tsar all manner of ethnographic and linguistic material to support his political theories. But again he was unsuccessful. Lefort was too busy to receive him or to mention his presence to Peter. The philosopher was left to Lefort's nephew, who accepted from him a memorandum requesting examples of all languages spoken in Russia, and a statement of the genealogy of the Russian Tsars. V. Guerrier, The Relations of Leibniz with Russia and Peter the Great, 12-16.

Chapter XII   Peter in Holland, 1697

1. The house in which Peter lived, or its neighbour, is preserved in Zaandam as a museum, known as Pieterhaus. Bogoslovsky, II, 133-34; S. N. Shubinsky, *Historical Essays and Sketches*, 27-33.

2. Bogoslovsky, II, 136.

3. *Ibid.*, 153.

4. When in Voronezh, on the eve of his departure on the second expedition against Azov, he had received news of the plot to assassinate William; it had made a strong impression on him and had probably contributed to the violence of his reaction to the Tsykler plot.

At a banquet, given by Lefort shortly afterwards, Peter, with great ceremony, had proposed a toast to the health and success of William. It was a toast that horrified the old Jacobite, General Gordon, who drank to the health of James. P & B, I, 551, 557; Bogoslovsky, I, 302-03.

5. Bogoslovsky, II, 174.

6. P & B, I, No. 186. This letter to the Patriarch was dated "September on the 10th day 1697" and is the first letter by Peter dated from the birth of Christ. The Orthodox calendar calculated from the beginning of the world and the year began on 1 September. The celebration of the New Year 7206 on 1st September a few days before had probably drawn Peter's attention to the difference between the Muscovite and Western calendars.

7. Ustryalov, III, App. xi, No. 3.

8. Bogoslovsky, II, 172-73.

9. Ustryalov, III, 78-81; App. xi, No. 3.

10. P & B, I, Nos. 189-90.

11. Bogoslovsky, II, 265; Ustryalov, III, 82-83; P & B, I, No. 207.

12. P & B, I, Nos. 181-82, 191, 193-95.

13. Peter always attached importance to the recruitment of Slavs for service in Russia and Ostrovsky's mission to "the Slavenian or Slovatskian and Sclavonian land" was almost certainly Peter's idea. Bogoslovsky, II, 266-68; P & B, No. 192; and Sumner, op. cit., 18-19, Note 2.

14. P & B, I, Nos. 196, 205-06.

15. *Ibid.*, No. 28; Ustryalov, III, 91; II, App. xv, No. 9.

16. Ustryalov, III, 92-93; App. iv.

17. P & B, I, No. 183.

18. This yacht is referred to as the *Transport Royal* in all books on the Tsar. In the log of the yacht, which is preserved in the National Maritime Museum, Greenwich, she is called the *Royal Transport*.

19. Ustryalov, III, App. iii.

20. B. H. Sumner and others state that the *Royal Transport*, Peter's new yacht, was sent to take him to England. It was not, however, until 2/12 March 1698 that the yacht was formally handed over to the Tsar by Admiral Mitchell; he sailed her for the first time on 13 March on the Thames. The log of the *Royal Transport* confirms that she could not have taken the Tsar to England.

Admiral Mitchell flew his flag in the *Yorke*, when he sailed to Holland; the *Romney* and the two yachts, *Mary* and *Henrietta* and *Isabella*, sailed with him. The account of the voyage to England is taken from the log of the *Mary*, preserved in the National Maritime Museum, Greenwich. B. H. Sumner, *Peter the Great and the Emergence of Russia*, 37; Bogoslovsky, II, 335.

Chapter XIII Peter in England, 1698

1. It is often stated that, while in London, the Tsar lived at 15 Buckingham Street, which would have made him a neighbour of Samuel Pepys. It is clear, however, that he resided in a house in Norfolk Street. This house has long since been demolished and the whole street has been completely and unattractively rebuilt. See London County Council *Survey of London* (London, 1937), XVIII, Part II, 74-75, explaining how this error may have occurred.

2. This wind-dial with the map painted by Richard Norderin in 1694 may still be seen in the King's Gallery in the State Apartments of Kensington Palace.

3. In King William's reign the Kneller portrait of the Tsar was hung in the Drawing Room of Kensington Palace. It was later moved to Windsor and then to Hampton Court. About 1900 it was taken back to Kensington Palace where it now hangs in the State Apartments.

4. Dew, *History of Deptford* (London, 1884, 2nd ed.), 182.

5. The story is told that the landlord of this inn in Deptford drew a picture of the Tsar and after his departure from England the picture was hung over the door where it remained until 1808 when it was bought by a collector. A copy was hung in its place. Later the inn was rebuilt and no portrait of Peter was hung outside, although it continued to bear the name The Czars of Muscovy. (Bogoslovsky, II, 317, and J. Barrow, *Memoir of the Life of Peter the Great*, 82-83). It has not been possible to trace this tavern. A list of "taverns and public houses" in an 1826 Directory of Deptford, the earliest available, makes no mention of a tavern which could possibly have any connection with Peter. The Czars of Muscovy may be one of those legends which grew up after his visit. Deptford still contains a Czar Street which runs from Evelyn Street almost to the dockyard gates, and was so named to commemorate Peter's visit.

6. The story that Peter himself ruined Evelyn's magnificent holly hedge by trundling through it in a wheelbarrow can hardly be true, although without doubt he played his part in causing damage to the bowling green, gravel walks, and other parts of the garden. Wheelbarrows were almost unknown in Russia at this time, and those in Evelyn's garden probably interested Peter as a novelty; George London's survey of damage included an item for "three wheelbarrows . . . broken and lost." W. G. Hiscock, *John Evelyn and His Family Circle* (London, 1955), 200.

7. *Diary of John Evelyn*, ed. by Austin Dobson (London, 1906), III, 334; Dew, op. cit., 33-38, 182-83.

8. Gilbert Burnet, *History of His Own Time* (London, 1818), III, 244-46.

9. Letter from Burnet to Dr. Falla, 9/19 March. Bodleian Library MS add D 23.

10. Thomas Clarkson, *Memoirs of the Public and Private Life of William Penn* (London, 1849), 253-54; J. Barrow, op. cit., 77-79.

11. Gilbert Burnet letter to Dr. Falla, 9/19 March, loc. cit.

12. Ibid.

13. The English Government was now paying greater attention to trade with Muscovy, and attached importance to this tobacco monopoly. A sign of this new interest was that on 30 October 1699, William III appointed Mr. Goodfellow to be his minister and consul-general in Moscow; Queen Anne renewed his commission in November 1702.

14. The contract was signed on 16 April 1698: P & B, I, No. 234; O. J.

Fredericksen "Virginia Tobacco in Russia under Peter the Great" in *The Slavonic and East European Review*, American Series II (Vol. XXI, No. 56, March 1943) contains a detailed and interesting account of the beginning of the tobacco trade in Russia. Also Bogoslovsky, II, 286-87.

15. P & B, I, pp. 702-03.

16. This account of Peter's visit to Portsmouth is taken from the Log of the *Humber* in the National Maritime Museum, Greenwich.

17. Peter watched the King give the royal assent to several bills, including one imposing a land tax estimated to produce £1,500,000, a sum considerably greater than the revenue of his own country. He was very surprised to learn that Parliament by a single Act could raise such a large amount, and he remarked that England was probably a very rich country. His surprise was considerably greater when he learnt that in the previous year a Bill had been passed, which had raised a sum three times as big. Huyssen, *History of Great Russia*, quoted by A. I. Andreev in *Peter I in England in 1698* in *Peter the Great: A Symposium*, ed. by A. I. Andreev, 82.

18. The tradition is that his meetings were with the eminent mathematician Halley, who succeeded Flamsteed several years later, but there is no evidence to support this. Andreev, *op. cit.*, 71-72. While there he also walked over the great naval hospital which William III was erecting in memory of his wife, Queen Mary: the building so impressed him that he suggested to William that he should move his court to Greenwich and turn Kensington Palace into the Naval hospital.

19. On his visit to the Tower, Peter was not shown the axe that beheaded Charles I "as it was feared that he would throw it in the Thames, so as to allow no opportunity to be reminded what impression was made on his father Tsar Alexei, and on the whole Russian people by the execution of the King, when the English merchants were deprived of all their privileges, which they had to establish trade in Archangel." Andreev, *op. cit.*, 82.

20. It is most probable that Newton received Peter and Jacob Bruce on their visits to the Mint. But no record of their meetings exists, unless among Newton's unpublished papers. Andreev, *op. cit.*, 85-86.

21. The records of the University contain no mention of his visit or of his receiving an honorary degree, as has been stated. Huyssen wrote that Peter was met by an archbishop and the University authorities and conducted over Christ's College, where he was presented with several books on mathematics, translated into Russian, Andreev, *op. cit.*, 79.

The only English reference to the Oxford visit appears to be in the diary of Narcissus Lutterall (IV, 368): "Last week the Tsar of Muscovy went privately to Oxford; but, being soon discovered, he immediately came back to London without viewing those curiosities he intended."

22. P & B, I, Nos. 228, 230, and notes.

23. *Ibid.*, p. 671.

24. *Ibid.*, Nos. 205, 214, pp. 670-71; Bogoslovsky, II, 333.

25. *Ibid.*, No. 229.

26. *Ibid.*, pp. 698-700.

27. Bogoslovsky, II, 350.

28. ". . . Sir Anthony Dean's son, an ingenious gentleman, whose father, Sir Anthony (being sent into France upon some occasion by King Charles II) was said to have learn'd the French the art of building ships, for which he was

several times mobb'd when he came back, and it had like to have cost him his life." Perry, op. cit., 165-66.

29. Perry's career in the Russian service was to prove far from happy; he could never obtain his salary and met with constant obstruction in his work, as he related subsequently in his book on Russia. Perry, op. cit.

30. P & B, I, No. 233.

31. N. Hans, "The Moscow School of Mathematics and Navigation" in The Slavonic and East European Review (Vol. 29, No. 73, June 1951).

32. Writing on 30 April 1698 to Dr. Charlett, Master of University College, Oxford, and then chaplain to the King, Wanley, who was a well-known antiquary, mentioned that the Tsar "gave the King's servants, at his departure, 120 guineas, which was more than they deserved, they being very rude to him; but to the King, he presented a rough ruby, which the greatest jewellers of Amsterdam (as well Jews as Christians) valued at 10,000 sterling; 'tis bored tho' and when it's cut and polished, it must be set upon the top of the Imperial Crown of England." In a subsequent letter of 3 May, Wanley added, "In the meantime, I take the boldness to say what I told you of the Ruby I had from a jeweller, who likewise added that it is the finest he ever saw, and that it is reputed to be one of the best in the world." Bodleian MS Ballard XIII f. 59 and f. 62V.

Peter rewarded Admiral Mitchell with a rich gift including forty sables, and six pieces of damask. Bogoslovsky, II, 389.

33. Perry, op. cit., 165.

34. Huyssen, quoted by Andreev, op. cit., 88-89.

Chapter XIV   Vienna and the Return to Moscow, 1698

1. Captain Ripley found his way to Moscow and there lost his life. General Gordon wrote from Moscow to Peter in Azov on 28 June 1699 that Ripley had vanished without trace on 20 June, "and it is feared that he has committed suicide, for he has been very melancholic for a long time and often wished for death. They have been searching everywhere for his body, but have not found it."

In his next letter, dated 6 July, Gordon reported that Ripley's body had been found in the Yauza River near Preobrazhenskoe. "From investigation," he wrote, "the back of his head was beaten in; there were bruises on his right hand; the silver buttons had been cut from his coat, and his pockets had been turned out; however, it is not known whether he died by his own hand, or was murdered." The state of the body certainly suggests murder. See Ustryalov, III, 495-96 for texts of Gordon's letters.

2. On 29 March Peter wrote to Streshnev, instructing him to arrange for the Royal Transport to be taken on arrival at Archangel through Lake Kubenskoe to Vologda, thence overland to Yaroslavl and down the Volga River. Peter intended that, as soon as the Volga-Don canal was finished, the yacht should proceed to Azov to become part of his Black Sea fleet. But Franz Timmermann, who was in charge of this operation, could get her no further than Kholmogory, because she drew nearly eight feet of water. The Royal Transport returned to Archangel where she remained until 1715 when, refitted and repaired, she sailed to join Peter's Baltic fleet and was lost in a storm on the Swedish coast. The Russian Fleet During the Reign of Peter the Great by a contemporary Englishman, ed. by Vice-Admiral Cyprian Bridges, 44; P & B, I, 719-20.

3. P & B, I, pp. 725-27.

4. *Ibid.*, pp. 708-09.
5. *Ibid.*, No. 238.
6. Bogoslovsky, II, 416-17.
7. The Tessings or Thessinghs were a wealthy family trading in Russia. In the 1690's three brothers handled the family business. Frederick Tessing lived in Vologda and Jan Tessing was often in Archangel, where he first met Peter. The Tessings gave considerable help to the Grand Embassy in Amsterdam by meeting bills of exchange and purchasing naval equipment. In Amsterdam, Peter visited Jan Tessing's house and there met an Englishman who, hearing his complaints about the Dutch lack of a science of shipbuilding, advised him to go to England. Peter later used to attribute his visit to England to this piece of advice. Bogoslovsky, II, 426, 428-29; IV, 293-96. The document formally conferring the monopoly was not given to Tessing until February 1700. P & B, I, No. 291.
8. This monopoly was subject to two restrictions: 1) religious books in church Slavonic or Greek were still to be printed by the presses in Moscow; 2) Elizar Izbrandt, the Holsteiner, retained the right, granted earlier, to publish maps and descriptions of Siberia and China. Solovev, Vol. XV, Chap. 2.
9. P & B, I, No. 242, p. 730.
10. *Ibid.*, No. 246.
11. *Ibid.*, Nos. 248-52.
12. Bogoslovsky, II, 475-76.
13. *Ibid.*, 526.
14. Ustryalov, III, 474-76.
15. P & B, I, No. 252.
16. Bogoslovsky, II, 558.
17. *Ibid.*, 563.
18. Ustryalov, II, 186-87.
19. Korb, I, 179-80.

Chapter XV   The Beginning of the New Era, 1698

1. Cf. V. Klyuchevsky, *Course of Russian History*, (1925, 2nd ed.), IV, 33, and Lecture LXVIII. M. M. Bogoslovsky, *Peter the Great and His Reform*, 68. B. H. Sumner, *Survey of Russian History*, 103.
2. In later years Peter himself thought of his reforms as beginning in 1699, and specifically with the creation of a regular army. But he overlooked or had forgotten the series of changes which, although apparently minor, amounted to a full-scale assault on old Muscovy. He launched these changes on his return from Europe in August 1698, and it is from this time that his great labours of reform should be dated.
Bogoslovsky considered that his reforming activities began on a large scale with the building of the Voronezh fleet. This was certainly a great and new undertaking, but it did not initiate his deliberate policy of reforming his country so that it could stand with the Western powers on terms of equality, Bogoslovsky, IV, 170-73.
3. Perry, op. cit., 197.
4. Ustryalov, III, 193-95.
5. The law imposing the beard-tax was re-enacted in 1701 and again four years later, when a new scale of taxes was laid down. In 1715 a single tax of

fifty rubles a year was imposed on bearded Orthodox and Old Believers. All the bearded paid this tax, except peasants who wore their beards tax free when in their own villages, but had to pay one kopek on entering and leaving a town. Klyuchevsky, op. cit., IV, 165.

6. The rich and exotic costume of the Muscovite ambassadors who came to England in 1662, impressed Samuel Pepys, but aroused such laughter among Londoners that Pepys was moved to write in his diary, "but Lord! to see the absurd nature of Englishmen, that cannot forbear laughing and jeering at every-thing that looks strange." Diary of Samuel Pepys, ed. H. B. Wheatley (London, 1893), II, 402, 408.

7. Korb, I, 257.

8. Ibid., 171.

9. Ustryalov, II, App. ii, Nos. 5, 6, 16.

10. Korb, V, 158-72; Ustryalov, III, App. i.

11. Korb, I, 188.

12. Ibid., I, 164-65, 188. The translation is misleading in this passage. It was Menshikov, not Lefort, who finally quietened Peter. See Ustryalov, IV (i), 211; Bogoslovsky, III, 20-22.

13. Bogoslovsky, III, 38; Ustryalov, III, 205-06.

14. Ustryalov, III, 216, but see also Korb, I, 177.

15. According to Korb, Peter himself wielded the executioner's axe, but Korb was not present and his evidence is uncorroborated. Korb, I, 177.

16. Ibid., 192-93.

17. Ibid., 194, 209.

18. P & B, I, No. 254.

19. Later, in 1702, and 1704, when he needed every soldier he could muster, Peter partially rescinded this law, and for a time some of the old streltsi were re-enlisted.

The streltsi regiments of other towns which had not shown the same mutinous spirit as the Moscow regiments, continued to serve and later won distinction in the war against Sweden. But they, too, were disbanded after the revolt at Astrakhan in 1705. See pp. 242-43.

Chapter XVI   The Voronezh Fleet, 1698-1699

1. P & B, I, Nos. 255-56.

2. Ibid.

3. Korb, I, 222-28.

4. Ibid., 257-58.

5. Ibid.

6. Ibid.

7. Ibid., 264.

8. Ibid., 265-66.

9. Ustryalov, III, 493-94; P & B, I, pp. 760-61.

10. Korb, I, 272; Bogoslovsky, IV, 9-10; Ustryalov, III, 264-65. Neither Bogoslovsky nor Ustryalov accept that Peter could have spoken in this sense, and they reject Korb's evidence. To the present writer, the incident seems most probable.

11. Even the funeral did not pass without incident. On leaving the church after the service, the boyars for some reason disturbed the order of the procession and displaced the foreign envoys. Peter noticed the change and, learning what had

happened, muttered, "They are dogs, my boyars!" After the funeral, Peter, accompanied by everyone went to Lefort's mansion. For a moment he went outside, and the boyars, thinking he had gone, prepared to leave. Peter returned and, meeting them face to face, shouted angrily, "Ha! You are made merry at his death! It is a grand victory for you that he is dead. Why can't you all wait? I suppose, because the greatness of your joy will not allow you to keep up this forced appearance, and the feigned sorrow of your faces." Korb, I, 279.

12. Bogoslovsky, IV, 18, 52-53; P & B, I, pp. 763-64; and Nos. 264, 269.

13. Under the Treaty of Karlowitz, Austria obtained Transylvania, Hungary, and Slavonia. Venice and Poland also gained under the treaty. But the Tsar "came off with empty pockets" and he never forgave the Hapsburgs for abandoning him at Karlowitz. This treaty was an important milestone in the decline of Turkey, which had begun with her repulse from the walls of Venice in 1683. Turkey was never again to menace Europe.

14. Ustryalov, III, 271-73.

15. E. I. Ukraintsev served in the Foreign Office at the same time as Voznitsyn, to whom he was senior. He rose to a position of great trust, although at one time charges of bribery and corruption nearly brought him down.

The Imperial government lodged a strong complaint against Voznitsyn for his unprincipled behaviour at the Congress. Peter never forgave the Imperial government but he apparently blamed Voznitsyn, at least in part, for his disappointment at Karlowitz. Ukraintsev on his return from Constantinople at the end of 1700, contrived to undermine Peter's confidence in Voznitsyn completely; he was not employed again and disappeared. Bogoslovsky, III, 342-43; Sumner, Peter the Great and the Ottoman Empire, 60-61.

16. Voskresensky, Document 7. Many of Weide's letters to Peter are printed in P & B, I, pp. 770-78.

17. Voskresensky, Document 2.

18. P & B, I, pp. 773-76.

19. A few days later an incident occurred that made the whole city tremble. Captain van Pamburg had invited a number of French and Dutch acquaintances to dine with him. They drank deeply and sometime after midnight Pamburg took it into his head to fire a salvo of all guns. The noise of the cannon fire echoed through the sleeping city. The Sultan and his wives awoke in terror. Everyone thought it was the signal for the Tsar's fleet to attack and when the Sultan heard that it was due to Pamburg's high spirits he was extremely angry. The Grand Vizier sent an official to Ukraintsev to demand his punishment. But Ukraintsev, while expressing polite regrets over the incident, maintained that he had no power to punish the captain. The Sultan then threatened to send Turkish troops to arrest Pamburg. Spiritedly Pamburg replied that he would blow up his ship the moment the Sultan's men set foot on board. And this was the last that was heard of the matter.

Chapter XVII   Preparations for War with Sweden, 1699-1700

1. Ustryalov, III, 305-22.

2. Ibid., 332-35.

3. Bogoslovsky, III, 163.

4. Ustryalov, III, 341-42.

5. On the eve of his departure for Voronezh in February 1700, Peter wrote to Ukraintsev authorizing him to yield completely over the lower Dnieper forts,

surrendering them to the Turks. Apparently the letter was not despatched, but it shows Peter's impatience, and the concessions he was prepared to make. Bogoslovsky, IV, 355; P & B, I, No. 294.

6. General Alexander Gordon and Baron Langen. Ustryalov, III, 346, 348.

7. *Ibid.*, 346 and App. xi, 5.

8. P & B, I, pp. 806-07, 814-16.

9. Ustryalov, III, 346 and App. xi, 5.

10. *Diary of Patrick Gordon*, quoted by E. Schuyler, *Peter The Great*, I, 429.

11. Bogoslovsky, IV, 166-69; Korb, II, 232-35.

12. Korb makes frequent references to the punishment of coiners; see, for example, I, 228-29.

13. *Ibid.*, 200.

14. The decree of 11 March 1700 was the first step in Peter's reform of coinage. He was to return to it several times. He introduced up-to-date minting techniques and then minted coins of new denominations. In part his coinage reforms were intended to increase the national revenue, and in part to assist trade. Inevitably his depreciation of the silver coinage to the extent of 42 per cent over his whole reign led to severe increases in prices. At the end of his reign the purchasing power of the silver kopeck was about half of what it was in Tsar Alexei's reign. James Mavor, *An Economic History of Russia*, I, 135-36.

15. Voskresensky, 30-33.

16. *Ibid.*, 33-34; Ustryalov, III, 12-13, 511.

17. Bogoslovsky, IV, 288-91; Hans, *The Moscow School of Mathematics and Navigation*, loc. cit.; Solovev, XV, ii.

18. Ustryalov, III, 551.

19. Bogoslovsky, IV, 358; P & B, I, Nos. 296-97.

20. P & B, I, Nos. 306, 320.

21. *Ibid.*, Nos. 321-22.

22. Bogoslovsky, IV, 366-67.

23. *Ibid.*, 464; P & B, I, No. 297.

24. Bogoslovsky, IV, 367.

25. Khilkov left Moscow in May, and never saw his native land again. He travelled by way of Narva on which he sent a full report, but, arriving in Stockholm he found that the King had already set out for Denmark. Khilkov insisted on presenting his documents to the King personally, and received every facility from the Swedes to continue on. He reached Malmo on 31 July and there was presented to Charles XII, who showed him special courtesy. Khilkov then returned to Stockholm where, as soon as the news of the Tsar's hostilities against Narva was received, he was arrested. He died in prison in Sweden after eighteen years' imprisonment. Bogoslovsky, IV, 409-423; Ustryalov, III, 555-56.

26. Bogoslovsky, IV, 405-06; Ustryalov, III, 369-70

27. P & B, I, Nos. 312-13, 314.

28. Ustryalov, III, 553-54; P & B, I, Nos. 320-22.

29. B. H. Sumner considered that this right was "perhaps the most important outcome of Peter's relations with the Ottoman Empire. It gave Russia much better chances of information and influence, and some possibility of direct action at Constantinople, and it put her on an equality with the other powers, which had regularly resident envoys there—France, the Empire, Great Britain, the Netherlands, and Venice." Sumner, *Peter the Great and the Ottoman Empire*, 59.

30. Ustryalov, IV, i, 1-5.

31. P & B, I, Nos. 324-25.

Chapter XVIII   Charles XII and the Northern War, 1700

1. Cf. Eugene Schuyler, Peter the Great, I, 468.
2. Ustryalov, IV (ii), App. ii, 1.
3. Estimates of the size of the Russian army have at times been fanciful. Some Swedish sources have stated that 80,000 and even 100,000 Russians were present. Alexander Gordon, who was at Narva, stated that the Russian army contained 34,000 men, while Hallart, the Saxon siege engineer, gave the figure of 30,000 men. Ustryalov's figure of 40,000 men based on the official records of the strength of each regiment is probably close to the truth. The number actually opposing the Swedes was less, as Alexander Gordon points out: "For the Russian army, whatever some authors have amused the world with, did not amount even to the numbers foresaid; considering that there ought to be some allowance made for the dead, killed and wounded, during a siege of above two months; and likewise, it is to be considered, that four thousand men were employed from the beginning, on the other side of the river before Ivangorod, who could not be attacked nor of use to those who were so, consequently they marched off with their artillery etc., undisturbed." Alexander Gordon, History of Peter the Great, 150-51; Ustryalov, IV, 9; Adlerfeld, I, 56.
4. Ustryalov, IV (ii), App. i, 4.
5. Charles Eugene, Duke von Croy, belonged to an ancient Netherlands House. He was forty-nine years old at the time of the battle of Narva, and had had wide military experience. At the age of twenty-five he had entered the service of Christian V of Denmark and had fought against Sweden, soon after winning the rank of Lieutenant-General. When peace was signed in the north, he entered the Imperial army and distinguished himself in fighting against the Turks. Finally he was given command of the Imperial forces in Hungary, but at Belgrade, learning of the approach of the Grand Vizir with a vast army, he raised the siege and retreated. He was strongly criticized for this action and, resigning his command, he left the Imperial service. Ustryalov, IV (i), 60-61.
6. Ustryalov, IV (ii), App. ii, 13.
7. Ibid., App. ii, Nos. 4, 6, 10, 18, 25-27.
8. In one of the skirmishes with a party of Swedes from the garrison at this time, Captain of Cavalry Bauer, who had been a prisoner at large in Narva, escaped to the Russians. He declared that he was a subject of King Augustus, and gave valuable information about the defences of Narva. Peter was suspicious and disinclined to accept Bauer's intelligence, until Hallart vouched for him. He was returned to Augustus, but subsequently enlisted in the Russian service in which he won distinction.
9. Ustryalov, IV (i), 20; IV (ii), App. ii, 17.
10. Ibid., IV (i) 21-22; IV (ii) App. ii, 35.
11. Jan Gummert, an Esthonian, had risen in the course of two years from sergeant to captain of the guards regiment, as well as receiving a house in Moscow and 4,000 rubles in gifts. Peter at first thought that he had been captured, for he could not believe that Gummert would defect. But it was soon beyond question that he had turned traitor. On his return to Moscow on 19 December 1700, Peter had a gallows placed in front of Gummert's house with him hanging in effigy, and a description in Russian and German of his crime.
12. Ustryalov, IV (ii), App. ii, 47.
13. P & B, I, Nos. 343-44.
14. Alexander Gordon, op. cit., I, 149.

15. Ustryalov, IV (i), 34.

16. *Ibid.*, and IV (ii), App. iv, 4-5.

17. Alexander Gordon wrote subsequently: "On hearing of the defeat and disaster of his army, [the Tsar] was much struck at first; but recollecting himself, said, 'I know very well, the Swedes will for some time beat us, but at length we may learn to beat them.' " Alexander Gordon, *op. cit.*, I, 155.

18. Ustryalov, IV (i), 49.

19. *Ibid.*

20. The official Swedish announcement of the victory claimed that Russian losses amounted to 18,000 men. Alexander Gordon estimated them at 12,000 men, while Hallart gave the figure of 8,000 to 9,000 men. Ustryalov calculated that from the regiments reassembled in Novgorod after the battle the losses were 5,700 men, to which must be added the 1,000 men lost from Sheremetev's cavalry detachment. It is improbable that the total losses were greatly in excess of 8,000. Adlerfeld, I, 56; Alexander Gordon, *op. cit.*, I, 154; Ustryalov, IV (i), 51, and (ii), App. iv, 1.

21. Ustryalov, IV (ii), App. ii, 107, C and D.

22. The Duke von Croy was heavily in debt at his death. Peter made enquiries about the amount he owed, intending to pay it himself, but apparently this was never done. His creditors in Reval invoked an old law which denied burial to insolvent debtors and the Duke's body was placed unburied in the vault of the church of St. Nicholas. Here it remained, clad in wig and uniform, and under glass for nearly two hundred years. The atmosphere of the church contained preservatives, for the body did not decay, but became mummified. Visitors to Reval were regularly taken to see this curiosity, until towards the end of the nineteenth century when the Russian Government had the body interred. Schuyler, *op. cit.*, 489; Ustryalov, IV (i), 60.

Chapter XIX   The Aftermath of Narva, 1700-1702

1. Ustryalov, IV (i), 69-70, IV (ii), App. ii, 54.

2. *Ibid.*, IV (ii), App. vi, No. 6.

3. P & B, I, No. 369.

4. No record of this ukaz exists in the state archives, according to Ustryalov, but Peter himself refers to it in the history of the Swedish war. Ustryalov, IV (i), 70-71.

5. *Ibid.*

6. P & B, I, No. 374.

7. *Ibid.*, No. 370.

8. *Ibid.*

9. Perry, *op. cit.*, 7.

10. P & B, I, Nos. 346-47.

11. Ustryalov, IV (i), 75.

12. R. Nisbet Bain, *Charles XII and the Collapse of the Swedish Empire* (1902 ed.), 79-80.

13. P & B, I, No. 350.

14. Ustryalov, IV (ii), App. ii, 94.

15. *Ibid.*, App. ii, 83.

16. Count MacDonnell, who made the English translation of the *Diary*, stated that the Imperial court "allowed the unsold copies to be destroyed," and that Peter's agents hunted down and destroyed stray copies. Not more than

a dozen copies of the original publication are still existing, of which one is in the British Museum.

The Diary is an invaluable and, on the whole, reliable source of detailed information, and it is free of malice and distortion. The Russians could hardly challenge its statements except possibly on some points of detail, although they had grounds for complaining that its publication at this time was an act of unfriendliness. See Count MacDonnell's Preface to Korb, iii-x.

17. Ustryalov, IV (ii), App. ii, 126.
18. Ibid., IV (i), 84-86.
19. The Patriarch was elected by an assembly of metropolitans, archbishops, bishops, archimandrites, and abbots, summoned by the Tsar's ukaz, and meeting in the Patriarchal Palace. The Tsar confirmed their choice. Without the Tsar's ukaz the ecclesiastical assembly did not meet, and without his approval the Patriarch-elect could not be consecrated. Often the Tsar himself selected the Metropolitan or Archbishop to be elected to the patriarchal throne, and the assembly gave effect to his wishes; Tsar Alexei, for example, virtually appointed Nikon to the patriarchate. Ustryalov, IV (i), 536-37.
20. Ustryalov, IV (ii), App. ii, 34.
21. Ibid., IV (i), 91-92.
22. P & B, I, No. 365; Ustryalov, IV (ii), App. i, 18.
23. Ustryalov, IV (i), 98.
24. Ibid., IV (i), 106-07; IV (ii), App. ii, 106.
25. Ibid., IV (i), 115.

Chapter XX   Catherine

1. Little is known of Catherine before she became a captive of the Russians. There are many conflicting accounts of her origin. Her birthplace has been said to be Livonia, Poland, Esthonia, Sweden, and Lithuania. Some have denied that she was of peasant stock and have claimed noble blood for her. A story so romantic invites embroidery.

The account followed here is that of F. C. Weber, the Hanoverian resident in Moscow. He obtained it from Gottfried Wurm, who in 1714 went from Moscow to St. Petersburg where he taught Russian to Weber and other foreigners. Wurm, as tutor to Gluck's children, lived in the house at the same time as Catherine and was thus in a position to learn both from the pastor and from Catherine herself. Wurm assured Weber that Catherine always behaved very correctly in the pastor's house and gave no trouble to anyone.

F. C. Weber, Das Veränderte Russland (1721), Part II, 24-25, Part III, 6-10. These passages have been omitted from the English translation, published in London in 1722 under the title The Present State of Russia. Ustryalov, IV (i), Chap. 5; W. Coxe, Travels into Poland, Russia, Sweden and Denmark (London, 1787, 3rd ed.), II, 398-434.

2. Waliszewski has written of the "legion of chance mistresses, who flit across the personal history of Peter the Great," and of his illegitimate posterity being almost as numerous as that of Louis XIV. He has even suggested that Peter was homosexual in his relations with Menshikov and with others; he gives no evidence for this statement which, like similar allegations concerning Peter's private life, is an echo of the gossip of the day.

Waliszewski is as unreliable in his selection as in his use of material and needs to be read with caution. K. Waliszewski, Peter the Great, I, 250-51, 236.

3. Catherine was known as Ekaterina Vasilevna, until she was accepted into the Orthodox faith, when she became Ekaterina Alexeevna, in honour of her new godfather, who was Tsarevich Alexei, Peter's son by his first wife. Alexander Gordon, op. cit., II, 258.

4. Ibid., II, 274-75.

5. Alexander Gordon states that Anna was soon afterwards married to Kaiserling, but that she was so chagrined by the Tsar's anger that she died a year later. It is not clear that she was married; certainly if she was, she was separated from her husband who was recalled to Prussia. Anna Mons did not die until August 1714, some ten years later. See Alexander Gordon, op. cit., II, 274-76, whose account of the fall of Anna Mons has been followed here.

6. Ibid., 258-59.

7. Four were sons, two named Pcter and two named Paul, all of whom died in infancy. Of the eight daughters, only two, Anna and Elizabeth, survived.

8. Campredon Despatches. Sbornik I.R.I.O., XLIX, 287.

9. Ernst Gluck reached Moscow with his family in January 1703. Peter received him with every kindness and two months later appointed him to establish a school in Moscow. He made Gluck a grant of 3,000 rubles, with which he was to engage suitable teachers, and he allotted as school premises the house on the Pokrovka of the Boyar Vasily Naryshkin, who had only just died. Gluck moved there from the Foreign Quarter, drew up in Russian an extensive programme of studies and appointed seven teachers, one of whom was Gottfried Wurm. The school was opened, but Gluck died before he could properly establish it. Ustryalov, IV (i), 142-44.

Chapter XXI   Reforms: Peter in Archangel, 1702

1. Ustryalov, IV (i), 155.

2. Ibid., IV (ii), App. (ii) 123.

3. Solovev, XV, ii, 1344; P & B, II, No. 421 & pp. 337-40; Ustryalov, IV (i), 162-63.

4. Ustryalov, IV (i), 184.

5. Solovcv, XV, ii, 1358.

6. Whitworth to Harley, 26 November 1706. Sbornik I.R.I.O., XXXIX, 342.

7. Whitworth to Harley, 3 May 1705. Ibid., 80.

8. P & B, II, No. 434.

9. A month later Afanasy died. He was widely loved and respected. Peter had been particularly attached to him since his first visit to Archangel nine years earlier. He had even at one time thought of elevating him to the patriarchate. Ustryalov, IV (i), 190.

10. P & B, II, No. 445.

11. Ibid., App. ii, 144.

12. P & B, II, No. 444.

13. Ibid., No. 448.

Chapter XXII   Conquest of Ingria, 1702-1703

1. P & B, II, Nos. 450, 452.

2. P & B, II, No. 458.

3. To mark the event he ordered a medal to be struck, bearing the inscription: "It has been in enemy hands for ninety years." In a note explaining the plan

of the siege of Noteburg, Peter wrote, "In this way, by God's help, our national fortress was recovered, having been unjustly in enemy hands for ninety-two years." (P & B, II, 110, 423.) Schlusselburg is now known as Petrokrepost.

4. P & B, II, No. 462.

5. *Ibid.*, No. 459.

6. *Ibid.*, Nos. 460-61, 463-65.

7. Pleyer, the Imperial resident in Moscow, reported to his Emperor that according to rumour, Menshikov was not of great birth. "Alexashka called himself Menshikov, perhaps, to hide his lowly origin or else to advance himself with the Tsar. Menshikov means minimus." (Ustryalov, IV (ii), App. vi, 17.) Whitworth reported that Menshikov was "of a very base extraction." Sbornik I.R.I.O., XXXIX, 124.

8. Ustryalov, IV (i), 207-08.

9. P & B, V, No. 1779.

10. Alexander Gordon, op. cit., II, 274.

11. It is strange that Menshikov should have remained semi-literate all his life. He could read, but wrote with difficulty. Ustryalov states that many thousands of his letters and papers have been preserved, all written by an amanuensis and bearing only his signature. To this there are only two exceptions; on one he wrote "Alexander Menshikov received," and on the other "Alexander Menshikov received and acknowledged"; in both cases the writing is laboured and shaky. (Ustryalov, IV (i), 210; Alexander Gordon, op. cit., II, 274.) Whitworth reported: "I am credibly informed he [Menshikov] cannot write or read and, as his birth deprived him of the advantages of education, so his stepping into the highest post without any subaltern employments, gave him no time to make his own observations or to get experience." Sbornik I.R.I.O., XXXIX, 125.

12. Alexander Gordon, op. cit., II, 277.

13. Solovev, XV, ii, Col. 1349.

14. *Ibid.*

15. Peter was at this time increasingly distracted by the war with Sweden and, having no real interest in the theatre, he did not give the attention to it that he gave to other ventures.

The theatre on the Red Square was closed down in 1706 and demolished in 1707. The properties and costumes were taken to Preobrazhenskoe where Tsarevna Natalya established her own court theatre, which she later moved to St. Petersburg.

S. S. Ignatov, "The Theatre of the Petrine Epoch," in *History of the Russian Theatre*, I, 69, 75.

16. P & B, II, Nos. 377, 379.

17. *Ibid.*, II, No. 395.

18. *Ibid.*, II, No. 419.

19. Peter Tolstoy became one of the most outstanding of Peter's officials, although he began under a cloud. He had been a strong supporter of Peter's opponents, Sofia and the Miloslavsky, and had taken an active part in stirring the streltsi to revolt in May 1689. After the fall of Sofia he came over to the side of Peter who did not trust him and gave him a minor post as voevod of Ustyug. But Tolstoy took part in the second Azov campaign and, although over fifty, he subsequently volunteered to study seamanship and navigation in Italy. Gradually he won Peter's trust and his appointment to Constantinople was the result. On his return to Moscow he was highly rewarded and thereafter Peter entrusted him with difficult tasks and made him head of the secret chancellery.

Unscrupulous, intelligent and able, sinister and cunning, Tolstoy was well
equipped for this office.
20. P & B, II, Nos. 490-93.
21. Perry, op. cit., 8-10.
22. P & B, II, Nos. 497, 511.
23. Ibid., No. 500.
24. Ibid., No. 513.
25. Ibid., No. 516.
26. Peter was the sixth knight of the Order of St. Andrew. The first was
Admiral Feodor Golovin; second, Hetman Mazepa; third, the Brandenburg envoy, Printzen; fourth, Field-Marshal Sheremetev; fifth, the Saxon Chancellor,
Count Beichling.
27. P & B, II, Nos. 523-25, pp. 547-49.

Chapter XXIII   The Foundation of St. Petersburg, 1703-1706

1. The story is told that Peter, taking the musket of a soldier, cut two sods
with the bayonet, and, laying them cross-wise, said, "Here shall be a town!"
Soldiers then dug a trench in which Peter buried a casket containing relics of
St. Andrew the Apostle, and gold coins. At this moment an eagle flew over
his head and alighted on two birch trees, which had been tied at the top to
form a kind of arch, marking the position of the future gate of the fort. Another
version is that the eagle, as it soared over the Tsar's head, was brought to ground
by a musket shot. Peter took the wounded bird, placed it on his wrist, where
it sat, as he set off in a boat to see the neighbouring island. M. I. Pylyaev, Old St.
Petersburg, 9.
2. Perry, op. cit., 300.
3. The Summer Garden, Summer Palace, and The Little House of Peter I,
by O. N. Kuznetsovaya and others (Leningrad, 1955).
4. Peter wrote Sankt-Peterburkh or Peterburkh in letters to those close to him,
Sanktpetersburg in communications with foreign governments, and occasionally
S-Petersburg. In later years the name of the city was written Sanktpeterburg or
S-Peterburg. Colloquially it was often known simply as Piter. During the 1914-
1918 War, the Germanic form was discarded and the city was officially called
Petrograd, the Slavonic form which Slavophils had used for some years. In 1924,
St. Petersburg was renamed Leningrad.
5. P & B, II, No. 588.
6. Adlerfeld states that the Russians numbered 25,000 men and that the
Swedish losses were slight. Peter's account of the size of his force is certainly more
reliable. In general Peter was always accurate in his reports, and disinclined to
exaggerate or distort. This applies neither to the Swedes, nor to the Russian
commanders. Adlerfeld, I, 239-40; P & B, II, Nos. 553-54.
7. Ustryalov, IV (ii), App. vi, No. 27.
8. P & B, III, No. 647; Ustryalov, IV (i), 250-51.
9. Ustryalov, IV (i), 252.
10. P & B, III, No. 723.
11. Ibid., No. 909.
12. L. A. Nikiforov, Russian-English Relations in the Reign of Peter I,
34-36.
13. P & B, III, No. 655.

14. Adlerfeld, III, 163-64.
15. Ustryalov, IV (i), 263-69; IV (ii), App. ii, Nos. 210, 304.
16. Ibid., IV (ii), App. ii, 215; P & B, IV (i), No. 1349; Ustryalov, IV (i), App. i, No. 162.
17. P & B, III, Nos. 636, 672.
18. Ibid., Nos. 1194, 1349.
19. Whitworth to Harley, 19 June 1706. Sbornik I.R.I.O., XXXIX, 279-80.
20. Ustryalov, IV (i), 274.

Chapter XXIV   Dorpat and Narva, 1703-1704

1. P & B, II, pp. 609-10.
2. Ibid., No. 566.
3. Ibid., No. 572.
4. Ustryalov, IV (i), 280, 283-84; P & B, II, No. 655.
5. Ustryalov, IV (i), 306-08.
6. Adlerfeld, II, 13.
7. P & B, III, No. 673.
8. Ibid., pp. 640-41.
9. Ibid., No. 679-81.
10. Adlerfeld, II, 22-23.
11. It is said that Peter struck Horn across the face for his insulting message sent in reply to Ogilvie's letter, but it was Horn's obstinacy in refusing to surrender, when the position was hopeless, that infuriated Peter, whose treatment of Horn contrasted with Charles XII's behaviour on a similar occasion. The incidents illustrate the difference between the two adversaries in their attitude towards war.

At Dunamunde, the Saxon Colonel Danitz had resisted to the last. Charles XII was delighted with his bravery and obstinacy, and had him brought into his presence. "You are my enemy," he said to him, "and yet I love you as well as my best friend, for you have behaved like a brave soldier in the defence of this fort against my troops; and to show you that I can esteem and reward valour even in my enemies, I make you a present of these five thousand ducats." Of the Saxon garrison of 1,700 men in the fortress at the beginning of the siege, there remained only seventy at the surrender. Adlerfeld, I, 102.

12. Whitworth to Harley, the Secretary of State, 14 March 1705. Sbornik I.R.I.O., XXXIX, 56.

13. P & B, III, Nos. 694-99, pp. 659-61.

14. Prepared to go to almost any lengths to avoid war with the Turks until he had defeated the Swedes, Peter even sent secret instructions to Tolstoy, in December 1703, to be acted on only as a last resort, to offer to withdraw Russian ships from the sea to Azov, or to sell them to the Turks, also to destroy the fortress of Kamenny Zaton, but not Taganrog.

Tolstoy did not have to make these concessions. In any case they were no more than a gesture. The Russian ships, built of unseasoned timber, were of little value, but Peter's shipyards at Voronezh were actively turning out new ships and his retention of Taganrog showed that he had no intention of abandoning his long term plans of challenging the Turks in the Black Sea. T. K. Krylova, "Russian-Turkish Relations During the Northern War" in Istoricheskie Zapiski (Moscow, 1941), 255, 267.

15. P & B, III, No. 755.

Chapter XXV   *Grodno, 1705-1706*

1. P & B, II, No. 560.
2. *Ibid.*, III, No. 788.
3. Ustryalov, IV (ii), App. ii, No. 39.
4. P & B, III, No. 387.
5. Subsequently a proclamation was also issued from Rome and circulated to all bishoprics. It gave a different account of the incident. It related that Peter, pressed by his own Orthodox bishops, finally agreed to destroy the Uniat church. He ordered the ikons of St. Josaphat to be torn down in Vitebsk, and arrived in Polotsk intending to burn the holy relics of the saint. On 11 July he went to the Uniat church and provoked the massacre in which nine (not five) priests were killed. Further, when a group of noblewomen came on the scene and, seeing the corpses of the priests, began to weep, Peter ordered his troops to cut off their nipples. He then sacked the altar and closed up the church, threatening to treat the Jesuits in the same way.

Of the two accounts of this incident, the Russian is the most acceptable, and there is confirmation of many of its details. The statement issued from Rome abounds in inaccuracies and improbabilities. Ustryalov, IV (i), 370-73, and IV (ii), App. ii, No. 298, prints both accounts in full.

6. P & B, III, No. 862.
7. *Ibid.*, No. 864.
8. *Ibid.*, No. 1005.
9. Ustryalov, IV (ii), App. ii, Nos. 352, 356.
10. P & B, IV (i), Nos. 1025-26.
11. Ustryalov, IV (ii), App. ii, No. 354.
12. *Ibid.*, Nos. 354, 357, 359.
13. *Ibid.*, No. 357.
14. P & B, IV (i), No. 1054.
15. *Ibid.*, Nos. 1064, 1067.
16. In his first excitement and anger on receiving this news, Peter believed that Patkul was responsible for this defeat, and wrote to Golovin that "in this very event [i.e. the defeat of the Saxons] the treason of Patkul will be clear." (P & B, IV (i), No. 1117.) It was a groundless and unjust charge.
17. P & B, IV (i), Nos. 1118-20, 1135.
18. Ustryalov, IV (ii), App. ii, Nos. 385, 390.
19. P & B, IV (i), No. 1212, and IV (ii), pp. 851-54.
20. *Ibid.*, No. 1220.
21. P & B, III, Nos. 927-28.
22. *Ibid.*, Nos. 1019, 1021-22.
23. Ustryalov, IV (ii), App. ii, 331.
24. *Ibid.*, 340.
25. *Ibid.*, and Sbornik I.R.I.O., XXXIX, 227-32.
26. Ustryalov, IV (ii), App. ii, 342.
27. *Ibid.*, IV (i), 415.
28. *Ibid.*, 423.
29. P & B, IV (i), No. 1017.
30. *Ibid.*, No. 1030.
31. On Peter's instructions, Feodor Golovin wrote to Straatman on 13 January

1706, cancelling the agreement, and stating that Patkul had acted wholly contrary to his orders; "he was ordered only in case of extreme need to negotiate the transfer of the troops to the Emperor." Patkul's interpretation of his orders, as contained in Golovin's letter of 3 October 1705 can only be considered honest and reasonable. Moreover, he had negotiated the agreement with Straatman after establishing that it was impossible to march through Poland, and that his officers were satisfied that the troops would die of cold or starve if they remained in Saxony. Ustryalov, IV (ii), App. ii, 342.

32. Ustryalov, IV (ii), App. ii, 341.

33. P & B, IV (i), Nos. 1110-12.

34. Ustryalov, IV (ii), App. ii, No. 407.

Chapter XXVI   The Treaty of Altranstadt, 1706-1707

1. Adlerfeld, II, 270-81.

2. The most illustrious of the ambassadors to appear at Charles's court was the Duke of Marlborough. He shared the general misgiving that Charles might disturb the balance between the Grand Alliance and France. He even had it in mind that he might have to check the Swedes in battle, and, from what he learnt of the Swedish army while in Saxony, he had no great fears of the outcome of such an action. But this proved unnecessary. On 16 April 1707, he had a meeting lasting four hours with Charles, and he left Altranstadt satisfied that Charles had no intention of assisting France, for his ruling purpose was to conquer Russia and to deal with Peter as he had dealt with Augustus. W. S. Churchill, Marlborough: His Life and Times (London, 1936), III, 247-56.

3. P & B, IV (i), No. 1304, and IV (ii), pp. 990-96.

4. Sbornik I.R.I.O., XXXIX, 124.

5. P & B, IV (i), No. 1391.

6. Ustryalov, IV (ii), App. ii, 452.

7. P & B, IV (i), No. 1361.

8. Ibid., Nos. 1417, 1404.

9. Menshikov reported that Mardefeld's army consisted of 5,000 Swedish cavalry, 3,000 Swedish infantry, and 20,000 Poles and that 5,000 Swedes and 1,000 Poles had lost their lives in battle. Adlerfeld stated that Mardefeld's Swedish troops amounted "to few more than 4,000 men." Adlerfeld, II, 292; P & B, IV (ii), 1195-1200.

10. P & B, IV (i), No. 1417, and IV (ii), pp. 1195-1200, 1211.

11. Adlerfeld, II, 270, 281.

12. Ustryalov, IV (ii), App. ii, 452.

13. Goltz joined the Russian service four months later (2 June 1707) as a General of Cavalry. P & B, V, p. 576.

14. Ibid., pp. 575-78.

15. Ibid., Nos. 1690-93.

16. Sbornik I.R.I.O., XXXIX, 347.

17. The Journal of Peter the Great states that the Saxon ministers handed over Patkul to the Swedes on 9 September 1706, but see Adlerfeld, II, 31. The Journal also relates that the Swedish officer in charge of the execution of Patkul was cashiered because he had Patkul's head cut off while he was alive; the King's order had been for him to die in agony, and then be executed and quartered. Journal, 161.

Chapter XXVII Discontent and Rebellion, 1700-1708

1. P & B, IV (i), No. 1428.
2. *Ibid.*, V, No. 1525.
3. Captain Perry observed that "many hundreds of coats were cut in this way at the gates of Moscow, and being done with good humour, it occasioned mirth among the people, and soon broke the custom of their wearing long coats, especially in places near Moscow and those other towns wherever the Tsar came." He also noted that the women took to the new fashions more readily than the men, particularly as, by the Tsar's orders, they could now take part in social entertainments. Perry, *op. cit.*, p. 198.
4. The usual method of reporting suspicion and denouncing treason was to cry out "Word and Deed of the Tsar." This simple formula inspired terror. The Secret Office carried out a thorough investigation of all allegations. Everyone concerned, no matter how remotely, was arrested and examined under torture. The investigation continued until the charge was proved false or the guilty had been executed.
5. The successor of the Secret Office was known as the Third Section of His Imperial Majesty's Chancery, and its descendants have been the OGPU, CHEKA, NKVD, and MVD.
6. Solovev, XV, ii, Cols. 1368-70.
7. *Ibid.*
8. *Ibid.*
9. *Ibid.*
10. *Ibid.*
11. *Ibid.*
12. *Ibid.*
13. *Ibid.*
14. *Ibid.*, Cols. 1371-72.
15. Sbornik I.R.I.O., XXXIX, 466.
16. P & B, VI, No. 2121, pp. 608-09.
17. *Ibid.*
18. *Ibid.*, No. 1852.
19. Solovev, XV, iii, Col. 1453.
20. P & B, VI, No. 2068.
21. *Ibid.*, VII (ii), p. 649.
22. Solovev, XV, iii, Col. 1457.
23. *Ibid.*
24. *Ibid.*, Col. 1459.
25. P & B, VII (i), No. 2553.

Chapter XXVIII The Year of Diplomacy, 1707

1. P & B, V, No. 1490.
2. *Ibid.*
3. *Ibid.*, Nos. 1505-06, 1491.
4. *Ibid.*, No. 1532.
5. *Ibid.*, No. 1528.
6. *Ibid.*, No. 1499.

7. *Ibid.*, No. 1573, pp. 453-54.
8. *Ibid.*, No. 1519, pp. 393-94.
9. *Ibid.*, Nos. 1602, 1631-32, pp. 404-05, 519, 548-49.
10. *Ibid.*, p. 551.
11. *Ibid.*, VI, No. 1944, and V, pp. 590-95.
12. *Ibid.*, V, pp. 676-78, No. 1669.
13. *Ibid.*, pp. 677-78.
14. *Ibid.*, pp. 575-78, Nos. 1526, 1647.
15. *Ibid.*, V, No. 1709.
16. *Ibid.*, Nos. 1721, 1773, 1833.
17. *Ibid.*, VI, pp. 295-97.
18. *Ibid.*, No. 1865.
19. *Ibid.*, No. 1885, p. 270.
20. *Ibid.*, No. 1977.
21. *Ibid.*, V, pp. 556-57.
22. *Ibid.*, p. 551.
23. Sbornik I.R.I.O., XXXIX, 24.
24. *Ibid.*, pp. 1-7.
25. *Ibid.*, pp. 49-50, 101-07, 134-42, and O. J. Fredericksen, "Virginia Tobacco in Russia under Peter the Great" (*loc. cit.*)
26. P & B, III, No. 787, pp. 770-71; Sbornik I.R.I.O., XXXIX, 88-89, 122-23.
27. Sbornik I.R.I.O., XXXIX, 112.
28. *Ibid.*, 115.
29. *Ibid.*, 39-40.
30. *Ibid.*, 92-93, p. 224.
31. Apparently Huyssen also approached Marlborough on the continent, for he reported that the Duke would like a Russian principality. A note in Peter's hand has survived, stating that Huyssen could offer him the choice of the principalities of Kiev, Vladimir, or Siberia. At the same time Huyssen was to induce him to persuade the Queen to help in obtaining a good peace with the Swedes, and he could promise Marlborough as a reward, if this peace was achieved, an annual pension of 50,000 ducats to the end of his days, a ruby without peer in Europe, and the Order of St. Andrew. P & B, V, No. 1551; IV (i), Nos. 1401, 1432-34, pp. 1145-54.
32. Coxe's *Memoirs of the Duke of Marlborough* (London, 1820, 2nd ed.), III, 165.
33. Solovev, XV, iv, Col. 1533.

Chapter XXIX   The March on Russia, 1707-1708

1. P & B, VI, No. 1921.
2. *Ibid.*, VI, Nos. 2004, 2960, 2999, 3015; Solovev, XVI, i, Col. 16.
3. P & B, VI, No. 2086.
4. *Ibid.*, No. 2081.
5. *Ibid.*, No. 2053, 2068.
6. Sbornik I.R.I.O., XXXIX, 464.
7. *Ibid.*, 448-49.
8. Solovev, XV, iv, Col. 1474.
9. Solovev, and other historians following him, have stated that Charles knew that Peter was in Grodno when he attacked. But Adlerfeld, who was with the

Swedish army, wrote that "the King of Sweden knew not that the Tsar was so near him." Adlerfeld, III, 1.

10. Solovev, XV, iv, Cols. 1475-76.
11. Ibid.
12. The Russians claimed 1,200 Swedes killed, while their own losses in killed and wounded were 336 men (Journal, 188-89). Adlerfeld claimed 3,000 Russians killed, and stated that Swedish losses were 81 officers and 255 men killed, and 1,219 wounded. (Adlerfeld, III, 28-29).
13. P & B, VIII (i), Nos. 2468, 2485-86; Sbornik I.R.I.O., XXXIX, 38, 40.
14. P & B, VIII (i), Nos. 2592, 2594-95, 2597.
15. Adlerfeld, III, 40-49.
16. P & B, VIII (i), Nos. 2660-61.
17. Ibid., Nos. 2667, 2669.
18. Ibid., No. 2681.
19. Ibid., No. 2732.
20. Journal, 205. This account of the battle of Lesnaya has been taken from the letters and reports of Peter. He was factual in his statements, not given to exaggeration, and always ready to pay tribute to his enemy. Apart from minor variations his reports are consistent and to the present writer they bear the stamp of truth. For some reason Western historians have usually accepted Swedish figures, although Swedish accounts of the Northern War, as exemplified by Adlerfeld, are exaggerated and extenuatory.

Adlerfeld stated that Lewenhaupt's force numbered 6,000 while the Russians were 30,000 strong (III, 59). Nisbet Bain wrote of Lewenhaupt's force of 11,000 men, although at Lesnaya they had become 8,000, while the Russians numbered 30,000 troops, reinforced by "some say as many as 15,000" (Nisbet Bain, Charles XII and the Great Northern War, 598-99, and Charles XII and the Collapse of the Swedish Empire, 171-72). B. H. Sumner, too, put Lewenhaupt's force at 11,000 men (Peter the Great and the Emergence of Russia, 70). The Journal stated that at first Peter had no intelligence of the size of the Swedish force, but rumour put it at 8,000 men. Prisoners taken by Menshikov and Pflug stated that it was 16,000 strong. This figure was confirmed by the captured Swedish Adjutant-General Knorring and other officers who reported that 13,000 Swedes were engaged at first, 3,000 having been sent on to Propoisk, whence they were recalled and they took part in the final action.

Peter also listed the Russian regiments, which comprised 14,001 men, including Bauer's reinforcement of 4,096 dragoons. The figure of 30,000 is fanciful. In fact the main reason for Peter's jubilation was that his troops, although inferior in numbers, had won a pitched battle against the Swedes. Journal, 200-09; P & B, VIII (i), Nos. 2681, 2723 26, 2731.
21. P & B, VIII (i), Nos. 2723-26, 2731-32, 2734.

Chapter XXX   Mazepa

1. P & B, VIII (i), No. 2759.
2. Ibid., Nos. 2760-63.
3. Ibid., Nos. 2767-72.
4. Ibid., No. 2764.
5. Ibid., No. 2786.
6. Solovev, XV, iv, Col. 1485.
7. Pushkin's poem, Poltava, describes dramatically the story of Matrena

Kochubei and her father's attempts to bring Mazepa down. Pushkin called her Maria, and it is by this name that she is usually known.
8. Solovev, XV, iv, Col. 1489.
9. Ibid., Cols. 1490-91.
10. Ibid., Col. 1518.
11. Ibid., Col. 1519.
12. Ibid., Col. 1520.
13. P & B, VIII (i), No. 2807.
14. Solovev, XV, iv, Col. 1527.

Chapter XXXI Poltava, 1709

1. P & B, VIII (i), Nos. 2887-88.
2. Ibid., No. 2816.
3. Alexander Gordon, op. cit., I, 289-91; P & B, VIII (i), Nos. 2910, 2912, 2929, 2941; IX, No. 2986.
4. P & B, VIII (i), Nos. 2760, 2772, 2793, 2800, 2845.
5. Solovev, XV, iv, Col. 1537.
6. P & B, IX, Nos. 3039, 3059.
7. Ibid., VIII (i), Nos. 2844, 2850, 2888.
8. Ibid., No. 2850.
9. Ibid., IX, No. 3062.
10. Ibid., No. 3177-79.
11. Ibid., No. 3185.
12. Ibid., No. 3191.
13. Solovev, XV, iv, Col. 1548.
14. P & B, IX, Nos. 3203-04.
15. Solovev, XV, iv, Col. 1548.
16. Journal, 234.
17. P & B, IX (i), No. 3251; (ii), pp. 980-83.
18. It is sometimes stated that only after learning that Charles had been wounded did Peter take the decision to throw his army across the Vorskla River and to engage the Swedes.
According to the Journal, news of Charles's wound reached Peter on 25 June, when his army was already entrenched in positions from which the attack on the Swedes was to be launched.
The Journal also states that Charles was wounded in an engagement with a band of Cossacks, whom he surprised when reconnoitering the Russian camp. Nisbet Bain, Charles XII and the Collapse of the Swedish Empire, 184. Journal, 235, and J. F. C. Fuller, The Decisive Battles of the Western World (London, 1955), II, 175.
19. R. Nisbet Bain and others have stated that at this point Peter was on the point of panic and flight. No evidence for the statement is given and the present writer has been unable to find any evidence. From Russian sources and from the subsequent action, when Peter displayed conspicuous bravery in command, it seems highly improbable. Nisbet Bain, Charles XII and the Collapse of the Swedish Empire, 188; Fuller, op. cit., II, 181.
20. Solovev, XV, iv, Col. 1553.
21. Journal, 241-42.
22. P & B, IX (i), No. 3266.
23. Ibid., IX (i), No. 3281, pp. 1021-22.
24. Ibid., IX, No. 3259.

Chapter XXXII The Aftermath of Poltava, 1709-1717

1. Prokopovich, the son of poor parents, managed as a youth to gain admission to the Kiev Academy. He had a flaming personality, outstanding ability, great eloquence, and a good voice. Soon he had absorbed all that Kiev could offer. He went abroad, studying in Lvov, Cracov, Florence, Pisa, and even in Rome, where he devoted his attention both to science and theology. He also studied under the Jesuits on whom he made a strong impression, but he rebuffed all attempts to convert him, and his investigations of Roman Catholicism not only confirmed him in his Orthodoxy, by made him an opponent of the papacy. From Italy he went for a time to Switzerland and then, in 1702, he returned to Kiev, confirmed in his Orthodox faith, but also convinced of the need for reform in the church and for education in Russia. P. Pekarsky, *Science and Literature in Russia*, I, 480-83.

2. *Ibid.*, 485; Solovev, XV, iv, Cols. 1558-59.

3. Solovev, XV, iv, Col. 1559.

4. *Ibid.*, Col. 1560.

5. *Ibid.*, Col. 1564.

6. Nostitz captured Elbing on 28 January 1710. Peter was delighted with this swift success and promptly rewarded him with promotion to the rank of Lieutenant-General. But this was not enough for Nostitz. He had managed to seize 250,000 Polish pieces of gold from the burghers of Elbing and he fled into Western Europe with this treasure. Peter had him condemned as a traitor and hanged in effigy. *Journal*, 283-85.

7. Solovev, XV, iv, Col. 1564.

8. In Moscow on this occasion Peter granted Sir Charles Whitworth, the English ambassador, a special audience to receive the formal apology of Queen Anne for the insult suffered by Matveev, the Russian ambassador, who in July 1708 had been arrested in London under a warrant issued by the Sheriff of Middlesex for failure to pay a debt of £50. This "crying insolence," as the English Secretary of State described it in a despatch to Whitworth (Boyle to Whitworth 23 July 1708, Sbornik I.R.I.O., L, 32-33), angered Peter; and Matveev, embittered by his failure to win English support against Sweden, did everything "to aggravate the blackness of his affront and raise the resentment of his master" (Whitworth to Boyle 22 Sept. 1708, *ibid.*, 84). The affair dragged on, although in April 1709 Peter gave orders to his ministers to make an end to it. Finally in February 1710 he granted this special audience for which Whitworth had been appointed ambassador extraordinary, and came armed with an illuminated copy of the Act of Parliament, passed as a result of this dispute and conferring diplomatic immunity from arrest, and also with a letter from the Queen. Peter expressed himself satisfied. Blackstone's Commentaries (London, 1830, 17th ed.), I, 254-56.

9. Solovev, XVI, i, Col. 38.

10. The Summer Palace is maintained now as a museum. The exterior with the bas-reliefs is in its original condition. Peter's successors made many changes in the rooms and furniture, but so far as possible these have been restored and are more or less as they were when Peter occupied them.

11. Solovev, XVI, i, Col. 42.

12. *Ibid.*, Col. 50.

13. The eight governments and their governors were: Moscow, Boyar Tikhon

N. Streshnev; St. Petersburg, Prince Menshikov; Kiev, Prince D. M. Golitsyn; Smolensk, Boyar Peter S. Saltykov; Archangel, Prince Peter A. Golitsyn; Kazan, Boyar Peter M. Apraxin; Azov, Admiral Feodor M. Apraxin; Siberia, Prince M. P. Gagarin.

14. Voskresensky, No. 240.

15. The ukaz refers to the absence of the Tsar from "Peterburg," not from Moscow which was still his capital. This and his letter to Romodanovsky after Poltava were not the earliest references to his intention of moving his capital from Moscow to St. Petersburg. Already in September 1704 in a letter to Menshikov, he was calling the new city his capital, but, one suspects, jokingly. P & B, III, pp. 161-62; Voskresensky, No. 241, p. 198.

16. Voskresensky, Nos. 242-44.

17. Ibid., No. 241.

Chapter XXXIII   The Campaign on the Pruth, 1711

1. Ustryalov, III, 280-81, 477-78.

2. Solovev, XVI, i, Col. 28.

3. Ibid.

4. Ustryalov, III, 471-72.

5. Bogoyavlensky, "On Russo-Serbian Relations in the Reign of Peter I" in Voprosy Istorii (1946), VIII-IX, 30-31.

6. Ibid., 25.

7. Solovev, XVI, ii, Cols. 60-61.

8. Ibid., Col. 57.

9. Ibid., Col. 58.

10. Ibid., Col. 59.

11. Ustryalov, VI, 25.

12. Solovev, XVI, ii, Col. 23.

13. Ibid., Cols. 64-65.

14. Ibid.

15. Ibid.

16. Ibid., Col. 66.

17. Peter is said to have written on 10 July to the Senate about his predicament, and to have instructed them that, if he should fall prisoner to the Turks, "You must not consider me your Tsar and Sovereign and you should not carry out orders from me, even if they are written in my own hand, until such time as I myself appear in person among you; but if I perish and you receive reliable information of my death, then choose among you the most worthy to be my successor."

This letter has apparently not survived in the original and its authenticity is open to doubt. Tsarevich Alexei was the heir to the throne and he had not yet incurred his father's wrath; it is highly unlikely that Peter would have disinherited him at this time and in this indirect way. In fact only a few weeks earlier the agreement for the marriage of Tsarevich Alexei to Princess Charlotte of Wolfenbuttel had been signed on the insistence of Peter, who was anxious to secure the succession to the throne. It is equally improbable that Peter would have allowed a successor to be chosen from among the senators, thus passing over Chancellor Golovkin, Admiral Apraxin, Prince Menshikov, and others who were closer to him and had better understanding of his policy. Solovev, XVI, ii, Cols. 73-74; cf. Golikov, IV, 265-66.

18. Solovev, XVI, ii, Col. 71.

19. Bruce and others relate that Catherine stripped herself of her jewels and going through the ranks collected money from the troops with which to bribe the Grand Vizir. The story is probably untrue. But it is certain that Catherine by her encouragement and support at this time of despair won Peter's boundless gratitude. P. H. Bruce, *Memoirs*, 144; Golikov, IV, 256-57.

"The sight of wagon loads of money that Peter sent into the Turkish camp" (Nisbet Bain, *Charles XII and the Collapse of the Swedish Empire*, 205) has often been given as the main reason for the Vizir's agreement to terms less severe than he might have imposed. Gifts were certainly usual in such circumstances and Baltadji would have expected them, but there is no evidence that Shafirov's promises influenced him.

When, on the night of 15 July, that is three days after terms had been signed, this money was brought into the Turkish camp, the Vizir refused to accept it, because he was afraid that Charles would make allegations of bribery, which would cost him his vizirship. His worst fears were realized a few months later, when he was displaced and charges of bribery, spread mainly by the Swedes in Constantinople, multiplied against him. But there is every reason for dismissing them as false. Solovev, XVI, ii, Cols. 78, 81; Sumner, *Peter the Great and the Ottoman Empire*, 40-41n.

20. Solovev, XVI, ii, Col. 75.

21. Charles had been a constant nuisance and expense to the Turks. At the beginning of 1713 the Sultan sent the Crimean Khan to Bender to persuade Charles to depart with a Tatar escort through Poland to Sweden. Charles refused to move. The Sultan sent a sharp order to him to leave as requested. Charles ignored it. The Turks stopped his food, burnt his stores, and surrounded his quarters. Charles with his small band of six officers and thirty-four men prepared for battle. The Sultan ordered him to be taken by force. Charles began firing when the Turks and Tatars approached. Even his own soldiers begged him not to stain Swedish honour by causing slaughter among hosts and benefactors. Two hundred Turks were killed before Charles was captured. But it was not until October of the following year that the unfortunate Turks were able to rid themselves of him finally.

Peter always spoke of Charles without bitterness, and even at times with a certain affection, and after Poltava usually referred to him as his "unfortunate brother Charles." But this incident saddened him. "I see," he said on learning about it, "that God has abandoned him, since he carried his ingratitude so far as to attack his benefactors." Staehlin, 247.

22. The Montenegrins and Serbs had won initial successes, but the defeat of the Russians left them to face the Turks alone. Peter sent word to them to cease hostilities and they agreed to an armistice with the Turks. Subsequently a Turkish army ravaged their land. Liberation by the Catholic Austrians, which they had dreaded, was their fate under the Treaty of Passarowitz. Despite their misfortunes they venerated Peter's name, and the moustachioed Tsar became a legend among them. The relations that Peter began with the Montenegrins, and made closer with the Serbs, were to continue with important results in the years to come.

Brancovan's loyalty to the Turks did not cancel their memory of his earlier treachery. In 1714 he was arrested, sent with his family to Constantinople, and there beheaded with his two sons.

Kantemir with twenty-four of his Moldavian Boyars was able to retreat with the Russian army. Peter bestowed on Kantemir the hereditary title of Prince and gave him large estates near Kharkov; other Moldavian boyars received similar grants of land. The Turks ravaged Moldavia, and it was many years before it recovered.

Chapter XXXIV The War in the Baltic: The Battle of Hango, 1711-1714

1. Ustrylov, VI, 27.
2. Guerrier, op. cit., 125-26.
3. Ibid., 159-60.
4. Ibid., 160.
5. Journal, 492. Golikov states that there is evidence that Peter publicly proclaimed his marriage in 1711 and that on 19 February 1712, he was then publicly married again. Golikov denies, however, that the marriage could have been celebrated a second time as it would have been disallowed by the Orthodox Church. Golikov, V, 48-49.
6. Solovev, XVII, i, Col. 308.
7. Ibid., 305-06.
8. Ibid., 306.
9. Journal, 403; Golikov, V, 106.
10. Golikov, V, 307.
11. Ibid., 311.
12. Ibid., 316.
13. Ibid., 320.
14. Ibid., V, 254-56.
15. Ibid.

Chapter XXXV The War in the Baltic: Peter in Paris, 1714-1717

1. Unpublished correspondence of Peter I concerning alliance with England in Voprosy Istorii (1946) VIII-IX, 101.
2. Ibid.
3. Ibid.
4. Solovev, XVII, i, Cols. 335-36.
5. Peter examined the English ships closely and gave Norris full leave to inspect the Russian fleet. Norris went over three new sixty-gun ships, built in St. Petersburg, which were, he considered "in every way equal to the best of that rank in our country, and more handsomely finished," and with superior arrangements in their powder rooms. He noted that Peter had "two English builders that have shown themselves great masters, all his want is to make seamen, which he labours to do out of his soldiers." Peter was greatly taken with Norris, and later offered him command of the Russian navy. Chance, George I and the Northern War, 92-93.
6. Solovev, XVII, i, Col. 340.
7. Golikov, VI, 54.
8. Ibid., 55.
9. Solovev, XVII, i, Col. 345.
10. Leibniz had sometimes been credited with first giving Peter the idea of establishing colleges on the Swedish model. But it is clear that this reform had already been in Peter's mind for some time. In April 1715, he had instructed Vasily Dolgoruky in Copenhagen to report fully on the names, functions, powers,

staff, and efficiency of the Danish Colleges, "for we have heard that the Swedes borrowed from them," Golikov, VI, 24; Guerrier, op. cit., 194-95.
11. Guerrier, op. cit., 187.
12. Ibid.
13. Solovev, XVII, i, Col. 349.
14. Ibid., Col. 363; Chance, op. cit., 131-39.
15. Solovev, XVII, i, Col. 351.
16. Ibid., Col. 353.
17. Ibid., Col. 354.
18. Chance, op. cit., 167-84.
19. Solovev, XVII, i, Col. 355.
20. R. K. Erskine, or Areskin as he was known in Russia, was born in Scotland about the middle of the seventeenth century. He studied at Oxford University, becoming a doctor of medicine and philosophy. He was in the Russian service from 1704 until his death in 1718. He was director or president of the Apothecary Department and Peter's personal physician.
21. Sbornik I.R.I.O., XXXIV, 150-51.
22. Ibid., 153.
23. Ibid., 164.
24. Ibid., 145-46.
25. Ibid., 174.
26. Ibid., 163.
27. Solovev, XVII, i, Col. 364.
28. Ibid., Col. 365.
29. Sbornik I.R.I.O., XXXIV, xxv.
30. Saint-Simon, Memoires, ed. by A. de Boislisle (Paris, 1920), XXXI, 374.
31. Peter was delighted at being elected an extraordinary member of the Academy as a result of his visit. In return for this honour he later had the Caspian Sea specially charted, sending the chart to be deposited in the Academy archives.
32. Saint-Simon, op. cit., XXXI, 387.
33. Sbornik I.R.I.O., XXXIV, 200.

Chapter XXXVI Peter and Alexei, 1717-1718

1. Solovev, XVII, i, Col. 411.
2. Ustryalov, VI, 16.
3. Solovev, XVII, i, Col. 414.
4. Ibid., XVII, ii, Col. 419.
5. Ibid., Cols. 421-22.
6. Ibid., Cols. 422-23.
7. Ustryalov, VI, 34.
8. Solovev, XVII, ii, Col. 426.
9. Ustryalov, VI, 42.
10. Ibid., 43.
11. Pleyer, the Imperial resident, reported that she had died of grief, caused by shortage of money, hostility of the Russian court, and persecution by Tsaritsa Catherine. Solovev points out that no evidence exists to support Pleyer's allegations. But clearly she was miserable in her married life in St. Petersburg and the main cause of her losing all desire to live must have been the neglect, indifference, and the drunken behaviour of Alexei.
Her relations with Peter were apparently excellent, apart from the incident

of her flight to her home in 1712, for which he had completely forgiven her. She was also on good terms with Catherine.

After her death a rumour circulated in Europe that she had fled to America, married a Frenchman in Louisiana, returned with him to Europe, living for a time in Paris and dying of old age in Brussels. Unhappily this story is not true. Solovev, XVII, ii, Cols. 439-40; Ustryalov, VI, 43, 45, 342-46.

12. Ustryalov, VI, 46-49, 346-48.
13. Solovev, XVII, ii, Col. 442.
14. Ustryalov, VI, 49-50.
15. Solovev, XVII, ii, Col. 443.
16. Ustryalov, VI, 50-51, 349-50.
17. Solovev, XVII, ii. Col. 445.
18. Ustryalov, VI, 51.
19. Ibid., 52.
20. Ibid., 53.
21. Solovev, XVII, ii, Col. 446; Ustryalov, VI, 52.
22. Ustryalov, VI, 54, 56-57.
23. Ibid.
24. Ibid.
25. Ibid., 79-80.
26. Ibid., 87.
27. Ibid.
28. Ibid., 111-12.
29. Ibid., 116-17.
30. Ibid., 119-20.
31. Solovev, XVII, ii, Col. 469.
32. Ibid.
33. Ustryalov, VI, 143.
34. Ibid., 239.
35. Vasily Dolgoruky was recalled and pardoned in 1724 on the occasion of the coronation of Catherine.
36. Evdokiya was sent to a convent at Old Ladoga near Schlusselburg and kept there under close guard. But she survived until 1731. She was taken to Moscow after Peter's death and lived at Novodevichy nunnery, but went to court from time to time during the brief reign of Peter II, and then during the reign of the Empress Anna.
37. Ustryalov, VI, 240.
38. Ibid.
39. Ibid., 241.
40. Peter exempted Efrosinia from torture and further examination. She was released and lived quietly in St. Petersburg, subsequently marrying an officer of the guards. Nothing is known of the fate of Alexei's child to which she gave birth in the Petropavlovsky fortress; it vanished without trace.
41. Ustryalov, VI, 273-76.
42. Various accounts of the death of Alexei have survived. The Journal of Menshikov states that on the morning of 26 June the Tsarevich was ill and that he died on that day. The Journal of the Chancellery of the St. Petersburg garrison states that the Tsar, Prince Menshikov, and eight others gathered in the garrison about 8 A.M. on 26 June, when torture was administered—to whom is not stated—and by 11 A.M. they had all departed. On the same day at 6 P.M. the Tsarevich died.

Neither of the above sources mention that the Tsar was present at his death, and it must therefore be presumed that he was not present. Nevertheless the French resident, de la Vie, reported on 11 July that on his deathbed the Tsarevich asked for his father. The Tsar went to him and Alexei, pleading his guilt, begged forgiveness. Peter gave him full pardon and left. Soon afterwards Alexei again asked for his father. Peter replied that he had already pardoned him. Shafirov persuaded him to return, but Alexei died before he could reach him. (Sbornik I.R.I.O., XXXIV, 354-55) Peter subsequently instructed his residents abroad to explain that the Tsarevich had received his father's forgiveness and died in a Christian manner. (Solovev, XVII, ii, Col. 490)

Pleyer reported that the Tsar cut off the head of his son with an axe at 8 P.M. on 26 June. Weber, the Hanoverian resident, reported that Alexei died of an apoplectic stroke. Alexander Rumyantsov in a letter dated 27 June, but probably a forgery written at a much later date, stated that he with four others suffocated Alexei on the night of 26 June. P. H. Bruce wrote that he was poisoned. De Bie, the Dutch resident, reported that his veins were opened and that he bled to death.

Ustryalov has listed all these accounts, and from the evidence assembled it is clear that the most acceptable version is that given by the Journal of the St. Petersburg garrison and confirmed by Menshikov's business journal. This account has been followed here. Ustryalov, VI, 283-94.

Chapter XXXVII   The Treaty of Nystadt, 1718-1721

1. Solovev, XVII, iii, Cols. 495-96.

2. So great was Swedish hostility to his policy of continued warfare that it was even said that one of his own men had killed him to save his country from further suffering. This rumour persisted for many years. In 1859 in the presence of King Charles XV and his brother the body of Charles XII was exhumed and from the position of the head wound it was considered proven that an enemy bullet had killed him.

On learning of the death of his enemy, Peter wept and was heard to say, "My dear Charles, how sorry I feel for you." Staehlin, 248.

3. Sbornik I.R.I.O., LXI, 537.

4. Ibid., 536-37, 561-66.

5. Chance, op. cit., 530.

6. "Our success" Carteret wrote, "is chiefly owing to the Tsar, he at the gates of Stockholm has reasoned best for us." Peter made a mistake in sending these raiding parties to Sweden, for they produced the opposite result to that which he had hoped. The Swedish party favouring peace with Russia, even on his terms, was very strong and might then have carried the day. Chance, op. cit., 338-39.

7. Solovev, XVII, iii, Col. 573.

8. Ibid., Col. 577.

9. Ibid., Col. 599.

10. Swedish prisoners of war in Russia were said to number more than 100,000. The majority remained in Russia, having married Russian women, and found good employment, especially in the new industries and government departments that Peter had established, and now service in the Tsar's army and navy was open to them. Most of those who returned sailed from St. Petersburg. Of them Vice-Admiral Ehrenskjold, whom Peter himself had captured, was

shown special honour. Although a prisoner of war he was accorded a farewell audience when the Tsar presented him with his portrait set in diamonds, and gave him a letter to his King, recommending him as a brave and skilful officer whose capture reflected in no way upon him, and who had won the Tsar's respect.
11. Solovev, XVII, iii, Col. 616.
12. Golikov, VIII, 240.
13. Ibid., 242.
14. Ibid., IX, 8.
15. Solovev, XVII, iii, Col. 626.

Chapter XXXVIII Reform in State and Church, 1714-1725

1. Voskresensky, 60; Solovev, XVI, iii, Col. 143.
2. Voskresensky, 214.
3. Ibid., 213.
4. Solovev, XVI, iii, Cols. 141-42.
5. Voskresensky, 216.
6. Ibid., 215; Solovev, XVI, iii, Col. 142.
7. The nine colleges with their presidents and vice-presidents as follows:
College of Foreign Affairs: Chancellor Count Golovkin, president; Baron Shafirov, vice-president.
Kammer College (responsible for collection of state revenues): Prince Dmitri Golitsyn, president; Baron Nirot, vice-president.
College of Justice: Privy Councillor Andrei Matveev, president; Brewer, vice-president.
College responsible for national income: Prince Yakov Dolgoruky, president; vice-president not appointed.
College of War: Prince Menshikov, president; General Weide, vice-president.
Naval College: Admiral Count Apraxin, president; Vice-Admiral Cruys, vice-president.
College of Commerce: Count Peter Tolstoy, president; Schmidt, vice-president.
Treasury College (responsible for national expenditure): Count Musin-Pushkin, president; vice-president not appointed.
College of Mining and Industry: General Bruce, president; vice-president not appointed.
Voskresensky, 219-20.
8. Ibid., 218-19.
9. Ibid., 225-26.
10. Ibid.
11. The General Regulation defined not only the functions and procedures of each college, but also the appointment and duties of every official from the highest to the lowest grades. The first draft was the work of Heinrich Fick, a German jurisprudent, who had made a study of the Swedish collegial system. The presidents and colleges had worked on the drafts and Peter with his capacity for detail had revised most of the articles (Voskresensky, 411-60).
12. Ibid., 245-46.
13. Ibid., 237-38.
14. Solovev, XVIII, iii, Col. 754.
15. Golikov, IX, 122.
16. Solovev, XVIII, iii, Col. 754.
17. Voskresensky, 308.

18. Shafirov was taken into the Kremlin early on the morning of 15 February 1723. The sentence was read out; his wig and old sheepskin coat were taken off, and he was led onto the scaffold. He crossed himself many times and then knelt, placing his head on the block. The executioner raised the axe. At this point Cabinet Secretary Makarov proclaimed that the Tsar, acknowledging his past services, had granted him his life and sentenced him to imprisonment in Siberia. Shafirov rose to his feet and stumbled off the scaffold with tears in his eyes. His friends and colleagues gathered to congratulate him on his pardon, but he was badly shaken by the experience. The doctors bled him and he commented, "It would be better to open my main artery and so put an end to my torments." Foreign ministers also congratulated him, for they liked and respected him despite his hot temper. Peter cancelled his imprisonment in Siberia and had him kept under arrest in Novgorod. He was subsequently pardoned and, living until 1739, he held many high offices. Solovev, XVIII, iii, Col. 765-66.

19. Voskresensky, 60.

20. Ibid.

21. Ibid., 73-74.

22. Ibid., 206.

23. Ibid., 384.

24. John Bell of Antermony, who went to St. Petersburg in 1714 and served in Russia for some years, wrote in his Journal: "I have more than once seen him [Peter] stop in the streets to receive petitions from persons who thought themselves wronged by sentences passed in courts of judicature. On taking the petition, the person was told to come next day to the Senate, where the affair was immediately examined and determined, if the nature of it would admit its being done in so short a time. It will naturally follow that such free access to his person was not only productive of great relief to many poor widows and orphans, but also a strong check upon judges, and tended very much to prevent any sort of influence prevailing on them to pronounce unjust sentences, for which they were so likely to be called to account." John Bell, Travels from St. Petersburg, II, 359.

25. Voskresensky, 342-45.

26. Golikov, V, 259.

27. Solovev, XVI, iii, Col. 181.

28. Ibid.

29. Ibid.

30. Ibid., 177.

31. Ibid., 191.

32. Ibid., XVI, i, Col. 10.

33. One day in the Senate, he was raging against the dishonesty of his subjects, and he ordered Yaguzhinsky to issue an ukaz condemning to death anyone who stole so much as would pay for the length of rope to hang him. Yaguzhinsky protested, but Peter angrily ordered him to do as he was told. Yaguzhinsky then said, "Does Your Majesty wish to be a master without servants, an Emperor without subjects? Do we not all steal, some more, some less, some privately, and some without disguise?" Peter laughed and let the ukaz drop. Staehlin, 159-60.

34. In 1719, as a reprisal for the expulsion of Abram Veselovsky, the Russian resident, from Vienna, Peter expelled all Austrian Jesuits from Russia. He took care, however, to inform the Pope that this was a political act, directed against the Emperor, and it did not mean withdrawal of the privileges granted to Roman

Catholics to pursue their faith in his dominions; but only French Jesuits would be admitted in future.

35. Solovev, XVI, iii, Col. 246.
36. Ibid.
37. Ibid., Col. 249.
38. Ibid., Col. 270.
39. Ibid., Col. 271.
40. Yavorsky was a divided unhappy man in whom humility and ambition, charity and bigotry, courage and faintheartedness were mingled. At times he appeared to be completely in the thrall of Peter's dominating personality, and he bowed with tearful humility to his will.

In 1712 he wrote to Peter in an outburst of despair and resignation: "Where shall I go from your spirit and how shall I flee from your face? I will not go to a foreign realm, for your power is given to you by God—in Nezhin, in Moscow, or in Ryazan—everywhere your sovereign power reigns over me; it is impossible to hide from it." Yu Serech, "Stefan Yavorsky and the Conflict of Ideologies in the Reign of Peter I," in Slavonic and East European Review (Vol. XXX, No. 74 December 1951); Solovev, XVI, iii, Col. 271.

41. Solovev, XVI, iii, Col. 276.
42. The Holy Synod endured until 1917 when it was abolished and the patriarchate was revived.
43. Travelling on the road from Spa to Aachen in July 1717, Peter noticed a man working in a garden, but not dressed as a peasant. Learning that the worker was a priest he went to talk with him. He asked why as a priest he was working instead of leaving it to servants and parishioners. The priest replied that his parishioners were busy earning their bread, while his calling gave him ample time for work in the garden and fields. Peter was tremendously impressed and said to his companions: "Remind me of this when we return to our homeland. I will try to arouse our village priests, who are often lazy, so that they, by working the fields and gardens, earn true bread and a better life than they have without working." Golikov, VII, 208-09.
44. Later generations of Russian Orthodox believers, and especially Slavophils, have charged Peter with depriving the church of its autonomy, subordinating it to the state, and, more serious, of degrading Muscovite Orthodoxy. His own contemporaries apparently felt less strongly and did not raise these charges. It is noteworthy that two men—Mitrofan, Archbishop of Voronezh, and Dmitri, Metropolitan of Rostov—who belong to the highest traditions of Russian Orthodoxy and whose example of simple piety and humility has been cherished through the ages by Russian believers, were among his ardent supporters. A. P. Stanley, Lectures on the Eastern Church, 452-93; cf. for example N. Zernov, Moscow the Third Rome (London, 1938, 2nd ed.), 77-94, and The Russians and Their Church (London, 1945), 115-124.

Chapter XXXIX   Social and Economic Reforms, 1714-1725

1. Voskresensky, 351-52.
2. Ibid., 352-54; Solovev, XVIII, ii, Col. 755.
3. Klyuchevsky states that it is not possible to estimate how many families were ennobled as a result of Peter's reforms. At the end of the seventeenth century there were 2,985 noble families, comprising 15,000 landowners. The Secretary of the Prussian Embassy at the Russian court in 1737 reported that at

the time of the first revision the nobles, with their families, numbered up to 500,000 persons and on this basis it may be estimated that there were 100,000 noble families. Klyuchevsky, op. cit., 104-05.

4. Solovev, XVI, iii, Col. 230.
5. Klyuchevsky, op. cit., 139.
6. Solovev, XVI, iii, Col. 234.
7. Ibid., Col. 152.
8. Ibid., Col. 235.
9. Historical Outline and Survey of Contents of the Manuscript Department of the Library of the Academy of Sciences, ed. by M. N. Murzanova and others, 5-34.
10. Solovev, XVI, iii, Cols. 238-39.
11. Ibid., Col. 802.
12. Ibid.
13. Ibid., Col. 242.
14. P. Pekarsky, Science and Literature in Russia, I, 226.
15. Sumner, Peter the Great and the Emergence of Russia, 207-08; cf. B. O. Unbegaun, "Colloquial and Literary Russia" in Oxford Slavonic Papers, I, 29.
16. Solovev, XVI, i, Col. 13.
17. Golikov, VI, 27.
18. Marie Hamilton who was of Scottish descent was the favourite lady-in-waiting of Empress Catherine, but she was found guilty of killing an illegitimate child by a court which sentenced her to death. Catherine used her persuasion and influence to wring a pardon from the Tsar. All at court added their pleas that she should be pardoned, for she was popular with everyone, including Peter himself. He nevertheless refused to commute or quash the sentence, believing that it was not within his power to do so. It is said that he was present at her execution and that he encouraged her to bear her punishment with fortitude. Golikov, VI, 66-68.
19. Ibid., 66-67.
20. Solovev, XVI, iii, Col. 164.
21. Ibid., Col. 166.
22. Klyuchevsky, op. cit., 137.

Chapter XL   Trade, Exploration, and the Persian Campaign, 1721-1722

1. Solovev, XVIII, i, Col. 645.
2. Golikov, VII, 266n and IX, 340.
3. Erket was almost certainly Yarkand, one of the principal cities of Sinkiang. The report that Peter had received from Gagarin, then Governor of Siberia, was confusing. It referred to a little town of Erket in Siberia on the river Darya, which might be taken to be the Amu-Darya (Oxus). The expedition of Buchholz, setting out from Tobolsk, penetrated farther south and, although unsuccessful, it was in the right direction. Solovev, XVIII, i, Cols. 645-66; V. Grigoriev, Russian Policy in Central Asia in II, App. iv, of Turkistan by E. Schuyler (London, 1876), 440-41.
4. Solovev, XVIII, i, Cols. 647-48.
5. Ibid., Col. 663.
6. One of his secretaries was John Bell of Antermony, who published in Glasgow in 1763 his journal of this journey and also of the journey to Derbent in 1722 when he accompanied Peter. His journal provides a valuable account

of both expeditions. He was frequently in the company of Peter for whom he developed a warm respect and even reverence.

7. Solovev, XVIII, i, Cols. 671-72.
8. Ibid.
9. Ibid., Col. 677.
10. Ibid., Col. 682.
11. Ibid., Col. 696.
12. In 1732 the Empress Anna restored these provinces to Persia. General Manstein, who was in the Russian service at the time, wrote: "The court who would have long before been highly pleased with any good pretence for getting rid with honour of those provinces which Peter I had conquered from Persia, and of which the keeping cost more than they were worth (a prodigious number of people having perished in them), an expedient was at length found. A negotiation was entered upon for this purpose with the Court of Ispahan, and the provinces were ceded to it in consideration of several advantages granted to commerce.

"Russia had been obliged to keep near thirty thousand men in garrison in those provinces, and not a year passed without it being necessary to recruit the deficiency of above one half, as the Russians, not being able to endure the climate, died like flies there. It was reckoned that from the year 1722 in which Peter I had entered that country, to the time that the Russians evacuated it, there had perished a hundred and thirty thousand men in it." Manstein, op. cit., 58-59.

In the following century, after nine years of war with Persia (1804-1813), Russia recovered these provinces as far south as Astara.

Chapter XLI   Emperor Peter the Great, 1722-1725

1. Neplyuev was one of Peter's "fledglings" and typical of the corps of young men whom he trained and inspired with his ideals. In his autobiography Neplyuev states that as a lieutenant he was placed in charge of ships under construction in St. Petersburg, a post which brought him into almost daily contact with Peter. Chernyshev, a member of the Admiralty College, advised him that to retain the Tsar's favour he must "be accurate and quick to tell the truth—God protect you from lying; although things may be bad for you, he'll be far angrier if you lie." Neplyuev was soon to put this advice to the test. He arrived late on duty and found Peter already there. Lateness, like laziness, earned Peter's displeasure. Terrified Neplyuev thought of fleeing to his home and sending word that he was ill, but then he summoned up his courage. "I'm already here, my friend!" said Peter on seeing him arrive. "I'm at fault, Your Majesty," answered Neplyuev. "Last night I was visiting and I sat far into the evening and I was late in rising." Peter seized him by the shoulder, looked him in the eye, so that he trembled, but then he said, "Thank you, little one, for telling the truth. God forgives. Who isn't the son of woman?"

In January 1721 at an assembly Peter, surrounded by his ministers and officers said, "I need a man who knows Italian to send to Constantinople as resident." Apraxin said that he knew a suitable man, but unfortunately he was poor. "Poverty's no handicap; it can be remedied quickly. Who is this man?" said Peter. Apraxin indicated Lieutenant Neplyuev. Peter turned and looked at him and then said, "He's a good man and I would like to keep him by me." But then Peter thought again and decided to give the young Lieutenant this important post. Neplyuev made a great success of it and for negotiating the treaty with the Turks after the Persian campaign was richly rewarded with promotion and estates. Solovev, XVIII, iii, Cols. 858-60.

2. *Ibid.*, XVI, iii, Col. 212.

3. Peter frequently remarked, "I am sensible that I have my faults, and that I easily lose my temper for which reason I am not offended with those who are on familiar terms with me when they tell me of it, and remonstrate with me, as does my Catherine." Staehlin, 266-67.

4. Golikov, IX, 296.

5. Solovev, XVIII, iii, Col. 839.

6. On the death of Peter, Catherine ruled alone as Empress until 1727 when Tsarevich Peter Alexeevich became Emperor, ruling until 19 January 1730. He was followed by Anna, daughter of Peter's half-brother, Tsar Ivan V, and then by his great-grandson, the infant, Ivan VI. Elizabeth, Peter's daughter, seized the throne from him. After Peter's death the Russian throne had a succession of four empresses, except for the brief reigns of Peter II and Ivan VI.

7. Bell, *op. cit.*, II, 359.

8. *Ibid.*, 360.

9. Golikov, X, 35-39.

10. Voskresensky, 58-59, 67-68, 88, and elsewhere giving extracts from the notebooks.

11. Solovev, XVIII, iii, Cols. 751-52.

12. S. P. Luppov, *History of the Building of St. Petersburg*, 25.

13. *Ibid.*, 36.

14. *Ibid.*, 81.

15. The Danish ambassador reported in 1710 that in building the Petropavlovsk fortress, "they say, 60,000 men perished from the work, from cold, and from hunger." The French consul reported in 1717 that the Tsar annually lost two thirds of the labour force in the city. The mortality rate was high enough, but these reports were both exaggerations. Luppov, *op. cit.*, 94.

16. Catherine knew that nothing gave her husband greater pleasure than new buildings which added to the beauty of St. Petersburg and its surroundings. During his absence in 1714-1715 she built for him a country palace of stone with an elaborate garden some eight miles from the city, and named it after the Livonian who had formerly owned the land, Sary, whence it became Sarskoe Selo or Tsarskoe Selo—the Tsar's village.

On his return Peter quickly inspected his city and expressed himself satisfied with progress. Catherine then mentioned that while he was away she had found a deserted but delightful place not far distant where he would undoubtedly want to build a summer residence. Peter at once asked where this place was and promised to build there if it was as pleasant as his wife claimed. He was impatient and they set out next day. Meanwhile Catherine had given orders for everything to be done in preparation for his visit. On the road, but still far off Peter espied the two-storied stone building, where no building had been before, and he was delighted. When they arrived Catherine led him through the gates saying, "This is the place which I told you about and here is the country palace which I have built for my master." She then showed him over the gardens and the palace and took him to a point where he could see St. Petersburg in the distance. During dinner soon afterwards Peter's delight was complete when, on Catherine proposing a toast to their host, eleven cannon fired a salute. Peter was enchanted with his wife's surprise and was heard to say that he could remember few days as happy as this one. Golikov, VI, 42-43.

17. *Ibid.*, IX, 262-65; "Story of the Boat Which Gave Peter the Great the First Thought of Building the Russian Fleet." Communicated by Sir Henry Ellis, Director of the British Museum. *Archaeologia*, XXXVI.

18. Sbornik I.R.I.O., XXXIV, 189.

19. Bell, op. cit., II, 362-63.

20. *Ibid.*, 356; Staehlin, 340-42.

21. Prince Pierre Dolgorukov, *Memoires* (Geneva, 1867), 44-45.

22. *Ibid.*, 39.

23. Ustryalov, VI, 187-88.

24. Solovev, XVIII, iii, Col. 801.

25. Catherine's request that Mons and Matrena Balk should be pardoned so angered Peter that he smashed a Venetian vase with his fist. "So can I destroy the most beautiful ornament in my palace," he exclaimed. It was an ominous remark, the meaning of which Catherine no doubt understood. But she did not lack courage as indeed she had shown in asking for their pardon, and she answered calmly, "But have you made the palace any more beautiful by doing so?"

Voltaire reported this incident which he had learnt from Bassewitz, the Duke of Holstein's minister in St. Petersburg. (Golikov, X, 107-08)

As a result of the Mons case, foreign ministers hastened to report to their governments that Mons was the lover of the Empress and that the Emperor had found them out. Prince Pierre Dolgorukov in his *Memoires* (p. 45) even alleged that Peter had caught them in the act of love. But there is no evidence whatsoever to support these statements, and nothing to suggest that Peter suspected or had grounds for suspecting Catherine of infidelity.

INDEX

493